EDUCATIONAL PSYCHOLOGY

A DEVELOPMENTAL APPROACH

FOURTH EDITION

Norman A. Sprinthall
North Carolina State University

Richard C. Sprinthall
American International College

RANDOM HOUSE NEW YORK
This book was developed for Random House by Lane Akers, Inc.

Fourth Edition

987654

Copyright © 1974, 1977, 1981, 1987 by Newbery
Award Records, Inc.

Library of Congress Cataloging-in-Publication Data

Sprinthall, Norman A., 1931–
  Educational psychology.
  Includes bibliographical references and index.
  1. Educational psychology. I. Sprinthall, Richard
C., 1930–   . II. Title.
LB1051.S6457 1987 370.15 86-24860
ISBN 0–394–36297–7

Manufactured in the United States of America

Cover Art: Carl Holtz, *Untitled* 1940. Courtesy of
the Graham Modern Gallery, New York. Photo by
Jeffrey Rosenbaum.

Cover and book design: Glen M. Edelstein

To children

Ye are better than all the ballads
That ever were sung or said
For ye are living poems
And all the rest are dead.

H. W. Longfellow

PREFACE

As if to prove the dictum that nothing worthwhile is permanent in the world of education and psychology, the time is ripe for this, our fourth, version of *Educational Psychology: A Developmental Approach*. Long ago (or so it seems, though it was only the late 1960s), we decided to create a text with a developmental theme. We had been very dissatisfied, in teaching at both the undergraduate and graduate levels, with the eclectic nature of most works on educational psychology. We decided to stop complaining and try our hand at the venture.

History since then has proved two points. First, there was a very substantial gap in the field, which our work has filled nicely in a succession of editions. Second, the generic theme of development has been the most important single feature of those several editions. So, for all those hundreds of institutions of higher education that have continued to adopt the text, the fourth edition carries on the tradition of the earlier versions. To those who have said "I'm sticking with Sprinthall" (words often overheard at professional conventions), your expression of allegiance has been heard. We have carefully reviewed huge amounts of new material and made selective and substantial changes. You will find, as a result, even more research and practical applications to comprehend our model.

To those, on the other hand, who may still be unsure of the value of a generic theme and are wavering between eclecticism and relativism, we invite you to take another look at our content and organization. The cognitive-developmental base for educational psychology has gone through two distinct periods since we started. With the publication of the first edition, the developmental approach was clearly "in" as the major new model for the field. The joining of a variety of developmental domains represented by such giants as Jean Piaget, Erik Erikson, and Laurence Kohlberg marked a new era. Then, as is often the case in intellectual history, there was a Thermidorian reaction (like the one following the French Revolution). Questions were raised concerning the model, and rightly so. Some of the earlier claims and suggestions were controversial and others were wrong. The research did not back up what the early theory implied. Thus, in the late 1970s an increasing number of articles cast doubt on the significance of some of the basic tenets. Is the transition between stages really so abrupt? Are women so different that the theories are sex-biased? What about cultural differences? Also, from a practical stance an additional series of questions surfaced: As the so-called direct-teaching model emerged, was there any relevance to understanding developmental stage differences? If teaching effectiveness was to be defined exclusively in direct terms, it could be that developmental concepts might be redundant.

It is instructive to see how the developmentalists have answered these criticisms. Rather than respond to each new study by debate and counterpoint, the field tended to business and produced a new generation of research-based studies. These studies now form the backbone of the revision. Shortly after Piaget's death, attempts were made to replace his entire framework because some studies questioned certain elements. One of the interesting reactions in social science to the death of a giant is often a new wave of highly critical commentary, a fate most recently experienced by Margaret Mead's theory for anthropology. So too for Piaget. The results, however, have been positive: a stronger research base for the overall framework and a more detailed understanding of the transition points. It is now clear that, except for the end of the first stage, there is more overlap between stages than was previously thought. Thus, there is some potential for concrete thought prior to age 5 to 7 when the shift was predicted to occur, just as there is some potential for abstract thinking prior to adolescence. This does not mean, as we note in the text, that we as educators should shift the main teaching focus to promote such premature development. Instead, we now have a greater appreciation for children's range of development, even while seeing the essential validity of the stages Piaget identified.

The same holds true for Kohlberg's system. There were many second thoughts voiced in the late seventies, particularly concerning sex bias and cross-cultural differences. The most recent research data, however, have strengthened the earlier contentions. The ability to understand and act on principles of justice is not sex-biased, and the framework for the development of moral behavior holds in both Western and non-Western industrialized countries. It does not hold, however, in tribal or feudal societies. So here, too, we now have a clearer understanding of theory as well as practice in the important area of value development.

The story of the challenges to developmental theory can go on and on. Since the greatest "sin" in education is to bore, we will not continue that story. Suffice it to say that if you want to know more about revisions to the approach, don't wait for the movie—read the book.

We decided to do some pruning, always one of the most difficult decisions because it means omitting some of our own writings. Yet, we had to face the music and set some priorities or risk a text much too long to cover in a semester. Based partly on a market survey and partly on our own reading of recent research, we decided to drop chapters on language development, creativity, and affective education. In the first case, it seemed that language development had become too technical and specialized for treatment in a text like this; we chose instead to focus on reading development in the context of Jeanne Chall's work. In the case of creativity, we felt that the questions of assessing creativity and applying what is known about it had not really been pursued in any more depth since the first edition. Rather than devote a complete chapter to covering very old ground, we have simply reviewed briefly the current state of the art in Chapter 13. Similarly, in the case of affective education, we thought there was almost no new material. Still, because aspects of the psychological education of the child or adolescent are important, we decided to delve into the meta-analysis research on effective teaching. That research shows the importance of classroom morale, a positive atmosphere, and using a variety of teaching models to boost academic achievement and promote a positive self-concept in students—topics covered in both Chapter 20 on discipline and Chapter 21 on mainstreaming.

Another change was our decision to write an entirely new chapter on information processing. What goes on inside the heads of pupils, so to speak, has always been a mystery wrapped in an enigma (as Churchill once said of Russia). The information-processing approach may provide a model of how pupils make connections between what they already know and what they are currently learning. Combined with developmental stage concepts, this new theory may help bring together theories of individual differences and stage theory to promote a fine-grained analysis, perhaps reducing both the mystery and the enigma.

One last point on changes: Since unusual progress has been made in the area of teaching effectiveness, we have completely revised two of the three chapters in Unit 3 and made considerable additions to the third. The synthesis we discuss, however, is not a simple-minded version of direct teaching for students at all ages and in all subject areas. Instead, we now think that a clearer basis than ever before exists for what we call teaching—the process of matching and gradual mismatching, or what is termed "attribute–treatment interaction." Together, the developmental understanding of pupil learning characteristics and this teaching model can be a guide to teaching and learning. Along with information processing, this model of effective teaching is an important new trend in the field.

Naturally, we would be remiss if we didn't thank those colleagues, both "old" and new, who have helped us immeasurably with the revision. The input from Jim Rest, Bill Bart, Maynard Reynolds, and Martin Haberman from the Midwest continues to inform our efforts as does the feedback we received from Larry Kohlberg, Jeanne Chall, and colleagues from the banks of the Charles River in Cambridge.

We have received help from others as well. Don Locke, an expert on cross-cultural development, and Sam Snyder, an expert on adolescence (both from North Caroline State University), have been very valuable. Marvin Berkowitz from Marquette University contributed many insightful new approaches to the moral-dilemma discussion. At American International College, important contributions were made to the information-processing section by Carol Spafford and Joanne Carlisle. Bob MacLachlan and Lee Sirois provided invaluable help in the learning and intelligence chapters, and Greg Schmutte and Art Bertrand added their expertise to the measurement sections.

So, after some 500 new pages of typed manuscript, and almost 500 new references, we have once again revised and updated the standard for the developmental approach to educational psychology. It's been a difficult and time-consuming task. We've had clerical and editorial help and we appreciate that very much. Robin Hughes and Pat Knowles in Raleigh, and Pat Cusing and Gwen Payne in Springfield, have done valiant work in preparing the manuscript. At Random House, a strong vote of apprecia-

tion must be given to both Lane Akers and Elaine Romano for their many helpful suggestions. They proved to be genuine experts in the overall production and supervision of the fourth edition.

Finally, we wish to thank our spouses for their assistance. We know that may sound somewhat conventional, yet in this case both Lois and Dianne have careers in their own right—in teacher education and art education. Their professional help was substantial, their personal support incalculable.

Norman A. Sprinthall
North Carolina State University

Richard C. Sprinthall
American International College

CONTENTS

BIOGRAPHIES

CONTEMPORARY ISSUES

OTHER
FEATURES

1

INTRODUCTION AND HISTORY

EDUCATIONAL PSYCHOLOGY: A BRIDGE STEPPED ON AT BOTH ENDS?

Educational psychology as a field of study has quite literally struggled throughout its history with an identity problem. Existing by definition somewhere between psychology and education, the discipline has experienced the crosscurrents and whirlpools often created when two great oceans meet. Psychology as the science of human behavior has as a major concern the discovery of laws. As such, it focuses on basic description and prediction to uncover gradually the nature of human beings. In this mode psychology is a science, a body of knowledge about ourselves. In the tradition of rigorous science, the questions it raises are generic. The rate of progress is slow. Human beings have been and will be more complex than psychological theories. Indeed, psychology as a science is forever limited by the size of the cerebral cortex of the investigators. Ultimately, we study ourselves. Breakthroughs are hardly a common outcome. Even at best, progress in basic theory proceeds more at the speed of a glacier than at that of great oceans on the incoming tide.

Psychology's theorists are commited to a careful and comprehensive analysis of what it means to be human. This is a long-term enterprise. The payoff is future oriented. As a professor of psychology and education puts it, "It's like investing in recreational land in Labrador. Don't expect an immediate return."[1] At the same time theorists are quick to point out that without theory, practice has nothing to guide it. Thus, those who wish to act without an informed theoretical basis do so at their own hazard. The traditions of science require a conceptual framework for practice.

On the other side, we have the profession of education. A profession generally has exactly the opposite agenda as a science. Education—like law, medicine, and business—has practice as its foremost concern. The practical world is completely different from the scientific realm. To many in a profession, applied knowledge is the only kind that matters. Otherwise, they claim, "It's too theoretical" or "It will never work." "It's another case of excessive navel gazing," they might say, or, "Remember that ac-

3

cording to theory the bumblebee can't fly." Such comments are quite understandable. Educators, like other professionals, confront the realities of practice every day. A teacher, counselor, or school principal cannot withdraw in the middle of a class, counseling session, or a budget proposal and say (perhaps wistfully?), "Well, we need more basic research on that point so I'll stop now, close the school, and go back to the drawing board. Class dismissed for the next three years." Nor can a doctor in the middle of an operation stop suddenly, look up, and say, "We don't have an absolutely scientific basis for this surgery, so tell the patient (when he comes to) to take a number and we'll get back to him as soon as we can." We cannot imagine a lawyer leaving halfway through his or her summation for the defense with the words, "We don't have a completely clear framework of precedents, so (members of the jury) put everything on hold. More research is needed."

THEORY AND PRACTICE: TWO CULTURES?

C. P. Snow in a famous volume denoted the problem of theory versus practice as a legitimate disparity between two cultures, the scientific and the humanistic.[2] The same split can be seen for educational psychology. Neither tradition is better, although the status of the two cultures may be different. In fact, the status problem has only clouded the central difficulty. In this country, and certainly in nearly all modern technological societies, scientific achievement is more highly regarded than professional activity. Science is more glamorous. Breakthroughs are announced in media blitzes. Money flows to basic research. However, the status difference is not really central to the problem. In our terms the difficulty is that the two traditions have different histories, different pressures, different procedures—indeed, fundamentally different ways of understanding what the problem is in the first place.

As you experience both scientific and professional courses, you will gain firsthand knowledge of the distinctions between these two different cultures. When C. P. Snow uses the term *cultures*, he means two different societies, or what the Germans call *Weltanschauung*—differ-

ent world views. The behavioral scientist may interview literally hundreds of subjects to uncover possible systematic variations in cognitive processes. The teacher wants to know what to do at a given moment with a student. The movement here is from the general, the scientific, and the objective to the particular, the active, and the subjective. Both groups can become easily annoyed with each other. The scientist often answers the professional with a shrug followed by a long, complex, and seemingly evasive nonanswer. The professional may retort in a situation, "Well, why don't you emulate the philosopher Bishop Berkeley. He isolated himself in a cave for a very long time trying to get his mind together. We will keep things going here as best we can, in the meantime."

As you enter the field of education, then, do not accept at face value any of the simpleminded statements that are made about educational psychology. The idea that we synthesize two diverse traditions with the wave of a hand does not hold up. Realize that comments such as "It's a connector science" or "It's an applied science" or "It's the science of education applied to the art of teaching" are oversimplifications. Educational psychology as a bridge between two different traditions is still being built. Indeed, the progress in the last decade has been substantial, but the discipline is still stepped on regularly at both ends. It isn't quite scientific enough for psychology nor is it quite practical enough for the profession.[3] On the other hand, the overall movement is positive. Just pick up some earlier reviews of teaching, for example. It was common to conclude in the past that educational psychologists didn't really know anything or have anything to contribute. Talk about a field in search of an accident about to happen! Researchers concluded after reviewing hundreds of studies on teacher effectiveness:

> Existing research has a long but disappointing history.
>
> We do not know how to define, prepare for, or measure teacher competence.
>
> Reviewers have concluded, with remarkable regularity, that few relationships between teacher variables and effectiveness criteria can be established.

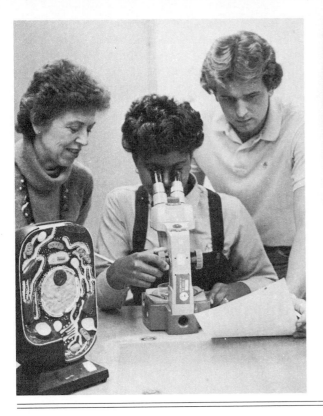

According to C. P. Snow, there is a disparity between scientific culture, which emphasizes objectivity, and humanistic culture, which is more subjective.

Research has not identified consistent replicable features of human teaching.[4]

We won't enumerate all of what we now know about teaching. That will have to wait for later chapters in this volume. We can say, though, that the current state of the art indicates a solid basis for both theory and practice.

Why Theory? Why Practice?

Let's look at another aspect of the two-culture question. In most cases science reserves the most important place for theory, while the profession takes the opposite position—that practice is the overriding concern. The purpose of theory, as any elementary text points out, is to provide a set of abstract, logically coherent explanations. Theory provides reasons and principles and is therefore descriptive. Practice provides a series of concrete behaviors—activities to do—and is therefore prescriptive. The question, then, is whether we really need both. Well, let's imagine for a moment that we don't. Then the following scenario might unfold: A new theory has been proposed. Preliminary evidence

shows that tall people may have a different learning style than short people. "So what?" you ask. "The new theory doesn't tell me anything about what I should do differently. I'm left with a general idea but no details. At best, all I can do is to speculate. Also, I just heard that another researcher claims that the only difference between tall and short people is in height, not learning style." So there you have it. The theory enables us perhaps to know something new about humans, yet the knowledge remains abstract.

Now, let's look at it the other way around. You are listening to some professionals. One says, "I decided to try something different in my class. I heard somewhere that another teacher had good luck in using the discovery method of teaching." That's it. By word of mouth, a promising practice is suggested. You have some specific details as to how to set up the room, ask open-ended questions, and use maps without cities designated. In fact, the suggestions for practice are very clear and very detailed. It is just the opposite of theory. As an educator you may instinctively feel that the second approach is clearly superior. You have the directions but you don't have any explanation. You don't know why the method works. The danger is that all teachers will use the same method on all students. Without theory, you have no way of knowing when to use it and when *not* to use it. The practical advice doesn't allow systematic prediction of the outcome.

The debate between theory and practice has a long history. Educational professionals and humanists often like to decry ''cold'' theory. Goethe, a great German dramatist, put the case clearly and emotionally: ''Theory is all grey and the golden tree of life is green.''[5] Sartre, a famous French philosopher, criticized scientists in this way: They build ''great theoretical cathedrals, but actually live in a small out-house next door.'' Theory without practice, then, can be abstract speculation. Practice without guiding theory, on the other hand, may be random—or even worse, frenzied—activity without point or consequence. One commentator remarked that practice by itself quickly becomes a fad wandering around, somewhere between the cosmic and the trivial, without knowing which is which.[6] We have scientific reasoning divorced from reality, or folklore separated from logic. Basic research can become sanctimonious aimlessness. Practice can become just aimlessness. Clearly, we need both even though each tradition works against an overall integration.

One Theory or Many?

Still another related question, if you are convinced of the need for both theory and practice, is which theory should be selected as a basis for informed practice. As any study of psychology quickly shows, there are many contending theories. How can you know which is best? Where is the supertheory for educational practice? Naturally, there is no easy answer. Many dedicated psychologists have literally given their entire lives to the search. Promising theories emerge but then do not stand up and so are replaced. The scientific community attempts to evaluate theory on the basis of two principles, parsimony and reductionism. Sometimes this is as difficult as serving two masters.

The first term means just what you think; *parsimony* equals stinginess. Like a person who spends money very carefully, theory should be succinct and compact. A parsimonious person doesn't throw money around needlessly. A theory should not be more elaborate or more abstract than it needs to be to explain the facts. To give an example, one of the current and largely justified criticisms of Freud's classical psychoanalytic theory is that it is based on a long series of assumptions that could not be tested out—assumptions such as unconscious motivation, the suppression of libido drives, castration anxiety, penis envy, the Oedipal complex, homosexuality and paranoia, the Electra complex, and others. A theory is not parsimonious if we have to accept, on faith, such numerous suppositions. The theory becomes more a set of beliefs or an ideology than a scientific basis for prediction. In order to make the theory fit, we are forced to add a number of qualifications. The theory becomes interesting in a sense yet ends as pure speculation.

A medieval philosopher, William of Occam, revolted against the wild theorizing of his day. You may have heard about a religious controversy concerning how many angels could dance on the head of a pin. Highly speculative and elaborate theories evolved to resolve this controversy in Occam's time. He wrote a scathing statement pointing out the need for parsimony. His work shook the scholastic world so severely that his thesis became known as Occam's razor, the tool to cut away needless elaboration and qualifications. Ideas had to be clear, concise, and to the point. Many a pseudotheory was slashed by Occam's razor.[7]

This is not the whole story. Other theorists, heeding (or fearing) Occam's razor, decided to go in a completely different direction from the wooly-headed theorists of Occam's day by paring theory to its bare bones. They eliminated as many assumptions, qualifications, and suppositions as possible. In psychological theory the best example was early behaviorism. All known human characteristics such as learning styles, temperament, feelings, stages of cognition, and so on were eliminated. In fact, everything in psychological theory was cut away except one principle, the law of effect. In its attempt to protect against meaningless elaboration, the drive to parsimony sometimes goes too far. In such an instance parsimony is called ''reductionism.'' In seeking to streamline theoretical thought, too many ideas are dismissed. This is sometimes called "tossing out the baby with the bath water."

Effective theory can be judged somewhere at a midpoint of an unusual continuum. The English scholar William of Occam sits in the middle, honing his razor, angels dancing on the head of a pin at one end, a baby in a tub of dirty water at the other waiting to be tossed. Naturally, as a new student to educational psychology you cannot realistically be expected to evaluate theories accurately on this continuum. However, you should realize that our current elaboration of theories for education does reflect our best estimates of the midpoint. The developmental approach provides a theory describing how students grow and change through a series of stages. This model for educational psychology does incorporate many of the best features of prior theories; in addition, it can and does change as new information is tested and found valid. We explain such a process in the succeeding chapters. The theories we will be examining have direct relevance to practice. You will find contributions from many theories joined together in the developmental framework. You will also find aspects of prior theories eliminated, ideas that were either too speculative or too narrow.

One final point of theory: Do not expect a theory to tie together all loose ends. Our theories represent our best current understanding, not the final solution. Human behavior is not a closed but an open system. As we learn more and test more ideas, our understanding changes. Theory is dynamic. In the process of moving forward, it leads to successive approximations as our knowledge of human development slowly evolves. It can never be complete because of the nature of human beings. There is always a lack of total understanding and of closure. However, each new generation of educational psychologists does stand on the shoulders (not the face) of previous generations. You will become accustomed to the idea that while certain actions or activities represent our best current understanding, they do not come with an absolute guarantee. We act on the basis of informed judgment. In the words of Harvard psychologist Gordon Allport, we are "whole-hearted but half-sure."

EDUCATIONAL PSYCHOLOGY: FOUR PROBLEMS TO SOLVE SIMULTANEOUSLY

One cause of difficulty in understanding educational psychology is the hybrid nature of science and education. Both theoretical and practical concerns are intrinsic to the nature of each field. Now, to up the ante, we turn to the problems that educational psychology seeks to solve. What is the world on which we focus? The simple answer is the teaching-learning pro-

Wooly-headed Thinking   Parsimony   Reductionism

cess. That has a nice clear ring to it—it couldn't be simpler. Yet, the moment we examine the question more closely, we immediately confront four interrelated concerns: the students, the teacher, the classroom strategies, and the content to be taught. We can refer to this as the four-way agenda of teaching (see Table 1.1).

First we need to know what pupils are like. After all, we are not dealing with pieces of wood or rocks but with real live human beings. Each human is unique—and yet is like some other humans and like all other humans in some ways. This statement, you will find, is quite often made by both psychologists and educators. But when you listen carefully, you may find that they quickly ignore their own words. It is a concept honored only in the breach. In other words, while offering three different versions of human behavior—the idiographic, which focuses on the uniqueness of individuals; the nomothetic, which looks for characteristics that all humans share; and an idiographic-nomothetic middle ground—both educators and psychologists all too often settle on one version. But you need to know about individual differences, group similarities, and the combination. So one part of the agenda is the often-times

bewildering variety of information on the nature of students, your classroom learners.

A second part of the agenda shifts the focus from pupils to you as a teacher, your own attitudes and understandings about learning. What are the goals of your classroom? What do you expect from your pupils? What is your level of self-understanding as a person and as a professional? The unspoken views of how a teacher really feels about his or her role and the students are sometimes called the "hidden agenda" of the classroom. In fact, research has shown just how powerfully some of the unintentional behavior that results from this hidden agenda affects the pupils. So while you are learning about pupils in the classroom, they are most likely learning about you, "where you are coming from," as the saying goes.

A third related part of the agenda is represented by the explicit set of teaching strategies, the actual classroom behaviors, you employ. Some years ago during the so-called know-nothing period when researchers kept bemoaning how little we knew about teaching, the solution to which teaching methods to use was breathtakingly simple. Since the experts didn't know, you could "just do your own thing." Be

TABLE 1.1   THE FOUR-WAY AGENDA OF TEACHING

STUDENT CHARACTERISTICS	*TEACHERS*
1. Physical	1. Attitudes to learning
2. Physiological	2. Attitudes to students
3. Cognitive	3. Attitudes to self
4. Personal	4. Understanding research
5. Moral/Value	
6. Motivations	
7. Individual and group behavior	
8. Special needs	
9. Cultural and gender	

TEACHING STRATEGIES	*SUBJECT MATTER*
1. Learning theories in practice	1. Structure of the disciplines
2. Teaching methods and models	2. Basic concepts of material being taught
3. Individual methods	3. Sequencing of subject matter
4. Lesson planning	4. Priorities in content selected
5. Variations in structure	5. Degree of specialized content
6. Student discipline	
7. Questioning	
8. Use of tests	

spontaneous and creative was the dictum. As you might suspect, that is easier said than done. Flying by the seat of one's pants has always had an attractive, romantic aura about it. But in the classroom it often led to disaster. There are a series of very important specific teacher "moves" that must be learned. However, they cannot simply be applied much as you would follow a cooking recipe. Certain specific skills must be mastered before you can achieve true flexibility as a teacher.

The fourth part of the agenda is represented by the content of your teaching—that is, language arts, math, science, social studies, and so on. Undoubtedly, it's hard to teach history if you don't know the field. As a teacher, knowing the field also means knowing how to divide up the content and sequence it in accordance with learning priorities. Clearly content stands on a par with the other three parts of the agenda. All four are involved in the process of teaching.

In this book, you may be relieved to know, we are concentrating *only* on the first three parts: students, teachers, and strategies. That makes it just a three-ring circus, you may be thinking as you review the enormous amount of material in those areas. This text will help you with three parts of the teaching-learning process. They are not the entire story, nor do they encompass all there is to know about teaching. Although we will not delve into the subject-matter area, we do not see it as less important than the other three. There are four problems and they must be solved simultaneously. Such has not always been the case. We will now turn to the history of educational psychology to give you a taste of its somewhat checkered past.

Students, teachers, subject matter, and strategy constitute the four-way agenda of teaching.

EDUCATION YESTERDAY AND TODAY

Yesterday: Trivia in the Classroom

In the late nineteenth century, a visitor to the public schools concluded that most classroom activity consisted of a game of recitation. The pupils and the teacher followed a systematic question-and-answer exercise. The teacher would ask a series of short, factual questions

with the rapidity of a machine gunner: "Now class, pay attention. . . . Tell me, who discovered America? What year? How many ships were there? What were their names? How long was the voyage? Each question was followed by a brief pause, and then students with hands raised were called on, again with the speed of light, until one student said the correct answer. At this point the teacher would fire the next question and skip around the class calling on pupils with hands raised until the next right answer was called out. The observer in the nineteenth-century classroom noted that the interaction between teacher and pupil seemed excessively mechanical. The process seemed to emphasize rote learning, the repetition of facts memorized from the teacher and the textbook. Inquiry was unknown. "In several instances when a pupil stopped for a moment's reflection, the teacher remarked abruptly, "Don't stop to think, but tell me what you know.' "[8]

These impressions of what we might call trivia in the classroom were given further credence by other observers. An English educator in 1908 noted the "time-honoured" tradition in American classrooms of question-and-answer recitation, in distinct contrast to the lecture method used on the continent of Europe. A study of classroom interaction further substantiated question-and-answer as the predominant approach to teaching in this country. Using stenographic notes of actual classroom discussions (this was in the days before tape recorders), a researcher in 1912 found that over 80 percent of all classroom talk consisted of asking and answering brief factual questions—questions that called for a good rote memory and an ability to phrase the answer in the same terms the teacher used. The teacher asked between one and four questions per minute, much like today's TV quiz games where contestants (pupils) are given a few seconds to come up with the right answer; if they don't have the answer at the tip of their tongue, they lose their turn, and the quiz master (teacher) moves on. The researcher noted:

> The fact that one history teacher attempts to realize his educational aims through the process of "hearing" the textbook, day after day, is unfortunate but pardonable; that history, science, mathematics, foreign language and English teachers, collectively are following in the same groove, is a matter for theorists and practitioners to reckon with.[9]

William James, one of this country's first and perhaps greatest commentators on the problems of teaching and learning, provided the following example of the recitation quiz game in the classroom.

> A friend of mine, visiting a school, was asked to examine a young class in geography. Glancing at the book, she said, "Suppose you should dig a hole in the ground, hundreds of feet deep, how should you find it at the bottom—warmer or colder than on top?" None of the class replying, the teacher said: "I'm sure they know, but I think you don't ask the question quite rightly. Let me try." So, taking the book, she said: "In what condition is the interior of the globe?" and received the immediate answer from half the class at once: "The interior of the globe is in a condition of igneous fusion."[10]

Today: Still Trivia in the Classroom?

Fully one-half century after the above observations were made, educational researchers studying classroom interactions between teach-

One researcher at the turn of the century found that over 80 percent of classroom talk consisted of asking and answering brief, factual questions.

ers and pupils made the following comments: (1) The teachers tend to do about 70 percent of all talking in the classroom. (2) Most of this talk is in the form of asking questions. (3) Between 80 and 88 percent of all these questions call for rote memory responses. (4) The teachers typically ask two questions per minute. (5) Pupil talk is almost exclusively a short response to the teacher's question. (6) Inquiries and suggestions from pupils are virtually nonexistent.[11]

In another study of 156 randomly selected elementary-school classrooms, these same results reappeared from grades K to 6. The authors noted of their 1974 study:

> At all grade levels, the teacher-to-child pattern of interaction overwhelmingly prevailed. This was one of the most monotonously recurring pieces of data. The teacher asked questions and the children responded, usually in a few words and phrases. . . . It is fair to say that this teacher-to-child interaction was the mode in all but about 5 percent of the classes.[12]

You may be struck by the remarkable similarity in the results of these studies—after seventy-five years the same mode persists. The state of affairs raises two questions: Is question-and-answer trivia an effective educational method? If it isn't, then why does it persist?[13]

Perhaps the best way to begin understanding the effect of rapid-fire question-and-answer procedures would be to ask you to remember such a situation in your own experience. You are in the third grade, sitting in a class of thirty children. The teacher towers over you physically, a difference exaggerated when she stands in front of the seated class. The class has been studying a unit on the American Indian. After a series of questions on Indian lore and myths, which you know about but don't get called on for (she had scolded you sternly, saying that you were to remain seated when you raised your hand), the teacher suddenly wheels around and looks directly at you: "What did the Navaho call their houses?" In the confusion (for you are still thinking about a previous question), you don't have the answer. The class falls silent. Twenty-nine children turn toward you. The teacher waits a few seconds that seem like years and then says, "Well?" "Tepee?" you say, hoping

that it's right, but mostly wishing there was a place to hide. "Hogan," the teacher replies. "Hogan—oh, that's what I meant to say," you add in a near-whisper. The moment does pass as the girl two seats away from you expertly fields the next question about how a hogan is constructed. A few minutes later recess mercifully arrives, and you manage to sneak out as unobtrusively as possible. So much for the question-and-answer quiz and the promotion of learning.

A series of studies has shown, perhaps not as dramatically or as personally as the above incident, that the classroom trivia quiz does not promote learning unless we really think that the recitation of textbook facts is equivalent to learning. If we view the objectives of teaching and learning more broadly, then we can only conclude that a form of "Button, button, who has the button?" or "Hogan, hogan, what's a hogan?" does not help students learn except in a negative way. You do learn to play the game after a while; that is, you learn to say the right thing and to act out of reflex. You do remember the acceptable phrases and terms, whether they concern the kind of a house a Navaho lived in or the state of igneous fusion in the center of the earth. But is this the process of inquiry we consider desirable? Is this the goal of human thinking? Is this the excitement of seeing new relationships among ideas? Is this the process through which we learn about ourselves.

EMERGENCE OF A THEORETICAL FRAMEWORK

Fundamentally, the problem faced by education and psychology has been to create a framework that is broad enough to provide working solutions to the four-part agenda of concerns we mentioned earlier. William James, this country's first psychologist, was also the first to grapple directly with the problem. The scope and depth of his vision provided initial and brilliant insights. Unfortunately, the field did not follow his views until very recently. Because of his

WILLIAM JAMES

Born in 1842 in New York City, William James showed little evidence of academic brilliance during his school years. In fact, his early education was meandering and informal. He attended several private schools in this country and abroad. The only consistent educational experience he had was with his family at the dinner table. Conversation abounded there on every conceivable topic. All members had the opportunity to test their wits against the others. His multiple talents seemingly prevented him from settling on any one career. His brother, Henry James, became a famous novelist. William in the meantime studied art for a while in Newport, Rhode Island, then decided to drop art and attend Harvard College, specializing in chemistry. After two years he switched his field again, transferring to comparative anatomy and physiology. At this point James wrote to a friend that the problem of career choice was limited to four alternatives, "Natural History, Medicine, Printing, and Beggary." He chose medicine but found, once again, some lack of meaning and so interrupted his studies first to collect specimens up the Amazon River and later to spend time recuperating from illness by a trip to Europe. Finally he did complete his medical studies in 1869 and was awarded the only academic degree he ever earned, an M.D. A scholar commented that it "seems a strange one for a man who was to make his mark as a psychologist and philosopher." But the real education of William James was not received in universities and did not lead to degrees. It had been in his home with his family.

When offered a position as instructor at Harvard at the age of thirty, James jumped at the chance to drop the sheer drudgery of medicine. He moved from the practice of medicine into the classroom. For James this was an important step; for psychology it turned out to be momentous. He thrived on academic life, worked hard at the craft of college teaching, and very early displayed a talent for both research and teaching. Once again, however, his enormous and restless talent stretched beyond the conventional and past the then recognized academic disciplines. In 1876 he created and began teaching the first psychology course ever taught in this country. His originality and creativity burst forth, and he poured out lectures that increased in popularity. Essentially he was creating a field of study, shaping the content, and outlining the sequence of topics all simultaneously. He wrote a monumental two-volume basic text for these courses simply titled *Principles of Psychology*. These outlined the basic tenets of psychology, the general themes. He started the first psychological laboratory and anticipated the theory of conditioning later demonstrated by Pavlov, as well as the importance of critical stages of learning, the so-called field theory, and the principles of gestalt psychology. His original book can still provide a modern reader with a relatively up-to-date version of psychology, so substantial was his vision.

For educational psychology James became both an educator and a philosopher. He saw the importance of tailoring educational material to fit the learner's true condition, not the condition that the teacher assumed the learner should be in. His pride in his own teaching meant that he could model effective instruction as well as tell others how to do it, a talent that few academic scholars can manage even today. In this way James was devoted to the idea of improving all teaching. Education, then as now, tended to be classed as slightly less respectable than some other disciplines. James's independence of

mind and his ability to go beyond the conventional once again were in evidence. As a Harvard professor, renowned scholar, and originator of the field of psychology, he devoted much effort and energy to improve the quality of classroom education. His famous lectures, *Talks to Teachers*, are very briefly quoted in the text to give you some feel for his flair with concepts as well as the significance of his thinking. His major point was that the entire enterprise of education is determined by the actual classroom teacher.

In these days of national curriculum projects and technological prescriptions for the classroom, we need to recall the central Jamesian theme: "Psychology is a science—teaching is an art; and sciences never generate arts directly out of themselves. An intermediary inventive mind must make the application, by use of its originality." James was convinced that the future of education depended directly on the quality of the intermediary

inventive minds of the teachers. It was they who would do the job in the classroom and they who needed to apply psychological principles humanely. By understanding the nature of children and adolescents as behaving organisms, James was convinced teaching could be improved.

An educational theorist, Paul Woodring, probably summed up James's significance to education most succinctly. He noted that if James had been read carefully by teachers and teacher educators over the past fifty years, many of our educational difficulties might have been avoided.

James's long and productive life ended in 1910 after some thirty-five years of teaching. The world lost that rare combination of talents that is so infrequent: teacher, scholar, leader, and philosopher able to go well beyond current thinking. With all this he had a personality so vivid that his sister described him as "born afresh every morning."

importance we will describe his work in detail, and some of the reasons for the long eclipse of his thinking, and his current relevance. After that, we will look at the contributions of some other theorists—E. L. Thorndike, John Dewey, and Maxine Greene.

William James: The Early Promise

William James exerted tremendous early influence on the whole field of psychology and was probably this country's most significant educational psychologist. In the nineteenth century, psychology was considered part of philosophy, not a separate discipline. It was William James at Harvard in the 1890s who began to give systematic attention to psychology as a discipline

in its own right and, more importantly for us, began to consider most seriously the question of applying psychology to the problems of the real world rather than leaving it in the laboratory.

James was concerned that the so-called scientific tradition would capture psychology and turn it away from its important purpose of helping us understand more about the processes of teaching and learning. He delivered a series of famous lectures (*Talks to Teachers on Psychology*) that are as relevant today as when they were originally delivered. At that time, "scientific" experiments were thought to be able to give us all the answers, including all the laws that govern human behavior. James feared the dangers of such an exclusive dependence on science. He warned that laboratory scientists "would go off by themselves and use apparatus and consult sources in such a way as to grind out in the requisite number of months some little peppercorn of new truth worthy of being added to the store of extant information on the subject."[14] Such efforts might produce a mound of peppercorns but not necessarily truth.

James wisely saw that psychology had to look to the natural environment for much of its information. Laboratory studies, especially animal studies, might not be such a great help when it came to teaching children. He therefore launched the effort to examine and understand the process of teaching and learning in the classroom. He observed classrooms (remember his igneous fusion anecdote) and also suggested positive alternatives to the state of affairs he observed. For example, he pointed to the central importance of starting lessons at a point just beyond the pupils' present comprehension. The famous dictum "Start where the learner is and proceed" was derived from this insight of William James.

> If the teacher is to explain the distance of the sun from the earth, let him ask . . . "If anyone there in the sun fired off a cannon straight at you, what should you do?" "Get out of the way," would be the answer. "No need of that," the teacher might reply. "You may quietly go to sleep in your room, and get up again, you may wait until your confirmation-day, you may learn a trade, and grow as old as I am—then only will the cannon-ball be getting near, then you may jump to one side! See, so great as that is the sun's distance!"[15]

James's most important effort was to try to convince educators that the observations, thoughts, and questions they brought out of their work with pupils would be a significant source of "scientific" feedback. He was particularly concerned to retain the human mind, or as he called it, "mental life," as a proper object for psychology; in fact, he deliberately defined psychology as the "science of mental life." What goes on "inside" a person's head—thoughts, feelings, interests, values, sentiments—these were what James thought psychologists should study in order to shed light on human strivings and motivations.

James was the first to warn teachers and educators not to depend on psychology to provide all the answers and to warn psychology not to present itself as a mirror-image of physical science. He saw psychology as a natural science, filled with uncertainty, an "open system" of questions concerning that most complex of all "systems," the human being. That was the problem, but it was also the challenge.

The difficulties of James's view were many. For example, to say that teaching is a process that we can never fully understand is unsettling to those in search of the truth. To say that we will have to be content with a series of approximations of good ideas and practices rather than perfect ideas or perfect practices is likewise unsettling.

Obviously it was, and still is, extraordinarily difficult to consider educational problems in such a broad perspective. James wanted educational psychology to study teaching and learning in the classroom in order to view educational problems in their real, or natural, environment. James wanted to focus on both the objective and the subjective nature of educational problems. For example, when he spoke of teaching methods, he discussed the teacher and his or her objectives on the one hand, and the pupils and their objectives on the other hand. He compared teaching to warfare:

> In war, all you have to do is to work your enemy into a position in which the natural obstacles prevent him from escaping if he tries to; then to fall on him in numbers superior to his own. . . . Just so in teaching, you must simply work your pupil into such a state of interest—with every other object of attention banished from his mind; then reveal it to him so impressively that he will remember it to his dying day; and finally fill him with devouring curiosity to know what the next steps are.[16]

So, from the teacher's perspective nothing could be plainer or simpler. The science of general pedagogics couldn't be clearer. Then James mentioned the other side of the classroom equation, schooling from the pupil's point of view. He reminded teachers:

> The mind of your own enemy, the pupil, is working away from you as keenly and eagerly as is the mind of the commander on the other side from the scientific general. Just what the respective enemies want and think and what

they know and do not know are as hard things for the teacher as for the general to find out.[17]

This clash, between what the teacher wants and what the pupils want, clearly is a difficult problem for science. In an attempt to develop answers, educational psychology moved into an era of laboratory investigations. That emphasis, however, has been something of a mixed blessing.

In rejecting James's views as too unwieldy, educational psychology headed in a logical direction. It seemed sensible when confronted with complexity to narrow the focus, to examine the effect of one variable at a time. And to add strength to this tendency, there was, at the time, an almost passionate desire for psychology to pattern itself after the physical sciences and to search for the "molecules" of human behavior. This meant that the emphasis shifted away from naturalistic studies of pupil and teacher behaviors in classrooms. There were too many uncontrolled variables operating in such settings; the open system of a classroom was not a scientifically researchable problem. The desire for precision in measurement and research design forced educational psychology into the laboratory. The era produced many useful pieces of information, especially about some aspects of learning. On balance, however, the focus was too narrow. Too much was left untouched. The classroom, as we noted at the beginning of this chapter, remained tragically similar to its early twentieth-century antecedent. To understand the impact of the new focus and its limitations, we will turn to the researcher whose name became synonymous with educational psychology, Edward L. Thorndike.

E. L. Thorndike: Scientific Education

The person most responsible for channeling education toward an emphasis on measurement was E. L. Thorndike, a famous professor at Teachers College of Columbia University. Thorndike sought to eliminate speculation, opinion, and naturalistic investigation. In fact, he considered visiting a classroom an extraordinary waste of time. It was much more "scientific" to understand the learning process by experimenting on cats in a laboratory than by observing children in a classroom. And experi-

ment he did. Thorndike studied the behavior of his famous cats in specially designed puzzle boxes. He was interested in discovering how long it took the cats to solve the puzzles (which usually involved getting out of the box) and in learning what rewards were the most effective in achieving the objective. (Will a hungry cat learn faster than a "fat" cat—or, in more scientific language, "an organism deprived of nutrition for forty-eight hours"—if food is the reward?) This procedure led to an almost endless number of empirical studies documenting how many trial-and-error sequences took place before the cat finally "learned" to stick a paw through the grating, lift up the latch to open the cage, and then stroll triumphantly over to the food.[18] As you can see, Thorndike was focusing on one aspect of learning—that which takes place by trial and error. By putting a cat through this sequence often enough, a bond would be formed, a stimulus-response connection in the nervous system, so that the cat would "remember" what to do.

It has been said that Thorndike was so influential that all subsequent research in education was merely a footnote to his work. His critics noted humorously of his influence that if one of Thorndike's cats behaved unpredictably, it would affect the curriculum for an entire nation.

On the positive side it should be stressed that Thorndike was an important influence because he exploded many of the educational myths of the day. The classical curriculum of the secondary school (four years of Greek, four years of Latin, and so on) had been justified on the grounds that such exercise would "train" the mind: Spending time and effort on Latin, for example, made it easier to learn French, while Greek would improve English usage. Using precise measurement procedures, Thorndike was able to show that little, if any, disciplining of the mind could be transferred from one subject to the other. In an almost singular way, he could proclaim, "If you want to improve your English, study English, not Latin or Greek." Thorndike believed that transfer occurred only when elements in a situation were identical or at least similar to elements in a second situation. Many a subsequent generation had Thorndike and his empirical research to thank for disposing of the mythical justification for the study of Latin and Greek. So Thorndike's contribution cannot be

EDWARD L. THORNDIKE

Born in 1874 as the son of a Protestant minister and brought up in the mill towns of Massachusetts, E. L. Thorndike completed his undergraduate studies in classics at Wesleyan University. A somewhat singular and solitary person, he demonstrated early in his life a capacity for hard work, long hours, and precision. Almost a personification of the Protestant work ethic, Thorndike simply abhorred making even the slightest error and consequently was always striving for perfection in his work. He had enormous amounts of mental energy and virtually threw himself into the task of defining a scientific base for psychology.

At Columbia University's Teachers College he completed his doctorate in the department of philosophy, psychology, anthropology, and education in the late 1890s. At that time departmental specialization was not yet established. The field of educational psychology was amorphous and resisted a generic definition. Academic psychology and the so-called brass-instrument laboratories and physical measurements represented one stance. At the other end William James at Harvard was lecturing on the art of teaching, separate from the science of psychology. In between there was a range of philosophers, educators, and psychologists all attempting to give definition and coherence to the field. This was educational psychology's moment of a "cultural revolution." A hundred flowers were blooming when the youthful but dedicated E. L. Thorndike appeared on the scene. Apparently he was not at all intimidated by the first-generation psychologists and educators. As a brand new assistant professor at Teachers College in 1898, he took pleasure in attacking his elders. He

referred to this period as his early assertive years. "It is fun to write all the stuff up and smite all the hoary scientists hip and thigh. . . . My thesis is a beauty. . . . I've got some theories which knock the old authorities into a grease spot." For such a fledgling, still in his twenties, to have the inner strength to attack the heroes of the day both in print and in association meetings was most unusual. Possibly within himself Thorndike transformed the Protestant ethic into a messianic vision not of religion but of scientific logical positivism. In other words, the dedication that a person might feel toward a religious mission was

apparently shifted so that science became his religion.

For the entire forty-one years of his professional life, Thorndike remained at Columbia Teachers College. He defined educational psychology as essentially the psychology of laboratory experimentation. His life work was to create a base of scientific knowledge through careful experiments, changing one variable at a time and using precise measures. He insisted that the operational definition was the only definition for science. If you couldn't see, measure, and directly record the phenomenon under investigation, then it was not scientific or even worthwhile. Look, see, and collect data were his words of advice for investigators. In fact, he really viewed himself more as an investigator than a scholar. He once noted that he had probably spent over 10,000 hours in reading and studying scientific books and journals, but he devoted even more time to his own experiments and writing. His bibliography runs to a prodigious 500 items. Science, he would say, was to be built by research, not proclamation.

When Thorndike finished his classic work on measurement for educational psychology, he sent a copy to William James. The amusing dialogue that resulted went as follows:

Thorndike, to James with academic modesty: "I am sending you a dreadful book which I have written which is in no end scientific but devoid of any spark of human interest."

James's reply: "I opened your new book with full feelings of awe and admiration for your unexampled energy. It was just the thing I had hoped for when I was teaching psychology. . . . I am glad I have graduated from the necessity of using that kind of thing any longer. I shall stick to 'qualitative' work as more congruous with old age!"[a]

His work, as we have noted in the text, became almost an endless series of studies on trial-and-error learning. His famous cats in the puzzle-box represented his observable data. He persuaded his university to create a psychological laboratory for him and there he remained, building the wall of scientific knowledge brick by brick. Thorndike reached the pinnacle of his career in 1934, when he was elected president of the American Association for the Advancement of Science. No psychologist had ever been so honored. In fact, only one social scientist had ever been elected to head the professional organization that represented the entire scientific community.

For Thorndike, then, this was truly the moment of glory. The years of hard work, the struggle to create a scientifically respectable basis for educational psychology, had at last achieved the ultimate recognition. His biographer Geraldine Jonçich has noted that an editorial in the *New York Times* in January 1934 pleased him above all else when it said of him, "But first and last, he is a scientist."

[a] Jonçich, G. (1968). E. L. Thorndike: The psychologist as a professional man of science. *American Psychologist*, 23(6), 444.

dismissed. However, his importance and influence were so great that educational psychology became almost preoccupied by trial-and-error learning and measurement techniques. All other ideas, perspectives, and theories were practically abandoned. The field grew more narrowly scientific, objective, and empirical. We began to be able to measure educational problems more effectively, but the problems we were measuring were increasingly less significant. In a word, we developed more precise ways of measuring increasingly insignificant educational problems. The range of what we could know was limited to what we could measure.

The single most significant effect of this emphasis on empirical measurement was that it was more suited to showing what was wrong than what was right. This is not to say that educational psychology does not need rigorous measurement procedures and evaluation systems, but it cannot progress as a field if that is its only focus. The movement was more and more to the laboratory, for more and more replications and refinements of essentially the same studies. When William James warned of grinding out peppercorns, he was predicting the direction the field actually took. Literally thousands of studies have been produced that have had little influence on learning and the practice of teaching. In the careful words of a contemporary educational theorist, "The fruits of this scholarship must appear quite disappointing."[19] Instead of a narrow focus, educational psychology needs to broaden its view to include again studies in the natural environment.

John Dewey and Human Interaction

One of this country's most important theorists, John Dewey, always used the phrase "some organism in some environment."[20] This was his way of emphasizing that you could not study learning in the abstract and ignore the broader context—the environment in which that learning took place. Here is one of his sardonic comments on traditional education:

JOHN DEWEY

Without question one of this country's major educational theorists, John Dewey has had a long and significant influence on the actual practice of education. Born in 1859, his life spanned almost a century, from the Civil War to 1952. Certainly this period was one of the most eventful for the country as a whole. The United States emerged from a predominantly rural and isolationist era to one in which we were the major industrialized power of the world. The education of American pupils went through a transformation that was almost parallel to these world-shaking changes, in large part because of John Dewey's ideas and his practice.

In some ways Dewey was a true product of nineteenth-century America. Naturally intelligent and serious about his educational mission, he wanted most of all to develop an educational philosophy that could be put into practice. The concepts had to be tested in the real world of schools and in the classrooms. Many philosophers were content to theorize about education and write learned essays. For Dewey, this was not enough. If the ideas were not translated and tested, then the practice of education would forever remain random or at a craft level. An American pragmatist, he had little patience with glossy educational rhetoric. He clearly was a doer.

Born in the heartland of New England, his early years as a Vermont Yankee fostered in him a great respect for natural growth and the critical relationship between person and environment. These themes recur throughout his educational writings. After graduating from the University of Vermont at the age of twenty, he completed his Ph.D. at Johns Hopkins some five years later.

His first professorship was at the University of Minnesota, followed quickly by moves to the University of Michigan and then on to the University of Chicago in 1894. He served as chairman of the department of philosophy and pedagogy. It was at Chicago that he established the first major educational laboratory school in the country. Here at last he had the natural learning environment he needed to test and revise his unique educational ideas. At that time the country's educators were convinced that children were to sit quietly in a classroom and learn by rote a classical curriculum. Instead of strengthening the mind, of course, such a learning environment placed the students in an exceptionally passive role. Anticipating the ideas of Piaget and the open classroom, Dewey developed learning environments which ensured that children would actively engage in learning. His dictum of learning through doing became famous. Experience should precede or at least be concurrent with educational concepts and ideas. This was a revolutionary stance to the educators of the day, because it turned the educational process inside out. An experience-based curriculum to promote both more effective learning and greater competence in living was his objective.

By this time in his career he was easily the most widely known educator of his day. It came as no surprise, then, for Dewey to move in 1904 to the center of educational thought on this continent, the famous Teachers College at Columbia University. He remained there until his formal retirement, twenty-six years later. He produced a multitude of books and lectured throughout the land. An innovator, he was one of those very rare educators who lived to see his ideas put into practice and become an educational doctrine.

Unfortunately, however, his most significant idea was also the most easily misunderstood. His concept of child-centered education was distorted in many instances into a laissez-faire curriculum, and in the late forties and early fifties it became quite fashionable to criticize Dewey as soft-headed. Fortunately for the country's children, this misunderstanding has now been cleared up. Learning by doing finds expression in today's schools in a multitude of ways. Learning laboratories and centers, workshops, lesson units, and school programs devoted to all aspects of human growth are reflections of his views in action. Perhaps Dewey's most important idea, or indeed vision, was the democratic ideal that always remained his goal. By developing significant education for all children, the American dream of free people in a free country might be realized. In his ninety-third year John Dewey died, the vision intact and the country closer to the goal.

The entire range of the universe is first subdivided into sections called studies; then each one of these studies is broken up into bits, and some one bit assigned to a certain year of the course. No order of development is recognized—it is enough that the earlier parts were made easier than the later. To use the pertinent illustration of Mr. W. S. Jackman in stating the absurdity of this sort of curriculum: "It must seem to geography teachers that Heaven smiled on them when it ordained but four or five continents, because starting in far enough along the course it was so easy, that it really seemed natural, to give one continent to each grade and then come out right in the eight years."[21]

Unfortunately, Dewey's important ideas were misinterpreted. He was thought to be advocating the so-called child-centered curriculum rather than the significant ecological concept of person-in-environment. Cafeteria-style education—in which a child was free to choose anything, even to play all day if he or she wanted—was supposedly the result of Dewey's work.

However, these "progressive" views on education clearly missed Dewey's point. What he advocated was careful, guided experience for children, arranged according to their interests and capacities. The importance of these concepts for educational psychology should not be missed.

The central idea of Dewey's work was that the child was not an empty vessel waiting patiently and quietly to be filled up with knowledge. In fact, Dewey's best writing took these traditional assumptions of education to task. For example, he tells of visiting a manufacturer of school furniture one day and having a difficult time finding what he wanted for his school. One dealer, apparently more intelligent than the rest, commented, "I am afraid we have not what you want. You want something at which the children may work; these are all for listening."[22]

In addition to the concept of active learning, Dewey also stressed the idea of stages of growth and development. In this he foreshadowed the now classic work of Jean Piaget. Dewey noted that the child was often assumed to be a small

Dewey developed learning environments that ensured children would actively engage in learning. His famous dictum of "learning by doing" became a byword.

version of an adult. "The boy was a little man and his mind was a little mind—in everything but size the same as that of the adult. . . . Now we believe in the mind as a growing affair, and hence as essentially changing, presenting distinctive phases of capacity and interest at different periods."[23]

Finally, Dewey's most significant assertion was that teaching and learning interacted, that the pupil was as much a part of the learning environment as the teacher. He constantly battled against what he saw as the artificial separation between learning and the pupil.

Dewey's central view, then, was to promote a balance between experiential learning and careful rational examination. He did not want pupils simply to experience in a vacuum. Supposedly, a teacher, in seeking employment at Dewey's laboratory school, said that he had ten years of teaching experience. Dewey quickly retorted, "Was it really ten years or was it one year ten times!" In other words, what had the person learned from the experience? How much reflection, examination, and analysis of the experience had occurred? Thus, learning through experience includes what is commonly called "intellectual analysis." Dewey viewed this process as a means of promoting cognitive thought structures. In this area he essentially anticipated a second Piagetian concept of cognitive structure, or schema, as the framework for understanding how children come to know and think. The classroom should be a natural environment in which living and learning occur together. In this way Dewey pioneered today's emphasis on education as an interactive process.

Maxine Greene: The Teacher as Stranger

Perhaps the best way to close such a far-ranging chapter is to focus on the individual teacher. Maxine Greene, one of this country's leading educational philosophers conceptualizes the role of teacher with a strikingly vivid metaphor, "the teacher as stranger." That concept may be somewhat unsettling at first sight. Teaching is intensely personal. How is it possible to think of a teacher as separated from students, as an alien or foreigner in a land of pupils? Greene would be the first to agree that teaching is an interpersonal process. It must involve heart and soul as well as the mind. Teaching is not divisible. Yet, the teacher cannot be one of the pupils. Instead, there is always a gulf, a separation. As a teacher you are the leader, the responsible adult. Our society grants a teacher special status. In fact, the pupils are not given the freedom of choice to attend school. Thus, there is fundamental asymmetry. Your purpose is clear—namely, to promote their growth. Their role is not to promote yours, even though it not only may but does occur. That is not, however, the primary agenda.

For the teacher the agenda is the pupils. Your role with the students is more that of a mentor than a colleague. You are constantly alert to individual differences, to signs of growth, to indicators of student interest, curiosity, or their need to know. This means you are with them, but part of you is separate. You can step back and review the process, ask yourself new questions, such as "What strategy should I try with Carolyn?" "What's the best way to reach Douglas?" "How can I help Jane gain confidence as a learner?" Somewhat ironically, your increasing reflective ability is the key element in becoming Maxine Greene's "stranger." By reflecting, you increase the depth of your understanding of teaching and children. Rather than simplifying, you come to appreciate your deepening wisdom. In the broadest sense Greene's teacher becomes a philosopher, but in a special sense. We usually think of a philosopher as someone almost hopelessly lost in abstractions. That's not Greene's definition. She sees the crux of teaching in the actual art of doing philosophy. The teacher is not a mechanic but a seeker of truth. Learning philosophy by doing teaching is her way of connecting art and science. As you grow in effectiveness through such a process, you will then experience what she means by stranger, a person who, by being somewhat removed from the others, has a clearer vision of the goals and the ability to stay on course. Greene puts the case more elegantly through metaphorical language. Read these lines and see what images you experience. First, think of the times when you as a student truly experienced deeper teaching with a particular

MAXINE GREENE

After completing her undergraduate program at Barnard College in 1938, with a liberal arts degree and a Phi Beta Kappa key, Maxine Greene began to follow what was then a traditional path: marriage, children, and a role as a suburban homemaker. However, in the late 1940s she made a mistake that changed the course of her life. She began graduate work at New York University in English, also a traditional area of study for females. The mistake was to take some work in philosophy with George E. Axtelle, whom she later described as a truly memorable teacher. It was the perfect match of person and ideas, and it provided a focus for the career she was to follow.

Combining philosophy with her intellectual interest in literary analysis from English, she soon saw philosophy as the master discipline. These two elements were the necessary foundations, but not the whole story. In addition, she had two other enduring interests, art and action. It was probably her interest in art as an aesthetic experience that provided the bridge between ideas and action. The result has been the careful development of a framework for educational philosophy that seeks to set forth a series of principles and actions, ideas and experiences, thoughts and feelings. In fact, the major goal of her publication record, which is quite vast, is to synthesize thought and action as a basis for a living philosophy.

Such was, of course, not the tradition of the so-called analytic school of philosophy. In that view, the goal of philosophy is analysis, in depth and logical—the philosopher as critic. The difficulty with such a conception as a goal for philosophy is that it can too quickly lead to criticism for criticism's sake and, indeed, render the obvious, obscure. In breaking through the traditional career roles for women, Greene has also broken through the traditional framework for educational philosophy. She approaches philosophical goals quite differently and with a refreshing vigor. Rather than delve into levels of increasingly arcane meta-analyses, she always holds up ideas and goals to the real world of practice and action. There is a vivid existential quality to her work, and it is not the negative existentialism of the "life is absurd" school of thought. Instead, she produces a positive existentialism in her continued insistence on philosophy as thought in action.

Her work began to enter the educational paradigm slowly at first. Analytic philosophy was, after all, the main school of thought, and it was not about to disappear overnight. But Greene's voluminous writings coupled with her frequent, powerful conference presentations and keynote addresses gradually created a major place for her ideas as a philosophy for education and educational psychology. In 1975 she was appointed to the endowed William F. Russell Professorship at Teachers College of Columbia University. A long series of honors and elections soon followed: Educator of the Year by Phi Delta Kappa, Best Educational Book of the Year from Kappa Delta Gamma, president of the American Educational Research Association, chairperson of the John Dewey Society, president of the Philosophy of Education Society, and election to the National Academy of Education.

For education the Greene philosophy becomes a set of guides to living the "good life" as a manager of child growth and development. As noted in the text, her idea of the teacher as stranger sets the role tasks clearly in the growth context. To act and reflect in the real world according to democratic ethical guides represent to her the means of living philosophy, of teaching as "doing philosophy." She sees the educator's role as not simply to teach subject matter or skills or to maintain discipline. Those are only intermediate objects. Instead, the framework suggests a far greater purpose, even though the purpose itself may be a paradox. As she says, "How can one act on one's commitment and at once set others free to be?" Her own career stands as the best answer.

adult. Second, imagine yourself in the role of teacher surrounded by pupils, your charges:

> If the teacher is able to think and do while being vitally present as a person, then others may be aroused to act on their own freedom. Learning to learn, some of those persons may move beyond the sheltered places until they stand by their own choice in the high wind of thought.

She concludes, employing the metaphor of children as growing trees:

> The teacher, too, must raise shadowy trees and let them ripen. Stranger and homecomer, questioner and goad to others, the teacher can become visible to one's own self by doing philosophy. There are countless lives to be changed, worlds to be remade.[24]

THE ART AND SCIENCE OF TEACHING

We have clearly pointed out the complexities of managing the four-way agenda of the teaching-learning process. We have also pointed out how, until recently, the science of educational psychology and the profession of education were more like ships passing in the night than interacting disciplines. We have shown how the scientific basis for psychology led to the laboratory and the professional basis for education led to the classroom. The traditions of both promoted separation. Then we noted the reasons for optimism, primarily a growing cumulative basis for theory and practice that forms the content of this book. In the end, of course, whether any of this makes a difference will depend on you, the teacher. For teaching as practice is fundamentally an art as is any human services profession such as law, medicine, or business management. In each case there are established scientific principles, or as one leading educational psychologist puts it, "the scientific basis for the art of teaching."[25] This means what it says. Art represents the skill, the art of putting it together in the real world of the classroom. Your own professional identity becomes the agenda for educational psychology.

By now you realize that our goal is to bridge the discipline of psychology and the practice of professional education. The solution is almost paradoxical: a theoretical practitioner, a practical theorist. To be successful in teaching requires both. There is the need for you to interact in the moment with students. There is also the need to reflect, to inquire, and to critique your own efforts. One of the unique characteristics of teaching as a career is that you rarely practice in the company of other adults. The isolation goes with the territory. Supervision, collegiality, and the analysis of teaching with other adults are highly unlikely. This only increases the need to develop a reflective capacity and a doing capacity. You cannot afford either as an exclusive mode. Acting and reflecting represent the key processes for professional growth, indeed a kind of Rosetta stone for teacher effectiveness. So the struggle you embark on is highly significant and difficult, filled with frustration, apparent contradictions, and at times overwhelming complexity. The two goals of becoming both artist and scientist can be achieved, however.

SUMMARY

In introducing you to the field of educational psychology, this chapter has presented a series of major issues with which the field has struggled. As Snow noted in the metaphor of two separate cultures, the scientific and professional traditions more often than not go their own way. The field of educational psychology attempts to bridge those traditions.

Both theory and practice are needed: Without theory, practice is aimless; without practice, theory is abstract speculation. Theory is nothing more than successive approximations that gradually increase our understanding. In arriving at theory, we must steer clear of the twin fallacies of wooly-headed thinking and reductionism. William of Occam expressed the ideal as one of parsimony: A theory should be neither more elaborate nor more abstract than it needs to be to explain the facts.

The teaching-learning process is a four-way

agenda. That is, its four main concerns are pupils, teachers, teaching strategies, and subject matter. These elements must be considered together to account for the complexity of the enterprise.

Educational psychology has not gained a foothold in the classroom until relatively recently. In the early part of the century, William James and others noted the presence of trivia in the classroom. To a certain extent, this emphasis on learning facts continues today. But there is a growing consensus on the need for theory and practice for effective teaching and learning. Thanks to the pioneering efforts of James, Thorndike, and Dewey, teachers now have a firm theoretical foundation on which to base their practice. The essence of good teaching, though, seems to be captured in Maxine Greene's metaphor of "the teacher as stranger"—the one who by reflective distancing learns to see the true needs of each student. That metaphor requires the teacher to become both scientist and artist.

KEY TERMS AND NAMES

theory practice
C. P. Snow
William of Occam
four-way agenda of teaching
trivia in the classroom

William James
E. L. Thorndike
John Dewey
Maxine Greene

REFERENCES

1. Quote from Ralph Mosher, Professor of Counseling Psychology and Education, Boston University. Personal note.

2. Snow, C. P. (1963). *The two cultures: And a second look.* New York: Mentor.

3. See Phillips, D. K. (1983). After the wake: Post-positivistic educational thought. *Educational Research, 12*(5), 4–14. Also Eisner, E. W. (1983). Anastasia might still be alive, but the monarchy is dead. *Educational Researcher, 12*(5), 23–25. These two scholars continued the debate. The scientist defended logical positivism as a major current force in education. The artist attacked it as a dead form of scholarship leading to meaningless laboratory research.

4. Quote 1: Sprinthall, N. A., Whiteley, J. M., and Mosher, R. L. (1971). A study of teacher effectiveness. In R. T. Hyman (Ed.), *Contemporary thoughts on teaching* (p. 279). Englewood Cliffs, N.J.: Prentice-Hall. Quotes 2 and 3: Doyle, W. (1978). Paradigms for research on teacher effectiveness. In L. Shulman (Ed.), *Review of research in teacher education,* Vol. 5 (pp. 69, 74). Etasca, Ill.: Peacock. Quote 4: Gage, N. L. (1978). *The scientific basis of the art of teaching* (p. 24). New York: Teachers College Press.

5. Goethe, as quoted in Liberman, A., and Miller, L. (1984). *Teachers, their world and their work* (p. iii). Alexandria, Va.: ASCD.

6. Quote from David Purpel, Professor of Curriculum and Instruction, University of North Carolina at Greensboro. Personal note.

7. See Sabine, G. (1937). *A history of political theory* (pp. 287–313). New York: Holt.

8. Rice, J. M. (1893). *The public school system of the United States* (p. 308). New York: Century.

9. Stevens, R. (1912). *The question as a measure of efficiency in instruction* (p. 66). Contributions to Education No. 48. New York: Columbia University.

10. James, W. (1958). *Talks to teachers on psychology* (p. 106). New York: Norton.

11. Bellack, A., Kliebard, H., Hyman, R., and Smith, F. (1966). *Language of the classroom.* New York: Teachers College Press.

12. Goodlad, J. I., and Klein, M. F. (1974). *Looking behind the classroom door* (p. 51). Worthington, Ohio: Jones.

13. Goodlad, J. (1984). *A place called school*. New York: McGraw-Hill. This recent national study of teacher-pupil interaction came to exactly the same conclusions on the persistence of rote recitation, especially at the secondary-school level.

14. James, *Talks to teachers* (p. 38).

15. James, W. (1968). *Psychology* (p. 333). New York: Macmillan.

16. James, *Talks to teachers* (p. 25).

17. James, *Talks to teachers* (p. 25).

18. Thorndike, E. L. (1932). *The fundamentals of learning*. New York: Teachers College Press. See also Thorndike, E. L. (1913). *Educational Psychology*, Vol. 2. New York: Teachers College Press. And Thorndike, E. L. (1898). Animal intelligence. *Psychological Review,* Monograph No. 2.

19. Shulman, L. S. (1970). Reconstruction of educational research. *Review of Educational Research, 40,* 378.

20. Dewey, J. (1938). *Logic: The theory of inquiry.* New York: Holt. See also Dewey, J. (1916). *Democracy and education.* New York: Macmillan.

21. Dewey, J. (1956). *The child and the curriculum: The school and society* (p. 103). Chicago: University of Chicago Press.

22. Dewey, *Child and curriculum* (p. 31).

23. Dewey, *Child and curriculum* (p. 102).

24. Greene, M. (1978). *The teacher as stranger* (p. 298). Belmont, Calif.: Wadsworth.

25. Gage, N. (1978). *The scientific basis for the art of teaching.* New York: Teachers College Press.

CHILD AND ADOLESCENT GROWTH

2

FUNDAMENTALS OF GROWTH AND DEVELOPMENT

Of all the species that inhabit the earth, the one whose growth and development is the slowest is *Homo sapiens*. The human being spends many long years in a state of physical immaturity, depending on the care and protection of others in order to survive. During the months the child is learning to walk and run with consistent steadiness, to communicate fears, joys, and needs, other species grow to full maturity. A two-year-old rhesus monkey has already attained sexual maturity, and a two-year-old rat may already be senile. "In the development of large muscles and the achievement of mobility, the typical child of two years is comparable to the chimpanzee of two months, the rabbit of two weeks, and the colt of two hours."[1]

Some years ago a study dramatically illustrated the difference in growth rates between species: A husband and wife psychologist team raised their infant son, Donald, along with a baby chimpanzee named Gua. Donald and Gua were treated as much alike as possible. They wore the same clothes, were fed the same food in the same way, and in general were given the same tender, loving care. They were also taught in the same way and given the same amount of practice in such things as standing, walking, eating with a spoon, and even toilet training.[2]

The whole situation must have been a competitive nightmare for poor little Donald, because Gua outstripped him at everything. When Donald was barely able to pull himself into an erect position, Gua was walking, running, and pirouetting around with the grace of a ballet dancer. When Donald still had difficulty even picking up a spoon, Gua was using the spoon to feed herself easily and with little spilling. When Donald was propped up and strapped to the seat of a swing, where he hung limply and loosely, Gua was performing like a trapeze artist on another swing.

The enormous difference in heredity and rate of maturation obviously allowed Gua to reach her genetic potential far sooner than Donald. Eventually, when Donald was nine months old (and the study was ended), he was beginning to catch up to Gua in certain areas, such as following verbal instructions, and to surpass Gua in others, such as speech development. But as for achieving physical mobility, Donald was still far behind.

In another attempt to find out whether environmental stimulation can compensate for heredity, another husband and wife team, with no children of their own, took a chimpanzee, Vicki, into their home and raised her as they would have raised a baby.[3] Above all else they wanted to see whether they could teach Vicki to talk. Despite their efforts, and despite the fact that Vicki did learn to respond to verbal commands, the attempt to teach her to speak ultimately proved to be futile. After three years Vicki could occasionally utter words like *cup, mama,* and *papa,* in an appropriate context, but that was as far as her language skills ever developed. In contrast, by three years of age the typical human infant has a vocabulary of almost 900 words.

In the early 1970s, an attempt was made to train a chimpanzee named Sarah in the use of symbolic communication.[4] Sarah obtained a vocabulary of about 120 symbols, the symbols being plastic shapes of various colors used to represent words. Although by chimpanzee standards Sarah's ability to communicate is fairly sophisticated, it is still a far cry from the language abilities demonstrated by even a two- to three-year-old human child. We have been warned to be extremely conservative in estimating Sarah's "human language ability."[5]

You may be wondering at this point why studies such as these were ever performed—they may seem as absurd as raising a human baby and an eagle together in a nest to see which one would be the first to fly. It may be obvious to you that different species mature at different rates and that chimpanzees achieve physical maturity more rapidly than humans. You may even wonder why anyone would bother trying to train chimps to talk, for if it were possible, it seems likely that someone, somewhere, would have observed chimps talking to one another.[6]

The best way to appreciate why these studies were conducted is to know something about psychology's brief but often stormy history. Our purpose is not to take you on a guided tour of dusty museum oddities but to give you a general historical background against which the present state of our knowledge will be more meaningful and, we hope, more appreciated.

THE NATURE-NURTURE CONTROVERSY

Of all the great debates in the history of psychology—and there have been many—the one that has generated the most heat and caused the greatest division in the field is the controversy over nature and nurture. More words have been written and more voices have been raised in anger over this issue than over any other.

The warring camps made their positions clear. The hereditarians, who favored nature, stridently claimed that all psychological traits were transmitted directly through the genes from generation to generation. Environment was of little consequence. If your father was a horse thief, you would be a horse thief, and if your mother's IQ was only 90, then you shouldn't make plans to go to medical school.

On the other side, the environmentalists as rigidly and shrilly claimed that a person's whole being was shaped by how and in what circumstances one was raised or "nurtured." Genetic endowment was a romantic myth, used to keep kings on their thrones, but of no use to science. The environmentalists held that all people were born genetically equal and that later differences among them were only a result of different environmental opportunities. Any baby could be molded into any kind of adult, provided the appropriate stimulus conditions were provided.

The Hereditarians Speak: Henry E. Goddard and the "Bad Seed"

In 1912, Henry Goddard published an account of the extremely damaging effects of an inferior genetic endowment, a "bad seed," on generation after generation of a family named Kallikak.[7] According to Goddard, who gleaned this material from books, newspapers, personal interviews, and other records, Martin Kallikak (a pseudonym chosen by Goddard to protect the family) was an American Revolutionary War soldier who was responsible for developing two completely different family strains. The "good" Kallikaks (and Goddard traced this strain through 496 descendants) resulted from Kalli-

Goddard's 1912 study of the two branches of the Kallikak family—the "good strain, resulting from Martin Kallikak's marriage to a worthy Quakeress," and the "bad" strain, resulting from an amorous adventure with a feeble-minded tavern girl—served to support the hereditarians' position.

kak's marriage to a "worthy Quakeress." She bore him "seven upright, worthy children," and from these seven children came "hundreds of the highest types of human beings"—doctors, lawyers, business leaders, and even college presidents. Only two of the nearly 500 "good" Kallikaks were of below-average intelligence.

Goddard also traced the descendants of an amorous adventure that Martin Kallikak had with a feeble-minded tavern girl. The result of this affair was an illegitimate son, later known to his friends and neighbors as "Old Horror." Fortunately for Goddard's story, even "Old Horror" apparently wasn't considered horrible by everyone, for he went on to father ten children of his own. Goddard identified 480 of these descendants, the "bad" Kallikaks, and found nothing but the lowest form of humanity—horse thieves, prostitutes, alcoholics, and so on. Also, of the bad Kallikaks, he found only forty-six who were of normal or near-normal intelligence. The rest, of course, were well below average.

Goddard wasted no time worrying about details, such as the dramatic environmental differences that existed between Kallikak's legitimate children and "Old Horror." The explanation was simple: The difference was hereditary.

Goddard's evidence, which was seriously cited in many psychology texts as late as the 1950s, is considered truly fantastic by modern geneticists. Even if intelligence were as directly and simply related to genotype as eye color (which it isn't), there would still have to be far greater numbers of intelligent members of the "bad" Kallikaks, and vice versa. After all, Martin Kallikak was himself half responsible for "Old Horror." But this was Goddard's point of view, and a cherished belief clouded scientific vision. Charles Davenport, one of America's leading geneticists at the time (1911), even went so far as to argue that human behavioral characteristics had straight Mendelian explanations—laziness being inherited through dominant genes and ambition through recessive genes, for example. Thus, according to Davenport, the genes we inherit from our parents account not only for how intelligent we are but also for how motivated we are.

The Environmentalists Speak: John B. Watson and "Give Me the Baby"

The strict environmentalists argued against the position of Goddard and the hereditarians. This group allied itself with philosopher John Locke (1691), who said that the mind was a blank slate upon which experience writes. As far as the environmentalist is concerned, the baby is nothing more than a lump of clay that can be molded and fashioned into any shape by the hands of that master artisan, the environment.

Perhaps the most eloquent advocate for the environmental position was the early behaviorist John B. Watson. It was Watson's belief that people are made, not born; that a baby can be shaped into any adult form—trapeze artist, musician, master criminal—through the judicious use of conditioning techniques. Watson began writing about the time (1913) that Pavlov's work in Russia on the conditioning of dogs was beginning to be recognized in the United States. Watson reasoned that if a dog could be conditioned, so too could a baby. In a now classic study, Watson and his colleague Rosalie Rayner tested this theory by conditioning a nine-month-old baby named Albert to fear a whole variety of objects (stimuli). This was done by presenting Albert with a certain conditioned stimulus (CS), a white rat, and then banging loudly with a hammer on a steel bar a few inches behind Albert's head. Watson assumed that the conditioned stimulus, the white rat, was originally neutral in its fear-inducing properties. Watson knew, however, that the unconditioned stimulus (UCS), the loud sound, would automatically produce a fear response in the baby. Because the CS was paired with the UCS, Albert formed an association between the two stimuli and reacted to the rat as he originally had responded to the loud sound. Albert had *learned* to associate the rat with the terrific din and, according to Watson, had thus learned to fear the rat. Later, Albert became afraid, through a process called stimulus generalization, of any stimulus which reminded him of the rat. By the time the study was completed, two months later, poor little Albert was intensely afraid of white rats, rabbits, dogs, fur coats, Santa Claus masks, cotton, wool, and anything else that remotely resembled animal fur. Watson also checked babies for other fear responses and found, for example, that if they were dropped they exhibited a fear response.

In order to "cure" Albert of these conditioned fears. Watson proposed, though never actually tried, presenting him with the fear-provoking object again, while "stimulating the erogenous zones (tactual). . . . We should try first the lips, then the nipples and as a final resort the sex organs."[8]

Not everyone has found Watson's evidence for emotional conditioning thoroughly convincing.

> It may be useful for modern learning theorists to see how the Albert study prompted subsequent research, but it seems time, finally, to place the Watson and Rayner data in the category of interesting but uninterpretable results.[9]

Recent evidence is also beginning to cast some doubt on Watson's assumption that Albert's conditioning had taken place in a mechanical fashion, or that any stimulus Albert was able to detect could be linked to any response Albert could make. As we shall see later, it may be that Albert was more biologically prepared, or genetically sensitized, to learn to fear a live rat rather than, say, a picture of a rat.[10]

Watson believed that he had come upon ultimate truth in psychology—that, no matter

© 1955 United Feature Syndicate, Inc.

what the genetic background, environmental stimulation in the form of conditioning could produce any behavior. Watson later said wryly:

> The Freudians twenty years from now, unless their hypotheses change, when they come to analyze Albert's fear of a seal skin coat . . . will probably tease from him the recital of a dream which upon their analysis will show that Albert at three years of age attempted to play with the pubic hair of the mother and was scolded violently for it.[11]

A few years later, Watson thundered his now famous words, ''Give me the baby,'' and this became the battle cry of environmentalists everywhere.

> Give me the baby and I'll make it climb and use its hands in construction of buildings of stone or wood. . . . I'll make it a thief, a gunman or a dope fiend. The possibilities of shaping it in any direction are almost endless. Even gross anatomical differences limit us far less than you may think. . . . Make him a deaf mute, and I will build you a Helen Keller. Men are built, not born.[12]

After reading about how Albert had been scared half to death by the sound of a steel bar being pounded behind his head and by being dropped, and how it was proposed to ''cure'' him by manipulating his genitals, the mothers of America did not line up to give Watson their babies.

Watson was striving to provide psychology with hard, scientific facts. His behaviorism was definitely not based on any humanistic view of human behavior or of society in general. Rather, he saw his mission as that of fact finder and cared little if his audience liked or disliked the facts. His approach was clinically aseptic and coldly detached.

Even today, behaviorists exhibit a similar disinterest. They often see their ultimate goal as far too cosmic to be constrained by any feelings of sympathy for a particular child. B. F. Skinner, today's leading exponent of behaviorism, was once criticized for having allegedly said that if given a choice he would rather burn his children than his books. Skinner's self-righteous answer was that he had not used the word *burn*.

> The word was *bury* . . . much as I admire my children and grandchildren and as dearly as I love them, I still believe that my contribution through my books will prove to be greater than that through my genes. How could a thoroughgoing environmentalist say otherwise?[13]

EDUCATIONAL PSYCHOLOGY: THE BATTLEGROUND

Nowhere were the lines between hereditarians and environmentalists more sharply drawn than in the field of educational psychology. The reason for this was that the measurement practitioners (those in the testing tradition) and the

JOHN BROADUS WATSON

American psychology's most vocal and possibly most influential environmentalist, John B. Watson was born near Greenville, South Carolina, in 1878. As a student in public school, the young John Watson was something less than spectacular. He later attributed his lack of early school success to his own "laziness," a rather subjective explanation from the man who demanded objectivity from everyone else. He later attended Furman University, where he studied such diverse topics as mathematics, Greek, Latin, philosophy, and chemistry. In 1900 he left Furman, having received a master's degree, and headed for the University of Chicago to study under the philosopher John Dewey. He soon found that Dewey was "incomprehensible" to him, and so he changed majors and began studying with James R. Angell, a psychologist, and H. H. Donaldson, a man of many talents: psychologist, biologist, and neurologist.

In 1903 Watson received the first Ph.D. degree in psychology ever conferred at the University of Chicago. For the next five years he taught psychology at the University of Chicago. During this period he taught straight Jamesian psychology in the classroom, but in the basement after class, he conducted numerous animal experiments on both white rats and monkeys.

In 1908 he left Chicago and went to Johns Hopkins University in Baltimore as a full professor. He immediately set up an animal laboratory at Johns Hopkins, and in 1913 he shook the world of psychology with the publication of a paper entitled "Psychology as the Behaviorist Views It." In this paper Watson attacked the orthodox psychology of the day, and he inaugurated a new school of psychological thought—behaviorism. He said that the only valid data in psychology was the behavior of the organism. He saw no room in psychology for mentalistic concepts like "mind" or "consciousness." The data of psychology should be the observable response, and the best approach to this, in order to rule out any mentalistic overtones, was to study the responses of animals. To be scientifically respectable, psychology must be behavioristic, objective, deterministic, mechanistic, and materialistic.

Watson then acquired a powerful ally. He had read of the work of I. P. Pavlov and the conditioned reflex, and Watson pounced on this concept and made it a central theme of his own behaviorism. In 1919 Watson began his now famous study on the conditioning of the baby Albert B. He conducted this study in collaboration with Rosalie Rayner. Together, Watson and Rayner showed how an apparently normal, healthy baby could be conditioned to fear virtually anything in his or her observable environment.

In 1920 Watson's career at Johns Hopkins suddenly ended. Amid great notoriety Watson was divorced by his wife and then asked by Johns Hopkins to resign his professorship. Later that year Watson married his research collaborator, Rosalie Rayner, and then, in 1921,

entered the advertising business. He began by working in New York City for the advertising agency of J. Walter Thompson. By 1924 he had become vice president of the agency, and he remained in that post for the next twelve years. In 1936 he joined the William Esty agency.

Despite leaving the academic world in 1920, Watson continued to write books and articles that advanced his views on childrearing and teaching. It wasn't until 1927 that Watson thundered forth his famous words, "Give me the baby."

Watson retired from the business world in 1946 and died in 1958, having exerted great influence on the fields of psychology and education. He made educational psychology more behavioristic, and he emphasized the role of conditioning in the classroom. The study of Albert caused him to believe that human behavior could be minutely controlled. It was Watson who set the stage for the work of B. F. Skinner and the proponents of behavior modification in the classroom.

---

learning theorists were the major influences on the field from psychology. The measurement practitioners (the IQ and achievement testers) were, by and large, hereditarians. The learning theorists, with very few exceptions, were behaviorists, and behaviorists were environmentalists. Thus it was inevitable that these two groups, both solidly entrenched in the field of educational psychology, and with diametrically opposed views in the nature-nurture debate, would be in constant conflict.

The IQ Testers

The testers had traditionally emphasized heredity, at least on the subject of intelligence. The history of the testing movement goes back to England and Sir Francis Galton, Darwin's cousin. During the later part of the nineteenth century, Galton created the first tests designed to measure intellectual potential. Galton believed that intellectual potential was a function of one's sensory equipment, one's power to discriminate among stimuli. He believed that sensory equipment was inherited. Parents who could detect slight differences among stimuli (could discriminate among subtle differences in tonal pitch, for example) were apt to have children with similarly keen powers. Furthermore, Galton believed, these sensory powers had sur-

vival value for the species. Cave dwellers who could detect the slight hiss of a rattlesnake were more likely to stay alive. James McKeen Cattell, who spent some time in Europe studying with Galton, brought this point of view back to the United States and, as Galton had done earlier, devised a series of sensorimotor tests (auditory range, visual range, reaction time, etc.) designed to measure a human's intellectual potential. It was Cattell in 1890 who first used the phrase "mental test." Cattell was also the key figure in early studies of reading, despite the fact that his major interest was in testing and individual differences. "His work on letter and word recognition, legibility of letters and print types, and stimulus intensity formed the groundwork for most basic reading research of the next 30 years."[14]

G. Stanley Hall, a distinguished psychologist and the first president of Clark University, had also studied in Europe and had also concluded that intelligence was primarily inherited. Hall became enormously important among the testers in America both because of the students he influenced (Goddard, Terman, and Gessell) and because he was the first to translate the Binet intelligence tests into English. Hall, perhaps more than any other American psychologist, influenced the testers in America to adopt a heredity posture.

G. Stanley Hall was the foremost American advocate of intelligence as an inherited trait.

The Stanford-Binet IQ test, which the testers used to obtain much of their data, was introduced into America by one of Hall's students, Lewis M. Terman. Starting with the original 1905 Binet scale, Terman created new norms based on American standardizing groups and revised so many of the original items as to practically create a new test (1916). The data collected in his later studies of gifted children seemed to support a genetic explanation of intelligence.

Thus the testers, whose influence on educational psychology was enormous, spread the hereditarian position they had "inherited" from Europe.

The Learning Theorists

The learning theorists, mostly Americans, were bound to be a strong influence on educational psychology. After all, what better contribution could psychology make to education than a more thorough understanding of the principles of learning? However, the major force among American learning theorists was behaviorism, and behaviorism was definitely an environmentalist position. Watson, the father of American

behaviorism, sounded the clarion call when he wrote, "The data of psychology is behavior."[15] And we have already seen ("Give me the baby") Watson's extreme environmental stance. The behaviorists—Watson, Thorndike, Guthrie, Hull, and Skinner—spread a kind of mechanical-person gospel. They spent little time studying the organism's growth and development. The emphasis was on how the organism learns, regardless of its inherited potential, regardless of its stage of physical or psychological development, and often regardless of its species. In brief, they saw learning as a result of associations formed between stimuli and actions, or impulses to act. These simple associations would accumulate and form larger groups of learned associations. Learning was seen largely as a result of conditioning, similar to Pavlov's dogs' learning to salivate at the sound of a certain tone. From his command post at Columbia Teachers College, E. L. Thorndike issued basic laws of learning that dominated the field of educational psychology, not to mention classroom practices, for over fifty years.

Few American learning theorists ever studied children in the classroom, or, in fact, ever studied any children at all. Thorndike and Guthrie worked primarily with cats, Hull with rats, and

Lewis Terman, Hall's student, revised Binet's original scale and introduced the Stanford-Binet tests in 1916.

Skinner with rats and pigeons, but the principles of learning derived from these studies were generalized to human beings. Not that these generalizations were always invalid. They too weren't! A child in a classroom can be conditioned to remain in his or her seat, just as a rat can be conditioned to press a lever. But it is the solid contention of this book that there is much more to human learning than mere conditioning.

The learning theorists certainly had their day, and from 1920 to well past the Second World War the learning theorists with their environmental bias were calling many of the shots in educational psychology in this country.

Why Was an Environmental Position So Attractive in America?

There are at least six ways to answer the question of why the environmental position appealed to American educators:

1. American psychology was dominated by liberals and, almost without exception, they lined up on the side of environmentalism. To their way of thinking, heredity doomed humans to a tooth-and-claw world, a racist society in which social change was impossible. The nature-nurture argument was rephrased in more "democratic" language as "instinct versus learning," or even "beast versus man." An ideology, a cherished tradition, was getting between the psychologist and his or her data.

2. Even among some of those psychologists who recognized the importance of genetic influences, they felt that heredity was fixed at conception and that there was no point in studying something that couldn't be changed. Environmental influences, on the other hand, could be manipulated, and heredity became unimportant simply because of its inaccessibility.

3. Genetics, as a discipline, is a relatively new field, and some of the major breakthroughs have occurred only fairly recently. For example, it was only in 1962 that Watson and Crick won the Nobel Prize for their pioneering work on genetic composition.

4. Very few psychologists were familiar with the information that was accumulating about genetics. Psychologists were more familiar with the related fields of sociology and cultural anthropology than they were with genetics. For example, Margaret Mead and Ruth Benedict were better known to students majoring in psychology than were Thomas Hunt Morgan or even Charles Davenport.

5. The special field of behavior genetics is of very recent origin. Although foreshadowed by a study published in 1924,[16] it was only in 1940 that Robert Choate Tryon of the University of California at Berkeley published a classic study that set the stage for the current work in this area.[17] Tryon had a large group of rats learn a maze, and then removed those animals that learned the maze quickly from those that learned slowly. By breeding the fast learners only with other fast learners, and the slow learners only with other slow learners, Tryon demonstrated that after seven generations he had created two significantly different groups of rats: maze-bright animals and maze-dull animals. Breeding experiments like this came *after* many of the behaviorists had already made their strong environmental statements.

6. The final reason for neglecting heredity was the long-term damage done by the instinct theorists at the turn of the century. Now thoroughly discredited, instinct theory attempted to explain behavior by describing it in other terms. Why do people fight? Obviously they have an aggressive instinct. Why do people get together in groups? They have a gregarious instinct. And, of course, the reason people twiddle their thumbs is because they have a thumb-twiddling instinct. This kind of reasoning commits what is called the nominal fallacy; it confuses description with explanation. As B. F. Skinner has pointed out, this tactic is extremely dangerous: If we assume that a redescription is an explanation, we may feel we have answers when in fact we don't; and we may give up the search.[18]

Do people have an inborn aggressive tendency that makes them fight? Yes claimed the instinct theorists, who confused description for explanation, a nominal fallacy.

ETHOLOGY

Although it was easy for American psychologists to dismiss the naive views of instinct theorists as unworthy of serious consideration, they could not ignore the carefully detailed work of the European ethologists. Ethology is the study of behavior, especially animal behavior, in the natural setting (as opposed to a laboratory setting). Ethologists are primarily interested in discovering innate behavior patterns, or, as they call them, innate releasing mechanisms (IRMs)—patterns many American psychologists overlooked, partly because they insisted on studying animals in aseptic, artificial laboratory situations. Releasers are those stimuli in an organism's environment that trigger unlearned behavior patterns. For example, if the male stickleback fish sees the color red, a rather violent attack response is released. During the breeding season all stickleback males develop bright red bellies, and if one red-bellied fish happens on another's nesting site, the intruder is roundly attacked and driven out of the nesting area.

The following story, possibly apocryphal, nevertheless makes the point. It seems that a graduate student in experimental psychology, unable to obtain a group of specially bred gentle, white Sprague-Dawley rats, undauntedly captured some wild rats from the local dump. To the dismay of the student, these rats, rather than learning the route through the complicated maze, simply ate their way through the wooden sides of the maze and quickly devoured the entire sack of food pellets. By the same token, it is highly improbable that a Sprague-Dawley rat, its IRMs bred out of it hundreds of generations ago, could stay alive for five minutes at the city dump. We can imagine this rat sitting passively trying to find a lever to push.

Imprinting

Perhaps the ethologists' most important findings—important from the point of view of forcing American psychologists to reevaluate their position on instincts and the role of heredity in determining behavior—came as a result of the work of Konrad Lorenz. Although it was noted

KONRAD LORENZ

If King Solomon had indeed "spake to the animals" in their own language, then it can truly be said that Konrad Lorenz has the wisdom of a Solomon. Ever since he was a child, Lorenz has been observing, studying, and learning to understand the ways of the wildlife, especially Austrian wildlife. During these many years Lorenz has learned to understand the "signal code," or language, of various animal species and has even learned to imitate this code in order to establish two-way communication.

Konrad Lorenz was born in Vienna, Austria, in 1903. His father, Adolph, was a world-famous orthopedic surgeon and a professor at the University of Vienna. His brother Albert followed in his father's footsteps and also became a professor of orthopedic surgery at the University of Vienna. During Konrad's childhood, the family spent the summer months at a country home in Altenberg. It was there that Lorenz became fascinated by the fauna of his native country. He explored the woods and ponds, and by age nine had set up his own microscope for studying the tiny wonder world of the freshwater pond. Says Lorenz, "For he who has once seen the intimate beauty of nature cannot tear himself away from it again. He must become either a poet or a naturalist . . . he may well become both."

His family merely tolerated young Lorenz's avid curiosity about animals. Lorenz brought into his home pet after pet, each more destructive than the last. The tolerance of his parents often wore thin.

As a result of his father's insistence, Lorenz became a medical student at the University of Vienna. In 1928 he received his M.D. degree, but his love of animals continued and so did his studies. In 1933 he received his Ph.D. degree in zoology, and for the next four years he continued his research on the behavior of animals in their natural habitats.

In 1937 he began his teaching career, receiving an appointment as instructor of comparative anatomy and animal psychology at his beloved University of Vienna. That same year he also published his now famous article in the journal *Auk*, titled "The Companion in the Bird's World." In this article Lorenz described the intricate biological mechanism of imprinting. During their first few hours of life, certain organisms will become imprinted on the first moving stimulus object in their visual field. They will then follow this object—usually, of course, their mother—with devotion and marching-band precision. This is how young organisms, especially birds, know which species they belong to, and it also accounts for their flocking behavior. Lorenz had revived the long discredited instinct theory and made it scientifically respectable.

In 1940 he became professor of psychology at the University of Konigsberg in Germany. By this time World War II was raging through Europe, and Germany was at the eye of the storm. The following year, Lorenz was called into the German army and later fought on the eastern front. In 1944 he was captured by the Russians, and after a long and arduous ordeal was released in 1948, three years after the war had officially ended. He immediately resumed his duties at the University of Vienna, but in 1950 he went to Germany again, this time as the assistant director of the Max Planck Institute for Behavioral Physiology. Lorenz is still at the Max Planck Institute, now as director. In October 1973 Lorenz and two other pioneers in behavioral science won the Nobel Prize in Medicine for their work in the comparative study of behavior.

Among his numerous publications are the following books: *King Solomon's Ring* (1952), *Man Meets Dog* (1954), *Evolution and Modification of Behavior* (1965), *On Aggression* (1966), and *Studies in Animal and Human Behavior* (1970).

Lorenz has established ethology, the study of animal behavior in the natural setting, as a serious and respectable discipline. In large measure because of his careful work, ethology no longer suffers from the early damage done by the naive instinct theorists. The message from Lorenz is: If you want to understand animal behavior, study the animal in its own environment, not in the artificial confines of the laboratory. And perhaps in educational psychology this message translates to the following: If you want to understand schoolchildren, study them in the classroom.

as far back as 1873 that newly hatched chicks seem to follow the first moving stimulus they see, it was not until 1935 that Lorenz revived the term *imprinting* to describe this form of learning. He also discovered that this phenomenon could occur only during one critical period in the chick's life. Lorenz noted that goslings would follow not only their mother but any moving stimulus that presented itself within the first few hours of their life. If Lorenz presented himself during this critical period, he found that the goslings would parade after him with a devotion usually reserved for their mother and that this habit would continue throughout the birds' lifetime.[19]

Although imprinting was noted in the organism's natural environment, it has also been demonstrated in the artificial world of the laboratory, proving that psychology and ethology are not at odds.[20] In fact, under laboratory conditions it was possible to show the exact point in time when imprinting had the most impact—imprinting in ducks, for example, can occur up to thirty-two hours after hatching, although the optimal time is between thirteen and sixteen hours of age.

Imprinting provided the perfect example of the careful blending of heredity and environment in producing behavioral change.

CHERISHED BELIEFS AND SCIENTIFIC FACTS

As we have now seen, psychologists in general and educational psychologists in particular have battled for years over the question of the relative contribution of heredity and environment to behavior. Each side felt that it had the answer. As often happens when narrow or even single causes are sought to explain anything, the search for this single cause results more in the creation of controversy than in the accumulation of knowledge. Each side becomes rigid and dogmatic, and cherished beliefs begin to cloud scientific vision. If Watson had been less zealous in the cause of environmentalism, he could not possibly have overlooked the importance of heredity. Nor could Goddard have overlooked the obvious environmental differences between the "good" and "bad" Kallikaks had not his cherished opinion, his "pride of authorship," clouded his vision.

Nor was his clouded vision totally innocent. Stephen Jay Gould has recently discovered that in the original volume of Goddard's Kallikaks, three of the photographs allegedly depicting "bad" Kallikaks had been obviously retouched. The pictures "were phonied by inserting heavy dark lines to give eyes and mouths their diabolical appearance."[21] If the bad Kallikaks hadn't really looked stupid and depraved enough, it now appears that Goddard saw to it that they would.

This problem is not confined to psychology or to education. In our long quest to gain knowledge about our environment and ourselves, we have often been blinded by cherished beliefs. Advances in astronomy were thwarted for centuries by our egocentric view that the earth, our habitat, must be at the center of the universe. Only slowly and grudgingly did we give up this notion and then only on the understanding that

Konrad Lorenz, the imprinted "mother" to these goslings, leads his charges on a morning stroll. Imprinted behavior depends on both inheritance and an environmental event in the life of the organism that has lasting effects.

These two photos of Kallikak family members are doctored. Note the obvious alteration in the mouths and eyes in order to dramatize an illusion of feeble-mindedness.

if the earth is not at the center, surely the sun, at the center of our solar system, is at the core of a revolving universe. Ptolemy's heliocentric view of the universe went virtually unchallenged for over a thousand years. Even today it is still for some a sore point to realize that the earth is only a dust spot in this vast and expanding universe. And if we struggled to preserve our special place in the cosmos, it was only a dress rehearsal for the real drama of preserving our glorified role on earth.

Despite our reluctance, we finally accepted our place in the universe—in the sixteenth century. Ptolemy gave way to Copernicus, the earth was put in its proper place, and the ground was prepared for the later theories of Newton and Einstein.

In other areas, however, we were even more backward: Physiology as a discipline did not really come into its own until the nineteenth century (it seemed even more threatening to our ego to learn that our bodies were open to the objective scrutiny of science). But the "most unkindest cut of all" was the thrust of the newest scientific discipline, psychology; it insisted on probing our very inner being.

It is thus no accident that our search to understand ourselves has only recently come under scientific observation. In the evolution of scientific disciplines there has been a fairly orderly sequence based on the degree to which each science has threatened our self-esteem. As we have seen, and will continue to see, cherished beliefs are hard to give up; this is certainly true of educational psychology in the twentieth century.

NATURE-NURTURE: A MODERN SOLUTION TO AN OLD PROBLEM

It is now clear, in the last two decades of the twentieth century, that the old question of heredity versus environment is unanswerable because it is meaningless. Behavior is not the result of a single cause, but of multiple causes. It is the result of heredity interacting with environment interacting with time (see Figure 2.1).

Our hereditary potential can be nourished or stifled depending on the type, amount, and quality of our environmental encounters and depending on when these encounters occur. (They can occur too early or too late to be of optimum benefit.)

In the chapters that follow we outline some of the major considerations that have moved educational psychology beyond the nature-nurture controversy. Since human behavior is determined by the interaction of both (recall Dewey's phrase, "an organism in some environment"), we need to look at nature and nurture simultaneously. We can then begin to consider, not in a single- or narrow-minded way, but within a broad context, how to educate children and adolescents. We need to know both how to strike and when the iron is hot. In Chapter 4 we present some of the central ideas about the significance and lasting effects of initial experience. In Chapters 5–7 we present the stages of cognitive and personal development to show, in our metaphor, just when the iron is hot. We can then shift our attention to arranging the environment for learning and teaching, to be discussed in the later chapters.

FIGURE 2.1   Behavior is the result of heredity interacting with environment interacting with time.

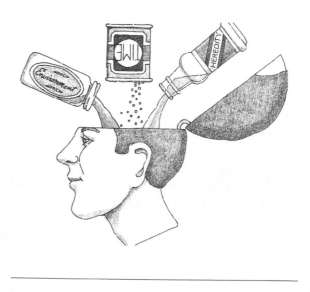

SUMMARY

The causes of behavior are multiple and complex, and it is dangerous to build a psychology of human behavior on the basis of animal studies alone. Growth rates differ markedly among species, and the rate of growth and development among humans is comparatively slow. Studies that compared the rate of maturation between humans and lower species found humans to lag behind.

The nature-nurture controversy created a great division in the field of psychology. Henry Goddard's study of the Kallikaks attempted to "prove" that heredity was the most important factor in determining a person's psychological makeup. John B. Watson argued that environmental influences, through the process of conditioning, were paramount in determining psychological traits.

In the field of educational psychology, the measurement practitioners (IQ testers) were typically strong believers in heredity, whereas the learning theorists were environmentalists. American psychology as a whole, however, tended to believe that environmental influences were more important than hereditary ones.

Ethology, the study of animal behavior in the natural setting as opposed to the laboratory, made the study of instinctive behavior (IRMs) more respectable as a legitimate scientific pursuit. The ethologists demonstrated a special form of learning called "imprinting," which occurs only during a critical time period in an organism's life.

Scientific objectivity has historically suffered as a result of the cherished beliefs and strong attitudes held by the scientists themselves or by society in general. Psychology has perhaps been the most affected by this, for it is the discipline concerned with probing our inner being and motivation.

The modern solution to the age-old nature-nurture controversy is that neither heredity nor environment is the sole cause of behavior. Behavior is the result of heredity interacting with environment interacting with time. This final point is critical to an understanding of the rest of the book, and is considered one of psychology's most basic principles.

KEY TERMS AND NAMES

nature-nurture controversy
Henry H. Goddard
John B. Watson
Kallikak family
Sir Francis Galton
James McKeen Cattell

instinct theory
nominal fallacy
ethology
innate releasing mechanism (IRM)
Konrad Lorenz
imprinting

REFERENCES

1. Wilson, J. A. R., Robeck, M. C., and Michael, W. B. (1969). *Psychological foundations of learning and teaching* (p. 165). New York: McGraw-Hill.

2. Kellogg, W. N., and Kellogg, L. A. (1963). *The ape and the child*. New York: McGraw-Hill.

3. Hayes, K. G., and Hayes, C. (1951). The intellectual development of a home-raised chimpanzee. *Proceedings: American Philosophical Society, 95,* 105–109.

4. Premack, D. (1971). Language in chimpanzees? *Science, 172,* 808–872.

5. Limber, J. (1977). Language in child and chimp? *American Psychologist, 32*(6), 285.

6. See Gardner, B. T., and Gardner, R. A. (1970). Two-way communication with an infant chimpanzee. In A. Schrier and F. Stollnitz (Eds.), *Behavior of nonhuman primates.* New York: Academic Press. The authors believe that chimps do communicate with each other, not verbally, but through a kind of sign language. Some years ago, a chimpanzee was trained in the use of the American sign language of the deaf, and the chimp's performance compared favorably with that of a three-year-old child who was deaf from birth.

7. Goddard, H. (1912). *The Kallikak family.* New York: Macmillan.

8. Watson, J. B., and Rayner, R. (1920). Conditioned emotional reactions. *Journal of Experimental Psychology, 3,* 8.

9. Harris, B. (1979). Whatever happened to Little Albert? *American Psychologist, 34*(2), 158.

10. Bolles, R. C. (1980). Ethological learning theory. In R. A. Hinde and J. Stevenson-Hinde (Eds.), *Theories of learning.* Itsaca, Ill.: Peacock.

11. Watson and Rayner, Conditioned emotional reactions, 14.

12. Watson, J. B. (1927). The behaviorist looks at instincts. *Harper's Magazine* (July), p. 233.

13. Skinner, B. F. (1975). Bury not burn. *A.P.A. Monitor, 6* (November), 2.

14. Venezby, R. (1977). Research on reading processes. *American Psychologist, 32*(5), 339.

15. Watson, J. B. (1913). Psychology as the behaviorist views it. *Psychological Review, 20,* 158–177.

16. Tolman, E. C. (1924). The inheritance of maze learning ability in rats. *Journal of Comparative Psychology, 4,* 1–18.

17. Tryon, R. C. (1940). Genetic differences in maze-learning ability in rats. *Yearbook of the National Society for Studies in Education, 39,* 111–119.

18. Skinner, B. F. (1953). *Science and human behavior.* New York: Macmillan.

19. Lorenz, K. (1937). The companion in the bird's world. *Auk, 54,* 245–273.

20. Hess, E. H. (1959). Imprinting. *Science, 130,* 133–141.

21. Gould, S. J. (1981). *The mismeasure of man.* New York: Norton.

3

PHYSICAL GROWTH AND DEVELOPMENT

Each of us begins life as a tiny, watery speck smaller than the period at the end of this sentence. This speck, technically a zygote, contains the genetic background that will shape and direct our development for the rest of our lives. The zygote is formed at the moment of conception, when the sperm cell of the male fertilizes the egg cell of the female. Half of the genetic background contained in the zygote comes from the father, half from the mother, so that the baby will be like both parents, but not exactly like either one. Thus the zygote contains the hereditary component that will be constantly molded and modified through environmental interactions. And these interactions begin immediately. If the zygote were to be surgically removed from the uterus and placed in a foreign environment, like a glass of water, it would soon perish. If the zygote remains in the uterus and the uterine environment remains healthy, then growth and development continue, and some nine months later the baby is born. It is important to recognize that all during the nine months environmental encounters are occurring. To be sure, the uterine environment is relatively constant, but not totally so. Toxic agents in the mother's uterus can modify, damage, or even halt the development of the zygote. One study even suggests that learning can occur in the uterus.[1] It has also been found that strong emotional arousal on the part of the expectant mother can be transmitted to the developing fetus.[2] Although there are no direct neural connections between mother and fetus, a mother's emotionality in the form of specifically released hormones can pass through the placenta and change the physiology of the yet unborn child. In short, our basic axiom that behavior is a result of the interaction of heredity, environment, and time covers one's entire life, from the moment of conception.

THE ABCs OF GENETICS

Our knowledge of genetics is of very recent origin. The science of genetics is based on the study of heredity, the biological transmittal of characteristics from parent to offspring. The nature-nurture argument was based in large part on the fact that not enough was known about

FIGURE 3.1   DNA and RNA.

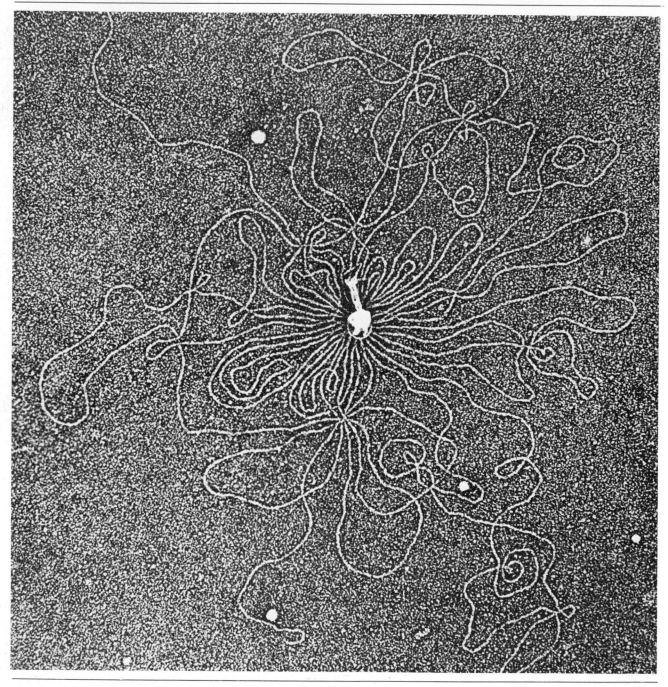

nature, and what was known about heredity wasn't fully understood by many psychologists, especially in America.

The fundamental unit of analysis in genetics is the gene. Genes are tiny particles that carry the hereditary characteristics. They are located in the nucleus of each of the body's cells, where they occur in pairs, one from each parent. Estimates of the total number of genes in any single human (the human genome) run anywhere from 5 to 10 million. Since at conception each parent contributes to this vast number of genes, there is obviously room for great genetic variation in the resulting offspring. Except for identical twins, every individual is genetically unique.

Genes are composed of the rather large organic molecules: DNA (deoxyribonucleic acid) and RNA (ribonucleic acid) (see Figure 3.1). These nucleic acids (DNA and RNA) are located in the chromosomes, which lie in the nucleus of every cell in the body. Chromosomes are fairly long, threadlike bits of protein, and each of the cells in the human body contains twenty-three pairs of these chromosomes (see Figure 3.2). However, the germ cells (sperm cells in the male and egg cells in the female) carry only twenty-three chromosomes, or half the number that exist in the body cells. At conception, then, the zygote receives half of its chromosomes from each parent, twenty-three from each, and thus achieves its full complement of twenty-three pairs.

The DNA and RNA molecules are located within the nucleus of each cell, where the chromosomes are arranged. The DNA molecule contains chains of atoms and simpler molecules that code and store information about growth and development. Their arrangement allows

DNA - archetypes
the DNA molecule to reproduce itself exactly—that is, to achieve precise self-duplication. For this to occur, the chemical environment must be appropriate. DNA acts as a blueprint or, as it is called by the geneticists, a template, for the formation of certain enzymes that help to guide the development of the organism. The coded information contained in the DNA molecule is transmitted to other parts of the cell by the RNA molecules. DNA may be thought of as the architect's blueprint, while the RNA would be the builder translating this blueprint into a finished home. It must be remembered, however, that these reactions do not occur in a vacuum. The chemical environment must be appropriate for the DNA "architect" and the RNA "builder" to work effectively.

From the moment of conception, then, the individual is a product of the interaction among heredity, environment, and time.

Dominants and Recessives

One of the first discoveries in the field of genetics occurred over a hundred years ago when

FIGURE 3.2   Human chromosomes.

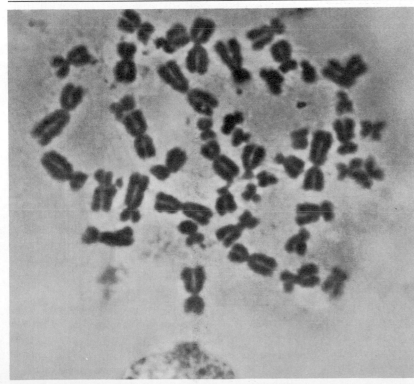

the Austrian monk Gregor Mendel (1822–1884) learned an important fact about inheritance. In his study of the flower color of garden peas, Mendel discovered that some genes are dominant and some recessive. Mendel found that if he crossed a red-flowered pea with another red-flowered pea, the resulting plant would have red flowers. Similarly, if he crossed a white-flowered pea with another white-flowered pea, the resulting plant would have white flowers. But if he crossed a red-flowered pea with a white-flowered pea, the resulting plant would have red flowers. Thus, the genes that determine flower color can be dominant or recessive, and in this case, red is dominant over white—that is, the trait carried by the dominant gene shows up in the flower. Crossing a red with a red, or a white with a white, produces a pure offspring, whereas crossing a red with a white produces a hybrid. When a dominant gene is paired with a recessive gene, the resulting hybrid always exhibits the dominant trait.

Among the human traits that follow this rule, perhaps the best example is eye color. Brown eyes are dominant over blue eyes. Thus, if both parents have blue eyes, their children must have blue eyes. This is because, for individuals to have blue eyes, they must be carrying only the recessive genes for eye color. If they were to have a dominant brown-eyed gene and a recessive blue-eyed gene, their eyes would have to be brown. If, however, both parents are brown-eyed, but both are carrying a recessive gene for blue eyes, their children still might have blue eyes. Chances are greater, however, that they will have brown eyes.

Two hybrid parents, each with brown eyes, have only a one-in-four chance of producing a blue-eyed child. The trait that shows up is the phenotype, whereas the one that remains hidden is the genotype. A person with a phenotype of brown eyes may have a genotype of two brown-eyed genes or a genotype of one brown-eyed and one blue-eyed gene.

A trait like eye color, in which a single pair of genes determines the phenotype, is a fairly rare case in genetics. Most behavioral traits, such as measured intelligence, result from the combination of large numbers of genes. This is called "polygenic inheritance" and again dramatizes the enormous potential for genetic differences among individuals.[3]

We can see from even this simplified excursion into genetics that heredity has lawful relationships, and it is certain that future discoveries in this field will uncover many more definite patterns and laws that influence physical traits and behavior. Studies have already shown that, in addition to motor skills and intelligence, schizophrenia and manic-depression have rather strong hereditary components. This is not to deny that environmental influences are important; they are! But the genes do carry constitutional predispositions toward various behaviors that the environment may stifle or nourish.

BEHAVIOR GENETICS

Psychologists are able to examine the possible effects of genetic endowment through both animal and human research. Though the results of animal studies cannot be directly generalized to humans, the animal data may be at least suggestive of hypotheses that might later be pursued when researchers attempt to understand the results of human studies. The studies in behavior genetics, both animal and human, have as their goal the discovery of lawful relationships between genetic endowment and observed behavior.

Animal Studies

The genetic studies of animals are typically of two types: inbreeding and selective breeding. Inbreeding studies usually involve the mating of brothers and sisters in order to obtain as much homozygosity in the population as possible. Homozygosity means that the gene pairs are identical. When animals are inbred, the like-sexed members come to have the same, or almost the same, genotype. Inbreeding experiments are commonly carried out on such organisms as mice and fruit flies (*Drosophila*). In one study, for example, fifteen different inbred strains of mice were compared on a number of characteristics.[4] Significant differences were found among the various strains on the behavioral characteristic of exploratory behavior. This tends to indicate that, among mice, willingness to explore new areas is at least partly genetically determined.

In selective-breeding studies, animals of a given strain are tested on some behavioral criterion, such as ability to run a maze. Then the animals demonstrating extremes of this behavior are selectively mated for generation after generation—the animals with the best performance on the maze, for example, are mated with one another, as are the animals with the lowest maze performance. In Chapter 2 it was pointed out that one study of this type, carried out by R. C. Tryon, established that after seven generations two significantly different groups of rats had been created: maze-bright animals and maze-dull animals.[5]

In another study white mice were separated according to the amount of aggressiveness they exhibited. The most- and least-aggressive mice were identified and then selectively bred. Again, after seven generations, dramatic differences in the aggressiveness displayed by the offspring became apparent.[6] In studies such as these, the pure effects of genetic endowment can be examined, since the animals' environments can be carefully controlled.

Human Studies

Since social taboos would argue against breeding experiments at the human level (not that there would be a shortage of student volunteers), psychologists must rely on after-the-fact, or *post hoc*, data in studying human genetic endowment. In some studies lineage records are traced backward in an attempt to establish the possibility of direct ancestry, a method used by Henry Goddard (Chapter 2) in his study of the Kallikaks. The problem with this kind of research is that genetic background and environmental influences are easily confounded: Martin Kallikak's "good seed" descendants were subjected to different environmental conditions than were the descendants of "Old Horror." Sir Francis Galton, the father of intelligence testing, was the first to use this lineage technique when he compared the achievements of successive generations of his own brilliant family with those of a less fortunate family.

In another type of human research in genetics, adopted or foster children are compared with both their biological and foster parents. If the children are behaviorally more similar to their biological parents (whose influence on the child's environment is presumed to be zero) than to their foster parents, the similarity is attributed to heredity.

Perhaps the most popular technique at the human level is to examine for behavioral similarities identical twins who have been reared apart. Since identical, or monozygotic (MZ), twins reared separately still have precisely the same genetic endowment, any remaining behavioral similarities are presumed to result from genetic causes. In one study, an attempt was made to discover whether or not there is a genetic component in schizophrenia.[7] In this study, members of MZ twin pairs (called the "probands") who had been diagnosed as schizophrenic were located and their co-twins then searched out. The percentage of co-twins of probands who are also schizophrenic is called the *"concordance rate."* When this concordance rate was compared with the concordance rate among fraternal, or dizygotic (DZ) twins, researchers found the MZ concordance rate to be substantially higher. Also, in the case of MZ twins reared apart, the concordance rate was roughly 60 percent, a figure that certainly lends some support to the author's genetic interpretation. The role of genetics in diseases other than schizophrenia is only beginning to be understood. One researcher, however, estimates that between 25 and 50 percent *of all common diseases* have a direct genetic cause.[8]

PSYCHOLOGY'S FIRST PRINCIPLE

Psychology's first principle and most fundamental axiom is that the organism is a product of heredity, interacting with environment, interacting with time, as shown in the following formula:

$$O = H \leftrightarrow E \leftrightarrow T$$

It is meaningless to ask whether intelligence, introversion, or any other psychological trait is inherited or learned. It's like asking which is more important in running a car, the engine or the gasoline; or which is more important in determining the area of a rectangle, the height or the width.

Even something as seemingly directly inherited as physical height is profoundly influenced by environment and time. An individual with the inherited potential for tallness will still be short if the environment prevents physical exercise or proper vitamin intake, especially if this deprivation occurs in early childhood (time).

Keep this first principle constantly in mind during the rest of this chapter. When we discuss developmental stages, we will give various age norms. However, it is crucial to remember that these are only averages, that there are large discrepancies between the averages and any individual case. For example, the averages show that children usually utter their first word at twelve months. But, in fact, some children say their first word at eight months, some at twenty-four months. A great deal depends on the amount and quality of environmental stimulation.

Environmental influences in the form of nutrition are also of great importance. The undernourished child may lag in both physiological and psychological growth. In one review of the work in this area, it was concluded that the nine months of prenatal life and the two or three years following birth are "most critical in the growth of brain tissue and are the periods of greatest vulnerability to malnutrition."[9] Mental deficiency was seen as one possible result of an inadequate diet during this critical period of life.

Though the time factor is given great importance in the following discussion, it must be remembered that time is only one factor. Though it is a convenient factor to utilize in discussing physical development, it is only part of the total equation. The organism is a product of heredity, environment, and time in constant interaction.

LIFE BEFORE BIRTH

At birth the human baby is already about nine months of age. As a matter of fact, during that first nine months, from conception to birth, more growth occurs than will ever occur again: That tiny speck, the zygote, has grown into a seven- or eight-pound baby by the time it emerges into what William James calls the "blooming, buzzing confusion" of the external environment.

The nine months of growth before birth can be conveniently divided into three periods.

The Zygote

The zygote floats freely in the fluid inside the uterus. After about two weeks it attaches itself to the wall of the uterus and becomes a parasite, receiving all its oxygen and nourishment from the mother's body. By the time the zygote attaches itself to the wall of the uterus, it has already begun to differentiate into three parts: the outer layer, or ectoderm, which will form the brain; the middle layer, or mesoderm, which will form the heart; and the inner layer, or endoderm, which will form the liver.

The Embryo

The second stage of prenatal development, the embryonic stage, begins two weeks after conception, at the time the zygote attaches itself to the uterus. At this point the developing organism is called an "embryo." The embryonic stage lasts until about eight weeks after conception, and during this stage the organism increases its weight by 2 million percent. Also during this period the heart begins beating, sex organs are formed, hands and feet are formed and can be flexed, and all the internal organs are formed. By the end of the embryonic period, the organism is clearly identifiable as human.

The Fetus

From eight weeks after conception until birth the organism is called a "fetus." Though the growth rate of the fetus is not as spectacular as the zygote's or embryo's, it is still extremely rapid by postnatal standards. The fetus is definitely a behaving organism, and its behavior can be studied.

Current medical techniques have established a fetal age of just over twenty weeks as the dividing line between whether or not the fetus can survive if prematurely born. At this age the fetus is capable of true breathing and can even vocalize a thin crying sound.[10]

With increasingly sophisticated medical care, it is likely that the dividing line between fetal viability and nonviability will be reduced from the current age of somewhat over twenty weeks. This may be especially true for the female fetus, who seems less susceptible to problems of prematurity, anoxia (abnormally low levels of oxygen in the blood), and maternal infection.[11]

Reactions to Stimuli   It is known that the fetus can react to stimuli as early as eight weeks after conception. At this time it is sensitive to stimulation of the nose, lips, and chin. The area of sensitivity gradually increases, and by the fourteenth week, the whole body is sensitive, except for the top and back of the head. The top of the head doesn't respond to stimulation until after birth.

Spontaneous Actions   Along with the ability to react to stimuli, the fetus can also act spontaneously. Certainly after the fourth month the mother is aware of fetal activity. This activity is quite diffuse—that is, movements are slow and involve several parts of the body at once.

All the preceding stages, from conception to birth, are collectively called the "prenatal stage of development." Prenatal development is characterized by its rapidity and by a maturation rate that enables the fetus to perform certain functions well before they are actually needed. For example, the fetus can make breathing movements by the fourth month, walking movements by the fifth month, and sucking movements by the sixth month. These activities are not needed until birth, yet they are ready months ahead of time.

PHYSICAL DEVELOPMENT IN CHILDHOOD

The newborn baby, or neonate, is certainly not a miniature adult. The baby's head and trunk are much larger, proportionally, than they will be at adulthood. For example, the head will only double in size from birth to adulthood, whereas the arms and legs may grow to five times their original length.

The Nervous System

In one sense the nervous system is complete at birth—that is, the number of typical nerve cells never increases after birth, but the size of these cells does increase. Also, although the neonate comes equipped with a fully structured nervous system, it is many years before this system can function efficiently.

Each nerve cell, or neuron, has two basic parts: fibers and cell bodies. Think of the neuron as a fiber with branches at both ends and a bulge (cell body) in the middle. The function of

Changes in body proportions as a function of age. The figures are adjusted to the same height.

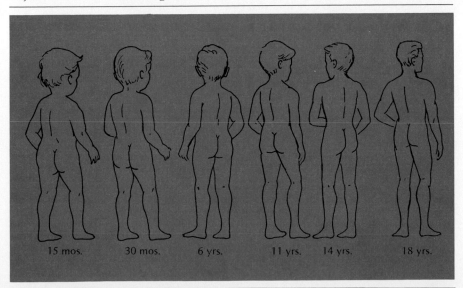

| 15 mos. | 30 mos. | 6 yrs. | 11 yrs. | 14 yrs. | 18 yrs. |

Data from N. Bayley, "Individual Patterns of Development," *Child Development* (1956), 45–74.

the neuron is to transmit messages (neural impulses) to and from all parts of the body. The branches, or fibers, pick up the messages and send them on their way. The receiving end of a neuron is the dendrite, and the transmitting end is the axon. In order not to short-circuit the electrically charged neural impulses, most of these fibers are insulated with a white sheath called myelin. The gray-colored cell body does not have this covering. Therefore, the myelin-covered neural pathways are called "white matter" and the uncovered cell bodies are called "gray matter." The myelinization of the nervous system is not complete at birth, so that a great deal of short-circuiting among the baby's neural impulses does indeed occur. This, in part, accounts for the mass activity that is characteristic of a baby's physical reactions. Touching a baby's foot doesn't result in just a foot response but is usually followed by gross movements of both feet, both arms, and even the trunk. It's as though you had no insulation on the wires leading to your electrical appliances, so that when you turned on the TV, the radio and stereo would go on, the alarm clock would buzz, the dishwasher would start, the coffeepot would begin percolating, and the doorbell would ring. Although the nervous system is structurally complete at birth, it is nowhere near functionally mature. The cerebral cortex, which is crucial for learning and complex behavior, doesn't become functionally mature until about age two, and some maturation continues until about age twelve or fifteen.

Sleep

Newborn babies spend most of their days asleep, averaging about sixteen hours a day. This time decreases rapidly until by age one year they are sleeping only a little over ten hours a day.

Motor Development

One of the most dramatic features of infancy is the development of motor skills. Compared to the neonate, the two-year-old child is a study

Newborn babies spend most of their days asleep, averaging about sixteen hours a day.

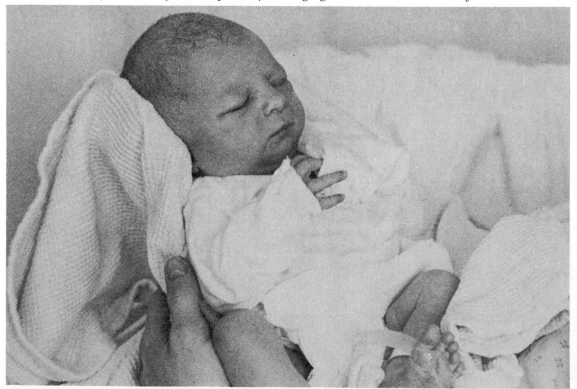

in grace and physical coordination. One psychologist, M. M. Shirley, studied the development of infants on a week-to-week basis. As can be seen from Table 3.1, Shirley's data suggest that there is a definite pattern to motor development. Infants can hold up their heads before they can sit alone, sit before they crawl, and crawl before they walk. This pattern of development is almost exactly the same for every human baby, and each child passes through each of these physical stages at almost the same age.[12]

Studies have shown that motor development occurs according to at least three general rules.

1. Cephalocaudal progression—meaning that motor ability develops from the head on down to the toes. The neonate's head is closer to its eventual adult size than is the rest of its body. Also, the infant has more motor control of the head than of the muscles lower down the body. The progression of motor control follows this pattern: first the head; then the shoulders, arms and abdomen; and finally the legs and feet.

2. Proximodistal progression—meaning that growth and motor ability develop from the central axis of the body on outward. Trunk

TABLE 3.1   STAGES IN MOTOR DEVELOPMENT The skills listed here illustrate the progressive development of control over different groups of muscles. This development proceeds in an orderly fashion from the head region down the body and out to the ends of the limbs.

DESCRIPTION OF STAGE	NUMBER OF CASES	AGE, WEEKS MEDIAN
First-order skills (control of the neck muscles)		
On stomach, chin up	22	3
On stomach, chest up	22	9
Held erect, stepping	19	13
On back, tense for lifting	19	15
Held erect, knees straight	18	15
Sit on lap, support at lower ribs and complete head control	22	19
Second-order skills (control of trunk and upper-limb muscles)		
Sit alone momentarily		
On stomach, knee push or swim	22	25
On back, rolling	19	29
Held erect, stand firmly with help	20	30
Sit alone one minute	20	31
Third-order skills (Beginning of body-limb coordination in prone position)		
On stomach, some progress	17	37
On stomach, scoot backward	16	40
Fourth-order skills (balance in upright position with support; locomotion in prone position)	22	42
Stand holding to furniture		
Creep	22	45
Walk when held	21	45
Pull to stand by furniture	17	47
Fifth-order skills (unsupported locomotion in upright position)		
Stand alone	21	62
Walk alone	21	64

Adapted from M. M. Shirley, The First Two Years, *Vol. 1,* Postural and Locomotor Development *(Minneapolis: University of Minnesota Press, 1931), p. 99.*

The sequence of motor development.

and shoulder movements occur earlier than separate arm movements. Control of the hands and fingers comes last.[13]

3. Mass- to specific-action progression—indicating that the baby's first actions are global and undifferentiated. Slowly, the infant's ability to make specific responses emerges. Refined activity of the fingers and thumb usually doesn't occur until the baby is about a year old.

Motor development is thus heavily influenced by biological maturation, though practice is certainly necessary for full development of the biological potential.

Sensory Development

Many studies have been done to determine what infants are able to receive through their sensory equipment. Since infants obviously cannot give verbal answers to questions, research in this area is much like animal research. If a researcher is trying to find out whether a rat can sense the difference between the colors red and green, the rat can be presented with a red light and food in one goal box and a green light with no food in the other. After a number of trials, if the rat goes consistently to the red light, even when it is randomly switched to the goal box that has no food in it, the researcher would know that the rat can discriminate between red and green. (Studies have shown that rats, in fact, cannot make this discrimination between red and green colors when the amount of illumination is held constant.)

Newborn babies have been shown capable of discriminating between sweet and sour tastes, taste being the most highly developed of all the senses at birth. Responses to different smells have been observed within a few hours after birth.

Some babies respond to sound almost immediately after birth, whereas others may take a few days to gain this sense. This difference is a result of the time it may take for the amniotic fluid to drain out of the newborns' hearing mechanism.

Vision develops more slowly than many of the other senses. Response to light and darkness (the pupillary reflex) is functional within two days after birth, and by ten days infants can follow moving objects with their eyes. By six months of age infants can discriminate between colors, between such shapes as circles and triangles, and between the faces of parents and strangers.

One classic study has demonstrated that six-month-old infants have the ability to perceive depth and thus to avoid situations in which they might fall.[14] In this study the babies were placed on a plate of glass that extended from a tabletop across a three-foot drop in space. When the babies reached what they perceived as the edge of the table, they refused to crawl across the rest of the glass. This perceived dropoff is called the "visual cliff," and it has been demonstrated not only with infants but also with lower organisms such as cats and rats. The ability to perceive a visual cliff obviously has value for survival.

Babies as young as six months can perceive depth.

Bonding

Some researchers believe that a process, similar to imprinting among birds, occurs between mother and child. This is called maternal-infant "bonding," and it is said to produce a strong emotional attachment between the mother and child. The bonding process requires direct physical contact between mother and child, and, apparently, must take place within the baby's first three days of life. Thus, a sensitive period has been hypothesized, suggesting a specific time frame in which bonding may appear. Some researchers have cited the failure to form this psychological bond as a possible reason for later episodes of child neglect and even child abuse.[15]

Speech Development

At birth, speech is restricted to general, undifferentiated crying, yet by the second month the baby can communicate both discomfort and contentment through the use of loud crying or gentle cooing. Of all the developmental factors covered so far, speech is obviously the one most influenced by learning. Yet even speech is built on a biological foundation. Studies of the various sounds made by infants throughout the world have found that certain sounds occur at about the same time and in about the same order in all infants. By listening to the sounds of a baby lying contentedly nearby, one can hear the basic sounds of all languages throughout the world, from the German guttural *r* to the singsong intonation of Chinese.

Learning theorists, such as B. F. Skinner, believe that babies keep some of these sounds—those reinforced by their parents—and slowly discard those that are not encouraged. By the ninth or tenth month they are able to imitate some of the sounds made by others around them.

Other theorists, such as Noam Chomsky, believe there is a heavy genetic component in language acquisition. Rather than learning language solely on the basis of reinforcement and imitation, Chomsky argues, children may acquire language as the result of an inborn "language acquisition device," which directs the infant's ability to learn.[16]

By about one year of age, babies can associate the sounds they make with specific objects and thus they begin to utter their first words, words such as *dada*, *mama*, or *bye-bye*. The young mother is often depressed over the fact that she's been through an uncomfortable pregnancy and has spent sleepless nights in feeding, changing, and comforting the baby, only to hear her baby's first word—*dada*.

After the first word, the infant's vocabulary increases slowly for the next few months. This slowness may be due to the total attention the infant is devoting to learning the intricacies of walking. Once the child has mastered walking, usually at about eighteen months, language development speeds up. In one study, 154 children below two years of age were tested on the ability to speak or understand certain test words. At twelve months of age, the average vocabulary was three words: by fifteen months, it was nineteen words; by eighteen months, twenty-two words. Then came a tremendous spurt, for by twenty-one months of age, the average was 118 words, and by twenty-four months, 272 words.[17]

These figures are, of course, only averages, and there are great individual differences from one child to the next. For example, children with high IQs begin talking, on the average, as much as four months earlier than the average child. Also, girls begin talking sooner than boys, use more words in each sentence, and have larger vocabularies.[18] Moreover, as they get older, girls have fewer speech problems than boys. Boys are more prone to stuttering, more apt to have difficulty articulating the consonants *l* and *r*, and more likely to fill up their speech with hesitation sounds such as "uh" and "er." Later in life there are still some dramatic speech differences between the sexes. Among stroke victims, for example, it is far more common for men to lose their ability to speak than it is for women.[19]

Speech and early experience   Speech, like other developmental abilities, is a product of heredity, environment, and *time*. The sensitive-period hypothesis illustrates the importance of time. If environmental stimulation comes too late, normal language acquisition is prevented. Evidence supporting a critical-period explanation of language acquisition comes from a true "horror story" about a young girl, reared in unbelievably improverished circumstances.[20] The girl, Genie, was locked by her father in a bare room when she was only twenty months of age. During the day she was strapped naked to a potty chair, and at night she was tied into her crib. On those occasions when she was visited, either by her brother or her father, she never heard the sounds of human language. The father and brother would only bark or growl at her, in mock imitation of a dog. Any attempts by Genie to make any vocalizations were severely punished by her father, who, as one author suggests, "lends renewed dignity to the notion of insanity."[21] When Genie was finally released *twelve years later*, she was, of course, unable to talk, but since that time she made great progress—further testimony to human resilience. Genie acquired some ability to talk—"Want think about Mama riding bus"— but her speech patterns have never come up to what could be called normal language ability. For example, she never uses pronouns, has no verb tensing, nor does her voice carry any inflections. In short, the study of Genie seems to indicate that at age thirteen, it's too late to acquire normal language, that the critical period for language acquisition has long since passed.

PHYSICAL DEVELOPMENT IN ADOLESCENCE

Although physical growth proceeds in fits and starts from two years of age to adolescence, it is not until adolescence that another really dramatic growth spurt occurs, and it occurs earlier in girls than in boys (see Figure 3.3). Though boys are typically taller and heavier than girls at age ten, by age thirteen the girls are taller and heavier than the boys. By age sixteen, the situation returns to the way it had been before the onset of adolescence, with the boys again taller and heavier.

In girls, adolescence is signaled by the occurrence of the menarche, or first menstruation. This happens concurrently with breast development, usually by age thirteen, though it is

FIGURE 3.3   The adolescent growth spurt typically occurs earlier in girls than in boys.

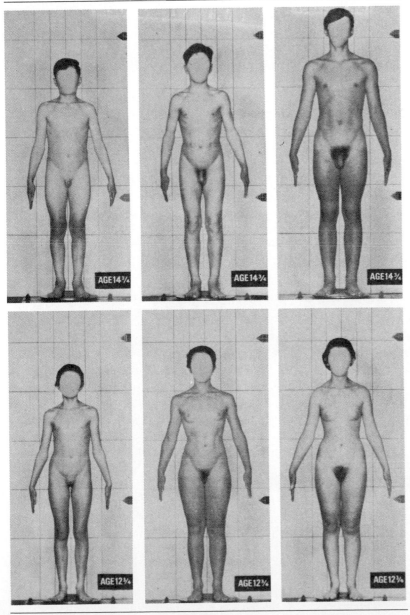

not uncommon for some girls to reach menarche as early as age ten or as late as age sixteen.

Adolescence in boys does not have such clear-cut criteria. If we use such indices as the appearance of pubic hair, the first seminal ejaculation, or increase in the size of the penis and testes, adolescence in boys usually begins between the ages of eleven and seventeen. Again, there is great variation in age among boys reaching puberty.

Special Problems for Girls

Menarche can be a traumatic event in the life of a young girl who is psychologically unprepared. This is especially true for the EM (early-maturing) girl. However, the girl who is secure in her sex identification and who has had adult support and guidance may regard her first menstruation with pride, as a sign that she is "grown-up" and is no longer a child. The girl whose parents have prepared her for this new experience is less likely to be anxious about her menarche.

Breast development has special psychological overtones in Western culture. America has been described as a breast-oriented nation, and certainly the popularity of the Playmate of the Month, the billboard ads for suntan lotion, the TV ads for "the slightly padded bra," and the direct stares of males of all ages do much to validate this description. During adolescence, then, breast development becomes a psychological symbol of approaching womanhood and sexuality. Typically, physical development of the breast from bud to full size occurs in about three years, from about eleven to about fourteen years of age. The bud stage almost always precedes menarche and the first signs of pubic hair.

Special Problems for Boys

Boys who begin puberty relatively late suffer psychological distress for a variety of reasons. LM (late-maturing) boys are apt to be shorter and physically weaker than the early maturers and are thus less apt to become outstanding athletes. Because social reinforcements are

Adolescent boys are often concerned with penis size. According to researchers Masters and Johnson, the size of the penis is not highly correlated with physical size.

fewer, the late-maturing boy more often turns psychologically inward, becoming introverted.

The size of the penis is also of great concern to the adolescent boy. In the shower room after gym classes the adolescent quickly glances from boy to boy, to see whether he "measures up." The boy with the small penis is often openly ridiculed and his masculinity challenged. He worries that he will be an unsuccessful lover. The facts, however, as reported by William Masters and Virginia Johnson, are that the size of the penis is not highly correlated with a he-man physique or with great physical size. The largest penis they measured (without erection or stretching) was five and a half inches and belonged to a man only 5 feet 7 inches tall. The shortest penis, just over two and a third inches, was found on a man almost 6 feet tall.[22]

Further, Masters and Johnson found little evidence for the widely held myth that the larger the penis, the greater the potential for giving sexual satisfaction. Because the vagina distends when excited in order to permit entry and then contracts around the penis in a snug grip, the size of the penis is of little importance.

Adolescent Sexuality

In his classic study on sexuality, Alfred Kinsey reached a series of conclusions concerning sexual behavior. Kinsey gathered his data in two major studies during the 1940s and 1950s. He reported the following:

1. Men reach their period of greatest sexual activity (defined as sexual arousals leading to orgasm) between sixteen and seventeen years of age.

2. Women tend to be less easily sexually aroused at any age, compared to men, and seem less preoccupied by sex than men.

3. Fifty percent of women and 85 percent of men had intercourse before marriage.

4. Forty percent of women and 95 percent of men masturbated to orgasm.[23]

A more recent series of studies of human sexuality has been conducted by Masters and Johnson. Their results are more up-to-date than Kinsey's and more comprehensive as well, since

CONTEMPORARY ISSUE

Sex Differences: Learned or Genetic?

Aside from the obvious anatomical differences between males and females, there is a question of growing concern as to whether psychological differences between the sexes are learned or innate. The question is indeed of momentous importance, for if the differences are learned, and if, as some suggest, they favor the male, then it is up to us, to society, to change the childrearing and educational practices that produce this lack of fairness. For example, if boys are trained and shaped at an early age to be better equipped to succeed in our competitive society, then it's time the rules and norms were amended so the girls can be given an equal opportunity to achieve success. If on the other hand, there are in fact physiological-psychological differences that are built into the species, then educational (and psychological testing) practices should be altered so that every member of each sex will be given full opportunity to make the most of his or her potential.

The differences that have been the most consistently noted over the years are the following:

1. During the first few months of life, boys are less sensitive to and less often startled by sounds and do not turn as often toward them.
2. Girls show superior development of fine-motor coordination, not just with their fingers, but even in the small muscles of the larynx and pharynx—hence, they even sing in tune at a younger age.
3. Girls learn to speak at a younger age, develop larger vocabularies, and generally retain a linguistic superiority throughout life. In school, they learn foreign languages more easily.
4. Boys suffer far more from speech difficulties, stuttering, stammering, and the use of "um," "er," interjections, and so on.
5. Boys are more overtly aggressive than girls, as children and especially as adolescents. Boys are less able to sit still for long periods of time—thus, they are far more apt to be diagnosed as hyperactive when they reach school age.
6. Boys are superior in tests of spatial relations such as indicating which of four rotated shapes is identical with an original model, or mentally traversing a maze.
7. On IQ tests, females consistently outperform males on a number of verbal subtests, especially those concerning vocabulary, whereas males do better in other areas, notably in those concerning arithmetic. David Wechsler has even provided a formula for a "Masculinity-Femininity" score (1958), based on comparing one's performance on subtests typically excelled in by males with those typically excelled in by females.

Environmentalists explain all these differences as a result of the way our culture treats and differentially reinforces the sexes. No wonder little boys are more active and aggressive: They are told to be by parents, teachers, and story books. Little girls are admonished not to run, jump, or be boisterous, because it simply isn't "ladylike." Through reinforcement, then, little girls condition themselves to sit more quietly and to develop their fine-motor coordination by drawing, learning to sew, or playing with dolls—all generally more passive pursuits. Boys are allowed to throw themselves into rough-and-tumble games, and because of their conditioning, they are less able to sit passively and exercise and develop their fine-muscle coordination. With language development, the situation is similar. Girls, having been *conditioned* to be more passive, are much better able to listen to language, imitate new sounds, and sit still long enough to read a book. Therefore, it's no wonder that they will acquire larger vocabularies. As for speech problems, again culture is the culprit. Society demands more of little boys, and when a three-year-old male misspeaks, the parents make a major issue out of it. So much pressure is put on the male child to speak correctly that he becomes overanxious. After all, isn't he eventually going to have to be the competitive breadwinner of the family? Anxiety then builds on anxiety and a snowball effect is produced with speech pathology as the result. As for spatial relations, boys are more encouraged to be curious about the world of nuts and bolts and hammers and saws. Therefore, it's no surprise that they learn to manipulate spatial concepts. They get more rewards for it. In short, the differences are due to cultural stereotyping, and the sooner we as a society do away with our preconceived notions, the better we'll all be. Girls will then be more able to reach their full potential—and boys will, too, since they will be less wracked by pressures to perform.

The geneticists, on the other hand, insist that the cultural argument, though valid to some extent, has been generalized far beyond the physiological facts. For example, neurologist Richard Restak says that there are indeed fundamental differences, both chemical and morphological, between the male and female brains. The left hemisphere of the female brain is more heterogeneous, more neurologically complex than the male's. (In right-handed persons, and even in 60 percent of left-handed persons, the left hemisphere contains the language centers.) Even among left-hemisphere stroke victims, far more women than men retain their ability to speak and to understand language. Problems based on spatial relations, however, are controlled by the right hemisphere, and here the male brain is more complex. There are, say the geneticists, innate sex differences in brain organization, and to ignore them is simply to escape into fantasy land. Society's task is really to adjust for these differences, not to deny them. Since boys do excel in right-hemisphere tasks, "then tests such as the National Merit Scholarship Examination should be radically redesigned to assure that both sexes have an equal chance. As things now stand, the tests are heavily weighted with items (spatial-relations and mathematics) that virtually guarantee superior male performance.[a] Also, elementary grades should be restructured to allow boys more freedom of action and thereby to reduce the stress that triggers hyperactivity, speech problems, and learning disorders.

[a]   Restak, R. (1979). *The brain: The last frontier* (p. 205). Garden City, N.Y.: Doubleday.

---

they studied both the psychological and the physiological aspects of sexuality. Also, while Kinsey depended almost exclusively on in-depth interviewing for his data, Masters and Johnson combined interviewing with direct observation and measurement of sexual activity. In general, their conclusions supported and extended Kinsey's position. They found, for example, that masturbation is a common sexual practice and that it is not harmful. Fears of "going crazy," ruining your complexion, becoming impotent, weakening physical capacity, and so on are all myths. In addition, they found that women are capable of numerous climaxes in a relatively short time and that female orgasms occur in the clitoris and not in the vagina, as had been previously suggested.

Probably their most significant conclusions were that humans can remain sexually active throughout life and that at least half of married adults suffer from sexual inadequacy.[24] Masters and Johnson point to the need for effective educational programs to help reduce feelings of sexual inadequacy and to eliminate some of the popular misconceptions about human sexuality.

There is no question that part of the so-called hidden agenda of education during the junior- and senior-high-school years is a concern about human sexuality. Accurate information alone, of course, will not solve the complex issues of sexual inadequacy, but it can be an effective first step.

Early and Late Maturation

Much research has gone into discovering what differences exist between early-maturing and late-maturing adolescents, differences other than the rate of physical maturity. One must be careful, in interpreting these studies, not to leap to the conclusion that these other differences between EM and LM adolescents are due only to the adolescent's changing biology. Personality variables, for example, are especially influenced by the way others perceive and, accordingly, treat us. A boy of seventeen whose voice hasn't changed yet, whose body proportions are still as they were when he was twelve, is all too often treated by those around him as though he were, in fact, still only twelve years old.

Similarly, the twelve-year-old boy who is speaking in a rich baritone, whose shoulders have broadened, and who shaves daily, is more apt to be treated with dignity and respect. Social psychologists tell us that the way people respond often depends on how others treat them. People who are treated like children very often respond in childlike ways, and those who are treated like adults respond with more maturity. Early maturity can itself be a problem, however. If teachers and parents see early maturity as a negative characteristic, the adolescent can be adversely affected. This topic will be covered in more detail in Chapter 18. Keeping these interactions in mind, however, we observe that studies on early maturers and late maturers reveal the following:

1. There are almost no differences in IQ, grade placement, or socioeconomic status between EM and LM adolescents. There is some evidence, however, that children with extremely high IQs tend to be early maturers.

2. EM boys were rated by their peers as being physically more attractive and better athletes, and they were more often elected to student office.

3. On personality tests, EM boys showed more self-control, more interest in girls, more extroversion, and were more apt to support cultural norms.

4. EM girls were rated by adults as below average on social and personality traits, whereas LM girls were rated above average.

5. In comparisons of the peer ratings of EM boys and EM girls, EM girls were perceived in a less favorable way.

Thus, early maturity is more apt to be an advantage to the boy, but it may be a disadvantage to the girl in our society.[25]

GROWTH PERIODS AND EDUCATIONAL PROBLEMS

At each age and stage of development children and adolescents need continued assurance from adults in order to accommodate themselves to and assimilate the effects of constant change. During adolescence, diversity and change are at peak intensity, and the differences between the sexes and within the sexes are at a maximum. The junior-high-school years, especially, represent diversity in such areas as physical growth, glandular-sexual changes, social changes, and cognitive shifts. Each individual student and each subgroup of students need extra support during this critical period. For example, the late-maturing boy needs help in developing confidence and needs assurance that before long he too will develop into full maturity. Similarly, the early-maturing girl needs special support to withstand some of the intense pressures she is under from both adults and peers. Handling this situation can be extremely delicate. Class discussions may often do more harm than good, especially when they focus attention on specific students in the class. A public discussion of a particular student's problem may be a humiliating and destructive experience for the individual on whom the spotlight falls. Teachers need to develop an extra awareness of and sensitivity to these aspects of this often hidden classroom agenda. Careful listening to student concerns and some judicious reading between the lines will provide the teacher with more than a few cues as to possible reasons for a student's sudden "unexplainable" upset, mood change, or rapid attention shift.

In physical education and health classes, posting pictures and charts showing growth curves during adolescence may indeed be a case where a picture is worth a thousand words. It should also be helpful to present the students with some facts of sexual growth and maturation. A few facts in this area may remove the mystery and correct some of the blatant untruths that students often pass on to one another. Information of this sort may often be followed by an audible and collective sigh of relief from the class. This is not to suggest that the teacher should deluge the seventh-grader with graphic illustrations from Masters and Johnson, for the student may confuse sex education with sexual encouragement. If a teacher overreacts to this information deficit, the students can be overstimulated. The object is to present information in a style that will help the pupils to become comfortable with their own and their peers' physical, emotional, and sexual growth and less preoccupied by it. The goal is anxiety reduction, not sexual trauma.

SUMMARY

An understanding of the biological basis of behavior is important to understanding developmental psychology. American psychology for too long ignored this important aspect of its own discipline. Little attention, for example, was paid to the emerging field of genetics. Genetics is a relatively new discipline. It is the study of how characteristics are biologically transmitted from parent to offspring.

The basic unit of analysis in genetics is the gene, a tiny particle of heredity located in the nucleus of each of the body's cells. Genes are composed of DNA and RNA molecules. The DNA acts as a blueprint—or template—and contains the coded genetic information within the nucleus of the cell. RNA transmits this information to other parts of the cell. One of biology's most spectacular recent achievements was the deciphering of this genetic code.

Since each offspring receives twenty-three genes from each parent, the new individual is genetically unique, except in the case of identical twins, who begin life as only one cell. Psychologists are able to examine the effects of genetic endowment through both animal and human research.

Psychology's basic principle is that behavior is a result of heredity interacting with environment interacting with time.

Before birth, the human organism goes through three basic stages of development: (1) zygote, (2) embryo, and (3) fetus. Tremendous changes occur during the prenatal period. The organism increases its size dramatically, from a tiny speck to a seven- or eight-pound baby in a period of nine months.

Maturation both before and immediately after birth occurs on a time schedule that is fairly consistent for all members of a given species. The maturation of various organs occurs safely ahead of the time when they must be used.

Reflex and motor development, such as holding the head erect, sitting, crawling, and walking, is heavily influenced by biological maturation, though environmental encounters at the appropriate time are important for full development of the biological potential.

Sensory maturation shows functional development either at birth or within a few days of birth. Touch, smell, taste, and hearing develop slightly before vision.

Bonding is a process that requires direct physical contact between mother and child and occurs within the baby's first three days of life. It is said to produce a strong emotional attachment between the mother and child, and failure to form this bond may cause later episodes of child neglect or even child abuse.

Speech develops from the grunts and cries of birth to a recognizable word by the age of one year. Once the child masters the intricate details of walking, the verbal repertoire increases dramatically.

Adolescence marks the beginning of another growth spurt, a spurt that occurs earlier in girls than in boys. The early-maturing girl and the late-maturing boy may have special problems in our culture. Adolescents need extra support and understanding during this critical period of development.

Sex education must be handled sensitively and with compassion. If a teacher spends too much time attempting to detail the intricacies of sex education, the adolescent may feel overstimulated. He or she may confuse education with encouragement and thus increase rather than decrease his or her psychological problems.

KEY TERMS AND NAMES

genetics
zygote
gene
deoxyribonucleic acid (DNA)
ribonucleic acid (RNA)
Gregor Mendel
dominant gene
recessive gene
phenotype
genotype
polygenic inheritance

behavior genetics
homozygosity
monozygotic (MZ) twins
concordance rate
dizygotic twins
$O = H \leftrightarrow E \leftrightarrow T$
embryo
fetus
bonding
visual cliff
menarche

REFERENCES

1. Spelt, D. K. (1948). The conditioning of the human fetus in utero. *Journal of Experimental Psychology, 38,* 338–346.

2. Lubchenco, L. O. (1976). *The high risk infant.* Philadelphia: Saunders.

3. Lerner, M. I. (1968). *Heredity, evolution and society* (p. 137). San Francisco: Freeman.

4. Thompson, W. R. (1953). The inheritance of behaviour: Behavioural differences in fifteen mouse strains. *Canadian Journal of Psychology, 7,* 145–155.

5. Tryon, R. C. (1940). Genetic differences in maze-learning ability in rats. *Yearbook of the National Society for Studies in Education, 39,* 111–119.

6. Lagerspetz, K. (1964). *Studies on the aggressive behavior of mice.* Helsinki: Suomalainen Tiedeakatemia.

7. Gottesman, L. I., and Shields, J. (1972). *Schizophrenia and genetics: A twin study vantage point.* New York: Academic Press.

8. Lederberg, J. (1971). Genetic engineering,

or the amelioration of genetic defect. *Pharos of Alpha Omega Alpha, 34,* 9–12.

9. Kaplan, B. J. (1972). Malnutrition and mental deficiency. *Psychology Bulletin, 78,* 330.

10. Scarr, S. (1966). Genetic factors in activity motivation. *Child Development, 37,* 663–673.

11. Mussen, P. H., Conger, J. J., and Kagan, J. (1979). *Child development and personality* (p. 95). New York: Harper & Row.

12. Shirley, M. M. (1933). *The first two years,* Vol. III, *Personality manifestations.* Minneapolis: University of Minnesota Press.

13. Munsinger, H. (1975). *Fundamentals of child development.* New York: Holt, Rinehart & Winston.

14. Gibson, E. J., and Walk, R. D. (1960). The visual cliff. *Scientific American, 202,* 2–9.

15. Marano, H. E. (1985). Biology is one key to the bonding of mothers and babies. In H. E. Fitzgerald and M. G. Walraven (Eds.), *Human development* (pp. 85–86). Guilford, Conn.: Dushkin.

16. Chomsky, N. (1959). A review of verbal behavior by B. F. Skinner. *Language, 35,* 26–58.

17. Smith, M. E. (1926). An investigation of the development of the sentence and the extent of vocabulary in young children. *University of Iowa Studies in Child Welfare, 3*(3), 5.

18. Mussen, P. H., and Conger, J. J. (1969). *Child development and personality.* New York: Harper & Row.

19. Restak, R. (1979). *The brain: The last frontier.* Garden City, N. Y.: Doubleday.

20. Curtiss, S. (1977). *A psycholinguistic study of a modern-day wild child.* New York: Academic Press.

21. Maratsos, M. (1979). Is there language after puberty? *Contemporary Psychology, 24*(6), 456.

22. Masters, W. H., and Johnson, V. E. (1966). *Human sexual response.* Boston: Little, Brown.

23. Kinsey, A. C., Pomeroy, W. B., and Martin, C. E. (1948). *Sexual behavior in the human male.* Philadelphia: Saunders. See also Kinsey, A. C., Pomeroy, W. B., Martin, C. E., and Gebhard, P. H. (1953). *Sexual behavior in the human female.* Philadelphia: Saunders.

24. Masters and Johnson, *Human sexual response.*

25. Wilson, J. A. R., Robeck, M. C., and Michael, W. B. (1969). *Psychological foundations of learning and teaching* (pp. 188–189). New York: McGraw-Hill.

4

EARLY EXPERIENCE

"As the twig is bent, so grows the tree." "You can't teach an old dog new tricks." "Train them during their formative years." These statements and others like them attest to the fact that we have long recognized the significance of early experience for growth and development. Yet it is only within this century that we have come to appreciate how important early experience really is. It is also only recently that we have begun to recognize in how many ways our psychological and physical beings are affected by the amount and quality of our early experience.

It is true that psychologists have for some time recognized the importance of early experience for emotional growth. Freud, for example, wrote many papers at the turn of the century indicating that personality development is a product of one's childhood. Many educators agreed with this, and special schools were designed to enhance emotional and personal growth during these crucial years. In England, A. S. Neill established Summerhill, a boarding school where the major emphasis was on encouraging healthy emotional adjustment.[1] At Summerhill every student participates in school and curriculum decisions. No classes, books, or exams are required. Free expression of ideas and talent is encouraged, and only minimal restraints are placed on the children in all areas of their lives. There are many schools like Summerhill throughout the world, and it is safe to say that most schools today, not just the Summerhills, have been influenced to some degree by this alternative to the traditional, more authoritarian approach to education.

The point is that as psychologists learn more about human development, educators do respond accordingly—and sometimes too zealously. An indiscriminate embracing of a new theory may produce a curriculum that emphasizes one particular area at the expense of other important areas. For example, it has been seriously argued that the Summerhills may be nurturing emotional growth at the expense of intellectual growth.

Despite the fact that for many years now early experience has been considered critical in shaping emotional development, psychologists have only recently come to recognize the importance of these same years to intellectual development.

CONTEMPORARY ISSUE

Free Schools: An Idea Whose Time Has Passed?

During the height of the anti-schooling movement in the middle 1960s, a new educational concept swept the land. Traditionally organized schools in both cities and suburbs seemed grossly inadequate to meet the needs of students. The "thunder on the left" mounted. Moderates who suggested adjustments and alternatives were shouted down. In the midst of a heady revolutionary atmosphere, new voices called for the destruction of schooling in its present form. The heroes of the new revolution were many. Jonathan Kozol's account of life in an urban school system titled *Death at an Early Age* seared the conscience of the country. Herbert Kohl's poignant account of *Thirty-six Children* electrified educators and laypersons alike with a grim and guilt-inducing portrait of the slow and painful destruction of schoolchildren. Similarly, Ivan Illich issued pronouncements that shook the very foundations of public education. Society, Illich declared, must be deschooled. Schools as we know them need to be eliminated. As institutions originally designed to educate, schools have failed and have become instead institutions of oppression. As a result, freedom is circumscribed rather than promoted.

On the basis of these ideas, some educators began to propose a new form, Free Schools. With A. S. Neill's famous Summerhill school as a model, and Neill himself as a combination guru and patron saint, the new format began to spread like wildfire. Abandoned storefronts in central cities became mini-meccas for the new approach. The hills of rural countrysides sprouted little Summerhills. At one point, a cynic commented that if any more Free Schools were established in Vermont, they would soon have more pupils than cows. Even somewhat reserved suburban systems, which had traditionally seemed more like corporations than schools, set up small but nevertheless genuine Free Schools. Of course, such school systems did have to recruit a noticeably different faculty: those who would be at ease in overalls, surrounded by potter's wheels, and physically capable of canoe trips. However, there was no dearth of applicants. Many of the factories of teacher education retooled and began recruiting and training a new breed of teacher in the spirit of the Peace Corps and the New Frontier. Young, idealistic college graduates largely from well-to-do backgrounds were attracted to the cause.

And a cause it was. Rhetoric and ideology abounded. The tough, ubiquitous, and almost unsolvable problems of education were miraculously solved. Throw out structure, lesson plans, schedules, textbooks, assignments, and, most of all, tests. Replace them with freedom. Teaching was seen as a process at the exclusive control and behest of the pupils. In this view, the adult *never* suggests and *never, never* coerces. Rather, the teacher waits, in some cases as long as two years, Neill noted, for pupil initiative. Then learning is organized by the pupils around their needs and desires.

So much for history. Where are we now? Is the Free School movement doomed? Some think so, including major rhetoricians like Kozol, who now travels the country with speeches filled with despair and pessimism. Others might say the movement itself was bound to fail, since it was a revolution without substance. In other words, the Free Schools knew what was wrong but not what to do about it. The requisite educational theory (and—perish the thought—research) was simply nonexistent. Thus, proclaiming the benefits of freedom was not the same as the educator's task. To say was easy, to do was not. Extolling the vir-

EARLY EXPERIENCE: THE KEY TO THE NATURE-NURTURE PUZZLE

The nature-nurture question remained unresolved for so many years because the issue was stated as an either/or proposition: The hereditarians emphasized heredity at the expense of environment, and the environmentalists emphasized environment at the expense of hered-

ity. Neither side fully recognized the importance of the third dimension, time. Development is a result of heredity interacting with environment, but a key question remains: Is there a critical or a best time for the interaction to take place?

With regard to imprinting, it must be remembered that goslings learn to follow the moving stimulus only if the stimulus is presented during a certain critical time of their lives: from

tues of a Che Guevara, the folk hero of the Cuban revolution, does grab one's attention, but then what?

On the other hand, is the movement really dead? Free Schools are clearly in retreat, but could they simply be suffering a temporary setback? After all, the history of all revolutionary movements indicates that progress is never linear. Even the mighty French Revolution was followed by the Thermadorian reaction. Are we merely experiencing a temporary pause or short-term setback? The ideas are still in place and potentially just as compelling in the 1980s as they were in the 1960s. Humans still yearn for freedom. The vision of pupils leading self-directing lives cannot help but remain attractively humanistic. Perhaps next time, the new leadership for Free Schools will have learned something from the failures of the recent past—namely, that effective education is something of a paradox, a balance between support and challenge. If Free School men and women are willing to forgo some of the excesses of rhetoric and genuinely grapple with the educator's basic paradox, we may yet witness a rebirth. Then Free Schools may once again move to center stage as a controversial challenge to traditionally organized schooling.

about ten to thirty hours after hatching. Presenting the stimulus thirty-five or forty hours after hatching is no good—no learning occurs. It is obvious that this form of learning requires a hereditary potential as well as an environmental encounter. But which is more important? In fact, neither matters at all until we mix in the third ingredient, the time at which the encounter occurs. If it happens too soon, no learning, or minimal learning, occurs, and the same is true if the encounter is too late.

Two Studies of the Critical-Time Hypothesis

A number of years ago, a forward-looking psychologist, Myrtle McGraw, did a comprehensive study of human development, using a pair of twin boys as subjects.[2] One of the twins, Johnny, was given a great amount of early training in a wide variety of activities. The other twin, Jimmy, was given no practice in these activities until months later.

McGraw found that special, early practice had little or no effect on some behaviors, such as creeping, hanging by the hands, grasping objects, or even walking. Though Johnny was given stepping practice almost from birth, both twins took their first halting steps alone at nine months and both learned to walk almost simultaneously at twelve months. McGraw called behaviors such as these "phylogenetic activities" and concluded that they are not influenced very much by the environment or special practice. However, with regard to certain special skills that McGraw called "ontogenetic activities," the trained twin, Johnny, learned faster than his brother. Johnny began learning to roller-skate when he was twelve months old, just when he was learning to walk, and by fourteen months he was both skating and walking with considerable grace. Jimmy did not begin skating lessons until he was twenty-two months old, and he did not profit nearly as much from this late training. McGraw found that delaying the training made it more difficult to learn this skill. The development of other motor skills, however, was actually damaged by early training. Johnny was given special training in tricycling when he was eleven months old and displayed little progress until he was about nineteen or twenty months old, when he suddenly improved rather dramatically. Jimmy began tricycling when he was twenty-two months old, learned the skill quickly and efficiently, and became superior to his pretrained brother. The twin with the early training formed poor habits and was unable to develop the skill as well as the twin whose training was delayed.

McGraw concluded that there are optimal time periods during development when special training will assure the full acquisition of various motor skills. Said McGraw, "There are critical periods when any given activity is most susceptible to modification through repetition of performance."[3]

There are critical, optimal periods when children can most easily be taught certain motor skills. For example, it is best to teach a child to roller-skate at the same time he or she is learning to walk. However, development of some motor skills is actually retarded by early training.

McGraw's research was carried out some five decades ago, and her conclusions were definitely ahead of their time. She was the first psychologist to speak of "critical periods" in human development and although her views were not widely accepted during the heyday of American behaviorism, they now have a modern ring. In childrearing she advocated a middle road between constantly urging the child to practice new activities and just sitting back, relaxing, and allowing nature to take its own sweet time. Forcing children into activities before the critical period, when their nerves and muscles are simply not ready, is not only useless but, more important, may even be damaging.

In another classic study, Josaphine R. Hilgard provided a special twelve-week practice period for a group of two-year-old children on such motor tasks as stair climbing and cutting with scissors. Another group of two-year-olds was given the training for only one week, the last week of the experiment. The children in the second group, older and presumably more ma-

ture when their training began, initially learned these tasks more quickly than did the other group, but they never fully caught up. The group with the early (and longer) training maintained superiority at the experiment's end.[4]

A great deal of research remains to be done in this important area. At this point there are few hard data to indicate precisely when the various critical periods occur. We do know, however, the critical periods generally coincide with periods of most rapid growth. John P. Scott has defined the critical period as a "time when a large effect can be produced by a smaller change in conditions than in any later or earlier period in life." Scott further states that "there must be changes taking place within the animal which are correlated with time and hence account for the existence of critical periods."[5] Thus, the concept of critical periods has profound importance in education. We must hope to catch the child at exactly that time when environmental encounters will most effectively allow his or her hereditary potential to flourish. Damage can be done, impairment can occur, if we are either too early or too late.

EARLY EXPERIENCE: OBSERVATIONS AND THEORIES

The Berkeley Growth Study

Beginning in 1929, Nancy Bayley and her colleagues at the University of California, Berkeley, began a long-term study of human growth and development.[6] This was a longitudinal research study in that the same subjects were followed and continually tested over the years. Actually, data are still being collected on the original group of subjects, all of whom are now approximately in their mid-sixties. Although the study has contributed vast amounts of new data and fresh insights on the flow of human development, we will focus on only four specific observations at this time.

1. *IQs are not constant.* Bayley's results have challenged the belief cherished by some psychologists that one's IQ score is immutable. Bayley found considerable variation in measured intelligence over long periods of time; in other words, one's IQ score is not indelibly carved in the brain at birth but is instead a human quality that ebbs and flows as a result of environmental circumstances.[7]

2. *IQ variability is greatest during the first few years of life.* By comparing correlations between IQs measured at various ages, Bayley found that the older the child, the greater the IQ stability. This evidence foreshadowed the main thrust of Benjamin Bloom's hypothesis, to be discussed in the next section.

3. *Intellectual ability may continue to grow throughout life.* Bayley's data also indicate that intellectual ability does not top out in the late teens or early twenties but may continue to increase at least up to age fifty, when Bayley's subjects were last tested. Again, whether an adult's intellect grows or declines seems to be a function of environmental stimulation. The high-school dropout who spends all his or her working life bagging groceries in a supermarket is less apt to experience intellectual growth than someone who works in areas requiring more strenuous mental exercise.

4. *The components of intellect change with age level.* Perhaps Nancy Bayley's most provocative contribution is her suggestion that intellectual development in childhood occurs in qualitatively different stages. In her view, the fact that a child's growth score gradually shifts in strength from area to area supports the notion that changes occur in the organization of intellectual factors from one age to another. This view is consistent with that of Jean Piaget, to be presented in the next chapter.

Bloom's Hypothesis

Benjamin Bloom (1964) in a classic book has analyzed, sorted, and sifted through virtually all the studies on intellectual growth.[8] Bloom plots a negatively accelerated growth curve for intellectual development—that is, with increasing age, there is a decreasingly positive effect from a beneficial environment. Three-year-old children profit far more from enriching experiences than seven- or eight-year-old children. Bloom argues that beneficial early experience is absolutely essential for cognitive growth. Almost two-thirds of our ultimate cognitive ability is formed by the time we are six years old, the age, incidentally, when most children are just entering school. By the time formal education begins, the child's potential for further intellectual development is beginning to slow. Earlier intervention is required, especially among the disadvantaged groups. Experience has its most profound effect very early in life, during the period of most rapid growth.

This finding is consistent with Scott's argument regarding critical periods. Scott feels that critical periods occur when rapid organization of some kind is going on within the individual. Those mental changes that take place during a period of rapid development often occur easily and accidentally and then become a fixed and fairly permanent feature of the newly stabilized organization. Scott also reasons that any time we form new relationships, especially social relationships, can be a critical period for that relationship. Since most new relationships occur in early childhood, this is when most critical periods should occur. However, major new re-

NANCY BAYLEY

the next two years, she taught at the University of Wyoming, and in 1928 began teaching at the University of California at Berkeley. During the following year she began her famous longitudinal Berkeley Growth Study, starting with sixty-one healthy newborn infants. Testing and retesting this group over the years, both psychologically and physically, she produced many fresh and startling insights into the complex phenomenon of human growth.

In 1954 Bayley left Berkeley to become chief of the Child Development section at the National Institute of Mental Health in Bethesda, Maryland but periodically returned to Berkeley to locate and test her sample subjects for the Berkeley Growth Study. In 1964 she returned to Berkeley to serve both as the administrator of the newly formed Harold E. Jones Child Study Center and as a research psychologist at the University of California. She retired in 1971.

In addition to being selected as the American Psychological Association's Distinguished Scientist, Nancy Bayley won the G. Stanley Hall award in 1971, a special award presented by the American Psychological Association's Division of Developmental Psychology. Though formally retired, Bayley continues her productive professional career. She has contributed nearly one hundred scientific publications so far, and it is clear that as her 1929 sample continues to ripen and mature, it will continue to enrich psychology's book of knowledge.

Nancy Bayley was the first woman ever to win the American Psychological Association's prestigious Distinguished Scientific Contribution award. Bayley received this recognition in 1966, and her citation included the following: "For the enterprise, pertinacity and insight with which she has studied human growth over long segments of the life cycle. . . . Her studies have enriched psychology with enduring contributions to the measurement and meaning of intelligence . . . her participation in a number of major programs of developmental research is a paradigm of the conjoint efforts which are essential in a field whose problems span the generations."[a]

Nancy Bayley was born in 1899 in a small town called "the Dallas" near the northern border of Oregon. She attended local schools there and went on to earn her B.S. and M.A. degrees from the University of Washington. She received her Ph.D. in psychology from Iowa State in 1926, just two years after completing her M.A. degree. For

---

[a] *American Psychologist, 21* (December 1966), 1191.

lationships also take place in adolescence and in adulthood. One of the most important critical periods, in fact, often occurs during adolescence, when young people may form their first sexual relationships. The sexual problems an adult suffers are probably the result of events happening during adolescence. Another major critical period may take place during adulthood, when many women bear their first child; and this may be a critical period for both parents.

Bloom concludes that not only does lack of an enriched environment itself hinder a child's intellectual development, but the loss of precious time is especially harmful because there is no way to compensate for it later on. Just as in the case of Konrad Lorenz's goslings, there may be critical periods for intellectual development: Once the period is over, new stimuli have less and less effect.

Stimulus Variety: The Basic Ingredient

J. McV. Hunt reviewed the literature on early experience and reported that early stimulus deprivation is more likely to prevent normal motor development than early motor restriction.[9] For example, Hopi children who are reared on cradleboards, which almost completely inhibit their movements, walk as early as Hopi children reared with full use of their legs. Thus, as far as walking is concerned, early motor restriction does not seem seriously to affect later motor development. However, the effect of early stimulus restriction is, as Hunt points out, dramatically different.

Not only is early stimulus deprivation damaging to later intellectual development, but it also appears to impair later motor development. Wayne Dennis discovered an orphanage in Teheran where the children were kept in a condition of extreme isolation, each one living in a separate, almost soundproof, white cubicle.[10] The result of this severe sensory restriction was that virtually all the children were mentally retarded, despite the fact that they came almost exclusively from the literate population of Iran. This, of course, is further evidence that intellectual development is a function of both environment and heredity. But perhaps the most re-

markable finding of the Dennis study is that these stimulus-deprived children who had complete motor freedom were also physically retarded. Sixty percent of the children were unable to sit up alone when they were two years old, and 85 percent could not walk when they were four years old. Compare this with the cradleboard-reared Hopi children. Hunt points out that "these Hopi children reared on cradleboards were often carried about on their mothers' backs. Thus, while their arms and legs might be restricted, their eyes and ears could feast upon a rich variety of input."[11]

As Hunt has been insisting for over two decades, the crucial ingredient in intellectual development is stimulus variety. The more the child hears, sees, and touches, the more the child will want to hear, see, and touch, and the more intellectual growth will occur. On the other hand, Hunt is careful to advocate that the child should not suddenly be overwhelmed with stimulus variety. In what he calls the "problem of the match," he points out that the variety of inputs must somehow be matched with the child's present growth. Too much stimulus heterogeneity, and the child withdraws in frustration; too little, and the child withdraws in boredom. Hunt insists that there is a point of optimum stimulus variety that children naturally seek; when this is reached, children display a joy, a spontaneous interest in learning, and continuous cognitive growth.

It is important to emphasize that Hunt and others are not implying that intelligence is fixed, nor that stimulus variety must be matched with innate potential. Quite the contrary! Intellectual abilities grow and are nourished by stimulus variety. The match is between stimulus inputs and the child's present position on the growth continuum, a position that itself results in large measure from the child's own past experiences and environmental encounters. These encounters begin at birth. There is even evidence that some learning takes place before birth, while the child is still in the womb.[12] But certainly during early infancy, stimulus encounters—for example, in the game of peek-a-boo, which always seems to entertain—enable the baby to gather experience for encounters in later childhood.

Piaget and Bruner on Early Experience

For over forty years at the University of Geneva, Switzerland, Jean Piaget was a student of human development, especially the development of concept formation. Through carefully detailed, hour-by-hour observation of the developing child, Piaget formulated a theory of how children go about the business of learning to know, learning concept formation. A more detailed account of Piaget's position is presented in Chapter 5. It is enough now to say that Piaget describes the child's attempts to develop concepts—such as a concept of self as an entity separate from the environment, and concepts of time, cause and effect, conservation, and number.

Perhaps the most famous of the concepts Piaget has described is that of conservation, which he illustrates in the following manner. A child is shown a short, wide glass of water, and then the water is poured into a tall, thin beaker. The water level is much higher in the thin container than it was in the wide one. The child who recognizes that the amount of water has remained constant regardless of the height is said to have developed the concept of conservation of volume. However, the child who says that the taller beaker contains more water is assumed not yet to have reached this stage of concept formation.

According to Piaget, children can form concepts such as conservation or number only after they have gone through a series of developmental stages that are sequential in nature. Certain cognitive structures, or as Piaget calls them, "schemata," must be formed before children can understand mathematics, for example. If they have not discovered certain logical relationships, such as that seven large blocks are equal numerically to seven small blocks, then their later understanding of geometrical concepts or even of number itself will be arrested to some extent.

Jerome Bruner fills in more of the details. Bruner, like Piaget, maintains that cognitive growth depends on a process of model formation: the formation of rules, or strategies, for

Bruner insists that a variety of stimuli and a changing environment are necessary for proper cognitive growth.

coping with the environment. As they develop, children learn various techniques that enable them to make maximum use of the information their environment provides.

It is also important to note that Bruner insists that, for proper cognitive growth to occur, the young child must be exposed to a variety of stimuli, a shifting environment. Stimulus heterogeneity at an early age is a crucial ingredient in intellectual growth. The cognitive growth of children who have been deprived of sensory stimulation for any reason will be arrested, possibly irreversibly so.

Bruner supports his case for environmental encounters by citing the physiological work of Karl Pribram and others.[13] Bruner's interest in the developing organism results not only in the formulation of an explanatory model but also in a search for physiological correlates. It is now known that the traditional concept of sensory-neural impulses connecting in the nervous system with the motor-neural impulses was an oversimplification. The new evidence, from within the organism itself, shows us that when the receptor is stimulated, there is a flow of impulses toward the central nervous system and a simultaneous neural flow back to the receptor. The receptor is not a mere passive recipient of any and all stimulation but a filter through which only certain stimuli pass. Bruner has maintained that the organism cannot take in all the information the environment contains. Physiological evidence supports this, and Bruner sees it as an adaptive phenomenon, the ability to minimize environmental surprises aiding the organism in its quest for survival.

THE BIOLOGICAL BASIS OF EARLY EXPERIENCE

Now that we have seen that psychologists such as Scott, Bloom, Hunt, Piaget, and Bruner have pointed to the importance of early experience in determining intellectual level, the next questions might logically be, "What is the biological basis for this argument? Are there corresponding physiological changes taking place as a result of a beneficial early environment?"

The eminent physiological psychologist D. O. Hebb has outlined a theoretical model of the organization of neural activity in the brain.[14]

Hebb contends that this organization depends on environmental stimulation, that proper development of the neural arrangements in the brain will not occur unless the developing organism has the opportunity to experience environmental changes.

The A/S Ratio

Hebb noted that there were significant differences among organisms in the proportion of association and sensory areas within the brain. Compared to the human, a lower organism such as a rat has fewer association areas and more sensory areas. Thus, the rat, that workhorse of American psychology, is more sensory-bound, more responsive to the stimuli in its environment than is the human. The human brain, with its greater number of association areas, is capable of far more and probably many different varieties of learning than the rat brain. Also, the relatively small sensory area makes the human less a creature of the moment, less apt to respond impulsively to every minute environmental change. It also means that as we go up the phylogenetic continuum, as the ratio of association areas to sensory areas (A/S ratio) increases, the developmental importance of pronounced stimulus heterogeneity also increases. Humans, after all, cannot perceive subtle changes in odor as well as some of the lower primates are able to.

Hebb emphasized the critical importance of early experience on later development, especially on cognitive development. Hebb saw the human brain as unorganized and capable of only relatively simple forms of learning during infancy and early childhood. As the child experiences more and more environmental stimulation, the brain slowly becomes organized. A group of neurons begins to work as a unit. Hebb called this organized pattern of brain cells a "cell assembly." With the formation of a variety of cell assemblies, new learning takes place more quickly. As this process continues, as more cell assemblies are formed, a larger organization takes place: A series of cell assemblies, called "phase sequences," are formed. Finally, as the phase sequences begin acting in concert, widespread organization of the brain results, and the child is now capable of extremely rapid learning. The difference between a young child in the cell-assembly stage, slowly and painstakingly learning a simple task, and an older child, with a series of smooth-functioning, integrated phase sequences already formed, quickly learning complex relationships and concepts, is similar to the difference between a do-it-yourself carpenter and an experienced prefab team. The do-it-yourself carpenter, to borrow an analogy,[15] could take months constructing a home that the professional prefab crew could complete in days.

Based on Hebb's hypothesis of cell assemblies and phase sequences, researchers at McGill University compared the performance of animals of enriched early experience with animals of impoverished early experience. The McGill researchers wanted to determine whether organisms provided with stimulus variety during the early period of cell assemblies would reflect this early enrichment in their performance as adults. The researchers found what they were looking for.

Using the Hebb-Williams maze, a kind of animal IQ test, Hebb compared rats raised in the impoverished environment of laboratory cages with rats raised in the home as pets and found the home-reared animals superior. Other investigators found an even greater difference when they performed the same experiment using dog litter-mates.[16] The results of this study also favored the home-reared pets, lending further support to the suggestion that as we go up the phylogenetic continuum (as we select species with higher A/S ratios), the beneficial effects of an enriched early environment increase.

Perhaps even more significant is the work of Bernard Hymovitch.[17] This investigation was conducted entirely within the controlled conditions of the laboratory and showed that stimulus variety during early life was more effective than the same experience in later life. Hymovitch also showed that early stimulus variety was more beneficial to later maze-learning ability than early response variety. Animals with enriched response experience failed to benefit as much, measured by their later performance on the Hebb-Williams maze, as animals with enriched stimulus experience.

Hebb is certain that the results are precisely the same at the human level. Children who are raised up to the age of six in impoverished slum environments can never make up for this crucial intellectual deficit. The lack of stimulus variety early in a child's life cannot be fully compensated for by later enrichment, "because such damage is not reparable."[18]

The Evidence from Krech

More direct and even more startling evidence supporting the early-experience position has been supplied by the exciting and innovative research of David Krech.[19] It had been shown that certain drugs, such as Metrazol, may increase an organism's ability to learn, and other drugs, such as magnesium pemoline, may increase the organism's ability to retain what has been learned.[20] Krech reasoned, however, that the reverse might also be true—that is, if chemical agents could effect changes in the learning process, then environmental manipulation might bring about changes in the chemistry of the brain. By selecting twelve pairs of rat twins and randomly assigning them to two groups, Krech was able to control for possible genetic differences. One group of rats was raised in a stimulating environment, in a cage equipped with ladders, running wheels, and other "rat toys." These animals were let out of their cages for thirty minutes each day and allowed to explore new territory. They were also trained to perform numerous learning tasks and in general received a rich and varied array of stimulus inputs. The other group of rats was raised in a condition of extreme stimulus homogeneity. These rats lived alone in dimly lit cages, were rarely handled, and were never allowed to explore areas outside the cage. All animals, however, received exactly the same diet.

After about three months all the animals were sacrificed and their brains analyzed morphologically and chemically. If Hebb's theory is valid the brains of the stimulated animals, the animals that had been exposed to a large variety of learning situations, should be anatomically different from the brains of the deprived animals. That is, if the act of learning does indeed form neural cell assemblies and phase sequences, there might be some physical evidence for this in the brains of the stimulated rats. In fact, Krech may have supplied the evidence. The brains of the enriched rats were chemically and structurally different from the brains of their siblings. The cortex (gray matter) was larger, deeper, and heavier in the stimulated rats. Three components have been identified as contributing to this increase in brain size: (1) an increased number of glia cells (possible repositories of memory traces), (2) increased size of the cell bodies and their nuclei, and (3) an increase in the diameter of the blood vessels supplying the cortex.

Chemically, the brains also differed. The brains of the enriched animals showed greater quantities of an important ezyme—acetylcholinesterase—an enzyme that readies the nerve cells for further neural transmissions. Krech has thus demonstrated that providing stimulus and response variety during the early life of these animals caused chemical and structural changes in their brains and increased their ability to learn and to solve problems. In a very real sense he may have identified some of the physiological correlates of Hebb's constructs.

Environmental Stimulation for Physiological Development

It is now clear that for proper physiological development to occur, environmental stimulation is necessary; the nervous system and the perceptual apparatus do not mature automatically according to some preset internal clock.

Critics of the early-experience position often fall back on the neurological argument that since no new brain cells are added after birth, the central nervous system must remain unchanged, with or without environmental stimulation. They argue that the baby comes into the world with a full complement of typical brain cells and that, since no new cells are added, the baby must make do with the original equipment. However, as Krech has shown, the way this original equipment is organized and modified is definitely a function of environmental interactions. Krech proved that structural and chemical changes within the brain resulted from the type of early experience provided.

Further evidence comes from the exciting research of Joseph Altman.[21] Altman has challenged the traditional view that newborn children have all the brain cells they will ever get. Altman has found that tiny nerve cells (micro-

neurons) do arise in the brains of young animals after birth. These newly discovered tiny neurons apparently provide interconnections for some of the larger, more typical brain cells.

Neurons send out branches—axons and dendrites—in order that the neural impulse can travel from one neuron to the next (see Figure 4.1). The junction between the axon of one neuron and the dendrite of the next is called the "synapse." The neuron sends a message out along one axon and the dendrite of the next neuron picks up the message at the synapse. Often, the dendrite, the receiving branch, sends out a physical projection called a "dendritic spine." This is something like adding another length to your TV antenna in order to get a

FIGURE 4.1 Neural impulses travel from one neuron to the next along the branches of the neuron—axons and dendrites.

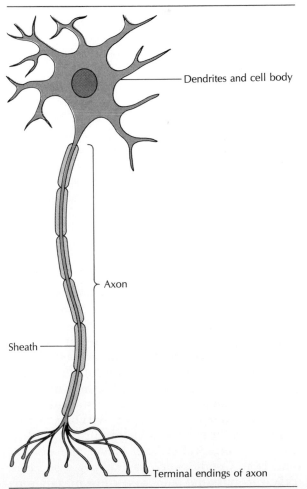

Dendrites and cell body

Axon

Sheath

Terminal endings of axon

better picture. Neurologists have found, however, that if these synapses are not used, the dendritic spines wither away and finally disappear. If a synapse is used frequently, new dendritic spines appear. It's as though the size and complexity of the antenna were a function of how often the TV set was used.

It has also been found that sensory apparatus must be stimulated by the environment in order to develop properly. Neurons on the retina of the eye may become damaged unless they are given visual stimulation.

A. H. Riesen reared chimpanzees in complete darkness and found that permanent damage was done to their visual apparatus.[22] Degeneration of the ganglion cells of the retina was noted in all animals, but if the period of darkness was twelve weeks or less, a physiological recovery was possible. One animal, kept in darkness for a year, showed more extensive damage and suffered a permanent loss of ganglion cells. Visual stimulation is therefore necessary for the proper development of nervous tissue. It is also necessary because, as Riesen has made clear, we really have to "learn" how to see. Using a similar design, Riesen raised cats in darkness, and although the resulting retinal degeneration was less severe than with the chimpanzees, it did occur.[23] Thus, we see that stimulation is more important as we progress up the phylogenetic ladder.

And what is behaviorism's answer to this wave of evidence in support of enriched early experience?

Skinner's Air Crib—Healthful but Unstimulating

B. F. Skinner, today's most important behaviorist, in an article entitled, "Skinner Agrees He Is the Most Important Influence in Psychology," urges parents to raise their children in his 1945 invention, the air crib.[24] The air crib is an "air-conditioned, temperature-controlled, germ-free, sound-proof compartment in which the baby can sleep and play without blankets or clothing other than a diaper."[25] While in this cubicle, the baby is less likely to catch cold or to suffer from heat rash. However, the air crib, or "Heir Conditioner" as Skinner also once called it, puts the baby in a constant environment and may not provide the enriching variety

of stimulus inputs so important to intellectual development. By the time the baby outgrows the air crib, it may be too late to compensate for this early deprivation.

HEAD START'S SUCCESS: THE PERRY PRESCHOOL PROGRAM

You may be wondering what all these studies of children raised on cradleboards, rats raised in enriched environments, chimps raised in darkness, and so on have to do with the intellectual growth of children. What proof do we have that these theories and studies have any validity in the real world of the schoolchild? Hasn't the early-experience theory been tested, for example in the Head Start program, and been found wanting?

In fact, Head Start was deemed a failure almost from its inception. The Westinghouse Learning Corporation and Ohio University released a highly critical evaluation of Head Start as early as 1969, only four years after the first Head Start program was put into effect. Later, there was general agreement with such statements as H. M. Levin's, that "good preschool programs are able to produce salutary increases in IQ for disadvantaged children, but these improvements *are not maintained* when the children enter the primary grades."[26] New evidence suggests that the critics may have spoken too soon.

The Head Start Synthesis Project of 1983, an analysis of outcomes from virtually all Head Start programs up to that time, found that they were indeed effective, that Head Start could be isolated as a causal variable in improving intellectual performance.[27] In fact, for Head Start the news gets even better. The report showed that Head Start programs have produced improvements over the years, in terms both of the intellectual gains found when the children entered regular school and, more important, in the tendency of those gains to persist.

The Perry Preschool Program of Ypsilanti, Michigan, has reported the results of a longitudinal study of Head Start participants who have been followed over the years from ages three and four to age nineteen.[28] This Head Start program was repeated each year for five successive groups of entering children. The evidence presented here is based on the first two

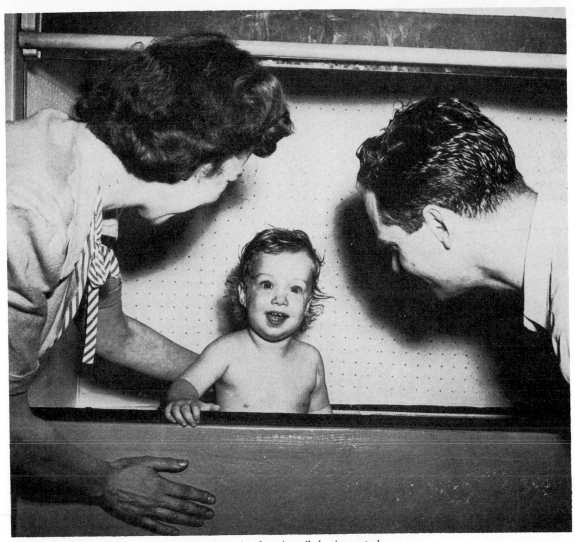

Skinner's daughter Debbie is shown here in the air crib he invented.

entering groups, those that began in the early 1960s.

The main finding, in brief, is that Head Start has a dramatic long-term effectiveness, and that a quality preschool program can change the lives of low-income, educationally at-risk children and their families.

Design of the Study

The Perry Preschool Program was set up as a true experimental design, with random assignment of matched subjects to the experimental group (who received the preschool program) or to the control group (who received no preschool program). The subjects, 123 black youths from families of low socioeconomic status, all had normal to below-normal Stanford-Binet IQs of from 60 to 90, and none showed signs of organic handicap.

The children in the experimental group participated in the program for two school years at ages three and four, and the children *in both groups*, experimental and control, received the same schedule of comparison tests and interviews (ruling out continuing evaluations as a confounding variable). Classes for the experimental group went for two and a half hours each morning, Monday through Friday, from October to May. Teachers (there was one teacher for every five children) also visited the homes of all their students for one and a half hours weekly, meeting with both mother and child together. Each mother was, therefore, kept aware of her child's progress, and the resources of the mother were strengthened in the hope that the child's development would be aided by the mother during after-school hours.

The curriculum for the program was especially designed to provide a wide variety of stimulus inputs, without overwhelming the child. Hunt's "problem of the match" was of vital concern to the framers of the curriculum, but, in their words, "program effectiveness is much more dependent upon the overall quality of program operations than on a specific curriculum."[29]

Outcomes of the Study

Although the experimental and control groups were repeatedly measured over the years, the outcome data to follow are based on the most recent measures, taken when the participants had reached age nineteen (see Table 4.1).

Increased school success   Those subjects who had attended the preschool program showed a significant increase in overall school success, as measured by a number of key factors:

1. Better academic grades

2. Fewer failing marks

3. Fewer absences in elementary school

4. Fewer special-education placements

5. Higher scores on the APL, the Adult Performance Level Survey, a standardized test developed by the American College Testing Program for assessing the skills needed for educational and economic success in modern society

6. Greater likelihood of graduating from high school

7. Greater likelihood of continuing their education after high school

8. A more favorable attitude toward high school (a particularly important finding, since it points to the fact that early childhood

TABLE 4.1   MAJOR FINDINGS AT AGE NINETEEN IN THE PERRY PRESCHOOL PROGRAM

CATEGORY	NUMBER[a] RESPONDING	PRESCHOOL GROUP	NO-PRESCHOOL GROUP	p[b]
Employed	121	59%	32%	.032
High-school graduation (or its equivalent)	121	67%	49%	.034
College or vocational training	121	38%	21%	.029
Ever detained or arrested	121	31%	51%	.022
Females only: teen pregnancies, per hundred	49	64	117	.084
Functional competence (APL Survey: possible score 40)	109	24.6	21.8	.025
Percent of years in special education	112	16%	28%	.039

[a] Total n = 123.
[b] Two-tailed p-values are presented if less than .100.

From J. R. Berrueta-Clement, L. J. Schweinhart, W. S. Barnett, A. S. Epstein, and D. P. Weikart. Changed Lives: The Effects of the Perry Preschool Program on Youths Through Age 19 *(Ypsilanti, Mich.: High/Scope Press, 1984), p. 2. Used with permission.*

education increases the efficiency of later schooling)

IQ differences   Although preschool participants in the Perry Program showed significantly higher Stanford-Binet IQs on entering first grade, the difference narrowed by the time the children reached fourth grade. It may very well be that ages three and four are too late to effect dramatic IQ improvement, but not too late to provide the enrichment for disadvantaged children to do better in school in the long run.

Socioeconomic success   Those who participated in the preschool program generally showed marked increases in socioeconomic success at age nineteen, as measured by two factors: (1) increased employment and (2) less reliance on welfare, food stamps, or other assistance programs.

Social responsibility   Another long-lasting consequence of the Perry Program showed up in an increase in social responsibility. Those

who participated in Head Start were found to have (1) fewer police arrests, both as juveniles and as adults, (2) fewer out-of-wedlock pregnancies, and (3) greater desire to undertake helping activities for family and friends, such as cooking meals, mowing lawns, making repairs around the house, and caring for children.

A Good Investment for Society

From these data the study's principal investigators build a strong case for the cost effectiveness of the preschool program. The cost of the Head Start program to the taxpayer is more than compensated for by the reduction in the later costs of special education, welfare, and, especially, the lower costs associated with crime, both to the state and to the potential victims. For a small up-front investment, society can reap enormous and recurring dividends in later years.

Finally, as Table 4.2 shows, in an analysis of seven separate longitudinal studies on the effects of preschool programs, Lawrence

TABLE 4.2   THE SEVEN STUDIES: PROGRAM INFORMATION

STUDY	BEGINNING AGE OF CHILD	PROGRAM DURATION IN YEARS	PROGRAM FOR CHILDREN	PROGRAM FOR PARENTS
Milwaukee	3–6 mo.	6	full-time year-round	educational/ vocational
Perry Preschool	3 or 4 yr.	2 or 1	part-time	weekly home visits
New York Pre-K	4 yr.	1	part-time	opportunities for classroom involvement
Rome Head Start	5 yr.	1	part-time Jan–Aug	opportunities for classroom involvement
Early Training	3 or 4 yr.	3 or 2	part-time in summer	weekly home visits during school year
Mother-Child Home	2 or 3 yr.	2	twice-weekly home visits	twice-weekly home visits
Harlem	2 or 3 yr.	1	twice-weekly 1:1 sessions	no separate program

From J. R. Berrueta-Clement, L. J. Schweinhart, W. S. Barnett, A. S. Epstein, and D. P. Weikart. Changed lives: The Effects of the Perry Preschool Program on Youths Through Age 19 *(Ypsilanti, Mich.: High/Scope Press, 1984), p. 99. Used with permission.*

Schweinhart reports that the documented effects of early childhood education show the following outcomes:

Early childhood—improved IQ scores

Elementary school—better scholastic placement (fewer children in special education) and improved academic achievement

Adolescence—less delinquency, higher rates of high-school graduation, and higher rates of employment following high school.[30]

THE FIRST THREE YEARS

One of today's most influential members of the early-experience position is Harvard psychologist Burton White. White contends that intellectual competence and psychological competence are largely determined during a very brief time in the individual's life span, the first three years.[31] Even the first three years is too broad an age-range category, since White is convinced that the critical period for psychological growth actually occurs during the eight-to-eighteen-month age period. Growth during the first eight months of life seems to take care of itself, for early development is so heavily influenced by biological factors that little can be done either to arrest or facilitate the growth process. From ages eight to eighteen months, however, environmental encounters become crucial, and here White focuses on the role of the mother. Mothers of competent children are alert and responsive to their children's needs, without being overly intrusive. The competent mother provides reassurance, guidance, and attention when the child needs this kind of encouragement but does not needlessly intervene just to prove to herself that she's a good mother. Although White suggests that the child be provided with suitable toys and materials, he believes the real key to sound growth is the quality of the child's interpersonal exchanges. Finally, White suggests that the mother encourage her child to adopt a certain amount of competitiveness and that this is best done in a nonthreatening context.

The BEEP Experiment in Early Intervention

Largely as a result of White's research findings, the Brookline, Massachusetts, school system introduced the Brookline Early Education Project, BEEP.[32] Working with White, Brookline set up a training program to teach parents the skills believed necessary for raising competent children. The basic premise of BEEP is that intervention must begin right after birth and in the babies' homes. Teacher-consultants visit the homes on a regular basis and are always on call during the periods between visits. The parents are guided into the use of the BEEP system. The teacher-consultants are never authoritarian—they train by example and the use of skillful questioning. Rather than telling the parent, "Do this," the teacher-consultant will ask, "Have you tried this?"

Along with the training program, BEEP also provides for a thorough series of medical and psychological examinations. Each baby is checked and rechecked for possible sensory impairments and psychological problems that might impede development. Great care is also taken to ensure the babies are on nutritionally sound diets.

Using BEEP as a model, other home-centered intervention programs are being set up in various cities throughout the United States. White's main message is that, in order to raise psychologically competent children, parents must be trained to excel in three key roles during the critical eight-to-eighteen-month period: "(1) as designers and organizers of their children's physical environment; (2) as authorities who set limits to dangerous or annoying behavior; and (3) as consultants to their children in brief episodes, according to need."[33]

The Milwaukee Project

Consistent with White's contention, the Milwaukee Project attempted to stimulate the cognitive growth of children by providing systematic and structured training to low-IQ slum children. This training began early, almost from the child's birth. Staff members began their interventions as soon as mother and child returned home from the hospital. After a few months the babies were brought to Milwaukee's Infant Education Center and were treated to a rich variety of teaching techniques and materials, all designed to stimulate cognitive growth.

In 1981 the project directors reported that the significant IQ differences between the children involved in the program and a control group of children not enrolled was being sustained in favor of the preschool group, at least up to age ten.[34]

It is now fairly certain that early experience is one of the key ingredients in cognitive growth. Had we known this years ago, the disparity between the "good" and "bad" Kallikaks might have been avoided.

The Critics Speak

Critics of the early-experience school of thought have not been quiet. Richard Herrnstein has argued that if we do provide a uniformly beneficial environment for a number of children, we will simply make intelligence more susceptible to hereditary influence than it would otherwise be.[35] Thus, according to Herrnstein, society should not expend either its funds or its energy in attempting to improve the lot of its poor or black citizenry. As one incredulous reader of Herrnstein's account phrased it:

> It is this present, imperfect society that Herrnstein, in the end, urges upon his black fellow citizens. They should abandon their agitation for equality lest they win the self-defeating victory that would expose the poverty of their genetic endowment. In sum, they should stop reminding us of their accusing presence.[36]

Admittedly, individual differences could in no way be caused by a uniform environment; whatever individual differences do arise have to be due to heredity. It should be added, however, that a uniformly bad environment would do exactly the same, make all the individual differences in intelligence the outcome of hereditary influences. But in the first instance, the IQs would fluctuate around a high average value, while in the second, the IQs would scatter around a low average value. Surely it would be more pleasant for the children themselves, and more beneficial to society in general, to let heredity decide differences among high IQs than among low ones.[37]

A related theory argues that the "bottom half is always below average."[38] Thus, or so the theory proclaims, if all intelligence quotients are raised by improved educational techniques, the lower class would still be at the bottom of the social order, and nobody's social status would be changed. This argument implies that society need not try to help the lower class by improving educational opportunities, for the result would only be to freeze present social arrangements. This requires comment.

A large factor in social status is occupation. Limitations of intelligence disqualify an individual from ever becoming a good engineer, physician, or attorney, for example. We might think of a threshold IQ for each occupation. With a very high intelligence one has all the intellectual requirements for being everything from a ditch-digger to an engineer. With a very low intelligence one cannot qualify for high- or middle-status occupations. Therefore, the higher the IQ, the more occupations the individual is qualified to fill. But here we arrive at an interesting point. When we consider IQ—the sheer ability to perform a given task—as an occupational requirement, it is the absolute level of intelligence that matters, not the relative level. If the whole IQ scale were lifted above the threshold for the job of power lineman, those jobs requiring less intelligence would all share the same low IQ status, but social-class standing might not seem as important. Many occupational differences would no longer be due to limitations of intelligence but to a difference of preference and interest, surely a more satisfying arrangement.

A WORD OF CAUTION

With all the recent evidence accumulating on the importance of early experience to cognitive growth, a word of caution to educators is in order. Although it now seems fairly conclusive that stimulus conditions can be provided that will allow for maximum intellectual development, the importance of providing conditions designed to promote emotional growth must not be overlooked.

A FINAL COMMENT

You may be wondering whether, if early experience is so significant in determining intellectual ability, there will be anything left for you to accomplish by the time the child reaches school age. Remember: The cognitive growth that takes place during those first critical six years simply provides the base for the intellectual structure the classroom teacher must build. The child should be allowed to begin formal schooling with the necessary background of cognitive skills to be able to take full advantage of the formal educational process. The goal of the early-experience theorists and practitioners is to prepare the child to profit fully from the educational experience. The job of the teacher, then, becomes more challenging, more stimulating, and less frustrating when the child enters school equipped with the necessary tools to learn. Educational experiences pick up where early experience leaves off, and studies have clearly shown that the quality of the educational experience influences both rate and maximum level of the cognitive growth achieved by an individual.[39]

SUMMARY

Though psychologists have for some time pointed to the importance of early experience for emotional growth, only recently has the same attention been paid to cognitive or intellectual growth. It was known, even as long ago as the 1930s, that early in a child's life certain activities could best be learned during certain critical periods. The work of McGraw on the twins Johnny and Jimmy made this point clear. Also, Bayley's Berkeley Growth Study was aimed at ferreting out some of the facts regarding changes that occur during the process of intellectual growth. A later attempt is the work of Bloom.

Bloom states that with increasing age there is less and less effect on intellectual growth from environmental influences. Children at age three, for example, profit more from enriching experiences than children of age nine or ten. Almost two-thirds of one's ultimate cognitive growth occurs by age six.

Hunt sees stimulus variety as the crucial ingredient in cognitive growth. In the "problem of the match," Hunt points to the importance of matching up the proper amount of stimulus variety with the child's present position on the cognitive-growth continuum.

Piaget and Bruner have developed explanatory systems of how and when cognitive growth occurs. Both indicate the importance of sensory inputs and environmental encounters during the child's early years.

Hebb stresses the internal, physiological changes that occur during cognitive growth and development. He cites the neural organization occurring within the brain as the child's ability to learn increases. At birth the brain cells are relatively unorganized, and the cellular organization occurs as a result of the child's own series of learning experiences.

The Krech study on rats shows that the structure and chemical composition of the brain results in part from the quality and quantity of an organism's early experience. Physiological development requires early environmental stimulation.

The long-term evidence from the Head Start programs is just now beginning to surface. In one study, the Perry Preschool Program, measures taken on nineteen-year-old youths who as children had been in the Perry Preschool Program were compared with a control group of youths who had not. In virtually every measurement category, the impact of the program had positive effects, ranging from an increase in academic ability and achievement to a decrease in criminal activity. Evidence from other studies, such as White's Brookline Early Education Project (BEEP) as well as the Milwaukee Project, has raised cautious hope that intellectual growth can be maximized through the use of innovative educational interventions during the early childhood years.

The early-experience school of thought contends that by providing a more beneficial environment during a child's preschool years, higher levels of intellectual functioning can be expected, especially from culturally deprived youngsters. Though providing more uniform environments does make hereditary effects more pronounced, the early-experience position is that the intellectual differences among adults will still be lessened, and people will thus have more occupational choices available to them.

The job of the teacher is in no way minimized by the efforts of the early-experience specialists. It is hoped that children will be more able to reach their intellectual potentials and thus be better able to profit from the educational experiences provided in the classroom. The teacher's job should, accordingly, be more challenging and less frustrating.

KEY TERMS AND NAMES

early-experience position
Summerhill school
critical periods
Nancy Bayley
Benjamin Bloom
negatively accelerated growth curve
stimulus variety

A/S ratio
Donald O. Hebb
cell assembly
Head Start: Perry Preschool Program BEEP
Milwaukee Project
Richard Herrnstein

REFERENCES

1. Neill, A. S. (1969). The idea of Summerhill. In R. C. Sprinthall and N. A. Sprinthall (Eds.), *Educational psychology: Selected readings* (pp. 194–198). New York: Van Nostrand-Reinhold.

2. McGraw, M. B. (1935). *Growth: A study of Johnny and Jimmy.* New York: Appleton-Century.

3. McGraw, M. B. (1939). Later development of children specially trained during infancy. *Child Development, 10,* 1–19.

4. Hilgard, J. R. (1932). Learning and motivation in pre-school children. *Journal of Genetic Psychology, 41,* 36–56.

5. Scott, J. P. (1968). *Early experience and the organization of behavior* (p. 68). Belmont, Calif.: Wadsworth.

6. Bayley, N. (1940). *Studies in the development of young children.* Berkeley: University of California Press.

7. Jones, M. C., Bayley, N., MacFarlane, J. W., and Honzik, M. P. (Eds.). (1971). *The course of human development.* Waltham, Mass.: Xerox.

8. Bloom, B. S. (1964). *Stability and change in human characteristics.* New York: Wiley.

9. Hunt, J. McV. (1969). Revisiting Montessori. In R. C. Sprinthall and N. A. Sprinthall (Eds.), *Educational psychology: Selected readings* (pp. 45–55). New York: Van Nostrand-Reinhold.

10. Dennis, W. (1960). Causes of retardation among institutional children: Iran. *Journal of Genetic Psychology, 96,* 47–59.

11. Hunt, Revisiting Montessori (p. 52).

12. Spelt, D. K. (1948). The conditioning of the human fetus in utero. *Journal of Experimental Psychology, 38,* 338–346.

13. Bruner, J. S. (1969). Cognitive consequences of early sensory deprivation. In R. C. Sprinthall and N. A. Sprinthall (Eds.), *Educational psychology: Selected readings* (pp. 34–36). New York: Van Nostrand-Reinhold.

14. Hebb, D. O. (1949). *The organization of behavior*. New York: Wiley.

15. Bugelski, R. (1964). *The psychology of learning applied to teaching*. Indianapolis, Ind.: Bobbs-Merrill.

16. Thompson, W. R., and Heron, W. (1954). The effects of restricting early experience on the problem solving capacity of dogs. *Canadian Journal of Psychology, 8,* 17–31.

17. Hymovitch, B. (1952). The effect of experimental variations of problem-solving in the rat. *Journal of Comparative and Physiological Psychology, 45,* 313–321.

18. Hebb, D. O. (1978). Open letter: To a friend who thinks the IQ is a social evil. *American Psychologist, 33*(12), 1143.

19. Krech, D. (1969). The chemistry of learning. In R. C. Sprinthall and N. A. Sprinthall (Eds.), *Educational psychology: Selected readings* (pp. 152–156). New York: Van Nostrand-Reinhold.

20. Grosser, G. S., Sprinthall, R. C., and Sirois, L. (1967). Magnesium pemoline: Activation of extinction responding after continuous reinforcement. *Psychological Reports, 21,* 11–14.

21. Altman, J. (1967). Postnatal growth and differentiation of the mammalian brain. In G. C. Quarton, T. Melnechuk, and F. O. Schmitt (Eds.), *The neurosciences.* New York: Rockefeller University Press.

22. Riesen, A. H. (1961). Stimulation as a requirement for growth and function in behavioral development. In D. W. Fiske and S. R. Maddi (Eds.), *Functions of varied experience* (pp. 57–80). Homewood, Ill.: Dorsey.

23. Riesen, A. H. (1961). Studying perceptual development using the technique of sensory deprivation. *Journal of Nervous and Mental Diseases, 132,* 21–25.

24. Rice, B. (1968). Skinner agrees he is the most important influence in psychology. *New York Times Magazine, 17* (March), 27 ff.

25. Rice, Skinner agrees, 27.

26. Levin, H. M. (1977). A decade of policy developments in improving education and training for low-income populations. In R. H. Haveman (Ed.), *A decade of federal antipoverty programs: Achievements, failures and lessons* (pp. 521–570). New York: Academic Press.

27. Hubbell, R. (1983). *Head Start evaluation, synthesis, and utilization project.* DHHS Publication No. OHDS 83–31184. Washington, D.C.: U.S. Government Printing Office.

28. Berrueta-Clement, J. R., Schweinhart, L. J., Barnett, W. S., Epstein, A. S., and Weikart, D. P. (1984). *Changed lives: The effects of the Perry preschool program on youths through age 19.* Ypsilanti, Mich.: High/Scope Press.

29. Berrueta-Clement and others, Changed lives (p. 108). For a detailed description of the program, see Hohmann, M., Banet, B., and Weikart, D. P. (1979). *Young children in action: A manual for preschool educators.* Ypsilanti, Mich.: High/Score Press.

30. Schweinhart, L. J. Preschool's long-term impact: Summary of the evidence. In J. R. Berrueta-Clement and others, *Changed lives: The effects of the Perry preschool program on youths through age 19* (pp. 95–105). Ypsilanti, Mich.: High/Scope Press.

31. White, B. L. (1975). *The first three years.* Englewood Cliffs, N.J.: Prentice-Hall.

32. Pines, M. (1975). Head Start. *New York Times, 26* (October), 17 ff.

33. Pines, Head Start, 58.

34. Garber, H. L., and Heber, R. (1981). The efficacy of early intervention with family rehabilitation. In M. J. Begab, H. C. Haywood, and H. L. Garber (Eds.), *Psychosocial influences in retarded performance,* Vol. II, *Strategies for improving competence* (pp. 71–88). Baltimore, Md.: University Park Press.

35. Herrnstein, R. (1971). I.Q. *The Atlantic Monthly* (September), pp. 43–64.

36. Piel, G. (1975). The new hereditarians. *The Nation, 19* (April), 458.

37. Grosser, G. S., and Sprinthall, R. C. (1972). A rejoinder to Herrnstein. *The Atlantic Monthly* (February), pp. 38–39.

38. Beihler, R. F. (1971). *Psychology applied to teaching* (pp. 470–471). Boston: Houghton-Mifflin.

39. Klausmeir, H. J. (1977). Educational experience and cognitive development. *Educational Psychologist, 12*(2), 179–196.

5

COGNITIVE GROWTH

As we pointed out in Chapter 1, it is very important to gain an understanding of how children actually think in learning situations. The pupil, one of the four concerns of the teaching-learning agenda, is the focus of this chapter. We will hold off other considerations such as teacher characteristics and teaching strategies in order to present a clear and detailed picture of the child as a learner. The framework we have selected comes from a long tradition of careful study of children through close observation. You will see just how the insights of this framework came to be and gain an understanding of the current state of our information base.

This chapter takes a special look at the kinds of cognitive stages or plateaus of development that occur during childhood and adolescence. Since cognitive development depends on interaction between the child and the learning environment, we will examine the problems of matching the child to the most appropriate learning tasks. This is another way of saying that we must have some informed basis for determining what we present to pupils and how we present it. Just as we know we cannot expect children to roller-skate before they can stand, we must also know when we can expect them to be ready to learn the various intellectual or cognitive tasks. If we understand how the cognitive systems develop, we can avoid both teaching children something before they are ready to learn it and missing a golden opportunity by waiting until well past the most sensitive moment. The major work of Jean Piaget will be featured throughout this chapter.

STAGES OF GROWTH AND DEVELOPMENT

Our understanding of the growth of brain power has changed so enormously in the past decade that a veritable "revolution in learning" has taken place.[1] Previously, the general view was that intelligence was, for all practical purposes, determined prior to birth. This meant that there was nothing to do but accept those inborn differences as natural and provide different educational experiences depending on whether the child was a fast or a slow learner. In other words, the erroneous assumption of

"Actually, I'm a little too old to believe in you, but I don't want to take any chances."
From *The Wall Street Journal*—permission, Cartoon Features Syndicate.

innate differences in intelligence produced an unfortunate educational assumption. We assumed that the differences in intelligence were largely differences in the speed of thinking. In fact "mentally retarded" was almost always translated as "slow learner." This meant that the differences in learning were seen as differences in degree, or more precisely, as quantitative differences. Pupils could be rated—much as if they were on a track team—from slow, to moderately fast, to superfast learners.

The most damaging effect of viewing learning differences as being fixed at birth and as being quantitative (slow to fast) was on educational programs. In general, the educational curriculum reflected this idea: The same material or the same curriculum was given to all students but at different paces, since the "slower" children would not be expected to learn as much or to go as far as the "faster" children. (The word *curriculum*, by the way, comes from a Latin word meaning a course to be run.) Starting from a standard curriculum, we would water it down for the "slow learners" and enrich it for the "accelerated learners." The "slow" children would cover, say, half the material that the "fast" children would cover in any given period. For example, the "slow" children would memorize only half as much poetry

as the "fast" children, learn fewer spelling words, less arithmetic, or hand in shorter compositions in English. Since there was little or no recognition of major stages of cognitive growth, the differences between a first-grade pupil and a twelfth-grade pupil were largely differences in how much they knew and how fast they learned it. In the same way, differences among first graders (as among twelfth-graders) were also quantitative—how much material they learned and how fast they learned it. It has, unfortunately, taken us a long time to get away from these ideas.

Arnold Gesell, who established the famous Institute of Child Development at Yale University during the 1930s, was the first to try to convince educators that growth and development occurred in an unvarying sequence. Many of his ideas and theories were later discarded because they were oversimplifications, but this one concept lasted. Growth stages are major periods of change. Each child goes through periods of major reorganization followed by periods of integration when a new stage is reached and the changes are assimilated. Al-

By understanding how and when cognitive systems develop, we can avoid, on the one hand, teaching children something before they are ready to learn it and, on the other hand, missing a golden opportunity by waiting to well past the most sensitive moment.

Arnold Gesell was one of the first to advocate that growth and development occur in an unvarying sequence.

though Gesell made a significant contribution with his idea of developmental growth stages, he erred in the details of his stages. He made the mistake of overgeneralizing from studying only a few children, and he presented an overly detailed "map" of development. For example, he made hard and fast statements about all two-year-olds, all two-and-a-half-year-olds, all three-year-olds, and so on. This created much confusion in the 1930s and 1940s. Parents were literally measuring their children every six months or so against Gesell's developmental graphs. Gross generalizations resulted: "All twos are terrible," "The threes are terrific," "At four and a half all children. . . ." For a time, parental demand for Gesell's truths outran his ability to produce books: *The First Years of Life* was followed by *The Child from Five to Ten.* One mother was heard to comment despairingly, "I don't know what to do with my children anymore. They are eleven and thirteen, and Gesell stopped at ten!" You are invited to read some of these now historical books. They may help you understand some of the influences on your grandparents as they raised your parents.[2]

The idea of sequential levels of development was most important in all the work of Gesell's

institute. He illustrated that growth took place in stages and that the stages themselves were like great leaps forward followed by periods of integration. Therefore, in order to understand cognitive development, you will have to understand more about the process of growth. At what ages do the major breakthroughs occur and when are the periods of consolidation?

JEAN PIAGET: THE LATE DISCOVERY OF HIS WORK

Throughout the period 1930–1960, while efforts to break away from the idea of fixed and quantitative intelligence were singularly unsuccessful (with the exception of Gesell's general concept of growth), Jean Piaget was working quietly and almost unnoticed at the J. J. Rousseau Institute for Child Study in Geneva. Using direct, careful, and systematic observation of children (including his own, the now famous Jacqueline, Laurent, and Lucienne), Piaget began to form a view that would revolutionize our understanding of intellectual growth.

Although there was some brief interest in his work here in the 1930s, it did not become fully known and appreciated until after the 1960s. There are two main reasons for such a long period of neglect by American psychologists. First, his ideas ran very much counter to the mainstream of educational psychology. He proposed that we start by investigating the child as opposed to the official Thorndike view that we research "laws" of learning in the abstract. What went on in the mind of a child, so to speak, was considered either too complex to understand or simply irrelevant. Thus, while Piaget was carefully observing and noting how children thought, most of the establishment in psychology considered his model inappropriate.

We cannot, however, place the blame just on this side of the Atlantic. Piaget himself made his own rather unique contribution. Steeped in the tradition of European scholarship, he seemed almost to enjoy writing his findings not only exclusively in French but in a brand of that language that almost guaranteed to obscure rather than enlighten. There is no way of knowing for sure, but enough stories have circulated to suggest that he enjoyed the independence of his views and held a kind of lofty indifference to the problem of clearly transmitting his ideas to the wider world of psychology. To be fair, of course, most innovators who singlehandedly move a field to a new level of understanding exhibit many of these same tendencies. The result, however, is most important. During most of his adult life, his work was unknown here. Now it is just the opposite. He is among the first group of psychologists cited in academic references. John Flavell, one of this country's renowned experts on child development, summed up Piaget's work as follows: "Piaget's contributions to our knowledge of cognitive development have been nothing short of stupendous, both quantitatively and qualitatively."[3]

Indeed, by the late 1960s (in part due to Flavell's excellent translation of Piaget's writings), when Piaget made one of his rare visits to this country, the occasion was like an astronaut's reception. As described by Maya Pines:

> It was a memorable occasion. With his fringe of long, straight white hair down the sides and back of his balding head, his high forehead, horn-rimmed glasses, gold watch chain and well-worn leather briefcase, he looked like a

stock character—The Professor. On the platform, he commanded instant respect. Speaking in a booming voice, in French, he began by describing some of the key stages of children's intellectual development.[4]

The Concept of Cognitive Growth

Piaget's contribution to our understanding of mental growth as a process of interaction accounts for his significance. Through an intensive study of children over long periods of time—a painstaking process of almost endless observation—Piaget began to chart the unexplored territory of the human mind and to produce a map of the stages of cognitive growth. He proposed, first of all, that cognitive growth takes place in developmental stages. This means that the nature and makeup of intelligence change significantly over time. The differences are not of degree ("slow learners" and "fast learners") but of kind (quality). The transformation of the human mind as it develops can be compared to the transformation of an egg to caterpillar to butterfly. The stages of growth are distinctively different from one another, and the content of each stage is a major system that determines the way we understand and make sense of our experiences (particularly the experience of learning from someone else). Obviously, if we wish to provide experiences that will nurture and facilitate growth, we must take into account the intellectual system the child is using at the time. Piaget's work provides us with the broad outlines of the different cognitive systems children use at different periods in their lives. Each new, evolving system is a major qualitative transformation.

Research Through Repeated Observations

It is important to know something about the way Piaget worked, how he was able to propose a system explaining such a highly complex problem as intellectual development. You might think, in these days of supertechnology, that he would have used a complicated computer-based program and enormous research teams. But you would be mistaken. As we have already mentioned, Piaget's work was based on careful and detailed observation of children in natural settings, like homes and schools. From a research methodology point of view, he was using repeated naturalistic observations. Thus, in some way his method is most like the kind of research a teacher or school counselor might do.

Starting almost like that other great "clinical" scientist, Sigmund Freud, Piaget very carefully examined the functioning of intelligence in a few children. On the basis of these subjective impressions, he began to ask himself some questions. Why, for example, did children become confused over family relationships? A child could readily acknowledge "I have a brother" but would still not understand that the brother also had a brother (or sister). He also found that children at certain ages seem to have great difficulty in understanding "simple" ideas.

It seems hard to imagine that children don't understand that when they pour beans from a short, fat glass to a tall, thin glass, the number of beans remains constant. In one of his classic experiments, Piaget found that if he took two piles of beans, had a child actually count both piles to be sure they had the same number, and then left one pile spread out on the table, and bunched the second pile together, that—well, see if you can guess what the child would say. Remember, the child goes by what seems biggest. For example, if you ask children of four or five whether they would rather have a nickel or a dime, they are likely to name the nickel, "because it's bigger."

In yet another observation, Piaget asked preschool children to draw a picture of a glass half-filled with water. He then asked a child to draw the glass upside down. Figure 5.1 shows what one child drew.

At each point in each successive experiment, Piaget would carefully reexamine his own questions (hypotheses) and then develop some further ways of testing them. As a result, it has taken almost an entire lifetime to convince skeptical researchers of his scheme. At first his studies were dismissed out of hand because he would try problems out on a single child or on three or four children. Also, because his sample was so small, he often did without statistics. (In this way he joined hands with such theoretically disparate researchers as Freud and B. F. Skinner.) To make matters even worse, he didn't follow a standard interview format: He wouldn't necessarily ask the same questions of each child, so that no two interviews were exactly comparable. It was almost too easy to criticize and dismiss his work on the grounds that his research designs were not standard.

Thus, partly because Piaget did not follow a standard research model and partly because his ideas, if understood, would have necessitated a major revision in our theories of cognitive

FIGURE 5.1   Piaget's experiments with preschoolers: The first shows a child pouring beans from a short, fat glass into a tall, thin one. The second is a child's drawing of a half-filled glass of water—right side up and upside down.

"Keep an eye on the kids for awhile, will you, Jean?"

From *APA Monitor*, September-October, 1974. Copyright © 1974 by the American Psychological Association. Reprinted by permission of the publisher.

growth, his work remained largely confined to Geneva. However, his findings were eventually noticed and have been widely accepted in the past ten to twenty years. Scientific skeptics began to take notice of his work. Piaget continued to direct a series of studies, including some that used large samples. Essentially, however, it wasn't the sheer number of subjects that mattered but the emergence, over and over again, of the same principles of intellectual transformation. Through repetition, rather than the single critical experiment, Piaget accumulated sufficient evidence to become the major theoretician of intellectual development today.

The Meaning of Cognition: Piaget's Definition

Before we describe the stages of cognitive development, it is important to explain just what Piaget meant by the term *cognition*. Essentially cognition, thinking, or rational processing is considered an active and interactive process. The mind in everyday language is not simply a blank sheet of paper on which the environment writes. But neither is it a totally separate apparatus that exists in splendid isolation. Flavell probably provides the clearest description when he says, "Thus the mind neither copies the world, passively accepting it as a ready-made given, nor does it ignore the world, autistically creating a private mental conception of it out of whole cloth."[5]

This means that cognition is the constant process of going back and forth between the person and the environment.[6] Another way to describe it is as a dialectical process, which means that cognition never takes place entirely "inside" the child nor is it entirely the result of outside stimulation. A third way to describe cognition is as the regulating mechanism that connects the person and the environment. The most important single point in all these different descriptions is that the cognitive process is active, not passive. A person affects the environment and the environment affects the person at the same time. When we describe the specific implications of this definition, we will continually come back to this same basic point. The child is not an empty organism. Learning is not passively filling up the empty vessel.

PIAGET'S STAGES OF COGNITIVE GROWTH

After examining the thinking patterns that children use from birth through adolescence, Piaget began to find consistent systems within certain broad age ranges. There are four major stages (see Table 5.1).

Since the four major stages are quite broad, each stage has subcategories. The important thing to remember, however, is that each major stage is a system of thinking that is qualitatively different from the preceding stage. Each stage is a major transformation in thought processes—compared to the preceding stage, a quantum leap forward, a breakthrough. It is also important to remember that the child must go through each stage in a regular sequence. It is impossible to skip or miss a stage or to bypass a stage: The stages of cognitive growth are se-

TABLE 5.1   *STAGES OF COGNITIVE GROWTH*

AGE	STAGE
0–2	Sensorimotor
2–7	Intuitive or preoperational
~7–11	Concrete operations
11–8 16	Formal operations

quential and follow an invariant sequence. Children cannot overcome a developmental lag or speed up their movement from one stage to the next. They need to have sufficient experience in each stage and sufficient time to internalize that experience before they can move on.

Our main concern as educators is to understand the major substance of each stage. Only then can we begin to consider what to teach and how to teach. Although the major substance of each stage is the main structure or scheme for the age span specified, these stages never exist in a pure form. There will always be some elements of the preceding and future stages mixed in. In other words, although a major intellectual activity does define each stage, bits and pieces of other stages will also be present.

In fact, most recent research has established that it is only the sensorimotor stage from birth to two years where universal agreement exists as to the starting point and the end. Sandra Scarr sums it up rather succinctly with the rhetorical question, "Do you know anyone who did

not make it through the sensorimotor stage?"[7]

Beyond that point, however, the stage-to-stage differences are not as great nor are the changes as abrupt as originally described by Piaget. Recent research, for example, has demonstrated that some symbolic thought, usually associated with later stages of development, actually occurs during the first stage.[8] Similarly, research has indicated that children in the second stage have a greater ability to classify numbers than was previously estimated by Piaget's research.[9]

What does all this mean to you? Is this just another case of researchers doing fine-grained studies designed to disprove some major Piagetian idea? Not really. Instead, the important point to remember as you read and learn about stage characteristics is that there are no pure types. You will not find any single child who will exhibit all the characteristics of a given stage, with the exception of the sensorimotor stage. Instead, you will see major trends and clusters of learning approaches that are truly consistent with the stage types. You will also see, as child development researchers are finding out, that some evidence exists of more advanced-stage thinking at earlier stages. In other words, you can expect some overlap. Children during elementary school will exhibit very clear cognitive trends of concrete thought, but there will be some foreshadowing of formal and abstract reasoning, though not much. The same foreshadowing of an advanced stage is true of the preschool child compared to the elementary child. So keep in mind that these two ideas are not contradictory but rather deepen our understanding: Each stage has major characteristics of its own that describe in a consistent manner how a child processes experience; at the same time the child also will exhibit some signs of the next stage as well as prior stages. With this in mind we can now turn to the stage descriptions.

Sensorimotor Experience (Birth to Two Years)

Cognitive activity during the sensorimotor stage is based primarily on immediate experience through the senses. The major intellectual activity of the stage is the interaction of the senses and the environment. Activity is practical. Without language to label experiences or to symbolize and hence remember events and ideas, children are dramatically bound to immediate experience: They see what is happening and feel it, but they have no way of categorizing their experience. Responses are almost completely determined by the situation. For example, a hungry child will literally scream the house down for food. It does no good to "tell" a six-month-old, "Now just wait a minute; I'm warming your bottle." The child has no way to represent the idea that in one or two minutes a nice warm bottle of milk will appear, and obviously he or she doesn't know what a minute is or, for that matter, what any of those other words mean. It's like speaking in English to someone who understands only Armenian. The child cannot, so to speak, go to the mental equivalent of an instant replay and say, "Oh, when she says that, it means something good is coming, so I won't be hungry much longer, and my yelling isn't going to make it come faster."

Being tied to immediate experience during this stage also means that there is almost nothing between the child and the environment. The mental organization lives in the raw, so that the quality of experience is unusually significant. Thus, what and how the child learns will remain an immediate experience, as vivid as any first experience. It would be fair to say that learning in the sensorimotor stage is a continuous peak experience. It is something like going through each day as if it were the first day of school, the opening night of a play, your first final exam, your first date, your first encounter with death, the first time you found yourself completely alone, and so on—all in the same day.

To give you some idea of how easily children at this age are bound by experience and can be victimized by it, we need only think of six-month-olds. This is the age at which children begin to be able to follow an object with their eyes (visual pursuit). Their eyes swing back and forth, following the path of a shiny object, fifty to a hundred times. They literally can't take their eyes off the moving object. Because this is the "first" time they have seen an object move from side to side, they will follow its visual path almost indefinitely unless we wisely choose to change the environment.

The development of visual pursuit (a sensorimotor behavior) is critical to mental development. Visual pursuit has to be learned before a very important concept called "object permanence" can be learned. As children begin to grow intellectually, they understand that when an object disappears from view, it still exists even though they can't see it. Whether it's a button hidden under a pillow, a person leaving the room, or a boy or girl hiding behind a door, children who have developed the concept of object permanence know the disappearance is only temporary and are thus liberated from endless visual pursuit.

The ability to notice and follow objects might be likened to a first stage of recognition. The growth of object permanence is almost like the beginning of an elementary memory. Children can "hold" in their minds a picture of the missing object; no longer is out of sight, out of mind. The experience of seeing things in the first few months of life and then of seeing those same things disappear and reappear plays an important role in mental development. Piaget has compared sighted babies with those born blind: "The inadequacy of the initial scheme [mental organization] leads to a lag in development of three to four years and more."[10] Lacking visual experience during the critical period of sensorimotor learning (birth to two years) prevents the growth of mental structures.[11]

The adage "There's no substitute for experience," best summarizes the sensorimotor period of cognitive development. This is so true of children from birth to age two that it accounts for the recent trend of providing babies with interesting crib mobiles and is also responsible for bringing back the popularity of some of the old-fashioned baby toys like rattles to shake and suck and blankets to hug. Linus, from the Peanuts cartoon, learning with his blanket in tow, stands as the prototype of a child in the sensorimotor stages. A rich and responsive sensory environment is the best means of developing the young child's intelligence.* Note how this relates directly to some of the research findings

---

* The implications for the recent growth of day-care centers in this regard are obvious. Failure to operate quality programs—rich and responsive sensory environments—will induce, at a critical juncture, serious developmental lags.

CONTEMPORARY ISSUE

What If Piaget Had Studied Animals?

Since so much of Piaget's work has been repeated with children from different backgrounds and different cultures, sooner or later the question had to be raised. What about animals? Do animals, especially those who are further along developmentally such as a chimp (versus a slug), exhibit Piagetlike progressions in growth? The main experiments as the child reaches two years focus on the establishment of object permanence. The tests become quite sophisticated. The child may be shown a small toy cat. The examiner holds the cat in his or her hand, then moves the hand underneath three separate napkins. The cat is randomly deposited under one. The empty hand is opened in full view of the child. Usually the child smiles and then quite systematically looks under each napkin until the hidden cat is fully and triumphantly uncovered. This ability to track the events, so to speak, mentally indicates the end of sensorimotor period and the onset of internal and symbolic thinking.

So far, research with animals using similar tests of object permanence indicates that cats progress partway through but stop short of full attainment. They can't track the shift from one hiding place to another. Monkeys, on the other hand, can achieve the same level of functioning as a two-year-old human but then seem to top out. Chimps clearly reach this level as well as some measure of symbolic thinking at the next stage. In this sense, then, the research evidence does support the idea of intellectual development in humans and in animals. Careful observation of different species shows some of the same progressions during the sensorimotor period. Thus far, it appears as if chimps and apes are the only species besides the human species that clearly make it all the way through the sensorimotor period.[a]

As we noted in Chapter 2, chimps can learn sign language and thus can communicate at a more human level than other animals. This development of language is the hallmark of the preoperational stage. In fact, for a while in the 1970s it was suggested that the chimps could master some of the elementary rules of grammatical sentences, a clear parallel to human development during the preschool years. At present, however, there is no firm evidence that the chimps really display the ability to create original sentences. Instead they apparently imitate adult repetitions.[b] If this finding is borne out through additional research, then we can mark a point somewhere in the preoperational period when chimps cease further cognitive stage growth, leaving the field of further cognitive development exclusively in the province of the human species.

---

[a] Flavell, J. H. (1985). *Cognitive development* (p. 37). Englewood Cliffs, N.J.: Prentice-Hall.
[b] Kalat, J. W. (1984). *Biological psychology* (p. 358). Belmont, Calif.: Wadsworth.

mentioned in Chapter 4 concerning the development of "intelligent" animals by exposing them to "creative" toys and "interesting" cages. The quality of experience during this first stage prepares the child to move to the next stage.

One final point: Babies during this stage are primarily learning through their senses and are most strongly affected by their immediate environment. However, as object permanence develops, especially between year one and year two, we now know babies are capable of some representational thought much like that of the next stage. Young babies can store information, even though their ability to do so may seem quite crude. We will make a mistake if we assume that because their talk, gestures, and manipulations are so poor, there is no thought during the sensorimotor period. As Flavell so cleverly puts it, "They just *look* incompetent to the naked eye."[12]

Intuitive or Preoperational Thought (Two to Seven Years)

During this period the quality of thinking is transformed. Children are no longer bound to their immediate sensory environment. They started to develop some mental images in the preceding stage (object permanence, for example), and in this stage they expand that ability by leaps and bounds. Their capacity to store images (words and the grammatical structures of language, for example) increases dramatically. Vocabulary development, including the ability to understand and use words, is especially noteworthy. The average two-year-old understands between 200 and 300 words, while the average five-year-old understands 2,000 words—a huge percentage increase.

During this stage, then, there is a major breakthrough in the use of language. Since this is the time when children are maximally ready to learn language, adults who talk a great deal to children, read to them, teach them songs and nursery rhymes—in other words, use language to communicate with them—have a significant effect on the children's language development.

The predominant learning mode at this stage is intuitive; preoperational children are not overly concerned with precision but delight in imitating sounds and trying out lots of different words. They are also unconcerned about the consequences of language. This is the time, for example, when preschoolers are hysterically funny over "bathroom" language, taking great glee in using choice expressions such as "poop face."

Obviously, the richer the verbal environment at this time, the more likely it is that language will develop. This is not to suggest that we should force-feed language teaching. In fact, teaching is almost unnecessary. The advantage of the intuitive mode is that children are capable of free associations, fantasies, and unique illogical meanings. They can pretend that stuffed toys are real, they can have imaginary friends, tell wild stories about their parentage, have whole conversations with themselves as well as with inanimate objects—these are all ways children have of trying language out, of teaching themselves. Intuition frees them to be experimental regardless of reality.

From the adult's point of view, the spontaneous nature of a child's language may have its

Piaget's second stage involves intuitive, or preoperational, thought. Oral vocabulary development is especially significant during this stage.

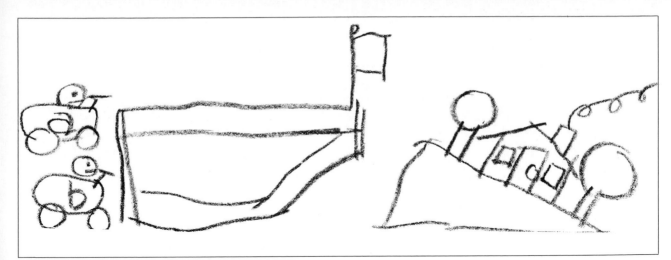

Intuitive preoperational reasoning. "If cars *A* and *B* get to the finish together, they go at the same speed" is one example of intuitive preoperational reasoning.

Preoperational child's drawing of a house on a hill.

drawbacks. Since the child doesn't worry about logic or reality, if it "feels" OK to talk to a tree, a dog, or a stranger in the street, you can be sure the child will be heard. How many stories have you heard about children who suddenly say something like, "Hey Daddy, look at that fat lady standing next to you." We have to remember that such comments are for the good of practice. In spite of embarrassing moments, the more extensive the practice the greater the future verbal facility and competency. Studies have shown that children who are deprived of speech to any significant degree during this period suffer a developmental lag that may be irreversible.

Piaget, in studying the use of language during this period, found that children seem to talk at rather than with others. We have all had the experience of realizing that other people weren't really listening to us; that they were talking over, around, and through us, mostly to hear themselves talk, as the old saying goes. With three- to seven-year-old children this is the predominant mode. Piaget has called it "collective monologue." If you ask a group of children to tell you a story, together, you will find as many different stories as there are children. Their speech patterns are egocentric; they bear little relationship to what others are saying. How-

ever, in terms of practice, the collective monologue is another means children have of trying out words without having to wait their turn.

The intuitive period is truly a golden opportunity for facilitating language development. But we should also make it clear that preoperational thought is a general mode during this time. This is why a child at this level would choose a tall, thin glass of water, rather than a short, wide one. Intuitively, it looks like more because it's taller. "Let's not worry that it's thinner," the child might say, "because being taller is enough. It looks bigger to me!" You may think this is a cavalier disregard of the facts, and that's just the point—it is. And it will do absolutely no educational good to tell a child of this age the "real" reasons why the amount of water is the same in both glasses. All you would accomplish would be to get the child to parrot back what you say, without the slightest understanding. There are literally thousands of uproariously funny stories that illustrate how children understand abstract concepts. Ask a six-year-old to say, and then explain, the pledge of allegiance to the flag ("the Republic of Richard Stands and One Naked Individual") or some biblical references ("Pontius the Pilot on the Flight to Egypt"; "The Father, Son, and Holy Smoke!"). These will remind us of another

A child who is thinking at a preoperational level and is asked to draw an upright pencil falling usually cannot draw the sequence of steps shown here. Similarly, if asked to draw a picture of someone dropping a ball, the child will usually draw the beginning and the end, but not the ball in the process of falling, as pictured here.

aphorism, "The child is not a midget-sized adult." A child's understanding is qualitatively different from an adult's.

Piaget has also shown that children at this age have difficulty realizing the reversible nature of relationships. He illustrates this fact with the following interview. A four-year-old girl is asked:

Have you got a sister?
Yes.
And has she got a sister?
No, she hasn't got a sister. I am my sister[13]

We can say, then, that the mental structures at the preoperational stage are largely intuitive, freewheeling, and highly imaginative. Do not assume, however, that because the process seems illogical it is necessarily inferior as a mode of thought. Indeed, much work in the area of creativity suggests that intuition and free association are an important aspect of creative or original problem solving. Intuition allows us to break out of the constraints imposed by reality. Inventors, artists, and other creative people commonly find that many of their ideas come to them intuitively or, as it is sometimes called, preconsciously. When we say, "From the mouths of babes, . . ." we are testifying to the importance of intuitive thinking.

Thus, we can say that the system of thinking that children typically employ during this pe-

riod is creative and intuitive. Puff the Magic Dragon lives. Yet remember there are some few signs during this time of an impending shift toward a greater recognition of reality. Recent research has shown a greater ability among preschoolers to distinguish between the real and the imaginary and to understand number sequences than was originally thought.[14] This means children can learn to count better than "one, two, three, ten zillion" and can learn letters better than "1 and emma p." There is also evidence that children at this stage can show some signs of self-discipline.[15] The increase in language ability essentially means that children can talk to themselves about resisting temptation. Some instruction in a formal sense will not damage children. This does not mean, however, that a teacher should structure any substantial portion of a preschool day on learning letters and numbers. Remember, just as was the case with the sensorimotor period, some attributes of the next stage are evident. These new characteristics, however, are very fragile.

The major significance of the period is best summed up by Flavell, who notes that while sensorimotor learning is slow, step by step, concrete, and tied to immediate experience. Preoperational learning is lightning fast and mobile. It is the beginning of symbolic thinking, with ideas replacing concrete experience. The child's ideation can range over the past, present, and future in a wink. The greatest single difference is, of course, the level of communication. Children can now share their cognitions socially. Sensorimotor experience is much more private and uncommunicative. "Each baby is imprisoned in her own separate cognitive world."[16]

Concrete Operations (Seven to Eleven Years)

Piaget's next stage represents another major reorganization of mental structure. In the preoperational stage children are dreamers, with magical thoughts and fantasies in abundance. Now, in the operational stage, they are young logical positivists who understand functional relationships because they are specific, because they can test the problems out. For example, if we show children at this age the pile of beans or the water-glass experiment, they will tell us there is no change in volume. This time around they understand the specific, or concrete, aspects of the problem. Now they can measure, weigh, and calculate the amount of water or number of beans so that an apparent difference won't "fool" them.

However, in their wholehearted abandonment of magical thinking, fantasies, and imaginary "friends," they become almost too literal-

In Piaget's third stage, concrete operations, activities now can have rules; schooling at this age should emphasize skills and concrete activity.

"You said we could paint anything we wanted to!"

© 1967 *NEA Journal.*

minded. Their ability to understand the world is now as "logical" as it once was "illogical." For example, they can easily distinguish between dreams and facts, but they cannot separate hypothesis from fact. Five-year-olds usually describe a dream as something that happens in their bedroom, that they watch like a movie, while nine-year-olds describe dreams as mental images inside their heads.[17] Also, once a nine-year-old's mind is made up on a question, new information will not easily change that point of view. In one study, seven- to ten-year-old children were presented with a number of reasons why Stonehenge (a prehistoric site in England) was a fort rather than a religious center. See the box on page 102 for the outcome.

In humor we also find evidence of the literal-mindedness of this stage. This is the time when children delight in using explicitness and literalness as a basis for their jokes. Slapstick and pie-throwing reach their zenith during this period. "When am I going to get my just desserts?" asks the fall-guy comedian plaintively. "Are you sure you want it now?" says the partner, holding a cream pie behind his back. You can fill in the balance of the dialogue and imagine the screams of delight from an elementary-age audience.

If, during the previous stage, children play around with fantasies, during concrete operations they play around with literal-mindedness.

Stonehenge: A Fort or a Religious Temple?

David Elkind, a leading Piagetian scholar, teaches a discovery unit in elementary-school social studies to illustrate the inability of concrete-thinking pupils to distinguish between facts and theories.[a] He shows a series of pictures of Stonehenge. He points out a large number of facts—the huge size of the stones, their placement in an open field, the circular trenches of outer and inner "defense" lines, and similar bits and pieces of information from which it is possible to conclude that Stonehenge was a prehistoric fort. He is careful to list a very large number of facts to back up the conclusion. He then presents just a few facts such as the open field and the two stones (the heel and the altar) that line up perfectly with the sunrise on June twenty-first each year, thereby suggesting that the site was really a religious temple. This second conclusion has fewer facts behind it yet essentially is more logical. The children, however, will not change their minds. To them, the large number of concrete facts, a quantitative difference, is more important than the smaller number of facts that "prove" the religious nature of the site. Essentially, for children at this age, there is no difference between theories and facts. What is important is how many. This means that the basis for complex scientific and logical reasoning is not yet available to elementary-age children.

---

[a]   Elkind, D. (1970). *Children and adolescents* (p. 54). New York: Oxford University Press.

One researcher illustrates this juvenile sophistry with the following story (again a favorite at this age): An eight-year-old boy comes to the table with his hands dripping wet. When his mother asks him why he didn't dry his hands, he replies, "But you told me not to wipe my hands on the clean towels." His mother throws up her hands and replies, "I said not to wipe your *dirty* hands on the towels."[18] Another reported the following as a most popular story, "A mother loses her child named Heine. She asks a policeman, 'Have you seen my Heine?' "[19] Usually by this time children are laughing so hard we never hear the punch line. And we must admit, compared to the previous period where the simple phrase "poop face" was considered hilarious, concrete-stage humor is more sophisticated, if not more appealing to adult tastes.

Schooling and concrete operations   In many ways schooling at the elementary age seems to fit the pupils' cognitive stage rather well. Where the school emphasizes skills and activities such as counting, sorting, building, and manipulating, cognitive growth will be nurtured. Field trips to historical sites or science through "kitchen physics" are additional examples. Activities can now have rules. In fact, you could almost say during this time that making the rules for a game, or classroom activity, is more significant than the activity itself. Whereas preschool children will obey rules without under-standing why we have them, elementary-school children understand rules because of their func-tional value. You cannot play real baseball with-out following the rules. However, we must also remember that they have a literal understand-ing of the concept of rules: Rules are given laws that cannot be changed. Adults understand that rules are a system of regulations that can be replaced by another system, but children see them as fixed, necessary, and arbitrary. The danger, then, is that we will exploit their literal-mindedness in order to manipulate rather than educate them.

Thus, although schooling at this age is gen-erally successful when it emphasizes skills and concrete activities, certain other aspects are not useful. For example, there is increasing interest in teaching elementary-age children the struc-ture of knowledge in the various disciplines—math, English, history, science—throughout the entire school sequence. Thus, we no longer teach history as facts or events but as a way of thinking. How does a historian think? What is the process whereby he or she knows (in our earlier example) that Stonehenge was a religious site? How does the historian examine artifacts? Given this broad objective, to teach structure, we then try to develop a spiraling curriculum. At each grade we present the concepts in a more sophisticated manner.

Where this process breaks down is precisely at the pupils' level of cognitive understanding. Since their mode of thinking is concrete and they don't have the mental equipment to grasp the cognitive abstractions, they translate the ab-stractions into concrete and highly specific terms. Boys and girls at this stage develop their own way of understanding the subjects in ac-cord with specific everyday experience. They learn to add in the first grade, take away in the second grade, fractions in the fifth . . . and so on for each subject and each teacher. In the case of subjects in the new curriculum, the same situation prevails but the words have changed. For example, in the "new" math they learn set theory in the second grade, rational and irra-tional numbers in the fourth, and so on. In other words, the compartments the children use are a reflection of the concrete operations they learn to perform every day in school. All they

have learned, in the meantime, is a new set of rote responses. Mary Alice White, a renowned school psychologist, observed the same situa-tion when it came to the question of what parts of the curriculum are considered most impor-tant by the children.[20] You can guess by now that they chose the subjects having the most tests and the most homework. Obviously, from a concrete point of view, that is the way to judge the importance or value of a subject. Even though teachers may say that all the subjects are important, actions speak louder than words, especially during this stage.

Parents of these children also get caught in the trap of the literal-minded thinker. Many par-ents report being upset and frustrated when they try to help their children with schoolwork. Children comment, "But that's not the way the teacher wants us to do it! She wants us to make the plus sign this way, not that way." "Teacher says we have to do spelling first, then arith-metic." "Fractions come before decimals." Usu-ally neither the parent nor the teacher realizes that the difficulty lies in the child's cognitive level. Instead, parents frequently get mad at their children for not realizing, for example, that decimals and fractions are equivalent. And they get annoyed at the teacher for teaching in such simplistic black-and-white terms. The teacher, on the other hand, gets equally annoyed at re-ports of such literal-minded parents. The chil-dren are caught in the middle between two equally arbitrary systems, neither of which they understand.

During the prior stage of intuitive reasoning, children exhibit a small amount of ability to reason concretely. So too, during the concrete stage children exhibit some fragile ability to rea-son abstractly, especially when the learning task is simplified. Thus, there is some foreshadow-ing of the next stage. This does not mean, how-ever, that it is worthwhile to spend large amounts of academic learning time attempting to promote formal thinking during the elemen-tary years. When such attempts were made in the 1960s, the programs did not succeed. Ele-mentary children could not develop the ability to think abstractly in learning concepts such as culture or society.[21]

Some cognitive-developmental researchers attempt to find evidence of potential for abstract thought during the elementary years. By simplifying the task and then intensively training the children, it is possible to "prematurely" bring about some aspects of growth. However, as Eleanor Neimark points out, these same training or teaching methods have vastly different effects on adolescents as compared to elementary-age pupils. She notes that concepts such as "love, country, parent change their meaning with age."[22] Also, prompting elementary children to say (i.e., memorize) such abstract definitions does *not* mean the children will generalize what they have learned. Thus, it is much better for teachers to wait for the onset of puberty and the start of formal operations to really begin instruction designed to promote abstract concept formation. Neimark concludes: "Practically all of the available research regardless of the task employed or the theoretical persuasion of the investigator shows a clear change in the quality and power of thought during the 11 to 15 years age range."[23]

Formal Operations (Eleven to Sixteen Years)

The shift to formal operations is quite noticeable to the teacher because of the remarkable differences in the characteristics of thinking. Table 5.2 outlines the four main differences.

Possibilities and hypothesis testing   To an elementary-age child the difference between a possibility and a probability is not particularly strong. This point can be illustrated by a study sometimes referred to as "The Las Vegas Game." It involves an apparatus with three buttons—red, yellow, and blue. When the correct button (red) is pressed, a reward or prize drops into a small chute. The catch is that the machine is adjusted so that it pays off only 66 percent of

In Piaget's fourth stage, formal operations, children can develop formal patterns of thinking and are able to attain logical, rational strategies.

the time. Thus, the most efficient strategy is to push the red button repeatedly. Both elementary children and adolescents have been tested on the game, and researchers have discovered marked differences from age to age in how they approach the game.

In one study conducted with this game, elementary-school children were puzzled by the fact that no matter which of the three buttons they pushed, the prize came out only part of the time. For example, Lisa, age nine, concluded that the best strategy was shifting from button to button—for example, "If you win you shift, and if you lose you shift." Once she and other nine-year-olds had settled on a strategy, they stuck with it, even when it was apparent that their strategy did not always lead to success. As a result, they received many fewer prizes than they would have had they simply pushed the red button repeatedly.

Fifteen-year-old Angie also entertained the

TABLE 5.2   COMPARISON OF CHILDHOOD AND ADOLESCENT THOUGHT

CHILDHOOD	*ADOLESCENCE*
Thought limited to here and now	Thought extended to possibilities
Problem solving dictated by details of the problem	Problem solving governed by planned hypothesis testing
Thought limited to concrete objects and situations	Thought expanded to ideas as well as concrete reality
Thought focused on one's own perspective	Thought enlarged to perspective of others

idea that the strategy might be a complex one. But once Angie saw that the strategies she tried were not successful, she abandoned them and fairly quickly came to the conclusion that the most efficient way to play the game was to push the red button repeatedly. Her score was much higher than Lisa's score.

Essentially, then, Lisa had decided that since there were three buttons, somehow all had to be pushed at one time or another. The teen-ager recognized the variety of possibilities and then logically focused on the sequence with the highest probable payoff. To put it another way, elementary-age children tend to think about what is; adolescents, about what might be.[24]

Such testing of hypotheses is another characteristic difference. This means the teen-ager has a greater potential for examining logical evidence before reaching closure. A classic demonstration of this characteristic of thought involves the task of finding the combination of five colorless chemicals that will produce a solution of a particular color. Most adolescents know immediately that the right answer is one of the logically possible combinations of colorless chemicals. Most of them proceed to solve the problem by simply trying each possible combination in turn until the right color shows up. Younger children, however, are less likely to conceive the possible combinations of so many liquids, nor can they proceed systematically through the possible combinations in search of the correct ones.[25]

Expanded thought: Metathinking   Another extremely important shift is adolescents' ability to think about their own thinking and the thoughts of others. This is what is meant by the term *metacognition*. This kind of self-reflection allows for a wide-ranging stretch of the imagination. Ideas can be tried out in the mind. In addition, teen-agers can become aware of *how* they know as well as what they know. Being conscious of a variety of learning strategies that might be used is another important characteristic of the teen-ager. This means the opportunity for self-correction in problem solving is much greater. The teen-ager can talk to himself or herself, a process sometimes called an internal dialogue, and reach new insights without actually needing to test each solution in concrete reality.

Perspectivistic thought   Closely related to metathought is the new awareness that different people have different thoughts about the same idea or situation. In other words, a kind of relativism develops. There is no longer one single and correct point of view. Not everyone understands the same way. In fact, Piaget demonstrated repeatedly that young children tend to think everyone views situations as they do. He described these young children as egocentric because they were centered or focused on their own view. Adolescents, however, are more likely to recognize that others' viewpoints are different from their own. It is as though they understand that others have different interests, knowledge, and ways of thinking than they have.

This characteristic of formal operational thinking (and the other three as well) may have a direct connection to the process of reading development. As the contemporary issue indicates, how students actually process and make meaning from the words they read may be significantly different, depending on their level of formal operations. When the potential for abstract thought is developed, students are able to attain logical, rational, abstract strategies. Symbolic meanings, metaphors, and similes can now be understood. Stories with a moral can be generalized. Games and simulations can be presented so that pupils understand their implications. For example, if we want to teach something about economic theories and principles, we can use a game like Monopoly, as long as we ask questions that point to the general principles. If we tried this at the elementary age, we would find that the children could understand the game only as a game; they could not generalize from it. Other powerful means of stimulating abstract thinking are viewing movies and film clips, and participating in art forms such as painting, drama, dance, and music. There are many sources of symbolic material besides that contained in the traditional school subjects. And the more active the symbolic process, the more it enhances cognitive growth. During this stage writing poems is more effective than reading poems; making films more effective than viewing them; taking part in an improvisational drama more effective than observing it. Probably the most creative and significant task confronting secondary-school

CONTEMPORARY ISSUE

Reading and Development: Jeanne Chall, Past and Present

It may sound unusual but most people do not remember learning to read. They may remember, quite vividly in fact, the first day they really understood what the words in a sentence meant but not how the process came about. Much like learning to ride a bicycle or to swim, it seems as if the day comes. We get the hang of it. We read.

To some degree either the vagueness of how reading develops or the seemingly automatic nature of the process itself has created a lag in understanding two important questions: How does a person learn to read, and what are the implications for instruction? For years arguments raged over what may sound like an easily resolvable question— how to teach young children to read. As so often happens, two theories emerged that took totally opposite approaches. One method was called "Ask and Guess." Whole words were presented, sometimes with pictures, and children went through the process of identifying single words and gradually words in clusters until they could read sentences and then paragraphs. In this mode little attention was paid to any of the formal aspects of language. Teacher training in reading was about as intensive as it was in music, physical education, or art—namely, short and superficial.

The other theory was the phonics method. Its adherents were (as you might guess) horrified by the "Ask and Guess" method since children were not taught how to recognize word sounds such as consonants, vowels, or diphthongs (two vowels

pronounced as one syllable). In a sense, the phonics model clearly took an opposite tack from "Ask and Guess," or the whole-word approach. The phonics proponents asked, Could a person learn the Morse Code (dots and dashes) by looking at clusters of dashes and dots? The answer was a clear no. It was necessary to teach the connection between letters and words early; otherwise, it would take longer to reach independence in recognizing words.

From the 1940s to the 1960s the debate raged, often looking more like the hostilities between two opposing armies than disagreements over reasoned differences. It wasn't so much that a research base was missing; the difficulties arose over interpretation of the studies. Remember that in educational research there is almost never a single conclusive study. In physics, for example, a single experiment under the stands of the University of Chicago's football stadium proved that atomic fission was possible. Educational research, as one cynic put it, more often generates lots of heat but little light. In the case of reading, each side was quick to point out the errors in the research the other side cited. Meanwhile, the nation's children were experiencing a variety of methods. One generation in one region might be taught to "guess"; their children in the same region, to break the code through phonics. Could there be no consensus?

To solve the reading problem, the Carnegie Corporation funded Jeanne Chall to become the mediator and indeed the arbitrator of the dispute. She literally poured

through all the research studies using the technique of meta-analysis. With objectivity, she clustered the available studies, reexamined the research designs, statistical treatments, and follow-up studies over a fifty-year period. Her conclusion was unequivocal: The better method was to teach young children the code, the alphabet and sounds. She also found that the evidence was not sufficient to say that direct or indirect teaching of phonics was superior. However, an update of her analysis of the research completed from 1967 to 1983 showed that direct teaching of the letters and sounds was better than indirect instruction in decoding.[a]

The result has been a major shift toward a consistent and effective method of reading instruction along with a new emphasis in teacher training. Perhaps most important, recent national statistics indicate that elementary children are learning to read more effectively than the pupils a generation ago. Whether in the future such children can recall the process of learning to read may be irrelevant, as long as the teachers remember.

In one sense, it might be pleasing to close this historical account on such a positive note. The reading issue is settled; we can turn to other educational problems. But can we? While the reading achievement scores in the early grades have improved as a result of more consistent and intensive instruction, other findings raise new questions. After breaking the code and being able to read words and sentences, what is the purpose of reading? Obviously, the answer is to communicate ideas—

in other words, reading for comprehension. It does little good for an oral reader to be able to zip through a passage with perfect word recognition and pronunciation, yet not understand the content. In tests of reading comprehension, the national findings are not so positive; in fact, they're almost the opposite: Very few students even in secondary schools can comprehend the meaning of abstract concepts in prose. The first set of bad-news findings came out in the 1970s with the nationally based Project Talent research (see text, p. 114). Findings from the National Assessment of Educational Progress were published more recently, showing in greater detail the relatively low levels of reading comprehension in secondary schools.

These findings quite clearly raise a new set of reading issues. We understand what might be called the mechanics of getting children started, and the mechanics lead to better comprehension. But for more mature reading, the results indicate that new theory and new practice will be required to solve the comprehension question. How will we make progress in this effort? Should we again call on Jeanne Chall? In fact, tackling this problem is one of her current efforts. She has recently published a book on a model of stages of reading development similar to Piaget's model of the stages of cognitive development. It proposes six stages, from prereading through the advanced reading needed for college.[b] The first three stages, through the primary grades, are characterized by learning to decode and to read fluently from texts that contain language and content largely known to the

reader. The last three stages, grades four through college, are characterized by reading texts that contain unfamiliar ideas and language and that require higher-level reading skills.

When compared to Piaget's theory, the first three stages of reading development require concrete operations, while the last three stages require ability to engage in formal operations. It is also during Piaget's shift to formal operations that the major breakdowns occur in reading development—at the junior- and senior-high-school levels. The students read the words, but their comprehension of abstract ideas lags.

We end this issue not with an answer but rather a call to "watch this space for further bulletins." Chall and her associates are working toward the goal of new theory

and new practice for reading development for all school pupils. Reading has always been considered one of the basic Rs. We know now that it involves more than the mechanics of letter and word recognition. General literacy requires the development of critical comprehension skills in reading. Chall's work will help us learn just how basic that process really is as a keystone for a democratic society.

[a]   Chall, J. (1983). *Learning to read: The great debate,* rev. ed. New York: McGraw-Hill.
[b]   Chall, J. (1983). *Stages of reading development.* New York: McGraw-Hill.

We wish to thank Joanne F. Carlisle, associate professor at American International College, for writing this issue. Also, we are indebted to Professor Chall for her review and editorial suggestions.

JEAN PIAGET

Jean Piaget was born in Neuchatel, Switzerland, in 1896. Piaget was a curious, alert, studious, and extremely bright child. By age ten he had published his first scientific paper, a description of an albino sparrow he had observed in a local park. Between ages eleven and fifteen Piaget worked after school as a laboratory assistant to the director of a natural history museum and in the process became an expert on mollusks and other zoological topics. When he was fifteen, he was offered the job of curator of the mollusk section at a Geneva museum. He received his degree from the University of Neuchatel at age eighteen and his Ph.D. in natural sciences three years later. Piaget had published more than twenty papers in the field of zoology before reaching his twenty-first birthday. In short, Piaget demonstrated a rare intellectual precocity during his childhood and adolescent years.

Despite his early interest in natural science, the young Piaget read widely in sociology, religion, and philosophy. While studying philosophy he became especially interested in epistemology, the study of how knowledge is obtained. With his background in zoology, Piaget became convinced that biological principles could be utilized in understanding epistemological problems. His search for a bridge between biology and epistemology brought him finally into the world of psychology.

After receiving his doctorate, Piaget sought training in psychology and so left Switzerland to study and gain experience at a number of European laboratories, clinics, and universities. During this time he worked for a while at Alfred Binet's laboratory school in Paris, where he did intelligence testing on French schoolchildren. He became fascinated, not by a child's correct answer to a test item, but by a child's incorrect response. He doggedly pursued the incorrect answers in the hope of learning more about the depth and extent of children's ideas and mental processes. His goal was to understand how children of various ages came upon their knowledge of the world around them. This became Piaget's lifework, to find out how children go about the business of obtaining knowledge.

Later Piaget took detailed, minute-by-minute notes of the mental growth of his own three children, Jacqueline, Lucienne, and Laurent.

In 1929 Piaget went to the University of Geneva, where he became the assistant director of the J. J. Rousseau Institute, and in 1940 he assumed the duties of director of Geneva's Psychology Laboratory.

Piaget wrote a tremendous number of books and articles on cognitive growth in children. He believed that intellectual growth is a direct continuation of inborn biological growth. The child is born biologically equipped to make a variety of motor responses, which then provide the framework for the thought processes that follow. The biological givens impose on the developing child an invariant direction to the development of cognitive processes. The ability to think springs from the physiological base. Clearly, Piaget kept his early training in natural science firmly in mind as he went on to develop his system of cognitive growth.

In his twilight years, Piaget actively sought answers to some of

---

teachers is the challenge that this theory of growth presents to building new approaches to curriculum materials.

EDUCATIONAL IMPLICATIONS OF PIAGET'S THEORY

Intelligence and Activity

A significant educational implication of cognitive development is that growth in any one stage depends on activity. In other words, the development of brain power is not fixed at birth but is a function of appropriate activity during any particular stage. Children must engage in appropriate activities to learn. This does not mean they should sit and listen to or observe others. In speaking of development in the first two years, Piaget has said: "Sensorimotor causality does not derive from perceptive causality; to the contrary, visual perceptive causality is based upon a tacticokinesthetic causality that is itself dependent upon the activity proper."[26] This quote, while demonstrating how difficult it can be to understand a passage from Piaget, also indicates the significance of his equation: Intelligence = Activity. Anthropological studies, especially studies of prehistoric humans,

psychology's most fundamental questions. According to his biographer, friend, and former student, David Elkind, Piaget rose early, about 4 A.M., and wrote at least four publishable pages before teaching his morning classes. His afternoons were devoted to taking long walks and thinking about his current studies and research, and his evenings were spent in reading. As soon as his classes were over for the summer, Piaget went to his mountain retreat in the Alps. As fall approached, the mountain air turned crisp, the leaves began to change color, and Piaget came down the mountain, laden with new material for several articles and books. Piaget came down that mountain for over fifty autumns, and the volume of his writing was enormous. In September of 1980, Piaget died in Geneva, Switzerland, in his eighty-fifth year.

Just as Freud's name has become synonymous with the study of emotional growth, Piaget has become known as psychology's foremost expert on cognitive growth.

have indicated that our brain power increased after the invention of tools. The manipulation of tools, acting or "operating" with axes, knives, and primitive shovels, induced the brain to grow. In a sense, primitive men and women, as they began to use tools, were almost challenged to come up with new uses for tools and to invent more efficient and effective tools. The effect of rising to the challenge posed by this activity, the manipulation of tools, itself increased our capacity to understand and become more sophisticated cognitively—the activity developed our mind. The critical point for us is the key phrase in all of Piaget's writings, that activity produces cognitive growth. Thus, over and over in his writings to educators, Piaget calls for the active school.

The American Question: Can We Speed Up Growth?

In a technologically oriented society such as ours, someone inevitably asks Piaget what he now calls the American question: How can we speed up development? "The first question which I am always asked in the United States is, 'Can one accelerate these stages?'" The answer obviously is no. Given all that Piaget has shown, we cannot speed up the process of intellectual growth.

Barnaby Barratt, an English psychologist, has actually researched the question.[27] He selected students aged twelve, thirteen, and fourteen from the top tracks in math and presented them with difficult reasoning tasks. Then he quite systematically instructed the students in how to solve similar problems. He taught them the steps to use and the reasons. The results indicated that the training "took" with the fourteen-year-olds but was ineffective with the thirteen-year-olds and even less effective with the twelve-year-olds. This means that such improvement was a result of two factors—the critical teaching *and* the stage of cognitive development. In everyday terms this means that pupils had to be far enough along developmentally in order to grasp the reasoning process and generalize it to similar word problems.

The study also substantiated a second point. How did the "trained" fourteen-year-olds compare to their same-age cohorts? Might not other fourteen-year-olds in the top math tracks also show a similar ability to solve the new problems? It turned out that the same-aged controls did *not* show the same level of reasoning. This is sometimes called the "other side of the American question." If we can't speed up growth, can we simply let students mature at their own pace, a kind of gradual unfolding? Barratt's second set of results, then, indicates that if left alone adolescents will not necessarily develop to their potential in employing formal operations. In fact, a series of studies from the University of Oklahoma demonstrates quite convincingly that educational programs can be effective at all ages.[28] For example, the researchers in these studies created materials to emphasize the concrete aspects of conservation during the early elementary-school years. These years are a time when children are at the transition between preoperational and concrete patterns. It is difficult for them to hold their perceptions constant on tasks such as transfer of liquid or solid amount (e.g., the spread-out versus bunched-up beans). The researchers systematically instructed such children by employing many hands-on experiences in six types of conservation: (1) numbers, (2) liquid amount, (3) solid amount, (4) weight, (5) length, and (6) area. In general, the results indicated that such careful teaching did improve the ability of children to conserve in problem solving in most of these aspects.

Thus, the answer to the American question is to nurture the process of growth at particular stages rather than simply attempt to accelerate constantly. Teachers do not need to carry the banner "Onward to Formal Operations." Rather, it is important to follow the suggestion of Piaget: "Present the subject to be taught in forms assimilable to children of different ages in accord with their mental structures."[29]

Accommodation and Assimilation

The broad outline of the stages of cognitive growth—sensorimotor, intuitive or preoperational, concrete, and formal—represents major transformations of mental organization. Each stage is qualitatively different from the preceding and is a new means of dealing cognitively with the world. However, it is important for educators to understand how cognitive growth occurs. We have already noted the critical importance of activity. Equally significant is Piaget's concept of accommodation and assimilation. Children at particular stages are maximally able to assimilate particular kinds of experiences. This means, for example, that sensorimotor experiences can be most fully taken in from birth to two years, preoperational from two to seven, and so on. And it also means the opposite, that it is difficult to assimilate experiences beyond the level of mental development. Thus, as teachers, we can get children to say they know, or force them to memorize, but we should not be fooled into believing that they really understand. Piaget might say, "To know by heart is not to know."

According to Piaget, the activity of assimilating certain experiences from the environment forces the child to accommodate, or internalize, those experiences. Internalizing experiences is critical to cognitive growth and cannot take place if experiences are allowed, literally, to go in one ear and out the other. Piaget suggests that the most complete development takes place when children assimilate experiences from their environment, since only then will they be able to accommodate, or internalize, those learnings. As we have indicated, this is the major new challenge facing educators—to develop an array of such experiences to provide maximal cognitive development.

Another way to think of the two processes is

suggested by Piagetian scholar Hans Furth.[30] He notes that assimilation by itself means that the person simply takes all new experiences into his or her mind without worrying in the least whether they really do fit. Thinking as assimilation is more like daydreaming or imagining. We don't check out our views. We take in new experiences and don't change our understanding. Furth calls this an "inside process," to take in experiences and ideas from the outside world without changing what they mean. Accommodation by itself is, of course, just the opposite. We may think about a new experience or idea, but we do not try to take it into our consciousness. We keep the new information at arm's length, so to speak. A student who dutifully memorizes a string of abstractions without any understanding is an example of a kind of pure accommodation. The words are said but the meaning isn't there. In fact, psychologists every once in a while run across a human being who exhibits monumental feats of memory such as reciting an entire Shakespearean play, reeling off all the Roman Emperors, or itemizing all the Körchel listings of records. When quizzed more closely it turns out these people do not really comprehend the meaning of any of the material that they spout forth. Some persons with this ability are called idiot savants, which means literally stupid wise people. The learning may have taken place by rote or by having a photographic memory. The information remains separated from understanding, a kind of splendid isolation, not to be confused with genuine learning.

If assimilation and accommodation remain as separate, isolated experiences, then no real mental growth occurs. In a manner similar to how two-years-olds play, in parallel, the two processes don't interact. When they do interact, however, a most significant learning activity takes place, the process of equilibration.

Equilibration: "Knowledge Disturbances"

As illustrated in Figure 5.2, equilibration is the process of balancing what we already know (assimilation) and what we may be asked to learn that doesn't quite fit (accommodation). Furth calls this a process of "knowledge distur-

bances." Remember that there is an important developmental assumption about the propensity to know variously termed "curiosity drive," "competence motivation," "the intrinsic need to master the environment," or "personal efficacy." Studies have shown that monkeys will "work" for long hours on interesting puzzles. So too will human babies. In fact, Flavell has pointed to recent research that shows that babies will also "work" in order to get at interesting pictures, sounds, and puzzles. This means that there is an intrinsic (built-in) drive, motivation, or personality disposition to learn new things. Children are not simply empty, waiting passively for outside stimulation. Instead Piaget's theory is just the opposite. Humans act on the environment. As we interact we become curious about any new event or unfamiliar idea. This is what Furth means by knowledge disturbances. Our natural bent doesn't allow us to be content just to exist; so when new things don't fit our past assimilations we ask why. Such is the basic learning motivation to master problematic situations. We learn by balancing the old information *and* the new—the process of equilibrating.

But how does the process work? Do we simply continually expose children to a wide variety of new experiences, a kind of force-feeding, to move the child to higher stages? Clearly not, because growth occurs slowly. New information and experiences are balanced (equilibrated) slowly so that the scales never dip too far. This is called "learning by exposure to a moderately discrepant environment." Another way to describe it is as a slight mismatch—new information not quite fitting with our old views. The end result of such experiences is the gradual development of more complex cognitive structures, or learning sets. First growth occurs within a particular stage as a result of small discrepancies and slow equilibration. Then there is movement to the next stage, followed again by a new set of mismatches and the slow incorporation for growth within the new stage. The slight imbalance on the accommodation side creates an adapting intelligence—not a fixed but an ongoing process. In this sense intellectual growth is the gradual development of more complex and more efficient rational prob-

FIGURE 5.2   Piaget's learning interaction: Equilibration is the process of balancing assimilation and accommodation.

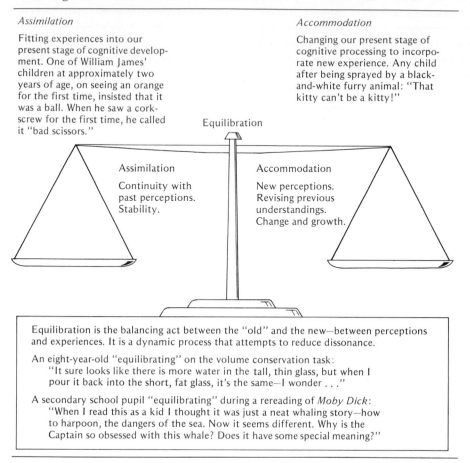

Assimilation

Fitting experiences into our present stage of cognitive development. One of William James' children at approximately two years of age, on seeing an orange for the first time, insisted that it was a ball. When he saw a corkscrew for the first time, he called it "bad scissors."

Accommodation

Changing our present stage of cognitive processing to incorporate new experience. Any child after being sprayed by a black-and-white furry animal: "That kitty can't be a kitty!"

Equilibration

Assimilation

Continuity with past perceptions. Stability.

Accommodation

New perceptions. Revising previous understandings. Change and growth.

Equilibration is the balancing act between the "old" and the new—between perceptions and experiences. It is a dynamic process that attempts to reduce dissonance.

An eight-year-old "equilibrating" on the volume conservation task:
"It sure looks like there is more water in the tall, thin glass, but when I pour it back into the short, fat glass, it's the same—I wonder . . ."

A secondary school pupil "equilibrating" during a rereading of *Moby Dick*:
"When I read this as a kid I thought it was just a neat whaling story—how to harpoon, the dangers of the sea. Now it seems different. Why is the Captain so obsessed with this whale? Does it have some special meaning?"

lem-solving capacities that we can generalize to new problems.

Furth provides an interesting description of a seven-year-old German boy starting to accommodate new information. His example illustrates that once the new information is taken in through equilibration, then the boy thinks in a new way. The boy learns that churches have steeples. Then, during a bike ride, he overhears a number of adults entering a house say they are going to church. The boy muses. A regular house can't be a church. It doesn't have a steeple. It seems nearly impossible to consider a simple house as a real church. His father tells him not to bike near the house on Sundays because of the traffic. Soon he hears other people nearby talking of attending services there.

He continues to deny the validity of the new insights. Gradually, however, the moderate discrepancy pushes him to reconsider his earlier impossibility. After talking, listening, seeing (and perhaps even peeking inside during a service), he comes to a new understanding of the idea of a church with or without special architecture. In his description Furth very carefully points out that no one tried to argue with the boy, nor did the situation become stressful. In fact, he pointedly notes that the boy was "in a relaxed state of mind" when he began to think through the discrepancies.[31]

It's clear you should not force accommodation. Equilibration takes place when there is a threshold of new awareness, or curiosity. There is some sense of uneasiness, an awareness that might be expressed as "Somehow my thinking doesn't quite handle the new information. Gradually I'll need to change my mind."

One final illustration: A small child in the first grade reported with a broad smile on arriving home each day, "I'm going to get a present for going to school!" After a few more days a parent asked, "Are you sure you're going to get a present?" "Oh, yes," came the answer brightly. "She said when she called our name you could say 'here' or 'present.'" So in time we know when a house is a church and, as one of the authors of this book so vividly remembers, when a present isn't a present. When such an accommodation takes place, there is a qualitative shift in thinking. We cannot go back to our old way of thought once the change is really incorporated.

Under conditions of accommodation and equilibration, we sense that a new explanation is better, or we intuitively begin to feel that a new level of understanding is beginning to dawn. We are not quite sure, and in fact may be a bit apprehensive, about exploring an unknown; part of us may be attracted to the change, while another part (our old comfortable way of thinking) resists. The feelings gradually have to be worked through during equilibration. Some of the old must be relinquished to make room for the new, a process that can involve anxiety.

As a teacher introducing new concepts, slightly better problem-solving methods, or somewhat more comprehensive theories, remember that you are inducing some equilibration within the pupils. They will need extra psychological and personal support during such transition periods.

In addition to giving the extra personal support during new learning, also remember that there is little sense in teaching preoperational or early concrete thinkers to think abstractly. If for the sake of equilibration we present information that is over the heads of the pupils, new learning will not take place—there will be no reconciliation of new ideas. In fact, the only notable increases may be in pupil frustration, anxiety, and perhaps rote memorization.

To sum up the phases of the learning of new concepts (that is, how we accommodate and

TABLE 5.3   PHASES OF DEVELOPMENTAL LEARNING

EQUILIBRATING THE NEW AND THE OLD

1. Awareness of a moderate discrepancy arises in understanding the meaning of an event or idea.
2. A feeling of puzzlement ensues: curiosity, uneasiness, affective arousal.
3. More new information accumulates that doesn't fit the prior understanding.
4. During periods of relaxed reflection, one tries to fit the new pieces of information into the old scheme; talking to oneself.
5. A new balance is reached. The new information moves from accommodation to assimilation.
6. After sufficient time the new information becomes "old" information and can be generalized to similar situations.
7. A new moderate discrepancy arises and the process continues.

then assimilate knowledge disturbances), Table 5.3 outlines a seven-step process that includes both the thoughts and feelings that the learner experiences. Gradualness, curiosity, and relaxed reflection lead eventually to a mastery of the new concept, self-confidence as a learner, and the ability to generalize the idea to other similar circumstances. This learning process is quite obviously different from rote memorization.

Teaching to Facilitate Cognitive Development

Certainly the major implication of Piaget's framework is that the curriculum should not take cognitive development for granted. On the contrary, the curriculum should provide specific educational experiences, based on the children's developmental level, to foster growth. This is particularly true for the final stage— formal operations. Just because adolescents are ready to develop formal logical thought processes does not necessarily mean they will think logically. For example, the secondary-school curriculum in science too often assumes that all pupils are already functioning at advanced stages of formal thought. Studies have shown, distressingly, that this is not the case. As Table

TABLE 5.4 FORMAL OPERATIONAL THINKING IN SCIENTIFIC PROBLEM SOLVING (SECONDARY-SCHOOL PUPILS)

Grade	N	Formal Thinking N	Percentage
9	94	17	18
10	94	26	27
11	99	29	29
12	97	33	33

5.4 indicates, out of a randomly selected research sample of almost 400 pupils in grades nine through twelve, only 18 to 33 percent were actually able to apply formal thinking to scientific problem solving.[32]

What the research sample suggests is that the great majority of pupils have difficulty in understanding the basic assumptions of math and science curricula in secondary schools. For example, in most biological and physical sciences the concepts of the atom and molecule represent the basic theoretical frameworks or the organizing principles upon which disciplined inquiry rests. If a student cannot grasp the abstractions, then the outcome is rote memorization minus any genuine understanding. The same is true for geometry, especially Euclidean.

Similarly, the picture in the humanities is no more encouraging. In English the requirement of diagramming sentences clearly involves formal thought. J. W. Renner's studies indicated that even by the ninth grade, only 18 percent of the sample were capable of this task. Other national surveys, particularly the huge Project Talent study, came to similar conclusions. Only 8 percent of a random sample in excess of 500,000 teen-agers could comprehend passages from Jane Austen. Only 33 percent could understand Robert Louis Stevenson (and that's *Treasure Island*—hardly the most complex metaphorical writing).[33] Thus the evidence from a wide variety of secondary-school subjects indicates a significant need to reexamine both the content and process of instruction in order to start where the learner is.

Each cognitive stage is like a switching station, where the pupil has the option of moving on to the next stage or staying in place. Whether movement occurs depends on the pupil's educational experience at that time. It is our view that much of the difficulty of teaching and learning, especially at the secondary level, arises from a lack of understanding of the process of cognitive development. If teen-age pupils cannot understand the curriculum materials they face day after day, we cannot blame them for losing interest completely. We would urge a careful examination of the cognitive assumptions of the curriculum materials. Further, we would urge an examination of the errors pupils make to see whether the material is clearly over their heads or beyond their present comprehension. It may be appropriate to revise lesson plans and use materials that are more within the pupils' level of understanding. Rather than assuming that high-school pupils are all competent in formal operational thought, we should provide experiences and activities to stimulate that development. A careful analysis of student "error" is highly recommended for development assessment.

PHYSIOLOGICAL DEVELOPMENT: BRAIN GROWTH?

In addition to the psychological aspects of stage change, the question of critical changes in the brain itself arises. This is a relatively recent area of research. At the moment research points to the fact that changes do take place that coincide with Piaget's stages. Children show two shifts—in head size and brain wave patterns. In other words, systematic changes occur in both size and function that coincide with the general shifts in thinking from sensorimotor to preoperational and so on. These findings add further evidence to support Piaget's theory since newer and higher-order thinking stages should be reflected both in psychology and biology. What is not clear, however, is whether the findings have new and unique educational implications. Some have suggested that such brain change, called "periodization," has direct importance for teaching. Since periods of rapid growth may even be followed by times of no growth, children may not really be capable of learning much of anything when growth ceases.[34]

At this point we must remember that no evidence supports such a position. As Kurt Fischer summarizes the findings, "They suggest that there is only a broad, nonspecific relation between brain development and Piagetian periods. They do not support the argument that children cannot learn new skills during times when their brains are growing slowly."[35] Thus, it is important to be alert to any suggestion that a child may be like a computer and be "down" and unable to learn just after the growth spurt periods. Growth depends on appropriate interaction before, during, and after stage shifts.

CHILDREN ARE NOT LIKE ADULTS

Piaget makes it clear that cognitive growth is a continuation of inborn motor processes—that is, the child comes into the world genetically equipped to make certain motor responses and these form the foundation on which later mental structures will be built. Thus, the biological givens inescapably direct cognitive growth. Further, Piaget considers the difference among his four major stages to be based on differences in how the child interacts with his or her environment and the child's own reality. Finally, though Piaget feels that in general the stages of development cannot be speeded up, he does concede that they may be retarded under conditions of low environmental stimulation. Thus, though the onset of the stages is, in a sense, predetermined, environmental stimulation is needed at the right time for the bud of each stage to come to full flower on schedule.

Piaget's theory of cognitive growth, in contrast to earlier views, shows how our thinking processes take dramatically different forms during different periods of growth. It also indicates the role of experience and active learning in generating growth and change. Above all, it stresses the importance of assessing the stage to which the pupil as a learner has developed, within the framework of developmental cognitive growth.[36] It is extraordinarily easy to assume that children think almost like adults. For

an educator, such a view is both simple-minded and somewhat dangerous.

Before we conclude the discussion on cognitive development, a final point should be made: We cannot assume that all teen-agers function at the formal level. Nor can we assume that all adults, including ourselves, function at the formal level in all domains. Thus, if we have not been exposed to a careful balance of experience and guided reflection in all areas of human activity, then it is highly likely that our own development may be incomplete. We may still operate at an intuitive or concrete level in certain areas. For example, it is often the case that graduate schools are filled with students who perform brilliant feats of theoretical syntheses in the areas of personality, abnormal psychology, history, and philosophy, and yet immediately revert to concrete or even preoperational thinking in their first required course in statistics. Similarly, we may be at the level of formal thought in literature yet preoperational in understanding simple principles of physics. Look at the number of college graduates well educated in the humanities who will pick out boxes in grocery stores because they seem larger. The bottle and box manufacturers of the country intuitively know that most adults apparently don't understand volume conservation. We adults merrily wend our way through the aisles picking out tall, narrow cereal boxes; tall, thin salad bottles; skinny soap-powder containers— all the while feeling that we're getting a bargain for our money. Actually, the list of such misconceptions is endless. In the aesthetic world, think how many of us really believe that taking photographs always involves carefully posing the subjects, or that symphonies must always be performed in the same concrete manner.[37] Table 5.5 gives a description of Piaget stages and examples of common adult behaviors. After looking at these descriptions, see if you can add a few based on your own experience. The point of the exercise is not only to remind ourselves of the need for humility but also to help us remember that human development is most likely never completed. Formal operations represent a laudable goal, even though few humans actually reach that level of functioning in all domains.

TABLE 5.5   ADULT BEHAVIORS ILLUSTRATING PIAGET'S PREADULT STAGES

PIAGET STAGE	ADULT BEHAVIORS
Sensorimotor: Emphasis on immediacy of feelings, inability to attend to consequences. The "here and now" is all.	Getting high on booze just before an important task.
	Smoking "pot" just prior to an important exam because it feels good.
	Going parachuting for thrills instead of meeting commitments at work.
	Throwing a temper tantrum instead of attempting to resolve conflicts.
Preoperational: Belief in intuition, magical thinking; fantasies are real. Superstitions abound.	Believing, as some athletes do, that each baseball bat has a magical number of hits (or that one must wear "lucky" clothes).
	Making significant life decisions according to horoscopes.
	Believing in mind-reading activities—for example, bending spoons with one's mind, reading a paper through one's nose, communicating with the dead (dialogues with Julius Caesar).
	Believing, as some bridge players do, that sitting parallel to the water pipes in the bathroom influences the cards.
	Giving away one's life savings to a total stranger who has a secret map locating Spanish gold (the flimflam).
Concrete: Emphasizing facts, routines; only one way to do things. Never vary any routine in spite of changed circumstances.	Always making the same sales calls on customers at the same time and day of the week.
	Repeating the same funny stories in lengthy and exacting detail to those who have heard them many times over (the "Ancient Mariner" routine).
	Always using the same play in game situations. (The Pittsburgh Steelers for years started each game with the fullback up the middle for three yards.)

Thus, we cannot assume that all elementary-school children function at the concrete level all the time, nor that all adolescents are at the formal level all the time, nor that we adults operate in all domains at the formal level. From an educational standpoint, however, this does not mean that as pupils or adults we are permanently relegated to less complex and complete systems of thought and action. Given the conditions of support and manageable new learning tasks, we can continue the process of growth. Accommodation and assimilation can proceed.

PIAGETIAN TASKS

Measuring Aspects of Concrete Operations*

The following tests are designed to assess children at the elementary-school level on their ability to conserve and to classify.

---

* The items in this section and item 3 in the next section were developed by Pisila Taufe'ulungaki, a specialist in tests and measurements at the University of Minnesota.

Instructions

1. Read each item carefully.
2. Answer all the items.
3. Mark the correct answer.
4. Explain your answer.

Practice item: Before you begin, look at the practice item below. Study it carefully to see how you are to find the right answer.

Shown below are two sets of fruit.

Set A has oranges. Set B has apples.

Set A:

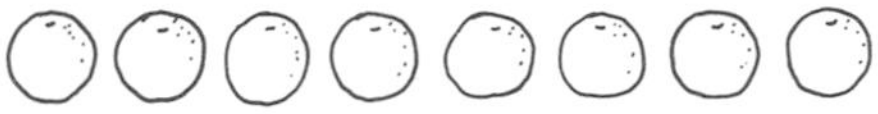

Set B:

A. Of the two sets, which set has the most fruit?

☐ a. Set A has the most fruit.
☐ b. Set B has the most fruit.
☐ c. They have the same number of fruit.
☐ d. None of the above answers is correct.

B. Explain your answer. *Set A has 8 oranges. Set B has 8 apples. Therefore, both sets have the same number of fruit. (or) Set A = 8. Set B = 8. Therefore, Set A = Set B.*

---

1. Shown below are two groups of marbles. Each circle represents a marble.

    Group A: ○ ○ ○ ○ ○ ○ ○ ○ ○ ○ 
    Group B: ○○○○○○○○○○

A. Of the two groups, which group has more marbles?

☐ a. Group A has more marbles.
☐ b. Group B has more marbles.
☐ c. Both groups have the same number of marbles.
☐ d. None of the above answers is correct.

B. _____

---

2. Show below are nine wooden blocks.

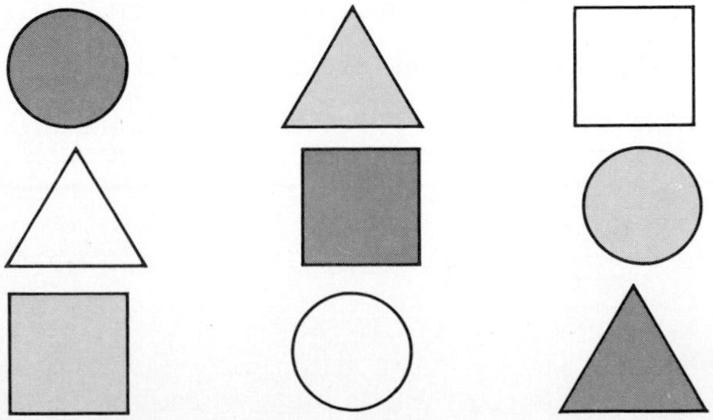

A. Two ways to sort the blocks into groups that are alike would be

☐ a. By color and by groups of two blocks.
☐ b. By shape and by groups of four blocks.
☐ c. By color and by shape.
☐ d. None of the above answers is correct.

B. Explain your answer. ――――――――

――――――――――――――――――――――――――――――

――――――――――――――――――――――――――――――

――――――――――――――――――――――――――――――

3, 4. Shown below in Picture A is a bottle half full of water.

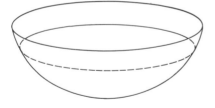

A   B   C

A. Suppose the bottle is tilted as shown in Picture B, and then placed flat as shown in Picture C. Draw the water levels on the bottles in Picture B and in Picture C.

B. Explain your answers. ――――――――

――――――――――――――――――――――――――――――

――――――――――――――――――――――――――――――

5. Shown below is a bowl half full of water. Beside it is an iron ball.

A. Suppose the iron ball is placed into the bowl of water. Will the water in the bowl go up or down, or will the water level remain the same?

☐ a. Remain the same.
☐ b. Go up.
☐ c. Go down.
☐ d. None of the above answers is correct.

B. Explain your answer. ――――――――

――――――――――――――――――――――――――――――

――――――――――――――――――――――――――――――

6. There are three girls named Jane, Mary, and Susan. Suppose Jane is taller than Mary and Mary is taller than Susan. Is Jane taller than Susan?

☐ a. Yes.
☐ b. No.
☐ c. Both are the same height.
☐ d. Not enough information is given.

Explain your answer. ――――――――

――――――――――――――――――――――――――――――

――――――――――――――――――――――――――――――

Answers: 1. c, 2. c, 3, 4. B   C   5. b, 6a

Measuring Aspects of Formal Operations

The following methods represent different approaches to measuring formal operations. The ability to think at an abstract level is the major element that separates people at this level from those at the prior stage.

1. *The meaning of proverbs and aphorisms.* Ask students to describe the meaning of any sayings such as:

    Still water runs deep.

    A stitch in time saves nine.

    A rolling stone gathers no moss.

    Make hay while the sun shines.

    Let no good deed go unpunished.

    Penny wise and pound foolish.

    The louder he proclaimed his honor, the faster we counted the silverware.

    Don't look a gift horse in the mouth.

    In my beginning is my end.

    Concrete thinkers will give literal descriptions tied very closely to the content: "When the water is very still, it means it's very deep," as opposed to "A quiet person often observes and understands the complexities of life." Or, "A farmer should gather in the hay before it rains" versus "When a good opportunity is at hand, act."

2. *Logic problems: The bean, bird, fish, snail islands puzzle.** This puzzle is about four islands in the ocean. People have been traveling among these islands by boat for many years, but recently an airline started in business. Students must listen carefully to the clues given about possible plane trips. The trips may be direct or they may include stops on one of the islands. When a trip is possible, it can be made in both directions between the islands. Here is how the puzzle should be presented:

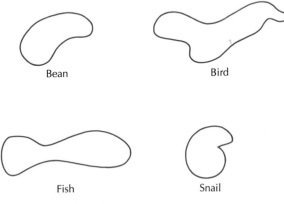

Bean   Bird

Fish   Snail

This is a map with the four islands, called Bean Island, Bird Island, Fish Island, and Snail Island. You may make notes or marks on your map to help you remember the clues. Raise your hand if you have questions about the clues.

First clue: People can go by plane between Bean and Fish Islands.
Second clue: People cannot go by plane between Bird and Snail Islands.

Use these two clues to answer Question 1.

---

*   This item is from *Research, Teaching and Learning with the Piaget Model*, by J. W. Renner, D. G. Stafford, A. E. Lawson, J. W. Mckinnon, F. E. Friot, and D. H. Kellog. Copyright © 1976 by the University of Oklahoma Press.

QUESTION 1: Can people go by plane between Bean and Bird Islands?

☐ a. Yes

☐ b. No

☐ c. Can't tell from the two clues.

Explain in your answer. _____

_____

_____

Third clue: People can go by plane between Bean and Bird Islands.

Use all three clues to answer Questions 2 and 3. Don't change your answer to Question 1.

QUESTION 2: Can people go by plane between Fish and Bird Islands?

☐ a. Yes

☐ b. No

☐ c. Can't tell from the two clues.

Explain in your answer. _____

_____

_____

QUESTION 3: Can people go by plane between Fish and Snail Islands?

☐ a. Yes

☐ b. No

☐ c. Can't tell from the two clues.

Explain in your answer. _____

_____

_____

Concrete thinkers will have difficulty remembering the combination of clues. Usually their explanations will indicate their inability to consider all the clues simultaneously.

Answers: 1. Can't tell; 2. Yes—take plane from Fish to Bean and Bean to Bird; 3. No—the second clue makes that impossible.

3. *Physical properties problems:* Ask students to answer the following physical science questions.

(a) The diagram below represents a scale. Beside it are several rings representing balls of different weights for balancing the bar of the scale.

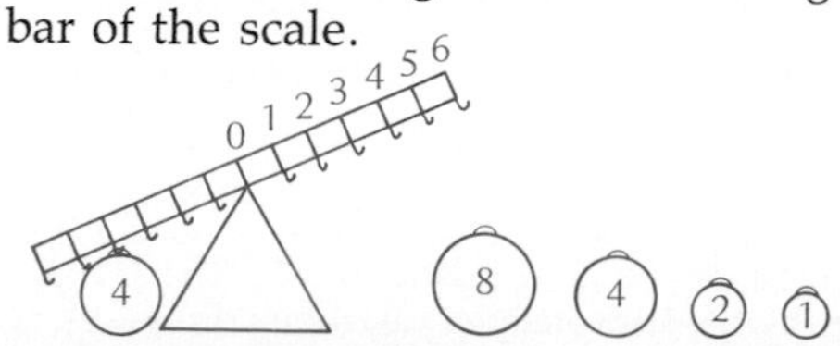

A. Suppose a four-ounce ring was placed on the scale as shown at point 4 in the diagram. By using one of the weights below, show how the bar could be balanced.

☐ a. Place the 8-ounce ring on 2.

☐ b. Place the 4 -ounce ring on 5.

☐ c. Place the 2-ounce ring on 2.

☐ d. None of the above.

B. Explain your answer. _____

_____

_____

(b) Shown below is a pendulum made in the form of an object hanging from a string. Also shown are pendulums with different string lengths and different weights.

A. A science class made some trials to see if the pupils could find out what made the pendulum swing faster or slower. The following is a record of the class observations of swing.

Length	Weight	Rate	Comment
short	light	slow	false
short	heavy	fast	true
long	light	fast	false
long	light	slow	true
short	heavy	slow	false
short	light	fast	true
long	heavy	fast	false
long	heavy	slow	true

By studying the above table of observations, select the choice that seems best.

☐ a. It is the weight.

☐ b. It is the length.

☐ c. It is the combination of both.

☐ d. None of the above.

B. Explain your answer. _____

_____

_____

Answers: 3(a). a, 3(b). b

SUMMARY

According to the definition of cognitive developmental stages presented here, growth is qualitative rather than quantitative. It is characterized by great leaps forward, followed by periods of integration rather than linear, step-by-step changes in degree. Piaget came to this conclusion based on repeated observations of children in natural settings.

Piaget's work created a new and significant theory regarding the process of cognitive growth stages. The stages are defined by system of thinking employed and by modal age. In the sensorimotor stage, from birth to twenty-four months, learning is tied to immediate experience; object permanence is learned at this stage. When a child moves into the preoperational stage, from two to seven years of age, language development allows the child to free-associate and fantasize; creativity is characteristic of this age. Children from seven to eleven years of age are usually in the concrete operations stage, when literal-mindedness reigns. Finally, children reach the stage of formal operations, from eleven to sixteen years, when thought enlarges to include possibilities, hypotheses, ideas, and the perspective of others. Although children usually operate at the stage appropriate to their age, they are sometimes capable of next-stage-up thinking, and teachers should encourage such development.

A basic Piagetian concept denotes the importance of activity as a central ingredient of intelligence at all stages. Active learning experiences tend to promote cognitive growth while passive and vicarious experiences tend to have minimal impact.

To the American question—Can we speed up growth?—Piaget's answer is that constant acceleration of learning is not possible because of the limitations of thought processes at various ages. But the process of growth can be nurtured.

To promote growth requires attention to accommodation and assimilation. When new information is presented that does not fit the learner's current understanding, a knowledge disturbance is created. Taking in such new information represents accommodation. The next phase involves making the new concept fit with previous knowledge, or assimilating. Equilibration involves a balancing of accommodation and assimilation. Furth has pointed out not only how this process works but also the feelings of anxiety and the worry that go along with the struggle between the old way of thinking and the changes needed to grasp the new concept. There is a relationship between the intellectual and the affective when the previous balance is upset.

There is also a relationship between intellectual development and physiological development. Current research on brain development supports Piaget's notion of stages of cognitive development, though educators should be cautious in how they interpret the findings.

What should be clear to teachers, however, is that children are not adults and should not be treated like miniature adults in the classroom. Realizing that activity is often neglected as a major mode of learning, you may find an additional way to reach children and teen-agers. The hands-on approach is highly recommended, whereas passive watching of plays, listening to orchestras, visiting museums, and so on are not viewed as having as much educational merit.

KEY TERMS AND NAMES

developmental stage
quantitative development
qualitative development
Jean Piaget
   sensorimotor stage
   preoperational stage
   concrete operations stage
   formal operations stage

active school
the American question
conservation
accommodation
assimilation
Hans Furth
equilibration
periodization

REFERENCES

1. Pines, M. (1970). *A revolution in learning.* New York: Harper & Row.

2. Gesell, A. (1940). *The first five years of life.* New York: Harper & Row.

3. Flavell, J. H. (1985). *Cognitive development* (p. 4). Englewood Cliffs, N.J.: Prentice-Hall.

4. Pines, *A revolution in learning* (p. 58).

5. Flavell, *Cognitive development* (p. 5).

6. Renner, J., Stafford, A., Lawson, J., McKimmon, J., Friot, F., and Kellogg, D. (1976). *Research, teaching, and learning with the Piaget model* (p. 22). Normal: University of Oklahoma Press.

7. Scarr-Salapatek, S. (1976). An evolutionary perspective on infant intelligence: Species patterns and individual variations. In M. Lewis (Ed.), *The origins of intelligence: Infancy and early childhood* (p. 185). New York: Plenum. Actually there is an answer to her rhetorical question. Severe and profoundly retarded children demonstrate characteristics of sensorimotor operations well past the age of two if not provided with adequate stimulation. See Walker, S. (1984). Issues and trends in the education of the severely handicapped. In E. Gordon (Ed.), *Review of research in education*, Vol. 11 (p. 105). Washington, D.C.: American Educational Research Association.

8. Flavell, *Cognitive development* (p. 39).

9. Gelman, R. (1982). Basic numerical abilities. In R. J. Sternberg (Ed.), *Advances in the psychology of human intelligence*, Vol. 1. Hillsdale, N.J.: Lawrence Erlbaum. See also Harris, P. (1983). Infant cognition. In M. M. Haith and J. J. Campos (Eds.), *Handbook of child psychology: Infancy and psychobiology*, Vol. 2. New York: Wiley. The article gives a major review of the current research on early cognition.

10. Piaget, J. (1970). *Science of education and the psychology of the child* (p. 30). New York: Viking.

11. Gibson, E. J., and Spelke, E. S. (1983). The development of perception. In J. H. Flavell and E. M. Markman (Eds.), *Handbook of child psychology: Cognitive development*, Vol. 3. New York: Wiley.

12. Flavell, *Cognitive development* (p. 39).

13. Piaget, J. (1964). *Judgment and reasoning in the child* (p. 85). Paterson, N.J.: Littlefield, Adams.

14. Gelman, Basic numerical abilities.

15. Mischel, W. (1981). Metacognition and the rules of delay. In J. H. Flavell and L. Ross (Eds.), *Social cognitive development*. New York: Cambridge University Press.

16. Flavell, *Cognitive development* (p. 28).

17. Piaget, *Science of education* (p. 30).

18. Wolfenstein, M. (1954). *Children's humor.* Glencoe, Ill.: Free Press.

19. Wolfenstein, *Children's humor.*

20. White, M. A. (1968). The view from the pupil's desk. *Urban Review, 2,* 5–7.

21. See Jones, R. (1968). *Fantasy and feeling in education.* New York: Harper. This is an interesting account detailing the failure of an attempt to employ a "high-powered' curriculum, "Man: A Course of Study," at the elementary-school level.

22. Neimark, E. D. (1982). Adolescent thought: Transition to formal operations. In B. B. Wolman (Ed.), *Handbook of developmental psychology* (p. 494). Englewood Cliffs, N.J.: Prentice-Hall.

23. Neimark, Adolescent thought (p. 493). The most comprehensive research on the nature of formal operations is being done by William Bart at the University of Minnesota. See Bart, W., and Mertens, D. (1979). The hierarchical structure of formal operational tasks. *Applied Psychological Measurement, 3*(3), 343–350.

24. Sprinthall, N. A., and Collins, W. A. (1984). *Adolescent psychology: A developmental view* (p. 92). New York: Random House.

25. Inhelder, B., and Piaget, J. (1958). *The growth of logical thinking from childhood to adolescence* (p. 122). New York: Basic Books.

26. Piaget, *Science of education* (p. 34).

27. Barratt, B. (1975). Training and transfer in combinational problem-solving: The development of formal reasoning during early adolescence. *Developmental Psychology, 11*(6), 700–704.

28. Renner and others, *Research, teaching, and learning* (p. 50).

29. Piaget, *Science of education* (p. 153).

30. Furth, H. (1981). *Piaget and knowledge,* 2nd ed. Chicago: University of Chicago Press.

31. Furth, *Piaget and knowledge* (p. 267).

32. Renner and others, *Research, teaching and learning* (p. 97).

33. Flanagan, J. (1973). Education: How and for what? *American Psychologist, 28*(7), 551–556.

34. Epstein, H. (1978). Growth spurts during brain development: Implications for educational policy. In J. A. Chall and A. F. Mirsky (Eds.), *1978 Yearbook of the National Society for the Study of Education.* Chicago: University of Chicago Press.

35. Fischer, K., and Lazerson, A. (1985). Research: Brain spurts and Piagetian periods. *Educational Leadership, 41*(5), 70.

36. Fisher, K. W. (1980). A theory of cognitive development: The control and construction of hierarchies of skills. *Psychological Reviews, 87,* 477–531.

37. See Nisbett, R., and Ross, L. (1980). *Human inference: Strategies and shortcomings of social judgment.* Englewood Cliffs, N.J.: Prentice-Hall. The book offers an extensive, distressing, and oftentimes hilarious set of examples of just how far from formal operations many adults are.

6

PERSONAL GROWTH

Although this chapter concentrates on personal development during childhood and adolescence, it is important to remember that the various areas of growth are not separate from one another. We indicated earlier that the mind is not a discrete entity, any more than is the body. Mind and body function together and are intimately interconnected. In the same way, we cannot really separate personal development (the growth of personality) from cognitive development (the growth of intellectual skills). For example, a basic part of our personality resides in our self-concept; how we perceive and think about ourself, especially in relation to other people, will certainly affect our personal development. Therefore, as you read this chapter, be careful not to assume that personal growth takes place in a vacuum.

To present ideas of growth and development in this very difficult area, we have based this chapter largely on Erik Erikson's elaboration of Sigmund Freud's original work. It was Erikson who transformed Freud's theories of emotional growth into a major developmental scheme as a means of understanding the process of healthy personal growth.

PERSONAL GROWTH: THE PRE-FREUDIAN VIEW OF MINDLESS CHILDREN

Before the earthshaking discoveries of Sigmund Freud at the turn of this century, it was generally assumed that, until they reached the age of six or seven, children were mindless creatures, more like animals than humans. It was important, naturally, to meet their physical needs, but beyond that they were thought to be in a kind of incubation period, too young to know or feel anything. There was little reason to take the early years seriously as a time when anything significant could occur.

Interestingly enough, this view of young children is common to many cultures throughout the world. In both modern and primitive societies, many practices are based on the notion that children are unthinking creatures, with no minds of their own, nor emotions of any consequence. These cultures sharply demarcate the beginning of the juvenile age (about seven years of age) from the age of mindlessness (birth to six). English common law and Catholic canon law, for example, both assume that children do not know anything before their seventh year. In non-Western cultures, a variety of initiation rites, performed between the ages of six and seven, are based on similar assumptions. In fact, one culture actually killed children who became seriously ill before the age of six, in the belief that they were not really children at all but snakes masquerading as humans.[1]

In this country, one of the pioneers in establishing childhood as a significant era in human development was Lawrence K. Frank. A child psychologist of particular eminence, he devoted his entire professional life to pointing out those practices within and across cultures that were designed to meet adult needs and ignore the needs of children.[2] He documented the entire array of child-rearing practices that assumed children were little more than pieces of clay to be molded into any shape by adult "master craftsmen." Molding and shaping had everything from physical to psychological manifestations. In some cultures heads are flattened, feet are bound, necks are stretched, skin is punctured or tattooed. In other cultures natural physiological functions, such as breathing, feeding, and sleeping patterns, are altered. The array of psychological practices is even greater, especially in the realm of what we could call character building. Using extreme forms of punishment, from beatings to severe scolding, adults have tried for centuries to defeat and deflect the process of personal growth. As L. K. Frank puts it, "Civilized man has survived *despite*, not because of, these methods of child care." The methods were too often created to suit the adult, not the child, and were based on an almost absolute ignorance of the special nature of childhood. As a result, "In the area of conduct and belief there apparently are no limits to the grostesque, the cruel and brutal, the diabolical ingenuity of man in warping and twisting human nature."[3] With these prior assumptions clearly in mind, we can now have some understanding of the impact, indeed shock wave, that was created by the works of Sigmund Freud.

SIGMUND FREUD: THE DISCOVERY OF CHILDHOOD

In searching for the causes of adult emotional difficulties, Freud began to create a revolutionary view of childhood that in no way resembled the prevailing view of benign emptiness. Freud, using the methods of clinical research, hypnotized his clients or asked them to free-associate ("Tell me the first thing that comes to mind") or to recount their recent dreams. He found, over and over again, that major aspects of his clients' personal development originated during their first six years of life. In fact, Freud discovered that he could understand the adult personality only by examining the kind of experiences and personal relationships the adult had had in childhood (before entering school). To know an adult, Freud would say, know the child. Hence the famous phrase, "The child is father of the man." In early experience could be discovered

Sigmund Freud: "The child is father of the man."

the foundations of later personal development. Uncovering significant childhood experiences is the essence of psychoanalytic theory.

Freud, with a kind of possessed genius, had to withstand enormous vilification as his theories became known. He was literally hated and feared, almost like the messenger in ancient times who was executed for being the bearer of bad news. Freud's bad news was simple: Adults must stop treating children as if they were too young to know or experience anything. There could be no justification whatsoever for child-rearing practices that mangle, distort, inhibit, and break young spirit.

Emotional Growth During Childhood: Freud's New View

Freud discovered that during their first years of life children go through a sequence of emotional stages, much as Piaget found them to go through a sequence of cognitive stages. In charting the course of emotional growth, Freud named three major stages of development from birth through seven years: the oral stage (birth to eighteen months), the anal stage (one and a half to three years), and the phallic stage (three to seven years).

According to Freud, this sequence of major emotional transformations leaves an indelible imprint on the adult personality. Also, as with cognitive growth, certain dimensions of personality are maximally affected at each of these stages. During the oral stage, for example, the quality of nurturing children receive, especially that related to feelings, will maximally affect their future feelings of dependence and trust in the world. During the anal stage (the name is derived from the universal requirement for bowel training), independence and control are

Training children as midget adults: Freud believed that children, far from being smaller images of adults, have a rich emotional life that can be divided into stages. In this sense, Freud "discovered" childhood.

Fingers firmly gripping the thin shaft of a quill pen, many a student in an early American school labored over his copy book, tracing the elaborate dips and swirls of the ABCs and struggling with the accompanying writing exercises.

Each page of the large, clothbound text contained examples of the exacting script of the teacher. On blank lines below the teacher's writing, the students meticulously sought to achieve the same effect, repeatedly tracing garnished letters of the alphabet and copying sentences of a relentlessly uplifting tone. Hour after hour they toiled, and some of the more gifted among them ultimately went on to achieve calligraphy so ornate as to be virtually unreadable.

The reward for this drudgery was the book itself, page upon page of the most elegant penmanship, often cherished for years by such scholars as Timothy Orne.

SIGMUND FREUD

If there is a single name in all psychology that is synonymous with personality theory, it is Sigmund Freud. Born on the Continent in 1856, he spent his early years as a member of a tightly knit family in Central Europe. Reportedly, his youth was marked by serious personality problems, including severe bouts with depression and anxiety states. These difficulties apparently started him on a journey of discovery aimed at understanding the roots of personality and gaining insight into the rela-

tionship between personality structure and actual behavior. It was to be a long and productive professional journey, beginning with his graduation from medical school at the University of Vienna in 1881. His career extended all the way to the beginning of World War II in 1939.

After completing his medical studies, he became increasingly interested in diseases of the nervous system. Instead of continuing to look for physical and physiological reasons, he shifted his attention toward a new arena, the mind. If diseases such as hysteria, high-anxiety states, and deep personal depression were not connected to a physical cause, then the usual types of medical treatment, from actual operations on nerves to prescriptions for drugs, were bound to fail. Such activities were merely treating symptoms. Often, after these treatments, patients simply developed a new set of symptoms. As a result of these ideas, Freud decided to study with Josef Breuer, a physician famous for his treatment of hysteria through hypnosis. Freud found that inducing hypnotic trances was somewhat limited as a treatment of choice. Some patients could not be successfully hypnotized and others simply shifted symptoms.

Freud began to experiment with unique treatment methods, primarily asking patients to free-associate

and to report on their dreams. In some ways this appeared an outrageous procedure for a physician to use. Imagine Freud asking a patient to stretch out on his soon-to-be-famous couch, then suggesting that he or she say whatever came to mind. (The first rule of psychoanalysis was to speak out and not repress any hidden thoughts.) All the while Freud himself was sitting behind the couch quietly jotting down notes, rarely speaking. Such a procedure seemed the work of a mad genius at best or of a charlatan at worst. Not only did Freud break with the traditions of his time completely, but he even went so far as to carry on psychoanalytically oriented treatment via the mail to the father of a child patient. In the famous case of "Little Hans," he successfully treated a young boy by writing to the father and explaining step-by-step how to cure the patient of a severe case of horse phobia. Since horses provided most transportation in those days, Hans's malady can be compared to a child who today would run and hide at the sight of an automobile.

Always an innovator, Freud continued to evolve creative treatment techniques throughout his life; however, his major contribution was his insight into the causes of behavior. Through hours of quiet listening to patients' free associations and dreams, he began to con-

at the forefront of development. In the phallic stage, sexual identity is the major aspect of personality formation.

Freud suggested that a period of latency (seven to twelve years) follows, in which the oral, anal, and phallic demensions are integrated and no new elements are added. However, during adolescence (the genital stage), the

period of so-called *sturm und drang* (a German expression meaning a period of extreme stress and strain), all the previous elements—oral, anal, and especially phallic—are brought back into play. During adolescence the basic elements are reworked into an adult character. This is a time for recapitulation, going back over the issues of dependence (oral period), indepen-

struct a theory of personality. He heard the same themes repeated over and over again and in time created his theory of infant sexuality. Adult patients were helped to gradually recall early feelings, thoughts, and sexual fantasies from their childhood. To suggest to the world that innocent little children had such sexual feelings was almost too much for the Victorian age to accept. Nevertheless, despite the enormous criticism generated and the departure of some of his closest associates, Freud continued to expand on the importance of sexuality as a determinant of personality during the early years of life. His three-part typology of the mind—the id, the ego, and the superego—combined with his three layers of conscious, preconscious, and unconscious led to his famous dictum that all human behavior was overdetermined. His clinical approaches demonstrated that our present behavior is related to a whole series of "causes." The task of the psychologist is to uncover great amounts of psychic material and then gradually help the patient understand how many of the factors from the past had been regulating his or her present behavior. In fact, Freud said that the psychologist is like an archaeologist—carefully and systematically digging through the past in order to slowly uncover the intrapsychic traumas of a person's early history. Here he found the structure of the past influencing present behavior; here was the repository of events, feelings, disconnected ideas, fantasies rooted in the unconscious.

The unconscious, according to Freud, is the key to human behavior. Even though individuals may try to suppress or repress inner thoughts and feelings and push them into the unconscious, the repressed material sneaks out in disguised form. Slips of the tongue, unfortunate "accidents," forgetting important events, getting names of familiar people mixed up, and similar unusual human behavior are not just incidental activities or randomly determined. He was able to show how such events are instead a direct expression of an individual's unconscious motivation. For example, a guilt-ridden criminal might "accidentally" leave a trail a mile wide from the scene of a crime in order to bring about his own punishment. Other examples abound in everyday life.

The insights of Freud changed our level of understanding in dramatic ways. It has been said that the greatest contribution was to end, once and for all, the age of innocence. Also, some have remarked that it would have been impossible to understand the horrors of the twentieth century without his theories of why and how people react. These theories demonstrated the importance of both sexual and aggressive human drives. The adverse interpersonal relationships so common in this age are current reminders of this insight. The desolation created by two major world wars, the total annihilation of innocent populations, the use of ultimate weapons from A-bombs to gas chambers—these products of a so-called advanced civilization can be better understood through his views. It is to be hoped that his insights will teach the world the importance of recognizing and gradually developing control over these destructive human drives. Ironically, he spent many of his last years as a captive of the most demonic human being of this century in Nazi Germany. His final year of life was spent in England in 1939. He watched the world he knew collapse once again in a paroxysm of hatred, tragic testimony to his deepest fears for humanity.

dence (anal period), and identity (phallic period) to prepare for a fully functioning adulthood in which, according to Freud, we can live and work productively—a simple but profound human objective.

Freud established once and for all that extremely significant personal and emotional aspects of our development are determined during the first seven years of our lives. It was no longer possible to assume that the young child has no mind or any significant emotions. Instead, Freud's theory provided valid information to buttress an old adage, "Just as the twig is bent, the tree's inclined." The adult personality is affected in major ways by the emotional experiences of childhood.

In other words, the interactions between the child and significant adults during the first six years determine whether or not the adult will be able to function efficiently. Inadequate or negative child-rearing practices will result in a personality that is flawed. The person might function adequately but show major deficiencies.

ERIK ERIKSON: THE SEQUENCE OF STAGES AND TASKS OF PERSONAL DEVELOPMENT

Erik Erikson, one of Freud's students, has done more than any other theorist to modernize Freudian theory and make it into a more complete theory of child and adolescent development. In a sense, one of the major difficulties with Freud's view was that it was too deterministic. According to Freud, by the time we are six or seven years old, personal growth is essentially all over.[4] Our basic personality structures are already set. As shown in Table 6.1, Erikson expanded the ideas of stages of development into a broader framework—a life cycle—and outlined the positive and negative dimensions of each period. This helped to clarify and balance the theory as a means of understanding personal growth.

Whereas Freud had emphasized the negative and pathological aspects of emotional growth, Erikson directed the theory into a broader context. He saw development continuing throughout one's entire life and yet gave special significance to childhood (birth to six years), the juvenile era (six to twelve years), and adolescence (twelve through the college years). Although he has suggested stages of development well into adulthood, we will concentrate on these three categories.[5]

The Epigenetic Principle: The Engine for Growth

You may recall that Piaget discussed the importance of equilibration as the mechanism that promotes cognitive development. There is a built-in drive to acquire more complex systems of thinking. In a parallel sense, Erikson says much the same for personal growth. His terms are different, but the assumptions are the same. Erikson refers to the epigenetic principle. Personality itself goes through structural elaborations in accord with a ground plan. Development is not random but proceeds according to the outline. Nor is development automatic; the ground plan is really a map of potential. If the child's interaction with the environment is healthy and the basic crisis of each stage of development is resolved, then the child will be ready for the next stage. We do not have to

TABLE 6.1   ERIKSON'S GROUND PLAN FOR PSYCHOSOCIAL GROWTH

AGE	BIPOLAR CRISES AT EACH STAGE (OUTLINED)				
Birth to twenty-four months	Basic trust vs. mistrust	Early autonomy, etc.	Early initiative	Early mastery	Early identity
Two to three years	Later forms of hope, etc.	Autonomy vs. shame	↓	↓	↓
Four to six years	↓	Later forms of will	Initiative vs. guilt	↓	↓
Six to twelve years	↓	↓	Later forms of purpose	Mastery vs. inferiority	↓
Thirteen to eighteen years	↓	↓	↓	Later forms of competence	Identity vs. diffusion
Eighteen years through college	↓	↓	↓	↓	Identity (moratorium and achievement) vs. continued diffusion
Resolution:	Hope	Will	Purpose	Competence	Fidelity

force a child to grow as a personality. The epigenetic principle means the potential for growth already is a given.

Originally Erikson posed his framework in terms of stages of crises, with bipolar definitions of the crisis at each stage—for example, trust versus mistrust. More recently, he has suggested that each of these opposites can be combined.[6] During the first years the child wrestles with the problem of how trustful or distrustful to become. Under appropriate conditions of nurture, these opposites are resolved into a new condition called "hope." Thus, as the first two years of life end, the child's personality disposition can be toward a basically positive outlook. Similarly, the resolution to the second stage, autonomy versus shame, is now termed "will." It is interesting to note that Erikson was quite uneasy denoting the resolutions in terms such as hope, will, purpose, competence, and fidelity. He apparently was worried that such "old-fashioned" terms might lead psychologists to dismiss his work as more philosophy than behavioral science. However, such terms actually clarify the goals of each stage as a meaningful synthesis, a new combination. For example, under the old system it was difficult to resolve the trust-versus-mistrust polarity as trust. Hope, on the other hand, represents more a resolution of two opposite tendencies than an either-or choice. The same is true of the other stages, as you will see in the following descriptions.

Childhood (Birth to Six Years)

Trust versus mistrust (birth to twenty-four months): Hope   Erikson subdivided the period of childhood into three categories that almost precisely duplicate Freud's. The first of these categories, from birth to twenty-four months, he labeled the stage of trust versus mistrust. In Freudian terms, this is the oral period, in which there is great emphasis on feeding, sucking, biting, drooling. The quality of nurture—the quality of care and affection that go into feeding, cuddling, bathing, and dressing the child—will develop feelings of trust or mistrust. The extent to which a baby's first experience of the world is of a dependable, warm place will create a general outlook, ranging from positive and trusting to negative and mistrust-

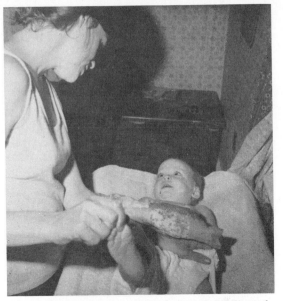

Erikson's periods of childhood almost duplicated Freud's. He labeled his first stage trust versus mistrust and felt that good nurturance would develop feelings of hope in the child.

ing. We are not talking about the old controversy of breast-feeding as opposed to bottle-feeding (for a long time that seemed to be the single controversy), but rather about the need for affectionate physical contact and comfort during feeding and other child-rearing activities. A cold, tense mother breast-feeding could be as lacking in good nurture as a bottle prop (a device that allows no human contact while feeding a baby).

Evidence for the importance of early experience has been provided by several researchers. Harry Harlow's continuing research has supported the concept of the importance of early nurturing patterns.[7] Harlow has been raising baby monkeys under different conditions of nurturing for numerous studies. Figure 6.1 depicts two types of substitute monkey "mothers": a warm, soft, cloth one and a cold, harsh, wire one. Both are capable of providing milk, but as you might expect, the wire mother's babies manifested substantial bizarre behavior as adults. They were unable to mate, to relate to strange or novel objects, and in fact, showed many behaviors reminiscent of schizophrenia. The cloth mother's babies, on the other hand, were able to explore strange and terrifying sit-

FIGURE 6.1   Harlow gave baby monkeys two kinds of substitute "mothers": a warm, cloth one and a cold, wire one. The wire mother's babies manifested bizarre behavior as adults—for example, they were unable to mate and exhibited characteristics similar to schizophrenia.

uations and demonstrated an ability to master their environment.

Equally dramatic was some clinical research conducted by Rene Spitz.[8] He studied the effects of orphanage experiences on very young children. Even though the children were given adequate physical care, washed, fed, and kept in warm, clean rooms, there was almost a complete lack of human warmth and contact. During an epidemic, the orphanage children were dramatically less able to withstand disease compared to other children of nearby families. In fact, when the figures were published, they were very hard for people to accept—thirty-four of ninety-one orphanage children died, compared to almost none of the other children in the area.

Erikson notes that maternal warmth and care teach children through the senses (as Piaget might say) that they can depend on the world.*

The mother is practically the entire world for very young children. Through her they learn that, although she disappears at times, she also always reappears. From the regularity as well as the quality of the experience, children develop their outlook on life and prepare to move to the second stage. As with the stages of cognitive growth, the stages of personal development are sequential. This means that if children's basic dependency needs are met during their first twenty-four months of life, they will be ready to move to the second stage of personal development. On the other hand, if these needs are not properly met, they may not be able to move on.

The dramatic studies of extreme cases of early deprivation of nurturance cited above indicate that the failure to develop could result in actual physical death (failure to thrive) or a kind of psychological death in the form of emotional withdrawal from the world (in so-called anaclitic depression). Children supposedly raised by wild animals such as the wild boy of Averyon, who was called a "feral child," exhibited similar irreversible disturbances.

---

* Erikson consistently refers to the indispensable role of the mother. He does not consider the role of the father in nurturance, though some commentators suggest that his theory can be accommodated to nurturers of either sex.

There is apparently no adequate compensation for nurturing during this period. In fact, for a while it was thought that the primary caregiver had to be the child's natural parents. The famous example in England during the 1940 bombing blitz was often cited as evidence. Young children were moved from the cities and placed in model child-care centers directed by experts, including Anna Freud and Dorothy Burlingham. In spite of the best efforts of these experts, the children separated from their natural parents showed definite developmental lags.[9] The problem, of course, is with the interpretation of causes. Wartime separation from parents for extended periods (sometimes parents could visit only once a month due to travel restrictions) is not really a fair test of substitute parenting. In an atmosphere of high anxiety and extended separation, it may be more significant that the children didn't regress more markedly. The caregivers were responsible for the children's well-being twenty-four hours per day, week after week, and the ratio of adults to children was far from ideal.

More recent evidence—namely, a careful review of early-childhood programs in the 1970s—seems to indicate that although babies are extremely sensitive to experience, they are also resilient. In other words, the negative effects of early deprivation are not quite as long-lasting nor as indelible as originally thought. The idea of critical periods was borrowed too directly from studies of ducks and other animals. Human babies are more adaptable. They can overcome the negative effects of deprivation.[10] Certainly that is welcome news. At the same time, this evidence in no way negates the importance of providing young babies with positive environments. A rich and stimulating experience is still the rule. In addition, the primary caregiver does not have to be the natural mother. As long as the primary care giver provides the child with a consistent, sensitive, and nurturant environment, the child will have a good chance to resolve the polar conflict between trust and mistrust as personal hope.

Autonomy versus shame (two to three years): Will   During this second period of childhood, emotional and personal development moves into what Erikson calls the stage of autonomy versus shame. This is when children emerge from their almost total dependence on a primary caregiver and begin, literally and figuratively, to stand on their own two feet. The physical maturation that allows them to crawl, walk, run, and climb provides the means for a great leap into personal autonomy. This is a time of intense exploration when they seem to be into almost everything. Physical maturation also frees them from dependence on the bottle or the breast and enables them to learn how to control their bowel and bladders. Thus, the positive aspect of this period is a fundamental sense of self-direction. However, Erikson makes it clear that there can be negative emotional development, too. We noted in the first stage that children are particularly sensitive to the way in which their dependency needs are met. In this stage they need to be independent, and the way in which that need is met will maximally affect their sense of personal autonomy. If children at this stage are punished excessively for exploring their house or neighborhood, if they receive particularly harsh and punitive bowel training, or if they are so overprotected that they are almost "smothered," then Erikson indicates that the major emotional lesson from this period will be personal shame. The growing sense of self-control ("I can do it myself!") can be impaired as easily as it can be nurtured during this second period of childhood.

It may be difficult for adults to learn not to interfere but rather to support the child's desire for freedom and autonomy. For example, if you watch a boy of three trying to tie his shoes, you may see him work with extraordinary motivation even though the loops aren't matched, and well over half the time as he tries for the final knot, he ends up with two separate laces, one in each hand. Then watch parents as they watch their children attempt a task like this. Too often the parent will step in and take over, tie the shoes the "right way" and defeat the child's growing attempt at self-mastery. The same goes for putting on boots, coats, and even playing with toys. It is terribly easy to fall into the trap of almost always responding negatively to a child at this age. Commonly a mother might say no up to 200 times a day at this stage. Such nagging not only is negative reinforcement in the extreme, but also a constant reminder to the child of his or her lack of self-control.

This is also the time when language begins,

CONTEMPORARY ISSUE

Is Day Care as Good as a Mother?

An issue of major importance is the question of the effects of day care on infants, especially in their first two years. Certainly both Freud's and more directly Erikson's theory strongly imply that there is no satisfactory substitute for a close bond between an infant and one primary caregiver. (It could be either parent or another adult.) In addition to theory, both experimental research (Harlow's monkeys) and clinical observations (the English children during World War II) support that view.

On the other hand, there have been major changes in child care both since World War II and since the experimental studies were completed. And from a sociological standpoint, the great majority of families in this country now have both parents working outside the home. Thus, the question of parenting takes on new theoretical and practical importance. As a result, Jerome Kagan and his colleagues at Harvard decided to test the effects of day care in a highly formal way.[a] They set up two matched groups of infants between three and six months old. During the two-year study, day care (from 8 A.M. to 5 P.M.) was provided for one sample, while the other sample was reared exclusively at home. The parents were largely from working-class backgrounds.

A wide variety of measures of child development indicated no major or even minor differences between the two groups of children. In fact, some clinical evidence indicated that the day care experience was somewhat better. The researchers noted a subtle difference. The natural mothers

tended to be somewhat overly emotionally involved with their own child (all were either first- or second-born children). The carefully selected and trained day-care workers, on the other hand, seemed able to provide a less intrusive yet not overly detached experience. Before you conclude, however, that all previous research and theory was wrong, there are some important factors to consider.

In the first place, the program was truly ideal. The day care workers were all carefully screened. Rather than relying on academic qualifications, the experts directly observed how sensitive the staff applicants were in handling real children. In addition, the workers were carefully trained in the latest techniques, and the program materials and physical space were state of the art. All the staff members selected

also had prior experience in raising their own children. Continuous supervision and staff development were also part of the ongoing program. Perhaps most important was the staff-to-baby ratio. Each worker was responsible for three babies for the first fifteen months. The ratio for toddlers was one to five. In a sense the most significant finding, then, was that there is no appreciable difference in development for babies between three and fifteen months as long as there is one effectively trained worker for every three babies. Any further generalization to either higher ratios or less than ideal conditions is not warranted during Erikson's stage of trust versus mistrust. In fact, Kagan was mightily impressed by these workers. They were truly gifted in providing just the right amount of nurturance to each of their three charges. When feeling distressed,

such babies would immediately pick out their own worker for comfort. When feeling pleased, they would turn to their own for contact.

Did such surrogate mothers actually replace the natural mothers? The results here also indicated no real differences between the two groups. The day-care children still viewed their mothers as the most "salient adult figure," so the pro-gram did not interfere with that process. From this we can conclude, at least tentatively, that an ideal or model program can provide young babies with a trust-enhancing psychological experience. Working parents who place their children in such programs do not have to feel pangs of guilt that somehow their baby will miss out on the resolution of trust-mistrust as an outlook of hope.[b]

a   Kagan, J., Kearsley, R., and Zelazo, P. (1980). *Infancy.* Cambridge, Mass.: Harvard University Press.
b   Naturally enough, such research doesn't really settle such an issue. Most recently, ignoring the Kagan results, Deborah Fallow has written extensively to prove the point that there is no effective substitute. See Fallow, D. (1985). *A mother's work.* Boston: Houghton-Mifflin.

and here again the child's sense of independence is clearly in the balance. Adults need to understand that their child's first attempts to speak will always be halting. All children stutter somewhat during this time, just as all tumble constantly as they learn to walk and run. Attempts to speak need encouragement and modeling: Adults should not baby-talk back to a child, nor should they overcorrect a child's use of language. The surest way to promote stuttering at this stage is to harp on the misuse of language. It will definitely promote a sense of personal shame if, when children first try to talk, they are criticized for not talking the "right way."

Professor Burton "Bud" White of Harvard has shown that patterns of mothering and fathering at this stage are clearly related to the child's sense of personal mastery, independence, and self-control. Even at this early stage, certain patterns of interaction between parents and children can accurately predict competence and future mastery.[11] The most successful patterns are found in homes where the parents do substantial indirect teaching. Effective parents talk clearly and do a great deal of "labeling" ("This is a dog," and then, gradually, "This is a big dog," and so on). Children in these homes are also allowed substantial initiative in selecting activities; there is a balance between activities initiated by a parent and activities initiated by the children. A mother or father may ask for children's ideas and ask questions to help them understand the activity (e.g., "Now what do you suppose will happen if I put the piece in the puzzle this way?" or "if you pour all the water from the big glass into this little cup?" "What will Little Red Riding Hood find when she goes into the bedroom?").

White has shown, then, that parents who provide an interesting, stimulating environment, talk frequently to their children, give them some initiative, and do a great deal of indirect teaching by asking questions and drawing out their perceptions and ideas have the most positive effect on their children's developing sense of competency. Their sense of being "doers" and being able to control and affect the environment receives a major boost during this time.

Quite recently, White's research has been applied in a special preschool project. His studies show that developmental delays in personal growth can be identified reliably as early as two years. He and other experts have concluded that effective programs to unlock growth can be started at the same time.[12] In this way his research has two sets of implications, one for parents in general and one for school systems. There is strong support for the idea that school-based projects can teach principles of effective parenting, and the results of a current longitudinal study provide further support for the concept. Parents who participated in the special preschool project were able to learn to encourage healthy personal development. From the point of view of this chapter, the most signifi-

ERIK ERIKSON

Born at the turn of the century, Erik Erikson spent his early years in Europe. As a son of well-to-do parents, he received an education that was both formal and informal. Like other upper-class children, when he finished his regular school work, he traveled the Continent. He described this period as his *moratorium*—a term he used in his later theory of human development to describe a temporary life space that adolescents go through between the completion of general academic education and the choice of a life career. He noted that at the time of his own young adulthood, it was fashionable to travel through Europe, gaining a perspective on civilization and one's own possible place in it. He chose the avocation of portrait painting as an activity during this time. It permitted maximum flexibility for travel and yielded some productive output as

well. Obviously talented, he soon gained a reputation as a promising young artist, especially for his portraits of young children.

The turning point in his life came when he was invited to a villa in Austria to do a child's portrait. He entered the villa and was introduced to the child's father, Sigmund Freud. There began a series of informal discussions as he completed his work. A few weeks later, he received a written invitation from Freud to join the psychoanalytic institute of Vienna and study for child analysis. Erikson has commented that at this point he confronted a momentous decision: the choice between a continued moratorium with more traveling and painting, and a commitment to a life career pattern. Fortunately for psychology and particularly for our eventual understanding of children and adolescents, Erikson ended the moratorium.

After completing his training, he migrated to this country and served from 1936 to 1939 as a research associate in psychiatry at Yale, and he worked with Henry Murray of TAT fame (Thematic Apperception Test) at Harvard. From 1939 to 1951 he served as professor at the University of California and then moved to the Austen Riggs Clinic in Pittsburgh. With each move, his reputation grew in significance. His theoretical framework was adopted *in toto* by the White House Conference on Children in 1950. The conference report, a national charter for child and adolescent development in this country, was almost a literal repetition of his thoughts. In 1960 he was offered a university professorship at Harvard in recognition of his national and international stature in the field of human development. The career that

started so informally that day at Freud's villa culminated with almost unprecedented eminence as a professor in one of the country's oldest and most prestigious institutions of higher education—all without the benefit of a single earned academic degree. Ironically, he was offered only associate status in the American Psychological Association as late as 1950. This oversight was partially removed in 1955 when he was elected as a Fellow of the Division of Developmental Psychology, without ever having been a member.

His work, as we have noted in the text, has made a major contribution to our understanding of healthy psychological growth during all aspects of the life cycle. In addition to the high quality of his insight, Erikson possessed a genuine flair in linguistic expression, both spoken and written. In fact, one could almost compare his command of the English language with the benchmark established in this century by Winston Churchill. In many ways Erikson's scope was as broad and comprehensive as that of Churchill. Erikson's genius has been his ability to see the threefold relationship among the person, the immediate environment, and historical forces. Thus, each human is partially shaped by environmental and historical events, but each human, in turn, shapes the environment and can change the course of history. Erikson is equally at home describing the balance of individual strengths and problems for a single "average" child or teen-ager as with an analysis of major historical figures such as Martin Luther and Mahatma Gandhi. He shows through personal history how events and reactions during childhood and adolescence prepare humans to be adults. Ralph Waldo Emerson said that there is no history, only biography. Erikson's work attests to this wisdom.

If there is a criticism of his overall framework, it would concern his differentiation between the sexes. As might be expected, he was conditioned and shaped by the major historical and psychological forces of his own time, following in the tradition of a predominantly male-oriented theory for psychology. This reminds us of the limits set by historical circumstances, which impinge on all humans. He was able to break with many of the limiting traditions of his time, particularly to move the concept of development from an exclusive pathological focus to a view that emphasized the positive and productive aspects of growth. He was, however, not successful in breaking with the cultural stereotypes regarding female growth.

Now well into official retirement, Erikson continues as an active leader in the cause of healthy development for all humans. In 1983 he addressed the annual meeting of the American Psychiatric Association. As you might guess, he was concerned with a broad and compelling issue of our time, namely, survival in the nuclear age. He closed his speech with a call for civilization to turn back from the brink of a nuclear holocaust and "learn to use our technological genius for the development rather than the destruction of mankind." At the age of eighty-two, he received a standing ovation. His vision for humanity has not dulled nor become myopic; instead, his life even in retirement epitomizes the life cycle completed, the stage of wisdom.

In sum, Erikson has personified his own theory of development in achieving a sense of personal and professional integrity. He reaches the end of life with a certain ego integrity, "an acceptance of his own responsibility for what his life is and was and of its place in the flow of history." These factors include his limitations as well as his many successes.

cant finding is that the project helped parents to work effectively during the autonomy-versus-shame stage to promote a resolution toward "will." Will is not willfulness in the usual sense. When we speak of a willful child, we usually mean one who is stubborn. However, what Erikson is referring to is really a stage of initial independence. Children learn to think for themselves as they shift from sensorimotor to symbolic thought at about this time. There is a similar potential change in their understanding of themselves as individuals. Will really means self-direction and individuality and, in fact, is the beginning of a sense of identity. The tension between autonomy and shame can be resolved. As Erikson puts it, "In balancing these two tendencies, rudimentary willpower supports a maturation both of free choice and of self-restraint."[13]

As you work with older children you may find some who have not adequately resolved the dependence–independence polarity and who alternate between willfulness and excessive compliance. In such cases it is very important to help the children develop appropriate self-control and direction. You may be sorely tried at times, but remember the epigenetic principle: The ground plan for growth is a given. We need to nurture each positive type of growth at each stage.

Initiative versus guilt (three to six years): Purpose   Personal development during the third stage of childhood takes place in the areas of initiative and guilt. This is the time when the child's identity as a boy or as girl is maximally affected. In the preceding stage the child discovers that he or she can be a person with self-direction. Now the task is to discover what kind of a person he or she is, especially with regard to a sense of maleness or of femaleness. Children at this stage begin to identify with the appropriate adult and to model, or copy, aspects of the adult's behavior. This can be seen most readily in those families that allow children to express themselves without a lot of censoring. In such an atmosphere boys will directly express their growing maleness by becoming unusually interested in their mothers. They engage in what becomes almost a rivalry with their father for their mother's attention and affection. The same is true of girls who, in discovering their femaleness, become very attached to their fathers. Many families report the humorous comments their children make at this age. A boy may say how happy he feels when daddy isn't home, all the while glancing rather obviously toward his mother. Similarly, a girl may wish to go off with daddy in the car. There are often pointed remarks concerning marriage: "I'm not going to marry anyone," a five-year-old boy might declare, "I am going to stay home and take care of mommy when daddy gets too old!" These are not simply humorous comments but reflect questions of sexual identity that are surfacing for the first time.

Adults often have difficulty understanding the importance of such issues. It seems, on the face of it, rather absurd for a four- or five-year-old girl to proclaim that she would like her mother to go away. But if adults punish such statements, the child is left with strong feelings of guilt concerning her identity. To punish her for expressing her natural desire to establish herself as a female will have lasting negative effects. And ridicule or sarcasm will be just as damaging as physical punishment, for it will make her feel very small and insignificant, guilty at having expressed some of her inner feelings about what kind of a person she hopes to become. As we have seen, particular aspects of personality are unusually affected during each stage. Between three and six years, it is the personal identity that is most affected. Thus it is especially important for children at this time to be reassured that they will become full-fledged adults and not to be made to feel guilty over these wishes. Erikson notes:

> Both the girl and the boy are now extraordinarily appreciative of any convincing promise of the fact that someday they will be as good as father or mother—perhaps better; and they are grateful for sexual enlightenment, a little at a time, and patiently repeated at intervals.[14]

In school itself, especially in kindergarten and the first grade, many of these same issues are plainly visible. Boys often become so enamored of their teacher that they "forget" and sometimes call their own mother by their teacher's name. "Some kids really know how to hurt a mother," one mother remarked, half humorously, when this happened to her. Recently, a first-grade teacher invited her class to her wedding. This happens every so often, but this par-

ticular wedding was featured in a television news broadcast. And there, for all the world to see, was the class—little girls in crinkly party dresses, bubbling over with excitement as they focused all their attention on the groom; and the boys, in coats and bow ties, weeping as the beaming bride swept down the aisle. This makes the point, perhaps melodramatically, that emotions and feelings at this stage are genuine, legitimate, and need to be accepted.

Children's physical size, compared to adults, can also increase any anxieties they may have at this age. In a world of adult "giants," they may fear that they will never grow big enough to be an adult. When Erikson used the phrase "perhaps better" in the previous quote, he was referring to children's need for reassurance that they will not only grow to become full-fledged adult men and women but that they will also surpass their parents. We can imagine nothing worse than growing up to be thirty- or forty-year-old "pseudoadults" who still live in the shadow of our parents. As in child rearing, so too in teaching—the ultimate test of how effectively we assist the formation of personal identity is the extent to which we help children outgrow their need for us. By deliberately reinforcing and nurturing children's male or female identities at this stage, we will help build a firm foundation for the next stage of emotional growth. And we will help them continue their general progress from dependence to independence.

Erikson is particularly concerned that at this stage of development children have ample time to play. In fact, his most recent writing called this time the "play age." Remember that from a cognitive view, preoperational, freewheeling fantasy thinking peaks at this age. He says that the child can well use this time to develop a sense of humor, the beginning of an ability to laugh at oneself. "The play age, furthermore, 'occurs' before the limiting advent of the school age, with its defined work roles."[15] What he seems to be saying quite directly is let's not move too far in the direction of early formal education for children during this stage. Extensive structured and basic education in reading, math, and writing may serve to inhibit the child, reduce a sense of healthy purpose, and constrain the growth of creativity. It is particularly unfortunate that some parents have been oversold on the idea of infant stimulation and have begun formal instruction at home well before even this stage. Armed with flash cards for numbers and letters, such parents seem to be drilling their children into premature socialization as midget-sized students. In a vain attempt to raise a child's IQ score through such artificial drill and practice, the parents may instead inhibit successful resolution of purpose by their children. As Erikson says:

> This long childhood exposes adults to the temptation of thoughtlessly and often cruelly exploiting the child's dependence by making him pay for the psychological debts owed to us by others, by making him victim of tensions which we will not or dare not correct in ourselves or in our surroundings. We have learned not to stunt a child's growing body with child labor; we must now learn not to break his growing spirit by making him victim of our anxieties.[16]

The Juvenile Period (Six to Twelve Years)

Mastery versus inferiority: Competence During the elementary-school years, Erikson indicates that personal and emotional development turns outward. Children enter a new "world"—the classroom, the neighborhood, the gang. These become the arenas for growth. The home remains an important base of operations, but the other arenas have special significance. In sheer number of hours, children now spend much more time (excluding sleeping) away from home than ever before. As juveniles they can fully participate as a member of a same-sex gang. We may recall from Piaget that not until they are six or seven years old can children genuinely listen to or talk with other children.

DOONESBURY   **by Garry Trudeau**

Now that "collective monologues" have been replaced by genuine discussion, important new groups can be formed.

During this time neighborhood and classroom gangs become major socializing agents. As opposed to adolescent cliques, the juvenile gangs are almost always made up of all boys or all girls. Occasionally a boys' gang will "allow" a particularly talented tomboy to join, but in general the juvenile world is stable and neatly stereotyped. Their world is divided into two camps on everything: boys versus girls, good guys in white hats versus bad guys in black hats, all infants are "babies," all adults are always right (including all teachers). There is no room for relativity in anything. Again if you will recall Piaget, this is the stage of concrete thought. From the personal point of view, this factor provides for a period of considerable emotional stability. The juvenile usually stands in an unambiguous relationship at home. He or she may have considerable freedom to roam the neighborhood. Adults are not overly concerned about academic performance in school, although the children at this age are, in fact, interested in learning many of the skills that are taught. At a concrete and functional level it is "fun" to decipher words, learn to write, add,

and subtract, since each of these skills makes a whole new realm of experience available to them—reading for comic books, writing for notes to pass around, adding for figuring out how much a new bike will cost, and so on. There is no need to lecture children at this age about the importance of learning these skills.

In addition to the many school-oriented skills, children during this period also develop a general sense of personal mastery. The sheer number of new activities and games they learn at this age is enormous—swimming, riding, sailing, skiing, roller skating, camping, boating, baseball, basketball, football, hockey, kick-the-can, sewing, cooking, collecting things (look in any child's pockets at this age!)—the list is almost endless and is testimony to the raw amount of energy and motivation for competence that exists at this age. The old saying that a child has 10,000 muscles that want to move and only one set to sit still is most appropriate. At the same time, we should understand Erikson's major point: This tremendous amount of energy can be put in the service of personal competence motivation. If children are not encouraged to engage actively with the surrounding world, their sense of personal industry will give way to personal inferiority. In other words,

The period between ages six and twelve (Erikson's stage of mastery and inferiority) presents a special challenge to both teachers and parents. During this period children have a natural desire to master new goals and control their environment. Robert White uses the phrase "competence motivation" to describe this attribute.

this is the time when the child's need to function and actively acquire multiple skills will *maximally affect* his or her sense of personal industry.

Erikson's term *competence,* to reflect the resolution of the industry, is unusually appropriate. In fact, it's possible to guess that Erikson's choice came from his association with another Harvard psychologist, Robert W. White. White actually coined the phrase "competence motivation" to describe what he considered a universal attribute of humans and other species. White reviewed all the major theories and research evidence for personal development and concluded that there is an inborn "drive" to master the environment. This drive is in our very bones, so to speak. We humans—and other animal species as well—are not the "empty" organisms, or so-called black boxes, that classic stimulus-response theory would suggest, nor are we passive agents who merely react to but never act on the world, as classic psychoanalytic theory would say.[17] White found, to the contrary, that humans and animals are naturally curious and seek to master and control the world around them. Just watch a child in a supermarket for a while, and you will see a perfect example of the need to explore and master the environment.

The reason the idea of competence is so important for educators is perhaps obvious by now. Personal and emotional development from six to twelve years of age takes place largely in school. Children spend more time in school than anywhere else. Thus, the classroom situation will be a major influence on their development at this stage. We too often overhear teachers making comments such as, "What can we do with a child who comes from a bad home environment?" The point is, we should not assume that we cannot have a positive effect on personal development and especially on the competence motivation of our pupils. In fact, elementary-school teachers are in a particularly strategic position to emphasize activities that can both nurture and, in some cases, restore a sense of mastery. Our elementary schools are gradually shifting away from rote learning, passive listening, and neatness ("Always color inside the lines!"), and are moving toward the open, active classroom. The so-called open classroom emphasizes many different activities and individual projects and absorbs great amounts of energy. By stressing doing instead of listening, the active school will do much to promote the pupils' sense of personal mastery. Erikson says that children are maximally ready for active learning between the ages of six and twelve. Our task as educators is to respond to this natural tendency so as to facilitate rather than impair healthy personal growth. We shouldn't worry so much about creating quiet, orderly, neat, and polite pupils. That objective will work directly against the opportunity to affect personal industry and mastery.

Adolescence (Thirteen Through the College Years)

Identity versus diffusion: Fidelity   Adolescence, in which the major issue is identity versus identity diffusion, is perhaps the most famous of Erikson's stages. The changes that take place during adolescence bring about a major shift in personal development. We have already seen (Chapter 5) that cognitive developments in this period mean that the adolescent has a completely new way to understand and think. We also have noted (Chapter 3) how the very substantial glandular changes at this time represent a major new system. Puberty obviously marks a major qualitative departure from the past. Changes of this magnitude in cognitive and physiological areas will by themselves create major psychological change. "How do I understand what is happening to me when so much is different?" someone in this stage might ask. It is no understatement to say that of all the stages of personal development, none is more radical than adolescence. Change is the name of the game during this period.

Early adolescence and self-concept   The changes in physiology, glands, and psychological systems experienced during early adolescence constitute the most substantial shift a human being undergoes. The adolescent can now experience the world in a major new way. He or she begins to think in relativistic terms and can appreciate the difference between objective reality and subjective perception. In addition, the adolescent develops the important ability to perceive feelings and emotions both in self and others, as well as the ability to take the perspective of another person (figuratively to place yourself in another person's shoes). And finally, he or she is now able to understand as-if situations and distinguish between symbolic and literal meaning. In short, the thinking system that begins to develop during this period provides the adolescent with a new and sophisticated mechanism for making meaning from his or her own experience, particularly in reference to understanding one's own identity as a person. To summarize, as an adolescent begins to think about self and identity, he or she can perform the following operations:

1. Differentiate feelings and emotions in self and others

2. Distinguish between objective and subjective reality

3. Adopt the perspective of another person

4. Understand symbolic meaning and role-play as-if situations

In one sense, then, it seems that personal development during adolescence represents a great leap forward, since one can now be more complex, comprehensive, empathic, and abstract and maintain a broad perspective on self and others. However, as one distinguished psychologist, David Elkind, points out, such is not the case. In fact, just the reverse takes place. The more complex thought system raises the adolescent to new heights of mental operations yet lowers him or her to new depths. On first entering this new stage, the teen-ager tends to become excessively egocentric in thought. The external world is no longer viewed as permanent and unchanging, but rather as relative, subjective, and phenomenological. Accordingly, the teen-ager may begin to perceive himself or herself as the center of the universe.

This egocentrism, unfortunately, is accompanied by excessive self-consciousness. The teen-ager is unusually vulnerable to going along with the crowd. As Figure 6.2 indicates, conformist thinking peaks during the junior-high-school years.[18]

The extent of social conformity in junior high was further demonstrated in a well-designed study specifically employing a developmental stage framework. The researchers predicted the level of conformity from stage of ego development. Their results indicated that eighth-grade pupils of both sexes had the highest scores on social conformity as well as on ego stage—the equivalent of Lawrence Kohlberg's Stage Three (see Chapter 7). Both younger students with lower-stage scores and older students with higher-stage scores were less other-directed. The pupils with the Stage Three scores were most strongly concerned with how others perceived them and with going along with the group.[19]

In another less formal study, researchers interviewed junior-high students on their personal perceptions of self and others. The results can be summed up in the words of one of the subjects. When asked, "What is the most real thing to you?" her unhesitating reply was, "Myself."[20]

Elkind on adolescence   Elkind has noted that how an adolescent views his or her "self"—that is, the self-concept—can be described along two basic dimensions of egocentric thinking: (1) the personal fable, and (2) the imaginary audience.[21]

The personal fable is a deep-rooted belief in one's own personal uniqueness—the notion

FIGURE 6.2   Level of conformity at various ages.

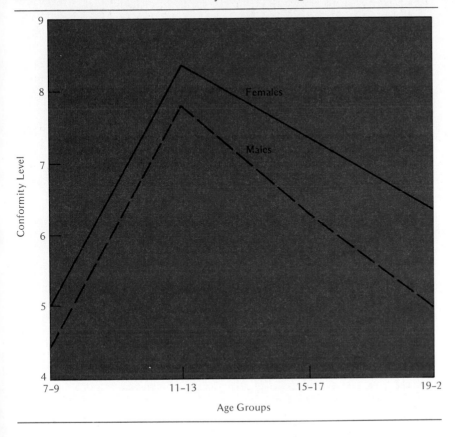

that no one else in the world can possibly understand how "I" really feel. As Elkind notes, the complex beliefs create an aura—"only he can suffer with such agonized intensity or experience such exquisite rapture." To retain this image an adolescent may create a personal fable, "a story which he tells himself (and others) and which is not true."

Possibly the best example of sexual fantasies and egocentrism can be found in the novel *Catcher in the Rye* by J. D. Salinger. Holden Caulfield, "everyperson as an adolescent," describes a classic dialogue with one of his near friends, "Old Ackley," in which the two were discussing sexual prowess. Holden narrates that he listened silently as Ackley described in monotonous detail how he "made it" with a girlfriend last summer. Holden is patient to a point, but he has heard Ackley's story at least a hundred times. Only each time it is different.[22] In Elkind's terms this is Ackley's personal fable—an

untrue story repeated ad infinitum (and ad nauseum, one might add).

Essentially, the imaginary audience refers to the belief that everyone else in the world is preoccupied with the personal appearance and behavior of the adolescent, as if the entire world pauses each morning to see how a teen-ager is dressed for school, or waits with hushed anticipation for the adolescent to speak his or her lines. In front of such imaginary audiences adolescents can swing from excessive self-criticism (admiring one's own martyrdom) to the other extreme—self-admiration to the point of boorishness. Elkind cites the famous passage from *Tom Sawyer* of Tom witnessing his own funeral as a universal fantasy of adolescents: "They will really miss me when I'm gone and be sorry too for all the mean things they said."

On an optimistic note, Elkind finds that adolescents can be helped to gradually distinguish between real and imaginary audiences, as well

Adolescents often hold the belief that everyone else in the world is preoccupied with the adolescents' personal appearance and behavior. In front of this "imaginary audience," teens may be excessively self-critical or self-admiring.

as to differentiate between themselves and others in both thoughts and feelings. Given the support of adult understanding, both the personal fable and the imagined audience are progressively modified and diminished. It is to be hoped that as adults, we can retain some of the positive aspects of this stage, namely, a healthy respect for our own individuality.[23]

The crisis of personal identity   Because adolescence represents such a major discontinuity in growth, Erikson has singled out one critical issue as the major task of this stage—resolving the crisis of personal identity. Our definition of self—how we see ourselves *and* how others see us—forms the foundation of our adult personality. If that foundation is firm and strong, a solid personal identity results; if it is not, the result is what Erikson calls a diffuse identity. Identity diffusion is something like suffering from amnesia or like perpetually wandering over a landscape trying to "find" a selfhood.

With no sense of past or future, the diffuse personality is like a stranger in his or her own land with no roots, no history. The sense of personal alienation prevents the establishment of a stable core for the personality.

Western societies have made it extremely difficult for adolescents to come through this stage with a firm sense of personal identity. Industrialized societies have exaggerated the marginal status of adolescents by grossly overextending the period of dependency. This is justified by the amount of special learning and training that is needed to survive in our complex world. However, it is easy to forget the negative personal effects of keeping a twenty-one-year old, or even an eighteen-year-old, in a position of dependency. To make matters worse, adults seem to be unable to decide just when it is that an adolescent becomes an adult. The age of legal adult responsibility is extremely inconsistent in this country: The legal age for marriage differs not only by sex (girls are permitted to marry without parental consent earlier than boys) but also according to state residency, with some states permitting legal marriage as early as fourteen years of age. And there are similar discrepancies in the legal age for going to work, driving a car, entering into a legal contract, voting in elections (for most of this nation's history adolescents were old enough to die for their country in war before they were old enough to vote in elections), drinking alcoholic beverages, and enlisting in the military services.

These few examples serve to highlight the problem of identity formation. Erikson notes that adolescents are caught between two major systems, both of which are in flux. They have to cope with internal, cognitive, and glandular changes at the same time that they are confronting a series of inconsistent and changing external regulations. And they go through all this while simultaneously discarding their identity from the previous stage, the age of mastery. Kick-the-can, bike riding, Boy and Girl Scouts, the "Three Stooges" on TV, tomboys, and most important, the view that adults are almost always correct because they are older and bigger—these dimensions of personal develop-

ment during the elementary age all have to be discarded. Adolescence is almost like entering a foreign country without knowing the language, the customs, or the culture; only it's worse because the "voyagers" don't even have a guidebook. It is truly a major shock during adolescence to find that adults are not always right and, in fact, are often working very hard to cover up their mistakes. The discovery of relativism, especially in the moral behavior of adults, further exaggerates the difficulties of personal development. On the one hand, adolescents learn that some police officers take bribes, some professors plagiarize, some teachers copy lesson plans, some major corporations "fix" prices, some elected officials solicit bribes, some professional athletes play under the influence of drugs, and so on. On the other hand, these same adults have a tendency to lecture adolescents on the subject of responsibility, the importance of obeying rules, and above all, of showing respect to adults. The resulting overreaction is well known. If you can't rely on some adults, don't trust anyone over thirty! If some businesspersons are overly materialistic, all businesspersons are Babbitts! If some adults are unfaithful, all marriages are institutionalized

Of all the stages of personal development, none is more radical than adolescence. Erikson singles out one critical issue as the major task of this stage—resolving the crisis of personal identity. The educator's objective is to provide real experience, genuine responsibility, and increasing amounts of independence during this time of stress and strain.

hypocrisy! The list is endless, and serves as a poignant reminder of how difficult it is to understand the highly complicated problems of living and personal development in a modern society.

College-age youth: Late adolescence   In one sense, adolescence officially ends at age eighteen or so, with graduation from high school. The process of identity formation definitely is an important hallmark of secondary-school years. However, some recent work by Alan Waterman indicates that the process continues for those who attend college. Waterman's studies show that less than 50 percent of college students in one sample actually reached identity resolution by their senior year.[24] While it may seem as if a relatively modest proportion make it through the stage, it is important to remember that successful resolution is a difficult psychosocial task. As the box on "Eriksonian Differences in College" also makes clear, such resolution is important.

The problem is clearly the difficulty inherent in combining the variety of self-images that are possible as a result of the ability to think abstractly about who one "really is" with all of the previous images one has had as a growing child. Those earlier identities retain at least their emotional components, and they usually work against a new integration. Also, recall that the growing identity integration also must be confirmed by the adult society—the interaction problem again, but in a slightly different form. The specific strength that emerges from resolution of the bipolar conflict is called "fidelity." The adolescent gradually transfers the need for guidance and direction from within the home and his or her parents to outside mentors (teachers, professors, leaders) and, in one sense, becomes "faithful" to a wider community. Thus, it is not really surprising that the majority of college students have not completed the process. It is important to note that the college years provide a healthy transition stage between the initial stage of identity formation and its resolution.

In keeping with his general stance to avoid hurrying personal development, Erikson has noted that the college years can serve as a moratorium—that is, they become a time of positive experimentation without the necessity of adult commitment. The purpose is to create some breathing space in order to explore more fully both one's own psychological self and objective reality. The surface difference between moratorium and diffusion may appear insignificant; yet underneath, the difference is substantial. In moratorium there is a genuine search for alternatives, not simply a biding of one's time. There is a major need to test oneself in a variety of experiences to increase in-depth knowledge of self. Commitments are temporarily avoided for legitimate reasons: "I need more time and experience before I can commit myself to a career such as medicine." Or "I am not ready to go for a Ph.D. in history. There are too many unknowns I need to explore first." Thus, a moratorium is not simply a cop-out or a time of aimless drifting. Instead, it is an active process of searching, with the major goal of preparing for commitment. Erikson's own life, as the biography points out, contained a very significant moratorium, as well as an even greater commitment. One flowed from the other, Erikson would say.

We should point out that it is not absolutely essential to attend college in order to reformulate and integrate a sense of an independent personal identity. Some research studies do indicate, however, that such a time for a moratorium is more likely to result in identity resolution. In studies of moral, value, and religious-concept development (all aspects of achieving an identity), there was a much greater probability for continued growth among college-going students than among their age cohorts who went into full-time employment.[25]

Psychological defenses during adolescence   Anna Freud has outlined the most common psychological defenses that adolescents employ.[26] She feels that much of the so-called pathology during this stage is in reality the normal upset that can be expected to accompany massive internal changes. In fact, she suggests that the only abnormality would be for adolescents to show no signs of psychological unrest. She points out that if we accept such turmoil as normal, we can avoid extreme overreactions. One parent typified these feelings when she said of adolescents, "We should bury them at twelve and dig them up again at twenty-one." Mark Twain allegedly commented on his own

Eriksonian Differences in College: The Inability to Take Hold

Erikson makes the point of the critical importance of identity formation during middle and late adolescence. He sees diffusion as a major setback. He often uses Biff, the son in Arthur Miller's play *Death of a Salesman*, as an example. Caught in the midst of a series of confusing and contradictory expectations, Biff appears aimless and lost. "I just can't take hold, Mom, I can't take hold of some kind of life." Bewildered, he exemplifies a person who has no identity. His self-definition is diffused—indeed, almost atomized.

Recently, a major study was conducted of college students in teacher training. Training programs require both skill and commitment, since the student teacher must learn academic material and then be able to present it to either high school or elementary school students in coherent and concise procedures. Student teachers regularly report how demanding and how personally stretching such a role is. Student teaching, particularly in junior and senior high schools, can often come close to the chaos described in William Golding's novel *Lord of the Flies* if the teen-agers decide that it's time to challenge a beginning teacher. Thus the stress factor is a major component of the student teacher's role.

If Erikson's theory has validity, then college students might perform in such a demanding role in accordance with their stage of identity formation. To test that hypothesis, Shirley Walter and Eugene Stivers sorted a large sample of student teachers (N = 319) by Erikson's level of identity versus diffusion.[a] They next assessed the actual in-class teaching effectiveness on an important series of elements: responsiveness to pupil questions, open-ended questions, empathy, use of positive reinforcement, accuracy of content—in short, characteristics of what is often called higher-order teaching.

The results were almost exactly as we would predict from Erikson's theory. The teachers with the highest scores on identity resolution were the most effective in responsive teaching and classroom management. The student teachers with high scores on identity diffusion were the least effective. Such student teachers had difficulty accepting pupil ideas, asked rote questions, and exhibited uneven classroom management. In fact, the Erikson identity score was the single most important predictor variable. The study included variables such as college board score (SAT), the cumulative grade point average, and IQ. None of those cognitive elements were as powerful as the measure of identity status. The student teachers, particularly the males, who were the most confused in the process of identity formation (i.e., who had the highest diffusion index scores) had the greatest difficulty in teaching. In Erikson's sense they apparently were still so far from resolving their identity conflicts that "they couldn't take hold."

[a]   Walter, S. A. and Stivers, E. (1977). The relation of student teachers' classroom behavior and Eriksonian ego identity. *Journal of Teacher Education* 38(6): 47–55.
From N. A. Sprinthall and W. A. Collins, *Adolescent Psychology: A Developmental View,* Copyright © 1984 Newbery Award Records, Inc., and Random House, Inc.

adolescence, "I thought my father was the dumbest person in the world, yet by the time I reached my twenties, he sure had learned a lot!"

Anna Freud lists the psychological systems in the following order:

Displacement: To transfer feelings and needs from one situation or person to another object. Commonly, adolescents may begin to feel attached to their parents, especially the parent of the opposite sex, and defend against this by becoming overly attached to other adults. Crushes on movie stars, rock singers, and attractive schoolteachers are well-known examples. Displacement also is often accompanied by substantial acting-up and heightened emotional expressiveness.

Reversal of affect: To turn needs and feelings inside out. This occurs when adolescents suddenly change the manifestation of feelings from one extreme to the other. Thus, instead of showing anger, an adolescent may display an exaggerated coolness. The desire for closeness may be demonstrated by withdrawal, alienation, and hiding out in one's room. Feelings and needs for excitement and curiosity may become inverted and appear as, ''But life is so boring.''

Withdrawal: To psychologically hide out. This is a more extreme defense in the sense that the adolescent begins to more actively separate himself or herself from both adults and peers. There is a greater use of fantasies and a decline in reality testing. Adolescents who see themselves as the new Messiah, capable of superhuman feats or reading others' minds, are examples.

Regression: To return to an earlier stage. This is quite simply the attempt to remain a child, to avoid ''growing up.'' Boys and girls, especially at the onset of obvious signs of puberty, may attempt to deny the changes and dress and play as if they are still in elementary school.

Asceticism: To deny pleasure. Some adolescents may attempt to deny the development of pleasurable feelings by becoming ascetic. The increase in the depth and range of emotions is checked by (metaphorically at least) putting on a hair shirt and rejecting food, sleep, and normal comforts. Shaving heads and putting on monks' robes are other manifestations.

Uncompromising: To rigidly adhere to a narrow prescriptive ideology. This is by definition an attempt to avoid accepting the complexities of life, the shades of gray, including compromise and cooperation. All issues become dichotomized into right and wrong. Dogmatic positions abound.

Anna Freud also wisely points out that these syndromes are common yet difficult for an adolescent to understand. We all are blind to certain aspects of our own behavior and dynamics, and know that such psychological blind spots don't suddenly disappear when we are told about them. Thus, although it is important for teachers to recognize these systems, it is not necessarily wise to then confront the adolescent with an interpretation. Such confrontations often make adults more defensive—and what is

Some adolescents may attempt to deny the development of pleasurable feelings by becoming ascetic.

true for adults is doubly true for this age group. Anna Freud suggests that educators understand these common defenses, realize when an adolescent is employing one, yet respond to the *person,* not the *defense.* Otherwise, we may find ourselves in long and unproductive arguments about whose interpretation is most accurate.

For example, probably the most common defense during adolescence is the displacement of sexual feelings toward a teacher. ''Crushes'' can develop in girls for attractive male teachers or in boys for particularly sensitive and understanding female teachers. It requires great tact by the adult in this situation to avoid either extreme of playing into the fantasy or putting down the adolescent with sarcasm and ridicule. On the one hand, playing into the fantasy is most inappropriate. Pupils at that age perceive sexual connotations in practically everything in the world anyway. If the teacher becomes coy and seductive in response to an adolescent's crush, then it's almost as if his or her wildest dreams may come true. The adolescent's non-verbal signs will be readily apparent, such as amorous looks, excessive volunteering of help, and putting down "immature" classmates. On the other hand, if the teacher chooses to ridicule these first stirrings of feelings of closeness and attraction, then the pupil may be genuinely shamed. Instead, as a teacher, you must be prepared to help the adolescent understand that it is quite normal and natural to have strong feelings of liking for a person just a "bit" older. This means that the adolescent is in the process of growing up. At the same time, however, you can also help him or her realize that it would be quite inappropriate for you as a teacher to play favorites and that eventually you are sure that someone closer in age will seem attractive. These are very sensitive moments as adolescents develop their initial impulses for tenderness and caring. Probably the least appropriate response by a teacher would be silence, since ambiguity actually increases projection and fantasy thinking. The so-called hidden agenda of sexual awareness by junior-high pupils is an extremely volatile issue that needs careful attention as well as tact and diplomacy. Classroom atmospheres charged with rampant sexual fantasies certainly, at a minimum, impede intellectual concentration and motivation for learning.

One final point to remember: All of the psychological defenses are methods (some better than others) of coping with the environment as the adolescent struggles to become an adult. It really is difficult for someone in the identity stage to "get it all together," or, in Erikson's words, to achieve ego integration. Yet it is essential to develop a healthy personal identity. In ringing phrases Erikson says,

> Indeed in the social jungle of human existence there is no feeling of being alive without a sense of ego identity. . . . The danger of this stage is identity diffusion; . . . Youth after youth, bewildered by some assumed role, a role forced on him by the inexorable standardization of American adolescence, runs away in one form or another; leaving schools and jobs, staying out all night, or withdrawing into bizarre and inaccessible moods.[27]

Other educational implications   As educators, we need to take special note of the challenge posed by the immensely complicated problem of adolescence. There are no easy solutions. But this does not mean that nothing can be done. For years it was fashionable to say that adolescence is a tough period, but everyone outgrows it eventually, so all you can do is grin and bear it. We now realize that such advice is mere rationalization and in no way excuses us from responsibility. The number of psychological casualties during adolescence is now too obvious to permit such an attitude. For example, we now realize that adolescent drug abuse is a symptom of the problem of personal identity formation, or in Erikson's terms, an attempt to solve the problem of identity diffusion. It is only an attempt because it is a nonsolution. The moment the drug wears off the same problems are still there, waiting to be attended to.

As we noted, educators are by definition in a strategic position to help guide personal growth. Adolescents feel a need to pull away from their own parents, so other adults can be of special significance. It is therefore our responsibility to develop effective ways to make this influence work. Erikson makes it obvious that to assist growth we need to provide them with increasing amounts of independence and responsibility. In the previous stage, mastery, we said that activity was the key. In this stage our objectives as educators should be to provide real experience and genuine responsibility.

Thus, the variety of school programs, especially at the secondary level, involving peer and cross-age teaching, community internships, peer counseling, and teen-age health "consultants" is important primarily because such role-taking can involve genuine responsibility. In these programs teen-agers learn to teach, counsel, and care for younger classmates. Such responsibility stimulates their own leadership development and psychological maturation. Thus, the potential for empathic understanding and human caring that is available for development during adolescence can be capitalized on in the service of healthy personal growth.

The results of a series of careful assessments indicate that such action-reflection methods at the secondary-school level really do have a significant impact on students. Table 6.2 summarizes the results from a large sample of over 4,000 students.[28] As you can readily see, the significant role-taking experience had very positive effects on the students' psychological identities. It would be wrong to conclude, however, that all we have to do is to set up experiential action-learning programs in the community. Both Daniel Conrad and Diane Hedin make a significant point: If such programs are to work, then a cognitive component is as important as the experiential. The students need to be guided into a careful examination of the experience through readings and keeping journals. Otherwise, there is no guarantee that experience by itself will have any positive influence at all.

In fact, as if to prove the point, a study of the impact of work experience on secondary students was recently completed. The results indicated that part-time after-school employment, aside from the monetary gain, produced highly dubious effects. The students were just as likely to learn the "wrong things" from the experience—for example, how to cheat on their boss, how to give away hamburgers to their friends, or how to "beat" the time clock.[29] While we may think that a real experience such as work helps students develop an identity, that doesn't necessarily happen. In an Eriksonian sense such experience by itself does little to help the adolescent resolve the identity formation-diffusion problem. Instead, if we do wish to nurture the resolution toward fidelity, it is im-

TABLE 6.2   WHAT STUDENTS LEARN IN EXPERIENTIAL LEARNING

Composite Profile of Students Responses from Thirty Experiential Programs (N = 4,000) (The first ten and last four of twenty-four items)

ITEM (IN RANK ORDER)	PERCENTAGE OF RESPONSES		
	Agree*	Disagree*	Don't Know
1. Concern for fellow human beings	93	4	3
2. Ability to get things done and to work smoothly with others	93	4	3
3. Realistic attitudes toward other people such as the elderly, handicapped, or government officials	88	4	8
4. Self-motivation to learn, participate, achieve	88	7	5
5. Self-concept (sense of confidence, sense of competence, self-awareness)	88	7	5
6. Responsibility to the group or class	86	7	11
7. Risk-taking—openness to new experiences	86	7	8
8. Sense of usefulness in relation to the community	85	8	6
9. Problem-solving	86	9	5
10. Risk-taking—being assertive and independent	86	9	5
21. Use of leisure time	60	26	14
22. Narrowing career choices	54	34	12
23. To become an effective parent	52	29	19
24. To become an effective consumer	46	32	22

* Strongly agree and agree are combined, and disagree and strongly disagree are combined.

From D. Conrad and D. Hedin, National Assessment of Experiential Education: Summary and Implications, Journal of Experiential Education, 12 (Fall 1981), 8. *Reprinted by permission of the Association of Experiential Education.*

portant to guide the experience and help the students reflect on what they are learning.

ERIKSON'S CONTRIBUTION

Each stage in personal development is characterized by certain aspects that can be maximally affected either positively or negatively. For too long, personal and emotional development was considered out of bounds for educators, as the exclusive province of child guidance clinics and of those specially trained to deal with pathological problems. Erikson's great contribution has been to bring the problems of personal growth out of the shadows of pathology and to integrate them into the overall process of healthy personality development.[30] Erikson spells out the major personal issues for us so that we can understand much more about our pupils at each

of the various stages. We hope that such insight will guide us to more effective ways of helping children and adolescents during important, indeed critical, times.

Erikson sums it up:

Each successive step, then, is a potential crisis because of a radical *change in perspective.* There is, at the beginning of life, the most radical change of all: from intrauterine to extrauterine life. But in postnatal existence, too, such radical adjustments of perspective as lying relaxed, sitting firmly, and running fast must all be accomplished in their own good time. With them, the interpersonal perspective, too, changes rapidly and often radically, as is testified by the proximity in time of such opposites as "not letting mother out of sight" and "wanting to be independent." Thus, *different capacities use different opportunities* to become full-grown components of the ever-new configuration that is the growing personality.[31]

SUMMARY

Personal development should not be regarded as a process separate from other aspects of development. There is a common tendency to pay lip service to the idea that aspects of development are not really separate but then to talk about these domains as if they were compartmentalized.

Prior to Freud, the common assumption about children younger than six was that they were empty, literally mindless creatures. Accordingly, little was expected of them. Freud was a pioneer in emphasizing the importance of sensitive growth periods for personal development during childhood.

This chapter focused on Erikson's theory of a series of stages extending over the period of the life cycle. Each stage is marked by psychosocial crises that require the resolution of opposite, or bipolar, traits. How adequately a person resolves the crisis of each stage helps to determine and promote strength for succeeding stages. The stages are linked together in an interdependent manner.

Trust versus mistrust, resolved as hope

Autonomy versus shame, resolved as will

Initiative versus guilt, resolved as purpose

Mastery versus inferiority, resolved as competence

Identity versus diffusion, resolved as fidelity

Evidence supports the importance of the specified major issue at each stage. For example, Harlow's work, Spitz's research, and Anna Freud's studies all suggest the critical importance of careful, warm, and consistent parenting in the first twenty-four months to establish hope in the infant.

White's studies detail the significance of patterns of parenting during preschool years as a means of building competence, autonomy, and initiative in young children. During the child's juvenile years, it is important for educators to encourage and facilitate personal competence.

Specific difficulties and challenges of adolescent development were also outlined. This stage is determined by a combination of "inside" changes (glands, physiological makeup) and "outside" changes (society's expectations and rites of passage). Common psychological defenses of adolescence as well as egocentric thinking patterns form a basis for understanding the interactions between the adolescent and the environment. The college years represent a continuation of adolescent development. These years often serve as a moratorium during which students experiment with aspects of their identity without making an adult commitment.

To promote healthy personal development during adolescence has always been difficult. But teachers can play a strategic role in fostering personality development by setting up action-learning programs for students.

KEY TERMS AND NAMES

Lawrence K. Frank
Sigmund Freud
   psychoanalytic theory
   oral stage
   anal stage
   phallic stage
Erik Erikson

epigenetic principle
competence motivation
David Elkind
   moratorium
   psychological defense
   student crushes

REFERENCES

1. White, S. (1968). Changes in learning processes in the late preschool years. Paper presented at American Educational Research Association Convention, Chicago.

2. Frank, L. K. (1966). *On the importance of infancy.* New York: Random House.

3. Frank, L. K. (1938). The fundamental needs of the child. *Mental Hygiene, 22,* 353–379.

4. Freud, S. (1960). *A general introduction to psychoanalysis.* New York: Washington Square Press.

5. Erikson, E. (1959). Identity and the life cycle. *Psychological Issues, I* (Monograph I). Quotes in footnotes 14, 16, 27, and 31 are reprinted by permission of W. W. Norton & Co., Inc. Copyright © 1959 by International Universities Press, Inc.

6. Erikson, E. (1982). *The life cycle completed.* New York: Norton.

7. Harlow, H. F., and Harlow, M. K. (1962). Social deprivation in monkeys. *Scientific American, 207,* 136–146.

8. Spitz, R. A. (1946). Hospitalism: A follow-up report. *Psychoanalytic Study of the Child,* Vol. 2. New York: International University Press.

9. Fraiberg, S. (1959). *The magic years.* New York: Scribner's.

10. Zigler, E., and Berman, W. (1983). Discerning the future of early childhood intervention. *American Psychologist, 38*(8), 894–906.

11. White, B. L. (1976). *The first three years of life.* Englewood Cliffs, N.J.: Prentice-Hall.

12. Pierson, D., Klien-Walker, D., and Tivnan, T. (1984). A school-based program from infancy to kindergarten for children and their parents. *Personnel and Guidance Journal, 62*(82), 448–454.

13. Erikson, *The life cycle completed* (p. 78).

14. Erikson, Identity and the life cycle, 78.

15. Erikson, *The life cycle completed* (p. 77).

16. Erikson, Identity and the life cycle, 100.

17. White, R. W. (1959). Motivation reconsidered: The concept of competence. *Psychological Review, 66,* 297–333.

18. Costanzo, P. R., and Shaw, M. E. (1966). Conformity as a function of age level. *Child Development, 37,* 967–975.

19. Hoppe, C., and Loevinger, J. (1977). Ego development and conformity. *Journal of Personality, 41,* 497–504.

20. Kohlberg, L., and Gilligan, C. (1971). The adolescent as a philosopher. *Daedalus, 100*(4), 1051–1086.

21. Elkind, D. (1978). Understanding the young adolescent. *Adolescence, 13,* 127–134.

22. Salinger, J. D. (1964). *Catcher in the rye* (p. 37). New York: Bantam.

23. Elkind, D. (1970). *Children and adolescents.* New York: Oxford.

24. Waterman, A. S. (1982). Identity development from adolescence to adulthood. *Development Psychology, 18*(3), 341–358.

25. Mischey, E. J. (1981). Faith, identity and morality in late adolescence. *Character Potential, 9*(4), 175–191. See also Sprinthall, N. A., and Collins, W. A. (1984). *Adolescent psychology: A developmental view.* New York: Random House. Chapter 2 gives a more extended discussion on this point.

26. Freud, A. (1958). Adolescence. *Psychoanalytic Study of the Child, 13,* 255–276.

27. Erikson, Identity and the life cycle, 90–91.

28. Conrad, D., and Hedin, D. (1981). National assessment of experiential education: Summary and implications. *Journal of Experiential Education, 12,* 6–20.

29. Greenberger, E., and Steinberg, L. (1981). The workplace as a context for the socialization of youth. *Journal of Youth and Adolescence, 10,* 185–210.

30. Snarey, J., Kohlberg, L., and Noam, G. (1983). Ego development in perspective: Structural stage, functional phase, and cultural age-period models. *Developmental Review, 3,* 303–338.

31. Erikson, Identity and the life cycle, 55.

7

VALUE DEVELOPMENT

It is perhaps quite ironic that in the area of value and moral development, there has been a major disagreement between professional educators and psychologists. From the very beginnings of the public or common school, educators have insisted that a pupil's character and values should be the proper object of teaching. Horace Mann, considered the architect of free public education, maintained stoutly in the early nineteenth century that veracity, probity, and rectitude were the significant goals for education. "Train up a child in the way he should go, and when he is old he will not depart from it."[1] Character and citizenship, then, were viewed as major objectives of schooling. Practically every public school had a printed curriculum objective extolling the virtues of character development. The Boston Public Schools' guide of a few years back was typical of many:

> We are unfit for any trust till we can and do obey.
> Honor thy father and mother.
> True obedience is true liberty.
> The first law ever God gave to man was a law of obedience.

On the other hand, psychologists had maintained, at least for the last fifty years, that attempting to inculcate traits and virtues was almost totally ineffectual. In other words, while educators were stoutly maintaining that schools mold character, psychologists were busily refuting all claims that values could be taught. In this chapter we shall review some of those classic character-trait studies and then turn to a relatively new framework for understanding the process of value development, with specific implications for curriculum strategies.

EXPLODING THE MYTH OF CHARACTER EDUCATION

In the 1920s two researchers, Hugh Hartshorne and Mark May at the University of Chicago, conducted a long series of studies, which they replicated again and again.[2] Their results were a bombshell. In every study they arrived at the same conclusion: Formal character instruction had no positive effect. They studied regular school classes in character education, special Sunday-school classes, Boy Scout classes, and others. After studying over 10,000 children and adolescents, they concluded that there was no correlation at all (essentially an *r* of o) between character-education/virtue training and actual behavior (such as cheating). They also found essentially no consistent moral behavior in the same person from one situation to another based on character education. This seemed to imply that people who cheat in one situation may or may not cheat in the next situation. (The sample honesty tests accompanying this discussion may help demonstrate such an assertion.) In general, moral behavior seemed unpredictable and moral character traits mythical. If ingrained character traits such as honesty or dishonesty did exist, then it would be possible to predict behavior accurately.

To make matters worse (Hartshorne and May were as dismayed as everyone else), the researchers also found no relationship between what people said about morality and the way these same people acted. People who express great disapproval of cheating or stealing actually steal and cheat as much as anyone else. Hartshorne and May concluded that the risk of detection was the single most important factor in deterring cheating. They also found that it was meaningless to divide people into simple categories and label them as either honest or dishonest. Like so many other aspects of human nature, cheating is normally distributed around a level of moderate cheating. A normal distribution means we can fit the results of tests that detect cheating on a bell-shaped curve. The distribution will look the same as that for measured intelligence, height, weight, or coin flipping for heads or tails. (See Chapter 15 for further discussion on the meaning of normal distribution.) Hartshorne and May found that what was true for supposed traits such as honesty/dishonesty was also true for traits such as altruism/selfishness and self-control/impulsiveness. What this does, of course, is to call into question the entire concept of character traits.

One of the criticisms of the Hartshorne and May research was that the situations set up in tests such as the Eye-Hand Coordination and Memory Test did not really create a battle of conscience. In other words the stakes were low,

so maybe the students didn't really care and merely opened their eyes out of curiosity or some other motive. If proved, that, of course, would be a fundamental flaw in the whole argument. In a quite ingenious study, a researcher built a special computerlike ray gun complete with video screen. The game was rigged to yield a score just below the level needed to win a special prize as a sharpshooter. In the first test over 80 percent of the students cheated on their reported score, thus confirming the original research findings. In a second study, however, the critical findings were completely different. More gadgetry was added to increase the battle of conscience—or at least that was the intention of the researchers. With additional computer equipment, a new sequence was rigged. Now the students would reach the very brink of success. Then they would miss. Under these new conditions only 15 percent of the one hundred children cheated. What happened? This was a total reversal of all previous findings—or was it? Interviews revealed that the students in the second study thought that the machine was indeed wired into a real computer that kept the actual score. There was no point in cheating. So with children, then, "Even if we are successful in arousing stronger emotional conflicts . . . we still have to conclude that moral behavior is essentially defined by situational factors, including expediency."[3]

What is true for Hartshorne's and May's seemingly old-fashioned virtues is equally true for the virtues we may cherish today. This means that if we ridicule the idea of teaching children to be "thrifty, brave, clean, and reverent," an antiquated bag of virtues, it is also meaningless to try to teach children to be "spontaneous, open, authentic, or genuine." A bag of virtues is a bag of virtues. None is particularly amenable to being taught. Merely changing the content of the virtues to be taught will not change the outcome. We may prefer the more modern traits, but this does not advance the educational problems of student growth and discipline. "Telling" is not teaching, and the same holds true for character development. Telling children and teen-agers to adopt particular virtues or manipulating them until they say the right words will not produce significant personal or cognitive development.

Sample honesty test: The eye-hand coordination and memory test. At the signal for each trial, place your pencil at point X. Study the circles, then *close your eyes* and write the number 1 in the first circle, the second circle, the third circle, and so on. For the second trial, open your eyes, place your pencil at point X, *close your eyes* and write the number 2 in the first circle, the second circle, and so on. For the third trial, follow the same procedure and write the number 3, and so on. Proceed for five trials.

   After each trial, put a check mark in the score box for each time you hit the correct circle. Count the checks and enter the total in column T. After the last trial, add up column T. This is your total score. The maximum is 50.

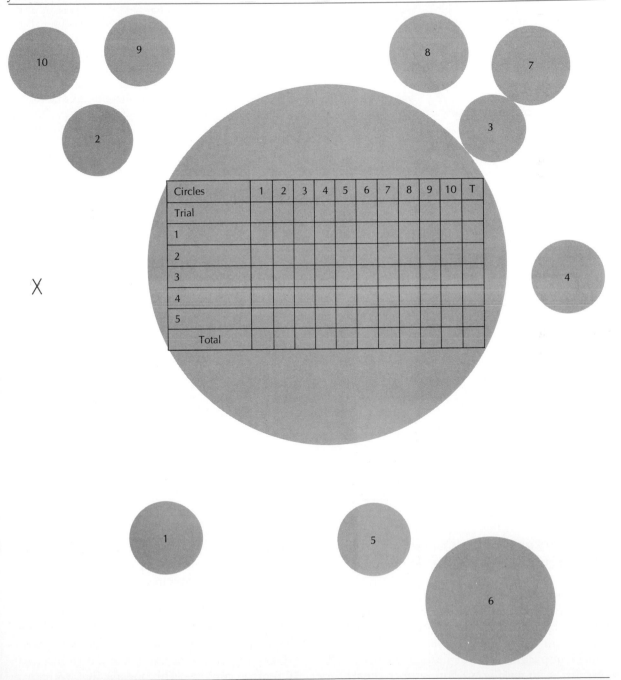

Circles	1	2	3	4	5	6	7	8	9	10	T
Trial											
1											
2											
3											
4											
5											
Total											

CONTEMPORARY ISSUE

Prayer in the Schools?

The Reverend Jerry Falwell contends that up until about thirty years ago the precepts of the Bible were at the basis of the curriculum of public schools throughout the country. Prayer was offered and passages from the Bible were read virtually every day, and, because of that, the country and its citizens were better off.[a] Falwell also claims that this was precisely what the founders of this country wanted. Quoting from President John Adams, who said that one means of preserving our Constitution was to "patronize every rational effort to encourage schools, colleges, universities and every institution for propagating knowledge, virtue and religion among all classes of the people," Falwell sees the recent elimination of school prayer as a contributing cause of the moral disintegration of society. Since in a democracy education is supposed to create better citizens, then schools must provide the moral foundation for that citizenry.

Senator John East pointed out that the phrase "separation of church and state" appears nowhere in the Constitution. If the government were required to eliminate all traces of religious practice, then "we could have no chaplains in the Armed Forces. We could have no religious facilities on military bases. We could not open the Senate or the House with prayer. We could not have 'In God We Trust' on our coins. We could not say 'God Save This Honorable Court' when the Supreme Court opens. . . . We could not allow the President, at the conclusion of his Presidential oath, to say '. . . So Help Me God.' "[b] In short, prayer in the schools was favored by the founders, and to eliminate it, as the Supreme Court has ruled, neglects a crucial component of every child's education.

Opponents of school prayer find major distortions in the current attacks against the "secularization" of schools and argue that the "materials [the opponents] advocate are consistent with historical traditions of character development while also being in tune with the present realities of the times."[c]

Opponents also maintain that prayer in the schools violates the principle of religious freedom, as enunciated in the First Amendment to the Constitution. Institutionalizing school prayer in the classroom in effect makes it no longer voluntary. Senator Lowell Weicker has said that this issue relates to "whether or not each of us will be able to find our own way to God, bound in our own way, or whether we go back to the history which we had denied and allow the State to do that for us. The one is the first step, the other, the last, in the career of intolerance."[d]

Opponents of prayer in the classroom are not unanimously against all prayer, but they feel that those who wish to pray together should do so in the privacy of their own homes or in their churches and synagogues. And finally, perhaps tongue-in-cheek, if children wish to pray in school, let them do so quietly and privately, since the Constitution's Fifth Amendment guarantees everyone the right to remain silent.

[a] Falwell, J. (1980). *Listen America.* New York: Basic Books.
[b] East, J. P. (1984). U.S. Senate debate (March 5).
[c] Noll, W. J. (1985). *Taking sides: Clashing views on controversial educational issues* (p. 43). Guilford, Conn.: Dushkin.
[d] Weicker, L. P. (1984). U.S. Senate debate (March 5).

KOHLBERG'S THEORY: A DEVELOPMENTAL VIEW

Lawrence Kohlberg, working first at Chicago and more recently at Harvard, has revolutionized our understanding of moral development. He found that people cannot be grouped into neat compartments with simplistic labels, "This group is honest," or "This group cheats," or "This group is reverent." Instead, he found that moral character develops. And this idea, that moral growth occurs in a developmental sequence, has completely revised our basic assumptions.

After conducting a long series of studies with children and adults, Kohlberg found that moral development occurs in a specific sequence of stages regardless of culture or subculture, continent or country. This means that we can no longer think of moral character in either/or terms, or assume that character is something we do or do not have. Instead of existing as fixed traits, moral character occurs in a series of developmental stages. In other words, what Piaget identified as stages of cognitive development, and what Erikson suggested to be stages of personal development, Kohlberg described as stages of moral development.[4] You may recall from the chapter on cognitive growth (Chapter 5) that a developmental stage, by definition, has four components. Each stage has the following features:

1. It is qualitatively different from the preceding stage.

2. It represents a new and more comprehensive system of "mental" organization.

3. It occurs in an invariant sequence.

4. It is age-related within general groupings.

With this definition in mind, we can now examine some of the specific aspects of this view.

KOHLBERG'S SIX STAGES OF MORAL GROWTH

Kohlberg identified six stages of moral growth, each distinctly different. He derived the stages by studying the system of thinking people actually employ in dealing with moral questions. By asking people from different backgrounds and of different ages to respond to problems involving moral dilemmas, he found that their responses fell into six judgmental systems, on which he based his six categories. The following two examples illustrate the type of problem he used:

1. Joe's father promised he could go to camp if he earned the $50 for it, and then changed his mind and asked Joe to give him the money he had earned. Joe lied and said he had earned only $10 and went to camp using the other $40 he had made. Before he went, he told his younger brother Alex about the money and about lying to their father. Should Alex tell their father?

2. In Europe, a woman was near death from a special kind of cancer. There was one drug

Lawrence Kohlberg

that the doctors thought might save her. It was a form of radium that a druggist in the same town had recently discovered. The drug was expensive to make, but the druggist was charging ten times what the drug cost him to make. He paid $200 for the radium and charged $2,000 for a small dose of the drug. The sick woman's husband, Heinz, went to everyone he knew to borrow the money, but he could only get together about $1,000, which is half of what it cost. He told the druggist that his wife was dying and asked him to sell it cheaper or let him pay later. But the druggist said: "No, I discovered the drug and I'm going to make money from it." So Heinz got desperate and broke into the man's store to steal the drug for his wife. Should the husband have done that?

As you can see, the problems are complex; they have no single, correct answer. In fact, the least significant part of the response is the direct answer "yes" or "no." Most significant are the reasons given for why the person should not behave in certain ways. In other words, the way in which suggested behavior is justified defines the respondent's level of moral development. Table 7.1 outlines the six stages of moral growth.

TABLE 7.1   KOHLBERG'S STAGES OF MORAL GROWTH

BASIS OF JUDGMENT	*STAGES OF DEVELOPMENT*
Preconventional moral values reside in external, quasi-physical happenings, in bad acts, or in quasi-physical needs rather than in persons and standards.	*Stage I:* Concern about self. Obedience to a powerful authority. Fear of punishment dominates motives. One sees oneself as being dominated by other forces. Actions are judged in terms of their *physical consequences.*
	Stage II: One-way concern about another person (what he/she can do for me, how we can agree to act so *I* will benefit). The basic motive is to *satisfy my own needs.* I do not consider the needs of the other person, unless I think it will benefit me to do so.
Conventional moral values reside in performing good or right roles, in maintaining the conventional order, and in meeting others' expectations.	*Stage III:* Concern about groups of people, and conformity to group norms. There is a two-way relationship (we are good to each other). Motive is to be a "nice guy/gal," to be accepted. Affection plays a strong role.
	Stage IV: Concern for order in *society.* Honor and duty come from keeping the rules of the society. The focus is on *preserving the society* (not just obeying, as in Stage I).

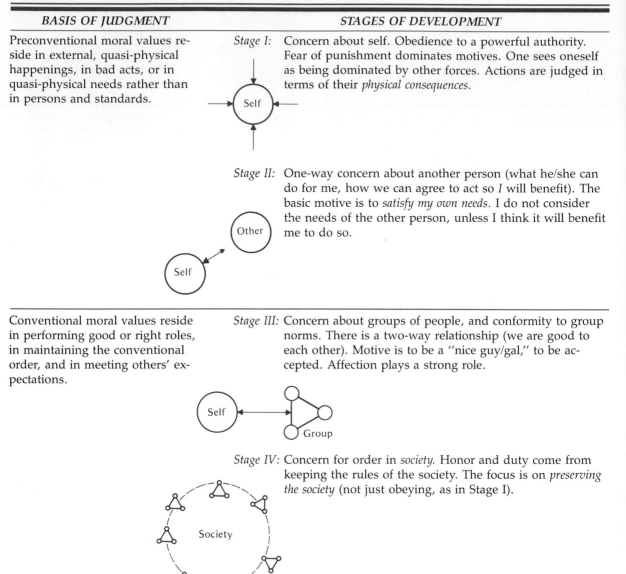

The pictorial diagrams were created by Philip Shaeffer, Ph.D., University of Minnesota.

Preconventional Morality: Stages I and II

Stage I obedience and moral decisions are based on very simple physical and material power—"Big fish eat little fish." "Might makes right." "The survival of the fittest." Stage I behavior is based on the desire to avoid severe physical punishment by a superior power.

Stage II actions are based largely on satisfying one's own personal needs, or "looking out for number one." The idea is to figure out ways to make trades and exchange favors—"You scratch

BASIS OF JUDGMENT	STAGES OF DEVELOPMENT

Postconventional moral values are derived from principles which can be applied universally.

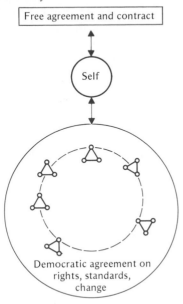

Free agreement and contract

Self

Democratic agreement on rights, standards, change

Stage V: Social contract, legalistic orientation. What is right is what the whole society decides. There are no legal absolutes. The society can *change standards* by everyone agreeing to the change. Changes in the law are usually made for reasons of the greatest good for the greatest number of people. Where law is not affected, what is right is a matter of personal opinion and agreement between persons. The U.S. Constitution is written in Stage 5 terms.

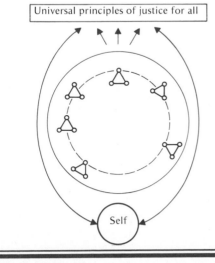

Universal principles of justice for all

Self

Stage VI: Universal ethical principles. What is right is a decision of one's conscience, based on ideas about rightness that apply to *everyone* (all nations, people, etc.). These are called *ethical principles.* An ethical principle is different from a rule. A rule is specific (Thou shalt not kill). An ethical principle is *general* (All persons are created equal). The most important ethical principles deal with justice, equality, and the dignity of all people. These principles are *higher* than any given law.

my back and I'll scratch yours''—but see if you can come out a little bit ahead on each trade. The orientation is materialistic in that moral discussions are expressed in instrumental and physical terms. If, for example, a person is caught stealing a car, punishment is determined by how much the car cost. This also means that it is perfectly permissible to use influence to fix any so-called wrongdoings. Fixing traffic tickets, bribing people, stealing from the boss, and similar misdemeanors are OK as long as you get away with it. If students alter their report cards,

Kohlberg's Stage II actions are based largely on satisfying one's own personal needs.

it's a Stage II response, providing they are successful. The clever con man or flimflam artist is a further example. In philosophical terms this category of moral thinking is referred to as instrumental hedonism, characterized by little human regard for the other person ("Nice guys finish last"). Genuine empathy is lacking.

In spite of the obvious shortcomings as a system of moral thinking, Stage II, "Let's make a deal," does represent an advance over Stage I. Gypping people financially, ignoring others' feelings, cheating at elections, and similar behaviors are not as bad as physical torture or death. Thus Stage II thinking represents a more adequate method of problem solving, but only when compared to Stage I, where right and wrong are determined by the fastest gun, the quickest fist, or the biggest bomb.

These first two stages are sometimes classified together as the preconventional stage of moral development. The reason for calling it "preconventional" will be obvious when we look at the next level, Stages III and IV.

Conventional Morality: Stages III and IV

These next two stages are classified as the conventional stage of moral development.

Stage III is the "social-conformity" orientation. At this stage a person makes moral judgments in order to do what is nice and what pleases others. At the same time, Stage III thinking is more comprehensive and more complex than Stage II. At this level a person does begin to take into account how others genuinely view the dilemma situation. The egocentrism of Stage II is replaced by the ability to empathize, to feel what others may be feeling, or, as it's called, an increase in social-role-taking perspective.

The problem with this stage, however, is that individuals may have great difficulty in resolving the conflicting feelings of all those involved in a dilemma situation. Thus, in the Heinz case mentioned above, a Stage III response would probably conclude that it was wrong to steal because almost all the people in the community say that stealing is wrong. "I will go along with the majority consensus, or social convention. I understand that most people hold that view and I would feel very uncomfortable going against the wishes of the majority." Thus, moral judgment is equated with following the leading crowd.

Stage III moral thinking depends on distinct stereotypes and sharp differences. Relativism and complexity are absent. In this sense, moral behavior is other-directed. Stage III behavior conforms strictly to the fixed conventions of the society in which we live. We don't look inward to the "self" and attempt to work through a

PEANUTS •   **By Charles M. Schulz**

decision independently. Kohlberg often illustrates Stage III behavior by referring to the comic-strip character, Charlie Brown. Charlie is usually caught in a hopeless predicament from trying to please everyone. His pleading with the iron-willed Lucy is both a comic and a poignant illustration of what it is like to try to live life always looking to other people for direction.

At *Stage IV,* the individual looks to rules, laws, or codes for guidance in dilemma situations. In one sense, civil- and criminal-law codes in our society represent a more stable and comprehensive system of resolving moral dilemmas than attempting to solve such questions on the basis of social conventions, community popularity, and what the leading crowd decides is the "nice" thing to do. Laws and rules as codified wisdom can be viewed as a positive glue, providing a society with stability and cohesion by guarding against rampant fads, quickly changing social customs, and societal anarchy or mob rule. The laws or rules represent society's attempt to set the same standards of conduct for all its citizens. Moral judgments are made by individuals in accordance with those rules. A person thinking at this level, then, does not simply look out for number one (Stage II) or follow the leading crowd (Stage III), but rather makes decisions that square with the existing legal codes.

Difficulties arise, however, with this rigid, law-and-order orientation. What do we do when the laws conflict or are unclear? Lawyers have a saying that difficult and complex social problems make for "bad" laws. In the Heinz case, for example, the law protects the druggist against stealing, but what about an equal-rights law that gives the wife a right to life? It is always possible to come up with exceptional cases to any comprehensive fixed law. For example, there are a few cases each winter where an electric or gas company has turned off the heat on a customer for nonpayment. Contract law is clear: If a person doesn't pay the bill, then the provider of the service is not obligated to continue service. But what happens when the non-payee dies from the cold? This may be an overly dramatic example, but such exceptional cases do occur. To handle such questions more comprehensively, we need recourse to a higher stage of reasoning.

Postconventional Morality: Stages V and VI

In the Kohlberg scheme, an individual at post-conventional morality, the highest stage of moral development, behaves according to a social contract (Stage V) or according to a universal principle such as justice (Stage VI). Moral thinking and judgments are complex and comprehensive. Diverse points of view are considered. Each situation is examined carefully in order to derive general principles to guide behavior appropriate for all. There are never any easy solutions to complex human problems and moral dilemmas. Judgments and decisions are neither simply situational and conveniently relative, nor easy and fixed in their application of a rule. At this level, we have to account simultaneously for all the situational aspects, motivations, and general principles involved.

The system of thinking at this level, then, represents a more adequate method of problem solving. Laws are viewed as a system of governance: Each law can be judged in terms of the extent to which it squares with the principles of the system.

At *Stage V* the principles are usually written as a document of assumptions or declaration of ideas. For example, the U.S. Constitution sets forth a series of principled rights as the basis for judging the adequacy of each law. As you can readily see, the key issue is to resolve dilemmas and conflicting laws by interpreting the intent of these written principles—justice, freedom, liberty, and equality of opportunity, to name a few.

It is also important to realize that problem solving on moral questions, social justice, or squaring my freedom with your freedom is not necessarily simpler at Stage V. Commonly, there is confusion on this issue: People believe that higher-stage reasoning is better because it's easier. Such is not the case. Reasoning at this level requires the ability to think abstractly (to view laws as a system of governance), to weigh competing claims, to take into account both the logical and emotional domains, to take a stand and yet remain open to future, more adequate interpretations of social justice.

At *Stage VI* the principles of social justice are universal, yet not necessarily in written form.

LAWRENCE KOHLBERG

Born in 1927, Lawrence Kohlberg spent three years as a junior engineer in the merchant marine before entering college. After those years at sea, he was ready to buckle down and push through the rigorous program at Chicago in record time. He completed the four-year B.A. degree in 1949 after only two years' work. He clearly demonstrated a great capacity for academic scholarship, and it was natural for him to enroll as a Ph.D. candidate at the same university. He completed his doctorate in 1958; after two years for his undergraduate studies, it took him nine years for the Ph.D. He remarked wryly that it only proved you couldn't accurately predict human behavior in all cases.

One of the major reasons for delay was his eventual topic, moral development in children and adolescents. A major portion of his doctoral work was in traditional areas of clinical psychology and child development, including a traineeship at the famous Children's Hospital in Boston. A substantial part of his difficulty was that all the time he was learning the traditional theories, including psychoanalytic views, he found in himself a growing skepticism. He began to evolve an alternative set of ideas to explain how children develop moral reasoning. What started as a traditional thesis on the relationship between the superego (the Freudian term for conscience) and moral behavior was transformed into a remarkably original framework for moral development in stages. It is rare for a young Ph.D. candidate to produce truly new insights into human behavior theory. It was uniquely creative for his thesis to force almost a complete revision of moral development theory as well.

With the completion of the thesis, finally, after nine years of work, he accepted an assistant professorship at the University of Chicago in 1962. Just six years later he was offered and accepted a full professorship at Harvard University and joined that faculty to form an innovative graduate program in human development. He was also awarded a special five-year Research Career Award by the National Institute of Mental Health to promote his longitudinal study on stages of moral development in adults as well as in children and adolescents. His major significance derives from the possible applications of the theory to promote psychologically healthy human beings. He is presently developing a series of intervention and teaching procedures that show promise of deliberately improving our level of moral judgment and moral maturity. Although so modest by nature that he suggests that his work is simply warmed-over Dewey, Kohlberg's work is much more than that. If we are concerned about improving the quality of interpersonal human relationships, his work at present represents the most helpful insights and processes to help us attain that objective.

It is always difficult to explain the exact difference between Stage V and Stage VI, because in some ways both systems are based on similar concepts. Also, analytical philosophers themselves are unclear as to the distinctions. The "official" definition of Stage VI is that the principles are abstract, ethical, universal, and consistent. As Kohlberg notes, "At heart, these are universal principles of justice, of the reciprocity and equality of human rights, and of the respect for the dignity of human beings as individual persons."[5]

Comparing the Stages

One way to see the different levels of complexity involved in judgments at each stage is to examine and compare the different response patterns associated with the preconventional (Stages I and II), conventional (Stages III and IV), and postconventional (Stages V and VI) levels. Let's look at some typical responses, at different levels, to the Heinz case.

A Stage I or II response (preconventional) would say that it was OK for Heinz to steal the drug because the druggist was himself a robber, or simply because Heinz needed it. However, he should be smart enough not to get caught. A Stage III or IV response (conventional) would say that Heinz was wrong in breaking into the store. Either it isn't nice to steal ("What if everyone went around just taking things?"), or the law must always be obeyed regardless of circumstance ("What happens to a society if we all break laws according to our own whim?"). In either case, the social convention or the rule says unequivocally, "Thou shalt not steal." Heinz should be judged the same way an escaped convict would be judged. There is no difference between Heinz and Clyde Barrow of *Bonnie and Clyde* fame. A Stage V or VI response (postconventional) would weigh Heinz's behavior against universal principles. How does the value of life compare to the value of property? What general rights do all people have? What constitutional provisions are there for such behavior? Also, what are the provisions for changing laws? Since there may be bad laws, what avenues are available for seeking redress? Is the law that allows the druggist to make whatever profit he can such a bad law? If so, does this justify, or does it simply rationalize, Heinz's theft? These are essentially Stage V considerations. Moral decisions are based on a system of laws themselves judged on the basis of the common good and social utility. This means that at Stage V we don't view the problem in terms of a single law, but in terms of the entire system.

At Stage VI the consideration would be based not so much on a system of laws (such as a written constitution), but on unwritten, moral, and universal principles. A moral principle would be something like the Golden Rule ("Do unto others as you would have them do unto you"), or it would be an ethical principle like Immanuel Kant's categorical imperative ("Act only as you would be willing that everyone should act in the same situation"). Stage VI principles apply across all social classes and cultures and, in fact, can be considered genuine principles only if they can be applied universally.

The idea of universal application is really the other half of "Love thy neighbor as thyself." In this case, then, it is irrelevant whether the woman in the Heinz dilemma is his wife. At Stage VI the concept of justice means that no matter who she is, rich or poor, friend or stranger, the respect for human life requires action to save her. Such a requirement, the philosopher John Rawls argues, is based on the concept of justice as equity.[6] This means that in a democratic society—where our creed calls for life, liberty, and the pursuit of happiness—each person has a responsibility to all others. We are not, at this level, individuals concerned only about ourselves or those whom we know well.

Thus, at Stage V decisions are made on the basis of a universal law, or a "higher" law that may not be written or even codified. However, the principles are implicit: value for human life, equality, and dignity. These are distinguished from static virtues and character traits because the values and principles are universal and dynamic. This also distinguishes such principles as "justice" from narrow and prescribed rules, such as "Thou shalt not steal." Stage VI requires that we consider the circumstances and the situation, as well as the general principles and the reasons behind the rules.

Thus, in the Heinz case, a Stage VI response might consider Heinz to be justified in stealing the drug since the value of human life is greater than the value of property—a universal principle. At the same time, Heinz should also be willing to accept legal punishment for stealing. The key here is the reasoning that makes it clear that Heinz deliberately challenged the law that allowed the druggist to make large profits, that he committed an act of civil disobedience and was willing to accept society's punishment for stealing. Socrates' refusal to alter his principles even to save his own life is an example of a Stage VI response. This is an important distinction. A certain behavior in and of itself is not necessarily an indicator of high-moral-stage thinking.

There needs to be a logical relationship between a person's behavior and the reasoning behind it. To steal the drug to please my neighbor is clearly not principled reasoning. On the other hand, to say that life is more important than property and yet not steal is just as clearly not principled behavior.

The accompanying excerpt from Martin Luther King, Jr.'s "Letter from the Birmingham City Jail" is an example of Stage VI judgment:

> You express a great deal of anxiety over our willingness to break laws. This is certainly a legitimate concern. Since we do diligently urge people to obey the Supreme Court's decision of 1954 outlawing segregation in the public schools, at first glance it may seem rather paradoxical for us consciously to break laws. One may well ask: "How can you advocate breaking some laws and obeying others?" The answer lies in the fact that there are two types of laws: just and unjust. One has not only a legal but a moral responsibility to obey just laws. Conversely, one has a moral responsibility to disobey unjust laws. I would agree with Saint Augustine that "an unjust law is no law at all."
>
> Now what is the difference between the two? How does one determine when a law is just or unjust? A just law is a man-made code that squares with the moral law or the law of God. An unjust law is a code that is out of harmony with the moral law. To put it in the terms of St. Thomas Aquinas: An unjust law is a human law that is not rooted in eternal law and natural law. Any law that uplifts human personality is just. Any law that degrades human personality is unjust.[7]

The Research Evidence

Figure 7.1 indicates the results of a series of cross-cultural studies conducted by Kohlberg in the 1960s. There are a number of important points to note. First, the trends are constant. Stage I and II behavior becomes less frequent as age increases, and Stage IV, V, and VI behavior increases during the same span. From this point of view we can say the sequence is developmental and invariant. The stages occur in order; that is, moral behavior develops from lower to higher stages, and no stages are skipped over. In this way, moral growth is similar to cognitive growth.

Since Kohlberg's original set of studies in the 1960s, there has been a substantial increase in the amount of research evidence in support of

the stage and sequence framework. These will be detailed throughout the chapter in the appropriate sections discussing the new longitudinal results, the relation between moral behavior and stage, the cross-cultural evidence, and the question of sex differences.

STAGES OF MORAL DEVELOPMENT AND AGE TRENDS

In 1979 all of the longitudinal data that formed the basis for the six-stage theory were rescored.[8] This rescoring was necessary as part of a large-scale effort to improve both the reliability and validity of the scoring system. An extensive measurement manual is now available that permits a much more exact assignment of student responses. There are more detailed examples of interview answers and more systematic rules for assigning "mixed" responses—that is, answers that contain different stage levels. The critics of the earlier, more or less intuitive scoring system have now been answered by the new scoring manual. However, important as this new manual is for the researcher, even more significant is what the new results say to the educator. The new norms substantially change some of the basic program goals. Essentially, the single most important change is a revision downward as to when postconventional Stage V reasoning and Stage VI reasoning occur in general.

Figure 7.2 presents the new age trends based on the rescoring of the research subjects' "old" responses—that is, their answers at ten, thirteen, and sixteen years of age—plus their "new" answers during their early and late twenties. Remember that the key to a longitudinal study is that the researchers work with the same subjects over a long time span—in this case, over a period of twenty to twenty-five years. The change in the system of reasoning, then, is based on the answers that the same subjects gave to the Heinz dilemma and to similar stories after being tested every three or four years.

The age trends, in general, are similar to those in the earlier studies previously discussed; that is, the sequence remains the same. There is no skipping of stages. The lower stages

FIGURE 7.1 Early cross-cultural studies.

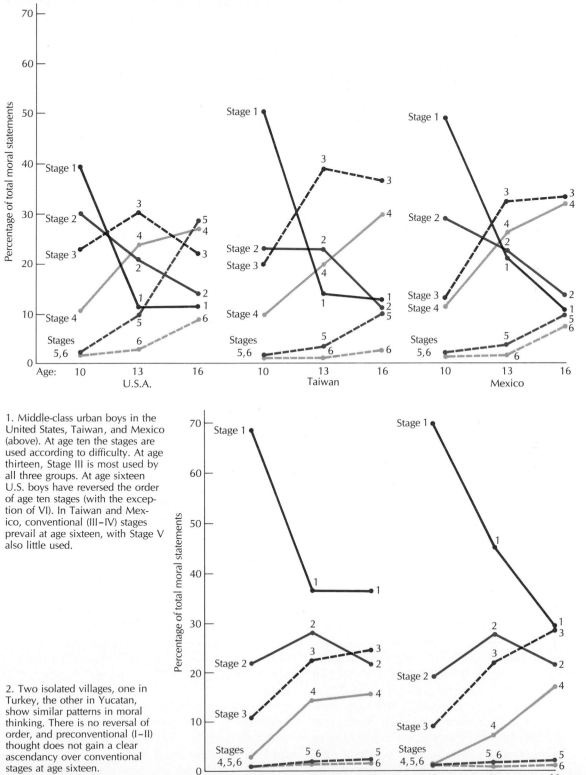

1. Middle-class urban boys in the United States, Taiwan, and Mexico (above). At age ten the stages are used according to difficulty. At age thirteen, Stage III is most used by all three groups. At age sixteen U.S. boys have reversed the order of age ten stages (with the exception of VI). In Taiwan and Mexico, conventional (III–IV) stages prevail at age sixteen, with Stage V also little used.

2. Two isolated villages, one in Turkey, the other in Yucatan, show similar patterns in moral thinking. There is no reversal of order, and preconventional (I–II) thought does not gain a clear ascendancy over conventional stages at age sixteen.

FIGURE 7.2   New norms: Percentage of moral reasoning at each stage for each age group.

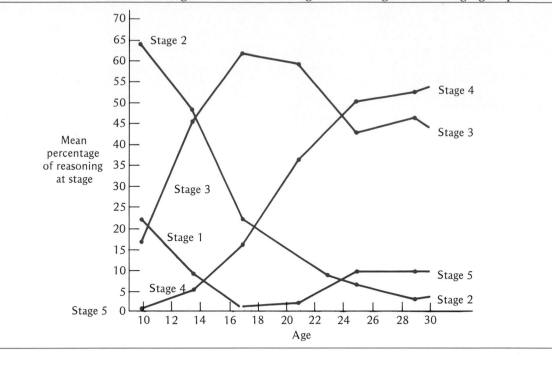

always precede the higher. However, it is now clear that principled reasoning (Stages V and VI) does not emerge in any substantial way during the secondary-school years. Earlier estimates suggested that 30 to 35 percent of moral reasoning during the period from sixteen to eighteen years could be classified as principled, that is, based on a clear understanding of the universality of democratic principles such as freedom and justice for all, the right to due process, the necessity of free speech, majority will and minority rights, and equality before the law. It is now clear that such reasoning is more complex than the earlier scoring system was capable of detecting. In other words, when the researchers compared the earlier responses given by a subject at age sixteen and then the dilemma resolutions posed by that same person at age thirty, they noted major structural differences in the thought processes. The responses scored "blind" indicated that much of the reasoning explained by the sixteen-year-old was pseudo-principled. The thinking was not generalizable at a principled level. In other words, the earlier scores were overestimates of the subjects' actual ability to process dilemmas.

The new norms indicate that at the junior-high level, the two most common modes of reasoning are Stage II and Stage III—almost 45 percent each. The lower stage, Stage I, accounts for about 7 percent, and the higher stage, Stage IV, for about 4 percent. This means that pupils have moved substantially beyond Stage I (almost 25 percent at age ten). Also, it is apparent that Stage II thinking is declining rapidly, while Stage III thinking is increasing in a major shift. The junior-high pupils are in the process of giving up an exclusive concern with their own materialistic rewards. Instead, more of the moral and value judgments are governed by a conformity to group norms. This finding indicates, in a manner similar to personal development outlined in Chapter 6, that the value choices are increasingly "other-directed" during this time.

During senior high school, the shifts that are apparent at ages thirteen to fourteen continue. Stage II declines further to less than 20 percent—almost equaling the rise in Stage IV to 15 percent. The major increase is clearly the emergence of Stage III. This form of moral reasoning now accounts for 60 percent of judgment at ages sixteen to eighteen. This is the peak. The power of the peer group as well as of other reference groups is strongest at this time. It is important to remember the second part of this point. It is almost common folk wisdom to agree that the peer group during middle adolescence helps mold value orientations. James Coleman's classic *Adolescent Society* clearly indicates the extent to which the high school "leading crowd" determines the value content. Most teen-agers follow the dictates of the group. However, Kohlberg's results indicate that such direction can come from sources other than the peer group. In other words, many teen-agers are other-directed in general. The source of direction may be the leading crowd of the peer group or certain charismatic adults. The power of pseudo-religious cults, gurus, and other adult-directed extremist groups has enormous appeal during this stage. The weakness of Stage III reasoning is particularly apparent under these conditions. Although it may not be the most important event of a lifetime for a teen-ager to process moral judgment according to the leading crowd in high school, there is no assurance that the adolescent would not be equally vulnerable to the exhortations of a cult that demanded shaved heads, public begging, and participation in drug-induced, religiouslike rituals.

During the early twenties, the shifts noted at junior and senior high continue. Stage I virtually disappears, and Stage II declines to less than 10 percent. Similarly, Stage III begins to turn down from its peak at sixteen to eighteen years. The most significant shift is the major increase in Stage IV judgment. By ages twenty-four to twenty-six, reasoning in accord with democratic laws becomes the major mode. Also, there is a small but highly significant development of principled reasoning to almost 10 percent at this time. In both cases, these two modes emerge much later than suggested by the earlier norms. The overall trends remain the same but the usage at the higher, more complex stages occurs much later than was previously reported. If anything, this indicates the need for more effective developmental programs to help stimulate the process of moral judgment. The new data on Piaget's norms indicated that secondary pupils were capable of but not using formal operations. The situation in moral reasoning is similar. Students are capable of Stage

IV reasoning at the secondary level, yet most do not use that mode. Similarly, students at the college level are capable of Stage V reasoning, yet rarely employ it. The potential, however, is there. It appears that more effective developmental experiences are needed in order to live as informed citizens in a democratic society.

Modal Stage "Plus One": A Preference for More Complex Reasoning

While the rescored norm results may be discouraging in the sense of lowered base rates, there is a very important and optimistic point. Two of Kohlberg's graduate students (now professors), James Rest[9] and Eliot Turiel,[10] demonstrated that students who reason in a modal sense at one particular stage actually understand and value reasoning at the next level "up" on the scale—that is, modal stage "plus one." We will discuss at greater length at the end of the chapter what implications these findings have for teaching. At this point, however, the main idea is to note that students usually reason

Moral development—like both cognitive and personal development—appears to proceed in an invariant sequence of developmental stages. A child cannot skip stages in moral development but, interestingly, will prefer moral judgments one level beyond his or her own. This fact has significant implications for the classroom teacher.

TABLE 7.2   VARIATION IN STAGE USAGE BY AGE GROUP (MODAL STAGE CIRCLED)

KOHLBERG STAGE	AGES			
	10	13–14	16–18	20–22
Stage I and II (Mix)	(47.6)	8.1	2.2	0
Stage II (Specific)	33.3	16.2	11.1	0
Stage II and II (Mix)	14.3	(56.8)	17.8	9.4
Stage III (Specific)	4.8	16.2	(44.4)	31.3
Stage III and IV (Mix)	0	2.7	24.4	(40.6)
Stage IV	0	0	0	18.8

in their modal stage about 40 to 50 percent of the time. Part of their reasoning is lower but part is higher; no one is totally "in" one stage at any single time. The higher reasoning component exerts a kind of pull and can gradually draw the student to a more complex level. Thus, it is important to remember two things about stage reasoning: First, the modal level is simply the most common system and is employed about half the time; there is variation. Second, there is a built-in preference for the next highest stage in the sequence. Table 7.2 summarizes both the modes and the "plus one" stages.

MORAL GROWTH: AN INVARIANT SEQUENCE

There is an important point to remember about the concept of development. To qualify as a developmental change, as we may recall from Chapter 5, a change can take only one direction: up. A developmental change can occur only from a lower to a higher stage. As Figure 7.2 suggests, not all people end up at Stage VI with Gandhi, Martin Luther King, Abraham Lincoln, Thoreau, or Socrates. However, there can be no reversals! With a few extreme exceptions (e.g., schizophrenics and other institutionalized patients), the researchers have found that major regressions in moral growth do not occur.[11]

The longitudinal results, in fact, showed a downward shift in scores only 8 percent of the time. Since the subjects had been tested a total of six times over a thirty-year period, the downward shifts noted fall within the acceptable error of measurement. The retesting also indicated that every case of reversal at one age was more than made up at the next. These results provided firm evidence supporting the direction of growth as a graduated sequence from less to more complexity. The results also showed quite clearly that the growth was systematic—one stage at a time. While there were no genuine reversals, neither did any of the subjects bypass or skip a stage.[12]

MORAL JUDGMENTS AND MORAL ACTION

A key element so far missing from this discussion is the connection between stages of moral growth and actual behavior in the "heat of battle," so to speak. This is an important issue, especially in this book where we have stressed that thinking about issues is no substitute for acting in real situations. The evidence for moral maturity and moral behavior comes from a series of studies. Naturally, if the theory of moral development has any meaning, we would predict significantly different behavior according to significantly different levels of moral judgment. For example, we would expect that almost everyone who responded to the Heinz dilemma at Stage I or II ("It's all right to steal, especially if you get away with it") themselves would cheat or steal if given any chance at all. And, at the opposite extreme, we would expect that almost no one who responded at Stage V or VI would himself cheat or steal.

To put this expectation to the test, a series of studies using "cheating" tests has been conducted. In one group of thirteen-year-olds, 75 percent of the lower-stage pupils (Stages I to II) actually cheated. At the same time, only 20 percent of the higher-stage pupils cheated in the same situation.

In an older population (eighteen-year-olds) the same trends occurred but, as we would predict, in different proportions: 42 percent of the lower-stage students cheated and 11 percent of the higher-stage students cheated. Thus, there is obviously a direct relationship between the rated level of moral judgment and behavior on the tests of cheating.

In another, more dramatic study, the moral-judgment tests were administered to subjects who had participated in the famous experiments of Stanley Milgram, in order to rate their level of moral maturity. Briefly, in the Milgram experiments research subjects were told to "follow orders" exactly as specified by a scientific investigator. The subjects were told that they were going to administer a series of strong electric shocks to an innocent "victim" in the next room. The subjects could hear the "victim"

pounding on the door, wincing, and screaming every time they pushed a button marked "high voltage." The experiment was set up to test how long subjects would follow orders and continue to administer increasing amounts of electricity to another human being. (In fact, of course, the supposed victim was part of the experiment and was not actually hooked up to the electric current.) The study itself caused a tremendous stir, because the results revealed that, in general, fully 65 percent of all subjects, regardless of age, background, or educational level, were willing to obey orders, no matter what! In other words, in spite of the screaming, pounding, and pleading from the "victim" in the next room, almost two-thirds of the subjects were willing to follow the scientist's directions. Figure 7.3 shows various phases of this classic experiment.

The results of the moral judgment testing showed that only 13 percent of the subjects rated at Stages I to IV actually refused to obey the orders, while 75 percent of the subjects rated at Stages V and VI refused to obey. This, of course, fits very closely the concept of moral maturity at the postconventional level. Only at that level would we expect a person to refuse to follow the rules and say, in effect, "I really don't care what the experiment is all about or whether a scientist tells me I must do what he says. I will not deliberately inflict harm on that guy in the next room. He is more important

Cheating test results.

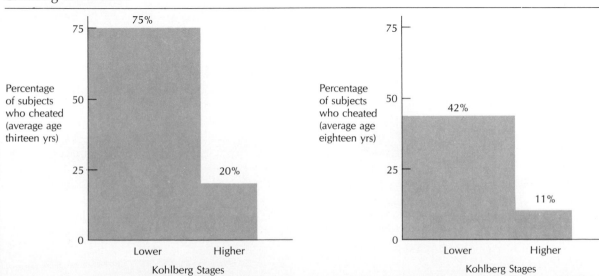

FIGURE 7.3 Various phases of Milgram's classic experiment: (a) A shock generator. (b) A subject being strapped into place. (c) A subject refusing to obey orders. (d) An obedient subject being introduced to his unharmed "victim." Below is a chart relating Kohlberg's stages to the results of this experiment.

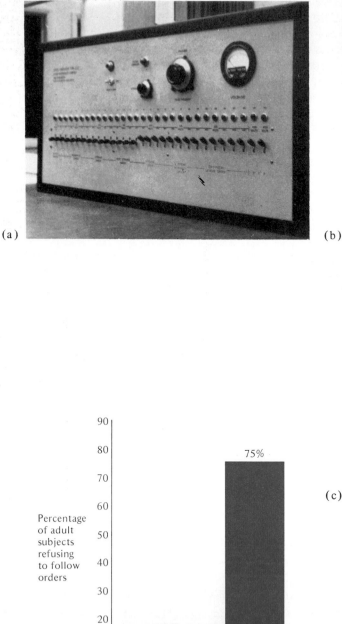

(a)

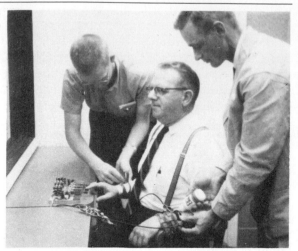

(b)

(c)

(d)

Photos: © 1965 by Stanley Milgram. From the film Obedience, *distributed by the New York University Film Library.*

than any experiment." In other words, only at that level could a person distinguish between obeying the "law" and valuing human life. We might recall at this point the number of times in history that humans have been willing to exterminate helpless victims on the grounds that they were "just following orders."

Another study of particular interest in detailing the relationship between moral thought and action was conducted by Shari McNamee. Sometimes referred to as a test of the Golden Rule and the parable of the Good Samaritan, her experiment was conducted with college students. They were to participate in a "psychology subject" program. She describes it as follows:

> Undergraduates who agreed to be interviewed on the standard moral dilemmas were led to a testing room. As they were entering the room they were intercepted by a student presenting himself as the next subject for the experiment. The student stated that he had just taken drugs and was having a bad time. He had come to the experiment because he thought that the experimenter, being a psychologist, could help him. The response of the experimenter was that she was a research psychologist, not a therapist. The drug-user persisted in soliciting aid, hoping that the experimenter could refer him to help. The experimenter replied that she had no experience with drugs and did not know what facility could help him. She told him to reschedule his testing session. The drug-user slowly left the room. The subject was faced with the choice of whether to remain an uninvolved bystander or whether to intervene.[13]

The results of the study are presented in Table 7.3. Almost three-fourths of the students who were rated at the principled level (Stage V)

offered to help the victim. There was a linear relationship between stage score and willingness to help, so that 38 percent of Stage IV, 27 percent of Stage III, and 9 percent of Stage II offered assistance. Thus, the relationship between stage score and actual behavior in a high-stress dilemma situation was clearly established. Two other points of interest: In McNamee's study the authoritative scientist was a female, and in Milgram's experiment the scientist was a male yet the outcomes were similar. Also, in both the McNamee and the Milgram studies, equal numbers of male and female subjects were used, and there were no sex differences in response by stage.

One final point on the McNamee study: In addition to observing actual helping behavior, McNamee also asked the subjects if they thought that they should help a distressed person. This is a kind of lip-service test to see if some of those who say they should help actually didn't. The results are most interesting. The greatest discrepancy occurs among those at Stage III. More than three-fourths of subjects at that level said they ought to help, but just over one-fourth actually did. This is a 50 percent difference between lip service and helping behavior. If you review the major characteristics of Stage III reasoning, you will see that the theory would predict exactly such an outcome. Since obedience to social conformity peaks at this stage, such subjects would agree to a socially acceptable statement yet be unable to resist the authoritative role of the scientist's social pressure. These results, then, further validate the Kohlberg theory.

A major review of over eighty studies of the relation of moral behavior to reasoning has been done by Gus Blasi.[14] He examined each study

TABLE 7.3   PERCENT OF COLLEGE STUDENTS HELPING A DRUGGED STUDENT ACCORDING TO MORAL STAGE SCORE (THE McNAMEE STUDY)

KOHLBERG STAGE SCORE	NUMBER	HELPED BY REFERRING VICTIM	THOUGHT THEY SHOULD HELP
II	11	9%	36%
III	29	27%	77%
IV	17	38%	69%
V	29	73%	83%

from the research design results and the theoretical assumptions. Although not all of the studies were well designed, Blasi concluded that on an overall basis the view that moral behavior and moral reasoning are definitely interrelated was strongly supported. Even more important was his conclusion that at higher levels of reasoning humans behave in a more consistent and altruistic manner than at lower levels of reasoning. The strongest finding of all was that at higher stages there was a much greater resistance to following the crowd or to going along in order to get along. Thus, as we've seen in both the Milgram and McNamee studies, the individuals who reasoned their way through hypothetical dilemmas at levels of principled thinking also behaved in an altruistic instead of a conformist manner.

SEX DIFFERENCES: GILLIGAN'S CRITIQUE

When the Kohlberg theory was first validated, there were two studies, one in Canada[15] and one in the United States,[16] that specifically examined the relationship between gender and stage. Both studies indicated that there was no gender difference, and the topic was largely dropped as a research interest. Carol Gilligan, however, challenged these findings and did so most dramatically. As a journal article (1977) that was soon expanded to book length, her *In a Different Voice,* published in 1982, created a major controversy. Relying mostly on historical evidence, case studies, and small-scale empirical research presented with a flair for the dramatic, she proclaimed that the Kohlberg theory was sex-biased. Not only did the scoring system penalize females, in her view, but his description of postconventional (Stages V and VI) reasoning systematically left out a concern for human caring. In other words, she claimed the Kohlberg theory defined principled reasoning as too objective and narrowly rational. Human compassion was absent from his system. She also was alert to point out that the original longitudinal sample was all male. Quoting from source material ranging from Portia in the *Merchant of Venice* and Nora in *The Doll's House* to characters from Mary McCarthy's novel *The Group,* she made a most persuasive case. She

claimed that psychological theory was only one instance of a pervasive sexism from a male-dominated society:

> As we have listened for centuries to the voices of men and the theories of development that their experience informs, so we have come more recently to notice not only the silence of women but the difficulty in hearing what they say when they speak. Yet in the different voice of women lies the truth of an ethic of care, the tie between relationship and responsibility, and the origins of aggression in the failure of connection.[17]

Her views had an immediate impact not only on psychology but also on the larger community. In 1984 she was named "Woman of the Year" by a leading national feminist magazine. Soon many theorists and researchers began to review their prior studies. How could so many have missed such an obvious bias? Could it really be true that all of Kohlberg's work was valid for only one-half of the population?

One of the first comprehensive reviews was published by James Rest, a professor at the University of Minnesota, where the tradition of precise measurement is extremely strong.[18] In fact, during the early days of Kohlberg's interview rating approach, Rest had created an objective paper-and-pencil test of Kohlberg's theory. Researchers used his instrument with teen-agers, college students, young adults, and professionals. The samples were large and represented both genders. Rest's quite startling finding was that there was no empirical evidence to support Gilligan's charge. By far the most frequent finding was no difference between male scores and female scores, regardless of the sample. Further, he found that when sex differences were found in a few studies, the differences were in favor of the females. For example, in a study of male and female law students, the females consistently scored higher on his test of principled moral reasoning (Kohlberg's Stages V and VI) than the males. In fact, whenever such characteristics as age, socioeconomic status, and educational/vocational status were controlled, the results were either no difference or in some cases differences favoring females. The Rest instrument as the major objective measure had clearly been validated, but what of the Kohlberg interview rating scale?

Gilligan had gone to special lengths to direct criticism to the interview method, claiming that whenever the raters came across comments suggesting the importance of ideas such as love, caring, or sympathy, those ideas would be immediately classed as Stage III, social conformity. This meant that the interview approach was still suspect. A recent examination of this aspect of Kohlberg's theory by two different researchers, Mary Braebeck[19] from Boston College and Lawrence Walker[20] from the University of British Columbia, refuted Gilligan's claim. For example, Walker reviewed 108 studies and a total of 8,000 subjects employing the Kohlberg assessment method. He found no differences according to sex. Braebeck's review reached the same conclusions. Somewhat ironically, in two of Gilligan's own earlier studies her results did not agree with her position. In a study with high-school boys and girls, both groups scored at the same level (Kohlberg interview method) on the standard dilemmas. When the dilemma content was changed, both groups had scores that decreased (from Stage IV to III).[21] And even in her now famous study of adult women confronting an abortion decision, she found that the women who demonstrated higher moral judgment stage scores also had "improved their life on follow up."[22] Thus, the Kohlberg interview level was an accurate predictor of significant life choices by women.[23]

To a major degree, then, the charge of sex bias has not been proven. To an even greater degree, Gilligan's claims continue to be a puzzlement. It is true that the original sample was male, but there have been an enormous number of studies since that time (including cross-cultural replications) with both sexes. The results are highly consistent with the claim of a universal sequence for both sexes. This does not mean, however, that there is nothing of substance to Gilligan's view. She has served as a valuable reminder that issues of caring and compassionate concern for others are important components of moral judgment. She has also correctly pointed out that the content of many of the standard dilemmas themselves (Heinz, Joe and the camp, and the Sergeant in Korea) routinely depict males as the key actors. As we move toward genuine sexual equality, fairness would require more females as the main figures. Kohlberg himself is certainly sensitive to Gil-

ligan's position and notes that the revised scoring manual avoids automatically classifying "caring" content as Stage III. Perhaps a less obvious but, in the long run, a more significant change is the definition of postconventional (Stages V and VI) reasoning. In his most recent writings, Kohlberg now describes the Golden Rule as having two elements: (1) Do unto others as you would have them do unto you, *and* (2) Love thy neighbor as thyself. The first part has been routinely mentioned in all his earlier writings and linked to the philosophy of Immanuel Kant. The newer focus on the second clearly reflects an ethic of caring, which is really Gilligan's central point. Fortunately, Kohlberg's theory and scoring system, as the research studies so clearly indicate, do include both the ethics of equity and caring.[24]

MORAL DEVELOPMENT: UNIVERSAL STAGES ACROSS CULTURES

Kohlberg originally demonstrated, both across cultures (from Malaysian aborigines to white middle-class Americans) and within cultures (lower- to upper-class Americans), that the sequence is the same not only within country, class, and caste, but also within major religious categories. Kohlberg's stages, like Piaget's and Erikson's, represent a systematic, one-way sequence from preconventional levels (Stages I and II) to conventional levels (Stages III and IV) and culminating in postconventional levels (Stages V and VI).

This means that the formal sequence of understanding and developing moral judgment is limited by developmental age and stage. The content may vary, but the structure of judgment may not. Thus, a ten-year-old Taiwanese village boy would say it was OK for Heinz to steal the drug, "Otherwise the wife would die and he'd have to pay for the funeral and they cost a lot"; and a ten-year-old Malaysian boy would say it was OK to steal the drug, "Otherwise the wife dies and he needs her to cook for him"; and an American middle-class boy the same age would say he should steal the drug, "Especially if the wife could turn out to be an important person— or if she died then he would have to go to the trouble of finding a new wife." The logical structure in all three cases is the same. The wife is viewed exclusively as an instrument of the husband in concrete and operational terms.

The cross-cultural question could not be completely settled on the basis of these studies, however. Cultural anthropologists had long maintained, starting with Margaret Mead's important research, that each culture was really unique. This so-called snowflake theory essentially said each society, like each snowflake, was different from all others. Cross-cultural universality was a myth. In fact, one researcher claimed that the Kohlberg system itself was only an example of cultural bias. The researcher cited case studies in order to prove her point.[25]

As with the charge of sex bias, the charge of cultural bias was dealt with by going to the newer research literature. Since research like Kohlberg's had been conducted in over forty-five countries in the past fifteen years, surely there must be some hard evidence to confirm or deny the case-study position of cultural anthropology. John Snarey of Northwestern University, in fact, did a careful, current, and exhaustive review.[26] One question of importance has to do with the content of the dilemmas. Snarey demonstrated how the stories were transposed to fit the specific cultural traditions and mores. Table 7.4 demonstrates three versions of the Heinz story—the original and adaptations to Kenya and Turkey. The general issues remained the same, but the form was changed so the issues were not exclusive to a Western culture such as ours.

The second issue Snarey checked was the so-called invariant sequence problem. Do the original trends from the longitudinal study still hold? Employing both cross-sectional and longitudinal studies from different cultures, he found that all stages of development were represented. Also there were no regressions in the major longitudinal studies, and none of the subjects skipped a stage. Thus, the major assumptions from the earlier studies were validated by current research. The subjects' level of moral reasoning shows the same sequence of development from the less complex to the more complex levels. The process is one stage at a time with no skipping. Also there were no regressions beyond that from measurement error.

In regard to the sex-difference question, Snarey examined eighteen cross-cultural studies

that assessed both males and females. He found clear sex differences favoring males in only one study—results that are virtually the same as in studies conducted in the United States.

One final point: Was there evidence of principled reasoning, Stage V or higher, in other countries? Here the results were most interesting. In all urban Western and in nearly all urban non-Western cultures, some subjects were found who reason at the level of democratic principled thought. In a review of eight tribal, rural, folk societies, Stage V or higher reasoning was completely absent. The main cross-cultural difference that now shows up is between urban versus tribal societies rather than Western versus non-Western. One such example of a tribal society is the Atayal culture in Malaysia. The elders arrange to prevent the development of abstract reasoning in their adolescents through a process similar to brainwashing. The elders insist during the rites of passage that the young adults maintain their beliefs in "black magic," the existence of demons, and other aspects of folklore.[27] Such aboriginal cultures are, of course, committed to maintaining myths to ensure the continuation of tribal cohesiveness; this is the opposite of our views on the importance of developing each person's individuality and human potential. Snarey's main point is that the cross-cultural research supports Kohlberg's developmental assumptions, with the exception of tribal cultures. This also proves another point. Development is not automatic but depends on interaction. If we do not provide humans with an appropriate learning environment, their development will not unfold, even in the area of value judgment. It is to that topic we now turn.

MORAL GROWTH: UNDERSTANDING AT YOUR OWN STAGE AND ONE STAGE UP

We have seen that children and adolescents generally understand moral judgments at their own stage and one stage above it. Generally, people operate out of one major stage (such as Stage III, the "social-conformist" orientation), but they also incorporate a few elements from the next higher stage (in this case, Stage IV, the "law-and-order" orientation). This enables

TABLE 7.4 THREE VERSIONS OF THE CLASSIC "HEINZ AND THE DRUG" DILEMMA

ORIGINAL UNITED STATES VERSION*

In Europe, a woman was near death from a special kind of cancer. There was one drug that the doctors thought might save her. It was a form of radium that a druggist in the same town had recently discovered. The drug was expensive to make, but the druggist was charging 10 times what the drug cost him to make. He paid $200 for the radium and charged $2,000 for a small dose of the drug. The sick woman's husband, Heinz, went to everyone he knew to borrow the money, but he could only get together about $1,000, which is half of what it cost. He told the druggist that his wife was dying, and asked him to sell it cheaper or let him pay later. But the druggist said, "No, I discovered the drug and I'm going to make money from it." So Heinz got desperate and broke into the man's store to steal the drug for his wife.

Should Heinz have done that? Why or why not?

ADAPTED KENYAN VERSION†

In a rural area of Kenya, a woman was near death from a special kind of heart disease. There was one kind of medicine that the doctors at the government hospital thought might save her. It was a form of medicine that a chemist in Nairobi had recently invented. The drug was expensive to make, but the chemist was charging 10 times what the drug cost him to make. He paid 80 shillings for the drug, and then charged 800 shillings for a small dose of the drug. The sick woman's husband, Joseph, went to everyone he knew to borrow the money, but he could only get together 400 shillings, which was half of what it cost. He told the chemist that his wife was dying, and asked him to sell it cheaper or let him pay the rest later. But the chemist said, "No. I'm the one who invented this medicine, and I'm going to make money from it." So Joseph got desperate and broke into the store to steal the drug for his wife.

Should Joseph have done that, broken into the store to take the drug? Why or why not?

ADAPTED TURKISH VERSION‡

A man and wife have just migrated from the high mountains. They started to farm, but there was no rain and no crops grew. No one had enough food. The wife became sick from having little food and could only sleep. Finally, she was close to dying from having no food. The husband could not get any work and the wife could not move to another town. There was only one grocery store in the village, and the storekeeper charged a very high price for the food because there was no other store and people had no place else to go to buy food. The husband asked the storekeeper for some food for his wife, and said he would pay for it later. The storekeeper said, "No, I won't give you any food unless you pay first." The husband went to all the people in the village to ask for food, but no one had food to spare. So he got desperate and broke into the store to steal food for his wife.

Should the husband have done that? Why or why not?

* Originally appeared in Lawrence Kohlberg, *Global Rating Guide: Preliminary Moral Judgment Scoring Manual* (Cambridge, Mass.: Center for Moral Education, 1969).
† Originally appeared in C. Edwards, Doctoral dissertation, Harvard Graduate School of Education, Cambridge, Mass., 1974.
‡ Originally appeared in E. Turiel, C. Edwards, and L. Kohlberg, "Moral Development in Turkish Children, Adolescents, and Young Adults," *Journal of Cross-Cultural Counseling*, 9 (1978), 75–85.

From J. Snarey, "Cross-Cultural Universality of Social-Moral Development," *Psychological Bulletin*, 97(2) (1985): 214.

them to understand judgments one stage up and also, because of the nature of development, to prefer it to their own mode. Each higher stage is more universal and less self-centered and so requires fewer rationalizations. At the same time, it is useless to present people with moral systems more than one stage beyond their own. Students, or adults for that matter, simply cannot comprehend that far in advance of their present level of understanding.

From an educational point of view, it is well to remember that we can get pupils or adults to make rote statements that sound like the very highest level of moral development. However, if they themselves are more than one stage "down" from the moral system embodied in such memorized statements, they will not internalize that system. Instead, we will succeed only in producing more lip service. Say, for example, that we wanted to coach the high-school debating team to present their arguments at Stage VI. We could teach them to mouth the concepts of universal principles of justice to support their position. However, unless they were already close to that level themselves, we would find, much to our chagrin, that when it came time for the rebuttal, our game plan would fail miserably. Once on their own, our debaters would immediately lapse back into their own level (probably Stage II, III, or IV), thereby undoing all our work. Instead of arguments based on principles such as justice, we would hear arguments in accord with their own natural levels. In the classroom, too, there is a need to match the level of discussion to the pupils' developmental stage. The research evidence on this point is supportive. All children were able to understand and represent correctly all stages below their own as well as those at their own level. Some children could spontaneously understand and represent thinking one stage up from their own level. Almost none were able to comprehend and translate thinking two or more stages above their level.

Moral Education in the Classroom

Recent evidence indicates that special classroom teaching techniques can affect the level of the pupils' moral maturity. It is also important to note the factors that make a difference. Because of the limits imposed by developmental stages, it makes little sense to start discussing moral dilemmas before students reach elementary-school age. There is the possibility, however, of starting discussions then to promote the idea of choosing from alternatives in everyday situations. Also, it is possible for pupils in elementary school to gain a sense of seeking reasons behind actions. Such discussions would help students become aware of a series of reasons for rules and would help them compare these ideas.

Most recent evidence strongly supports the dilemma-discussion approach. A major review by Stephen Thoma indicated that the discussion method was consistently effective.[28] He also found that there were some important characteristics to bear in mind in separating the effective methods from the ineffective ones. First, time was generally an important variable. Twelve- to sixteen-week courses were effective;

short-term workshops, two-week "units," or one-shot presentations were not. Second, he found that the discussion method worked well with all age groups, from early adolescents to adults, and generally the older the students, the greater the positive change. Finally, he found that the gains were modest. In other words, we should not expect students in any age grouping to demonstrate huge stage gains.

Since the process of moral reasoning is closely related to age, stage of cognitive development, level of experience, and the ability to reflect from different points of view, such a reasoning process cannot be changed overnight. One of the possible frustrations that teachers often experience in running such discussions is the slow growth rate. Students generally will maintain their own modal level, especially in dealing with difficult dilemmas. If you do decide to lead such discussions, it's important to remember that a slow pace is to be expected. You can, of course, interrupt at any point and teach them to say the "right answers" at a principled level. You will find, however, like the coach of the high-school debating team, that once back on their own resources in discussing a different dilemma, their modal levels will reappear.

The Berkowitz Approach: Support and Challenge

A further refinement of the discussion method comes from the work of Marvin Berkowitz from Marquette University.[29] He had the good idea of examining different methods of group leadership in the discussion format. What Berkowitz found out has direct relevance to the teaching question. First, he found that effective discussion requires flexibility and the use of indirect teaching strategies. (See Chapter 12 for a further discussion on indirect methods.) This meant quite simply that lecturing, telling, or reading to students *about* moral dilemmas has little impact. Just think of how many times lecture material goes in one ear and out the other. Second, he found that the leader needs to balance the ratio of questions between supportive questions and challenging ones. This means that sometimes the leader restates, reflects back, and paraphrases what the student says. This helps the student think out loud, so to speak. At other times, however, the leader needs to challenge the student's statement (and remember, you are challenging the idea and not the person). By asking the student to carry an illogical view to its logical conclusion, the weakness of the argument may be revealed to the student and others in the class. The student may be asked to refine and extend a view and even to defend the view against competitive or alternate points of view. Table 7.5 contains some examples of questioning designed to test and challenge the student's view as well as questions designed to paraphrase and clarify. The effective leader uses both techniques. The one thing the effective

---

TABLE 7.5   *LEADING MORAL DILEMMA DISCUSSIONS: THE QUESTIONING METHOD*

A. Starting
  1. First, getting the facts straight:
       Be sure the content is accurate.
       Paraphrase what the issues are.
       Make sure all are tuned in.

  2. To start the actual discussions, use open-ended questions:

       "What should Person X do? Why, or what are the main reasons?" Survey the group.

       If any of the reasons aren't too clear, then ask *clarifying questions*. For example:

           "Would you say a little more . . . ?"
           "Do you mean . . . ?"
           "Let me see if I can paraphrase . . . ?"

OR

       Ask others in the group if they understand Person X's reasons.

   Goal
   Make sure everyone has the chance to make an opening statement. Use "wait time" if needed in questioning.

B. Continuing the discussion
   To continue the discussion and help develop greater elaboration, the following techniques are helpful:

   1. *Alternative consequences:* What might happen if the person did A, or B, or C?

   2. *Role switch:* What would your reasons be if you were Person X, Y, or Z? Put yourself in the shoes of the other person.

   3. *Feelings and emotions:* How do you suppose Person X is feeling? How might you feel in such a situation? What might be some consequences of those feelings?

   4. *Personal experience:* Has anything like this ever happened to you? What were your thoughts, feelings, actions? Looking back, is there anything you would change?

   5. *Change a key element:* "Let's say that the person in the situation is someone you didn't even know, rather than someone very close to you. How might that change things?"

   6. *"Some people say":* "Some say there is never a good reason to break a law. How would you answer that view?"

   7. *Have discussants talk back and forth to each other:* "Henry, how would you answer Amy?" "Jill and Troy seem to be on opposite sides . . . "

C. Reaching closure
   1. *Issue-related questions:* "Now that we viewed it from so many different positions, what are the *key elements,* or most persuasive issues? Is there any particular element that would cause you to switch your view?"

   2. *Justice-related questions:* "From a justice and fairness to all perspective, what solution would be best?"

leader never does is to "put down" a student. Sarcasm, belittling, making fun of a student's view serves to hamper discussion. Excessively critical teaching in general (see pp. 300–301) has been shown to reduce both academic achievement and positive self-concepts. The same is true in moral-dilemma discussions. So remember that a ratio of supportive questions to challenging ones is essential for student growth. Challenge in this case is not license to cut off a child at the ankles, so to speak, with withering ridicule.

Discipline and moral development can become a direct part of a positive educational program. Discussions of moral dilemmas can be introduced to classes by use of headline stories from newspapers, everyday incidents, popular moral issues (e.g., capital punishment, civil disobedience, an "attractive" nuisance), or incidents from movies or readings. The teacher's job is to present the case material in a systematic and provocative way by asking questions. The idea is to promote a flow of ideas about what actions might be proposed. If, for example, children say that capital punishment should be abolished, their reasons should be explored. Reasons for and against capital punishment can be outlined by moral stage (see Table 7.6).

Of course, you may need practice in identifying the levels of response. But, in most cases, the differences in stages become quite apparent as long as you resist the temptation to take over and do all the talking. By rephrasing and clarifying certain reasons produced by pupils in the class, you can help them begin to hear and understand one stage up.

A further point: Don't wait until a student in your class does something wrong before starting discussions of moral values. That is the worst possible time educationally; from the child's point of view, it's like being caught with one hand in the cookie jar. Shaming does not teach.

Another teaching point to remember: Stifle your own tendency to overreact. You may be more than surprised, and somewhat dismayed, if you succeed in getting the children to say what they really think about certain issues. For example, elementary children frequently express highly racist and narrow-minded views. It may be quite natural to want to challenge and ridicule such ideas and insist that they stop talking "that way." For example, in a recent sixth-grade class in social studies, the children were discussing welfare. They unanimously agreed that some people were not able to work through no fault of their own. The students' middle-class backgrounds made it proper to say things like, "We should help those less fortunate than we." They had also done extensive reading, watched films, and even interviewed economically "poor" people. They all agreed that in most cases, through a series of often dramatic and poignant events, the grinding cycle of poverty acted as an overwhelming social force. Individuals have been destroyed, their will to act energetically has been broken, and so on.

At this point, the teacher presented a hypothetical case of a welfare family, a mother with six children, ages fourteen to two, and an institutionalized husband. The class was asked to develop a budget of needed financial assistance. At this point all empathy vanished from the classroom. The pupils decided that the family

TABLE 7.6   REASONS FOR AND AGAINST CAPITAL PUNISHMENT BY MORAL STAGE

	PRO	CON
Stage II	An eye for an eye—to put a murderer to death is a fair trade.	It takes too much time, energy, and money to convict a person of a capital offense. It's too expensive.
Stage III	Society shouldn't keep any "bad apples" around—they infect others.	Civilized societies shouldn't themselves murder humans. Group pressure to socialize criminals can be used instead.
Stage IV	A law declares that if a murderer is tried and convicted, then electrocution is simply carrying out the law.	A law declares that cruel and unusual punishment is not justified. It's the law.

didn't need a dining room table or chairs ("They could eat sitting on the floor"); that they needed only a few beds ("They could take turns sleeping"); that all children above the age of eight could go to work, even though this meant dropping out of school; and that the mother could work at night when the older children returned from their jobs ("It's good for people to make their own money and not beg")! Obviously the entire objective had been missed; there was a total lack of comprehension. As you might guess, the teacher then got angry at the class. She sermonized for the balance of the period. The next day the pupils were back in class talking about the need for welfare programs to help unfortunate poor people.

The teacher, of course, had really missed the key opportunity in the lesson—the opening to discuss the discrepancy between the students' "budget" and their high-sounding ethics, and then to gradually move them to a higher stage of moral awareness. Had she discussed the legal framework (Stage IV), for example, she could have led them to step beyond the Stage II and III arguments they had presented. Child-labor laws, compulsory-school-attendance laws, and so on could have become a means of examining the reasons for such laws and the need to protect individual rights. In this way a slightly "higher" explanation could have been introduced and thought about.

Kohlberg's developmental framework, then, suggests that children between nine and twelve years of age are maximally ready to discuss and examine questions of moral judgment, decisions concerning the value of life versus property, and others. This is the time, both cognitively and personally, for them to move into Stages III and IV of moral judgment. This is when it makes most sense educationally to provide experiences and classroom discussion to ensure growth beyond Stages I and II, that is, past the level where moral judgments are exclusively self-serving or egocentric.

For adolescents, the problem of moral education is similar to that of children in upper elementary and junior high school, yet it is more complex. The modal system employed by most adolescents at this time is a major Stage III orientation with the beginnings of Stage IV. In other words, this is the time for a major examination of social conformity versus soci-

ety's laws and beyond that, the reasons or principles behind the laws. It is an enormous challenge to educators to help stimulate reasoning beyond the level of social conformity. There is an increasing number of highly sophisticated, very helpful curriculum materials available in disciplines such as English and Social Studies. The curriculum project at Carnegie-Mellon is extraordinarily promising. Both in English literature and historical events, a moral-dilemma format is employed to help students learn the processes of value analysis and moral judgment.[30] Other projects, notably one in the Boston area, are even more ambitious in setting up a school-within-a-school for a prototype of democratic decision making.[31] Such experiences create an important atmosphere for serious examination of significant general and personal dilemmas.

One of Kohlberg's associates, Moshe Blatt, has conducted an original set of studies demonstrating the usefulness of classroom discussions of moral dilemmas. An actual transcript of a classroom interaction involving high-school students appears in the accompanying box. Note how Blatt does not put down, criticize, or judge each pupil's comments. Also note how he clarifies responses, asks for elaboration, gently probes, and suggests alternative views.

Dilemma

There was a case in court the other day about a man, Mr. Jones, who had an accident in his house. His child, Mike, was wounded in the chest. He was bleeding heavily; his shoes and pants were soaked with blood. Mike was scared. He began screaming until he finally lost consciousness.

His parents were scared, too. His mother began screaming, crying. She thought her child was dying. The father no longer hesitated; he lifted Mike up, ran down the stairs and went outside in hopes of getting a cab and going to the hospital. He thought that getting a cab would be quicker than calling an ambulance. But there were no cabs on the street and Mike's bleeding seemed worse.

Suddenly, Mike's father noticed a man parking his car. He ran up and asked the man to take him to the hospital. The man replied, "Look, I have an appointment with a man about an important job. I really must be on time. I'd like to help you but I can't." So Mr. Jones said, "Just give me the car." The man said, "Look, I don't know you. I don't trust you." Mr. Jones told Mrs. Jones to hold Mike. She did. Then Mr. Jones punched the man, beat him up, took his keys, and drove away toward the hospital. The man got up from the street, called the police, and took them to the hospital. The police arrested Mr. Jones for car theft and aggravated battery.

Mr. Blatt: What is the problem? Was the man legally wrong for refusing to drive Mr. Jones and Mike to the hospital?

Student A: It's his car, he doesn't have to drive.

Mr. B: Well, Mike was hurt. You said no, he's not legally responsible, because, why not?

Student A: Because it's his car.

Mr. B: It's his car. It's his property, and he has the right of property and he can legally—

Student B: But a life is at stake.

Mr. B: Okay. It's not so easy. Like here is property, but here is life, so the conflict here is between life, Mike's life, or that man's car.

Student B: But if Mike died, then that guy could be charged with murder, because, you know . . .

Student C: No, he couldn't. . . .

Mr. B: But do you people think this man has a right, a legal right, to refuse to give Mr. Jones the car?

Student D: Does that man have children? He probably has to support a family, he's got a family, he can't just—

Student E: So? He can always find a job—

Mr. B: The question is, do you think that the man who had the job, wouldn't he understand if you came up to him and said, "Look, I was here, I wanted to be on time, but I saw this boy bleeding, and I wanted to help him out." Don't you think he would understand?

(Chorus of "yes" and "no")

Student F: No, because if you're supposed to go on the job—

Student G: You could make him show some proof.

Student F: Bring the kid there when he's well.

Mr. B: All right. This man who refused to give the car was not legally wrong. You couldn't take him to court. But do you think he was wrong in any way? (Chorus of "yes")

Student B: He was just all wrong because if that kid died, I don't know what he'd be charged with, but he'd be charged with something. There's something, I don't know what it is, but there's something they could charge him with.

Mr. B: I don't know if they could charge him legally, but you're right; there's something very wrong with that, because what is this man doing? Which is more important: property or life? (Chorus of "life") Why? (Confused answers, on the principle that life is irreplaceable) Life is

The power of this process really depends on the teacher's ability to lead discussions using such an indirect format. (See Chapter 12 for further information on indirect teaching.)

Blatt's studies have shown that pupils improve in their ability to think at more comprehensive and empathic levels as a result of moral dilemma discussions through indirect teaching. Whether or not this process actually works depends on the teacher's skill in facilitating participation, creating a supportive atmosphere so all can talk, and helping pupils actually listen to each other's points of view. The process is complex, as the transcript demonstrates.

something you can't replace, right? Everybody wants to live. Now this guy, what was he putting first, life or a job? What do you think is more important, losing a job and maybe getting another one, or saving a life? (Answers: "Saving a life") Helping to save a life. But this guy refuses to help Mr. Jones and Mike out, to take them to the hospital. What was he doing? He was putting his property before somebody else's life. He said, "This is my car." Mr. Jones asked him, "Look, I'd like you to lend me your car; I'll bring it back." The guy said, "No, I don't trust you."

Student A: Well, he didn't know Mr. Jones; maybe he didn't trust him.

Student D: What did he look like?

Student A: Yeah, I wouldn't trust nobody with my car.

Student H: Well, I would trust him if I knew him. (Confused comments about whether they would or would not trust somebody with their car)

Student B: Would you care if you trust him or not?

Student E: Well, I wouldn't go so far as to beat him up and to take his car. He might still need it. (Conversation on beating up somebody)

Mr. B: So what you're saying is, this man's value, what he thought was most important was his property. His property was more important to him than somebody else's life. You said legally he was right. Right? (Agreement) Can you say morally he was right? (Indistinguishable answers) What do you mean by morally?

Student C: It's—there's not a law but—

Mr. B: What kind of a law may be involved? It's not a legal law; although it may be, it doesn't have to be. What kind of law is it? What were you saying before, about your mother? What did she say?

Student B: God's law.

Mr. B: God's law, what does it say about killing?

Student B: Thou shalt not kill.

Students B and F: God's law is moral law.

Mr. B: What do you mean?

Student B: 'Cause this is the law of his

country and God has moral laws for everybody.

Mr. B: Oh, so what you're saying is—did you listen to what he's saying? Would you repeat what you said? It's very important.

Student B: God's law is for everyone and there's different laws in different countries, so God's law, his moral laws are for everyone.

Student D: God's laws include more people than laws down here, yes.

Mr. B: Now what you're saying is that God's laws are for all people regardless of where you live. And so, they're universal laws, right? They're for the whole universe, is what you're saying. All right. Now you said, from the legal point of view he was right, from a moral point of view he was wrong. He had a legal right to refuse his property but no moral right to do so. Now what about Mr. Jones? Was he justified, from a legal point of view, in beating up the man and taking his car? (Chorus of "no") Why not?

Student B: Because there's a law like that, that guy's car, you know, he can say whatever he likes about it, he has a right to do what he wants with it, but with the moral law [Mr. Jones] was doing pretty good.

Mr. B: He was doing right? do you agree with him? He says that Mr. Jones was doing right from a moral point of view.

Student B: But it still went outside God's law, going against the law. Thou shalt not steal.

Mr. B: So what you're saying is—

Student D: There's a problem. It's still stealing.

Student F: Yes, he should have asked him. If the man said no, that should have been the answer.

Mr. B: Did he have a moral right to beat up the man and take his car? (Chorus of "no") Why not?

Student F: He didn't have no right to do it.

Student B: There's another moral law. . . .

From L. Kohlberg's *Collected Papers* (Cambridge, Mass.; Harvard Graduate School of Education, 1974). Reprinted by permission.

SUMMARY

The theoretical breakthrough provided by Kohlberg revolutionized our understanding of moral development. His work parallels Piaget and Erikson in that it includes specific, age-related stages of growth. Each stage represents a system of thinking defined by how we process moral/ethical and value questions. Each stage is also part of an invariant sequence and represents a qualitatively more comprehensive system of understanding than the previous one.

Kohlberg's framework "emerged" from interviews with his research subjects. By presenting moral dilemmas to people from different backgrounds, he was able to sample the system of reasoning, thinking, and judging—the reasons behind their decision. In analyzing these reasons, Kohlberg formed the six-stage category system. Then he set out to cross-validate the system both cross-sectionally and now longitudinally. Snarey's review has validated the cross-cultural nature of moral development. Recent research has not supported Gilligan's critique of the system as sex-biased.

The stages are defined by the major set of assumptions a person uses to think through, reason, and rationalize or justify an important ethical decision. Each stage is "better" than its preceding one; higher stages take into account an increasingly broader perspective, represent more complex and abstract thought, contain more personal empathy, and "solve" social problems more on the basis of principles. Thus, the direction of the system is highly congruent with the principles of a democratic society—values and ethics based on principles of justice.

There is not an exact one-to-one relationship between moral stage and actual behavior. However, the trends in practically all studies are almost always consistent with the theory—whether it be performance on "cheating" tests or behavior in the Milgram and McNamee studies.

In relating the Kohlberg system to the classroom, the teacher's job is to present or to encourage statements and reasons that are slightly ahead of those of the majority of the class. This means that the teacher must do a great deal of probing, asking clarifying questions, and seeking elaboration of the pupils' thought processes. It also means the teacher has to withhold his or her own judgments and not get overly angry or lecture the pupils. Exhortation, though tempting, is not teaching for moral development.

The teaching for moral development needs to be understood as a slow and complex process. We cannot really accelerate moral development beyond the limits set by the stage concepts. On the other hand, we cannot just sit by and beg the value question.

Undoubtedly the most important aspect of the entire chapter is that it confronts educational psychology with questions of character education in the form of stages of moral maturity. For almost half a century such questions of moral education and general education have been avoided or not considered a legitimate area for inquiry. Kohlberg has changed all that. We now must think through the value questions as part of a developmental sequence.

KEY TERMS AND NAMES

Hugh Hartshorne and Mark May
Lawrence Kohlberg
moral development
invariant sequence
"plus one"

Stanley Milgram
Carol Gilligan
John Snarey
Moshe Blatt

REFERENCES

1. Cremin, L. A. (1957). *The republic and the school* (p. 100). New York: Teachers College Press.

2. Hartshorne, H., and May, M. (1928–1930). *Studies in the nature of character*, Vols. 1, 2, 3. New York: Macmillan.

3. Kohlberg, L., and Candee, D. (1984). The relationship of moral judgment to moral action. In L. Kohlberg (Ed.), *Essays on moral development*, Vol. II (pp. 498–581). New York: Harper & Row.

4. Kohlberg, L. (1969). Stage and sequence: The cognitive-developmental approach to socialization. In D. Goslin (Ed.), *Handbook of socialization theory and research*. New York: Rand McNally.

5. Kohlberg, L. (1975). The cognitive-developmental approach to moral development. *Phi Delta Kappan, 56*(10), 671.

6. Rawls, J. (1971). *A theory of justice.* Cambridge, Mass.: Belknap Press.

7. King, M. L. (1963). Letter from Birmingham jail. In *Why we can't wait* (pp. 84–85). New York: Harper & Row. Copyright © 1963 by Martin Luther King, Jr. Reprinted by permission of Harper & Row, Publishers, Inc.

8. Colby, A., Kohlberg, L., and Gibbs, J. (1979). The measurement of stages of moral judgment. *Final report to the National Institute of Mental Health*. Cambridge, Mass.: Center for Moral Development and Education.

9. Rest, J. R. (1973). Patterns of preference and comprehension in moral judgment. *Journal of Personality, 41*, 86–109.

10. Turiel, E. (1966). An experimental test of the sequentiality of developmental stages in the child's moral judgment. *Journal of Personality and Social Psychology, 3*, 611–618.

11. Rest, J. R. (1973). The hierarchical nature of moral judgment. *Journal of Personality, 41*, 86–109.

12. Kohlberg, L. (1984). The meaning and measurement of moral judgment. In L. Kohlberg (Ed.), *Essays on moral development*, Vol. II (pp. 415–422). New York: Harper & Row.

13. McNamee, S. (1977). Moral behavior, moral development and motivation. *Journal of Moral Education, 7*(1), 27. Reprinted by permission of NFER-NELSON on behalf of the Social Morality Council.

14. Blasi, G. (1980). Bridging moral cognition and moral action. *Psychological Bulletin, 88*(1), 1–45.

15. Sullivan, E., McCullough, G., and Stager, M. (1970). A developmental study of the relationship between conceptual, ego, and moral development. *Child Development, 41,* 399–411.

16. Turiel, E. (1976). A comparative analysis of moral knowledge and moral judgment in males and females. *Journal of Personality, 44,* 195–208. Actually, in this study the females scored higher than males at the outset; the differences disappeared by midadolescence.

17. Gilligan, C. (1982). *In a different voice* (p. 173). Cambridge, Mass.: Harvard University Press.

18. Rest, J. R. (1979). *Development in judging moral issues.* Minneapolis: University of Minnesota Press.

19. Braebeck, M. (1982). Moral judgment: Theory and research on differences between males and females. *Developmental Review, 3,* 274–291.

20. Walker, L. K. (1984). Sex differences in the development of moral reasoning: A critical review. *Child Development, 55,* 677–691.

21. Gilligan, C., Kohlberg, L., Lerner, M., and Belenky, M. (1971). *Moral reasoning about sexual dilemmas: Technical report of the U.S. Commission on Obscenity and Pornography.* Washington, D.C.: U.S. Government Printing Office.

22. Gilligan, C., and Belenky, M. (1980). A naturalistic study of abortion decisions. In R. Selman and R. Yando (Eds.), *Clinical-developmental psychology: New directions for child development*, Vol. 7. San Francisco: Jossey-Bass. In the study Gilligan and Belenky concluded that most women (N = 21) on follow-up "advanced in their moral judgment over the intervening year and reported improvements in life circumstance. . . . A correlation of r = .61 was found between moral development and improvement in life circumstance" (p. 80).

23. The study most frequently cited as evidence of sex bias has been: Holstein, C. B. (1976). Irreversible, stepwise sequence in the development of moral judgment: A longitudinal study of males and females. *Child De-*

velopment, 47, 51–61. The author studied adult males and their spouses. She did not control for occupational level, and the results favored the males. More recently two similar studies were conducted and when higher education/job status were controlled, the sex differences disappeared. See Kohlberg, L. (1984). *Essays on moral development,* Vol. II (p. 348). New York: Harper & Row.

24. See Kohlberg, *Essays* (p. 347).

25. Simpson, E. (1974). Moral development research: A case study of scientific cultural bias. *Human Development, 17,* 81–106.

26. Snarey, J. (1985). Cross-cultural universality of social-moral development. *Psychological Bulletin, 97*(2), 202–232.

27. Kohlberg, *Essays,* Vol. II (p. 123).

28. Thoma, S. (1984). Do moral education programs facilitate moral judgment? A meta-analysis of studies using the Defining Issues Test. *Moral Education Forum, 9*(4), 20–25. See also Leming, J. (1981). Curricular effectiveness in moral/values education: A review of the research. *Journal of Moral Education,*

10(3), 147–164. This article compares the dilemma approach with "values clarification."

29. Berkowitz, M. (1984). Process analysis and the future of moral education. Paper presented at the Annual Meeting of AERA, New Orleans, La., April 23, 1984. See also Berkowitz, M., and Gibbs, J. (1983). Measuring the developmental features of moral discussion. *Merrill-Palmer Quarterly, 29*(4), 399–410.

30. Carnegie-Mellon Civic Education English Curriculum under the direction of Edwin (Ted) Fenton with Linda W. Rosensweig. A senior research associate has created a series of highly interesting and provocative classroom dilemmas in both English and social studies.

31. See R. L. Mosher (1979). *Adolescents' development and education.* Berkeley, Calif.: McCutchan. The "just community" high-school model has been developed both in Brookline, Massachusetts, under the direction of Ralph Mosher, and in Cambridge, Massachusetts, by Kohlberg.

UNIT 2

LEARNING THEORY

8

LEARNING BACKGROUNDS

The study of learning has been at the very heart of psychology, especially American psychology, since its origin about a hundred years ago. During the 1870s the great Harvard psychologist William James discussed the importance of learning, and later he called habit that "enormous fly-wheel of society, its most precious conservative agent. . . . It keeps the fisherman and deckhand at sea through winter; it holds the miner in his darkness. . . . It keeps different social strata from mixing."[1] James felt that learning, especially during childhood, shapes and directs our later lives: "Could the young but realize how soon they will become mere walking bundles of habits, they would give more heed to their conduct while in the plastic state."[2] We might paraphrase James by saying that if society realized how soon its children would become walking bundles of habits, that society would give more heed to the importance of its early childhood education programs.

Though the study of learning has been the core area of American psychology, the pursuit of this study has been anything but serene. Great debates, full of sound and fury, over the nature and process of learning all but shattered the foundation of the fledgling discipline. Some psychologists, rigid behaviorists like John B. Watson, felt that learning involved the patterning of overt responses. Knowledge, to these psychologists, resides in muscular reactions, not in cerebral exercise. As you drive to your favorite ice cream store, it would be your arms and legs that would "know" the route, not your head. These psychologists were correct—to some extent. Certain kinds of learning do occur as a result of response patterning. For example, try explaining to a youngster how to tie a necktie. It is almost impossible to transmit this knowledge through words alone, for it doesn't exist completely at the conceptual level. You will probably find that you have to demonstrate and, even then, you will stand behind the child, since your responses are so restricted and rigid that you can't tie a necktie while facing it. In playing the piano, knowledge of certain intricate passages seems to reside in your fingers. You may have forgotten a certain tune, but after fiddling around on the keys for a few minutes, your fingers suddenly "remember." Or in sports like skiing and golf, despite hours of verbal instruction, you ultimately have to learn a certain "feel," a certain muscular patterning.

Other psychologists, cognitive theorists like Max Wertheimer, Wolfgang Kohler, and Kurt Lewin, felt that learning required thinking and insight. As you drive to your favorite ice cream store, to return to a previous example, your arms and legs wouldn't be any help without a more general cognitive map, probably located in your brain. To the cognitive theorists, teaching children by drill or rote is like training a bunch of parrots. Children really learn only when they discover solutions for themselves, only when they "understand."

ASSOCIATION LEARNING AND COGNITIVE LEARNING

Now that the dust has settled on some of the great theoretical debates of the past, two main schools of thought on learning have emerged, though many variations still exist. These two main schools of thought are association learning and cognitive learning.

Association theorists see learning as the result of connections (associations) between stimuli (sense impressions) and responses. Dogs salivating when they hear the can opener opening their food, babies waving "bye-bye" on cue from their mothers, or fifth-graders saying "seventy-two" to the stimulus "nine times eight" are all examples of association learning. A bond has been formed between two elements, a stimulus and a response.

Cognitive theorists, on the other hand, view learning as a reorganization of a number of perceptions. This reorganization allows the learner to perceive new relationships, solve new problems, and gain a basic understanding of a subject area. A fifth-grader suddenly realizing that multiplication is successive addition; an ape suddenly understanding that by putting two short sticks together, a banana that was out of reach is now obtainable; or an eighth-grader discovering a way to calculate the area of a parallelogram—these are all examples of cognitive learning.

These two views of learning parallel the two sides of another controversy that has historically split the field of psychology: behaviorism versus gestalt psychology. The behaviorists have typically been associationists, whereas the gestaltists have been cognitive theorists.

THE ORIGINS OF LEARNING THEORY: WILLIAM JAMES AND WILHELM WUNDT

It must be remembered that psychology as a separate discipline was a product of the late nineteenth century. Its origins are philosophy and physiology. For example, many philosophical overtones are apparent in the work of the first major American psychologist, William James. In fact, James had great difficulty deciding whether to cast his lot with philosophy or with psychology, being first in one deparment and then in the other at Harvard. And this vacillation occurred in spite of the fact that he created Harvard's psychology department.

Wilhelm Wundt, who set up the first experimental psychology laboratory in Europe around 1879, was also strongly influenced by philosophy. However, he was influenced by physiology as well, having begun his career as a physician and having later become a physiologist. Like the philosophers who preceded him, Wundt was interested in studying conscious experience, and he sought to do this by analyzing consciousness into its smallest components. He was looking for the basic elements of psychology, the smallest parts of analyzable consciousness. This was analogous to the physicists having, at roughly the same time in history, constructed the atomic table. As physics had its elements, so, too, thought Wundt, would psychology. Wundt felt that by analyzing consciousness into these tiny elements, or "atoms," he could make psychology as respectable a science as physics.

The main thesis of Wundt's work was that these basic elements of the mind are connected through association; that is, the mind is composed of individual elements, or atoms of experience, linked by associations. The problem was to ferret out these elements for study. To accomplish this, Wundt used the technique of introspection. He trained subjects to look within themselves and report all their most fleeting and minute feelings and sensations.[3] Both behaviorism and gestalt psychology began in reaction to Wundt; he set the stage for the great controversy to come.

The Gestaltists Attack Wundt

A group of psychologists, led by Max Werthei-mer, got together around 1910 at the University of Frankfurt and began the school of psychology known as gestalt psychology.* The gestaltists felt that Wundt had led psychology down the primrose path—that in order to produce his neat atomic chart of psychology, Wundt had lost sight of the reality of human experience. They felt that by analyzing experience into its small-est parts, Wundt had, in effect, destroyed the total experience. He was like a musician analyz-ing each note separately and never hearing the melody. "The whole is more than the sum of its parts," thundered Wertheimer. You must study the whole, the totality, the entire config-uration, or, to use the German word, the *Gestalt*. The gestaltists felt that the study of the associ-ations formed between tiny elements, whether they are elements of consciousness or stimuli-response connections, is misleading. It is mis-leading because elements often act and look dif-ferently when they are taken out of context. For example, Wertheimer would say that if you were to study each frame in a motion picture, you would never see movement, which is what a motion picture is all about.

The Behaviorists Attack Wundt

The school of behaviorism was born under the impetus of John B. Watson at Johns Hopkins University. The behaviorists attacked Wundt be-cause of his use of introspection as a scientific tool. The behaviorists believed in elements, all right, but they didn't like the way Wundt went about finding them. In the now classic paper, "Psychology as the Behaviorist Views It," Wat-son proclaimed that behavior is the real data of psychology.[4] According to Watson, introspec-tion is as useless to psychology as it would be to chemistry or physics. The only thing that is really observable and therefore the only thing that really allows for the use of the scientific method is the subject's overt behavior. Watson also announced to the world what would and what would not be proper areas for psycholo-gists to study. If consciousness can be studied only through introspection, and if it has no be-havioral correlates, then throw it out of psy-chology. As we have seen, Watson was not one to equivocate.

Behaviorists and Gestaltists Attack Each Other

Although these two powerful schools of psy-chology began by fighting independent battles with Wundt, the scene of battle soon shifted and they began fighting each other. Watson fell in with a powerful ally, Ivan Pavlov, the Russian whose work on the conditioned reflex was being recognized at about the same time Watson was preparing for combat. Watson found just what he needed when he needed it—the con-ditioned reflex, something observable to replace Wundt's nonobservable elements. Watson soon felt that all learning could be explained on the basis of conditioning, that is, the association of stimuli with responses. A new unit of analysis had been found that was both observable and consistent with the principle of association. Watson was ready to take over American psy-chology, and through his direct influence and through the indirect influence of those who followed—Edwin Guthrie, Clark Hull, E. L. Thorndike,* and B. F. Skinner—Watson cer-tainly did manage to shape and direct the course American psychology was to take. Learning was a matter of accumulating a series of stimulus-response associations. There is no need to study insight, or even thinking in the traditional sense, for conditioning pretty much explains it all.

The gestaltists did not agree. Wertheimer, and later Kohler and Lewin, felt that learning could not be dissected into little stimulus-re-sponse associations and still be consistent with what they saw as reality. Children could be con-ditioned ad nauseam, trained to recite the mul-tiplication tables, the state capitals, the major agricultural products of each country—but without insight or real understanding, the in-formation would be virtually useless. According to the gestaltists, if you want children to learn nonsense, go ahead and condition them; but if

---

* Schools of psychology refer to schools of thought, not specific colleges and universities.

* Even though some of Thorndike's writings predate Wat-son's, Watson's influence on Thorndike became very pow-erful.

In his work on the conditioned reflex, the Russian Ivan Pavlov provided Watson with evidence to support his contention that learning was the result of associations between stimuli and responses. Pavlov discovered the phenomenon of the conditioned reflex in the course of his research on his major interest, the digestive ability of dogs. He won a Nobel Prize in 1904.

you want them to learn meaningful relationships, then a different approach is needed—a cognitive approach.

Hermann Ebbinghaus: The Pioneer

The experimental study of learning had quiet beginnings. In Germany during the 1880s, Hermann Ebbinghaus carried out the first of these studies, pioneering work that eventually earned him the title "father of learning psychology." Because he wanted to study learning in its pure form, he had to control for the influence of meaningfulness. In order to do this Ebbinghaus used long lists of nonsense syllables (cav, lek, pum, etc.) which, he felt, allowed him to control for difficulty. Since many words have past associations or inherent interest, they might be easier to learn than others, whereas all lists of nonsense syllables would be of comparable difficulty and would have to be learned from

Ebbinghaus hoped to lay the basis for a scientific study of learning by memorizing long lists of nonsense syllables and then measuring his retention capacity. His pioneering research on learning earned him the title of "father of learning psychology."

scratch. Ebbinghaus was his own subject and he spent many hours learning these meaningless words. His work led him to draw two major conclusions:

1. Once something is learned, it is not forgotten at an even rate. Most of what is forgotten is lost very quickly, and the rest is lost at a slow and fairly stable rate.

2. In order to learn new material, it is more efficient to space practice than to mass it. For example, if you had one hour to learn something, you would retain more by taking four fifteen-minute practice sessions spread over a few days, than by spending one full hour working without a break.[5]

The results of these studies, although interesting to the learning theorist, have limited practical use in the classroom. Laws governing the learning of meaningless information may not be generalized to the learning of meaningful material. Material learned in the classroom should be meaningful, though unfortunately students are still being made to memorize vocabulary, passages from poems, and grammatical rules—material that may be no more meaningful to them than the nonsense syllables were to Ebbinghaus.

The Associationists Versus The Gestaltists

We now turn to a discussion of how the association learning and cognitive learning positions were formed and eventually translated into action. We begin with those theories that dominated the first half of the twentieth century, spotlighting the early associationists Thorndike, Pavlov, and Guthrie, in that order. Watson, though not singled out for independent coverage in this section, is intermittently mentioned in the discussions of the other three. Watson's influence on the early behaviorist-associationist movement was very significant.

The discussion of the early cognitive theorists focuses on Wertheimer and Kohler, two gestaltists who made important contributions to our current knowledge of cognitive learning. In Chapter 9 we examine in some detail the two current spokesmen for each position: B. F. Skin-

Ebbinghaus's retention curve. Most of the learned material is lost very rapidly and the rest more and more slowly.

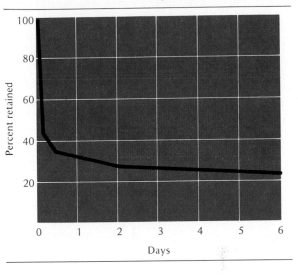

ner and Jerome Bruner. The present chapter provides a background for appreciating the significance of Skinner and Bruner in education today.

THE EARLY ASSOCIATION THEORISTS

E. L. Thorndike

In 1899 Edward Lee Thorndike published a paper entitled "Animal Intelligence" and thereby was catapulted to the forefront of the emerging field of learning psychology. From his headquarters at Columbia Teachers College, Thorndike issued his concepts and laws of learning for many years thereafter. For most of the first half of the twentieth century, he was truly Mr. Educational Psychology in the United States. His studies of cats learning to escape from puzzle boxes are now legendary.

Thorndike viewed learning as a series of stimulus-response (S-R) connections, or bonds. His theory of learning described the ways in which these S-R connections could be strengthened or weakened. He felt that learning was basically a trial-and-error enterprise, and he paid little attention to the possibility of concept formation or thinking.[6]

The three major laws   Thorndike postulated three major laws of learning:

1. *The law of readiness.*   When an organism is in a state in which the conduction units (S-R connections) are ready to conduct, then the conduction is satisfying. If the conduction unit is not ready to conduct, then conduction is annoying. Thorndike was speaking here of a brief, neurological readiness, not the kind of maturational readiness that, as we saw in Chapter 4, was of concern to Myrtle McGraw. Thorndike was referring to a more momentary phenomenon, a kind of neurologically teachable moment.[1]

2. *The law of exercise.*   This law, also called the law of use and disuse, states that the more an S-R connection is used, the stronger it will become; the less it is used, the weaker it will become. This law is obviously based on the old maxim about practice making perfect. Thorndike, especially in his later writings, made it clear that practice led to improvement only when it was followed by positive feedback or reward. Blind practice, with no knowledge of the consequences of the act, had no effect on learning.

3. *The law of effect.*   This was by far Thorndike's most important law. It states that when an S-R connection is followed by satisfaction (reward), the connection is strengthened. Also, if the connection is followed by annoyance (punishment), it is weakened. In later years Thorndike played down the importance of the second part of the law. In fact, he changed his mind about the significance of punishment as a means of weakening learned associations. He came to feel that reward strengthened learning far more than punishment weakened it. His evidence for changing his position on this issue was, to say the least, rather flimsy. It was based on a study of symbolic reward and punishment, where the reward consisted of saying "Right" to the student and the punishment consisted of saying "Wrong." The results might have been quite different if the reward had been a candy bar and the punishment a mild electric shock.

There is no doubt that Thorndike had a dehumanizing effect on American education. His first work involved the study of how cats solve problems. He saw little basic difference between

Thorndike first stressed the importance of motivation in learning, an aspect overlooked by Ebbinghaus.

animal and human learning—never mind the qualitative differences in learning that Piaget insists occur at different periods during human development. Thorndike spread a kind of mechanical-person gospel that viewed animals and children as akin to robots.

His contribution to education, however, cannot be minimized. He was, through his law of effect, the first psychologist to stress the importance of motivation in learning. When an individual is rewarded for learning, then learning is far more apt to occur. This aspect of learning seems to have been overlooked by Ebbinghaus. Since he was so close to his experiments (he was, after all, his own subject), Ebbinghaus could hardly take note of his own fantastically high motivation. If you have any doubts about the strength of Ebbinghaus's motivation, try spending a few months doing virtually nothing but learning lists of nonsense syllables.

In addition to stressing the importance of motivation in learning, Thorndike also made much of another crucial concept, that of transfer. His law of identical elements specified that the learner is better able to confront new problems if these new problems contain elements similar to those the learner has already mastered. This, after all, is largely what schooling is all about. If we learned how to use an encyclopedia while we were in school, we are more likely now to be able to diagnose what is wrong with our car by looking it up in our owner's manual, or to prepare a gourmet meal from the directions in a cookbook, or to plan an advertising campaign by making use of appropriate library resources. Transfer will be discussed in greater depth in the next chapter.

Ivan Pavlov

The laboratory work of the Russian physiologist Ivan Pavlov was of great importance to the study of learning. Though most modern physiological psychologists consider his theory of the neurological process of learning a historical curio, his laboratory techniques and findings are still of great significance. In 1904 Pavlov won the Nobel Prize in medicine for his work on the digestive activity of dogs. His lasting fame, however, resulted from what at the time were incidental and chance observations regarding digestion in his dogs. Pavlov noted that the dogs salivated not only when meat powder was placed directly in their mouths, but also well before that (for example, when they heard the trainer's footsteps coming down the stairs). Pavlov later coined the term "conditioned reflex" to describe this phenomenon.[7]

A reflex must have an identifiable stimulus that automatically elicits the response, even though no learning has occurred. For example, when a bright light shines directly into a person's eyes, the pupils automatically contract. No learning or training is required for this to occur. Similarly, when food is placed in a dog's mouth, salivation automatically occurs. Reflexes are therefore directly caused by an unconditioned stimulus (UCS), much as pulling the trigger of a loaded gun automatically causes the gun to fire.

Pavlov also noted that if a neutral stimulus—one that does not elicit a certain response—is repeatedly paired with an unconditioned stimulus—one that does automatically elicit a certain response—the neutral stimulus will eventually take on the power to elicit the response. This is now called "classical conditioning," and an example will illustrate. When meat powder is placed directly in a dog's mouth, the dog automatically salivates. This is a reflex action and does not have to be learned. However, if a 2,000-cycle tone is presented immediately before the meat powder, the tone soon comes to evoke the salivation. Through association with the meat powder, the tone begins to act as a signal that meat powder will follow, and the dog eventually learns to respond to the signal the same way it used to respond only to the meat powder. Technically, the meat powder is called the "unconditioned stimulus" (UCS), since responding to it does not depend on prior experience or learning. The tone or signal is called the "conditioned stimulus" (CS), since the response to it must be learned. For the same reasons, salivating to the meat powder is called the "unconditioned response" (UCR), and salivating to the tone is called the "conditioned response" (CR).

When John B. Watson studied the acquisition of fear in the baby Albert, this was the technique he used (see Chapter 2). When Watson first presented Albert with a white rat, Albert showed no sign of fear. Then Watson struck a steel bar right beside Albert's head, and this loud sound (unconditioned stimulus) automatically made Albert cry (unconditioned response). After repeated pairings of the white rat and the loud sound, Albert began crying as soon as the rat came in view, even when he heard no loud sound. The rat (conditioned stimulus) took on the power to elicit the crying (conditioned response). Note that the conditioned and unconditioned responses are the same: salivation in the case of Pavlov's dogs and crying in the case of Watson's baby. The difference is what brings them about. The conditioned response is one that is elicited by a stimulus that has to be learned through association.

One reason educators must know about conditioning is that a great number of autonomic reflexes can be conditioned while the child is still in school. Just as Albert was conditioned to fear a rat, so the schoolchild may be conditioned to fear math, science, spelling, or any other school subject. Autonomic responses, such as sweating, rapid heartbeat, or general feelings of anxiety, may be conditioned by certain cues that come to be associated with various aspects of the school setting. Children who have been conditioned to such an extent that they are literally paralyzed by fear at the mere sight of a math problem are unlikely to be able to learn much math. They might sincerely try to learn the subject, but because of a great and crippling discomfort, they are not able to.

This is not to say that teachers deliberately create these fears, but they can unwittingly set the stage for such conditioning. For example, a math problem is presented, followed by some other action of the teacher that may already be associated in the child's past experience with feelings of tension, and now the math problem itself triggers autonomic reactions of anxiety on the part of the child. After a few associations of this kind, the mere presentation of the math problem (CS) begins to elicit anxiety (CR). Sometimes this process occurs because teachers themselves have a conditioned fear of math and unwittingly transmit it to their students in the form of scolding, bullying, or a generally "uptight" approach to learning the subject.

Stimulus generalization   Pavlov found that reflex conditioning had some extremely impor-

tant by-products. For example, once a dog was conditioned to salivate to a 2,000-cycle tone, it would also salivate to a 1,300- or 2,700-cycle tone, even though these new stimuli were never used in training. In other words, once a given conditioned stimulus is associated with a reflex, other similar stimuli also take on the power to elicit the response. This is called stimulus generalization. The original conditioned stimulus becomes generalized, and the organism begins responding to other stimuli that are in some way similar to the original one. Once Watson's young subject, Albert, was conditioned to fear the rat, he was also afraid of a Santa Claus mask, a sealskin coat, human hair, a dog, a rabbit, and cotton wool. The point is, reflex conditioning has wide-ranging effects. A child who is conditioned to fear math problems may generalize this fear to many other school subjects, perhaps even the entire school situation. Phobic reactions can be understood in this way. Suppose an unruly child is punished by being locked in a closet. The conditioned stimulus might be generalized so that the child becomes fearful of any enclosed area. The result, claustrophobia, could carry over into adulthood, and the person so afflicted might live a severely restricted life.

Pavlov found that the only way to break the association between a conditioned stimulus and a conditioned response was through a process called "extinction." Extinction is achieved when the CS loses its power to evoke the CR; it is accomplished by repeatedly presenting the CS without following it with the UCS. If the 2,000-cycle tone is consistently presented without the meat powder, the dog eventually stops salivating when he hears it. It is important to note that for extinction to occur, the conditioned stimulus must be repeatedly presented by itself. Unfortunately, when the conditioned reflex is fear, the afflicted individual naturally avoids the conditioned stimulus, and extinction is never allowed to occur. Joseph Wolpe, a famous psychotherapist, uses techniques of classical conditioning and extinction in treating phobias.

Edwin Guthrie

The last of the early associationists we will cover here is Edwin Guthrie. Guthrie was the behaviorist-associationist par excellence. Following directly in Watson's footsteps, he rejected any psychological concepts that might have "mentalistic" overtones. He postulated one law of learning: learning by association or, as he called it, "contiguity." According to Guthrie, if a certain stimulus (or pattern of stimuli) is followed by a response, then the next time that stimulus appears, the same response will follow. That's all there is to it—stimuli and responses in sequence. There is no need to call on reward, reinforcement, or "effect" in order to explain how learning occurs. He also believed that learning occurs the first time the stimulus and response become associated.[8]

To create conditions that will promote learning, Guthrie believed that the teacher should provide the stimulus and the student should respond. For example, the teacher might point to a map and the students would then reply with the name of the city. The important thing is for the appropriate stimulus to be presented before the desired response occurs.

A frenzied mother once brought her child to Guthrie. The child had been in the habit, on coming home from school, of opening the door of his home, taking off his coat, and throwing it on the floor. The mother told Guthrie that no matter how many times she told her child to pick up the coat and hang it in the closet, the child continued this behavior. Guthrie did not reach for any deep psychological explanation, like finding out what throwing the coat on the floor symbolized, what it "meant" to the child. He simply told the mother to rearrange the stimulus-response sequence. When the child throws his coat on the floor, he should not be told to hang it up. He should instead be told to put the coat on, go back outside, come through the door and, only then, hang up the coat. Thus hanging up the coat could become a response to the stimulus of entering the house, rather than to the stimulus of the mother's command, "Take your coat off the floor and hang it up."

The advice apparently worked, for from then on the child hung up his coat correctly. Fortunately for Guthrie, and especially for the child, a longer sequence of S-R associations did not form. That is, according to Guthrie's system, the child might have forever learned to come home, open the door, throw the coat on the floor, pick it up, put it on, go back outside, come back in, then hang up the coat!

THE EARLY COGNITIVE THEORISTS

Max Wertheimer

Max Wertheimer, as noted earlier, founded the school of psychology called gestaltism, or configurationism. Wertheimer insisted that it was useless to study small parts of psychological concepts, like perception or learning. Studying parts in isolation was unjustified, because changing any single part necessarily changes the whole. Similarly, the whole may remain, even when all the parts have changed. For example, if we play a tune in two different keys, even though the individual notes are different each time, the tune retains its integrity.

Wertheimer was concerned with the way children learn, particularly in school. He was against the use of rote memorization, especially when it so often seemed to be an end in itself. Above all else, he wanted children to achieve understanding, to have insight into the nature of the problem.

Wertheimer explained that there are two kinds of solutions to problems, type A and type B. Type A solutions are those that use originality and insight, whereas type B solutions are those that make use of past associations in a rigid, inappropriate way. Wertheimer used the example of teaching a child how to find the area of a parallelogram (see Figure 8.1).

The child is first taught how to find the area of a rectangle, not by memorizing the formula but by understanding why the formula works. The rectangle is divided into smaller squares, and the child sees that the total area is composed of the number of squares in a row times the number of rows. Wertheimer then cut a parallelogram out of paper and asked the child to determine its area. Some children persisted in multiplying the length times the height, a type B solution. Others used type A solutions, like cutting off one of the triangular ends and fitting

MAX WERTHEIMER

Max Wertheimer was born in Prague in 1880, the son of a schoolteacher. As a student, young Wertheimer's interests were far ranging. He studied law for awhile, then switched to philosophy, and finally began to study psychology. After attending a number of schools and universities, Wertheimer received his Ph.D. degree at Wurzburg in 1904. For the next six years he continued his work in psychology at Prague, Vienna, and Berlin.

Wertheimer had been schooled in the structuralist psychological tradition, which held that all psychological phenomena could be broken down and analyzed into their smallest parts or elements. In 1910, while traveling by train from Vienna to a Rhineland vacation resort, Wertheimer was suddenly struck by an idea. He began to ponder this structuralistic viewpoint, and the more he pondered, the more he doubted. Suddenly he decided to forget his planned vacation and left the train at Frankfurt. He rushed to the nearest toy store and purchased a child's stroboscope.

This was in the days before motion pictures, and a stroboscope was a device that, when turned at a constant speed, exposed a series of still pictures that appeared to move. In his hotel room Wertheimer examined his new purchase. He spun the stroboscope, fascinated by the apparent movement that the device produced, and in one of the history of psychology's great examples of insight, thought, "Aha, Wundt and the structuralists must be wrong." Here was a psychological perception, apparent movement, which simply could not be explained or understood by analyzing the individual still pictures. When the elements of this perception were studied individually, the total phenomenon of perceived movement was lost. The whole must be more than just the sum of its parts. In order to understand this perception of movement, one had to study all the parts together in their particular *Gestalt*, a German word that means whole, or totality, or configuration.

Wertheimer went to the University of Frankfurt and began a series of controlled experiments. His first subject was Wolfgang Kohler, who was later joined by Kurt Koffka. Early in 1912 Wertheimer explained to Kohler and Koffka the results and meaning of his studies. Gestalt psychology had been born. Both Kohler and Koffka became zealous advocates of this new school of thought, and both went on to produce many experiments, articles, and books in support of it. Both became famous gestalt psychologists in their own right.

In 1912 Wertheimer published his now famous article, "Experimental Studies of the Perception of Movement." As a result of this single, revolutionary article, a tremendous new movement in psychology was under way, and thousands of articles and books were written and are still being written on this important subject.

In 1916 Wertheimer joined the faculty at the University of Berlin, where he worked with another soon-to-be-famous gestalt psychologist, Kurt Lewin. In 1933 Wertheimer came to the United States, where he taught at the New School for Social Research in New York City. He remained at the New School until his death in 1943.

Wertheimer was a man with a cause, but he was not arrogant or authoritarian. He was a gentle, warm, deep-thinking man. He had a close personal relationship with Albert Einstein, and he was deeply concerned with the social and ethical issues of his times.

Wertheimer was also interested in education and the techniques of good teaching. He pointed out the importance of gestalt principles as they apply to learning in the classroom. He criticized the use of repetition and rote memorization, explaining that such procedures lead only to blind, nonproductive learning on the part of students. He insisted that educators should teach for understanding, and this is made possible when the teacher arranges the material so that the student can see the "whole," or the *Gestalt*, and not just a series of seemingly unrelated parts. In his book *Productive Thinking*, Wertheimer stressed the importance of gestalt theory in the practical problem of educating children.

Whereas Watson and Guthrie were concerned with overt responses, stressing always what the student *did*, Wertheimer placed his emphasis on the child's process of mental organization, stressing instead what the student *understood*.

FIGURE 8.1 Wertheimer's parallelogram problem. Part A shows Wertheimer's way of explaining why the area of a rectangle equals the product of length times width, in this case sixteen by five. Part B shows the parallelogram for which he asked subjects to find the area. Part C shows one person's solution to the problem—cutting off one end, moving it to the other end, and thus converting the parallelogram into a rectangle.

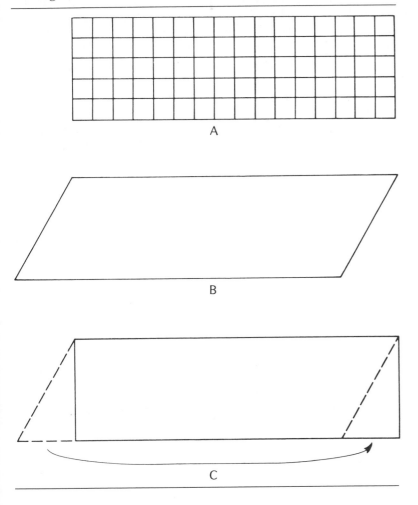

A

B

C

it against the other end. At this point, the child had created a rectangle and could correctly utilize the previously learned formula. Another type A solution involved bending the parallelogram into a loop with the two angular ends abutting each other, then making one vertical cut which would also create a rectangle. The children using type A solutions had obviously discovered a real geometric relationship.[9]

Wolfgang Kohler

Wolfgang Kohler, who had worked with Wertheimer at the University of Frankfurt, spent a few years during World War I on the island of Tenerife off the coast of Africa. There he performed gestalt psychology's most famous animal studies. Kohler arranged an ape's cage so that there were bananas hanging from the top and a couple of boxes on the floor. In order to reach the bananas, the ape had to stack one box on top of another and then climb to the top. The ape's solution to the problem appeared to Kohler not to be one of blind trial and error. Instead, the ape seemed to size up the situation and then, almost in a flash, it understood the problem and "saw" the solution. The ape displayed what Kohler called insight, and Kohler felt that this was more typical of learning, especially human learning, than Thorndike's concept of blind trial and error.

In another experiment, Kohler put food outside the cage, beyond even an ape's long reach. Inside the cage, however, there were some sticks. At first the apes would throw the sticks at the banana. Then they "realized" that by using the stick as a kind of tool they could reach out and rake the banana in. One especially intelligent ape, named Sultan, was even able to join two short sticks together to rake the food in.

Kohler's explanation was that the apes were able to see the problem as a unified whole. In the box-stacking problem, the ape did not see the boxes and bananas as separate elements but came to realize that they belonged together as part of a whole. Similarly, the sticks and bananas were perceived as belonging together, and it was only after this reorganization of perceptions that insight into the solution to the problem occurred.

Insight has been called the "a-ha" phenomenon. Kohler made much of the concept of insight, perhaps too much. He felt that insight learning did not depend on past experience, that it was not just a special case of transfer. As we shall see in a later chapter, Harry Harlow's studies on learning sets have since cast some doubt on the validity of Kohler's interpretation.

NEW DIRECTIONS IN PSYCHOLOGY AND EDUCATION

You may now be wondering why nobody tried to bridge the gap between the two learning theory traditions, for both positions evidently have some merit. The behaviorists did have a strong case for insisting that overt responses are the appropriate data for psychology. If you were trying to judge people's attitudes toward some

issue, you would, in all probability, be more influenced by what they did than by what they said. For example, if your boss constantly bragged of being an equal opportunity employer and yet never hired black applicants, you might rightly feel that "actions speak louder than words."

Yet you probably feel equally sure that the gestaltists also had a good case; learning, understanding, discovering new relationships must be more than just the mere conditioning of certain responses. Some reorganization of perceptions, something going on within the organism, must account for understanding and discovery.

In fact, some psychologists did attempt to bridge the gap. E. C. Tolman, for example, produced a theory called purposive behaviorism. It was called purposive because Tolman insisted that, far from being random and chaotic, learning was goal directed. The learning organism is a striving organism, striving to give meaning to behavior. Yet Tolman's theory was also behavioristic because he believed that scientific validity could be achieved only by observing objective behavior.

Tolman stated that both rats and humans learn by forming cognitive maps of their environment.[10] This explains how organisms get from place to place. They form hypotheses, see relationships, and then select out appropriate responses on the basis of their cognitive maps. Although Tolman did not emphasize stimulus-response connections as the basic units of analysis, he was still an associationist because he saw learning as a result of bonds formed among a number of stimuli. The learner forms an association between some new stimulus, or sign, and a previously encountered and therefore meaningful stimulus, or significate. Tolman's behaviorism is therefore an S-S (sign-significate) psychology, rather than a Watsonian S-R psychology.

Tolman was more responsive to the work of the developmental psychologists than were most of the other behaviorists. He postulated his famous H-A-T-E variables (Heredity, Age, Training, Endocrine) as of crucial importance in understanding and predicting behavior. Heredity sets certain limits on what environmental manipulation can accomplish. Age determines how much impact training can have. Training is, of course, vital, since learning cannot occur in a static environment. Endocrine, or internal physiological, factors also play an important role in learning. Thus Tolman, perhaps more than any other learning theorist, understood the importance of individual differences. Recent studies, such as those by David Krech, have shown how strong the relationships between training variables and the internal physiology of the organism are.[11]

With all its sophistication and thoroughness, Tolman's system never really caught on in education. Tolman never exerted the influence on teachers that Thorndike or Watson did. Though he may be rediscovered in the next decade, and in the long run may have more influence than Thorndike, this is not yet the case.

Why was Tolman so ignored by the field of education during his lifetime? There are a number of reasons, but it is primarily because he never translated theory into practice. The teacher might learn from Tolman that a rat at a choice-point in a maze hypothesizes a solution before acting, but this hardly helps the teacher in the classroom. The teacher wants answers to specific questions regarding learning and discipline in the classroom, not sophisticated and elegant theorizing. Further, Tolman failed to develop his theory to its fullest potential. He didn't do enough experiments to make his cognitive position firm enough to generate precise predictions. As Winfred Hill, a modern expert in the field of learning, has said of Tolman, "His system is more a road sign or a pious hope than it is an accomplished fact."[12]

And so educational psychology turned away from the old-line theorists and turned toward psychology's "new breed" theorists, psychologists who talked to teachers, who told teachers what to do in given situations, who told teachers how to produce desired behavior changes or set up conditions that aid discovery. Educational psychology turned to B. F. Skinner and Jerome Bruner.

SUMMARY

The study of learning has been of utmost importance in psychology for over a century. Though psychologists agreed on the importance of learning as an object of study, they disagreed on the mechanics of how the learning process occurred.

The major schools of thought were:

1. *Behaviorist-associationists:* those who viewed learning as resulting from the forming of connections between stimuli and observable responses

2. *Cognitive-gestaltists:* those who believed that learning resulted from the reorganization of perceptions and the forming of new relationships

Both the behaviorists and the gestaltists began their schools of thought as reactions to Wundt's associationist-introspectionist brand of psychology. The gestaltists, led by Wertheimer, challenged Wundt's associationist position, while the behaviorists, led by Watson, attacked Wundt's use of introspection.

Wertheimer and the gestaltists argued that psychological phenomena could not be understood by studying simple associations among tiny elements but must be viewed as a total configuration or, to use the German word, as a *Gestalt.* Wertheimer argued that the whole is more than just the sum of a group of separate parts. Learning was seen as the understanding of a total, meaningful relationship, and the only acceptable approach to the study of learning was a cognitive one. Watson and the behaviorists, although not objecting to the study of separate parts, did denounce Wundt's use of introspection. Watson argued that the only true scientific data in the field of psychology were observable responses. Thus, if a concept such as "consciousness" could not be seen, touched, or observed in any way, it should be thrown out of psychology. Watson believed that learning could be thoroughly understood on the basis of Pavlov's principles of classical conditioning.

The first experimental studies of learning were conducted by Ebbinghaus during the late nineteenth century. In order to control for past associations, Ebbinghaus studied the learning of nonsense syllables. He discovered that the forgetting of learned material does not occur at an even rate, that most of what is forgotten occurs very quickly, and that the rate of forgetting eventually slows down to a fairly even pace.

Thorndike, an early associationist, posited three major laws of learning: (1) the law of readiness, showing the importance of neurological anticipation; (2) the law of exercise, showing the importance of practice; and (3) the law of effect, indicating the importance of motivation.

Pavlov, a Russian physiologist, discovered some lawful relationships between stimuli and responses. He showed how learning could take place through conditioning, a trained association among stimuli and a certain response. Pavlov's system is now called "classical conditioning" and applies only to reflex activity. Pavlov also introduced such concepts as extinction, stimulus generalization, and discrimination learning.

Guthrie, a psychologist in the behaviorist-associationist tradition, felt that all learning was a result of stimuli and responses in sequence. Guthrie saw no need to use concepts such as motivation or reinforcement to explain learning.

Wertheimer, the first of the cognitive-gestalt psychologists, was concerned with how the learner achieved understanding and insight when confronted with a problem. He felt that rote memorization did not lead to real understanding.

Kohler, also of the cognitive-gestalt school, performed several important animal studies. Kohler's studies on apes led him to conclude that learning was a result of a series of insightful solutions, not blind trial and error.

Tolman attempted to bridge the gap between behaviorists and gestaltists by creating a type of psychology called "purposive behaviorism." Tolman thought that striving toward a goal gave meaning to the resulting behavior. Learning occurs when a new stimulus (or sign) is associated with a previously encountered and therefore meaningful stimulus (significate).

The two basic positions, behaviorist-associationist and cognitive-gestaltist, have their contemporary proponents in B. F. Skinner and Jerome Bruner. Skinner (the behaviorist) and Bruner (the cognitive theorist) are especially important in educational psychology today, for each devotes a great deal of time to talking directly to the classroom teacher.

KEY TERMS AND NAMES

learning
  stimulus-response learning
  cognitive learning
Wilhelm Wundt
  introspection
gestalt psychology
behaviorism
Hermann Ebbinghaus
Edward L. Thorndike
  law of readiness
  law of exercise
  law of effect

Ivan Pavlov
  classical conditioning
  unconditioned stimulus
  conditioned stimulus
  unconditioned response
  conditioned response
  conditioning
  extinction
Edwin Guthrie
Max Wertheimer
Wolfgang Kohler
  insight
E. C. Tolman

REFERENCES

1. James, W. (1890). *The principles of psychology* (p. 79). New York: Henry Holt.

2. James, *The principles of psychology* (p. 83).

3. Wundt. W. (1910). *Physiological psychology,* 5th ed. New York: Macmillan.

4. Watson, J. B. (1913). Psychology as the behaviorist views it. *Psychological Review, 20,* 158–177.

5. Ebbinghaus, H. (1913). *Memory: A contribution to experimental psychology,* trans. by H. A. Ruger and C. E. Bussenius. New York: Teachers College.

6. Thorndike, E. L. (1898). Animal intelligence. *Psychological Review, Monograph Supplement, 2,* No. 8.

7. Pavlov, I. P. (1927). *Conditioned reflexes.* London: Oxford University Press.

8. Guthrie, E. R. (1935). *The psychology of learning.* New York: Harper.

9. Wertheimer, M. (1945). *Productive thinking.* New York: Harper.

10. Tolman, E. C. (1948). Cognitive maps in rats and men. *Psychological Review, 55,* 1–4.

11. Krech, D. (1969). The chemistry of learning. In R. C. Sprinthall and N. A. Sprinthall, *Educational Psychology: Selected Readings* (pp. 152–156). New York: Van Nostrand-Reinhold.

12. Hill, W. F. (1971). *Learning: A survey of psychological interpretations* (p. 129). Scranton, Pa.: Chandler.

9

LEARNING THEORY TODAY

Now that we have had a look at some of the positions learning theorists have taken over the years, you may be questioning whether there is anything in all these theories for you, the future classroom teacher. If the study of learning is so complicated as to have generated so many different and often conflicting explanations, how can the prospective teacher begin to understand the learning process, let alone stand up in front of a roomful of children and help them learn? Is the study of learning really as complicated as the controversies that we have outlined seem to indicate?

Part of the reason there are so many theoretical positions is that learning means so many different things—from a child memorizing a poem, to a rat finding its way through a maze, to a baby trying to imitate an adult saying "bye-bye," a smoker choosing one brand of cigarettes over another, a teen-age boy fearing and thus avoiding all contact sports, a young geometry student suddenly seeing the solution of a difficult problem, and on and on. Almost all our thoughts and behavior have been learned. Learning may be adaptive or maladaptive, conscious or unconscious, overt or covert. Feelings and attitudes are learned just as certainly as facts and skills. Learning means so many different things that controversies sometimes result merely because different theorists are studying different aspects of learning. Like the blind men feeling the elephant, each one describes only that part with which he happens to come in contact. And yet, our present knowledge of learning is neither so incomplete nor so complicated that the classroom teacher can't profit from it. There are scientific principles of learning that can be translated into classroom use in order to make learning more efficient and productive.

In this chapter the spotlight falls on two contemporary theorists, B. F. Skinner and Jerome Bruner. Each has a different philosophical lineage: Skinner is today's most eloquent behaviorist-associationist; Bruner is the most influential cognitive-gestaltist. Each also has a great deal to say to the practicing classroom teacher. Part of the problem in the past was that some learning theorists were of virtually no help to the educator. It may have been glorious to contemplate the elegance of Clark Hull's "oscillation of

BURRHUS FREDERICK SKINNER

B. F. Skinner was born in Susquehanna, Pennsylvania, in 1904. His father was a lawyer in Susquehanna, and young Skinner attended the local schools, graduating from high school in 1922. He then went to Hamilton College in New York, where he majored in English and also took several courses in Greek. In 1926 he graduated from Hamilton and was awarded the coveted Hawley Greek Prize.

During his senior year in college, Skinner had written some poetry which he sent to Robert Frost for comment and evaluation. Frost's response was so flattering that, following college graduation, Skinner took time out to do some serious writing. He was not pleased with the result. Says Skinner of this experience, "I discovered the unhappy fact that I had nothing to say, and went on to graduate study in psychology, hoping to remedy that shortcoming." And remedy it he apparently did, for Skinner has not been at a loss for something to say ever since.

The young Skinner showed an early interest in utopian societies. He had been born only a short distance from where Joseph Smith had written the *Book of Mormon*, and as a young man he had read Thoreau's *Walden Pond*—a book about getting away from the world as it is and creating one of your own.

In 1928 Skinner entered Harvard, where he found himself attracted to the ideas of John B. Watson. Watson, though not at Harvard himself, was very influential in American psychology, especially in the 1920s and 1930s. Skinner pursued a degree in experimental psychology and received his Ph.D. in 1931. He remained at Harvard under various research fellowships until the fall of 1936. At this time he went to the University of Minnesota as an instructor. In 1937 he was made an assistant professor and in 1939 an associate professor. In 1944 he won a Guggenheim Fellowship. During World War II Skinner participated in a government research project, the results of which were not made public until 1959. He had been conditioning pigeons to pilot missiles and torpedoes. The pigeons were so highly trained that they could guide a missile right down into the smokestack of a naval destroyer.

In 1945 Skinner went to the University of Indiana as chairman of the psychology department, a job he held until 1948. During this time he developed the now famous air crib, a soundproof, air-conditioned, germ-free, glass-enclosed box for raising children in a scientifically controlled environment. One of his daughters, Deborah, spent much of her first two years of life in an air crib. Skinner later attempted to market the box as the "Heir Conditioner," but the device was not widely acclaimed by the mothers of America. Skinner's grandiose plans for mass-producing the box were quietly dropped. Deborah was also toilet trained by another of Skinner's contraptions—a music box that was placed inside the toilet and played the "Blue Danube" whenever it got wet.

In 1948 Skinner was appointed to the faculty at Harvard, and from his command post in Cambridge he has influenced a whole generation of students in experimental psychology. While at Harvard he developed the experimental chamber, or Skinner box, for the study of learning in rats and pigeons. This

reaction potential" or Kenneth Spence's paper on the transposition controversy, but neither gave much comfort to the teacher trying to find out why Johnny couldn't read.

This chapter focuses on the theories of Skinner and Bruner. Another important theoretical model of learning, information processing, will be covered in Chapter 11.

B. F. SKINNER AND RESPONSE ANALYSIS

No psychologist ever dominated American behaviorism to the extent that B. F. Skinner does today. John B. Watson commented that behavior is the data of psychology and felt that responses, not conscious experience, should be

device has enabled American psychologists to study animal responses with a precision and ease never before possible. While the animal is in the Skinner box, its every movement can be recorded and made ready for analysis by automated equipment.

Skinner later became very interested in educational psychology, after visiting his daughter's arithmetic class in elementary school. He says of that visit that he had been a witness to "minds being destroyed." He felt that human beings could be trained in much the same fashion as the rats and pigeons that he had conditioned in the Skinner box. Children, too, could be conditioned, step by step, each correct response followed by reinforcement, until they acquired complex forms of behavior. He developed and tested his first "teaching machine" in the 1950s and as a result has been credited with creating a revolution in the technology of education. Many teachers saw the

teaching machine, or programed instruction, as a threat to their jobs. Skinner has assured teachers that programed instruction is a learning aid, not a substitute teacher. He has also assured educators that the children trained with this device will not become mechanized little robots but instead will be more likely to reach their intellectual potential.

Skinner's analysis of the learning situation into operant responses and reinforcing stimuli also led to the development of behavior modification techniques in the classroom. Under this system, teachers are trained to wait for their students to emit appropriate responses and then to reinforce these responses speedily and consistently. Behavior modification is the second revolution in teaching technology attributed to Skinner.

Skinner has been a most prolific researcher and writer. His books and papers are far too numerous to summarize here, but his best-known works are: *The Behavior of*

Organisms (1938); *Walden Two*, a novel about a utopian society where everyone's behavior has been shaped according to conditioning principles (1948); *Science and Human Behavior* (1953); *Verbal Behavior* (1957); *Schedules of Reinforcement* (1957); *Cumulative Record* (1959); *The Technology of Teaching* (1968); and *Beyond Freedom and Dignity* (1971). Skinner also wrote a lively autobiography, *Particulars of My Life* (1976), in which he discusses many of the intimate details of his life history. This has since been followed (1979) with a second autobiographical account, *The Shaping of a Behaviorist*.

In 1958 Skinner received the American Psychological Association's Distinguished Scientific Contribution Award. Skinner is an avowed behaviorist in the tradition of J. B. Watson. Though now retired from active teaching, Skinner is today America's most important and honored behaviorist psychologist.

studied and analyzed. Skinner wholeheartedly agrees, and since the 1938 publication of his *Behavior of Organisms*, he has outlined a system of response analysis that is far more thorough and detailed than anything seen before. Although behaviorists were already preoccupied with response analysis up through the mid-1930s, Skinner's arrival changed this preoccupation to a near-obsession. To the Skinnerians every little squiggle on the cumulative recorder that records the responses of an experimental animal is fraught with profound significance.

Skinner's work is not concerned with what goes on inside the organism, the organism's motivational or emotional state, or even its neurology. Skinner's psychology is an "empty organism" psychology, a psychology of environmental conditions (stimuli) associating with and affecting the organism's response repertoire.

Skinner's line of descent, back through Watson, Thorndike, and the other early associationists, is clear and direct. He views learning as an association between stimuli (S) and responses (R), although not always in that order, and emphasizes R-S associations as much as S-R associations; that is, he has found that conditioning takes place when a response is followed by a reinforcing stimulus.

Skinnerian psychology is based on a totally environmental view of behavior. Since the consequences of a response influence further action, and since these consequences occur in the outer environment, it is the environment that causes changes in behavior. This is essentially Skinner's "theme song."

Throughout our discussion of Skinner's system, we focus on the conditioning of rats and pigeons. Although his data were derived primarily from work with these animals, Skinner's findings are, nonetheless, relevant to education. A fairly thorough knowledge of Skinner is essential to the classroom teacher, for as we shall see later, Skinner believes that his techniques do work in the classroom just as surely as in the aseptic confines of the Skinner box.

Reinforcement

Skinner picks up the behaviorist-associationist tradition about where Thorndike left off. You may recall that one of Thorndike's three major laws of learning was the law of effect, which stated that learning is an association between a stimulus and a response as a result of the consequences of an act. If the S-R sequence is followed by a satisfying state of affairs, the association is strengthened; that is, learning takes place.

Skinner borrowed the law of effect, streamlined it somewhat, and called it "reinforcement." Thorndike had spent considerable time defending his law of effect against the charge that it was subjective and mentalistic (a charge leveled by behaviorists who were even more tough-minded than Thorndike). Skinner's concept of reinforcement needs no such defense. He totally stripped his concept of any subjective or mentalistic overtones. Reinforcement neither offers a reward nor creates a feeling of satisfaction in the learner. Reinforcement, like all of Skinner's concepts, is defined strictly in operational terms, that is, in terms of the way it is observed or measured. Thus, a positive reinforcement is any stimulus that, when added to the situation, increases the likelihood that the response will occur. Similarly, a negative reinforcement is any stimulus that, when removed from the situation, increases the probability that the response will occur. That is all there is to it. There is no mention of subjective feelings, only a description of the observed events. If a pellet of food is a positive reinforcer to a hungry rat, it is only because the rat pressed a lever to get another pellet. Reinforcement is defined as something that is observed to increase the likelihood of a response recurring. Skinner is no hedonist basing his concepts on the search for pleasure but an objectivist defining his concepts in operational terms.

Responses: Two Types

Skinner, like the earlier behaviorists, bases his system on the observation of overt responses. He divides all responses into two categories: respondents and operants.[1]

Respondents   Respondents are those responses that can be automatically triggered by a specific unlearned or unconditioned stimulus; Pavlov called them "reflexes." Pavlov, and later Watson, based a whole system of learning on the fact that reflexes can be conditioned. Skinner accepts the fact that respondents can be conditioned in precisely the manner Pavlov described, but he doesn't consider respondent conditioning nearly so important as Pavlov and Watson did. The reason is that so many living organisms have so few respondents. To generalize the laws of classical conditioning to the whole range of human behavior is to carelessly overwork a fairly restricted formula. As Skinner pointed out, a human being is far more than a mere jack-in-the-box with a list of tricks to be elicited by pressing the correct button. The bulk of an individual's response repertoire takes another form.

Operants   Operants are all those responses that cannot be classified as respondents. An operant is a response that occurs spontaneously, without having to be triggered by an unconditioned stimulus. For example, when you stretch your legs, raise your hand, or shift in your seat, there are no known unconditioned stimuli that automatically force those responses.

An operant is therefore a response for which the original stimulus is either unidentified or nonexistent; it may be loosely thought of as voluntary behavior. The consequence of operant behavior can be observed, even though the stimulus is not known. In operant conditioning, reinforcement is contingent on the operant first being emitted. Thus, the organism must "operate" on the environment in order that the reinforcement will follow. Earlier psychologists called operant responding "instrumental responding." Skinner believes that most human behavior is of the operant type.

Some responses we first think are respondents turn out not to be when they are subjected to further analysis. For example, putting your foot on the brake pedal to the stimulus of a red traffic light is not a reflex. You had to learn the significance of a red traffic light. You didn't come into the world already equipped to press your foot down automatically at the sight of a red light. This response is an example of a conditioned operant.

Operant Conditioning

The best way to understand operant conditioning is to examine the experimental situation Skinner has used over the years. Figure 9.1 is an illustration of the experimental chamber or, as it is so often called, the "Skinner box." It is a small box, the sides and top of which are made of clear plastic. A lever protrudes from one side and there is a tube that empties into the food cup next to the lever. The experimenter decides which operant to condition; in this case it will be pressing the lever. The experimenter then simply waits while the rat explores the cage. Since there aren't that many things to do in a Skinner box, the rat eventually presses the lever. A pellet of food (a reinforcing stimulus) immediately drops down the tube into the food cup. The rat pounces on the food, and conditioning has begun. It is important to note that when the rat, after wandering around the cage for a while, chances to press the food-producing lever, the response is not a reflex action trig-

gered by a particular unconditioned stimulus. Skinner says that operants are emitted by the organism, whereas reflexes or respondents are elicited by unconditioned stimuli.

Thus, the sequence of events for operant conditioning is:

1. The emitting of the free operant (the rat chancing to press the lever); followed by

2. The presentation of a reinforcing stimulus (the rat is given a pellet of food); followed by

3. An increase in the probability that the response will occur again

The response is now becoming controlled, or predictable. Note that the events must follow in the order specified above. The food must come after the response is emitted. How long after? The sooner the better. For optimum conditioning, the reinforcement should immediately follow the response. This is an important Skinnerian principle. Skinner believes that in the classroom the student should be reinforced as soon as the appropriate response is emitted. One commentator on Skinner's approach gives this example:

A student in a class contributes very little to classroom discussions. The teacher is concerned and wants to increase the student's active participation. Finally, the student asks a

FIGURE 9.1 The experimental chamber, often called the "Skinner box."

question. The teacher, using Skinnerian psychology, looks at the student, pauses a while, and then proceeds to comment on the good quality of the question and adds that if more questions of such quality were introduced the sessions would be more profitable to the whole class. The episode is followed by a dramatic increase in the asking of questions on the part of this student. The teacher's commendation is hence deemed reinforcing (rewarding). But for some students, approval from the teacher may act as a negative stimulus. Consequently, the art of teaching, according to Skinner, must include the identification of events that reinforce each student and the setting up of conditions that provide the opportunity for each to experience reinforcement upon making desired responses and showing progress.[2]

Note that, unlike reflex or respondent conditioning, the experimenter cannot force the response to occur. The experimenter may have to wait a while until the rat chances on the lever and emits the appropriate operant. Pavlov had no such wait, for he could automatically trigger the desired response (salivation) by simply presenting the unconditioned stimulus (meat powder).

In operant conditioning, although the experimenter might have to wait as long as fifteen or twenty minutes before the rat presses the lever for the first time, after a few reinforced responses the rat begins pressing ever more frequently. It is not unusual to see a conditioned animal pressing the lever 300 to 400 times in the space of one hour. With a highly conditioned rat, the sound of lever-pressing emanating from the Skinner box is reminiscent of the sound of a high-speed typist.

The law of operant conditioning   We may now state Skinner's general principle: If the occurrence of the operant is followed by a reinforcing stimulus, the rate of responding, for that particular operant, will increase.

Remember that the free operant originally had no connection with a stimulus. In operant conditioning, the response produces the reinforcing stimulus, or in Skinner's terms, the reinforcement is contingent upon the occurrence of the response. In this case, then, a response-stimulus connection is formed, not a stimulus-response connection.

We have said a number of times that as conditioning proceeds, the rate of responding increases. Increases over what? The rate increases over what is known as the operant level, or the frequency with which the response typically occurs in the untrained animal. For conditioning to take place, a response must occur before it can be reinforced. The experimenter must therefore select a response that the animal is apt to make on its own, such as rising on its hind legs, stretching its neck, or more commonly, pressing a lever. When first placed in the experimental chamber, the naive rat may happen to press the lever three or four times during the course of an hour, even though the lever is not producing any food. That is, the animal will occasionally press the lever even without positive reinforcement. The operant level is, therefore, the rate with which the free operant is typically emitted prior to conditioning.

Extinction

Extinction may be loosely thought of as a kind of forgetting process. For example, as has been seen, an animal may be conditioned to the point where it is pressing the lever 400 times per hour. Similarly, the response may be extinguished, or the animal "deconditioned" back to the point where it will press the lever only three or four times per hour. The technique is simple. Allow the conditioned response to occur, but do not reinforce it. With the Skinner box, this means that pressing the bar no longer produces a food pellet. After enough nonreinforced lever presses, the animal "gives up," and the rate of response returns to its preconditioned, or operant, level. Note that extinction does not cause the animal to stop pressing the lever completely, but it does cause the response frequency to return to the operant level.

It is important to remember that extinction requires that the animal emit the response and that the response not be reinforced. If the animal were somehow prevented from making the response, extinction would not occur. For example, if a conditioned animal were removed from the Skinner box and returned to its home cage, where there was no lever to press, the animal would retain the conditioning. If the animal were returned to the Skinner box, even a year later, lever-pressing would be resumed.

The first time a conditioned animal's response is extinguished, spontaneous recovery of the response will occur. This requires time, though sometimes as little as an hour. If the animal whose behavior has been extinguished is taken out of the Skinner box for an hour or so and then returned to it, lever-pressing will resume, even though no new training has taken place. These spontaneously recovered responses will extinguish more quickly, however, than did the original extinction. Several extinction–spontaneous recovery sequences may be necessary before extinction is complete to the point where the animal remains at the operant level with no further evidence of spontaneous recovery.

Discrimination

Although in its original state the free operant is not attached to a stimulus, it may become so through training. This technique is called "discrimination training," and the operant that has become associated with the stimulus is called a "discriminated operant." Discrimination training is accomplished in the following manner: We introduce a new stimulus to an animal that has been conditioned to press the lever, such as a light that we turn off and on in a random time sequence. We now reinforce the animal only for pressing the lever when the light is on. Since any lever-pressing that takes place when the light is off is not reinforced, the response is extinguished as far as periods of no light are concerned. The animal emits the response only when the light is on; that is, the operant has become attached to the stimulus "light on." At this point the operant is no longer free, but is firmly controlled by the stimulus.

Technically, the stimulus for which responding is reinforced is called the "discriminated stimulus," or the S^D—in this case "light on." The stimulus for which responding is extinguished is called the "stimulus delta," or S^Δ—in this case "light off." Responding to the discriminated stimulus (pressing the lever) is fol-

lowed by reinforcement (food pellets). This sequence of events is crucial to the development of discrimination: (1) stimulus, (2) response, and (3) reinforcement.

Stimulus Generalization

Once discrimination training has been completed—that is, once the animal has attached an operant to a certain stimulus—the stimulus may become generalized. Stimulus generalization means that other stimuli similar to the one used in training may take on the power to produce the response. If the animal has been trained to respond to a bright light, through generalization it may also respond to a dim light, even though the dim light was never used in training. Or perhaps a buzzer was used as the stimulus; through generalization, the animal may also be found to respond to a clicking sound or even a bell.

When generalization is noted, further discrimination training may be used to train the animal to respond only to a fairly specific stimulus magnitude. For example, if the original discrimination training used "light on" as the S^D and "light off" as the S^Δ, the animal will eventually respond only when the light is on. However, because of generalization, responses will occur at many different light intensities. Perhaps the original S^D was a fairly bright light, but because of generalization the animal also responds to a dim light. We may now "correct" for this generalization by a new discrimination series in which the bright light is the S^D and the dim light is the S^Δ. That is, we continue reinforcing responses to the bright light, while extinguishing responses to the dim light. This procedure allows the experimenter to determine the animal's capacity for distinguishing between rather subtle stimulus differences. For example, we can probe such questions as how small a difference in light intensity the animal is capable of identifying. Experiments have even been carried out in which the S^Δ was a card printed with the words "Don't Press," and the S^D a card with the word "Press." The experimental animal, in this case a pigeon, then displays the seemingly uncanny ability to "read" by rushing over to the lever and pecking whenever the "Press" card is shown. The pigeon reacts on cue, much in the way that a studio audience on a TV show frantically claps when the "Applause" sign is presented. As one TV narrator said in describing such an experiment, "It gives new meaning to the term *birdbrain*."

Conditioned Reinforcement

A stimulus that is not originally reinforcing may become so through repeated presentation with one that is. For example, if lever-pressing produces both a light and a food pellet, the light, by association with the food, will take on the power to reinforce. The sequence of events for establishing conditioned reinforcement is (1) response; (2) neutral stimulus, such as a light or buzzer; followed by (3) the primary reinforcement. It is important that this order of events be followed, for if the neutral stimulus is presented before rather than after the response, discrimination, and not conditioned reinforcement, will result. If a light is presented before the response has been emitted, the light will become an S^D, whereas if it follows the response, it becomes a conditioned reinforcer. In a sense, discrimination training teaches the rat to respond *to* the light, whereas conditioned reinforcement teaches the rat to respond *for*, or in order to get, the light.

Schedules of reinforcement   The way in which the reinforcers are arranged determines in large measure the strength of the resulting conditioning. Responses that are reinforced periodically, rather than each time they are emitted, tend to be conditioned more strongly and are thus more difficult to extinguish. Though there are many variations on the major themes, Skinner has identified five major schedules of reinforcement:

1. *Continuous Reinforcement (Crf).* As the name implies, the Crf schedule provides for reinforcement each time the operant is emitted. For example, a rat in a Skinner box will receive a pellet of food every time the lever is pressed.

2. *Fixed Ratio (F.R.).* Under the F.R. schedule the reinforcement occurs only after a fixed number of operants have been emitted. For

Although the teacher may sometimes use primary reinforcers such as candy, conditioned reinforcers such as good grades, promotions, prizes, and teacher approval are usually more appropriate.

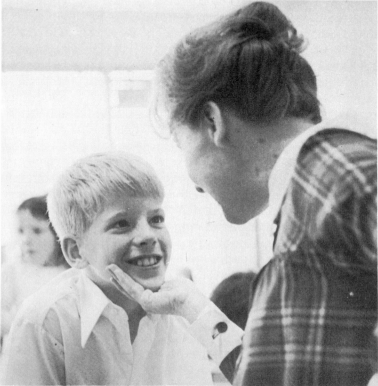

example, on an F.R. schedule of 3:1, the rat in a Skinner box must press the lever three times in order to get one pellet of food. Skinner has demonstrated that the ratio can go as high as 196:1 and still maintain the conditioning.

3. *Fixed Interval (F.I.).* Rather than being based on the number of responses being emitted, the F.I. schedule is keyed to a fixed *time* interval. That is, a given period of time must elapse, regardless of what the organism is doing, before the reinforcement is presented. For example, on an F.I. schedule of thirty seconds, this thirty-second time period must be allowed to elapse before the organism's next response will be reinforced.

4. *Variable Ratio (V.R.).* Like the F.R., the V.R. schedule is also based on the number of responses being emitted. Under the V.R. schedule, however, the ratio is constantly being varied so that the organism never knows which response will be reinforced. The rat might be reinforced after five responses, then after fifteen responses, then after the very next response, and so on.

5. *Variable Interval (V.I.).* On this schedule the time periods, rather than numbers of responses, are varied. The rat may have to wait thirty seconds, then five seconds, then fifty seconds, and so on before the pressing of the lever will deliver the reinforcement.

Analysis of the reinforcement schedules
Each of the reinforcement schedules creates differences in the way the resulting conditioning is exhibited. The Crf schedule, though extremely useful for the acquiring of new behavior, does not result in a great deal of perseverance. Extinction can occur rather rapidly when a response has been conditioned on the continuous schedule. Parents in the United States may be guilty of using too much reinforcement in bringing up their children, and consequently nurture such qualities as a lack of perseverance, low frustration tolerance, impulsiveness, impatience, and a generally low level of ego strength.

Children at home, or rats in the Skinner box, tend to give up easily (have a low resistance to extinction) when the reinforcers are continuous.

This is especially true in a highly industrialized nation in which continuous reinforcement is built into the society.

> The conveniences provided by technological gadgets work in concert with parental indulgence by providing immediate gratification with great consistency while requiring little effort. Coke machines, television sets, automobiles, and many other devices yield rewards quickly and consistently with a minimum of sweat. Indulgent parents, who readily provide their children the means for making life easy and convenient, should not be surprised to find that their children lack some of the old-fashioned traits that the parents were taught to admire in their early lives.[3]

The other schedules, F.R., F.I., V.R., and V.I. are all of the intermittent type: They require that the organism learn to wait out the hard times. Responses conditioned in this way become highly resistant to extinction. Intermittent reinforcement does condition perseverance and perhaps "hope."

Life outside the Skinner box creates many conditions that are analogous to the various intermittent schedules. For example, factory workers or farm laborers who are paid on a piecework basis are being conditioned on an F.R. schedule. In piecework one's pay is based on a set number of items produced or apples picked. Workers who are paid by the hour or by the week illustrate the F.I. schedule. An example of the V.R. schedule might be a door-to-door encyclopedia salesperson who is paid on a commission basis. The salesperson knows that he or she must emit a number of responses but never knows which response is going to lead to a payoff. Slot machines and other forms of gambling are set up on a V.R. basis. Because the V.R. schedule creates responses that are highly resistant to extinction, people can often become addicted to gambling. This helps explain why the gambler can persevere through long dry spells and still go back to the game. The V.I. schedule also creates strongly conditioned responses that are maintained at a rapid rate and are highly resistant to extinction.

The variable schedules are typical of most social situations. Human interaction is characterized by inconsistent reinforcement, and the result is a repertoire of responses that may become almost extinction-proof. Habit, as William

James has told us, that great fly-wheel of society, keeps people doing the same things over and over again, even when the habits are self-destructive.

THE ENGINEERING OF SOCIETY

Skinner suggests that through the judicious use of reinforcement schedules, a society free of war, crime, poverty, and pollution could be behaviorally engineered. The individuals in the society could be shaped to reflect the best of human traits: honesty, altruism, ambition, and so on. It is Skinner's conviction that this not only could be but should be done. A culture should be designed in which the behavior of the individuals is systematically controlled. As Skinner has said, "A refusal to use the knowledge we have could mean the difference between the survival and the destruction of our civilization or even the species."[4]

Skinner feels that a democratic society cannot provide true justice because it must ignore minority opinion. A society should be planned and managed by someone (presumably Skinner) who is interested in the good of all. Skinner does not seem overly concerned about who will decide which behaviors are to be reinforced and which are to be extinguished.

The relation between the controller and the controlled is reciprocal. The scientist in the laboratory, studying the behavior of a pigeon, designs contingencies and observes their effects. His apparatus exerts a conspicuous control on the pigeon, but we must not overlook the control exerted by the pigeon. The behavior of the pigeon has determined the design of the apparatus and the procedures in which it is used.[5]

Thus, just as the scientist in the laboratory is to some extent under the control of the pigeon, so too will the controller of a society be influenced by the members of that society. Despite Skinner's view on the apparent equality between the controller and controllee, some of you may feel you'd prefer the role of experimenter to that of pigeon.

Environment: The Master Controller

The heart of Skinner's message is that we are all at the mercy of environmental controls. What

Even though Skinner's data came primarily from working with rats and pigeons, he thought the results could be applied to humans.

we do, who we are, what we become—all result from the particular set of environmental stimuli that has impinged on us and that will impinge on us. We humans are yoked to our environment just as rigidly as animals are to theirs. Environment—and only environment—controls behavior. People are directed not by cherished ideals, strong emotions, or the forced will of profound ideas, but by the environment. Humans and animals differ, not because of varying complexities of perception or ideation, but only because of varying environmental complexities. The environment and the reinforcement schedules provided by the environment are the true and only prime movers.

Verbal Behavior

Skinner uses his system to explain all animal and human learning. For example, Skinner believes that learning to talk follows the principles of operant conditioning. Picture for a moment a one-and-a-half-year-old baby contentedly lying in a crib. The baby is cooing, gurgling, uttering a whole series of disconnected sounds. Suddenly, from out of the babble, and surely by accident, the baby chances on the sound "da-da." The parents, who have been listening intently, are beside themselves with joy. They heap praise on the baby and, sure enough, the baby soon says "da-da" again.

In technical Skinnerian terms, from the entire repertoire of possible verbal operants, the baby has emitted the operant "da-da." This is immediately followed by positive reinforcement, increasing the probability that the operant will be repeated. After more "da-da" responses are followed by more reinforcements, the baby will emit the operant at a fairly frequent rate. Conditioning of the operant has occurred. Now, however, the parents' expectations are raised so that reinforcement no longer follows each and every utterance of the magic word. The parents begin teaching the baby to discriminate, so that only when the father himself is presented as the stimulus does baby get reinforced. When the baby says "da-da" to the mother's presence, no reinforcement follows, and the response to that stimulus is extinguished. In this case the father is the S^D, the stimulus for which responding will be reinforced, and the mother is the S^Δ, the

stimulus for which responding will be extinguished.

This discrimination will occur quickly, but because of stimulus generalization, the family may be in for an embarrassing moment. A few days later the postman stops in with his delivery. The baby, seeing the male figure, proudly calls out "da-da." Obviously, further discrimination training is in order. When the baby says "da-da" to other male figures, reinforcement is withheld. Finally, the father is perceived as the only appropriate S^D for that operant, and the family perhaps breathes a sigh of relief.

Attaching a verbal response to an S^D in this manner is called, by Skinner, "tacting." Skinner believes that language is acquired in this general fashion, and he has added other terms, such as *mands* for verbal responses that specify their own reinforcers, *echoics* for verbal responses that parrot the speech of others, and *autoclitics* for verbal responses that provide grammatical framework. In short, during language acquisition, what are learned are the verbal responses, not the thoughts lurking behind them. An operant is conditioned so that it occurs regularly, and then, through discrimination training, it is attached to its appropriate stimulus. Perhaps the child later generalizes the word *car* to include all wheeled vehicles. Through discrimination training, the child then learns the appropriate responses that will correct for this stimulus generalization.

Skinner's contention that verbal behavior is learned strictly through operant conditioning has not gone unchallenged. Specialists in the field of psycholinguistics believe that language acquisition is not a mere matter of conditioning. Noam Chomsky, for example, sees the child as genetically prewired, born with biological givens that direct the course of language development. In this way Chomsky can explain how children learn sentence structure and the complex grammatical sequencing of words—both of which he feels children learn far more easily than the principles of operant conditioning would predict.[6] Evidence in support of Chomsky's notion has been provided in a number of studies. One researcher has found that motor and language development occur hand in hand "(or is it foot in mouth?) and this development is independent of culture."[7]

Operant Conditioning in the Classroom

Only Skinner's general approach to the problem of classroom teaching will be treated in this section. Specific techniques, such as teaching machines and the arrangement of reinforcements to promote student control, will be covered in the next chapter.

Education is the learning of certain responses that will be useful later in life. How can this best be accomplished? The teacher, says Skinner, should use the techniques that produce meaningful behavioral changes. Though the teacher may sometimes use primary reinforcers such as M&M candy, conditioned reinforcers such as good grades, promotions, prizes, and the generalized social reinforcement of approval are usually more appropriate. One of the real problems with the use of conditioned reinforcers, however, is that they are often too distant. As we have seen, operant conditioning is most effective when reinforcement is immediate. This is one of the reasons why Skinner strongly favors the use of the teaching machine. It can provide immediate reinforcement and help bridge the gap between student behavior and the more distant conditioned reinforcers such as promotion or grades. Skinner is against the use of punishment in the classroom, not because it won't control behavior—it will—but because it may produce a host of negative emotional reactions. Negative emotional reactions, conditioned through the use of punishment, may prevent further learning and even further school attendance. Punishment always leads to attempts to escape, and when children do escape from the classroom situation, formal learning in the classroom is obviously impossible.

Just what is the goal of education according to Skinner? Skinner believes that education should maximize knowledge. This is done through operant conditioning, through building up a student's repertoire of responses. Understanding a subject, such as history, is simply the result of having learned a verbal repertoire. Skinner insists that when students can answer questions in a given area, and speak and write fluently about the area, then, by definition, they understand that area. A verbal repertoire is not a sign of knowledge—it is the knowledge. In order to teach a knowledge of biology, one must teach the specific behavior from which the knowledge is inferred. That is, in order to say that students know something, we must observe certain responses: how they speak, the diagrams they draw, the equations they can solve, and so on. These, then, are the very responses that should be trained into the students who don't display this knowledge.

Good teaching is thus the ability to arrange the proper sequence of reinforcements and to make sure that these reinforcements are contingent upon students emitting the appropriate responses.

BEHAVIORISM TODAY: THE FUNCTIONAL VIEW

Traditional behaviorism generally adhered to three underlying principles:

Skinner is against aversion techniques since punishment always leads to attempts to escape the classroom situation.

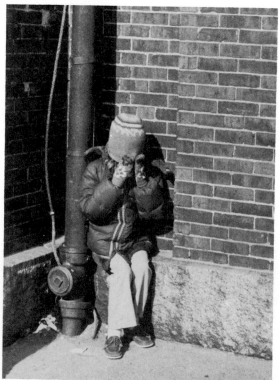

1. Organisms enter the world, come into any new situation, as virtual blank slates. Under the leadership of Watson, behaviorists as a group were extremely strong environmentalists. They clung to the cherished belief, previously espoused by English philosopher John Locke, that the mind was a "blank slate upon which experience writes," or "nothing in the intellect not first in the senses." And in a way they clung to this belief in a manner that probably would have made John Locke blush, since Watson most certainly would have considered Locke a mentalist for having used such terms as "mind' and "intellect." Behaviorists paid little attention to internal cognitive structures and even less, of course, to genetic predispositions.

2. There are few important differences in learning and/or conditioning styles across species. An understanding of rat and pigeon behavior could be easily extrapolated to the human condition.

3. Any response an organism is capable of producing could be linked through training with any stimulus the organism could be made aware of. Learning was seen as occurring in an automatic fashion, and the learner was typically seen as a recipient of environmental stimuli, not a selector of stimuli.

Given these premises, it is little wonder that behaviorism had to adhere to a robot model of learning and that the twin concepts of growth and development had to play, at most, a secondary role. In large measure the behaviorists painted themselves into a corner. Because of their almost slavish insistence on these three fundamental principles, they had to overlook, or attempt to explain away, empirical data that ran counter to their position. Anomalies began to appear, and traditional behaviorism went into what Thomas Kuhn would call a "crisis" stage.[8] Attempts to stem the flow soon gave way in the face of a virtual torrent of new evidence.

The Challenge Today

More recent work in conditioning is offering a strong challenge to the traditional behaviorist position. Martin Seligman, for example, has shown that responses to some stimuli are much easier to condition than responses to others. Seligman's position is that each organism comes into the world biologically prepared to be conditioned more quickly to certain environmental stimuli than to others and that this preparedness differs from species to species. Birds, for example, are conditioned easily to visual stimuli, whereas human infants are conditioned more quickly to verbal stimuli. Seligman says that the organism carries within itself "certain equipment and predispositions [which are] more or less appropriate to that situation."[9]

Seligman believes, therefore, that since organisms have evolved a variety of adaptive behavior sequences over millions of years, it is unlikely that today's conditioning procedures can countermand these built-in predispositions. For example, was Watson's conditioning of little Albert really as automatic as it appeared, or was Albert already biologically prepared to learn to fear the white rat? In one study, usually overlooked by the behaviorists, E. O. Bregman attempted a replication of this experiment of Watson. Her finding, an obvious anomaly for orthodox behaviorism, was that fear in a child could indeed be conditioned if the CS was a *live animal*, but conditioning did not take place if the CS was an *inanimate object*.[10] It is therefore highly likely that humans are born biologically prepared to suspect that live animals might do them harm and, because of that tendency, learn quickly to fear and avoid them. Seligman also believes that common phobias, such as the fear of snakes, enclosed places, or speaking in public, undoubtedly have biological roots in an evolutionary survival system.[11] Although few of us have ever actually been bitten by a snake, locked in a closet, or pelted with stones from an angry crowd, these extremely common phobias are too easily acquired to be explained on the basis of the traditional principles of conditioning.

Keller and Marian Breland have also discovered serious anomalies in the behaviorists's paradigm.[12] Using operant conditioning techniques, the Brelands trained raccoons to pick up coins and deposit them in a slot in order to receive a food reinforcer. Although the raccoons dutifully learned this routine rather easily, the conditioning soon decayed and literally drifted into a different behavioral sequence. The raccoons, despite continued reinforcement, soon began rubbing the coins together as part of an instinctive washing ritual (as though they were preparing to eat them). This action broke up the conditioning sequence. The Brelands called this phenomenon "instinctive drift" and stated that many of the artificial conditioning routines produced so easily in the laboratory will soon drift back toward the organism's natural behavioral repertoire.

Could it be that the behaviorists have consistently been lucky in arranging their studies in such a way that the conditioning environment just happened to meet the organism's preparedness? As we have seen, Watson was certainly lucky in choosing a live rat as a CS, since Albert would not have been conditioned nearly as easily, if at all, to a stuffed rat or a picture of a rat. Were Thorndike and Skinner also as lucky? Certainly a rat can be conditioned quickly to pressing a lever for food. But what if one of Thorndike's cats were substituted for one of Skinner's rats? Cats, although they can learn that pressing a lever delivers food, soon stop pressing and simply sit and wait—and the hungrier they get, the more they crouch down and wait. The difference is in the types of food-gathering techniques utilized by the two species. Rats actively seek out food in their environments, whereas cats are great ambushers that normally crouch patiently while awaiting their prey. Also, note that the lever in a Skinner box is always made of metal, not plastic or wood; nonmetallic levers would probably simply be eaten by the rats rather than pressed.

With pigeons, the typical Skinnerian arrangement is to substitute a small, lighted key *to be pecked*, rather than a lever to be pressed. High-speed photographs of this pecking response show clearly that the pigeons are, in fact, not simply pecking the key but trying to eat it.[13] In a summary statement of the pigeon studies, R. C. Bolles said:

> The picture that emerges from this work is that key pecking in pigeons, which surely must be the most studied and most characteristic of all operant responses in the Skinnerian tradition,

is not an operant after all, and is not even learned because of reinforcement. It is simply another instance of the misbehavior phenomenon; the pigeon pecks the key because, when the discriminated stimulus is on (the light), the key is evaluated as food.[14]

A Message to Educators

What should we, as educators, derive from this evidence? Traditional behaviorism should no longer be accepted at face value. What seemed like an almost noninteractive model of conditioning should now, most assuredly, be viewed as extremely interactive. The environmental manipulations that produce conditioning interact decidedly with the particular organism's innate predispositions. Again, we see behavior as resulting from the interplay of heredity and environment. Conditioning should not be seen as completely automatic in its nature, nor as permanent in its result, as the behaviorists have led us to believe. Instinctive drift can override and even countermand conditioning sequences that attempt to compete with innate predispositions. Just as with the raccoons, children who have been conditioned to act in a particular way through the use of tokens or whatever may quickly "drift' out of that conditioned behavior, *especially if the situation changes.*

Conversely, we should not glibly use the "instinctive drift" argument to give up on changing behavior we can't seem to control. It becomes all too easy to say "This kid was born to be bad" when his or her disruptive behavior continues despite efforts to change it. We must keep in mind that whatever the genetic basis might be for a particular set of responses, the innate predisposition is still being expressed *in learned ways.*

Perhaps the most provocative of the new research is the work relating learning and conditioning to what we now know of age-related changes in capacity. No longer can we afford to smugly set forth universal laws of associative learning; we must instead attempt to identify the adaptive importance of particular instances of learning, found at particular stages of development. The human organism is, after all, biological as well as psychological.

MEDIATION THEORY AND VERBAL LEARNING

Before turning to Bruner, it should be pointed out that some of today's association theorists do try to bridge the gap between response learning and cognitive learning. These theorists, for example, Howard Kendler, explain a large part of learning by the use of what they call "mediation theory." Mediation theory suggests that much of our learned behavior can be explained on the basis of internal, nonobservable S-R systems that are chained to overt stimuli and responses. The internal mediators can be such things as words, concepts, sets, and images. This can be most easily seen in the case of words. As children begin to develop the use of language, they can use verbal labels to expedite the learning of everything from visual discriminations and generalizations to motor responses; that is, children (or adults) will make learning easier by inserting a word (a mediator) between the stimulus and the response. For example, if three-year-old children are trying to learn the differences between a circle, a triangle, and a square, they will learn far more quickly if they are given verbal labels for each form. The verbal labels help make the stimuli more distinctive and, therefore, easier to learn and remember. Also, there are certain kinds of learning that can be explained far more simply by mediation theory than by any other current theory. This is true, for example, in the case of paired-associate learning. In this situation, pairs of words, typically up to a dozen pairs, are presented to the subject for memorization. Subjects learn the associations far more quickly when the pairs of words are mediated by some meaningful connection than when random pairs are presented. For example, a subject will learn to associate "cat-dog" more easily than "cat-inch."

In summary, the more that verbal labels make stimuli more distinctive, the easier it is to learn a discrimination. Conversely, the more that verbal labels make stimuli equivalent, the easier it is to learn a generalization.

Finally, some theorists believe that the association of the verbal label and the stimulus forms a linkage within the central nervous system.[15] Much more will be said on this important issue during our coverage of information processing in Chapter 11.

JEROME BRUNER AND THE PROCESS OF THOUGHT

Whereas Skinner has presented a behaviorist-associationist account of learning, borrowing heavily from Watson and Thorndike, Bruner's position is more consistent with the cognitive-gestaltist position. For example, Bruner insists that the final goal of teaching is to promote the "general understanding of the structure of a subject matter."[16] When the student understands the structure of a subject, he or she sees it as a related whole. "Grasping the structure of a subject is understanding it in a way that permits many other things to be related to it meaningfully."[17] These are hardly the words of a behaviorist-associationist. Bruner stresses the importance in learning of forming global concepts, of building coherent generalizations, of creating cognitive *Gestalts*. Bruner tells the teacher—and he constantly aims his message at the working classroom teacher—to help promote conditions in which the student can perceive the structure of a given subject. When learning is based on a structure, it is more long-lasting and less easily forgotten. The student who once studied biology, for example, may forget many of the details over the years, but these details can be more easily and quickly reconstructed if the general structure is still there.

Bruner calls his position a theory of instruction, not a learning theory. He feels that a learning theory is *descriptive*; that is, it describes what happens after the fact. A theory of instruction, on the other hand, is *prescriptive*: it prescribes in advance how a given subject can best be taught. If a learning theory tells us that children at age six are not yet ready to understand the concept of reversibility, a theory of instruction would prescribe how best to lead the child toward this concept when he or she is old enough to understand it.

Bruner's theory has four major principles: motivation, structure, sequence, and reinforcement.

JEROME BRUNER

Jerome Bruner was born in 1915 in New York. He was born into a successful upper-middle-class family that fully expected young Bruner to become a lawyer. Bruner, however, had other ideas. He graduated from Duke University in 1937 and immediately entered Duke's graduate school in psychology. The following year he transferred to Harvard, where he received his Ph.D. degree in psychology in 1941.

When Bruner first arrived at Harvard, his interest focused on the investigation of perception in animals. Harvard had only recently (1933) created an independent department of psychology, and under its chairman, E. G. Boring, the research emphasis was aimed at experimentation in animal learning and perception. Bruner studied under the great Harvard researcher and physiological psychologist Karl S. Lashley. With the outbreak of World War II, Bruner's interests shifted to social psychology, and he wrote his doctoral thesis on the techniques of Nazi propagandists. During the war, Bruner entered the army and worked on psychological warfare in General Eisenhower's headquarters in SHAEF (Supreme Headquarters Allied Expeditionary Force). He returned to Harvard in 1945, and in 1947 he published a significant paper on the importance of needs as they influence perception. In this study he showed that poor children are more likely to overestimate the size of coins than are well-to-do children. From this study he concluded that values and needs strongly affect human perceptions and also that people make meaning out of their perceptions by making them consistent with their past experiences. People are thus able to reduce the possibility of mental strain by viewing the world in such a way as to reduce environmental surprises. These findings led to what became known as the "new look" in perception theory and also laid the groundwork for an American school of cognitive psychology. Cognitive psychology deals with the human being's ability to obtain knowledge and develop intellectually. Although the field of cognitive psychology had been important in Europe, America, under the heavy influence of the behaviorist tradition, had turned a deaf ear to anything as subjective and "unscientific" as the study of thinking. Bruner changed all that. By 1960 he had helped found Harvard University's Center for Cognitive Studies, and although he didn't invent cognitive psychology, he certainly went a long way toward making it systematic and consistent with the rules of science.

Always the empiricist, Bruner kept science's basic rule clearly in mind: Begin by observing the data from which the conclusions are to be drawn. Once when a group of academic psychologists was debating the possible impact a certain film might have on children, Bruner was brought in as a consultant. After listening to this group of armchair speculators for a while, Bruner suddenly interrupted them and said, "I've got it! We'll get a child, show him the film, and then we'll ask him what he thought of it."

This is also Bruner's approach to the problems of educational psychology. If you want to know how children go about the business of learning in the school situation, then study children in the classroom, not rats and pigeons in cages.

In 1960 Bruner published the important work *The Process of Education.* As *Harper's Magazine* said, "To people starved for reasonable comments on education in intelligible English, Bruner's writings are above reproach." In this book Bruner developed three important points. First, schools should strive to teach the general nature, or the "structure," of a subject rather than all the details and facts of a subject. Second, any subject can be taught effectively in some intellectually honest form to any child at any stage of development. And finally, Bruner stressed the importance of intuition in learning. Intuition is a problem-solving technique whereby a child relies on insight or immediate apprehensions rather than planned steps of analysis.

Bruner's work has not gone unnoticed by his colleagues. In 1963 the American Psychological Association awarded him the Distinguished Scientific Award. In 1965 Bruner was elected president of the American Psychological Association.

When the spring semester at Harvard came to a close, Bruner would leave the summer heat of Cambridge for the fresh winds of the sea. On his sailboat, Bruner and his wife and children confronted the natural forces of wind and tide. He is as skilled a navigator as he is psychologist and researcher.

In 1972, more than thirty years after his arrival at Harvard as a graduate student, Bruner left to begin the newly created duties of Watts Professor of Psychology at Oxford University in England.

Jerome Bruner has made things happen in educational psychology. Says *Harper's*, "He is the first person to come along in years—perhaps the first since John Dewey—who can speak intelligently about education to his fellow scholars as well as to educators."

Bruner's First Principle: Motivation

Bruner's first principle, motivation, specifies the conditions that predispose an individual to learn. What are the critical variables, especially during the preschool years, that help motivate and enable the child to learn? Implicit in Bruner's principles is the belief that almost all children have a built-in "will to learn." However, Bruner has not discarded the notion of reinforcement. He believes that reinforcement, or external reward, may be important for initiating certain actions or for making sure they are repeated. He insists, however, that it is only through intrinsic motivation that the will to learn is sustained. Bruner is far more concerned with intrinsic motivation than with what he believes to be the more transitory effects of external motivation.

Perhaps the best example of intrinsic motivation is curiosity. Bruner believes that we come into the world equipped with a curiosity drive. He feels this drive is biologically relevant, that curiosity is necessary to the survival of the species. Bruner suggests that young children are often too curious; they are unable to "stick with" any one activity. Their curiosity leads them to turn from one activity to another in rapid succession, and the curiosity must therefore be channeled into a more powerful intellectual pursuit. Games like Twenty Questions help develop a sense of disciplined curiosity in the child.

Another motivation we bring into the world with us is the drive to achieve competence. Children become interested in what they are good at, and it is virtually impossible to motivate them to engage in activities in which they have no degree of competence.

Finally, Bruner lists reciprocity as a motivation that is built into the species. Reciprocity involves a need to work with others cooperatively, and Bruner feels that society itself developed as a result of this most basic motivation.

According to Bruner, the intrinsic motivations are rewarding in themselves and are therefore self-sustaining. How can the teacher take advantage of this in the classroom situation? Bruner's answer is that teachers must facilitate and regulate their students' exploration of alternatives. Since learning and problem solving demand the exploration of alternatives, this is at the very core of the issue and is critical in creating a predisposition to the long-term pursuit of learning.

The exploration of alternatives has three phases: activation, maintenance, and direction.

Activation In order to activate exploration, in order to get it started, children must experience

Teen-agers playing in a high-school orchestra exemplify two motivating factors: a drive to achieve competence and a need to work with others cooperatively.

a certain level of uncertainty. If the task is too easy, they will be too bored to explore alternatives, and yet if it is too difficult, they will be too confused to explore alternatives. This is similar to J. McV. Hunt's problem of the match, already discussed in Chapter 4. The teacher must provide students with problems that are just difficult enough for the children's intrinsic curiosity motivation to itself activate exploration.

Maintenance   Once activated, exploration must be maintained. This involves assuring children that exploration is not going to be a dangerous or painful experience. Children must view exploration under the guiding hand of the teacher as less risky, less dangerous than exploration on their own. The advantages of exploration must be made greater than the risks.

Direction   Meaningful exploration must have direction. The direction of exploration is a function of two factors: knowledge of the goal, and knowledge that the exploration of alternatives

is relevant to the achievement of that goal. Children must know what the goal is and how close they are to achieving it.

Thus, Bruner's first principle indicates that children have a built-in will to learn. Teachers must manage and enhance this motivation so that children will see that guided exploration is more meaningful and satisfying than the spontaneous learning they can achieve on their own. In short, Bruner's first principle is a justification for formal schooling.

Bruner's Second Principle: Structure

Bruner's second principle states that any given subject area, any body of knowledge, can be organized in some optimal fashion so that it can be transmitted to and understood by almost any student. If appropriately structured, "any idea or problem or body of knowledge can be presented in a form simple enough so that any particular learner can understand it in a recognizable form."[18] This is not to say that all of the nuances of Einstein's theory of relativity can be fully mastered by a six-year-old child. It does mean, however, that if properly structured, Einstein's general position could be understood by the child, and that under questioning the child could convey to a physicist a recognizable account of the theory.

According to Bruner, the structure of any body of knowledge can be characterized in three ways: mode of presentation, economy, and power.

Mode of presentation   Mode of presentation refers to the technique, the method, whereby information is communicated. One of the reasons teachers fail to convey some fundamental point to a seemingly uncomprehending child is that the teacher's mode of presentation simply does not fit with the child's level of experience. The child will remain uncomprehending as long as the message is incomprehensible. Bruner believes that a person has three means of achieving understanding: enactive, iconic, and symbolic representation.

Enactive representation is needed for very young children, who can understand things best in terms of actions. For example, children can demonstrate their understanding of the principles of a balance beam by referring to their experiences on a seesaw. If the child on the other end is heavier, you compensate by sliding farther back on your own end; if the other child is lighter, you push yourself farther forward. Young children also define words in terms of the actions that are associated with them: A chair is to sit on, a spoon is to eat with, and so on. When children are in the enactive stage of thinking, it is important that the teacher's messages somehow make contact with their muscles. Even adults may revert to enactive representation when learning something new, especially a new motor skill. Teaching an adult to ski is best accomplished wordlessly. A skilled ski instructor doesn't just tell students to "edge into the hill" but will instead ask them to imitate her own stance. In short, when young children are in the enactive stage of thinking, the best, the most comprehensible messages are wordless ones.

Iconic representation may be used with somewhat older children. They learn to think at the iconic level when objects become con-

ceivable without action. Children can now draw a picture of a spoon, without acting out the eating process. They may even be able, at this stage, to draw a diagram of a balance beam, for they now possess an image of it that no longer depends on action. This is a significant breakthrough in the development of intellect, for the use of pictures or diagrams allows children at this stage to be tutored in simpler ways.

Symbolic representation can be used at the stage when children can translate experience into language. The balance beam can be explained through the use of words rather than pictures. Symbolic representation allows children to begin making logical derivations and to think more compactly. Bruner says that through symbolic representation "powerful representations of the world of possible experiences are constructed and used as search models in problem solving."[19]

Which of these modes should the teacher choose in order to facilitate the learning pro-

At the iconic level subjects become conceivable without having to be acted out.

During the symbolic stage the child can translate experience into language.

cess? It depends on the learner's age and background and on the subject matter itself. For example, Bruner believes that teaching a problem in law demands symbolic representation, whereas geography is well suited to the iconic. New motor skills are often best communicated by enactive representation, especially at first. Mathematics can be represented, and often should be, by all three modes.

Economy of presentation   Economy in communicating a body of knowledge depends on the amount of information the learner must keep in mind in order to continue learning. The fewer bits of information, the fewer facts the learner must bear in mind, the greater the economy. The best way to provide economy in teaching is to give the learner concise summaries. For example, Bruner feels that it is more economical to "summarize the American Civil War as a battle over slavery than as a struggle between an expanding industrial region and one built upon

a class society for control of federal economic power."[20]

Power of presentation   Bruner believes that nature is simple; hence, to be powerful, a presentation of some aspect of nature should reflect nature's simplicity. Teachers often make difficult what is inherently easy. A powerful presentation is a simple presentation, one that is easily understood. It allows the learner to see new relationships, to find connections between facts that may at first seem quite separate. Bruner feels that a powerful presentation is especially important in the field of mathematics.

Bruner's Third Principle: Sequence

The extent to which a student finds it difficult to master a given subject depends largely on the sequence in which the material is presented—Bruner's third principle. Teaching involves leading the learner through a certain sequence of the various aspects of the subject. Since Bruner believes that intellectual development is innately sequential, moving from enactive through iconic to symbolic representation, he feels it is highly probable that this is also the best sequence for any subject to take. Thus, the teacher should begin teaching any new subject with wordless messages, speaking mainly to the learner's muscular responses. Then the student should be encouraged to explore the use of diagrams and various pictorial representations. Finally, the message should be communicated symbolically, through the use of words. This is obviously a very conservative approach. Some children, because of their age and background, may seem to be able to begin a new area at the symbolic level. But, though conservative, this sequence is safe. Children who seem ready to handle new material at the symbolic level may suddenly become lost and

confused if they haven't been given the basic imagery to fall back on.

Bruner's Fourth Principle: Reinforcement

Bruner's fourth principle is that learning requires reinforcement. In order to achieve mastery of a problem, we must receive feedback as to how we are doing. The timing of the reinforcement is crucial to success in learning. The results must be learned at the very time a student is evaluating his or her own performance. If the results are known too soon, the learner will become confused and his or her explorations will be stifled. If they are known too late, the learner may have gone beyond the point where the knowledge would have been helpful, and by this time the child may have incorporated false information. The teacher's role is indeed sensitive. If the learner has gone on to

Teaching involves leading the learner through a certain sequence of the various aspects of a subject.

incorporate false information, this must now be unlearned in order for the learner to get back on the right track.

Not only is the timing of the reinforcement important, but the reinforcement must also be in a form that the learner will understand. If the learner is operating at the enactive level, reinforcement at the iconic or symbolic level may be useless. To be helpful, feedback must be made understandable to the learner.

Discovery Learning

Though it is possible to memorize a poem, the multiplication tables, or the state capitals, meaningful learning often requires actual discovery. The facts and relationships children discover through their own explorations are more usable and tend to be better retained than material they have merely committed to memory. Teachers can provide the conditions in which discovery is nourished and will grow. One way they can do this is to guess at answers and let the class know they are guessing. The students can then analyze the teacher's answer. This helps prove to them that exploration can be both rewarding and safe, and it is thus a valuable technique for building lifelong discovery habits in the students.

Bruner is not saying that discovery learning is the only form of learning. Nor is he saying that students must discover for themselves the solutions to every problem in a given field. That would be extremely wasteful, if it were even possible, for it would mean that each generation would have to rediscover the ideas and technology of their culture. Beginning physics students, for example, shouldn't have to discover the technology of radio transmission, as Marconi once did. Students can, however, through insightful questioning and prompting by the teacher, discover for themselves some of the basic principles that account for radio transmission. Learning through such discoveries enables the student to reach a level of understanding that far surpasses the rote memorization of a radio chapter in an electronics book.

Discovery learning is more conceptual, and studies have repeatedly shown that conceptual learning has longer-lasting consequences than nonconceptual activities. Also, conceptual re-

tention promotes greater feelings of self-esteem on the part of the learner.[21]

Teaching for discovery is obviously not easy. The teacher must be bright, flexible, and really know the subject matter. In order to communicate knowledge, the teacher must have mastery of that knowledge. Finally, the good teacher is a patient teacher, for discovery teaching cannot be hurried. It is often frustratingly slow, but the goal of real student understanding is well worth the wait.

A FINAL COMPARISON

At times it may seem that Skinner and Bruner are from two different worlds, that they discuss entirely different concepts. In part, this is true. Skinner's data came primarily from his work with rats and pigeons; Bruner's from his observations of children in learning situations. Skinner is an associationist; Bruner a cognitive theorist. Skinner is an avowed behaviorist; Bruner speculates on events occurring within the child's mind. Yet both are discussing learning, and both are talking to working teachers. Skinner speaks of the laws of conditioning, and Bruner, acknowledging that the teacher is a potent reinforcer, insists that the teacher should know these laws.

Piaget has stated that there are really two kinds of learning, P learning and LM learning. P learning is physical learning, learning that takes place when physical things act on us. LM learning is logico-mathematical learning, learning that results from our actions on things.[22]

That distinction of Piaget's is similar to the distinction between associative and cognitive learning. P learning is, in effect, conditioning, and it's the kind of learning that has been so thoroughly analyzed by Watson, Thorndike, and Skinner. P learning is externally motivated; it is the properties of the physical objects that act on us (the sweetness of candy or the aversive properties of a slap on the hand) that have a potential reinforcing effect. This, of course, is precisely the way the behaviorists have described motivation in learning; and indeed this is exactly the way they should have described it, since they have been describing P learning almost exclusively. When Skinner tells us that learning is the result of a given response followed by a reinforcing stimulus, he is in effect defining P learning— a physical event acting on the learner. LM learning, on the other hand, has been more the province of the cognitive-gestaltist theorists. LM learning is the result of our continuous experience of organizing and reorganizing our actions as we proceed toward the goal of understanding. Piaget says that LM learning is intrinsically motivated; that is, the discovery of a new relationship is self-rewarding. When children experience new LM relationships that they have discovered through their own actions, they feel pleasure, a joy that swells up from within.

After examining the positions of Skinner and Bruner, can we now say which one is right— which theory says it all? The answer, of course, is that both are right, though neither one is likely to have the supertheory. Skinner's laws of conditioning are certainly valid. The evidence with regard to operant conditioning overwhelmingly supports his position. Skinner has much to teach us about how to teach. He has simplified and made more efficient the learning

of the informational background children need in order to think creatively. It must be remembered that P learning, though perhaps not as glamorous as LM, is crucial to intellectual growth. Skinner has given us invaluable aids for transmitting this P-learning base.

Bruner, too, has made an extremely important contribution, but at a different level. In his theory of instruction he has pointed out ways of carrying children beyond mere conditioning, or P learning. Bruner's interest is more in the area of cognitive organization, understanding, LM learning. To some extent, Bruner's theory may be more speculative than Skinner's, but exciting advances in science have often in the past been foreshadowed by sophisticated speculation. This isn't to imply that Bruner's position is not perched on an empirical base. After all, Bruner has spent long hours watching children going about the business of learning.

It is certainly true that all the answers are not yet in on this complex phenomenon called learning, but it is also true that Skinner and Bruner have pointed us in the direction of knowing more about what the questions are.

SUMMARY

Two major theorists in educational psychology are spotlighted in this chapter; Skinner, representing the behaviorist-associationist tradition, and Bruner, representing the cognitive-gestalt tradition. Both Skinner and Bruner discuss issues in learning that are of practical importance to the classroom teacher.

Skinner bases his concept of learning on the experimental facts of operant conditioning. Operant conditioning occurs when a response is followed by a reinforcing stimulus. The rate of responding then increases. Skinner distinguishes between operants (responses that need no stimuli to set them off) and respondents (responses that do need unconditioned stimuli to be activated). Skinner uses the term *respondent* to describe the same kind of behavior that Pavlov had previously described during his conditioning studies on dogs—that is, Skinner's *respondent* is synonymous with Pavlov's *reflex*.

The operant conditioning system also in-

cludes such other concepts and techniques as extinction, spontaneous recovery, discrimination, stimulus generalization, and conditioned reinforcement.

Skinner has also conducted research into the schedules of reinforcement—that is, the methods by which reinforcers are arranged. Responses that are reinforced periodically, either on the basis of time or the number of responses emitted, are conditioned more strongly and are thus more difficult to extinguish.

Skinner indicates that language is learned via the principles of operant conditioning. Also, such cognitive-sounding concepts as understanding and knowledge are really examples of operant conditioning. In order to gain knowledge, one must be equipped with the specific set of responses from which that knowledge may be inferred.

Good teaching, according to Skinner, is the ability to arrange the proper sequences of reinforcements for the student and then to be certain that the presentation of these reinforcers is contingent on the student emitting the correct response.

Behaviorism today faces two important challenges, one due to internal, experimental anomalies (experimental results that are not consistent with the theory), and the other due to the rise of a more ethological and functional interpretation of behaviorism's known facts. Any theory faces a severe test when another theory can predict outcomes with more accuracy and entails fewer assumptions.

Somewhere between the behaviorist-associationist position and the cognitive-gestalt position lies a theory of learning called "mediation theory." Mediation theory tells us that much of learning can be explained on the basis of internal, nonobservable S-R systems, such as words and images, which are attached to the overt stimuli and responses. Learning is aided immeasurably by the use of internal mediators.

Bruner's position regarding learning is in the cognitive-gestalt tradition. His goal is to create a theory of instruction that will allow a teacher to prescribe how a given subject can best be taught.

Bruner's theory has four major principles: (1) motivation, (2) structure, (3) sequence, and (4) reinforcement. These four principles are aimed at producing a learning based on understanding and meaning, rather than on the conditioning of facts and details.

Bruner insists that meaningful learning requires the child to search actively for solutions. Such discovery learning is far more long-lasting and useful than learning based on memorization and conditioning. Good teaching demands that the student be encouraged to explore alternatives and discover new relationships. Bruner also insists that when presented appropriately, any subject matter can be understood by almost any child.

The theories of Skinner and Bruner, though seemingly diametrically opposed, share a common framework when viewed from the position of Jean Piaget. Piaget distinguishes between P learning, learning that takes place when physical things act on us, and LM learning, learning that results from our actions on things. Skinner's position seems consistent with Piaget's P learning, while Bruner may be discussing Piaget's LM learning.

KEY TERMS AND NAMES

B. F. Skinner
  reinforcement
  positive reinforcement
  negative reinforcement
  respondents
  operants
  operant conditioning
  respondent conditioning
  operant level
  spontaneous recovery
  discrimination
  stimulus generalization
  conditioned reinforcement
  schedules of reinforcement

Noam Chomsky
mediation theory
paired-associate learning
Jerome Bruner
  motivation
  structure
  enactive representation
  iconic representation
  symbolic representation
  discovery learning
  P (physical) learning
  LM (logico-mathematical) learning

REFERENCES

1. Skinner, B. F. (1938). *The behavior of organisms: An experimental analysis*. New York: Appleton-Century-Crofts.

2. Carpenter, F. (1974). *The Skinner primer* (pp. 8–9). New York: Free Press.

3. Carpenter, *The Skinner primer* (p. 28).

4. Skinner, B. F. (1978). Why don't we use the behavioral sciences? *Human Nature, 1* (1), 32.

5. Skinner, B. F. (1971). *Beyond freedom and dignity* (p. 169). New York: Knopf.

6. Chomsky, N. (1957). *Syntactic structures*. The Hague: Mouton. See also Chomsky, N. (1965). *Aspects of the theory of syntax*. Cambridge, Mass.: MIT Press.

7. Gentile, J. R. (1978). A cross-cultural, multidisciplinary proof of the newly discovered developmental linguistic law of concordance of speech, and motor development in children. *American Psychologist, 33* (8), 761.

8. Kuhn, T. S. (1970). *The structure of scientific revolutions*, 2nd ed. Chicago: University of Chicago Press.

9. Seligman, M. E. P. (1970). On the generality of the laws of learning. *Psychological Review, 77,* 410.

10. Bregman, E. O. (1934). An attempt to modify the emotional attitudes of infants by the conditioning response technique. *Journal of Genetic Psychology, 45,* 169–178.

11. Seligman, M. E. P. (1972). Phobias and preparedness. In M. E. P. Seligman and J. L. Hager (Eds.), *Biological boundaries of learning*. New York: Appleton-Century-Crofts.

12. Breland, K., and Breland, M. (1961). The misbehavior of organisms. *American Psychologist, 16,* 681–684.

13. Moore, B. R. (1973). The role of directed Pavlovian reaction in simple instrumental learning in the pigeon. In R. A. Hinde and J. Stevenson-Hinde (Eds.), *Constraints on learning*. New York: Academic Press.

14. Bolles, R. C. (1980). Ethological learning theory. In G. M. Gazda and J. Corsini (Eds.), *Theories of learning* (p. 199). Itsaca, Ill.: Peacock.

15. Kendler, H. H., and Kendler, T. S. (1962). Vertical and horizontal processes in problem solving. *Psychological Review, 69,* 1–16.

16. Bruner, J. S. (1962). *The process of education* (p. 6). Cambridge, Mass.: Harvard University Press.

17. Bruner, *The process of education* (p. 28).

18. Bruner, J. S. (1966). *Toward a theory of instruction* (p. 44). Cambridge, Mass.: Harvard University Press.

19. Bruner, *Toward a theory of instruction* (p. 14).

20. Bruner, *Toward a theory of instruction* (p. 46).

21. Deci, E. L., Scheinman, L., Wheeler, L., and Hart, R. (1980). Rewards, motivation and self-esteem. *Educational Forum, 44,* 429–433.

22. Piaget, J. (1959). Apprentissage et connaissance (première partie) (pp. 21–67). In P. Greco and J. Piaget (Eds.), *Etudes d'épistémologie génétique*, Vol. 7. Paris: Presses Universitaires de France.

10

LEARNING IN THE CLASSROOM

"In an American school, if you ask for the salt in good French, you get an A. In France you get the salt." This statement by B. F. Skinner illustrates perhaps the major feature of the educational process.[1] The concepts, skills, and techniques we teach are not only useful in the present, but more important, will also be useful at some later time. One of the major goals of education is to equip us to transfer what we learn in the classroom to future situations. Learning to add, subtract, and spell has the immediate advantage of good grades, a gold star, a promotion to the next grade, or perhaps a teacher's or parent's general approval. Eventually, however, the advantages become more compelling. In later life we learn that our ability to spell or multiply or derive square roots has enormous practical consequences, for example, in helping us earn a living. Some of us learn this too late. "If only I had paid more attention in school," we moan. And, we might add, we might have paid more attention if our classroom experience had been structured differently.

TRANSFER

Transfer is the key to classroom learning. Transfer takes place when learning task A influences learning task B. Transfer may be positive or negative. When learning A facilitates learning B, positive transfer is said to have taken place; conversely, when learning A inhibits learning B, negative transfer has occurred. Here are a few examples of positive transfer: Learning to ride a motorcycle is easier if you already know how to ride a bike; learning Italian is easier if you already know Latin; writing a letter to Santa Claus is easy if you have learned your second-grade spelling. Here are some examples of negative transfer: Learning to lean forward while snow-skiing may cause you to fall on your face when you learn to water-ski; learning to keep your elbows away from your body to hit a baseball may cause a disastrous slice when you learn to hit a golf ball; studying a French assignment until the wee hours may wreak havoc with the Spanish exam you take the next morning.

There is also a special case of negative transfer in which the influence works in reverse. You successfully learn A and then learn B; when you

233

try to recall A, you draw a complete blank. This is called "retroactive inhibition," and it happens when the second task works retroactively to inhibit recall of the first task. More will be said on this important topic when we discuss information processing in Chapter 11.

Formal Discipline

Current theories of transfer can be traced back to the early Greek notion of formal discipline. According to this view, the role of the school is to discipline the students' minds. It was thought that the mind, like an athlete's muscles, must be systematically exercised until it becomes so strong it can learn and understand virtually any new material. The theory of formal discipline remained in vogue until the early twentieth century. Subjects such as logic, Latin, and Greek were taught not for their practical value, but because they were thought to strengthen the student's mind to the point where all later problem solving would be easy.

The challenges to formal discipline   The theory of formal discipline was challenged around the turn of the century by three important psychologists. The first, William James, put the theory to the test.[2] He spent 132 minutes, over an eight-day period, memorizing a long segment of poetry (Victor Hugo's *Satyr*). He reasoned that if the theory of formal discipline was correct, exercising the mind by memorizing another poem would make further memorization easier. He therefore spent the next thirty-eight days memorizing Book I of Milton's *Paradise Lost*. Finally, he tried to memorize another segment of the *Satyr*, equal in length to the first segment he had memorized, only to find that it took him even longer than it had previously. The results of this rather informal test led James to suspect the validity of the theory of formal discipline.

The second challenger, E. L. Thorndike, had subjects practice estimating the length of lines one-half to one-and-one-half inches long.[3] When these subjects achieved a certain degree of accuracy in this task, Thorndike introduced a different, though similar task: estimating the length of lines six to twelve inches long. Thorndike found that there was little, if any, improve-

ment on the second task as a result of the practice gained from the first task. Although he believed that he had thoroughly refuted the theory of formal discipline, Thorndike still maintained that transfer could occur. Thorndike based his explanation of transfer on the existence of certain elements in the second task that were identical to those in the first task.

The third challenger, Charles Judd, took on both the theory of formal discipline and Thorndike's "identical elements." In a classic experiment, Judd trained two groups of boys to hit a target submerged in twelve inches of water.[4] One group of boys, the experimental group, was instructed in the general principles of refraction; the control group was not. Although both groups did equally well while the target was at the twelve-inch depth, when it was later raised to a depth of four inches, the boys in the experimental group performed significantly better. The boys in the control group, who had not been given any of the principles of refraction, responded to the new task as though it were a completely new problem. On the basis of this experiment, Judd postulated the theory of transfer by generalization, which stated that transfer is far more efficient when the theory or the generalization behind the task is learned. The boys who had simply learned to hit a target submerged in twelve inches of water transferred this skill only to other targets also submerged twelve inches deep. When the target depth was changed, no transfer took place.

Judd thus insisted that classroom students should be taught abstractions and generalizations as well as the details of a subject. Students should still learn certain facts and possess certain information, but their ability to transfer depended equally on a basic understanding of the theoretical generalizations that allow those facts to be interpreted. Robert Travers says:

> The student of geography must have certain essential information about a nation, such as location, population, resources and economy. . . . Yet, mastery of this knowledge for the sake of mastery is insufficient. The instructor should guide his students to realize that economic diversity, for instance, in modern society is a necessity for any nation. Dependence on one crop is disastrous if the world market would shift its need for this single item.[5]

The Learning Curve

Many studies of the learning process have shown that the acquisition of new information or of a new skill proceeds in a predictable fashion. When first confronting a new subject, we begin learning slowly and then pick up speed rather dramatically. Finally, our pace slows down and begins to level off.

Figure 10.1 shows a typical learning curve. It is said to be negatively accelerated because as the number of trials increases, there is less and less increase in the amount learned. After the first few trials, in which the learner is "catching on" to the basic procedures, rather huge gulps of new learning are quickly assimilated. As time goes on, however, improvement becomes less and less pronounced and finally levels off. This leveling off is called a "plateau." Novice golfers may score 150 their first few times around the course, but after their fourth or fifth round they may be down to around 120. At this point they may feel that it's easy to excel at golf and that, if they can continue lopping 30 strokes off their score, they will soon be ready for "the tour." They soon learn, however, that lowering their score from 100 to 90 is far more difficult than lowering it from 120 to 110.

Students learning a new skill may reach a whole series of plateaus. Typing students, for example, may proceed fairly rapidly at first and then level off. Perhaps they were learning the keyboard letter by letter. Suddenly, they notice another increase in performance, for now they have learned certain letter sequences like *ing*, or *tion*, or *the*, which can be rattled off as though they were single letters. This is actually an example of positive transfer, in which the previous learning finally builds up to the point where a

sharp increase in new learning has become possible.

Learning Sets

Harry Harlow has done some important research in learning, using monkeys as subjects. Harlow coined the phrase "learning set" to describe the phenomenon of learning how to learn. He found that with practice his monkeys became increasingly skilled at solving discrimination problems. They improved not only on the previously learned problems but on novel problems as well. The fact that the monkeys developed these learning sets freed "them from the restrictions of the slow, trial-and-error process of the original attempts."[6]

Using straight reinforcement techniques, Harlow trained monkeys to respond to an odd item among a set of three items. For example, the monkey would be presented with three geometric shapes, two circles and an "odd" item, in this case a triangle. Once the monkey learned to respond to the triangle, a different three-item set was presented, say two knives and a fork. With enough previous training, the monkeys would show the ability to select the fork, the new odd item. In short, the monkeys had learned a rule or a relationship rather than a simple discriminated response to the triangle.

Harlow feels that his concept of learning sets has explained what the gestalt psychologists had labeled "insight." He sees the sudden spurt in learning, the so-called a-ha phenomenon, as just another extension of the theoretical concept of transfer.

Students can also be trained in learning how to learn. Through instruction, students have demonstrated an increased ability to learn relationships, which aided them in the retention of both classroom and textbook materials.[7]

Massed Versus Distributed Learning

If you had four hours to parcel out any way you wished, how could you make the most of this time to learn a new skill? In learning new motor skills, the evidence is fairly clear—distributed practice of, say, sixteen fifteen-minute segments is more efficient than a massive dose of four straight hours. When learning to skate, ride a

FIGURE 10.1   A typical learning curve.

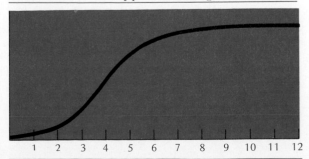

| 1 | 2 | 3 | 4 | 5 | 6 | 7 | 8 | 9 | 10 | 11 | 12 |

bike, or perform a new skill in a physical education class, this distributed practice prescription is indeed sound advice. Not only are the shorter sessions less fatiguing but by their very nature, motor skills are best learned a step at a time. When it comes to more intellectual tasks, however, the situation is somewhat different. To learn a simple problem or a passage of poetry, it is probably best to use a single sitting of massed practice, since breaking this kind of material down into smaller units makes it less meaningful. Bruner has stressed the importance of keeping a subject internally coherent and meaningful when setting up efficient learning conditions. When longer material must be learned, a compromise can be worked out; the material can be divided into meaningful units and learned in several massed-practice sessions.

Whole versus part learning   The question of whether the material to be learned should be carved up and doled out in small units, or whether it should be presented as an integrated whole, if only sketchily, is of great concern to educators. Is it more efficient for you, the reader, to try to master the material in this chapter by reading three pages a day, or by reading through the whole chapter first and then going back and attempting to iron out the details? The message from Jerome Bruner is clear—the more meaningful the material, the easier it is to learn. Therefore, breaking it down into parts is a risky venture, unless the material to be learned is something like Ebbinghaus's nonsense syllables. The trouble with learning material in parts is that the parts eventually have to be pieced back together, and this can be extremely time-consuming. In many learning situations the best approach is to work first on the whole and then to go back to the various parts. When presenting a new unit in, say, social studies, the teacher should spend some time discussing the general point of view of the whole unit before introducing the details. Giving the student an overview of the whole unit makes even the use of a teaching machine more effective.

SOCIAL LEARNING OR MODELING

Albert Bandura, an important contemporary psychologist, has suggested that a significant part of what a person learns occurs through

The more meaningful the material, the easier it is to learn. When introducing new material to students, give a general overview of the subject matter before introducing the details.

imitation or modeling. Bandura has been called a "social learning theorist" in that he is concerned with the learning that takes place in the context of the social situation. During social interactions an individual may learn to modify his or her behavior as a result of how others in the group are responding.

Bandura's social learning theory is truly an all-inclusive psychology, borrowing as much from behaviorists as from cognitive theorists. Bandura sees behavior, internal cognitive structures, and the environment as interacting so that each acts as an interlocking determinant of the other.[8] People are to some extent products of their environments, but they also choose and shape their environments. It's not simply a one-way street.

Modeling Versus Operant Conditioning

Though recognizing the importance of Skinner's operant conditioning, Bandura insists that not all learning takes place as a result of the direct reinforcement of responses. People also learn by imitating the behavior of other people, or models, and this learning takes place even though these imitative responses are not themselves being directly reinforced. For example, a young child may stand up when the "Star-Spangled Banner" is played because he sees his parents stand. The child's response in this instance is not immediately followed by an M&M candy or any other primary reinforcer. The child simply imitates the response made by his parents.

Learning new responses   In the previous example, the child's abilty to stand up was, of course, already a part of his behavioral repertoire. Bandura further says that people can also learn *new* responses simply by observing the behavior of others. A child learns to ski, or an adult learns a tennis stroke, simply by imitating the behavior of the instructor. The language-lab method of teaching a foreign language is based on the premise that people can efficiently learn to imitate the sentences and phrases that are electronically reproduced for them to hear. The list of new forms of behavior that can be learned through modeling is virtually endless, and though the previous examples stress positive

forms of learning, modeling may also create undersirable responses. A child may learn to become overly aggressive, or deceitful and dishonest, through the modeling mechanism.

In a now classic study, Bandura subjected a group of young children (ages three to six) to the improbable spectacle of watching adult models punch, kick, and yell at a large, inflated "Bobo" doll.[9] When later allowed to play with "Bobo" themselves, these children displayed twice as many aggressive responses as a control group of children who had not witnessed this performance. The form of imitation in this study was indeed direct. The children even yelled the same phrases the adults had used: "Kick him," "Sock him in the nose," and so on. One might speculate that had the adults danced with "Bobo" rather than punching him, the children, too, would have behaved in this gentler fashion.

Reinforcement and modeling   Though, as has been shown, learning through modeling does not require direct and immediate reinforcement, Bandura has suggested that reinforcement may still be involved. In the first place, many of the significant models in the child's world, parents and teachers, are also in charge of the child's reinforcement schedule. The parent may not only provide the modeling stimulus but may also reinforce the child when the behavior is imitated. Second, Bandura has demonstrated that a child is more apt to imitate an adult model's response when the adult is being reinforced for that response.[10] In other words, the child who observes an adult being praised for a certain action is more likely to respond in the same way than is a child who views the action but not the subsequent reinforcement. Bandura calls this "vicarious" learning, since the learner in this instance is not being reinforced but is merely witnessing the reinforcement.

Thus, reinforcement and modeling can together create very potent conditions for behavior change. Many of our most persistent habits and attitudes are a result of this combination of powerful forces.

Modeling and retention   Reproducing the behavior of the model when the model is no longer present is facilitated when the learner

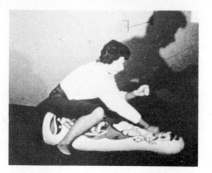

Bandura exposed a group of young children to adults who punched, kicked, and yelled at an inflated "Bobo" doll. Later, in playing with doll, these children displayed twice as many aggressive responses as children who had not seen the aggressive behavior.

uses verbal coding to symbolically store the behavior sequence in memory. That is, modeled behavior is retained longer if the learner can describe the behavior in words. This allows for internal rehearsal and organization. Although the learner can still model on the basis of visual imagery, verbal coding encompasses a far wider range of the kinds of activities usually found in schools.[11]

Modeling as a therapy technique   Bandura has also shown that the modeling process can be used as a technique in psychotherapy. Just as persons can learn certain fears through modeling, so too can these fears become unlearned. A child, for example, may learn to fear snakes by observing his father recoil in horror at the sight of a snake. In one study, Bandura attempted to cure a group of individuals, all of whom had severe snake phobias.[12] The subjects in one group watched, in various stages of agitation, while the experimenter or model handled and played with a king snake. The experimenter then urged the subjects to imitate his behavior, asking them first to touch the snake while wearing gloves, and later with their bare hands. After ten sessions, the cure rate was a phenomenal 100 percent. All of the subjects in the "Live Modeling" group were able to pass the criterion test, that is, sit quietly for thirty seconds while a large snake was allowed to crawl all over them.

Significance in the Classroom

Other than the parents, the classroom teacher may be the most important model in the child's environment. Many children have been known to model their teacher's behavior so closely that they in a sense "become" the teacher when interacting with younger brothers and sisters at home. In some cases, these children demand that the younger siblings call them by their teacher's name—"I'm not Debbie, I'm Mrs. D." The teacher's likes and dislikes regarding subject matter may become obvious to the students and result in imitative attitudes. The teacher who loves music but hates math may, through vicarious learning, transmit these feelings to the class. So-called math blocks may be created in

this way, and the student can be permanently affected.

Other types of negative teacher behavior may also be imitated by the students. A first-grade teacher was having a very difficult time maintaining what she considered to be proper discipline in her classroom. She began spending more and more time screaming at the children. The parents of one of the children found that each day, after school, the child would shut herself up in her room and scream at her dolls (even using the same words the teacher had used). A teacher's attitude toward minority-group students can also have a significant effect, both on how the minority student learns to perceive himself or herself and on how the student is perceived by the other members of the class. In short, teachers provide conditions for learning in the classroom, not only by what they say but also by what they do.

OPERANT CONDITIONING IN THE CLASSROOM

As we saw in the previous chapter, Skinner's principles of operant conditioning can be translated into specific classroom techniques. The Skinnerians feel that colleges have failed to equip prospective teachers for the actual day-to-day job of educating children. The new teacher, no matter how knowledgeable in educational theory, is usually at a complete loss when it comes to putting theory into practice. The teacher may understand the importance of recognizing individual differences, and may know full well that learning requires motivation and that students' interest must be captured, but then what? What happens when, in order to motivate students, the new teacher proudly displays the best student's written work on the bulletin board, only to find the next day that the essay is on the floor and the thumbtacks have been stolen? What happens when the new teacher, steeped in the philosophy of "fairness," leaves the room and asks the students to cover their eyes so that the one guilty child can come discreetly forward and return a dime that has been stolen from another child? Not only is the dime not returned, but one young philanthropist, missing the teacher's point entirely, loudly offers to contribute a dime to the aggrieved child so that the class can go on to important matters. What happens when the new teacher demands that an unruly child sit down and be quiet, only to have the child stare back coolly and say, "Make me!"? What happens when . . . and on and on.

The current popularity of operant conditioning techniques is due in large measure to the fact that operant conditioning offers the teacher a precise prescription for handling specific classroom situations. The Skinnerians do not resort to such clichés as "seizing the teachable moment" or being an "educational provocateur." The Skinnerians are specific, and they urge the teacher to be just as specific.

The Case for Behavior Modification

Some of the essentials of this thing we now call behavior modification have probably been with us since time immemorial. As soon as people "discovered" that their behavior could be affected by environmental conditions, some aspects of behavior modification came into being. Many of today's college students, on hearing their first lecture on behavior modification, respond with a smug yawn and ask, "So what else is new?"

The fact is, however, that despite its apparently long history, and despite its obvious overtones of "mere common sense," behavior modification as it is technically understood and used today is of fairly recent origin. The *American Psychologist* distinguishes between behavior influence and behavior modification.[13]

1. *Behavior influence*: a very general phenomenon that occurs anytime one person is able to exert some degree of control over the behavior of another person. "This occurs constantly in such diverse situations as formal school education, advertising, child-rearing, political campaigning, and other normal interpersonal interactions."[14]

2. *Behavior modification*: a specific type of behavior influence that translates the theories and principles of learning derived from experimental psychology into an applied technique for behavior change. The technique should always be used in the pursuit of pos-

itive goals, that is, to reduce human suffering and increase human functioning. "Behavior modification emphasizes systematic monitoring and evaluation of the effectiveness of these applications . . . and is intended to facilitate improved self-control by expanding individuals' skills, abilities, and independence."[15]

Thus, behavior influence occurs normally whenever people interact and may result in either positive or negative consequences for the people involved. Behavior modification is a precise form of influence, based on research findings and used to promote positive behavior changes.

Finally, it should be pointed out that behavior modification, unlike Freud's theory of psychoanalysis, assumes that the most important forces affecting any individual are the current life experiences, not the memories of childhood events and traumas.

Defining objectives   Every teacher has a general idea of educational goals for the class as a whole or for individual students. It is crucial that these goals be specifically stated in objective, behavioral terms, so that both the teacher and the students know what the goals are and when they have been reached. Furthermore, goals should be specified not just for the term but for each day of the term.

Behavioral terminology avoids words such as *understanding*—that is, words that do not describe a demonstrable behavior. A behaviorally formulated objective is one that describes the behavior that will result when the objective is attained. For example, students can be said to have learned multiplication when they can recite the multiplication table with no errors. In terms of daily goals they may be expected to make no more than five errors the first day, no more than two the second day, and none at all the third day. Each time a goal, or terminal behavior, is reached, a new goal is set so that the first goal is just a step in a continuing process toward an overall goal.

Say the goal, or the terminal behavior, for a certain child is to develop better study habits in the classroom. This must then be defined in behavioral terms. Perhaps the teacher wants the child to not gaze into space, to talk and fidget less, and to read and write more. When objectified in this way, it can be accurately judged whether or not the terminal behavior is achieved, and if it is, exactly when.

Reading skills can be objectified as the ability to recognize correct definitions for a hundred selected words. Music appreciation can be objectified as the ability to identify the composers of twenty musical compositions. The proponents of behavior modification argue that anything that can be taught can be objectified, and that all educational goals can be stated in behavioral terms. Critics may argue that being able to recognize twenty composers "isn't what we mean by musical appreciation," or that recognizing definitions of a hundred selected words "isn't what we mean by reading skills." If so, the Skinnerians would say it is up to the critics to state clearly what they do mean in order that these goals can be knowingly reached:

> Mathematical behavior is usually regarded, not as a repertoire of responses involving numbers and numerical operations, but as evidences of mathematical ability or the exercise of the power of reason. It is true that the techniques which are emerging from the experimental study of learning are not designed to "develop the mind" or to further some vague "understanding" of mathematical realtionships. They are designed, on the contrary, to establish the very behaviors which are taken to be evidences of such mental states or processes.[16]

Establishing the operant level   Once the goal has been defined (and nobody says this is easy, but then, good teaching is not easy), the teacher must observe the student and establish the operant level, or the rate at which the behavior occurs naturally in the classroom. Since student responses are so often specific to the stimulus situation, it is important that the operant level be established by observing the classroom. Many children who are disruptive in class are as good as gold in the counselor's or principal's office. If unruly students are sent to the psychologist's office, they are not as likely to display their disruptive behavior, since the releasers for this behavior remain back in the classroom.

Let's visit a fifth-grade classroom and observe the behavior of an eleven-year-old boy, Walter

S. An art lesson is in progress. As the teacher begins giving the directions for today's project, Walter stands on top of his desk and calls out his own name, "Wally, Wally, Wally," and makes strange, grunting sounds for two minutes. After the teacher's tenth request, Walter sits down and remains silent for just over one minute. The students then file toward the front of the room to pick up their supplies. Walter spends the next two minutes running back and forth, occasionally sliding, as though going into home plate. The teacher brings Walter's supplies to his desk, where Walter remains seated quietly for almost three minutes. Among the art supplies are some elastic bands which he suddenly discovers can be put to use in an aggressive way. He flicks them at the other students for the next thirty seconds, or until he runs out. One girl receives a direct hit and calls loudly to the teacher, who is three rows away helping another student. Walter laughs at the girl's discomfort but immediately takes his seat when the teacher comes over to investigate the uproar. Walter finally gets down to work and remains quietly at his seat for almost ten minutes. Suddenly, he discovers that a certain piece of cardboard, which he had previously cut, doesn't quite fit where he had planned to glue it. He leaps back up on top of his desk, makes loud noises, and contorts his face. The class seems to enjoy his performance, and despite the teacher's pleas, he remains on top of his desk for almost three minutes.

Out of twenty-two minutes of class time, Walter has now spent just over seven minutes engaging in disruptive behavior. His operant level for disruptive behavior is, thus, a little over 34 percent.

What should be done with Walter? Behavior modification experts, like Charles and Clifford Madsen, say that the teacher has the responsibility to help Walter. He is obviously a problem child. In testing Walter, the school psychologist discovers that Walter's home life is extremely bad: He has no father, his older siblings engage in delinquent behavior, there is no supervision in the home at all, and so on. Walter's test scores show him to be "precariously adjusted." Perhaps the teacher now feels a sense of compassion toward Walter and even some guilt for having disliked him so. Walter is probably headed for real trouble and may someday spend a great deal of time in a more structured institution than a school. Should the teacher throw up her arms in dismay and give up trying to interact meaningfully with Walter? The proponents of behavior modification say "no."

In discussing the problem child, in this case the proverbial "Johnny," Madsen and Madsen say:

> The truly pathetic situation is that no one will teach Johnny. The one place where there is some hope for Johnny is the school. Yet, many teachers quickly abdicate responsibility once his history is known. Johnny can discriminate. He can be taught new responses to deal with that world outside the home. He can learn to read, write, spell; he can learn new rules of social interaction and thereby break the cycle of the past. If cooperation (with the home) is impossible, he can even learn these responses in spite of a bad home. It is not easy to deal with the Johnnies [or the Walters]. They take time, energy and a disciplined teacher. All the Johnnies do not survive; yet for these children the school is their only hope. Who has the responsibility of discipline?—The teacher.[17]

The modification of behavior   Once the educational goals have been defined behaviorally and the operant level assessed, one can begin the job of modifying behavior. The techniques used are those outlined in Chapter 9. In order to change responses, in order to modify behavior, we must allow the operant to occur and then provide an appropriate stimulus situation. For example, if we wish to strengthen a certain response (i.e., increase the rate of a given operant), the response must be allowed to occur and then be followed by positive or negative reinforcement. Recall that a positive reinforcement is a stimulus that, following a given response, increases the rate of that response. A negative reinforcement is a stimulus that, when removed, increases the response rate. Both positive and negative reinforcement increase rather than decrease the strength of a given response. Punishment, on the other hand, is an aversive stimulus that reduces the rate of the response. We will discuss punishment in detail later in the chapter, but it is important to note now that punishment and negative reinforcement are very different kinds of stimulus situations that have exactly opposite effects on response rates.

The Use of Reinforcement

Positive reinforcement   In the classroom, positive reinforcement may be provided by a primary reinforcer, such as milk, cereal, or candy, or it may be a conditioned reinforcer, such as gold stars, high grades, social approval, or, in the case of younger pupils, physical contact.

> A certain student, John D., would not remain attentive or even attempt to do his numerical reason problems. The teacher set the behavioral goal of nineteen correct solutions out of twenty problems. Observation of the student indicated that his operant level was zero; he simply would not do the work. After a conference with his parents, the boy was sent to school each morning without any breakfast. The teacher used milk and cereal as the positive reinforcers for correct math solutions. The student reached the desired goal on the fourth day.

> Tommy L., a third-grade student, was boisterous and noisy in class and prevented other students from concentrating on their own work. The first behavioral goal was set at thirty minutes of complete silence. Tommy was presented with an M&M candy each time he remained quiet for forty-five seconds. On the eighth day the goal was reached. At this point a new goal was set for sixty minutes of silence. Also the reinforcement schedule was altered so that Tommy had to remain silent for two minutes in order to receive the M&M reinforcement. This new goal was reached in only three days.

Such primary reinforcers as food for the child who has had no breakfast or candy for the child who loves sweets are obviously of a positive nature. When it comes to conditioned reinforcers, however, the teacher must observe the situation closely, for, as the proverb states, "One man's meat may be another man's poison." What the teacher may consider a positive reinforcer will not necessarily be such for each and every student. Usually, however, the teacher can select from conditioned reinforcers. Madsen and Madsen suggest the following:

1. Words—spoken and written
2. Expressions—facial and bodily
3. Closeness—nearness and touching
4. Activities and privileges
5. Things—materials, awards, toys[18]

Negative reinforcement   Negative reinforcement—the removal of an aversive stimulus in order to increase response rate—has been used in a variety of school settings. One fairly common use of this is the so-called time-out procedure, a technique, incidentally, that is commonly used by parents in the home.[19] In a study conducted at the University of Kansas on preschool children with poor cognitive, language, and social skills, the time-out procedure has produced some dramatic results. A child who exhibits low self-control is placed for brief periods of time in a small room next to the classroom. When the child's behavior becomes more positive and less hyperactive, he or she is allowed to return (aversive stimulus is removed) to the regular classroom. This technique is combined with the use of various positive reinforcers to enhance the build-up of desirable responses.[20]

Negative reinforcement has proved successful in shaping a variety of desired responses. In one instance a student who had not done his homework assignment was placed in a time-out room and told to complete the work. Only when the assignment was finally completed was the student allowed back in the classroom. In this case, the removal of the aversive stimulus (escape from the isolation room) acted to strengthen the behavior (doing the assignment).

Negative reinforcement should be used only with great caution. An example cited by Madsen and Madsen involved a second-grade boy whose teacher made him wear a girl's ribbon in his hair until he began acting in a more controlled fashion. Whenever his behavior improved, the hair ribbon was removed. Madsen and Madsen question the advisability of this particular technique on the grounds that it might affect the child's perception of his sex identification.

A teacher should examine carefully the possible disturbing consequences whenever considering the use of negative reinforcement. There is a real difference between placing children in a time-out room, where they have the opportunity to finish their work, and shoving them into an unlighted closet with the door closed. It is obviously very easy for the teacher's intended negative reinforcement to become simple punishment. When that occurs, as Skinner has pointed out, the whole purpose of reinforcement is defeated.[21] Control by aversive means may provoke a counterattack; daydreaming, dropping out, vandalism, refusal to learn assignments are all common indications of an attempt to avoid aversive control.

Consistency   Perhaps the major premise underlying the technique of behavior modification is that consistency should be observed at all times. Once a child is placed on a reinforcement program, the teacher must not waver. As Skinner's research on animals has shown, behavior that is intermittently reinforced is the most difficult to extinguish. If children are told that every time they act in a certain way they will be sent to the principal's office, they must be sent to the office every time they act that way. There can be no exceptions. Inconsistency teaches just that—inconsistency. As Madsen and Madsen point out:

> The child does not remember the 1,321 times he went to bed at 8 P.M., he remembers the two times he got to stay up. The third grader does not really believe that the teacher will send him to the time-out room (isolation) for ten minutes. This is already the sixth time the teacher has threatened and nothing has happened yet. The ninth grader cheated before and didn't get caught; why should he get caught this time? The college student has turned in late papers before; why should this professor be such a hard nose?[22]

Consistency is a key ingredient in the success of any behavior-modification program. The cute little student who pleads, "Can't you make an exception just this once?" may be hard for the teacher to resist, but resist the teacher must. Once the teacher breaks the rules, the children learn only too well that the rules are there for the breaking.

> A ninth-grade creative writing class was slowly but surely getting out of control; assignments were not being turned in, the students were becoming increasingly boisterous and rude both to the teacher and to each other. The teacher, Miss W., pleaded with the students to be fair and meet her half way, but this had no effect. It was suggested to Miss W. that reinforcement principles might be applied. She thereupon informed the class that if they behaved well for two successive days, they would go on a trip downtown to see the movie "Hamlet." The next two days found the class no different, just as rowdy, just as out of control. Virtually every five minutes Miss W. shouted (to those who could hear her) that if they didn't behave, the trip would be cancelled. In fact, she actually cancelled the trip three times, but on the third day, the class pleaded with her and she relented. They saw the movie, and the next day the classroom situations became even more deteriorated. Miss W. was beside herself. "I've tried everything, even behavior modification, and nothing works." She went back to class and pleaded with the students to be fair.

In her discussion of discipline in the classroom, one educator has recently suggested two basic rules:

1. Be consistent.

2. Know your subject matter.

From personal experience, this educator discovered these rules as she went through her first year of teaching. She found that initially children will not give back kindness for kindness; they must be shown rules, and these rules *must never be relaxed*. Nor can a threat of punishment be made unless it will be carried out—every time. As she notes:

> That second year of teaching, I began the first classes with a quiet statement of the rules: no one could leave his or her seat without permission; no one could communicate with a fellow student without permission; no one could call out an answer without first being recognized. The penalty for the smallest infringement of the rules was to remain after school in my room

from three until five o'clock. No exceptions would be permitted. Invariably, some inoffensive student would open his mouth by mistake. He would be given a note on his desk, unobtrusively, to report at three. The next morning, after a dull session of gazing at me or resting his head on the desk, the student "got the word around." "She's tough, be careful." Two or three students slipped—and suffered utter, long boredom. The result was a quiet room, not of surly students, but of careful, somewhat surprised young people.[23]

The timing of reinforcement   To modify behavior effectively, the reinforcement must be timed to occur after the desired response has occurred. The teacher should never, never deliver the reinforcement on the promise that the behavior will occur later. For example, a teacher asks the students in his class to turn in their assignments at the beginning of each class period. At the start of the next class period no assignments are handed in. The teacher then tells them that if they promise to begin turning in their assignments the following Monday, they can have a record party for the last half hour of today's class period. The class quickly promises, has the record party, and the teacher is still waiting for the homework.

A seven-year-old boy enters his house muttering an innocuous swear word. His mother becomes upset and urges the boy never to say that word again. In exchange for his promise to obey her, the mother gives him a quarter. An hour later he returns demanding a dollar, saying, "If you think that word was bad, wait 'til you hear this!"

Reinforcement must follow actual behavior. We learn by doing, not by talking about doing or by promising to do. As the behavior modifiers argue, the reinforcement must be made contingent on the appropriate response.

Punishment

The use of punishment to control behavior has been a controversial issue among both learning theorists and educators. Thorndike, for example, changed his position on the question of punishment. His original law of effect stated that reward and punishment had equal but opposite effects, reward strengthening and punishment weakening a learned stimulus-response connection. Later in his career, Thorndike revised this law drastically, saying that reward was far more effective in reinforcing learning than punishment was in weakening it. Later still, the Skinnerians demonstrated that if a rat was reinforced, say, a hundred times for pressing a lever and thus had a rather large build-up of responses waiting to be emitted, punishment would temporarily slow down the response rate but would not reduce the number of responses that would be emitted once the punishment was removed.

The typical experiment used a rat in an experimental chamber. The rat was reinforced with a food pellet for each lever press, until lever-pressing became highly resistant to extinction. (The rat's lever-pressing response was strengthened until he would emit, say, 200 responses without being further reinforced.) The lever was then electrified so that the rat now received a punishing shock every time he pressed the lever. The rat learned very quickly to stay away from the lever. However, once the shock was removed, he went determinedly back to the lever and all 200 responses were finally emitted. Punishment had merely held the responses in abeyance, suppressing them temporarily until the aversive stimulus was removed.

Because of Thorndike's changed position, the rat data from the Skinnerians, and other studies and theoretical positions, many psychologists and educators assumed that punishment had no real effect on learning. This scientific news was greeted with some skepticism, especially by older teachers who recalled the effect of the hickory stick on class control. Many parents and grandparents also found it difficult to mesh this "scientific breakthrough" with their own experiences in raising children.

More recent psychological studies, especially those carried out in the past ten years, have shown that punishment is indeed an effective technique for controlling behavior. The problem with the previously mentioned rat study was that it was an extremely artificial situation. In the first place, the rats were exceptionally highly motivated to press the lever—the lever was the route to life-sustaining food for these poor starving creatures. In the second place, no alternative response would produce the reinforcement. If a rat is given another response

option during the time the punishment is in force, the original lever-pressing response does indeed weaken very rapidly. Punishment may not be a human conditioning technique, and it may create some serious side effects, but it does control behavior. Even the most humanitarian parent seems to know this in moments of crisis. A child who is playing on a busy highway is quickly punished and then shown another area where he can play safely. A baby is not "reasoned with" when she is found poking her fingers into a light socket.

Punishment in the classroom usually takes the form of disapproval or of withholding a positive reinforcer. Severe disapproval by the teacher may often be an effective form of controlling behavior, but it does not instill a love of learning. Withholding a positive reinforcer, if the rule of consistency is religiously followed, is also an extremely effective behavior modifier. This method of aversive control takes such forms as the loss of privileges, objects, or pastimes the students value. The purist should note that withholding a positive reinforcer when used as punishment is not the same as extinction.

> In extinction, consequences that ordinarily follow the behavior are simply discontinued; in punishment, behavior results in the application of aversive consequences through forfeiture of positive reinforcers. Thus in extinguishing aggression sustained by peer attention, the behavior is consistently ignored; under the punishment contingency, however, the rewards of peer attention are pitted against the negative effects of confinement to one's room, loss of television privileges, or some other type of negative outcome.[24]

Proponents of behavior modification have made extensive use of punishment in psychotherapy. For example, male homosexuals have been treated by showing them slides of nude men and women. While viewing the slides of male nudes the patient receives an unpleasant shock through electrodes attached to his leg. While viewing the female nudes, no such punishment is administered. The proponents claim this technique has been successful in changing the sexual orientation of a number of subjects.

Children who suffer from stuttering have also been treated by the administration of electric shock whenever they begin stammering. Fairly dramatic recovery rates, of two weeks or less, have been attributed to the use of this technique. Punishment has even proved effective with severely disturbed children, children who unless restrained bang their heads against hard objects, tear and bite off pieces of their own flesh, pummel their own faces, and so on. Despite the fact that these children might be assumed to enjoy being hurt, they apparently don't enjoy being hurt by others. Research in this area indicates that the use of shock, administered whenever self-injurious behavior is observed, can drastically reduce and even eliminate self-destructive responses.

There is, however, growing concern that the use of electric shock on people may be ethically wrong and an infringement on the individual's civil liberties.[25] No doubt, there are moral issues and even problems of possible physical harm to be considered. In one report, a psychotic child was given painful electric shocks with a cattle-prod device for self-injurious behavior. This technique resulted in the total elimination of such behavior after *167 days of treatment.*[26] American companies are even advertising radio-controlled "Remote Shockers" that can "deliver a painful shock from up to 300 feet away." These devices have been displayed at psychology conventions. Recently a plea has been advanced that if a person, who may not have the capacity to give full and informed consent, is to be subjected to such aversive conditioning procedures, then an outside, objective advocate should be called in to determine the person's best interests.[27] Thus, retarded or psychotic children and adults will be protected from the possible abuses arising from the indiscriminate use of a painful shock as an aversive stimulus.

Does punishment cause emotional disturbance?   The question of whether the use of punishment causes any long-term emotional damage is one that has as yet not been fully answered. The traditional, almost legendary view, is that punishment is very much involved in the origin of behavioral disorders. One theorist has outlined a long series of punishment-provoked problems, including rigidity, social deviance, poor adjustment, and regression.[28] However, other psychologists are not so sure.

One expert in the field of punishment argues that many punishment procedures produce no long-term emotional outcomes. The real question to be argued is not whether some forms of aberrant behavior can be produced by certain punishment procedures but whether these reactions are typical results of punishment. "The answer to this question is clearly 'no,' although specific circumstances can be contrived to produce such effects."[29]

Aversive Stimuli in the Classroom

The use of aversive stimuli in the classroom, whether as negative reinforcement or as punishment, should be viewed with extreme caution. Although certainly an effective means of controlling behavior, it rarely instills in the student a joyful attitude toward learning. Aversive stimuli can also act to classically condition emotional responses that can cause "blocks" to future learning (see Chapter 9). Punishment's effect on behavior, although possibly very depressing in the presence of the aversive stimulus, may not generalize at all beyond that stimulus. As has been stated elsewhere, punishing a student for a certain behavior does not necessarily mean that the student stops engaging in the behavior. "Rather, the student may simply learn not to engage in that behavior in the presence of the teacher. The behavioral pattern may remain with the student in all other environments."[30]

If punishment is to be used, it should be used sparingly and only in conjunction with a positive reinforcement of some alternative response. That is, while the punishment is suppressing an undesirable response, positive reinforcement should be used to strengthen a socially approved alternative response. Punishment has only a short-lived effect on people who have few response options. This is why it is so often ineffective in the case of criminals—they have few, if any, socially approved means of achieving the material things our society values. In short, behavior modification brought about through positive reinforcement is more likely to be lasting and, eventually, self-perpetuating than that brought about through the use of aversive controls.

reinforcement, it may in the long run decrease a student's intrinsic motivation to learn. Second, it may be that once the tokens are withdrawn (and a student cannot be kept on a token system forever), the resulting behavior changes may be extinguished.[34]

Perhaps token systems in school settings are best employed when they are viewed from the outset as temporary arrangements. Token systems in the classroom should only be started, says one educator, "when teachers know how and plan to remove the system. Books and things learned from exciting teachers maintain interest, not the tokens."[35]

The Premack Principle

The Premack principle states that behavior that occurs at a naturally high rate of frequency may be used to reinforce behavior that occurs at a naturally low rate of frequency.[36] For example, if left to their own devices, many children will spend far more time watching TV than reading. According to Premack, when such children

have finished a given amount of reading, allow them to go watch TV for a while. The teacher should carefully observe the children during free-choice periods and note the behaviors that naturally occur most frequently. These behaviors can then be used as positive reinforcers for low-probability responses. Teachers usually find that academic behavior has a low natural frequency, meaning that, when given a choice, most children prefer not to do schoolwork.

PROGRAMED INSTRUCTION

The general concept of programed instruction is probably as old as formal schooling itself. Each grade level has a certain small portion of our accumulated knowledge allotted to it, and each child is expected to master that segment before being allowed to proceed to the next grade. Children who don't keep up with the rest of the class are held back and repeat the year. Children who are not challenged by the content in their grade are skipped ahead to a

Activity that children enjoy can be used to reinforce low-frequency activity.

level more consistent with their ability. The proponents of behavior modification agree with this practice in general (except in cases where the pressure of the social promotion pushes all the children ahead, regardless of achievement), but they argue that the practice is too general and not tailored to the needs of the individual child. The individual child, they urge, needs a system of precision teaching, an educational prescription written just for him or her.

Programing is the arrangement of the material to be learned in a sequence of steps designed to lead the students to the final goal. The steps are usually quite close together, ensuring a gradual increase in difficulty. The material being presented is broken down into small units called frames. The entire program may have hundreds of frames, and the frames are written in such a way as to maximize the possibility of success. They may sometimes seem repetitious, but this is the result of a deliberate attempt to prevent any misconceptions from forming in the student's mind. A good program is one in which the students make very few errors, no more than 5 percent. This means, of course, that they are constantly experiencing success, or that they are on what is close to a continuous reinforcement schedule. Teachers can add their own reinforcers (such as prizes or desired activities) for the completion of, say, every twenty-five items. This puts the students on an intermittent schedule of reinforcement (fixed ratio) for the external reinforcers, while they remain on a continuous reinforcement schedule for the intrinsic, success reinforcer.

A good academic program may employ various techniques in the construction of frames. Certain frames may consist basically of words which serve as prompts through familiarity and experience. Other frames may merely introduce new material and ask easy questions about it. Logical order is another criterion used to determine the next frame to be presented, and degree of difficulty is still another consideration. At various times in the program a word might be requested which requires a synthesis of earlier concepts. From time to time frames may review previous material or require that it be used in new contexts. Programing, then, is not a sterile, mechanized technique, but offers a wide range of possible responses.[37]

Almost anyone with some degree of literacy can go through a program. Students will not all proceed at the same rate, but that, after all, is the story of individual differences. The first frame is always very easy, and the students are led by small steps into more complicated frames until the unit is completed or until the students have achieved the desired "terminal behavior."

Programs can be written in book form, with the questions on one page and the answers on the facing page. The students cover the answers, respond, and then uncover the answers as a self-check. Programs may also be placed in machines which are set so as not to move from one frame to the next until each one in turn has been successfully completed. Some machines are even equipped with a buzzer or a bell that sounds when a correct response has been given. The buzzers and bells act as further conditioned reinforcers for correct responses.

Programed instruction has several key advantages.

1. The student must pay attention, for if the program is to continue, responses must be given. The student is, therefore, an active participant in the learning process, not a mere passive observer.

2. Each student proceeds at his or her own rate. One student may finish in one hour a program that takes another student five hours to complete.

3. Reinforcement, to use Skinner's term, or feedback, to use Bruner's, is immediate. There are no delays between the response and knowledge of results.

4. Learning that takes place in a programed setting is always by positive reinforcement. Aversive techniques are never used. Machines don't shout, or hit, or "tell parents."

5. Machines can be set automatically to keep track of errors. These can be discussed later with the student, and in this important student-teacher dialogue, any misconceptions about the subject matter can be allayed.

Probably the main disadvantage to programed instruction is that many students report finding it boring. "If that same question is asked

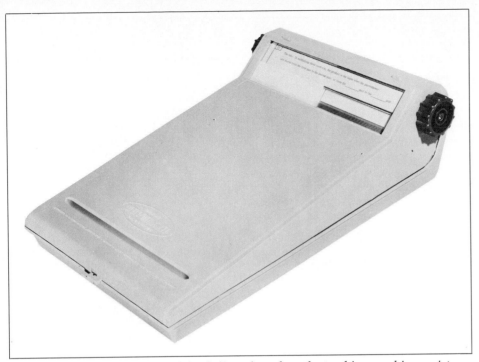

Rather than taking the place of the dedicated teacher, the teaching machine assists the teacher in the job of communicating with students.

one more time, I'll scream," said one student facing the seventeenth successive frame making the same point. In their zeal to increase frame difficulty ever so slowly, certain programers have simply not increased the frame difficulty at all for long periods in the program. This is often resented by the alert student.

Computer-Assisted Instruction

Even the teaching machine may be phased out and replaced by what is called "computer-assisted instruction (CAI). With the advent of the microcomputer, CAI has taken a great leap forward. In past years CAI was restricted to fairly wealthy school districts. It consisted of using a computer (usually just one) together with TV screens and typewriters to allow groups of students to try their hands at programing in BASIC or to go through fairly stilted preprogramed lessons. These earlier computers were expensive and had very limited internal memory. In the 1980s this somewhat cumbersome technique

has almost completely disappeared, replaced by the inexpensive yet powerful microcomputer.

The increase in capacity and the decrease in cost of the computer has been dramatic. Only a scant fifteen years ago, one of the major mainframe manufacturers was selling a computer called the "Century 200." It sold for what at the time was hailed as a breakthrough price of only $250,000. Of course, there were a few necessary extras, such as a $95,000 "clean room," a special, dustfree environment with built-in monitors for constant temperature, pressure, and humidity control. The machine's internal memory was 64K, or about the same memory capacity as today's $100 microcomputer. It has recently been estimated that had automobile technology advanced at the rate of computer technology over the past thirty-five years, a Rolls Royce would now cost $2.50 and would get 2 million miles per gallon of gas.[38]

The microcomputer, the small, stand-alone, desk-top computer with its own central processor, has now found its way into virtually every school system in the country. To be sure, some microcomputers are still being used to promote

CONTEMPORARY ISSUE

Computer Literacy: How Much Is Enough?

Without a doubt, the computer revolution is upon us. Computers and their "magic" chips do everything from making out the payroll and scanning income tax returns to running cars, watches, and cameras. It's little wonder that educators have begun insisting that every educated person should become "computer literate" and that no self-respecting classroom should be without at least a couple of these electronic miracles.

Even first-grade children are being introduced to the computer and are being taught some elementary programing skills. They are also learning what not to do, such as never removing the floppy disk while the little red drive light is still on. Thrilled parents bask in the reflected glory of their children's computer accomplishments and secretly dream of the day when their children will be winning a Nobel prize for having created some new and exotic technological breakthrough. In short, "computer literacy" has become the catchword phrase of the 1980s and a given in our various curricula. To argue against computers is viewed as akin to seeing the first automobile roll down the road and saying. "I'd rather have a horse," or "The only accelerator I'll ever need is a buggy whip."

What has made the computer revolution even more compellingly dramatic has been the advent of the microcomputer, that incredible little desk-top machine. The micro is a stand-alone computer with its own input device (the keyboard), internal memory (RAM), central processor, memory storage system (usually a floppy disk), and output display (the screen). The memory capability of even the least expensive of today's micros exceeds that of many of the mainframes fifteen years ago.

But the question is not whether today's computers are extraordinary marvels of electronic wizardry—they are. It is whether every child should become computer literate and, if so, how literate.

Computer literacy seems to have several definitions, but most are some variation of the following:

> By computer awareness and literacy is [sic] meant a general understanding of computers, their uses and applications to everyday living. Knowing what a computer can and cannot do, how they [sic] are used in today's world, and how they may affect our lives are central themes which run throughout a program in computer awareness and literacy.[a]

Problems begin, however, as soon as we begin to operationalize the generalities in this definition. For example, to some experts, knowing what computers can and cannot do demands expertise in programing.

> To tell a computer what you want it to do, you must be able to communicate with it. To do that, you will need to learn a language for writing your ideas down. . . . if you can tell a computer how to do the things you want it to do, you are computer literate.[b]

To others, learning to program the computer is not essential:

> Computer literacy is a familiarity with a device that enhances one's ability to live in and cope with the modern world. This does not mean, however, that students must acquire the ability to program, but rather the ability to manipulate computer technology.[c]

The issue of whether or not to include programing in the definition of computer literacy is, therefore, one that divides the experts. Some experts, mercifully of the minority, claim that computer literacy is virtually synonymous with achieving a degree in computer science. The student should have courses in everything from machine language to FORTRAN, from computer architecture to advanced Pascal, and much much more. Admittedly, some students should probably follow this rigorous path, but all students?

A more modest goal of those advocating programing is that each student learn at least one programing language, usually either BASIC or LOGO. Their argument is not that learning to program is an end in itself but that it teaches the student how to think. Learning to create logical algorithms and translate them into a programing language is alleged to produce, in a sense, a strong and disciplined mind. Even those holding this view, however, issue this warning:

> A certain amount of elementary programing—in LOGO or BASIC—might also be introduced in the early grades. However, there is danger in carrying this too far. Without competent, informed computer teachers, students often pick up very bad programing habits that must be broken later. This is a well-documented fact. It

may be better, therefore, to postpone the bulk of programing instruction until students reach a junior high class taught by the specialist.[d]

Advocates of programing also urge that students be taught the binary numbering system. Since computers can only respond to on-off commands, to understand what a computer goes through, one must learn to convert base 10 to base 2, and at least be able to add and subtract in base 2. A thorough knowledge of the binary system, it is felt, is essential for understanding the rudiments of any programing technique.

On the other side of this issue are those who feel that programing skills are not necessary, that computer literacy is like automobile literacy: You only have to learn how to make it go, not the physics involved. Those who hold this view define computer literacy as being able to turn on the machine, insert a disk, and follow a "user friendly," menu-driven program. And since the use of a computer demands entering data of some sort, they argue the student is far better off taking a course in typing than one in base 2 math. A parallel argument is that taking courses in BASIC is like taking a course or two of French. It might be fun to then go to a French restaurant and order your meal directly from the menu, but if you need a highly accurate translation of more difficult material, you'd better hire an expert. Besides, in programing, a little learning can be dangerous: If you start breaking into a prepackaged program in order to change a line or two, you can ruin the whole program. This

position also sees the learning of base 2 as a waste of time. The machine may have to "think" in on-off terms, but the student doesn't.

A final antiprograming argument is that in a very few years BASIC and LOGO will be dead languages, important historically, but of little relevance to students entering the job market in the 1990s. The computers of tomorrow will still be programable, "but nobody except the experts will do the programming. . . . the final custom-fitting of all commercial programs will be done by the user, but in English, not in BASIC."[e]

What can we expect of students in the 1980s in the way of computer literacy? The consensus among those holding the middle-ground view is that minimal computer literacy should include the following:

1. Knowing a little about the history of computers, the sequence from giant, vacuum-tubed mainframes of yesterday to the miniaturized microcomputers of today
2. Knowing the basic parts of the computer, from input to output
3. Knowing how to handle format and copy disks as well as how to protect them from damage
4. Knowing at least one word-processing program and one math program (Research strongly suggests that the use of at least these two types of programs enhances a student's writing and math skills.)[f]
5. Knowing how to handle the computer safely and

intelligently, and, as much as possible, learning the basic damage-prevention techniques

Obviously, some students should be provided with more than just these minimal competencies. The choice of what to include should also take into account each student's own special aptitudes and interests. Students interested in science, for example, should be exposed to laboratory simulations on the computer, whereas those preparing for an office career should be trained in data-base and spreadsheet techniques.

In short, the ultimate goal of computer literacy should be to provide students with skills they can use in all their traditional courses in order that they may be better students today and better citizens tomorrow. In the words of one expert, "The schools, relying primarily on computers and teachers for instruction, will play a central role in the moral and intellectual development of U.S. youngsters."[g]

[a] N. Watts. (1981). A dozen uses for the computer in education. *Educational Technology* (April), p. 20.
[b] A. Luehrmann. (1982). Computer literacy: What it is; why it's important. *Electronic Learning* (May/June), p. 162.
[c] R. Scher. (1984). The computer backlash. *Electronic Learning* (January), p. 48.
[d] A. Luehrmann. (1984). The best way to teach computer literacy. *Electronic Learning*, (April), p. 39.
[e] F. D'Ignazio. (1983). Beyond computer literacy. *Compute* (September), p. 41.
[f] G. Bracey. (1982). Computers in education: What the research shows. *Electronic Learning* (November/December), pp. 51–54.
[g] P. Wagschal. (1984). A last chance for computers in the schools. *Phi Delta Kappan* (December), p. 57.

computer literacy and programing skills (see the box on computer literacy), but many have become supplemental teaching tools in such traditional subjects as math, geography, history, and English grammar. Thus the microcomputer has taken on the role of personal tutor, aiding students in sharpening their skills and increasing their understanding of basic curriculum mainstays. And, as with any personal instructor, the student can proceed at his or her own pace.

The earliest software programs were designed to promote drill and practice; that is, they were much like flashcards on a screen. Then came the software tutorial, a program for taking a student through a discrete lesson unit. The latest software has as the final goal the mastery of global concepts. The student makes many choices throughout the running of the program and, in effect, is prodded into discovering a concept for himself or herself. A student's error automatically triggers a program review of the material not fully comprehended. Thus CAI is constantly interactive, forcing the student to respond, to make choices, to participate. Unlike TV instruction, CAI does not allow the student to become a passive recipient of information.

The research on CAI has so far been virtually unanimous in its positive findings. Children are learning more and liking it better. In an analysis (meta-analysis) of over fifty different studies, James Kulik has shown the striking effectiveness of CAI in grades six through twelve.[39] Computer-based teaching, Kulik found, raised final exam scores from the fiftieth to the sixty-third percentile, and these gains were maintained in follow-up examinations given several months after the completion of instruction. CAI was also found to be more efficient than traditional instruction in that it significantly reduced the amount of time the students needed for learning. In addition, CAI was shown to be more effective at the secondary level than it had proven to be among college students. Because of this, Kulik wondered if CAI might be even more effective with elementary-school children than older students.

A study performed by the Educational Testing Service (ETS) appears to lend substance to Kulik's suspicion. Using a sample of several thousand elementary-school children divided into CAI (experimental) and non-CAI (control) groups, the ETS found that at the end of the first year CAI students scored at the sixty-fourth percentile while the control groups scored at the fiftieth percentile on a standardized math test. At the end of the second year, the CAI students had jumped to the seventy-first percentile, and after the third year to seventy-sixth. "In other words, the increase in their test scores was steady over several years."[40]

It may very well be that learning through computer interaction has both developmental and cumulative effects. The earlier the child begins, the better the learning strategies being incorporated; hence CAI may have a snowball effect as training continues. Finally, aside from the achievement outcomes, CAI has proven to have produced other important effects.

Affective/motivational outcomes   Gerald Bracey reported that from kindergarten through grade twelve students consistently display positive attitudes toward computers.[41] Students almost unanimously report that they enjoy working at their own pace and appreciate the elimination of public embarrassment over making mistakes. Students are more willing to try, to take chances in the secure knowledge that a wrong guess is never going to expose them to public scorn. In Jerome Bruner's analysis of learning, for true discovery learning to occur, the student must be willing to take chances and explore new areas. This can only take place when the student knows that exploration is both rewarding and safe.[42]

Because students feel more in control of their educational destinies when CAI is involved, they are less likely to explain away poor performance as just a matter of bad luck. They gain a feeling of mastery, which may be at least as important an outcome as academic achievement itself (if indeed the two can be separated).

Social outcomes   The dire warnings that CAI will dehumanize the classroom, usually issued by an educational philosopher who has never seen students busily working *together* on a personal computer, are beginning to appear groundless. Bracey reported that CAI often fosters a cooperative group atmosphere. When two or three students are working together on a single computer, there is more "collaboration, or cooperative problem solving, than there is anywhere else in the school."[43] The students are typically immersed in trying to get the program to run and are not blatantly competing to be the first person with a hand in the air signaling the teacher that "I won."

The prevailing consensus is that CAI is an asset in the classroom. It tends to promote achievement, motivation, and a spirit of cooperation—an extremely powerful academic mix. Also, as a teaching aid CAI can provide simulations of activities the student otherwise might never experience. This is probably most pertinent in science courses, where laboratory supplies might be scarce or where running a particular experiment could be too dangerous, expensive, or time-consuming. Perhaps CAI simulations can reverse the trend, reported by the National Science Foundation, of students' dropping out of science and science-related courses.[44] Obviously, a great deal more research is needed in this important area. As M. R. Lepper points out, the influence of this new technology "is likely to have more important effects on the lives and the social and psychological functioning of children than any other technological advance in the past century."[45]

The Teacher's Role

Although computers have proven effective in transmitting facts and, to some extent, even concepts, the teacher is needed to tie these facts and subconcepts into more global abstractions. The teacher can use current examples of certain principles, thus helping to make the computer lesson seem more alive and thus more effective. Bruner has said that the student must have a background of facts, the "stuff of learning," before discovery learning can take place. A computer can obviously supply that "stuff." Knowing a few names and dates does allow for a certain level of understanding, which will aid a student in further exploration and discovery. A student who thinks that John Dewey and Aristotle were classmates together at Columbia, for example, may find it difficult to appreciate the significance of the historical succession of philosophical ideas. There are, however, some areas that simply can't be fully taught by the computer. History and literature would be reduced to a pile of bits and pieces (or perhaps even bits and bytes) without the teacher to integrate the material into a living picture.

As we saw in the beginning of this chapter during the discussion of whole versus part learning, when material is learned in discrete units, the parts must be put back together. No programer can ever anticipate all the ways in which children may misinterpret the way the separate parts should be glued back together into a meaningful whole. The teacher is there, on the spot, guiding, motivating, doing the real job of teaching in its true sense.

SUMMARY

Learning in the classroom involves the concept of transfer. What is learned in class is thought to transfer into later-life situations, so as to enable the learner to earn a living and enjoy a fuller life.

Theories of transfer date back to the early Greek notion of formal discipline, in which the mind, considered comparable to an athlete's muscles, was thought to require systematic exercise if it was to grow. Even as late as the early twentieth century, proponents of this position created academic curricula that stressed such subjects as logic, Greek, and Latin, not because these subjects had any practical value, but because they "strengthened" the mind.

Formal discipline theory was seriously challenged by a number of psychologists, including William James, E. L. Thorndike, and Charles Judd. All of their studies pointed to the fact that "training the mind" had little if any lasting benefits.

Educators today are no longer concerned with the theory of mental discipline, but they are concerned with promoting positive transfer between learning in the classroom and living effectively in later life.

The learning curve, a plotting out of one's learning speed, is typically negatively accelerated, which means that when confronted with a new subject, students learn a great deal of the material in a relatively short time and then, with increased practice, add less and less new learning.

Harlow coined the phrase "learning sets" to explain what gestalt psychologists had previously labeled as "insight."

Massed versus distributed practice involves the question of how the learner should allocate his or her time for maximum efficiency. In learning a new physical skill, distributed practice (an hour a day for a week) is more efficient than massed practice (seven straight hours in one day). On intellectual tasks, however, distributed practice may destroy the meaning of the material. In this case it is best to divide the material into meaningful units and then work on each unit in a massed-learning session.

Whole versus part learning involves the question of whether learning is most efficient when the material is broken down into small, discrete units or left in a total, organized whole. The best method seems to be to work first on the whole in order to gain a general overview of the material and then go back and work on the various parts.

Albert Bandura has suggested that a large part of what a person learns occurs through imitation, or modeling. This is called "social learning theory," since it is concerned with learning that takes place within a social situation. Bandura has shown that learning that occurs through modeling need not be based on direct reinforcement of the response. Other than the parents, the teacher may be the most important model in the child's environment. Conditions for learning are thus established not only by what the teacher says but by what he or she does.

The current popularity of operant conditioning in the classroom is due in large part to the fact that the teacher is presented with a very precise prescription for handling specific classroom problems. Changing a student's behavior through the use of conditioning techniques is called behavior modification.

To use behavior modification techniques, the teacher must first define the educational objectives in behavioral terms, that is, determine exactly *what* the student should learn and *how* the student is to show that the learning has taken place. The teacher can infer that learning or

understanding has taken place only by observing the *behavior* of the student.

Once the objectives have been defined, the teacher observes the student's initial rate of response, or operant level, for the activity in question. The operant level, or base rate, for the given activity should be observed in the classroom situation.

After the behavioral goal is set and the student's operant level is established, the teacher can use reinforcement to strengthen (condition) some student behavior and withhold reinforcement of (extinguish) other student behavior. Reinforcement always increases response rate. Positive reinforcement occurs when the response rate increases by adding the reinforcer (giving the student M&M candies, gold stars, or high grades), and negative reinforcement occurs when the response rate increases by taking away the reinforcer (removing an aversive stimulus when the desired behavior is emitted). Aversive stimuli should be used as negative reinforcement or punishment *only* with great caution since they can result in the student's acquiring not only the goal behavior the teacher intended but also other potentially damaging responses.

The key to the successful use of behavior modification techniques is *consistency*. The teacher must follow through on the established reinforcement schedule without exception.

Reinforcement must *follow*, not precede, the student's response. Usually, the sooner the reinforcement follows the response, the more impact it will have in changing behavior.

Behavior modification proponents also make use of the token system, a system based on the use of conditioned reinforcers, or tokens. The token system has two main advantages: (1) It maintains a high daily rate of desirable responses, and (2) it teaches delayed gratification.

The Premack principle states that behavior that naturally occurs at a high rate can be used to reinforce behavior that occurs at a naturally low rate. Thus, one set of responses may be used to reinforce another set of responses. If a student has a higher rate of TV-viewing responses than reading responses, then viewing TV can be used as reinforcement for a certain amount of reading.

In programed instruction the material to be

learned is arranged in an orderly sequence of steps designed to reach a certain goal. A good program is one in which level of difficulty increases very slowly, so that students make very few errors (less than 5 percent). The material to be learned is broken down into small units, or frames, and can be presented to students by mechanical means (the teaching machine). The basic advantage of programed instruction is that each student can proceed at his or her own rate. However, some students, especially brighter students, become bored with the long succession of similar items. Also, when material is learned in bits and pieces, it is often hard for the student to integrate it back into a meaningful whole.

Even now, teaching machines may be in the process of being phased out in favor of computer-assisted instruction. With the advent of the microcomputer and the recent upgrading of instructional software, CAI has proved to be an important teaching adjunct. Research findings indicate that CAI has been effective in increasing academic achievement. It appears also that CAI has other personal benefits, especially in the affective/motivational and social areas.

Despite its apparent success as a "private tutor," CAI can never replace the teacher. He or she must remain as the major component in the total educational enterprise. The teacher's role becomes even more critical during this technological age of bits, bytes, and chips. Without the teacher to explain relationships and integrate concepts, CAI's long-term success may turn out to be shallow. Critics suggest that CAI may be in danger of producing a generation of child robots, whose knowledge base, though admittedly large, will be superficial and perhaps even random.

KEY TERMS AND NAMES

transfer
  positive transfer
  negative transfer
learning curve
learning sets
massed learning
Albert Bandura
  social learning theory
  modeling
terminal behavior

punishment
shaping (successive approximation)
token system
Premack principle
programed instruction
teaching machine
behavior modification
verbal coding
computer-assisted instruction (CAI)

REFERENCES

1. Skinner, B. F. (1953). *Science and human behavior* (p. 402). New York: Macmillan.

2. James, W. (1890). *The principles of psychology.* New York: Henry Holt.

3. Thorndike, E. L., and Woodsworth, R. S. (1901). The influence of improvement in one mental function upon the efficiency of other functions. *Psychological Review, 8,* 247–261, 384–395, 553–564.

4. Judd, C. H. (1908). The relation of special training to general intelligence. *Educational Review, 36,* 28–42.

5. Travers, J. F. (1972). *Learning: Analysis and application* (p. 166). New York: McKay.

6. Harlow, H. F., McGaugh, J. L., and Thompson, R. F. (1971). *Psychology* (p. 301). San Francisco: Albion.

7. Brown, A., Campione, J., and Day, J. (1981). Learning to learn: On training students to learn from texts. *Educational Researcher, 16,* 14–21. See also Novak, J. (1980). *Handbook for the learning how to learn program.* Ithaca: New York State College of Agriculture and Life Sciences.

8. Bandura, A. (1978). The self system in reciprocal determinism. *American Psychologist, 33*, 344–358.

9. Bandura, A., Ross, D., and Ross, S. A. (1963). Imitation of film-mediated aggressive models. *Journal of Abnormal and Social Psychology, 66*, 3–11.

10. Bandura, A., and McDonald, F. J. (1963). Influence of social reinforcement and the behavior of models in shaping children's moral judgements. *Journal of Abnormal and Social Psychology, 67*, 274–281.

11. Bandura, A. (1982). Self-efficacy mechanism in human agency. *American Psychologist, 37*, 344–358. See also Bandura, A. (1980). Self-referent thought: The development of self-efficacy. In J. Flavell and L. D. Ross (Eds.), *Cognitive social development: Frontiers and possible futures.* New York: Cambridge University Press.

12. Bandura, A., Blanchard, E. B., and Ritter, B. (1969). Relative efficacy of desensitization and modeling approached for inducing behavioral affective and attitudinal changes. *Journal of Personality and Social Psychology, 13*, 173–199.

13. Stolz, S. B., Wienckowski, L. A., and Brown, B. S. (1975). Behavior modification: A perspective on critical issues. *American Psychologist, 30* (11), 1027–1048.

14. Stolz and others, Behavior modification, 1027.

15. Stolz and others, Behavior modification, 1028.

16. Skinner, B. F. (1954). The science of learning and the art of teaching. *Harvard Educational Review, 24*, 86–87.

17. Madsen, C. H., and Madsen, C. K. (1970). *Teaching-discipline* (p. 14). Boston: Allyn & Bacon. This quote and the ones on pp. 243 and 247 are reprinted by permission.

18. Madsen and Madsen, *Teaching-discipline* (p. 116).

19. Sears, R. R., Maccoby, E., and Levin, H. (1957). *Patterns of child rearing.* Evanston, Ill.: Row, Peterson.

20. Baer, D. M. (1973). The control of developmental process: Why wait? In J. R. Nessebroade and H. W. Reese, *Life-span developmental psychology: Methodological issues.* New York: Academic Press.

21. Skinner, B. F. (1969, originally 1965). Why teachers fail. In R. C. Sprinthall and N. A. Sprinthall (Eds.), *Educational psychology: Selected readings* (pp. 164–172). New York: Van Nostrand-Reinhold.

22. Madsen and Madsen, *Teaching-discipline* (p. 34).

23. Spettel, G. B. (1983). Classroom discipline—now. *The Clearing House* (February), p. 267. Reprinted with permission of the Helen Dwight Reid Educational Foundation. Published by Heldref Publications, 4000 Albemarle St., N.W., Washington, D.C. 20016. Copyright © 1983.

24. Bandura, A. (1969). *Principles of behavior modification* (p. 338). New York: Holt, Rinehart & Winston.

25. Davison, G. C., and Stuart, R. B. (1975). Behavior therapy and civil liberties. *American Psychologist, 30*, 755–763.

26. Tate, B. G., and Baroff, A. S. (1966). Aversive control of self-injurious behavior in a psychotic boy. *Behavior Research and Therapy, 4*, 281–287.

27. Koocher, G. P. (1976). Civil liberties and aversive conditioning for children. *American Psychologist, 31*, 94–95.

28. Maurer, A. (1974). Corporal punishment. *American Psychologist, 29*, 614–626.

29. Walters, G., and Grusec, J. (1977). *Punishment* (p. 158). San Francisco: W. H. Freeman.

30. Hurt, H. T., Scott, M. D., and McCroskey, J. C. (1978). *Communication in the classroom* (p. 32). Reading, Mass.: Addison-Wesley.

31. Madsen and Madsen. *Teaching-discipline* (p. 26).

32. Ayllon, T., and Azrin, N. H. (1968). *The token economy.* New York: Appleton-Century-Crofts.

33. Meacham, M. F., and Wiesen, A. E. (1969).

Changing classroom behavior, Second Edition (p. 50). This quote and the one on p. 250: Copyright © 1969, 1974 by Harper & Row, Publishers, Inc. Reprinted by permission of Harper & Row, Publishers, Inc.

34. Levine, F. M., and Fasnacht, G. (1974). Token rewards may lead to token learning. *American Psychologist, 29,* 816–820.

35. Stephens, T. M., and Cooper, J. O. (1980). *The educational forum* (November), p. 112.

36. Premack, D. (1965). Reinforcement theory. In D. Levine, *Nebraska symposium on motivation* (pp. 123–180). Lincoln: University of Nebraska Press.

37. Meacham and Wiesen, *Changing classroom behavior* (p. 100).

38. Rochester, J. B., and Gantz, J. (1983). *The naked computer* (p. 15). New York: William Morrow.

39. Kulik, J. A., Bangert, R. L., and Williams, G. W. (1983). Effects of computer-based teaching on secondary school students. *Journal of Educational Psychology, 75,* 19–26.

40. Ragosta, M. (1983). Computer assisted instruction and compensatory education: A longitudinal analysis. *Machine Mediated Learning, 1* (1), 108.

41. Bracey, G. W. (1982). Computers in education: What the research shows. *Electronic Learning* (November/December), pp. 51–54.

42. Bruner, J. S. (1966). *Toward a theory of instruction.* Cambridge, Mass.: Harvard University Press.

43. Bracey, Computers in education, p. 54.

44. *Science & engineering education for the 1980's and beyond* (1980). National Science Foundation Report. Washington D.C.: National Science Foundation of the Department of Education.

45. Lepper, M. R. (1985). Microcomputers in education: Motivational and social issues. *American Psychologist, 40* (1), 18.

11

INFORMATION PROCESSING

The cognitive theorists, using the computer as their basic model and E. C. Tolman as their ancestral hero, have provided another important theory of learning and memory, called information processing. Tolman, as we have already seen, was essentially a behaviorist, but a behaviorist with a decided difference. He held that maze learning could not be explained as a mere collection of tiny S-R connections but must instead be based on the organism's internalization of a cognitive map of its environment. Even a rat could therefore incorporate a picture of its surroundings and find its way through the maze on the basis of that picture. The cognitive map, then, was viewed as an internal representation of environmental *information*. These are clearly not the thoughts of a Watsonian behaviorist.

Although at first glance the information-processing model may seem like a step backward into the era of Wilhelm Wundt, who attempted to analyze consciousness into its various components, it is in reality far more empirically based. Wundt presumed to be using empirical techniques when he instructed his subjects to look within themselves at the elements of their own conscious awareness. Wundt called this technique experimental introspection, but from the viewpoint of science it was far too subjective and unreliable. Introspective reports varied from subject to subject and, worse, from laboratory to laboratory. The data were too inconsistent to provide psychology with anything resembling a firm foundation. The information-processing theorists, on the other hand, analyze mental events in terms of their behavioral effects—effects that can be reliably observed and measured. Such overt measures as reaction times (chronometric measures) and verbal recognition of various stimuli can be and are used to verify inferred mental constructs.

Although the information-processing theorists take a behavioral stance with respect to measurement, they have traditionally leaned toward the gestalt orientation when it comes to theory. They have been addressing such issues as the organization of thinking, the role of meaning in learning, cognitive strategies in problem solving, the structure of human awareness—in short, most of the same areas that had earlier been studied by such gestaltists as Max Wertheimer, Wolfgang Kohler, and Kurt Lewin.

LEARNING AS INFORMATION PROCESSING

Information-processing theory is loosely modeled on the way in which computers process information.

Just as data to be entered into a computer must be encoded in a form that the computer can store and process, information that flows through the sensory receptors and is attended to must also be encoded before it can be stored and processed. At the psychological level, encoding involves the creation of memory traces, which are abstractions based on the salient features of the incoming information. It is also thought that at the physiological level the nervous system adopts an internal code that represents the external stimulus. In this way, the encoded representation of the external object or event becomes internal information and is, thus, readied for storage.

Although there are several variations in the specifics of how the information-processing model of learning appears to work, the consensus view is that learning and remembering are based on the flow of information that passes *within* the organism. The sense organs respond to and pass along incoming information, which is encoded in the memory and nervous system. The encoded information is then stored and processed in a manner that allows it to be retrieved and acted on. Thus, as with the computer, the information-processing model consists of input of encoded information, storage and processing, and finally output, or retrieval. The model to be presented in this chapter will be focused on intentional learning, which is, after all, the major mission of the schools.

Storage refers to internal memory, or the persistence of information over time. In one form, it is analogous to the computer's use of disks or tape to save information for future use. Unless

The first phase of information processing is encoding, which involves the formation of memory traces that may entail physiological changes.

damaged, of course, a computer's disk stores information that does not change over time, whereas there is considerable debate over whether human memory possesses that type of etched-in-stone immutability.

Retrieval is the output end of the memory process. It refers to the utilization of the stored information, loosely comparable to accessing the computer's data base. To be retrieved, stored information must be not only available but also accessible to the individual. That is, although stored information may be theoretically available, it may not always be easily located and utilized.[1]

With this brief analogy in mind, we will now turn to how learning is acquired, in the view of information-processing theorists. Figure 11.1 shows in diagram form the main features of the information-processing model of learning.

The Sensory Register

When information from the environment first impinges on a receptor (sense organ), there is an extremely brief moment, half a second to perhaps as many as four seconds, when it is held in sensory memory. This memory, also known as the sensory register, is called "iconic memory" for visual items and "echoic memory" for auditory items.[2] Because the sensory memory holds only raw, unprocessed sensory information, it is sometimes seen as a sensory buffer, or way-station, situated between the external environment and internal memory.[3] Although both iconic and echoic memory are based on neural traces (electrochemical changes in neurons) in the receptors and the nerves leading from the receptors to the brain, it seems that the traces are held for a slightly longer period in echoic memory than in iconic memory.[4] Other sensory memories may also exist, such as touch, taste, and smell, but the evidence regarding sight and sound is now more direct. Regardless of the sensory mode involved, the activation produced by incoming information may create a recognition pattern, or an internal connection between the external stimulation and previously encoded information. The brief and volatile sensory memory trace disappears almost immediately unless it is attended to. It's a literal case of the old adage "in one ear and out the other."

It should be pointed out that there is currently some debate among the information-processing theorists regarding the status of sensory memory. Since the sensory register is based on the activation of the sense organs and sensory neurons leading to the brain, and therefore not in the brain itself, it may not be a true memory process. Also, even if there is a sensory register that momentarily holds information about the physical environment, it may have little relevance to the information-storage process over longer periods of time.[5]

If the individual is paying attention to the incoming stimulation, the information is encoded and moved along from the sensory memory register into storage. A critical component here is attention, for if the information is not attended to immediately, it most likely will be

FIGURE 11.1   The information-processing model of intentional learning.

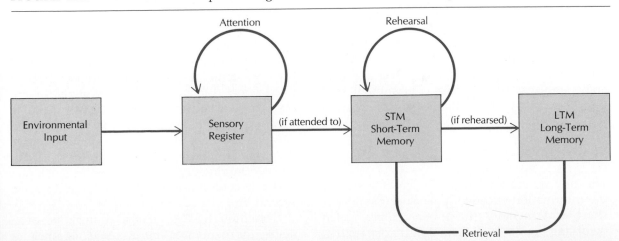

Sight and sound are the most direct routes for sensory input.

lost. For example, if you are introduced to someone at a party and don't really pay attention to the introduction, moments later you may not even recall the person's name.

Some theorists do suggest, however, that under certain conditions it is possible to activate a kind of incidental-acquisition process, where some information from the environment may be automatically encoded in the sensory register without either attention or intention.[6]

Short-term Memory

The first of the two main systems for storing the information encoded in sensory memory is short-term memory (STM)—sometimes called "working" or "active" memory.[7] It appears that

short-term memory can only encode about seven separate items (plus or minus two) and can hold them for only a limited time.[8] Estimates of how long information may be retained in STM vary from about a few seconds to almost a minute. Since seven is the typical number of separate items in a telephone number, STM is often referred to as "telephone number" memory. Thus, if you were verbally given a phone number, you could most probably hold it in STM long enough to pick up the phone and dial the number. However, if the other party didn't answer the ring or there was a busy signal, you probably couldn't recall it long enough to dial a second time.

Even though STM is restricted to about seven items, the items may be grouped together, or

Children can increase their capacity to remember by chunking items of information.

chunked. In this way, several items may be packaged together and processed as a single element. For example, you might be asked to repeat a series of nine digits, a number that is pushing the limit of the "magical" value of seven plus or minus two. By chunking the digits into groups of three, however, you then only have to hold three separate items in mind, not a difficult task. The same is of course true for letters. Whereas a random set of seventeen letters pushes STM far beyond its limit, by chunking the letters, retention can be made easy. Take the letters OPECIBMSONARRADAR, which is a total of seventeen letters. If you chunk them into OPEC, IBM, SONAR, and RADAR, the task of remembering them falls far short of STM capacity. Radio and TV commercials make use of this strategy, especially when giving telephone numbers. They tell you that telephone operators are standing by to receive your call. Rather than presenting you with eleven separate numbers to dial in order to get your volume of *Art Treasures of the World*, you are told to dial 1-800 ART INFO, which is at most only three separate units. The toll-free 1-800 has probably already been chunked and encoded by the listener, leaving only ART and INFO to be retrieved when getting to the phone. It has also been shown that chunking, especially around gestalt laws of perception, can aid in the recall of visual as well as auditory stimuli.

Long-term Memory

The information from STM can be passed along to be processed and consolidated into long-term memory (LTM). LTM has the potential for holding encoded information for a lifetime. However, not all information from STM enters LTM. The key to LTM storage is in being motivated enough to rehearse the items from your STM. If, at a party, you were introduced to an extremely attractive person, your level of motivation might automatically be high enough to prod you into saying over and over again to yourself not only his or her name but also the phone number (if you were lucky enough to get it).

According to the popular dual-code theory, information in LTM is coded into both visual images and verbal representations.[9] There have also been suggestions that auditory representations may be encoded in LTM. Even though they may not have been in your consciousness for years, you can still probably recall the visual picture of your childhood home and perhaps the sounds you heard while playing in your backyard; you may also recall the *names* of some of your childhood friends. Verbal representations play the major role in our LTM. In fact, some theorists believe that we can retain few, if any, memories of events that occurred prior to our acquisition of language.

Retrieval from long-term memory   Once information has been stored in LTM, it is available but, as was mentioned earlier, it is not always easily located and utilized. John P. Houston, an expert in the area of learning theory, gives the example of the student who knows (has stored) the names of all of the states of the Union, but at any given moment in time, he may not be able to retrieve all of them.[10] Therefore, even though the information is in storage and available, it may not always be accessible. The student may know the names of all the states abutting, say, Indiana, but explains forlornly that he just doesn't seem to have the names handy or that they have momentarily escaped him. Prompting, by providing cues, aids the student in his or her storage search and eventual retrieval. This is why, when meeting a long-ago acquaintance, you may find it so much easier to remember the person's face than his or her name.

Some people feel they are unique in that they have "a good memory for faces but not for names." That, of course, is true of all of us. Remembering the face is a recognition task (the face is right there in front of you), but the name is strictly a matter of recall. This is also why multiple choice and true-false tests are easier than exams that require unaided recall. For example, compare the following items:

1. Who was president of the United States immediately after Franklin D. Roosevelt?

2. True or False: Harry S. Truman was president of the United States immediately after Franklin D. Roosevelt.

Item 2 should be easier, because you are being offered more ways to search your memory. Item 1, the recall item, demands that you access your memory of Franklin Roosevelt and then search for Truman. But for item 2, the recognition item, you could search from Truman to Roosevelt, even if you could not access it the other way around, from Roosevelt to Truman.

Concept formation   Information processing is more than just the shuffling of stimulus inputs from sensory memory to short-term memory to long-term memory, then retrieving the bits of information. Information is also processed into conceptual form. Concept formation is based on identifying the characteristics of stimuli that have been presented and then *organizing* them in such a way as to provide encoded meaning. Since memory for the meaning of events lasts longer than memory for specific, physical details, once information is processed into concepts, it is not only more easily stored in LTM but, perhaps more important, more easily accessed for retrieval. According to David Ausubel, concepts can be formed with or without verbal representations. In fact, Ausubel suggests that concepts are learned in two stages. First, the child learns the representative image of the concept and then later learns the verbal representation.

Ausubel describes the cognitive activity of a child who has been handling some cubes and thereby forms the concept of a cube before learning the name of the concept:

> These cubes, we will suppose, differ in size, color, and texture. As a result of this concrete experience, the child discovers inductively the criterial attributes of the cube. Moreover, these attributes are embedded in a representative image of a cube, an image that the child has developed from his experience and can recall in the absence of real cubes. This process of inductively discovering the criterial attributes of a class of stimuli is called *conceptual formation*. When it is complete, the child is said to possess the concept of a cube, and the meaning of this concept is the representative image comprising the criterial attributes of this class of objects.[11]

This view portrays language as adding additional meaning to an already acquired concept. Because of its focus on both images and language, Ausubel's position on concept formation is consistent with the dual-code theory of information processing. Ausubel clearly recognizes that the two stages, imaging and verbalizing, may occur simultaneously, especially in older children, though it need not. Harry Harlow's study of learning sets (see p. 235) showed dramatically that chimps could learn to form concepts and that these concepts were based strictly on image (considering the chimps' rather restricted vocabulary).

As children learn to increase their verbal-conceptual bases, their ability to comprehend written material also increases. One expert in the area of reading, Joanne Carlisle, has found that children can be trained in the use of strategies

CONTEMPORARY ISSUE

Is Computer Thinking Like Human Thinking?

The difference between human and artificial intelligence can be summarized this way: Humans think; computers compute.

Since the information-processing theorists have typically used the computer as their model, it is little wonder that research has been generated in the area of artificial intelligence. Artificial intelligence is predicated on the belief that human thinking can be simulated by computer programs, *if we understand how human beings think*. Typically, a theory on thinking is first devised, and then a computer program is written that simulates the theory. Allen Newell and Herbert Simon wrote a program called the "Logic Theorist," which attempted to simulate a series of rules for solving problems in formal logic.[a] The program worked well enough to solve most of the complicated problems that had been advanced by the logicians Alfred Nash and Bertrand Russell in their 1925 masterpiece, *Principia Mathematica*.

The question at issue really shouldn't be whether computers can think but rather whether computers can be programed to parallel, even roughly, the human thought process. So far the answer is a decided "no." Despite more than twenty years of research, no program yet written approaches the human ability to display intelligent behavior. To some extent this is due to the obvious fact that even the most technologically sophisticated computer is hopelessly naive when compared to the intricacies of the human mind. It is also due, alas, to the fact that psychology has still not gained a full understanding of how human intelligence is organized.[b]

In short, our human ability to extract meaningful information from the environment and form abstractions and high-order cognitive structures has so far been only roughly approximated by the computer. Top chess players can still beat a computer, and computerized chess is one of the better programs to have been developed. In fact, even though computers can play a decent game of chess, they still cannot incorporate information and abstractions of the environment as well as the average three-year-old child. One group of artificial intelligence programers did try to teach a computer some motivational sequences, including what to do when hungry. The computer learned a variety of ways to react to hunger instructions, and finally when asked what it would do when it wanted a mid-afternoon snack, the computer replied that it would go to the nearest pizza stand. When asked what it would do when it got there, it responded, "I'll eat the pizza stand." Thus, a critical difference between artificial intelligence and human intelligence is that although computers can obviously compute better than humans, they are much worse than humans at matching. The computer can only match incoming words against those stored in its memory if those words are exact counterparts. As Morton Hunt says, "Any two-year-old child could do better."[c] Can the computer ever be expected to account for the complex patterning and economy of the human mind?

[a]   Newell, A., and Simon, H. (1972). *Human problem solving*. Englewood Cliffs, N.J.: Prentice-Hall.
[b]   Anderson, J. R. (1980). *Cognitive psychology and its implications*. San Francisco: W. H. Freeman.
[c]   Hunt, M. (1982). *The universe within* (p. 333). New York: Simon & Schuster.

designed to increase reading comprehension.[12] Carlisle's technique is based on a "learning how to learn" concept, where children are provided with numerous examples and lots of practice in forming abstractions, looking for relationships, and then retrieving the concepts. In short, the children are deliberately provided with learning sets.

THE INFORMATION-PROCESSING THEORY OF FORGETTING

Forgetting, to the cognitively oriented information theorist, is defined as the inability to retrieve information. The two major reasons for forgetting, according to these theorists, are decay and interference.

Decay

Decay is the passive loss of the memory trace due to inactivity or lack of rehearsal. Actually, this is not a new idea. Thorndike, an early S-R theorist, postulated as one of his three major laws of learning the law of exercise. In this law, Thorndike stated that the more an S-R connection is used, the stronger it becomes; conversely, the less it is used, the weaker it becomes. Hence, through inactivity, the S-R connection simply rusts away, or passively decays over time.

The information-processing theorists accept decay as an important influence on forgetting, especially at the input stage of the processing sequence. Sensory memory, you will recall, decays in a matter of less than a few seconds, and information in STM, if not rehearsed, is lost in less than about a minute. But what about LTM? Here the evidence is not totally clear. Some theorists claim that once information is brought into LTM, it is stored quite permanently. For example, Wilder Penfield feels that the brain is like a recording tape and that all its memories are *permanently* stored.[13] While performing brain surgery, Penfield stimulated, with a slight electrical current, various areas of a patient's cerebral cortex. (The patient was conscious.) As long as it persisted, each stimulation produced in the patient extremely vivid memories of long-past events. When the stimulation ceased, so too did the memory. The images and memories

reported by the patient were so dramatically distinct that the patient felt as though they were being relived. The patient also believed that these memories had been completely forgotten. Thus, Penfield argued that the memories had remained organically intact and would remain so for life but that under normal circumstances the patient simply couldn't retrieve them.

This experiment, provocative though it may be, doesn't absolutely close the book on the case for permanent LTM. Critics suggest that Penfield's patient may not have been recalling actual events but instead was experiencing new sensations that only resembled past events.[14]

Other theorists believe that decay does take place in LTM, but *at a much slower rate* than in STM. Estimates of the decay rate in LTM vary somewhat, but most theorists concede that once in LTM, information will probably remain relatively intact for many years.

Interference

Forgetting also occurs on the basis of interference, which takes place when the recall of one event is inhibited by the incursion of another event. Again, this is not a brand-new explanation. For example, S-R theorist Edwin Guthrie, in his 1930s learning theory, put forth interference as the sole reason for forgetting. Interference is viewed as being of two types: proactive inhibition and retroactive inhibition.

Proactive inhibition   When you learn A, then later learn B, only to discover that your previous learning of A has in some way disrupted your recall of B, that is called "proactive inhibition" (PI). The previously learned, older material (A) has worked forward in time to hamper your efforts to retrieve that newer material (B). You might take a French course one semester and a Spanish course the next. On the Spanish final, your recall might well be disturbed by the interference effects produced by having previously taken the French course.

Retroactive inhibition   When the learning of new material (B) works backward and prevents the recall of older material (A), that is called "retroactive inhibition" (RI). To use the foreign language example again, after finishing the Spanish course you might now find your recall of French disrupted. You might very well confuse your *estar*s with your *être*s. Your knowledge of French would have remained more solidly intact had you not spent the intervening semester working on Spanish. Some students cram for a final until they drop off to sleep in the early morning hours in a state of exhausted confusion. On awakening, just before the exam, the material suddenly seems less confusing and more understandable. Some students attribute this to the fact that they have continued learning in some mysterious fashion while asleep. Though this theory is admittedly seductive, a simpler explanation is that sleeping helped to prevent retroactive inhibition. Going to sleep, rather than adding to the store of knowledge, simply prevents a large degree of interference. Also, on awakening, the student is obviously less tired and more alert for the retrieval process. In general, the best way to take a break while studying for an exam is to do something as different as possible from the exam material. For example, if you are studying for an educational psychology exam, it's better to take a fifteen-minute Ping-Pong break than to read over your sociology notes.

Houston has prepared an exercise that should give you a quick, first-hand impression of how retroactive inhibition works.[15] Cover the three telephone numbers on the right side of Table 11.1, and concentrate on the number to the left. Spend about thirty seconds looking at and rehearsing that number. When you're satisfied that you know it, cover the entire table and wait for about forty-five seconds. During this waiting period, *do not rehearse the number*. Think of other things, like how many different brands of soft drinks you can name. After the forty-five seconds have elapsed, try to recall that phone number. You will probably be able to repeat it correctly. Now prepare yourself for the demonstration of retroactive inhibition by

covering the left-side number that you just learned. Concentrate on memorizing the three numbers on the right side. When you think you have them down pat (it should take about a minute), try to recall that left-side number. Unless you encode and process information at a level far beyond the ability of the average person, that first number is now virtually impossible to retrieve.

Offsetting the effects of interference   The process of storing information (learning), then, can disrupt both past and future learning. Says Houston, "The very act of learning itself constitutes an ironic source of forgetting."[16] Don't make too much of this accurate, though somewhat restricted, statement, however. You needn't assume that you'd better not learn too much now or it will make it that much more difficult to learn new material later. Nor should you be wary of tackling new material for fear of forgetting what you've already learned. As we shall soon see, the facilitative action of positive transfer may more than compensate for the inhibitory effects of interference. In fact, it has been shown that a background of information, especially when that information is *organized*, can offset the effects of interference.[17]

Aids to Retrieving Learned Material

Processed information is of little use unless it can be retrieved. What, therefore, can be done to increase a student's ability to recall and utilize processed information and to compensate for interference?

Overlearning   Studies show that retention is longer and retrieval easier when material is overlearned—that is, learned to a point beyond which it appears to be mastered.[18] Teachers should encourage students to keep at it, even though the students feel the material has been fully learned. Overlearning is especially valuable with those areas that students find difficult. The alert teacher will spend extra time going over such material.

Understanding   Teachers should stress the understanding of concepts, rather than concentrating only on the repetition of facts. When provided with categories of understanding, stu-

TABLE 11.1 *TESTING RETROACTIVE INHIBITION*

NUMBER TO BE LEARNED FIRST	NUMBERS TO BE LEARNED SECOND
562-7201	617-5317
	413-2096
	783-0301

CONTEMPORARY ISSUE

The Debate over Bilingual Education

Approximately 10 percent of the school-age population in the United States speaks a native language other than English. These "second-language learners," or bilinguals, present special problems to educators. Until the early 1960s, such children were typically placed in the traditional English-language curriculum alongside their native-English-speaking counterparts in the belief that all ethnic groups should be forced to blend into a single "all-American" cultural group. During this decade public schools suddenly experienced an influx of several thousand Cuban children who had immigrated to the United States with their families. These non-English-speaking children were dropping out of school at what soon became alarmingly high rates.[a] The educational establishment was confronted with several major issues.

Because schools had experienced great difficulty in obtaining valid evaluations of their academic ability, many of these bilingual children were being incorrectly placed in classes for the mentally retarded. This rather widespread, and certainly unfortunate, practice led in part to the 1974 Supreme Court decision (*Lau* v. *Nichols*),

which set careful guidelines and regulations designed to reverse this trend. School districts were required by the Department of Health, Education and Welfare (HEW) to develop bilingual education programs whenever they had twenty or more students from a single language background.[b] Then, in 1984, federal legislation reauthorized school systems to amend these programs to include placing bilingual children in regular school programs with the proviso that instructional aides be available to assist the classroom teacher.

There has been a lively debate among educators over which method is best for educating these children. Two very different approaches are currently in use. One method, the native-language approach, provides reading instruction in the child's native language. Proponents of this approach claim that children learn to read and understand concepts best by having their own native-language structures reinforced. A. L. Gutierrez proposes that establishing a firm base in the child's native-language structures allows reading skills to be more readily transferred into the second language, English.[c]

The second approach, the di-

rect method, totally immerses the bilingual children in the language of their new culture. Its proponents believe this will more fully prepare the children for the language demands inherent in their later career and life responsibilities. Advocates of this approach are not concerned with the development of reading skills in the children's first language. Because the numbers of bilingual students are increasing, the prevailing federal and local philosophy appears to be in line with this "direct" approach.[d]

R. D. Milk argues for an integrative approach to close the gap between these two methods. Simultaneous access to both languages would enable students to use the verbal skills they already possess in their native language in order to acquire needed concepts that can be expressed in both languages. Two key elements are apparently critical to an integrative approach: (1) the integration of second-language (English) goals into content area classes, and (2) the fostering of classroom conditions that allow students to receive the input necessary for second-language acquisition.[e]

Experts in the field would agree that not enough evidence is

dents are more likely to learn new information quickly and efficiently. When equipped with a conceptual framework, students are more apt to be able to deduce solutions to new problem areas. Also, abstractions are easier to develop when an underlying understanding of a concept has been incorporated. Conceptual learning becomes self-perpetuating, since each new concept provides an anchorage that makes the acquisition of new information and new concepts

more efficient. It's as though entering new information into a computer literally expands the computer's internal memory. Learning then requires less effort and becomes more enjoyably efficient. Also, as a myriad of studies have shown, the more meaningful the material is, the greater the likelihood of both its acquisition and retrieval. It is virtually impossible to teach for understanding if the material seems random and meaningless.

available to show us which is the better method. There are problems inherent in both models currently in use, and the integrative method is a viable but still unsubstantiated alternative. The direct method, for example, is not always being implemented effectively, especially among Spanish-speaking children. In addition, there appears to be a growing interest in the maintenance of ethnic languages, identities, and cultures to sustain a pluralistic society in this country. For these and other reasons, some educators have leaned toward the native-language approach. However, because of certain methodological problems—including the lack of adequate control groups and the possibility of the Hawthorne effect (see Chapter 17)—studies have failed to fully support the superiority of this approach.

Part of the difficulty inherent in resolving the bilingual issue is that more research is needed in learning and information processing to shed light on double-language learning in early childhood. As we have seen, the problems produced by proactive and retroactive inhibition are significant under the best of circumstances and may be especially acute for the young child faced with having to learn two languages at the same time.

Currently no answer exists to the question of how best to teach bilingual children. We are a long way from having enough evidence to show us the most effective method. And so the controversy continues, particularly in regions where the concentration of immigrant families is especially high.

[a] Natalicio, D. S. (1979). Reading and the bilingual child. In L. B. Resnick and P. A. Weaver (Eds.), *Theory and practice of early reading*. New Jersey: Lawrence Erlbaum.
[b] *The Linguistic Reporter* (1975). *18*(2), 5–7.
[c] Gutierrez, A. L. (1975). Bilingual education: Reading through two languages. In D. E. Critchlow (Ed.), *Reading and the Spanish-speaking child*. Waco, Texas: Texas State Council of the International Reading Association.
[d] Enright, D. S., and McCloskey, M. (1985). Yes, talking: Organizing the classroom to promote second language acquisition. *TESOL Quarterly, 19*(3), 431–452.
[e] Milk, R. D. (1985). The changing role of ESL in bilingual education. *TESOL Quarterly, 19*(4), 657–672.

This contemporary issue was especially prepared for this volume by Carol S. Spafford, American International College.

Retention is easier when material is overlearned.

Building an organized knowledge base The acquisition and retrieval of new information can be made easier when it builds on previously incorporated information. The evidence from studies on positive transfer as well as Harry Harlow's data on learning sets show that acquisition improves when it is built on an existing knowledge base. Just as new motor skills are improved by positive transfer (learning to ride a bike aids in learning to ride a motorcycle), so too are more cognitively based skills. Concepts build on facts, and *concepts build on concepts*. Knowing how to add, subtract, multiply, and divide is obviously helpful to the student taking a course in algebra. Having taken algebra, in turn, makes a course in physics more understandable. The ability to access and utilize information is a direct function of the number of previously incorporated categories available to a student. Recalling that Truman succeeded Roosevelt is facilitated by stored information about Truman, Roosevelt, or any facts relating to the United States at the end of World War II. These encoded facts also increase the likelihood of a student's acquiring organized concepts relating to that historical time period. These concepts, in turn, help ensure a more complete understanding of such concepts as the restructuring of the postwar economy or of the sociopolitical justifications for the establishment of the United Nations. Thus, as students acquire more different *organized* categories into which information may be processed, the information becomes ever more accessible to retrieval and use.

Relating new material to the existing knowledge base   The teacher should always strive to interweave new material with relevant existing learning. When new material is tied into the student's existing knowledge base, teaching effectiveness is increased.[19] Part of the reason for this is that information is then stored in several categories, and each of the associations then serves as a cue to a source of retrieval. Thus, the more categories under which new information is indexed, the more readily it can be retrieved. The student should constantly be reminded of these related categories as new information is presented.

Using cue associations   When attempting retrieval, the student should be taught to work on actively producing as many cue associations as possible. Since retrieval of stored information is often cue dependent, an *active* search of all relevant cues often brings the information back into working memory. For example, in trying to retrieve the name of Abraham Lincoln's assassin, the student should think of as many things as possible about Lincoln, perhaps the fact that he was assassinated at a play, the name of the theater, or even the quotation "*Sic semper tyrannis.*" The more associations the better, since eventually one of them might cue the name, John Wilkes Booth. This technique is often called "associative searching," since it usually makes use of less commonly used pathways among the various concepts and facts related to the information being retrieved. Its opposite is active searching, in which information is accessed along more practiced pathways.[20] Obviously, the student should be encouraged to utilize the associative search only if a direct search comes up empty.

Mnemonics   Mnemonic devices are aids to retrieval and are typically employed during both acquisition and retrieval. These may be visual or verbal. Suppose, for example, you wanted to remember to pick up some ice cream, bread, and milk. As an aid to memory, you might attempt to produce a vivid visual image of your grocery list, perhaps by imagining a gigantic ice cream cone, soaking in milk and surrounded with slices of bread. With that bizarre picture fixed firmly in mind (in fact, the more outlandish the image, the better), your grocery list should be secure. Or, instead, you might choose a verbal mediator and simply think of the letters IBM—ice cream, bread, and milk. Just don't make the mistake of forgetting what the letters stand for and inadvertently bring home instant coffee, bananas, and margarine.

The ancient Greek and Roman orators used to employ imagery to help them memorize the key points in their speeches. The orator would imagine himself strolling down some well-known path and then tie the image of a passing landmark to each successive rhetorical point. This is now known as the method of loci, and as many after-dinner speakers will attest, it still works today as well as it did in the early Greek days. You might even use it on your way to take an educational psychology exam. Suppose, for example, you need to do some last-minute cramming on Thorndike's three major laws of learning. As you leave the dorm, the flagpole is on your left, and on top of the pole you picture a gymnast going through an "exercise" routine. Next, as you pass the library, you visualize a large cat at the main entrance poised to pounce on a mouse; the cat appears to be coiled in "readiness." Finally, before entering the classroom building where the test is to be given, you walk by the Campus Snack Bar and remember the "effect" the cold french fries had on you the last time you were there. As you mentally rewalk the route during the test, you recall the laws.

Verbal mediators are also used as mnemonics. Fifth-graders, for example, may learn the acronym HOMES in order to remember the names of the five Great Lakes: Huron, Ontario, Michigan, Erie, and Superior. Such acronyms are called "first-letter mnemonics," since the

peg word HOMES, contains the first letters of all the items to be recalled. Research in this area has shown rather convincingly that if the peg word itself is not too complicated, the use of the first-letter mnemonic definitely aids recall.[21] The novice boatsman might learn to use the mnemonic "red, right, returning" in order to recall that the red buoys should be kept to the right when returning to the harbor. Many so-called memory experts utilize long and intricate mnemonic devices when performing their amazing feats of recall.[22]

Mnemonic devices, however, may be so complex that recalling the original stimuli is even more difficult than it would have been without it. One college student had learned a long poem which was designed to ensure the memorization of all the U.S. presidents in order. The first letter in each word of the poem corresponded to the first letter in the last name of the president. Sometimes, however, the student would forget a word or line from the poem, and at other times he would forget the name the letter had designated. For example, once when asked who the thirteenth president was, he paused, repeated the poem to himself, and then proudly answered, "Franklin." (This is not to suggest, of course, that he also believed that Fillmore was the name of a stove.)

Another use of the peg word mnemonic combines the verbal mediator with a visual image. The following example, one of the simplest peg systems, uses rhymes for numbers.[23] First, re-

hearse and put into memory storage the following words:

1. Gun
2. Shoe
3. Tree
4. Floor
5. Hive
6. Sick
7. Heaven
8. Gate
9. Wine
10. Hen

Now have some other person give you a verbal list of ten items, slowly and in order, such as:

1. Book
2. Football
3. Bathtub
4. Coke
5. Candle
6. Orange
7. Track Meet
8. Rose Bowl
9. Professor
10. Dice

As each item is announced, create a mental picture associating the item with the peg word. Here's an example, although you can probably do this far more creatively yourself.

1. Gun—a *book* that has been hollowed out and contains a gun

2. Shoe—a large shoe kicking a *football*

3. Tree—a *bathtub* perched high in the limbs of a large tree

4. Floor—a bottle of *Coke* spilled all over a kitchen floor

5. Hive—a beehive with flaming *candles* inserted in it

6. Sick—eating an *orange* and becoming violently sick from it

7. Heaven—a *track meet* in heaven, with angels competing in each event

8. Gate—a large gate at the entrance to the *Rose Bowl*, festooned with admission tickets

9. Wine—your *professor* drinking too much wine and acting in a foolish fashion

10. Hen—a large hen laying a dozen *dice* instead of eggs

Once you've stored these images, the other person can either give you a number, say four, and you'll respond with "Coke"; or an item, say track meet, and you can respond with the number "seven." It's not hard to do, and you'll definitely impress your friends and relatives with your "amazing" powers of memory. Students have even been known to wager against such feats.

The pros and cons of mnemonics in the classroom   Mnemonic devices are unquestionably effective in aiding the recall of specific information. They may be troublesome at the start of a learning sequence, since they take time to initiate, but once in place they allow information to remain systematically stored—like an office filing system. In fact, one study, which reported on a technique first used by Japanese students called "Yodai mnemonics," suggested that third-graders in the United States may learn to manipulate fractions in a few hours—a feat that typically takes two to three years. According to the study, once manipulative math procedures are acquired, understanding naturally follows.[24]

This seemingly bright picture has another side, however. Too much reliance on mnemonics may actually prevent understanding and especially creativity. Advocates of this view believe that mnemonic devices are merely tools for rote memorization, better used for training parrots than children. Material learned in this fashion is difficult to relate to larger concepts. As one critic notes, "Mnemonics may help children learn arbitrary associations but are likely to be less helpful when the material to be learned has conceptual links not expressed by the mnemonic cover story."[25]

IQ AND INFORMATION PROCESSING

Dating back to the 1920s, studies have consistently shown that IQ and the acquisition/retention of new material are highly correlated. A child with an IQ of 130 will typically learn and retain more information than a child whose IQ is only 100. But what about forgetting? In a series of studies, first reported in 1959 by Herbert Klausmeir and John Feldhausen, children with high, average, and low IQs were shown to retain about the same *proportion* of what they had learned.[26] That is, although in absolute terms the high-IQ children learned and retained the most, the percentage of what was retained over time remained the same for all three IQ

groups. Thus, the proportion of information retained seems to be a constant across a wide range of IQ values.[27]

Yale psychologist Robert Sternberg has also studied intelligence as it relates to information processing.[28] Sternberg has found that people who score highest on IQ tests are not necessarily the persons who are the fastest responders at all stages of the information-processing sequence. In fact, the highest IQs are registered by persons who spend *more time* encoding the relevant cues in a given problem and then *less time* in strategically processing the information during the solution phase. The greater time spent during the early encoding stage is, thus, compensated for by a lessening of the time spent later in the sequence and in an increased likelihood of finding the correct solution.

DEVELOPMENTAL ASPECTS OF INFORMATION PROCESSING

There are, of course, obvious differences between the infant's and the adult's ability to process information. And once again, we find the nature-nurture controversy arising. At the two extremes, one view states that cognitive development is a straight function of genetic unwinding (nature); the other view is that it is based solely on experience. The position that we will take falls between these two poles—that is, that the human information processor develops increasingly sophisticated strategies as a result of the overall interaction of heredity, environment, and time. Cognitive maturity thus depends on a genetic predisposition interacting with environmental encounters occurring within a range of specific age levels. The developing child acts on and reacts to his or her environment, and, as a result, the quality of the child's information-processing system is transformed.

On average, older children obviously have better memories than younger children. Much of this has to do with language. As language acquisition progresses, the older child has more categories of verbal representations to use to encode and retrieve information. Also, as we have seen in our discussion of Jean Piaget, qualitative differences in the child's cognitive style and level develop over time. As the child's cognitive base broadens and matures, higher and more abstract levels of thought processing typically become the rule. In fact, the latest studies have even pointed to the fact that the child goes through critical periods in the development of processing capacities.[29] Each passing day brings fresh evidence demonstrating the linkage between the information-processing model and the currently accepted parameters of cognitive growth. Let's now examine some of the developmentally related components of the information-processing model.

Differences in Processing Input

Earlier studies had suggested that younger children were less able to take as much information into their sensory registers (or hold it as long) as older children and adults could. But doubt is now being expressed about this finding. More recent studies have indicated that five-year-old children do not differ from adults in the amount of information they perceive or the time they hold it in the sensory register. What the earlier studies had interpreted as a sensory difference now appears to be a difference in how much information can be encoded into STM before it simply decayed in the sensory register. It is at this stage of the process that older children show superiority. Nor can this advantage be explained solely on the basis of language differences.[30] The mature learner's apparent superiority in the amount of information recorded in sensory memory may actually be due to a more refined strategy of sensory rehearsal. In fact, the literal sensory image (icon) is believed to persist even longer in the young child than in the adult. Thus, at least with regard to visual memory, the infant is simply *processing* the information more slowly, even though the actual duration of the icon may remain intact somewhat longer.[31]

Processing speed   Again, although earlier studies seemed to have found that processing speed was a direct function of age, the current view is more cautious. In the earlier studies investigators had typically presented the subjects with a simple stimulus, then measured the time it took for recognition to occur. But what had at first appeared to be a difference in processing speed may instead have been an artifact of the experimental methodology. Perhaps older children were more willing to take a guess as to what the stimulus might be and, because of their broader knowledge base, were more accurate when they did guess.

Thus, the evidence on processing speed is still unclear. Its importance from a developmental point of view, however, should not be minimized. As Robert Solso states, "If children indeed process individual stimuli more slowly, the cumulative effect of this deficit across large numbers of stimuli could be substantial."[32]

Attentional processes   Since the ability to attend to or focus on relevant stimuli is a key element in the transfer of information from the sensory register to STM, the study of the growth of attentional processes is of major significance to developmental psychologists. The evidence in this area is fairly straightforward. Numerous studies have shown that older children are indeed better able to focus and control their attentional processes than are younger children. A child's potential ability to attend to relevant cues and ignore the irrelevant seems clearly to be a direct function of growth and development.

Encoding   The ability to internally encode incoming information also seems to have a substantial developmental component. Whereas young children typically incorporate only a small number of stimulus dimensions, sometimes only one or two, older children engage in what is called "multiple encoding."[33] In the processing of complex stimuli, which have a large number of encoding alternatives, multiple encoding becomes especially important. A stimulus may be encoded on the basis of its size, distance, density, color, shape, texture, name, and so forth. In short, older children tend to encode by using many of these alternatives; younger children focus on only a few.

Differences in Storing Information

Rehearsal strategies   Age-related differences have also been found in rehearsal strategies.[34] This is an obviously important factor, since rehearsal allows STM codes to be processed into LTM. The major findings in this area indicate that as children get older, they develop more organized rehearsal strategies, which, because of their cumulative effects, allow significantly more information to be consolidated into LTM. Younger children, although still attempting to rehearse, do so in a less systematic fashion than older children.

Chunking techniques   Closely related to rehearsal strategies are chunking techniques, since both depend on organizational skills and the ability to form abstractions. A list of words—such as *airplane, train, bus, couch, table, chair, piano, guitar, trumpet*—are easy to remember when chunked into the three categories of modes of transportation, furniture, and musical instruments. If the list is encoded as nine separate and seemingly random items, retrieval becomes far more difficult. Younger children, even when prompted as to the obvious chunking categories, have difficulty memorizing this type of list. Up to about third grade, children seem not to do any better on easily categorized items than they do on unrelated items.

Retrieval skills   Retrieval skills have also been found to be based on age-related strategies. As children mature, they develop what appears to be almost a spontaneous increase in the use of retrieval strategies. This, after all, should not be surprising. Since the developing child is encoding and organizing information in an increasingly sophisticated manner, it is little wonder that he or she can access that processed information more efficiently. The older child utilizes more categories, more information storage bins, and because of this is better able to use retrieval cues to facilitate the search. It has also been suggested that older children possess more knowledge about their own memory skills and thus are better equipped to know when certain retrieval skills are appropriate. This concept of having internal knowledge about memory has been called "metacognition," or "metamemory," by John Flavell and others.[35] Thus, younger children may not use as many retrieval aids, either because they don't yet have them or, if they do, don't know that they have them— or even that the aids might be helpful in retrieval. The difference between cognition and metacognition is in the students' self-awareness and control. Cognitive processes often grow over time, with little awareness or effort on the part of learners. Metacognition involves definite awareness, and even conscious monitoring and control. Elizabeth Bondy puts it this way: "A student who summarizes the chapter he/she has just read exercises cognitive skills. When the student constructs a summary as a means of obtaining feedback on his/her understanding of the material, the student engages in metacognition."[36]

Metacognition is thus defined as thinking about thinking, and Bondy believes that these metacognitive strategies can be taught, that classroom teachers can promote the development and use of metacognitive abilities. Among other strategies she suggests are:

1. Providing opportunities for feedback

2. Having students keep a daily learning log

3. Providing instruction in self-questioning techniques

4. Teaching students to rate their own abilities to comprehend

Studies aimed at the direct instruction of children on the use of these metacognitive strategies have consistently reported increases both in their usage as thinking tools *and in memory performance.*[37]

Finally, retrieval sometimes takes a rather concerted effort on the part of the learner, and younger children may not be as willing to exert themselves in the search for cues. Also, retrieval takes more effort when the incoming information is relatively new and unorganized. The younger child probably has to exert *more* effort in retrieving information simply because it is not as easily accessed.

In summary, then, the evidence emerging from the information-processing studies has confirmed the developmental aspects of this important theory.

THE PHYSICAL LOCUS OF MEMORY

In Search of the Engram

Before closing this chapter, we should take a brief look at the physical side of the learning

Students can be helped to develop their metacognition, or their ability to think about thinking.

organism. As prospective teachers, your appreciation of the overall information-processing model in general and the learning child in particular should be enhanced by developing some awareness of recent research into the biological correlates of learning and memory. How does a memory form in the physical sense? And if we can find out how it is formed, can we also discover its physical location? Finally, are there any physiochemical procedures available for enhancing one's memory capabilities? Implicit in all discussions of the memory process is the ghost of the "black box." Even the most ardent behaviorist cannot allay the gnawing thought that when learning is identified at the behavioral level, even as a new squiggle on a Skinnerian cumulative record, somewhere, someplace, somehow changes are taking place within the organism's nervous system. The actual, physical location of the memory trace has been called the "engram."

During the height of behaviorism, in the 1940s and 1950s, those researchers who dared give voice to these nagging thoughts, such as the great Harvard physiological psychologist, Karl Lashley, usually spoke of electrical reverberating circuits and saw the brain as a direct analog of the electronic computer. But when these researchers tried to find the precise location within the nervous system of these reverberating circuits and failed, Karl Lashley uttered his plaintive, though tongue-in-cheek comment, "Learning is just not possible."[38]

Beginning in the mid-1950s, however, a different approach was taken, one based on a biochemical model. Theorists began to focus on chemical changes. The Swedish biochemist Holger Hyden was one of the first, in 1959, to put forth the RNA theory.[39] In order to support a biochemical account, it seemed essential to find molecules large enough and complex enough to store the millions of memories that an individual might accumulate over the years. Logic seemed to dictate, therefore, that the enormously large, life-controlling nucleic acids, RNA and DNA, might possibly be the storage sites. Hyden suggested that since we are born with roughly 10 billion brain cells, and that within each of these cells there are millions of RNA molecules, then the RNA theory could logically account for trillions of images and memories. Hyden then did an experiment and found that changes in the RNA within nerve cells occurred as a *direct result of environmental stimulation*. Although this, of course, did not prove that memories are encoded in RNA molecules, it certainly suggested that RNA might play a role. Since his early work, Hyden has turned to a more complex account of memory storage, though still maintaining the importance of RNA. Hyden has since stated that the retrieval of stored learning depends on three things: electrical patterning, the transfer of RNA from the brain cells called "glia" to neurons, and the presence of unique proteins in the neuron.[40]

About the same time as Hyden's early work, James V. McConnell began reporting some rather astonishing findings, so astonishing in fact as to create some skepticism among many of his colleagues.[41] McConnell, working with flatworms, or "planaria," had first succeeded in training these tiny organisms to respond to a conditioned stimulus. He then cut the worms in half, allowing the heads to regenerate new tails and the tails to regenerate new heads. Both sets of "new" planaria retained the conditioned response, indicating that perhaps memory could be chemical in nature. If this were the case, McConnell reasoned, then it might be possible, in effect, to transplant a memory from one organism to another if the right chemicals from the trained worm could be injected into an untrained worm. This approach simply did not work. McConnell then recalled that under certain conditions flatworms will eat one another, and since they have only a rudimentary digestive tract, it might even be possible that tissue from one worm could pass into the body of the cannibal worm in a relatively unchanged state. The new experiment was a success: After grinding up trained worms and feeding them to untrained worms, McConnell found that the untrained worms responded to the conditioned stimulus. He felt sure that memory had been chemically transferred from one organism to another.

Also working from a biochemical model, William Corning and E. Roy John trained a group of planaria, cut them in half, and allowed the halves to regenerate, some in normal pond water and some in a solution of ribonuclease, an enzyme that is known to break up RNA.

Under both conditions, pond water and ribonuclease, the heads that regenerated new tails retained the conditioning. However, only the pond-water tails that regenerated new heads retained the learning. The tails that had regenerated heads in the ribonuclease failed to show evidence of conditioning.[42]

This was a fairly significant finding in that it showed a direct link between RNA and learning. Since the heads of planaria contain about 75 percent of their nervous systems, the fact that the RNA inhibitor did not affect them is not surprising, since most of the coded RNA was simply retained in the head. However, the tails, which had to regenerate the bulk of their nervous systems, were affected by the ribonuclease. The ribonuclease apparently prevented the coded RNA from being duplicated in the new head cells. Again, it must be underscored that although this is not definite proof that memory resides in the RNA molecule, it does point a tantalizing finger in the direction of RNA's being at least involved in the memory process. John further believes that memory is not localized to one section of the brain but is more probably spread throughout the brain.[43]

The Two-Stage Memory Process Revisited

During the late 1950s and early 1960s, it became increasingly evident that memory could not be explained on the basis of a single process. The concept of reverberating electrical circuits was especially vulnerable when attempting to explain long-term memory, yet it was clear from our knowledge of the neural impulse that its electrical properties were somehow involved.

The two-stage memory process system was originally foreshadowed by the work of William James. (What, in modern psychology, is not?) James had said that consciousness occurred in two stages, transitive and substantive. James hypothesized that all ideas first enter consciousness in a transitive state, that is, as fleeting, will-o'-the-wisps of only marginal existence. The idea then *may* or *may not* proceed into substantive form. If it does, the idea gains stability because of its transformation into a physical substance.[44] Then much later, in 1949, D. O. Hebb set forth his famous dual-trace memory theory. As Hebb stated it:

The conception of a transient, unstable reverberatory trace is therefore useful, if it is possible to suppose also that some more permanent structural change reinforces it. There is no reason to think that a choice must be made between the two conceptions; there may be traces of both kinds and memories which are dependent on both.[45]

As we have seen, current theories imply that memory is governed by at least two stages, short-term and long-term, and perhaps, as James and Hebb had suggested earlier, these stages are qualitatively different. Short-term memory is probably largely electrical, whereas long-term memory may be largely chemical. STM may be fleeting because no permanent change takes place within the organism. The short-lived electrochemical process decays rapidly. But sometimes, before the short-term trace disappears, a second series of events occurs in the brain that may involve the production, as Hyden has suggested, of new proteins. Thus, although STM is accompanied by transient electrical changes in the brain, LTM may be accompanied by the physical production of new, permanent brain proteins. Interestingly enough, this theory is not inconsistent with the previously mentioned RNA theory, in that the RNA is needed for protein synthesis.

Some familiar phenomena seem to support this position. People who suffer head injuries with loss of consciousness usually sustain a loss of memory for events just preceding the trauma. This is called retrograde amnesia and indicates that when the brain is jolted, a long-term memory may somehow be prevented from consolidating.[46] Some experimental evidence has been supplied by Murray Jarvik and his associate.[47] In a series of studies, they demonstrated that if organisms are given a jolt of electrical current to the brain, a current just strong enough to scramble the brain's electrical circuitry, the organisms are unable to recall the training that preceded the shock. There have, however, been some questions raised concerning the interpretation of these data. For example, is the memory permanently gone, or is it simply currently irretrievable due to emotionally induced interference factors? It has been found, for example, that human amnesia patients may sometimes have their seemingly lost memories restored under conditions of sedation. Using a different approach, Bernard Agranoff, another advocate of the two-stage memory theory, has

Researchers have suggested that there is a qualitative difference between short-term memory, which we may use to remember a phone number just recited to us, and long-term memory, which we may use to recall an experience from the past as we glance at a photo. Short-term memory probably involves fleeting electrical changes in the brain, whereas long-term memory involves more permanent chemical changes.

worked with the antibiotic puromycin, which inhibits the formation of new proteins.[48] When puromycin was injected into the brains of trained organisms just prior to learning, they showed no memory impairment at first. However, when tested a few hours later, they evidenced far less retention of the task than did a control group that had not received puromycin. The action of the puromycin, it appears, prevents the short-term memory from consolidating into the more permanent long-term memory. Other researchers have validated this finding, and the general phenomenon is now called the "puromycin effect."[49] In addition, just as some chemical agents have been shown to inhibit memory, others such as Metrazol and magnesium pemoline have been shown to facilitate the consolidation process.[50]

And the search goes on. In 1983 James V. McConnell reported on a study conducted by Ewen Cameron in which elderly senile patients were found to have significantly higher levels of ribonuclease in their bloodstreams than did nonsenile elderly persons. Since ribonuclease is an enzyme that, as we have seen, breaks up and destroys RNA, an attempt was then made to lower the ribonuclease levels in the senile patients by injecting them with yeast RNA. It was hoped that the ribonuclease would then destroy the yeast RNA rather than the RNA produced in the brain. Also, in order to enhance RNA production in the brain, other patients were given the drug magnesium pemoline. The results in both cases proved promising. Some of the patients given yeast RNA did recover memory, though not all. The patients who had been injected with magnesium pemoline also showed improved memory, but as soon as they were taken off the drug, memory deterioration again set in.[51]

In an animal study, conducted by Michael Warren, two groups of "elderly" mice were kept in dramatically differing environments. One group was constantly stimulated, trained, and handled, whereas the other group was confined to sensory isolation chambers. The stimulated mice proved to be better problem solvers and also had *more RNA in their brains*. Warren, extrapolating this finding to the human level, suggested that older persons who continue to lead an active and challenging life have less chance of developing intellectual impairments than do those who sit around in gloomy silence.[52] Another study by Japanese investigators showed that the neurotransmitter cholecystokinin octapeptide had positive effects on memory in rats.[53]

To summarize, the old electrical model of learning and retention, which was most vulnerable when attempting to explain long-term memories, has been revived to explain short-term memories in a way that fits the empirical data. Permanent, possibly lifelong memories, however, are better explained via the biochemical model, and this too fits with the experimental data.

As David Krech notes:

> Both the biochemist and the teacher of the future will combine their skills and insights for the educational and intellectual development of the child. Tommy needs a bit more of an immediate memory stimulator; Jack could do with a chemical attention-span stretcher; Rachel needs an anticholinesterase to slow down her mental processes; Joan, some puromycin—she remembers too many details and gets lost.[54]

The story of the physical side of memory is just now unfolding. Despite the evidence being supplied by physiological psychologists, our knowledge in this exciting and provocative area is still extremely limited. The point is, however, that researchers are now looking for answers within the organism, and the old admonition to avoid "stuffing the black box" is today as anachronistic as a portrait of George Washington seated happily in front of a computer terminal.

SUMMARY

The information-processing model of learning and memory has a cognitive-gestalt orientation and is loosely based on the known parameters of the computer. The theory attempts to correlate the psychologist's understanding of thought processes with what is known of computer operation. Learning and remembering are seen as resulting from the flow of information that passes through various stages within the organism.

The model presented in this chapter was focused on intentional learning. Incoming information is encoded within the organism both at the psychological level (in the form of a conceptual representation) and the physiological level (in the form of the neural memory trace). The stimulus information first enters the sensory register, where it is held for only a few brief seconds. If the learner is attending to these stimuli, they enter the first of two storage compartments—short-term memory, or STM. STM has only a limited capacity, about seven separate items, and only a limited duration, roughly less than a minute. If the learner is motivated enough to rehearse the contents of STM, the information may then be passed along into the second storage compartment—long-term memory or LTM. LTM has the potential for holding information for up to a lifetime.

On the output side, information becomes available for retrieval when it can be located and accessed. There are a number of retrieval strategies that can aid the learner's storage search, but in general the greater the number of organized categories into which information has been stored and the more meaningful these categorizations, the more accessible the information becomes. Memory for the general meaning of events is both longer lasting and more easily accessed than is memory for specific details.

Forgetting occurs as a result of both decay and interference. Decay is thought to occur passively over time. Two important interference factors are proactive inhibition, where past learning interferes with the processing and recall of new information, and retroactive inhibition, where new learning interferes with the recall of past learning.

Studies prove that retrieval can be facilitated by the following: (1) overlearning, (2) understanding new information, (3) building an organized knowledge base, (4) relating new material to the existing knowledge base, (5) using cue associations, and (6) using mnemonics. Mnemonic devices, such as visual imagery, peg words, and rhyming, can be used as memory aids both for learning new information and retrieving already processed information. But some critics warn that mnemonic devices should not be overused since material learned in this way may not be easily related to other concepts.

Studies of the relation of IQ to information processing show that those with higher IQs learn and retain more information than those with lower IQs, though the percentage of what is retained over time remains the same. Also, those with high IQs spend more time encoding and less time processing information than those with lower IQs.

The sequencing of information processing has extremely important developmental aspects, and researchers are now proposing a number of age-related correlates of the processing model. The developing child is seen as acting on and reacting to his or her environment, and, as a result, the quality of the child's information-processing system is transformed.

Finally, physiological psychologists are examining the physical components of this learning model. The search for the biological underpinnings of memory has led researchers to believe that the production of cortical RNA (ribonucleic acid) and the synthesis of new brain proteins are important links in the internal chain of neurologically grounded memory events. These researchers now suggest that chemical agents may soon be used to enhance the information-processing abilities of both children and adults.

KEY TERMS AND NAMES

information processing
encoding
storage
retrieval
sensory register
short-term memory (STM)

chunking
mnemonic devices
artificial intelligence
engram
RNA theory
long-term memory (LTM)

rehearsal
concept formation
proactive inhibition (PI)
retroactive inhibition (RI)

dual-code theory
two-stage memory process
protein synthesis
retrograde amnesia

REFERENCES

1. Murdock, B. B. (1974). *Human memory: Theory and data*. New York: Wiley.

2. Sperling, G. (1960). The information available in brief visual presentations. *Psychological Monographs, 74* (Whole No. 498).

3. Rozenzweig, M. R., and Leiman, A. L. (1982). *Physiological psychology*. Lexington, Mass.: Heath.

4. Kolers, P. A. (1983). Perception and representation. *Annual Review of Psychology, 34*, 129–166.

5. Haber, R. N. (1983). The impending demise of the icon: A critique of the concept of iconic storage in visual information processing. *Behavioral and Brain Sciences, 6*, 1–11.

6. Hasher, L., and Zacks, R. T. (1979). Automatic and effortful processes in memory. *Journal of Experimental Psychology, 108*, 365–388.

7. Wickelgren, W. A. (1981). Human learning and memory. *Annual Review of Psychology, 32*, 21–52.

8. Miller, G. A. (1956). The magical number seven plus or minus two: Some limits on our capacity for processing information. *Psychological Review, 63*, 81–97.

9. Paivio, A. (1971). *Imagery and verbal processes*. New York: Holt, Rinehart & Winston.

10. Houston, J. P. (1986). *Fundamentals of learning and memory*, 3rd ed. New York: Academic Press.

11. Ausubel, D. P., and Robinson, F. G. (1969). *School learning: An introduction to educational psychology* (p. 62). New York: Holt, Rinehart & Winston.

12. Carlisle, J. F. (1983). Training in reading comprehension. *Annals of Dyslexia, 33*, 187–202.

13. Penfield, W. (1969). Consciousness, memory and man's conditioned reflexes. In K. Pribram (Ed.), *On the biology of learning*. New York: Harcourt Brace Jovanovich.

14. Houston, *Fundamentals of learning and memory* (p. 132).

15. Houston, *Fundamentals of learning and memory*.

16. Houston, *Fundamentals of learning and memory* (p. 226).

17. Reder, L. M., and Ross, B. H. (1983). Integrated knowledge in different tasks: The role of retrieval strategy on fan effects. *Journal of Experimental Psychology, 9*, 55–72.

18. Keppel, G. (1968). Retroactive and proactive inhibition. In T. R. Dixon and D. L. Norton (Eds.), *Verbal behavior and general behavior theory* (pp. 172–213). Englewood Cliffs, N.J.: Prentice-Hall.

19. White, R. T., and Gagne, R. M. (1976). Retention of related and unrelated sentences. *Journal of Educational Psychology, 68*, 843–852.

20. Klatzsky, R. (1984). *Memory and awareness: An information-processing perspective*. New York: W. H. Freeman.

21. Nelson, D. L., and Archer, C. S. (1972). The first letter mnemonic. *Journal of Educational Psychology, 63* (5), 482–486.

22. Lorayne, H., and Lucas, J. (1974). *The memory book*. New York: Stein & Day.

23. Kantowitz, B. H., and Roediger, H. L. (1980). Memory and information processing. In G. M. Gazda, and R. J. Corsini (Eds.), *Theories of learning: A comparative approach*. Itasca, Ill.: Peacock.

24. Higbee, K. L., and Kunihira, S. (1985). Cross-cultural application of Yodai mnemonics in education. *Educational Psychologist, 20*, 57–64.

25. Kilpatrick, J. (1985). Doing mathematics without understanding it: A commentary of Higbee and Kunihira. *Educational Psychologist, 20,* 65.

26. Klausmeir, H. J., Feldhausen, J., and Check, J. (1959). *An analysis of learning efficiency in arithmetic of mentally retarded children in comparison with children of average and high intelligence.* U.S. Office of Education, Research Project No. 153. Madison: University of Wisconsin.

27. Gentile, J. R., Monaco, N., Iheozor-Ehofor, I. E., Ndu, M., and Ogbonaya, P. K. (1982). Retention by fast and slow learners. *Intelligence, 6,* 125–138.

28. Sternberg, R. J. (1982). Who's intelligent? *Psychology Today, 16,* 30–39.

29. Kail, R. (1984). *The development of memory in children,* 2nd ed. New York: W. H. Freeman.

30. Solso, R. L. (1979). *Cognitive psychology.* New York: Harcourt Brace Jovanovich.

31. Lasky, R. E., and Spiro, D. (1980). The processing of tachistoscopically presented visual stimuli by five-month-old infants. *Child Development, 51,* 214–225.

32. Solso, *Cognitive psychology* (p. 362).

33. Solso, *Cognitive psychology* (p. 363).

34. Ornstein, P. A., Naus, M. J., and Liberty, C. (1975). Rehearsal and organizational processes in children's memory. *Child Development, 45,* 818–830.

35. Flavell, J. H. (1985). *Cognitive development.* Englewood Cliffs, N.J.: Prentice-Hall.

36. Bondy, E. (1984). Thinking about thinking. *Childhood Education* (March/April), pp. 234–238.

37. Lodico, M. G., Ghatala, E. S., Levin, J. R., Pressley, M., and Bell, J. A. (1983). The effects of strategy-monitoring training on children's selection of effective memory strategies. *Journal of Experimental Child Psychology, 35,* 203–277. See also Paris, S. G., Newman, R. S., and McVey, K. A. (1982). Learning the functional significance of mnemonic actions: A microgenetic study of strategy acquisition. *Journal of Experimental Child Psychology, 34,* 490–509.

38. Lashley, K. S. (1950). In search of the engram (pp. 454–482). *Society of Experimental Biology Symposium,* No. 4, Cambridge University Press.

39. Hyden, H. (1959). Biochemical changes in glial cells and nerve cells at varying activity. In O. Hoffman-Ostenhoff (Ed.), *Biochemistry of the central nervous system.* London: Pergamon Press.

40. Hyden, H. (1970). The question of a molecular basis for the memory trace. In K. H. Pribram (Ed.), *Biology of memory.* New York: Academic Press.

41. McConnell, J. V., Jacobson, A. L., and Kimble, D. P. (1959). The effects of regeneration upon retention of a conditioned response in the planaria. *Journal of Comparative and Physiological Psychology, 52,* 1–5.

42. Corning, W. C., and John, E. R. (1961). Effect of ribonuclease on retention of conditioned response in regenerated planaria. *Science, 134,* 1363–1365.

43. John, E. R. (1976). How the brain works. *Psychology Today, 9,* 48–52.

44. James, W. A. (1890). *The principles of psychology.* New York: Holt.

45. Hebb, D. O. (1949). *The organization of behavior.* New York: Wiley.

46. Crovitz, H. F., Horn, R. W., and Daniel, W. F. (1983). Interrelationships among retrograde amnesia, post-traumatic amnesia, and time since head injury: A retrospective study. *Cortex, 19,* 407–412.

47. Jarvik, M. E., and Kopp, R. (1967). An improved one trial passive avoidance learning situation. *Psychological Reports, 2,* 221–224.

48. Agranoff, B. W. (1965). Molecules and memories. *Perspectives in Biological Medicine, 9,* 13–22.

49. Flexner, J. B., and Flexner, L. B. (1970). Further observations on restoration of memory after treatment with puromycin. *Yale Journal of Biology and Medicine, 42,* 235–240.

50. Grosser, G. S., Sprinthall, R. C., and Sirois, L. (1967). Magnesium pemoline: Activation of extinction responding after continuous reinforcement. *Psychological Reports, 21,* 11–14.

51. McConnell, J. V. (1983). *Understanding human behavior,* 4th ed. New York: Holt, Rinehart & Winston.

52. Warren, J. M., Zerweck, C., and Anthony, A. (1982). The effect of environmental stimulation on old mice. *Developmental Psychobiology, 15,* 13–18.

53. Katsuura, G., and Itoh, S. (1985). Prevention of amnesia by cholecystokinin octapeptide, as studied by passive avoidance behavior in the rat. Paper presented at the 16th International Congress of the ISPNE, Kyoto, Japan.

54. Krech, D. (1969). The chemistry of learning (p. 156). In R. C. Sprinthall and N. A. Sprinthall (Eds.), *Educational psychology: Selected readings.* New York: Van Nostrand-Reinhold.

TEACHING EFFECTIVENESS

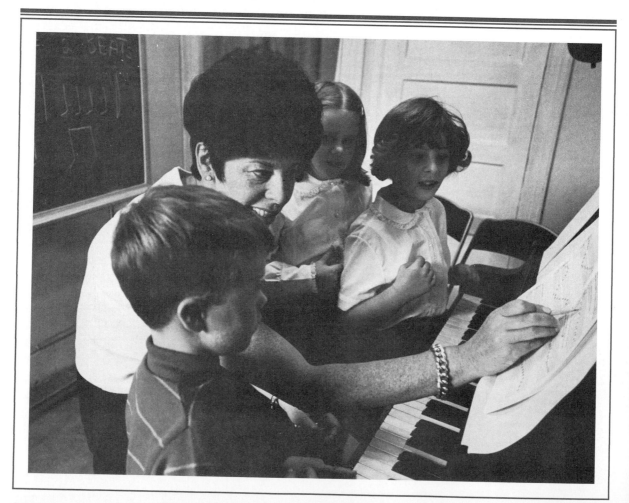

12

METHODS AND MODELS OF TEACHING

As we noted in Chapter 1, a research basis for understanding the process of teaching effectiveness has expanded rapidly in the last decade. In this chapter we will review and generalize the research suggestions. We will also show how these results, single pieces of research evidence, can be incorporated into a broad framework to guide your practice. A model of teaching basically represents a specific cluster of teaching strategies designed to reach a particular type of learning outcome with pupils. However, no single model represents the best way to teach. Instead, overall effectiveness will depend on your ability, first, to master specific techniques and, second, to combine them within a particular model. Finally, you must develop the ability to use a variety of models. When you have reached that point, you will be on your way to mastery of a repertoire of teaching models.

In Chapter 13 we will switch focus from the teacher to the students, addressing the question of how to apply the different models according to your goals as well as the needs of the students. For now, however, we will concentrate on discrete teacher skills, then move from specific skills to models. We will start with a review of elements of teaching effectiveness, then look at the use of a system of analyzing teaching as a bridge to the more general models.

ELEMENTS OF TEACHING EFFECTIVENESS

The most comprehensive review of elements of teaching effectiveness has been completed by Herbert Walberg from the University of Illinois.[1] Using the techniques of statistical meta-analysis, he compiled more than 3,000 studies, then carefully analyzed them to determine just how important each particular element was in student learning. From his results, he compiled a list of weighted factors. In Table 12.1, we have selected from his overall list the elements that are most closely related to teacher behavior in the classroom—in other words, the kind of procedures a teacher may actually employ. Each will be discussed here in turn. In subsequent chapters we will focus on other factors not so directly related to teacher behavior yet that do contribute to student learning.

TABLE 12.1   THE EFFECTS OF SELECTED TEACHING TECHNIQUES AND PROCESSES

TECHNIQUE OR PROCESS	SIZE OF EFFECT ON ACADEMIC ACHIEVEMENT*
Engaged academic learning time	+.38
Use of positive reinforcement	+1.17
Cues and feedback	+.97
Cooperative learning activities	+.76
Classroom atmosphere morale	+.60
Higher-order questioning	+.34
Use of advance organizers	+.23

* The size represents units of standard deviations; for example, in the case of "cues and feedback," teachers employing this mode had students whose achievement scores averaged one standard deviation higher than those in control classes.

Data from H. Walberg, "Improving the Productivity of America's Schools," Educational Leadership, *41 (1984): 19–27.*

Academic Learning Time

Although it may seem too obvious to note, academic learning time in the classroom has emerged as an important variable. Recent studies have shown that the amount of on-task behavior can vary as much as 40 percent from one classroom to the next.[2] Even how quickly a teacher calls the class to order can vary all the way from one to ten minutes. Thus, how efficiently you plan your lessons, how long you take to get started, how you handle digressions, off-task behavior and discipline, and how you handle transitions will have an effect on student learning.

Important as academic learning time is, there is not an exact relationship between time on task and learning outcome. Moreover, it is difficult, if not impossible, to measure what is going on in a student's mind at a specific moment. In fact, one study showed that students who appeared to be paying attention (engaged in academic learning time) were actually thinking about nonacademic issues.[3] Students soon learn the importance of putting on a good face in order to protect their privacy. As a result of these and other factors, time is an important necessary condition but far from the whole story. In measurement terms the efficient use of instructional time has an impact equal to about 40 percent of one standard deviation. (See Chapter 15 for more information about what this

means). Basically, academic achievement was moderately affected by the efficient use of time.[4]

Use of Reinforcement

By far the single most significant discrete instructional variable was the use of positive reinforcement. The careful and consistent use of Skinnerian reinforcement techniques, both verbal and nonverbal, had an effect greater than one standard deviation. This means, for example, if one class scored an average of 80 points on a hundred-item test and the standard deviation was 10 points, then a similar class without positive reinforcement would score one standard deviation below, or an average of 70 points. The reinforced class on the average would be at a B level, versus a C level for the other class.

Does this mean, then, that the teacher should apply principles of positive reinforcement to all students all the time? As was the case with academic learning time, it's not quite that simple. The relationship between positive reinforcement and achievement is nonlinear. You must be selective; indiscriminate praise doesn't work. The effect will wear out if the students hear you praise all activities and products, even those of marginal competence.

Table 12.2 gives some important guidelines for the effective use of praise. Jere Brophy has

TABLE 12.2   GUIDELINES FOR EFFECTIVE PRAISE

EFFECTIVE PRAISE	INEFFECTIVE PRAISE
1. Is delivered contingently	1. Is delivered randomly or unsystematically
2. Specifies the particulars of the accomplishment	2. Is restricted to global positive reactions
3. Shows spontaneity, variety, and other signs of credibility; suggests clear attention to the student's accomplishment	3. Shows a bland uniformity, which suggests a conditional response made with minimal attention
4. Rewards attainment of specified performance criteria (which can include effort criteria, however)	4. Rewards mere participation, without consideration of performance processes or outcomes
5. Provides information to students about their competence or the value of their accomplishments	5. Provides no information at all or gives students information about their status
6. Orients students toward better appreciation of their own task-related behavior and thinking about problem solving	6. Orients students toward comparing themselves with others and thinking about competing
7. Uses students' own prior accomplishments as the context for describing present accomplishments	7. Uses the accomplishments of peers as the context for describing students' present accomplishments
8. Is given in recognition of noteworthy effort or success at difficult (for *this* student) tasks	8. Is given without regard to the effort expended or the meaning of the accomplishments (for *this* student)
9. Attributes successes to effort and ability, implying that similar successes can be expected in the future	9. Attributes success to ability alone or to external factors such as luck or easy task
10. Fosters endogenous attributions (students believe that they expend effort on the task because they enjoy the task and/or want to develop task-relevant skills)	10. Fosters exogenous attributions (students believe that they expend effort on the task for external reasons to please the teacher, win a competition or reward, etc.)
11. Focuses students' attention on their own task-relevant behavior	11. Focuses students' attention on the teacher as an external authority figure who is manipulating them
12. Fosters appreciation of and desirable attributions about task-relevant behavior after the process is completed.	12. Intrudes into the ongoing process, distracting attention from task-relevant behavior

carefully outlined and compared different methods.[5] To add to the complexity, it turns out that the effect of praise, even when properly applied, varies according to student characteristics. Students from middle-class backgrounds are not as susceptible to praise as are students from lower- and/or working-class backgrounds. The method still works but not as powerfully. Lower- and working-class parents tend *not* to use positive reinforcement as frequently as do middle-class parents. As a result such children are more affected when praise is used. Praise by itself, then, has to be used carefully in order to produce the desired effects.

Cues and Feedback

To some extent the use of cues and feedback is related to the process of questioning. Through cueing, the teacher provides some help in student answers. In the so-called good old days many a famous university professor would earn a reputation for tearing students apart in the process of questioning. In the now classic movie *The Paper Chase*, Professor Kingsfield was shown again and again carefully dissecting a quivering student. Intimidation and sarcasm were the stock in trade. Current research in teaching effectiveness shows the opposite. Good teachers

HERBERT J. WALBERG

If you were to ask any educational psychologist to list the ten most productive and influential scholars in the field, you would be sure to find Herbert Walberg's name in that select group. In fact, he is often referred to as Mr. Educational Psychologist II, having inherited the position from the now retired Ralph Tyler.

To some extent it may be surprising that such a quiet, unassuming scholar has become so eminent in a relatively short time. Actually there is no special secret to his success. From the early days of his career to the present, he has simply outperformed his colleagues. His particular genius has been policy research and his mastery of educational psychology's three components of theory, research, and practice. Thus, his work speaks to all educational psychologists. The theorists see in his work a synthesizing of ideas, a means of combining previously separate conceptual frameworks into a more cohesive cluster of directing concepts. The researchers follow very carefully his new system of meta-analysis as a means of combining empirical results from a wide variety of studies. No longer are educational studies dependent on one or a dozen or even a hundred studies. Walberg has shown the field how to review 2,000 to 3,000 studies and end up with meaningful conclusions. In the pre-Walberg era, many reviews of the research literature would suggest that there was little in the way of substantial knowledge and (often with a whimper) conclude that "more research is needed." A few years later, another review would be published with similar results and end with the same call.

To some degree the most important aspect of his work may be its implications for practice. His recent summarization of the research on teaching effectiveness is a clear example of just how practical research can be in the hands of such a brilliant man. He avoids any allegiance to a particular school of thought and instead reviews all studies on the basis of parsimony both theoretically and empirically. Indeed, in some quarters he is viewed as a modern-day version of William of Occam, separating faith and ideology from reason and fact. One of the continuing complaints about educational psychologists in general is that if you know their theoretical framework, you can safely predict their conclusions without even looking at the data. Walberg, however, stands apart from any specific tradition and lets the actual analysis of the findings determine what elements really make a difference in distinguishing effective from ineffective teaching.

Shortly after completing his Ph.D. at the University of Chicago in 1964, he joined an outstanding team of researchers at the Harvard Graduate School of Education, "Harvard Project Physics." Over a three-year period the group developed and evaluated an innovative approach to teaching physics in secondary schools. While at Harvard he authored or coauthored thirty-four journal articles, and thirteen were immediately reprinted by other authors. With his career off to such an auspicious start, he was much sought after as a speaker, consultant, and editor. Since he was a midwesterner at heart, it was not surprising that he quickly accepted a professorship at the University of Illinois, Chicago Circle. He had learned a great deal on the East Coast, among other things how much he missed Lake Michigan and the proper midwest English. Soon after his return to Chicago, he was named, in rapid succession, associate professor, professor, and then research professor. In fact, one of the difficulties in reporting on his progress is how quickly any comment is outdated. As we go to press, he has written or edited 25 books, 26 chapters, 4 encyclopedia articles, 21 monographs, and 230 research articles, all the while retaining not only his youthful vigor but looks as well. Colleagues envy his reputation and his ability to resist the aging process.

Professor Kingfield's withering inquisition of his law students has been shown to be less effective than cueing students so they can develop their own answers.

cue the students. They help a student develop an answer. For example, such a teacher will pick up part of an answer and then ask for clarification or elaboration—for example, "Yes, Columbus did lead the expedition in 1492, and do you remember who sponsored the voyage?" Such prompting can reduce the anxiety of the classroom trivia methods (Chapter 1) and expand the students' thinking.

A second component of effective cueing is sometimes called wait time, which gives the student some time to think about the question. By providing time and then helping a student elaborate an answer, the teacher will increase academic achievement and decrease anxiety.

Providing constructive feedback is the other part of this strategy. Ever since the famous Ellis Page study, it has been shown conclusively that feedback improves academic achievement. Page demonstrated this by systematically providing brief written comments on assignments.[6] When teachers merely collect assignments and then either say nothing or simply make a checkmark, then an opportunity for growth has been missed. The same is true for homework. In fact, Walberg found that graded homework with comments was 50 percent more effective than homework by itself. Constructive feedback obviously provides the student with information on which to build learning.

Cooperative Learning

The effectiveness of cooperative learning is a most interesting new finding. We will provide a substantial discussion on this approach in Chapter 14. The main point here is the importance of employing small-group techniques in the classroom with cooperative objectives. Such a procedure encourages student participation and also results in improved academic performance. Bascially such an approach requires a blend of techniques, and hence it is not really a single technique.

Classroom Morale

This is another process that, like cooperative learning, is not strictly a teaching strategy. Still it is important not to lose sight of the fact that classroom atmosphere obviously has a significant impact on learning. This isn't to say that a kind of happy-go-lucky, do your own thing, laissez-faire atmosphere is appropriate. That would be as bad as the other extreme, an authoritarian, teacher-controlled room where strict attention is always required. Walberg's research found that the old-school view of strict discipline and tight control is not effective nor is the casual "laid back" approach. Instead, feelings of cohesiveness, satisfaction, goal direction, and student perceptions of a friendly atmosphere make a positive difference in learning. These findings were cross-validated by Thomas Good's research.[7] He found that one main element of effective teaching is the need to create a relatively relaxed learning environment within a task-orientation focus. We will have more to say when we move to models of teaching that illustrate the relation between class morale and methods. At this point it is clear that positive class morale cuts across specific techniques as a general factor producing student achievement.

Higher-Order Questions

Since teacher questioning has an unusually long history, it is clearly important to examine it as a strategy.[8] Generally, as we illustrated in the opening chapter, the common questioning approach is more like a game of Trivial Pursuit than education. But asking rapid-fire questions calling for rote, almost robotlike answers does not increase achievement. It obviously makes a difference how the questions are posed. A higher-order question is basically a query that requires the student to analyze and produce a reasoned response, not a mimic of the teacher's words. In other words, there is not an already prescribed factual answer to the question. Asking a student to name the year of the Columbus expedition is clearly a lower-order question. Asking the student to explain why Columbus was able to convince the monarchy of a country different from his own to support his voyage calls for greater intellectual work, and thus it qualifies as a higher-order question.

Recently there has been a remarkable upsurge in the "teaching of thinking."[9] Such a process, which involves logical analysis and argumentation principles, is most encouraged by higher-order questioning. Thus, an idea that had lost favor in the 1970s—namely, to distinguish between the lower- and higher-order questions—has returned as a result of newer research evidence and a general interest in formal instruction designed to promote "thinking."

Advance Organizers

The final skill involves the use of the deductive approach. The student is told in advance what the main point or the main concepts to be covered will be. Such advance organizers have been shown to help students focus attention on the key points. On the other hand, the effect is positive but not particularly strong, representing about a 25 percent improvement in the standard deviation. In all probability, then, an advance organizer is a good method to get a class clued in. Since some learners need a clear road map of the main points in a lesson in advance, the method should not be ignored.[10]

THE FLANDERS SYSTEM: BRIDGING TO MODELS

One of the weaknesses of such a massive meta-analysis as Walberg's is that the results cannot depict actual patterns of teaching. A robot could be programed to use certain elements in a sequence, but student learning wouldn't necessarily be affected. Classroom interaction between teacher and students would be frozen

Peanuts   by Schulz

TABLE 12.3   CATEGORIES FOR FLANDERS INTERACTION ANALYSIS

<table>
<tr><td rowspan="7">TEACHER TALK</td><td rowspan="4">INDIRECT INFLUENCE</td><td>

1. **Accepts feelings.**   Accepts and clarifies the tone of feelings of the students in an unthreatening manner. Feelings may be positive or negative. Predicting or recalling feelings are included.
2. **Praises or encourages.**   Praises or encourages student action or behavior. Jokes that release tension, but not at the expense of another individual; nodding head and saying ''um hm?'' or ''go on'' are included.
3. **Accepts or uses ideas of students.**   Clarifies, builds, or develops ideas suggested by a student. As teacher brings more of his or her own ideas into play, shift to # 5.
4. **Asks questions**   Asks a question about content or procedure with the intent that the student answer.

</td></tr>
<tr><td rowspan="3">DIRECT INFLUENCE</td><td>

5. **Lecturing.**   Gives facts or opinions about content or procedure; expresses his or her own ideas, asking rhetorical questions.

6. **Giving directions.**   Directions, commands, or orders that students are expected to comply with.

7. **Criticizing or justifying authority.**   Statements intended to change student behavior from unacceptable to acceptable pattern; bawling someone out; stating why the teacher is doing what he or she is doing; extreme self-reference.

</td></tr>
</table>

<table>
<tr><td>STUDENT TALK</td><td>

8. **Student talk—response.**   Talk by students in response to teacher. Teacher initiates the contact or solicits student statement.
9. **Student talk—initiation.**   Talk initiated by students. If ''calling on'' student is only to indicate who may talk next, observer must decide whether student wanted to talk.
10. **Silence or confusion.**   Pauses, short periods of silence, and periods of confusion in which communication cannot be understood by the observer.

</td></tr>
</table>

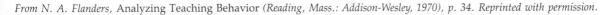

From N. A. Flanders, Analyzing Teaching Behavior *(Reading, Mass.: Addison-Wesley, 1970), p. 34. Reprinted with permission.*

while the machine cranked through its program. To understand how the elements fit together more clearly, we turn to the work of Ned Flanders.[11] He and his associates did extensive classroom observations of teachers at different levels and across different content areas. He found that teacher talking behavior could be clustered into seven categories (and student talk in three), as shown in Table 12.3. You can also see how much of his system, developed in the 1950s and 1960s, still relates to current research on teaching behaviors, as is shown in Table 12.4.

The seven categories represent the most commonly observed teaching behaviors, which brings us to the next question. What is the relation between these behaviors and student achievement? Actually a major analysis of the Flanders studies was done by Nate Gage in his book *The Scientific Basis of the Art of Teaching*.[12] Rather than examine one element at a time, however, Gage grouped the system into two broad categories: indirect teaching—types 1, 2, 3, and 4—and direct teaching—types 5, 6, and 7. You can see that the main difference between the two modes is basically whether teaching is viewed as asking questions or giving directions and lecturing.

In comparing the modes Gage also wanted to examine possible differences according to grade level, elementary versus secondary. He found very clear evidence that teachers who employed the indirect mode at the secondary level produced greater academic gains on the part of their pupils than teachers who used the direct mode. This means that the academic performance of teen-age students will be enhanced through the effective use of questioning and

NED A. FLANDERS

Born in 1918 and raised on the West Coast, Ned Flanders gradually migrated eastward. He completed an A.B. degree at the University of California in 1940 and received a B.S. from Oregon State College in 1944. He then left the Coast and completely changed his field of academic interest. From his undergraduate work of chemistry and a B.S. in electrical engineering, he shifted to educational psychology, completing both a master's degree and a Ph.D. at the University of Chicago. He remained at Chicago for a brief period and then, from 1949 to 1962, he served as an assistant and then associate professor of educational psychology at the University of Minnesota.

It was during this period at Minnesota that his research focus matured. He began to successfully crack one of the most difficult problems in education—a theoretical and practical model to define teaching effectiveness. Prior to his work, hundreds of research studies had been conducted in this area, almost always yielding insignificant results. Researchers had tried to correlate personality characteristics, temperamental traits, personal interests, cultural backgrounds, social and economic status, marital state, birth order, and similar variables to effective teaching performance. Attempts had also been made to relate measures of a teacher's "warmth" or knowledge of subject matter to effective performance in the classroom. These so-

called characteristic studies produced very little valuable information; instead, the results were inconclusive and often contradictory. One study might find a small but statistically significant correlation between a trait such as friendliness and teaching effectiveness; the next study was just as likely to show no relationship.

When Flanders began to develop the concept of direct versus indirect teaching, he also started a series of field studies to test the possible relationships. As we have noted in the text, his central findings remained consistent through a long series of studies. With various subject matters, at different grade levels, and in different school settings, teachers employing indirect teaching styles were producing higher levels of academic learning in their pupils than were those using direct methods.

As we move toward educational accountability, with the general public demanding increasing documentation of teaching effectiveness, the Flanders system gives evidence of becoming a major index of effective teaching. In 1962 Flanders moved from Minnesota to the University of Michigan, where his work continued. He has published *Teaching with Groups* and *Analyzing Teaching Behavior*, as well as numerous articles reporting his research on teacher interaction analysis. In 1970 Flanders returned to California, where he was with Far West Laboratory for research in teaching. Now enjoying retirement atop one of San Francisco's most beautiful hills, he has maintained an active professional interest in teacher behavior.

TABLE 12.4 A COMPARISON OF TEACHER EFFECTIVENESS: FLANDERS AND WALBERG

FLANDERS' TYPES	WALBERG'S ELEMENTS OF TEACHING EFFECTIVENESS
(6) Gives clear directions	Academic learning time
(2) Praises or encourages	Use of positive reinforcement
(3) Accepts and builds on student ideas	Use of cues and feedback
A combination of indirect modes plus (6), gives clear directions	Cooperative learning
(1) Accepts feelings (2) Praises (3) Accepts ideas	Classroom morale
(4) Asks questions (3) Accepts and builds on student ideas	Higher-order questions
(6) Gives clear directions (5) Lectures (4) Asks questions	Advance organizers

open inquiry. The finding held true across subject matter. However—and this is most important to remember—this research does not mean that the secondary teacher must stay exclusively in the indirect mode. The evidence is based on ratios of time expended in one mode versus the other. At the high-school level effectiveness is increased if the teacher uses the indirect mode more than half the time. Obviously, there will be times to give careful directions, to lecture, and to criticize students for misbehavior; yet for the most part, employing the other modes of questioning, reinforcing, cueing and responding to feelings will produce academic gains to a greater degree.

To further buttress this approach to teaching and learning, researchers conducted a series of independent studies at the college level. Although the actual Flanders system was not used, the overall results were quite similar. The college researchers found that professors who provide time for student questions, allow students to question each other, and encourage students to make statements in class fostered cognitive growth and greater complexity of thinking on the part of their students.[13] So, results from both high-school studies and college studies indicate the advantage of the indirect

mode with older students. Certainly if you think about Piaget's work, you will remember that during adolescence students can develop greater capabilities for abstract reasoning and greater independence in thinking than earlier in their development. This is probably a main factor favoring the indirect mode. We will have more to say about the interaction between teaching method and pupil development in the next chapter.

At the elementary level, Gage's review yielded somewhat different results. He found less of a relation between the indirect modes and pupil learning. There were some positive outcomes in the indirect mode but also many in the direct mode. In fact, more recent research especially at the elementary level seems to indicate that the more directive approach to teaching can be quite significant in producing student achievement.[14] For example, in elementary-school instruction in both reading and mathematics, the teacher-directed approach yielded stronger gains. Actually it took reading teachers and researchers a very long time to finally understand that young nonreaders need to be taught to "break the code" and learn the letter symbols (instead of learning through the ask-and-guess technique). Similarly, direct methods in math are necessary to teach the rudiments of the number system. Again it is important to underscore the point of these findings. The results indicate a ratio is desirable—spending more time on direct methods, but not focusing exclusively on them. To use direct methods exclusively would miss the point. The effective elementary teacher needs to ask questions, praise, build on ideas, and respond to feelings. However, the elementary teacher may well use the more direct methods more than half the time. The careful use of advance organizers and a low level of ambiguity provides younger students with helpful guidance for learning.

One of the most important researchers in the direct teaching approach has recently suggested that we replace the phrase "direct teaching" with "active teaching." Thomas Good says that such a concept is broader than direct teaching and suggests much greater flexibility in classroom practice. It reminds us that we are concerned with changing ratios, not states and unchanging single modes as a basis for teaching. In summarizing the findings at the elementary level, he states: "Teachers whose students made greater gains were more active in presenting concepts, explaining the meaning of those concepts, providing appropriate practice, and monitoring those activities prior to seatwork."[15]

With this background we can now move to the next level of generality in regard to teaching, namely, comprehensive models of teaching. A model is a cluster of strategies that is logically consistent with a certain set of assumptions about how students best learn. Another way to view it is as a "school of thought" regarding how best to manage the development of the pupil. So now to models.

MODEL ONE: THE TRANSMITTER OF KNOWLEDGE

Probably the most common teaching model, and certainly the one with the longest tradition, is that which views teaching as the transmission

Teaching is interactive, and the teacher's job is to manage and direct the instructional process, not the telling process.

of knowledge. This view assumes that there exists a well-known and finite body of knowledge from which the teacher selects certain facts and concepts to pass on to pupils. In a metaphorical sense, the teacher looks over all the knowledge "stored" in the Library of Congress, pores through books and pamphlets, reads and digests everything, and takes some of it to school, where it will be disseminated.

This model emphasizes the need to give pupils basic facts and information before they can be expected to think for themselves. They must learn what is already known before they can come up with any new ideas that might fit in with the existing knowledge.

The assumptions are clear. Learning new information is essentially a linear step-by-step sequence. The teacher's expertise is needed to arrange both the content material to be mastered and the method of presentation. Probably the most obvious distinguishing characteristic of this model is the high degree of structure employed.

In Model One, the teacher uses advance organizers.[16] At the outset of a lesson the teacher presents the pupils with the general rule, the generalization, or the main "point" of the activity. For example, a social studies unit might start with, "Today we are going to study about the origins or beginnings of civilization—the early settlements on the banks of two rivers in the Middle East." Thus, at the outset, the goal of the lesson is described at a generalizable, conceptual level—learning about the origins of civilization. This technique helps the students tune in immediately to the overall objective. It creates, at least theoretically, a set of expectations that is clear and explicit. The pupils are ready.

Immediately following the presentation of the generalized idea, the teacher then changes the level of abstraction to concrete examples. The rule or principle stated at the outset creates a readiness in the pupils. Their cognitive attention is focused. The concrete examples help them understand the connections between the facts and the general point. Thus, in the social studies example, the teacher would now present a series of concrete facts and examples: "For many thousands of years tribes would wander from place to place; food was gathered as it grew naturally; as the seasons changed the tribes would pick up and move on, seeking less

hostile climates." These examples would set the stage for the understanding of the generalized idea. The teacher would proceed to a presentation of a long series of facts: "Gradually, as groups of tribes were settling temporarily all over the globe, the group that settled in Mesopotamia happened to hit upon a most fortuitous set of circumstances—a benign climate and incredibly rich soil. These circumstances, together with a series of other factors, led to the permanent establishment of cities and government, to economic specialization, to the beginning of architecture, even to the establishment of schools—in short, to all the elements of what we call civilization."

The presentation of examples, finally, is followed by the restatement of the generalized principle. In this sense, the transmission-of-knowledge model is often called "guided discovery." Through various examples, all pupils are led to the same generalization. Ambiguity is low. It is clear from the outset what the goal is; concrete examples are carefully selected to support the point; and at the end, the pupils are reminded what rule or generalization they have learned.

Probably the strongest example of this model of transmitting information is the lecture format. Although it can be used with other teaching strategies, this model is most effectively used as a format for lectures, or for minilectures. If you recall your own experience as a pupil, you will readily remember instances of hopelessly disorganized lectures that did not follow this model. Look back at your own notes, or the lack of them, from these lectures. You may find a few random comments in your own writing, lots of questions and false starts, perhaps even a scribbled memo to yourself: "But what's the point of today's lecture? He can't seem to make up his mind. Where is it all going? He must have eighteen hands—on the one hand this, on the other hand that—I hope the period ends soon!"

Thus the transmission-of-knowledge model, through the use of advance organizers, can provide a clear and systematic approach to teaching. One of the disadvantages of the model is that so much of the work of learning is controlled and directed by the teacher.

This is why, as we noted in the previous section, the effective use of advance organizers and teacher-led instruction also requires much attention to maintaining pupil activity. If teachers aren't careful, then pupil passivity can increase markedly for some students, particularly the low achievers. One study found that low achievers did not understand the directions, spent most of their time watching their peers speed through the assignment, turned in incomplete work, and were frequently criticized. Such a cycle was repeated, often to the distress of both the students and the teacher.[17] Also it is clear that some students will do better under learning conditions that are less teacher directed and controlled.

MODEL TWO: INDUCTIVE INQUIRY

Another common teaching model that came into vogue in the 1960s suggests that the teacher's role is to reveal or unveil the fundamental structure of a discipline. The idea here is to teach concepts or the process of inquiry, not facts. In some ways this is like teaching for problem solving, whereby we learn to solve problems by understanding the framework or the structure of the concepts. For example, pupils used to learn to cross-multiply fractions to solve a division problem. In Model Two, the teacher focuses on the concepts of fractions and divisions so that the pupils understand that cross-multiplying is really dividing both sides of an equation by a common number. Similarly, in a social studies class, or what used to be called geography, pupils are no longer asked to memorize the principal cities and products of a state. Rather, they might be given a blank map showing topographical features such as hills, mountains, valleys, rivers, and lakes and then be asked to figure out where cities might be located. In other words, they go through an inquiry process that helps them understand why big cities grow in certain locations. The Model Two teacher produces minischolars in the various disciplines.

According to this model, the sheer intellectual excitement of discovering the reasons behind events—for example, the logic a historian or a mathematician actually uses—motivates the

pupils to further activity and exploration. Teaching and learning resemble an archaeologist's uncovering of one fragment after another of some mysterious object. The archaeologist's curiosity about the fragments naturally makes him or her want to make sense of the puzzle; this curiosity produces both activity and excitement. The discovery method of teaching is based on this model. The teacher, by analyzing material and asking questions, but not giving answers, spurs the pupils to learn by helping them discover the answer. The experience and the insight resulting from having put the puzzle together nurture the entire educational process.

There are a variety of specific methods that enhance discovery learning such as the inductive-thinking strategy of Hilda Taba, the inquiry-training method of Richard Suchman, and the scientific-inquiry technique of Joseph Schwab.[18] These methods are related to John Dewey's original project method, which emphasized the process of inquiry rather than content acquisition as central to learning. In each case, the teacher arranges material that is open-ended in order to stimulate the processes of asking questions and exploration by the pupils.

It is, of course, possible to overemphasize learning by discovery. It can be exasperating to never have any of your questions answered. It isn't necessary to discover everything for yourself in order to learn. Most important, however, it is difficult to know, especially at the elementary level and in junior high, exactly how much the pupils genuinely understand about the structure of a discipline taught in this way. The idea of a structure is itself abstract and therefore beyond the comprehension of the concrete stage of thinking in which most of these children are. To understand such concepts and such processes, substantial cognitive sophistication is necessary. For example, to learn how a historian "thinks," we must understand concepts such as a fact, an opinion, a value, cultural relativism, subjectivity, and objectivity—to name a few.

A major debate has been going on between those who advocate this approach and those who hold other views. Jerome Bruner, formerly a professor at the Harvard Center for Cognitive Studies, is a leading advocate for teaching for the structure of knowledge. One of his most provocative statements promotes this view: "Any subject can be taught effectively in some intellectually honest form to any child at any stage of development."[19] Thus, according to Bruner, the six-year-old minischolar can learn to think like a historian or a mathematician.

We have already mentioned (Chapter 5) some of the problems inherent in the so-called spiraling curriculum, a system that teaches children the same concepts, with increasing sophistication, throughout their entire schooling. The difficulties, especially at the elementary level, are enormous. The cognitive structure of elementary-age children makes it difficult for them to understand abstract concepts, and therefore they tend to translate the abstractions into concrete terms and miss the connections altogether. Jean Piaget has said that Bruner's statement "has always filled me with the deepest wonderment." Imagine, for a moment, trying to teach a three- or four-year-old the structure of algebra or the idea that historical knowledge is relative and biased.

Nor is the educational problem strictly limited to the elementary ages. Much secondary-school material is based on the assumption that all teen-agers are already well into formal operations, which we know is not the case. Model Two teaching, though it has a laudable objective, rests on a doubtful assumption. There is a difference between assuming the ability to think abstractly and carefully creating a series of experiences that will nurture and promote the development of this ability. Teaching to reveal the abstract structure of the disciplines may often result in a mismatch between the curriculum on the one hand and the pupils on the other.

Thus, an important component of the inductive method is to work at developing the student's potential to reason more openly and independently. This means, in addition to substantial cueing in questioning, that use of structure and advance organizers may also be necessary, especially at the outset. We should also point out that the inquiry or discovery method can be modified for the elementary level. Certainly, the revised research findings concerning open education (see the box, p. 300) indicate that elementary-school children can benefit from some experiences with the inductive discovery model.

MODEL THREE: INTERPERSONAL LEARNING

While the first and most common teaching model emphasizes learning the facts and the second stresses the discovery of concepts, the third and most recent model, interpersonal learning, stresses the development of warm human relationships between teacher and pupil. If the teacher can convey a genuine affection and empathy, a warm, facilitative classroom climate will be created, and the pupils will take it from there. The quality of the human interaction, especially the degree to which the teacher treats the pupils with sincerity and honesty, is the key to creating the best environment for learning.

A leading exponent of this third model is Carl Rogers. Rogers has said that teaching as deliberate instruction is a vastly overrated function. The educator should instead concentrate much more attention on creating the conditions that will promote experiential learning. Rogers emphasizes experience and feeling rather than thinking or reading as the proper pathway to knowledge—an odd thought, no doubt, as you sit reading a textbook! Rogers is convinced that traditional learning is so impersonal, cold, and aloof that it really goes in one ear and out the other. According to him, we learn only what is really important and relevant to us as people. In his classic work *Freedom to Learn*, Rogers presents three necessary and sufficient conditions for the promotion of learning: empathy; unconditional positive regard; and congruence, or genuineness.[20] Empathy allows us to communicate to our pupils that we really understand the emotions they are experiencing and permits us to accurately "read" their feelings. Unconditional positive regard allows us to accept our students for what they are without passing judgment. This acceptance is unconditional and involves none of the usual bargaining. ("If you do this for me, then I will like you.") Rogers repeatedly says that teachers must place no conditions on these relationships and must accept students without reservation. Congruence, or genuineness, means being "real," honest. Going through the motions and pretending we like children or listening to their feelings and emotions half-heartedly is not enough.

CONTEMPORARY ISSUE

The Fall and Rebirth of Open Education

During the 1960s teacher education began to deemphasize the traditional teacher-directed, self-contained classroom and to stress open education. Classrooms and indeed entire buildings were rebuilt to accommodate the new approach. Learning centers, reading corners, and science (kitchen physics) areas were installed. Children moved freely through a sequence of activities individually and in small groups. The lock-step approach of twenty-five or so pupils all learning the same material at the same time was abandoned. Excitement was high. It seemed as if the old mold for education was at last about to break. Optimism was further increased by some early research findings that suggested positive outcomes in academic achievement. Equally if not more important was the suggestion of gains in pupil autonomy and responsibility. It seemed as if open education was able to achieve two simultaneous objectives, achievement and growth in self-concept.

Then the bomb fell. In 1976 Neville Bennett, a British psychologist, published the results of a single study that concluded that open education was a failure.[a] Since England itself had been a prime mover in the innovation, it seemed as if the home ground

was now fatally shaken. One of our country's most prestigious newspapers, the *New York Times*, did a feature giving the claim even greater exposure and, indirectly at least, validity. In addition, Nathaniel Gage, one of our country's most respected educational psychologists, published a summary in 1978 that also concluded that open education was a failure.[b]

Of course, these three events by themselves could not account for the shift away from open education. The country as a whole was moving toward a more conservative viewpoint. Both conservative politicians and conservative educators happily seized upon these findings. We should return to the basics in education—no more "frills," no more experimentation, no more "liberal" philosophy. Open education became almost a lightning rod, a convenient target for those in both arenas who wanted to keep schools as they were in the "good old days." The results of their efforts were all too successful. In the public's mind open education was just another failed innovation.

Although the public and conservative politicians may still adhere to that view, educational psychologists don't. A careful reanalysis of Bennett's original findings uncovered basic statistical

errors.[c] Then Gage himself undertook a more complete and careful review. He also noted his earlier errors: "I reviewed a small and regrettably haphazard set of some seven of those studies and concluded that they showed that students learned less."[d] His more complete review of 150 studies came to the opposite conclusion. He found that there were no real differences in academic achievement. The students did not learn less. Also the open-education students demonstrated greater creativity, more independence as problem solvers, and had more positive attitudes toward school and teachers.

Whether the general public will again accept and support open education remains to be seen. Fortunately, the integrity of educational psychologists shows through clearly in this case. Errors in analysis can be corrected and policy issues reevaluated.

---

[a] Bennett, S. N. (1976). *Teaching styles and pupil progress.* London: Open Books.
[b] Gage, N. (1984). *Hard gains in the soft sciences.* Bloomington, Ind.: Phi Delta Kappa.
[c] Aitkin, M., Bennett, S. N., and Hesketh, J. (1984). "Teaching styles and pupil progress: A re-analysis." *British Journal of Educational Psychology, 51,* 37–41.
[d] Gage, *Hard gains* (p. 17).

If teachers provide these conditions, then, according to Rogers, the children will be free to learn. The natural makeup of children and teenagers is such that if we remove the inhibitions imposed by outside direction, then self-directed learning will follow.

Model Three teaching is not as concerned as

Model One is with disseminating appropriate information, nor does it worry too much about understanding concepts or discovering the structures of a discipline. Model Three teaching is primarily concerned with human interaction. This may also be its major drawback.

We realize that classroom atmospheres are

important; clearly, pupils have difficulty learning anything if the anxiety level is high. Under such conditions our perception, how much we can "see," becomes narrow. Studies have shown that nonsupportive, critical, and negative classroom "climates" have adverse physiological and psychological effects on the pupils: Heartbeats increase, the galvanic skin response (GSR is a scientific term for sweaty palms, etc.) goes up, the resistance level (measured in ohms) increases. In the psychological domain the pupil's self-concept as a learner decreases, and self-direction in learning declines. Also, as one might expect, negative attitudes toward the teacher increase. Finally, and perhaps most important, the academic achievement of the pupils declines under the stressful directive-critical teaching atmosphere. Even pupils' voices—both the content of what they say and how they say it—reveal differences clearly in favor of supportive classroom atmospheres. Thus, the quality of the interpersonal relationship between the teacher and pupils does have an impact on many facets of classroom interaction, and how much the pupil actually learns is related.[21]

On the other hand, we cannot necessarily conclude that teaching and learning can be explained exclusively by the three Rogerian conditions. We can all think of examples from our own experience in which ideas, directions, and other types of academic content were important, and a skeptic might be quick to conclude that love alone is not enough. We are not suggesting either extreme. Obviously unconditional positive regard is not sufficient; but just as obviously, such facilitating conditions are important and necessary.

One final point: Recall that Walberg's massive summary of pupil achievement outcomes denoted classroom morale as a key factor in learning. In this sense, the atmosphere or climate can enhance morale or do just the opposite. If pupils feel prized as persons instead of feeling unworthy, then the learning outcome is positive. There are always exceptions, of course. Someone is bound to say, "I really felt put down all the time in that class but I learned the material." Individuality is such that a few can learn even under the worst possible conditions. Remember, these are exceptions, not the rule.

SYNTHESIZING TEACHING

From a developmental view, each of the three general models of teaching we have discussed has assets as well as liabilities. It would be a great mistake to settle exclusively on any one of these methods. There is something to be said in favor of each one, as well as something to be said against each one. Certainly, from the point of view of the pupil, the deficits are clear. Bruce Joyce, one of the country's leading researchers in the teaching-learning process, has commented that the actual teaching styles of most teachers are extremely limited. As a result, it is most important to "add and blend" a repertoire of models—that is, synthesize teaching—in order to enhance effectiveness. In other words, the old advice that advocated finding your own model, learning it, and sticking with it no longer holds. Joyce notes a series of personal experiences to underscore the need for variety. His account, which follows, illustrates how a teacher may so overuse one approach that the student soon becomes sick of the subject matter.

> When I was in high school, I was one of the poorest members of a good swimming team. The coach used drill-and-practice methods to teach us the strokes and how to increase our speed. He was tremendously encouraging to all of us, including those who really were not doing the team that much good. We loved him, enjoyed each other, and felt good about ourselves. As my body matured in college, I showed some promise as a long-distance swimmer and was taken under the wing of a fairly genial but hard-driving coach who emphasized practice rather than instruction. Given the academic demands of college, our little group had keys to the pool and were asked to swim for four to six hours sometime during each evening or night. It was, of course, not his fault that he couldn't be there to provide variety, but one of the side-effects of that experience is that I have not swum five consecutive laps since I was 20 years old. I love to play in the water, but I have an incredible aversion to anything remotely resembling swimming practice.[22]

Avoiding Rigidity

Having learned to use the various Flanders categories outlined in Table 12.3, you will be able

CARL R. ROGERS

Born at the turn of the century in a Chicago suburb, Carl Rogers spent his early years deciding how to focus his career. In 1919 his first interest at the University of Wisconsin was in scientific farming. Simultaneously, he was extremely active in church work, including attendance at a Christian youth conference in Peking, China. Upon his return to this country he shifted his undergraduate major to history. He felt that such a change was more in line with his emerging desire to go into evangelical work. He received an A.B. in history in 1924 from Wisconsin. Ironically, in view of his subsequent eminence in the field, he had but a single academic course in psychology as an undergraduate, and that by correspondence.

To prepare for the ministry, Rogers attended Union Theological Seminary in New York. There he began to change his emphasis once again, in this case from the dogma of religion to more general questions concerning the nature of the helping relationship. His interest in the healthy personal and psychological development of each person as an individual became more important than the formal, organized practice of religion. It was here that one of his key concepts took shape, the unique and special nature of "personhood." Much later, this idea was actualized with the establishment of his famous Center for Studies of the Person. With this shift in focus, it was not surprising for Rogers to transfer from Union to Columbia Teachers College. He received his Ph.D. in 1931, having spent much of his time in doing field work in Rochester, New York, with the city's child study department for the prevention of cruelty to children.

His interest in preventive treatment for mental health problems, another lifelong theme of his professional career, had its roots in this early work. One of the major difficulties that psychological treatment as a concept has grappled with almost from its inception has been this matter of preventive treatment. To provide help after a person becomes emotionally upset—that is, treatment after the fact—had been a major model of psychotherapy. It was really borrowed from the practice of medicine. Psychological help, then, in this view, takes the form of diagnosis, prognosis, treatment, and the cure process. People with problems would be classed into categories of mental illness, become patients, and, if the psychotherapy was successful, would be cured. Rogers felt almost from the beginning that this approach had severe limitations. Diagnostic

categories easily became negative labels. Focusing on mental disturbance could cause therapists to overlook the positive forces for growth inside each person. Treatments designed to help people often encouraged dependency or became a purchase of friendship. Rogers waged a long battle with the traditional psychological and psychiatric establishment on these issues. In his view, it was most important to prevent personal problems from being treated as long-term mental illness. An ounce of prevention is always worth more than a pound of cure. In this vein, he tried to develop counseling techniques that would encourage the positive growth forces within each person. To grow psychologically strong people was his answer to the treatment question.

Essentially the entire career of Carl Rogers has been a pilgrim's progress toward the goal of personhood for all. After spending almost a decade at the Rochester Clinic, he moved into the university setting, first at Ohio State from 1940 to 1945 and then at the University of Chicago. At Chicago he created a now famous client-centered counseling agency for the university. With this as a laboratory, he began to provide not only a significant new approach to college counseling but also a research base to document his work. He was the first counselor therapist to record his sessions on tape.

By analyzing the actual transcripts of the counseling interactions, he was able to dispel many of the myths surrounding psychological treatment. He was not well received by the more orthodox establishment. His openness in providing a public record of counseling challenged therapists to examine their own work and attest to its effectiveness. Up to that time, treatment failures were almost always blamed on the patient. If the patient didn't get well, there were three possible explanations: He might be too disturbed, he might be untreatable, or he might have a chronically weak ego. Rogers was able to show that many treatment problems were actually derived from the therapists.

Research on the counseling process began to show that particular conditions were absolutely essential if the person was to be helped. In a series of significant research studies started first at Chicago and then moved to Madison, Wisconsin, Rogers concluded that three conditions represented the core of the therapeutic relationship: unconditional positive regard, empathy, and congruence. (These are explained in the text.) The famous Rogerian triad became the central ingredient in the helping process. What was true for psychotherapy, he felt, applied equally to counseling and teaching.

Throughout his career, he has stressed the importance of the quality of interpersonal relationships, that how we relate to each other as human beings is central to the development of the person. Too often, he would say, we neglect this fundamental truism. Just as John Dewey can be thought of as the major proponent of education as a democratic ideal, so Carl Rogers can be viewed as a lifelong fighter to democratize counseling and psychotherapy. He saw and still sees today the need to develop equal and genuine relationships between people. The ability to help and care, according to Rogers, is an important resource within each human being, and we all have a responsibility to use it, as part of our mutual human interdependence. His work has always focused on that goal.

In his invited address to the American Psychological Association in 1972, he once again challenged psychologists to move out of a narrow scientific and even narrower professional stance and teach the principles of healthy growth to all people. "If we did away with 'the expert,' the 'certified professional,' the 'licensed psychologist,' we might open our profession to a breeze of fresh air, to a surge of creativity, such as it has not known for years." Now in his ninth decade, Carl Rogers still stands for the same principles of helping and caring in interpersonal relations that he has always advocated.

to combine clusters that will most naturally fit the major teaching models presented at the outset. Employing advance organizers in the transmission-of-knowledge model (Model One) means that Category 5 (lecturing) would be the most common technique used. Similarly, the inductive modes associated with Model Two would rely heavily on Category 4 (asking open-ended questions) plus Categories 2 and 3. The interpersonal model (Model Three) would include a strong emphasis on Category 1 (accepting feelings) as well as on Categories 2 and 3. The goal, then, is to learn to apply these models with skill in order to increase the variety of learning experiences for the pupils. However, Joyce warns that it is very important to avoid a

All three models—the transmittal of knowledge, inductive inquiry, and interpersonal learning—are important to the classroom teacher, and effective teaching demands a combination of the three. Certainly it would be a mistake to depend exclusively on any one.

heavy-handed or singular reliance on any one mode day in and day out.

When I am working with my classes, there are certain days when I simply have a terrific urge to get things clarified or when I want to express myself and the way I think about material. On those days, I am very likely to lecture with the use of advance organizers. There are other days when I would be bored silly by that same approach, and use another to stay lively and help the students stay with me. Pretending that we are not people would be a serious error in teaching, and our intuition about what feels right on any given day should be listened to, even though we select models on an analytic basis much of the time.[23]

A rigid adherence to a single teaching strategy as a means of achieving a unique goal is to be avoided at all costs. The following is a classic example of excessive rigidity.

A beginning teacher was presenting a lesson he had just worked up. The lesson was titled "World War I Armaments: The Machine Gun." The objective was to convey information (the technological development of a rapid-continuous-firing gun) and comprehension (the effect of this new weapon on strategy). He wanted to show the students that the development of the machine gun helped created a stalemate. To emphasize his point, the teacher had assembled pictures showing infantry and cavalry futilely attempting to charge machine-gun nests and being cut to ribbons in the process.

However, as is almost always the case in good teaching, the presentation was making the pupils think. One boy in the third row raised his hand, "I see what you mean about the machine guns. It meant it was easier to defend than attack. But didn't that lead to the tank? Wasn't it near the end of the war that they brought tanks in?"

At this point the teacher got himself trapped in his own lesson plan. Since the subject was machine guns, he said brightly (after a few anxious moments of silence), "Yes, that's right, tanks were also introduced in World War I, and on top of each tank, they put a machine gun."*

NONVERBAL BEHAVIOR

In addition to the need for blending in Joyce's sense, there is yet another important component of teaching effectiveness. To an ironic degree the nonverbal aspect of being human is so obvious that we often overlook it. In fact, until the work of theorists such as Charles Galloway, of Ohio State University, and a few others, the area of body language or nonverbal communication was largely ignored in teaching and teacher education.[24] This happened in spite of earlier and pioneering research work that indicated most clearly just how significant the phenomenon was.

It's hard to imagine, but from 75 to 90 percent of a message's impact is transmitted nonverbally. The actual verbal content turns out to be far less important than tone of voice, facial expression, and posture. In the classroom how you stand or sit, move, gesture, and raise and lower your voice, for example, will convey what you really mean to your students. But unfortunately, as Galloway points out, too often we are almost totally unaware of our own nonverbal modes. We rarely see ourselves in interaction and hence do not really understand what impact we may be having on others.

Perhaps even more important is the extent to which we convey how we really feel about others without words. Studies have shown that teachers who have positive attitudes toward the world actually employ an important set of facilitating nonverbal cues to encourage student participation and involvement. Those with negative attitudes displayed nonverbal behavior designed to discourage and inhibit student involvement.[25] Researchers could predict which type of nonverbal behavior a teacher would use if they knew the teacher's attitude set. Moreover, it was obvious that the children understood the meaning of the different body language systems.

As a result Galloway and his colleagues developed a nonverbal version of the Flanders system. Instead of coding verbal messages, however, they rated the body language of the teachers. Table 12.5 outlines the main elements of the patterns of communication divided into two main areas: nonverbal behavior that (1) facilitates students' development or (2) constricts their growth. He has also organized the nonverbal categories according to indirect methods and direct approaches.

The results of Galloway's research have two major implications. First, there is a clear connection between a teacher's nonverbal behavior and the classroom atmosphere. We noted both in the teaching model focused on interpersonal relationships and from the meta-analysis on the importance of classroom morale that such elements have an important effect on learning. Essentially, your nonverbal behavior will set the tone in the classroom.

Second, teachers should make a deliberate attempt to become more aware of their own

---

* We are indebted to Professor Ralph Mosher for relaying this classroom incident to us.

TABLE 12.5   NONVERBAL BEHAVIORS: THE GALLOWAY SYSTEM

Direct Influence	**1, 2**	**CONGRUENT** Nonverbal behavior is consistent with words. No "mixed messages" are given. Body language demonstrates an appropriate range of feelings.	**INCONGRUENT** Behavior contradicts words; for example, smiles when annoyed. Body language is overcontrolled. Feelings are rarely if ever shown.
	3	**IMPLEMENT** As teacher uses ideas of pupils, nonverbals are consistently encouraging; for example, leans toward, smiles.	**PERFUNCTORY** Nonverbal behavior indicates no genuine interest in student ideas; for example, bored posture or facial expression.
	4	**PERSONAL** Teacher maintains face-to-face eye contact, is "connected" with the class, maintains a comfortable "psychological" distance.	**IMPERSONAL** Teacher avoids eye contact; for example, talks to the floor or ceiling or maintains excessive distance.
Indirect Influence	**5**	**RESPONSIVE** Tone, pace of talk are designed to keep student interest.	**UNRESPONSIVE** Teacher drones on and on, with little variation in tone, and screens out student cues.
	6	**INVOLVE** Nonverbal behavior encourages student participation in clarifying directions and rules.	**DISMISS** Nonverbal behavior cues students to avoid participation.
	7	**FIRM** Nonverbal behavior is consistent with firm language in controlling misbehavior.	**HARSH** Nonverbal behavior is severe, aggressive, genuinely intimidating.

basic repertoire of nonverbal behavior. This doesn't mean you need to enroll in a method acting school. It does mean you should recognize and improve areas where your nonverbal behavior may be inhibiting student growth. Obviously, the use of videotapes of classroom performance is one major way of gaining awareness and seeing the effect of a new behavior. Another is to ask a good friend to observe and write down examples of how your behavior fits into the Galloway system.

The most difficult problem is that there can be no exact prescription of how to behave. You need to find a comfortable middle ground between a cold, aloof, restricted set of behaviors and their opposite—a rushing, gushing, overpowering, and hectic nonverbal repertoire. If you are naturally inclined to be quiet and limit your nonverbal behavior, then you will want to work on adding to your repertoire. If, on the other hand, your nonverbal behavior seems to indicate that you are running the class like a fire drill and a two-minute warning in sports,

then you'll want to relax more and express less of yourself nonverbally. Incidentally, this also holds even in the area of discipline. The old truism used to be "Don't smile 'til Christmas" if you were a new teacher.[26] The idea was to keep the students in line right from the start through stern composure. We now know that's wrong. Effective teachers are skillful not only in stating their expectations but also in demonstrating a genuine interest in listening to and working with the student, thus conveying an atmosphere of mutually shared expectations. They can even smile before Thanksgiving.

It is important to add the component of nonverbal behavior as a general element to all models of teaching. In fact, if you want to try an interesting experiment in the classroom, put together a brief lesson (ten to fifteen minutes) on any subject and then teach it nonverbally. Many years ago when the microteaching approach was first adopted (a method of concentrating on one teaching behavior at a time), the final unit was a nonverbal one. You could use the black-

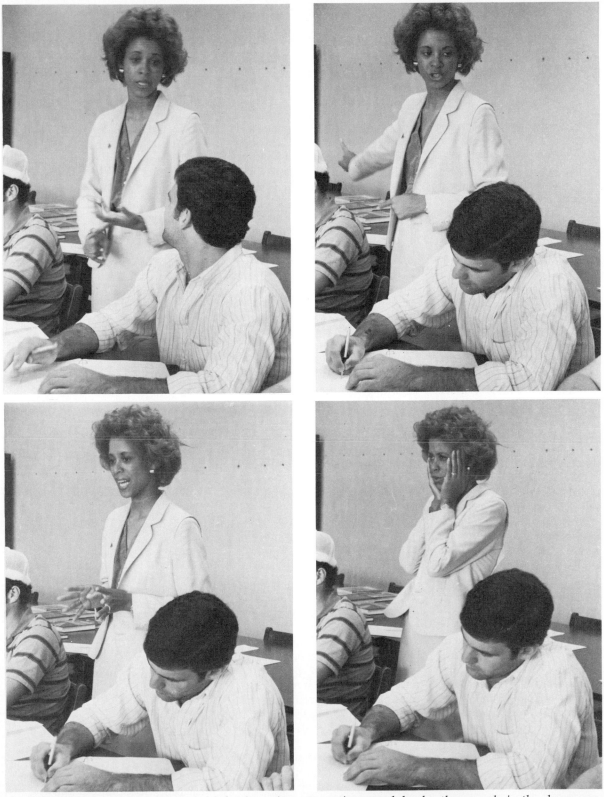

As Galloway's research on nonverbal behavior points out, actions speak louder than words in the classroom.

CONTEMPORARY ISSUE

Teacher Enthusiasm—From Kounin to Rosenshine to Dr. Fox

Whenever we think of teaching effectiveness, a question frequently asked is: What about enthusiasm? Doesn't it make a difference if the teacher is genuinely interested in and eager to convey the subject matter? Certainly Thomas Good's concept of active teaching seems to indicate the need for well-paced instruction.[a] Obviously, a teacher who labors over each point in a slow, pedantic manner must have a negative effect. Such a teacher, humorless, plodding, and somewhat out of touch with reality, represents almost a Hollywood version of an ineffective educator.

It was Jacob Kounin who first formalized a framework to help understand the concept of teacher enthusiasm.[b] How alert, wide awake, or "with it" a teacher is does make a major difference, particularly in handling discipline and in moving from one subject to the next. In other words, one of the keys to a good learning environment is the avoidance of "down time," when nothing seems to be happening in the classroom. Thus, managing a group involves a pace or tempo. From a logical viewpoint, then, teacher energy is clearly important. What does the research say?

The first series of studies was done by Barak Rosenshine through careful observations of actual classroom instruction. Through such naturalistic study, Kounin's ideas were validated. The enthusiastic, "with it" teachers outperformed their cohorts. The pupils gained in academic achievement. The positive correlations to achievement ranged be-

tween .30 and .60.[c] But since such findings weren't particularly surprising, they received only modest notice in the educational psychology literature. It remained for a new group of researchers to put the concept at the forefront through a series of provocative and somewhat controversial studies, the "Dr. Fox studies."

Every once in a while, a group of behavioral scientists will come up with a startling new approach to a phenomenon. D. H. Naftulin, J. E. Ware, and F. A. Donnelly decided to push the study of enthusiasm to the limit.[d] At a professional conference they hired an actor to give a lecture. Introduced with all the appropriate (though "fake") expert credentials, the actor used charisma, enthusiasm, and style in delivering a basically meaningless talk. At times, it even verged on double talk. Of course, by now you may have guessed the outcome. The audience solemnly proclaimed through evaluations that the talk was well organized, clearly presented, and "stimulated thinking." The redoubtable Dr. Fox had indeed outfoxed his audience. National newspapers and the media quickly picked up the study.

Naturally, there is and has been much debate about what such a study actually proves. It does not suggest that in a real classroom over the course of an entire school year students will learn meaningful content from meaningless lectures. After all, you can't fool all the people all the time. Further studies have shown that when real content is included, the "expressiveness" of

the teacher continues to have a significant effect not only on student ratings but on achievement as well. So what is now being referred to as "an extended visit with Dr. Fox in the classroom" essentially agrees with Kounin's original contention and Rosenshine's first series of naturalistic studies.[e] The experimental studies help to cross-validate the original findings.[f] Enthusiasm makes a difference. The Dr. Fox experiment serves as a reminder of a truism from early folklore in teaching, "The greatest sin of an educator is to be boring."

[a]   Good, T. L. (1983). "Recent classroom research: Implications for teacher education." In D.C. Smith (Ed.), *Essential knowledge for beginning educators* (pp. 55–64). Washington, D.C.: American Association of Colleges of Teacher Education.
[b]   Kounin, J. (1970). *Discipline and group management in the classroom.* New York: Holt, Rinehart & Winston.
[c]   Rosenshine, B. (1970). "Enthusiastic teaching: A research review." *School Review, 78,* 499–514.
[d]   Naftulin, D. H., Ware, J. E., Jr., and Donnelly, F. A. (1973). "The Dr. Fox lecture: A paradigm for educational seduction." *Journal of Medical Education, 48,* 630–635.
[e]   Williams, R. G., and Ware, J. E., Jr. (1977). "An extended visit with Dr. Fox: Validity of student satisfaction with instruction after repeated exposure to a lecturer." *American Educational Research Journal, 14*(4), 449–458.
[f]   See Larkins, A. G., McKinney, C. W., Oldham-Bass, S., and Gilmore, A. C. (1985). Teacher enthusiasm: A critical review. In H. S. Williams (Ed.), *Educational and Psychological Research.* Hattiesburg: University of Southern Mississippi. This is an excellent comprehensive review of the concept of enthusiasm, including a detailed examination of the research design employed.

board, overheads, and handouts as well as eye contact, hand gestures, nods, and the like—but no words. As you teach the lesson, you'll quickly realize how much we overrely on verbal messages. And with practice, you'll find out how much you can accomplish without words. Actions, after all, do speak more loudly than words.

The final point here is a question. If the teacher's nonverbal behavior influences students, does the converse also hold true? As you've probably guessed, it does work both ways. Teachers can be clearly influenced by a student's physical appearance, posture, and tone of voice.[27] As a result some students receive frequent approval while others not only receive less approval but also less eye contact, fewer smiles, and more disapproval. We'll comment more on this when we discuss the personal aspects of teaching (Chapter 14), since it relates very much to the basic attitudes a teacher may have toward pupils and the self-fulfilling prophecies that result.

Cross-Cultural Differences

If you think about it, you will quickly realize that body language varies considerably according to a person's cultural background. Some nonverbal behavior may have a very different meaning in different cultures. As a result, when the cultural background of the child and the teacher vary widely, nonverbal messages may be misinterpreted. Two examples illustrate the point. Some Native American children are taught not to maintain steady eye contact with an adult. In some tribes an adult who looks straight into another person's eyes is seen as untrustworthy. This does not mean that you can't look at Indian children; however, if you force the child to look directly into your eyes, you may be sending a very mixed message. Similarly, the amount of physical space that is psychologically comfortable varies considerably among cultures. A newly arrived student from Great Britain may require more "personal space" than a student from Mexico. At the same time, however, it is most important not to overgeneralize. Many English children and Mexican children would welcome either closer or more distant contact. What they are accustomed to may also depend on how "Americanized" their family has become.

In dealing with children from culturally different backgrounds, it is wise to watch for signs of incongruity. When their behavior is incongruent, it may indicate that whatever you are attempting to communicate nonverbally is being misunderstood. In other words, they may be decoding your nonverbal message in a way you didn't intend. Because of the enormous complexity of cross-cultural differences, it may be impossible for research to develop a definitive list of them. As a teacher, you should be sensitive to their existence and observe the nonverbal responses to your own behaviors as an index of effective communication.

SUMMARY

Recent research on teaching effectiveness based on large-scale meta-analyses conducted by Walberg indicates that the following factors are key elements: engaged academic learning time, positive reinforcement, cues and feedback, cooperative learning, positive class atmosphere, higher-order questioning, and the use of advance organizers. The system of instruction developed by Flanders shows how these elements fit together in actual classroom interaction.

Teaching elements can also be grouped into general models of teaching. In Model One the emphasis is on the transmission of knowledge. Use of advanced organizers and direct teaching methods are the main features. Model Two involves inquiry or discovery-based teaching. It emphasizes the indirect methods of open-ended questions and building on student ideas. The focus of Model Three is the quality of interpersonal relations. A positive classroom atmosphere is a central component of the model.

Joyce emphasizes the need for a variety of teaching models. Instead of relying exclusively on any single model, he suggests synthesizing methods. Teachers thus need to practice the different skills involved with each method in order to achieve teaching effectiveness.

One of the main criticisms of the teaching models has been the absence of any emphasis on teacher nonverbal behavior. Based on Galloway's system, a new method of analyzing teacher nonverbal behavior has been developed which parallels Flanders' framework. Galloway's work underscores the importance of teacher awareness of how actions often do speak louder than words in the classroom. In the area of cross-cultural differences, there are few, if any, consistent nonverbal differences. It is important, however, for teachers to become aware of possible incongruities between pupil words and body language. Thus, teachers need to learn about not only their own nonverbal channels of communication but those of their pupils as well.

KEY TERMS AND NAMES

Herbert Walberg
David Ausubel
Ned Flanders
Nate Gage
Carl Rogers
   empathy
   unconditional positive regard
   congruence

Bruce Joyce
Charles Galloway
   nonverbal behavior
   teacher enthusiasm

REFERENCES

1. Walberg, H. (1984). Improving the productivity of America's schools. *Educational Leadership, 41,* 19–27.

2. Good, T. L. (1983). Classroom research: A decade of progress. *Educational Psychologist, 18*(3), 127–144.

3. Peterson, P., and Swing, S. (1982). Beyond time on task: Students' reports of their thought processes during classroom instruction. *Elementary School Journal, 82,* 481–491.

4. Fisher, C. W., and Berliner, D. (1985). *Perspectives on instructional time.* New York: Longman.

5. Brophy, J. (1981). Teacher praise: A functional analysis. *Review of Educational Research, 51,* 5–32.

6. Page, E. B. (1958). Teacher comments and student performance. *Journal of Educational Psychology, 49,* 173–181.

7. Good, T. L. (1983). Recent classroom research: Implications for teacher education. In D. C. Smith (Ed.), *Essential knowledge for beginning educators* (pp. 55–65). Washington, D.C.: American Association of Colleges of Teacher Education.

8. Redfield, D. L., and Rousseau, E. W. (1981). Meta-analysis of experimental research on teacher questioning behavior. *Review of Educational Research, 51*(2), 237–246. The effect size quoted in the text, however, comes from Walberg's more recent (1984) analysis, cited in note 1.

9. See *Educational Leadership* (1985), *42*(8) (special issue on direct instruction and teaching for thinking).

10. See Gage, N. L. (1985). *Hard gains in the soft sciences.* Bloomington, Ind.: Phi Delta Kappa. There are other effects on learning that we have not included in this review, such as acceleration (special programs for the gifted), mastery learning, reading, tutoring, and personalized instruction. These are largely not within the immediate control of the classroom teacher and are related to more basic policy and/or administrative

questions. Also (and unfortunately), we do agree with W. L. Gage's commentary on the persistence of conventional classroom teaching as the mode in something like 90 percent of the secondary-school classes and 75 percent of the elementary classes (p. 49).

11. Flanders, N. (1970). *Analyzing teacher behavior*. Reading, Mass.: Addison-Wesley.

12. Gage, N. L. (1978). *The scientific basis for the art of teaching*. New York: Teachers College Press.

13. Chickering, A., and McCormick, J. (1973). Personality development and the college experience. *Research in Higher Education, 1,* 43–70.

14. Gage, *Hard gains in the soft sciences*.

15. Good, Recent classroom research. It is also interesting and important to note that results even from the "heartland" of the directive teaching approach have recently caused a shift in overall recommendations. As Good has noted, "Active teaching also connotes a broader philosophical base and *should* become somewhat less direct as students become more mature and instructional goals more focused on affective and process outcomes" (pp. 58–59).

16. Ausubel, D. P., and Sullivan, E. V. (1970). *Theory and problems of child development*, 2nd ed. New York: Grune & Stratton.

17. Good, Recent classroom research (p. 56). See also Berliner, D. C. (1984). The half-full glass: A review of research on teaching. In P. L. Hosford (Ed.), *Using what we know about teaching* (pp. 51–77). Alexandria, Va.: Association of Supervision and Curriculum Development.

18. Joyce, B. R. (1978). *Selecting learning experiences: Linking theory to practice*. Washington, D.C.: Association of Supervision and Curriculum Development.

19. Bruner, J. (1966). *Toward a theory of instruction* (p. 44). Cambridge, Mass.: Belknap Press, Harvard University.

20. Rogers, C. R. (1969). *Freedom to learn*. Columbus, Ohio: Merrill.

21. Flanders, N. A., and Morine, G. (1973). The assessment of proper control and suitable learning environment. In N. L. Gage (Ed.), *Mandated evaluation of educators*. Stanford: California Center for Research and Development in Teaching.

22. Joyce, *Selecting learning experiences* (p. 18). This quote and the one on p. 304 are reprinted with permission of the Association for Supervision and Curriculum Development and Bruce Joyce. Copyright © 1978 by the Association for Supervision and Curriculum Development. All rights reserved.

23. Joyce, *Selecting learning experiences* (pp. 18–19).

24. Galloway, C. (1977). "Nonverbal." *Theory into Practice, 16*(3), Entire Issue.

25. Smith, H. (1981). Nonverbal communication in teaching. *Review of Educational Research, 49*(4), 631–672.

26. The phrase is from Kevin Ryan's (1970) classic study of the experiences of novice teachers, *Don't smile until Christmas*. Chicago: University of Chicago Press.

27. Woolfolk, A. E., and Brooks, D. M. (1983). Nonverbal communication in teaching. *Review of Research in Education, 10* 103–150.

13

TEACHING OBJECTIVES

Sooner or later all those involved in the educational enterprise confront the question of teaching objectives. What is the point and purpose of the curriculum content? Is it content mastery, academic acquisition? Is it personal growth? Or are process goals the ultimate purpose? Essentially, the basic problem involves examining the question, education for what? And, as you may have guessed, there are as many proposed purposes as there are questions. In this chapter, we shall discuss the problem in a global sense, then outline a framework that provides significant guidance for the choices that teachers face.

We will also present information on the general principles involved in lesson planning. Such planning can become an important vehicle for attaining specified objectives. Without it your goals as a teacher and your pupils' learning may miss one another like ships passing in the night.

OBJECTIVES: THE PROBLEM OF WHAT TO TEACH

What objectives do we want to achieve in teaching anybody anything? A few years ago this very question was given perhaps its best portrayal in *The Saber-Tooth Curriculum*, a book written under the pen name of J. Abner Peddiwell. It was a spoof, but it made its point most dramatically and effectively. In Paleolithic times a tribe developed an educational curriculum based on survival needs. The young were taught how to scare away saber-toothed tigers with firebrands, how to club woolly horses for clothing, and how to fish with their hands. However, as time passed and the Ice Age began, the survival needs changed: The tigers caught cold and died, the woolly horses ran away, and the fish disappeared in muddy water. In their places came big, ferocious bears that weren't scared by firebrands, a herd of antelope that could run like the wind (the woolly horses had been slow-footed and clumsy), and new fish that hid in the muddy water. It soon occurred to the tribe that their educational curriculum was, in today's parlance, not relevant. Scaring tigers, clubbing horses, and catching fish by hand were relics of the old days. The tribe now

CONTEMPORARY ISSUE

Academic Content Mastery Versus Personal Growth: Incompatible Educational Goals?

As we pointed out through the example of *The Saber-Tooth Curriculum*, the question of educational goals usually raises a heated debate. Since education is a public enterprise and the American public almost never speaks with one voice, it is quite natural that different views abound. On the question of overall purpose, such divergence is quite visible.

Generally, policy groups favor quite separate goals. For example, the back-to-the-basics movement wishes to foster schooling for the single purpose of subject-matter mastery in traditional areas. Its goals are to teach the three Rs, eliminate electives and frills, roll back grade inflation, and promote fundamental content acquisition. At the other extreme are some of the so-called humanistic educators. In their view, personal growth and humane sensitivity are far more important than content. To be fully human requires process, spontaneity, authenticity, and genuineness.

You can just imagine how different the schools would be under each policy group. Mastery tests, highly structured material, and memorization would predominate under the one group; schooling would become almost a grim, joyless enterprise. Under the other group, there would be a kind of quiet anarchy, with groups of pupils and adults gathering and dispersing in an almost whimsical manner. Must this apparent controversy always yield such diametrically opposite positions? Will we find in the year 2000 a revisitation of the saber-tooth, only in galactic terms?

In the last decade, a series of research studies raised the possibility of a new synthesis of goals for education. It just may be possible to have our basics "cake" and, in the humanistic spirit, to "eat it too." Rather than choosing the mind or the heart as ships passing in the night, a developmental approach may combine both. Thus, instead of an either-or problem, the educational goal could be the promotion of both views in the form of general psychological maturity.

What are the elements that make up psychological maturity? On the intellectual side, the elements would include the general ability to symbolize experience, to relate ideas with logic and rationality, and to think in a field-independent way. Those intellectual competencies, however, are not sufficient by themselves. Douglas Heath, who conducted a longitudinal study of the factors that predict success in adult life, found that a second major factor of psychological maturity was required. The ability to act allocentrically (altruistically), with compassion, and with a disciplined commitment to humane democratic values constitutes this second factor. Heath made the following surprising observation:

> Adolescent scholastic aptitude as well as other measures of academic intelligence do not predict several *hundred* measures of the adaptation and competence of men in their early thirties. In fact, scholastic aptitude was inversely related in this group to many measures of their adult psychological maturity, as well as of their judged interpersonal competence.[a]

In other words, academic achievement by itself is not sufficient to predict psychological maturity.

Lawrence Kohlberg also reviewed a large number of such life-success studies and came to similar conclusions. Academic content mastery by itself made no independent contribution to predictions of successful life adjustment. However well a student achieved academically did not predict how competently that student would function after graduation. Instead, Kohlberg found that measures of developmental stage did predict success in occupation and other indices of adult maturity.[b]

Finally, David McClelland also provided substantial evidence in favor of psychological maturity and competence as a goal. He investigated the relationship between grade-point achievement and scores on scholastic aptitude tests on the one hand and success after formal education on the other. Included were a wide range of job groups: factory workers, bank tellers, air-traffic controllers, scientific researchers, and medical personnel. Within each job group, grades and scholastic test scores bore no relation to successful performance, while psychological maturity and competence did. McClelland, in fact, felt that the whole idea of scholastic aptitude testing was a cruel hoax.[c] High test scores seemingly predict only more high test scores, not life-success outcomes. It's kind of an educator's version of *Catch 22*.

McClelland suggests that we should develop methods to assess psychological maturity and personal competence.

What are you to make of all this? Perhaps the next time you hear the battle lines being drawn up between the "thinkers" versus the "feelers," between those who espouse content acquisition versus those who promote personal development, you can step into the controversy. "Neither side is correct," you can announce. "What we need is an educational program that stimulates both intellectual and personal development. Both sides of the human condition require development in order that people may be able to live significant, successful lives." If such an educational program works, the saber-tooth tiger will disappear as an insurmountable educational dichotomy. If it doesn't, the debate will continue.

[a]   Heath, D. (1977). *Maturity and competence* (pp. 177–178). New York: Gardner.

[b]   Kohlberg, L., and Mayer, R. (1972). Development as the aim of education. *Harvard Educational Review* 42(4), 449–496.

[c]   McClelland, D. (1973). Testing for competence rather than for intelligence. *American Psychologist* (January), pp. 1–14.

needed to learn how to trap bears, snare antelopes, and build fish nets. However, the "educational establishment" of the tribe declared in august tones:

> Don't be foolish. . . . We don't teach fish-grabbing to grab fish; we teach it to develop a generalized agility which can never be developed by mere training (in net-making). We don't teach horse-clubbing to club horses; we teach it to develop a generalized strength in the learner which he can never get from so prosaic and specialized a thing as antelope-snare setting. We don't teach tiger-scaring to scare tigers; we teach it for the purpose of giving that noble courage. . . .[1]

The debate on educational objectives has a long history. The controversy usually covers the same terrain; namely, advocates of teaching skills for survival are in opposition to those who would teach for intrinsic and general education. Each side has some merit. We certainly do need to learn survival skills, but if that is all we learn, it is obvious that our skills are destined to become obsolete. Critics compare this approach to training a generation of dinosaurs—animals that, because of their inability to adapt to changing times, were unable to survive.

In addition to the time-limited nature of specific skill training, a second aspect of education as content acquisition is almost always raised by critics of that approach. Memorizing facts and mastering information generally have almost no long-term effects. In a series of classic studies conducted in the 1930s, Ralph Tyler demonstrated quite clearly that pupils unlearned almost as fast as they learn. He studied the amount of content retained. The pupils "forgot" almost 50 percent of the content taught after one year. The figure shot up to 80 percent after two years. As an aside, he ironically noted that most pupils in this country in the 1930s thought that all banks paid 6 percent compound interest since that was the figure commonly used in arithmetic word problems.[2] So much for the argument that the goals of education should be to inculcate specific skills and content! When Jean Piaget said that "to know by heart is not really to know," he neatly summarized the fundamental flaw in this educational goal.

On the other hand, proponents of learning for its own sake claim that a "classical education" will train the mind for disciplined thought. Mind training could never become obsolete, because skills we have developed can be brought to bear on any problem we meet in life. However, as you may recall from Chapter 1, E. L. Thorndike conducted a series of studies showing that the theory of mind training through the study of Greek and Latin was false. Such learning did not generalize. Such a classical general education for the disciplining of the mind seemed as nebulous a goal as memorizing specific concrete skills.

BENJAMIN BLOOM

This eminent psychologist and scholar was born in 1913. After completing his undergraduate work and master's degree at Penn State, Benjamin Bloom moved to the University of Chicago. He was named instructor of educational psychology in 1940, completed his Ph.D. in 1942, and remained there for over thirty years. He rose through the ranks to a full professorship, all the while building a reputation for careful and significant scholarship. His insistence on precision in educational thought soon led to the now famous taxonomy for educational objectives in both the cognitive and affective domains, scholarship that literally revolutionized the process of lesson planning for classroom teaching. His category system soon became the standard for describing objectives and the process of achieving those specified goals. Not content to rest on these laurels, Bloom next stepped into the raging controversy concerning the nature of intelligence. His scholarship and care were once more tested. He published the classic *Stability and Change in Human Characteristics,* in which he attempted to resolve the nature-nurture controversy. His work clearly indicated the significance of early experience and the critical nature of early learning as factors that promote intellectual growth. He has also created a new approach to teaching, mastery

learning, in search of methods as effective as individual tutoring. His most recent study is on the process of gifted and talented performance.

A lifetime of significant scholarship for educational psychology perhaps best sums up his valuable contributions to the field.

EDUCATIONAL GOALS: BENJAMIN BLOOM'S TAXONOMY

Education has always been unable to decide between those who advocate a curriculum of relevance and those who desire a program of general education. In the mid-1950s a team led by Benjamin S. Bloom of the University of Chi-

cago bravely decided to settle the matter once and for all, and developed the now famous taxonomy, or classification, of educational objectives.[3]

Bloom felt that one of the major difficulties confronting anyone interested in education was the definition of goals, that is, what we want to strive for as teachers, counselors, or educational administrators. If you ask any of your friends to define their goals as teachers, you are likely to receive either an impossibly abstract statement ("I want to help students realize their full potential as individuals—to become self-actualizing") or some very explicit and narrow statement ("My job is to teach the multiplication tables").

Bloom examined this problem of considering educational objectives from either an impossible cosmic or hopelessly trivial point of view. He came up with a scheme that classifies educational objectives and relates each objective to specific classroom procedures. Bloom's approach has a very healthy effect in that it forces teachers to specify their goals and the means of getting there; it fits procedures and materials to instructional strategies. Bloom's system also specifies a sequence of six stages or levels of objectives that are matched to a sequence of assessment strategies. We will describe each level of his system by defining its content and briefly discussing its associated assessment procedures.

Level One: Basic Knowledge

Definition: Students are responsible for information, ideas, material, or phenomena. They have to know specific facts, terms, and methods.

Assessment: Direct questions and multiple choice tests. The object is to test the students' ability to recall the facts, to identify and repeat the information provided. The teacher doesn't ask the students to form new judgments or to analyze ideas; he or she simply tries to find out how much material they can recall.

Level Two: Comprehension

Definition: Students must show they understand the material, ideas, facts, and theories.

Assessment: A variety of procedures are applicable. Students can restate the material in their own words, reorder or extrapolate ideas, predict or estimate. In other words, at this level students are assessed on the basis of their capacity to act upon, or process, information. As-

sessment at this level requires more activity from the pupil than assessment at level one. Objective or multiple choice questions can still be used, but they would be of a different order, since they must provide evidence that the pupils have some understanding or comprehension of what they are saying.

Level Three: Application

Definition: Students must be able to apply their knowledge to real situations. At level two we are satisfied if they understand the ideas. At level three we want them to demonstrate that they can actually apply their ideas correctly.

This particular level has been one of the stumbling blocks of educational psychology itself. In Chapter 1 we raised the question of why, after fifty years, the mode of classroom teaching has changed so little. We also cited the research showing the predominance of what we called trivia in the classroom. Educational psychology, as a field, contains much basic knowledge (level one) and understands much of it (level two) but has been unable to apply the ideas to real situations (level three). The application of knowledge is critical because it means putting knowledge into action, rather than merely talking about what might be done.

Assessment: We have to go well beyond the usual procedures in order to assess how well students apply what they learn. If, for example, we are teaching them to play volleyball, the test would be obvious: Put them on either side of a net and evaluate their performance. It is easy to see whether children can apply their knowledge of addition or subtraction: Just give them some money, have them "buy" things in a mock store, and see if they end up with the correct change. In geometry, have them construct a right-angled triangle out of wood and then measure the length of each side. In physics, children can wire a bell and see whether or not it will ring. However, the one drawback to tests of this sort is the possibility that pupils may learn by rote how to apply the information. The teacher needs to be aware of this possibility and to vary application tests to ensure that pupils can genuinely put their knowledge into practice.

Unfortunately, testing for application at ad-

CONTEMPORARY ISSUE

Creativity: The State of the Art or the Ark?

Certainly one of the most over-used words in the English language is *creativity.* Hardly a day goes by but that you hear it used as a universal modifier—a creative solution, creative financing, a creative design. As a result it is not unusual to find that the goals of schooling often contain the same phrase, namely, to promote pupil creativity.

What exactly is creativity? The definitions are, in fact, almost as broad as the use of the word itself, and a word that may have so many meanings can end up as meaningless. Creativity seems to involve three distinct cognitive operations: (1) fluency, (2) flexibility, and (3) originality. Fluency is the ability to express meaning through multiple ideas and concepts—in short, to be able to symbolize experience broadly. Flexibility implies the ability to change your "mind set," to search for alternative solutions when the obvious answers are wrong. Originality is the ability to come up with unique or new solutions or concepts. In-

ventions are the most common example of this aspect of creativity. The first person to put a light bulb inside a refrigerator, attach an eraser to a pencil, or bend a wire in the form of a paper clip showed originality.

Sometimes the entire process of creativity may be referred to as divergent thinking—coming up with unusual solutions or different uses for ordinary pieces of material. (For example, how many uses can you think of for a brick?) This does not mean, however, that anything goes. Eventually someone has to judge whether or not the new idea, a new use, or an unusual suggestion is really creative. In spite of many advances in measurement, there are still major controversies concerning the reliability and validity in assessment of creativity.

In addition to the assessment problem there is also the instruction or teaching question. Obviously, any educator would want to help children develop abilities such as fluency, flexibility, and

originality, but that may be easier said than done. Some years ago a number of interesting approaches to encouraging creativity emerged, notably the original work of Paul Torrance and Calvin Taylor. Both based their work on a similar assumption—namely, that all (or almost all) humans possess the potential for creative performance. In other words, they did not consider creativity a special talent found in only a tiny percentage of the population. Nor in their view should creativity be confused with gifted development. This democratic or populist view suggests that the teacher's role, then, is to find and promote creativity in each child.

The theory and research on this important question have lagged in the past decade.[a] The national focus for educational policy has switched from concerns about such questions as creativity to much narrower concerns such as the size of the Scholastic Aptitude Test score decline. As a result schools are now under pressure to

vanced levels of courses in the humanities is more complicated. In fact, it is interesting to note that Bloom and his associates could find no examples from the humanities. Perhaps as we develop more active methods of teaching in the humanities, we will find it possible to test applications.

Level Four: Analysis

Definition: Analysis is essentially a more advanced aspect of level two (comprehension). Analysis requires that pupils classify or break material down into its components, understand

the relationship between the components, and recognize the principle that organizes the structure or the system. (As you can see, it becomes increasingly difficult to describe the levels as we move from the simple and the concrete to the complex and abstract.)

Assessment: The ability to analyze material can be assessed in a number of ways. For example, we might see whether students can identify the assumptions behind an argument or a debate. Thus, an advocate of the use of preventive nuclear war might argue that "in times of extreme danger, with national survival at stake, a coun-

revise their curricula to produce SAT score improvement. An array of computer-based SAT test preparation programs, special classes, and particularly in suburbia, "coaching" schools have sprung up. These efforts, of course, directly drain off interest and resources for educational programs focused on creativity. The SAT does not measure creativity; in fact, it does not measure problem solving. Yet in the present era it will be difficult for teachers and researchers to work on the instructional problem while the nation wants higher achievement scores, not creative thinking.[b]

There is, however, some hope. The issue of creativity has been taken up by Howard Gardner at Harvard University.[c] He is the first to examine the question from a developmental perspective. If children demonstrate stages of growth in intellectual, emotional, interpersonal, and value areas, do they also demonstrate growth in creativity? A director of Project Zero, he has been engaged in the needed basic research. Using a developmental model similar to that of Piaget, he has started to chart the process. Some of his initial findings are quite provocative. For example, it appears that pupils between the ages of ten to fourteen (just prior to the full onset of formal operations) are developmentally most ready for creative artistic competence. If such findings are borne out in future research, we may have a real breakthrough for the teaching of creativity. Schools, especially middle schools, would have a strong reason to offer serious programs in the arts. At this point, of course, this work is speculative. There is hope, however, that through such research the creative process will be more clearly understood. Then teachers can start on the task of building programs that effectively promote the development of creative competencies. We know that appropriate interaction promotes growth. We now need programs designed especially for that purpose.

[a]   Wallach, M. (1985). Creativity testing and giftedness. In F. D. Horowitz and M. O'Brien (Eds.), *The gifted and talented: Developmental perspectives* (pp. 99–124). Washington, D.C.: American Psychological Association.
[b]   Frederickson, N. (1984). The real test bias: Influences of testing on teaching and learning. *American Psychologist, 39*(3), 193–202.
[c]   Gardner, H. (1982). *Art, mind and brain: A cognitive approach to creativity.* New York: Basic Books.

try has to defend itself by striking at and destroying the enemy before the enemy attacks it." Students would be asked to identify the assumption from which this person's argument is constructed. In order to analyze the statement, students would have to ask some of the following questions: How extreme is the danger? Does the end (survival) justify the means (a nuclear war)? In everyday language, this kind of analysis is called "critical thinking." Critical thinking allows us to separate fact from opinion and to compare theories so that we can take a position based on logic. Piaget's stage of formal operations involves just this kind of logical thinking.

Level Five: Objective Synthesis

Definition: The educational objective at level five is to learn to synthesize material. This means making something new, bringing ideas together to form a new theory, going beyond what is now known, providing new insights. This is a "tall order" since it means guiding pupils beyond our own level of understanding—to help them create new ideas and outgrow ours!

Assessment: Assessment should be designed to produce new ideas, methods, or procedures. Some obvious examples might be writing an original short story, play, or poem; painting a picture; composing music. In other areas, term papers or essays might be vehicles for synthesis. Unfortunately, it is often difficult to judge whether an essay or term paper is a genuine synthesis, one that is indeed a novel or creative approach to a topic. Creativity itself is a highly subjective matter and very difficult to measure. You might just see whether or not you find yourself saying, "Now, why didn't I think of that?" One of the major rewards of teaching comes when we realize that one of our pupils is breaking new ground, advancing our knowledge.

Level Six: Objective Evaluation

Definition: Level six, the learning of value judgments, involves all the previous levels to some degree. Pupils are developing the ability to create standards of judgment, to weigh, to examine, to analyze, and most of all, to avoid hasty judgment. Evaluation requires a lengthy process of scholarly care, of minute examination.

Assessment: Although it may sound circular, it is possible to evaluate evaluation—there are standards for judging the way others pass judgments. For example, we can judge the performance of an umpire at a baseball game (the fans, managers, and players do so all the time). In the same way we can judge the performance of a trial judge or a labor arbitrator or a newspaper editor. It is possible, but it is also difficult.

The basic principle of assessment at level six, then, consists of developing critical evaluation skills. Essay exams, especially at the college level, often ask for a critique of a particular theory, literary work, or historical interpretation. To do this successfully students need a comprehensive, logical framework as a basis for judgment. In writing such an essay they provide a sequence of reasons extensively spelled out so the reader can follow a train of thought each step of the way to the conclusion. Thus, the judgment cannot remain intuitive. To say that a painting by a master such as Picasso is great because it makes you feel more deeply is not an adequate enough basis for your conclusion. In a critique you must consciously describe the standards you use for such a judgment call.

Table 13.1 summarizes the different Bloom levels and provides examples of questions that best reflect each level.

Taxonomy and Developmental Stages

Although Bloom and his associates did not directly connect their objectives to developmental and Piagetian cognitive stages, there is an implicit relationship. Bloom's levels one, two, and three—basic knowledge and facts, comprehension, and application—are all clearly within the grasp of elementary-age concrete thinkers. When we reach levels four, five, and six, we are moving toward the need for symbolic and logical thinking in Piaget's formal-operations sense. As you read the descriptions of the style of thinking required at these levels, you realize the importance of a careful instructional sequence to promote the growth of abstract thinking. We cannot assume that adolescents are automatically able to use formal operations at Bloom's levels four to six without deliberate teaching that is aimed at this objective.

DAVID HUNT: EDUCATIONAL OBJECTIVES AND DEVELOPMENTAL STAGES

The work of David Hunt represents a more direct connection between educational objectives and developmental stages. Hunt has been able to specify the interaction between the conceptual level of the pupils and the expectations, learning atmospheres, and conceptual level of the teachers. We have stressed throughout this text that a developmental approach to education means that we have to look both ways, so to speak: at the pupils and their levels of development, and at the teachers. Hunt suggests that if it is important to assess the levels of the pupils, it is equally important to assess the levels of the teachers (and as we will note later, the level of the curriculum material itself). Thus, Hunt presents a three-stage framework for educational objectives and instructional strategies.[4]

Conceptual level proceeds through three general stages, characterized as follows:

STAGE A—Low conceptual level: Generally, thinking is concrete and stereotyped. There is a single "right" way to learn. Rules are fixed and unchangeable. Obedience to authority is unquestioned. Problem solving tends to be rigid. Social desirability and pleasing others are strong. Students are anxious for closure and seek highly structured learning activities.

STAGE B—Moderate conceptual level: Students exhibit some evidence of toleration for uncertainty and ambiguity and

TABLE 13.1   BLOOM'S TAXONOMY: KEYING QUESTIONS TO LEVELS

BLOOM LEVEL	QUESTIONS
Level One—Factual knowledge: Questions require factual recall of material.	How much is . . . Who is . . . What is . . . When was . . . How did . . .
Level Two—Comprehension: Questions require the student to think more broadly, to show more in-depth understanding, to explain using his/her own words.	Demonstrate the meaning of . . . Paraphrase, in your own words, . . . Give an example . . . How are these ideas similar to . . . Explain the meaning of (the story, a graph, etc.).
Level Three—Application: Questions ask the student to apply learning to a new situation or to develop a product.	What would happen if . . . Apply the formula to the following problem . . . Teach your friend the meaning of . . . Using your knowledge of angles, build a toothpick tower . . . Using the story as a basis, write . . .
Level Four—Analysis: Questions are designed to ask students to take the material apart and examine the pieces.	How are _____ the same, and how are they different? List the basic assumptions . . . Describe the variety of motives . . . Distinguish between theory and facts . . . Separate the major and minor themes . . .
Level Five—Synthesis: Questions attempt to get the student to go beyond our present knowledge.	Describe the three major theories, and show how they may be combined . . . Write an essay proposing a new solution to the problem of . . . Write a play (paint a picture, do a musical score, construct a formula, etc.) which best illustrates a new way to understand . . .
Level Six—Evaluation: Questions are designed to require the student to evaluate ideas according to an explicit and detailed set of reasons. The system of judgment employed must be clearly explained.	Write a careful critique of _____ theory. Detail the strengths and weaknesses. Justify your conclusion. Evaluate the recent decisions by _____ , according to democratic versus expedient principles. Compare and contrast the approaches to _____ according to the following ethical principles . . . Detail the logical inconsistencies in theory X as an example of an inadequate scientific paradigm.

Young children tend to think concretely.

awareness of alternatives. There is some openness to new ideas, increased independence in thinking (inner-directedness), awareness of emotions, and increased inductive inquiry.

STAGE C—*High conceptual level:* Students exhibit evidence of integration and synthesis both in complex intellectual and interpersonal arenas. They weigh and balance alternatives and can simultaneously process their own view and that of others. Closure is temporary. Students employ successive approximation and principles in decision making, and they will not compromise those. They accept full responsibility for the consequences of their own behavior.

Young children tend to think very concretely (stage A) and need careful and explicit directions. Pupil "growth" proceeds in a developmental sequence from concrete to abstract, from simple to complex, and from being dependent on others toward self-direction. Most impor-

tant, Hunt shows that such developmental growth *does* depend on how the teacher structures the learning experiences. To facilitate the pupils' achieving increased levels of intellectual complexity, teachers need to match the learning tasks with the actual developmental functioning of the pupils. Thus, for stage A pupils, teachers need to provide high structure, explicit assignments, frequent feedback, and consistent and concrete rewards. For stage C pupils, of course, a significantly different environment, characterized by low structure, substantial freedom for pupils to develop their own assignments, less frequent feedback, and more abstract and intrinsic rewards, would be required.

Attribute-Treatment Interaction

The idea of matching teaching goals and methods to pupils' level of development is denoted as the attribute- (or attitude-) treatment interaction (ATI) model. The current system of thinking (a pupil's attribute) interacts with the teaching method (the treatment). The outcome of the experience, then, does not result from one or the other by itself. In a sense what this means is that no generic teaching methods can be applied across the board. Some pupils learn more material and develop positive attitudes with one particular method while other pupils do better with a different method. In this model teaching is not a one-way transaction nor is learning. This also explains why a teacher-proof or pupil-proof curriculum is impossible. The experiments with specified national curricula content and method in the 1960s showed the inadequacy of the single-mode approach. On the other hand, where attribute and treatment meet and match, the interaction determines the end result.

To illustrate the different effects of a learning environment and pupils' conceptual level (CL), Hunt demonstrated some aspects of variation.[5] Figures 13.1 and 13.2 indicate that learning outcomes vary, especially for the low-CL pupils. Both figures show that stage A pupils understand learning material in significantly greater amounts when teachers employ advance organizers and the rule-example-rule sequence. The stage C pupils, on the other hand, learn best under methods using low structure (examples only) and discovery. They also comprehend under high structure, but composite concept learning declines under the rule-example-rule sequence. Also, and this doesn't show in either of the figures, the stage C pupils are less motivated under either condition of high structure. Thus, according to Hunt, the teacher employs variable structure to achieve significant educational objectives. He uses the phrase "accessibility channels" to denote the meaning of developmental stages. The teacher tunes up the material and method in accordance with the different channels the pupils prefer to use.

In everyday terms you can think of this as "different strokes for different folks." Some students need a great deal of structure, concrete

FIGURE 13.1   Comprehension of academic content.

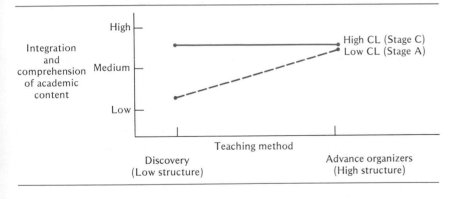

FIGURE 13.2   Composite concept learning.

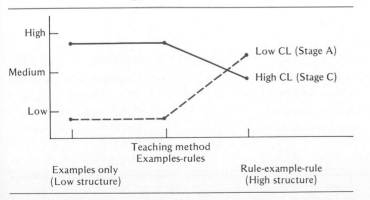

directions, immediate feedback, and so on; others don't.[6] Table 13.2 summarizes some of the main differences according to the stage of development of the pupil. With pupils at the concrete level of cognitive functioning (low conceptual level), a systematic sequence carefully directed by the teacher is appropriate. With pupils at a less concrete and more abstract level, a more interdependent approach is appropriate.

As you might guess, ATI is an idea that has been around a long time. In fact, when it was first proposed by Hunt, the early research summaries seemed to indicate that the idea itself was found wanting.[7] The research base was thin. However, more recent research, especially that of Penelope Peterson and her associates at the University of Wisconsin, has provided a solid basis for Hunt's earlier view. What Peterson found in a number of classroom investigations is a definite trend of interaction between pupil characteristics (such as different levels of ability, levels of anxiety, and attitude) and teaching method.[8] She also found an interaction between pupil attributes and the kind of examination employed.

Thus, the whole approach to teaching effectiveness and educational goals needs to include the concept of ATI. A single approach to teaching is obviously not justified. For pupils of high ability, low anxiety, and positive attitudes, an approach more consistent with small-group instruction, open-ended questioning, and greater student initiative is called for. The opposite is true for those of lower ability, greater anxiety, and less positive attitudes. Such pupils much prefer a more highly structured and teacher-directed method. Peterson's research does support the general ATI model. The work, however, did not explicitly employ Hunt's conceptual stage assessment of pupils' attributes or characteristics.

The most comprehensive review specifically of the Hunt model was conducted by Alan Miller.[9] He examined, as did Peterson, different teaching methods, particularly variation in levels of structure, as the "treatment." His measure of aptitude, however, was a direct assessment of the students' stage of conceptual development; thus, his summary provides more direct support for the ATI theory. Basically, his conclusions are similar to Peterson's. Pupils who process information and experience at a more advanced conceptual level prefer greater involvement in learning, more exploratory "indirect" teaching, and participation in discussions; they can resist premature closure (or coming to a conclusion) in problem solving. However, such an open-ended or low-structured approach does not foster learning with pupils who are at a less advanced conceptual level.[10] This overall conclusion is not "all there is to know" about teaching. The ATI theory also forces educators to take a closer look at what we mean by "matching."

TABLE 13.2   DIFFERENTIATION OF STRUCTURE

FACTORS	HIGH STRUCTURE	LOW STRUCTURE
Concepts	Concrete	Abstract
Time span	Short	Long
Time on task	Multiple practice	Single practice
Advance organizers	Multiple use of organizers	Few if any advance organizers
Complexity of learning tasks	Learning tasks divided into small steps and recycled	Learning tasks clustered into "wholes"
Theory	Concretely matched with experiential examples	Generalized, including collaborative classroom research
Instructor support	Consistent and frequent	Occasional

Matching or Mismatching: The Art of Teaching

As we indicated in the opening chapter, the goals of education almost always include a reference to enhancing human development. Indeed, a developmental view clearly suggests growth as an outcome. If we view the ATI model from this perspective, then an immediate question arises. Suppose we match teaching methods to the pupils' conceptual level and the short-term outcome is improved academic achievement and positive attitudes. Does this aid the process of growth? Or does such a match keep a pupil in place, so to speak? Particularly for students who enter your class with low CL styles, wouldn't the continued use of a high-structured approach rob them of initiative? Wouldn't there also be times when even students with high CLs would need a more directive approach? In answering such questions, there are two important points to keep in mind: how CL is defined and how growth can be encouraged.

The initial preferred style   In the first place CL refers to the *current preferred style of learning*; it is not a permanent classification. In Chapter 5 we indicated that Piaget described learning as a process of equilibrium, balancing the old (assimilation) and the new (accommodation). At any stage of development, we use a relatively coherent system to maintain consistency, or a steady state of equilibrium. Even when "knowledge disturbances" occur (recall the boy who was trying to reconcile his idea of church with a building that looked like a house), we try to maintain our present system. This is what we mean by a preferred method. We are used to thinking and problem solving in particular modes. These modes work best when matched with appropriate learning environments. To match the pupil's preferred style, then, is another way to say, "Start where the learner is." This also means starting with and accepting the pupils' current methods of problem solving—starting with how they think, not what they think. Hence, the first rule from ATI is to match, or start teaching in concert with, the pupils' level of development.

Graduated mismatching   The second principle is to begin to mismatch—gradually shift to a slightly more complex level of teaching in order to help the student develop. Recall that students have a potential or an intrinsic drive to learn, as Robert W. White and others have shown us. However, they will not shift quickly or suddenly to higher levels of conceptual development. Remember how long it took the boy to accommodate to the new concept of church, and that was a relatively simple "new" learning. You need to be prepared to present and review new material in a recycled manner, listening carefully to your students' questions. In this way you will understand who is "getting it" (accommodating to the new material and methods) and who needs further experience at his or her present level.

Another way to view the problem of matching and then mismatching is to recall information from Chapter 7, Kohlberg's research on "plus one." In moral-dilemma discussions, leaders found that under relaxed conditions (a nonpunitive atmosphere) pupils would gradually understand and support reasoning just slightly ahead of their current preferred mode. The slightly higher level of complexity creates a kind of knowledge disturbance, or dissonance. In resolving the dissonance the pupils end up with a more complex level of thinking; in other words, they experience developmental growth. So we can answer the first part of the earlier question: In dealing with pupils whose current conceptual levels and styles are low, the teaching strategy is to match the low level with high structure and very gradually shift. What about other students, those further along? Do we just stick with the low-structure approach? Not quite—and we'll describe why.

Two qualifications   Certainly, the general rule with students who function at more complex levels would be to use less structure, more participation, more discovery, and so on. However, there are two important qualifications. First, development varies according to domain. A particular student may be an advanced thinker/reasoner in one area, yet not in another. When we discussed Piaget's stages of cognitive growth, we cited examples of adults not always

CONTEMPORARY ISSUE

Gifted Development: What's the Price?

One of the continuing unanswered questions in education concerns gifted development: How far do we push and at what cost? Throughout history we have all read biographies featuring prodigious achievement, often at a very early age. Every four years the entire nation watches our Olympic athletes excel. We gasp in awe when we learn of some of their ages. We often hear in the interviews male teen-age voices still in the process of maturing, and in some cases, especially in female gymnasts, see female bodies at the developmental level of junior high school. So too in other domains, we read about a teenage chess "phenom" who can match the masters or a teen-age math whiz who discovers testing errors committed by a national assessment service. We then wonder about the process of development on the one hand and the process of education on the other. Are these "special" people who would have achieved no matter what, or are they ordinary people who have been "specially" educated? Once again, we face the nature-nurture question but in a slightly different form.

To discover answers Benjamin Bloom, as he has done before in so many other areas, assembled a research team and did an intensive investigation of over a hun-

dred subjects. They preselected their subjects in a way to ensure the inclusion of enormously talented young persons from a wide variety of fields such as music, art, science, athletics, and research. All subjects had achieved national and/or international eminence prior to age thirty-five. The subjects were selected to represent outstanding performances in one of three areas: psychomotor, aesthetic, or cognitive. They originally posed a fourth area, interpersonal relations, but dropped it because of the difficulty of defining objective criteria.

Their major findings indicate that a series of coordinated factors were quite similar across the domains. At the outset, as the child exhibited some unique achievements, parents provided careful and consistent encouragement. Some early chance factors also pointed the child toward a specific area—the team needed an extra swimmer, a local violin teacher was available at low cost, the child had an unusually gifted elementary-school teacher. After the initial period, chance factors faded almost completely. From then on, the secret to Olympic performance on the field, the stage, or the classroom was the same. In the words of a TV commercial, "They made it the old-fashioned way. They earned it." In fact, the case

reports are all similar: long hours of practice with a carefully selected mentor. Local coaches and/ or teachers were no longer involved. Some families moved to new areas to provide their child with special teachers. Others willingly purchased expensive special equipment. Although the training was a cooperative effort of the child and the mentor, often the entire family and in some cases neighborhoods were involved as positive supporting elements. At this point the third crucial element appeared, the evaluation by the mentor.

Bloom's group found that eminent performance could not be predicted up through early adolescence. The early and middle years are certainly important, but it was the later years (adolescence and early adulthood) that made the difference. During those years the individual's life became almost totally consumed with the special activity and the relationship with the mentor. The mentors were in many cases products of a similar upbringing. This meant they evaluated harshly. They would not continue working with a person unless they were convinced that he or she really had both talent and commitment. Their standards were indeed Olympian and their work requirements Herculean. If the person did not show signs of

thinking like adults. An advanced thinker in history or agronomy may be at a more concrete level in statistics, art, and music. Variations also exist within any subject matter. In psychology some students may quickly understand a variety of theories of personality at an abstract level yet have problems understanding, say, physiological or experimental psychology. So even

with so-called more advanced students, you may have to deviate from the general rule of low structure in your teaching because of systematic gaps in students' understanding of different subjects as well as different topics within one subject. When you discover such gaps, it's a sign to shift the teaching to higher structure and more direct instruction.

international giftedness, he or she was dropped. Those that did show such talent were worked even harder. Such is the picture of *Developing Talent in Young People.*[a]

This study, of course, raises a number of interesting questions. First, it is clear that so intensive an approach is appropriate for only a tiny fraction of the nation's youth. In fact, Bloom's general rule was only one special child in each family. Genes have an influence, but even within a single family there would be only one with world-class potential. Also given the amount of family time and effort, there might not be sufficient "nurture" for a second or third prodigy.[b] Thus, it is clear this approach isn't a model for general development. Parents and educators must be careful not to generalize. These young people are by definition extremely rare. Most of us will never encounter such children. A second issue, however, is even more provocative: What happens to those who don't quite make it?

No study can answer all questions, and Bloom's group did not have a second and/or control group consisting of those who went through parallel experiences yet didn't quite measure up, or who momentarily made it, then burned out or flamed out. Thus, we can't assess the potential psychological costs of such intensive education. Basically, we can only talk to the winners, the medalists, the summas. Did they survive while others, almost as good, fell into despair and felt a major sense of time wasted, other opportunities missed, or other roads not taken? We simply can't say. We read media accounts of such fallen idols or near-misses that raise questions as to the psychological expense of intensive education. In fact, just recently an international tennis association was considering the effects of tennis burnout on teen-age stars. Both Tracy Austin and Andrea Jaeger were cited as examples of the negative physical consequences of intensive training during the growth years. The po-

tential for psychological scars is at least as great; they just don't show from the outside.

The overall question, then, is not with training and/or development but with goals and objectives. The paradox is the eternal one of benefits versus costs. Any nation needs gifted humans. We need the new knowledge, the new techniques, the new performances that are unique to such special children. Until we understand the other side more fully, however, we must be careful not to promote a new fad, a shift from excessive "infant stimulation" to excessive "adolescent stretching."

---

a   Bloom, B. S. (1985). *Developing talent in young people.* New York: Random House.
b   In educational literature this is sometimes referred to as the "Matthew effect": "Unto everyone that hath shall be given and he shall have abundance." Of course, this may not be entirely fair to the gospel writer since he also wrote, "Many that are first shall be last; and the last first."

The second qualification has to do with pupil anxiety. Under stress, many students will lower their preferred style of solving problems. This is certainly understandable when we realize that when stress is too high, humans tend to narrow their perceptual field; that is, they screen out more and more information and experience. An extreme example is the story of a victim being quizzed by detectives immediately following an armed robbery. "All I saw was the barrel of the gun pointed at my face," he said when asked to describe the assailant. Of course, a classroom should never be quite that stressful. Yet in introducing new material and/or new learning strategies, pupils can be quite anxious. In specific cases, such as students who face excessive parental pressure for achievement, the anxiety level may be even higher. Under such conditions it is highly appropriate to shift modes and provide more advance organizers, more explicit directions, and quicker feedback.

One final point on anxiety: Remember that during specific developmental transitions, anxiety also can be quite high. In other words, changes taking place within the pupil can be as anxiety producing as any changes you make in the teaching material and problem-solving work. In discussing Erik Erikson's work (Chapter 6), we noted particular psychological/personal milestones of development. During each of these transition stages of personal growth, anxiety tends to be higher than usual. The most obvious example is puberty, accompanied by egocentrism, the personal fable, and the magical audience. Yet starting the first grade, leaving home, and shifting to the stage of mastery is also an important transition with its own anxieties, the "little worries" common to children. Certainly the same is true for entrance to high school and to college. Resorting to a more structured approach to teaching at such times is simply another way to start where the learner is. You will soon be able to move to a more open-ended approach, especially with secondary students, as the anxiety from the personal transition subsides and the teen-ager becomes accommodated more adequately to the new level of psychological maturity.

To summarize, then, the general rule of using an open-ended approach with abstract thinkers has some important qualifications: (1) There is variation across and within academic subject matter. Pupils may not excel in all areas. (2) Pupils may experience high levels of anxiety when confronted with new material and/or when going through transitions in personal growth. In any of these situations, switching to higher structure in teaching will not impede pupil growth. You need not worry that you are robbing students of their chance for initiative by more adequately matching your method to a lowered ability. Instead, you are more likely to find that students experience a sense of relief. They can get back on the learning track and then resume their growth toward a more complex mode.

In an overall sense, then, the ATI model, by suggesting flexibility in teaching mode, helps you avoid two kinds of educational failures. First, you avoid the prospect of boring the students with a single "tried and true" teaching method. Second, you avoid the problem of either overmatching or undermatching. Overmatching is teaching at a level well beyond the pupils' current preferred mode, such as expecting fourth-grade children to understand the symbolic meaning of Ahab and the white whale from *Moby Dick* or succumbing to the current fad of "infant stimulation" with flash cards for six-month-old babies. Undermatching, on the other hand, presents not "plus one" but "minus one" material to students: ideas and problems they already know and techniques that require "old" learning methods. Asking adolescents to memorize long lists of material when they should be learning to draw inferences is an example of undermatching. With either over-

matching or undermatching, growth is not an outcome. Effective teaching from an ATI perspective requires a quite different approach, one that is more responsive to pupil needs and is more likely to nurture their growth and achieve the general educational goals of Bloom's taxonomy.

LESSON PLANNING: THE VEHICLE FOR EDUCATIONAL GOALS

So far in this chapter we have been stressing the need for a careful analysis of pupils' conceptual level as a basis for selecting particular modes or models of teaching. We have focused on the interaction between how you teach as a process and how the students make meaning from your strategies. There is, in addition to this ATI, another important part of teaching—namely, lesson planning. Sometimes it is best to think of planning lessons as similar to drawing a road map. The purpose of the plan is to provide you with a sequence of routes or steps to follow as you teach the material. Naturally, there is no single best way to organize a lesson or unit in a plan. Research and practice have shown, however, that some basic steps are effective. These fundamental components of a good plan are based on the work of Madeline Hunter.

Hunter's Seven Steps

Using a metaphor from cooking, Hunter has outlined seven basic components of a plan. She calls this a "basic white sauce of teaching."[11] Her point is that teaching, like good cooking, is built on some fundamentals. (A culinary artist such as TV's Julia Child still uses white sauce as a starter.) After years of observing classroom instruction, Hunter denoted the following as her white sauce of lesson planning.[12]

Step one: Anticipatory set   The first step is to increase the students' interest in and motivation to learn the material. It's an attempt to get the students to "lean toward" you with an orienting question. For example, in a high-school unit on social studies, the teacher might say, "Today's topic will focus on the question of what the

American Indians experienced during Manifest Destiny. Why do many Indians regard Thanksgiving as a national day of shame?"

Creating an anticipatory set does not mean spending large amounts of time setting the students up, so to speak. Rather, Hunter suggests a relatively brief yet somewhat provocative beginning to gain attention. Even relatively "dry" subjects can be introduced in a manner designed to nurture interest. A professor of geology introduces a lesson on conservation by showing a slide of a toilet and asks, "How much water do we use with each flush?" A philosophy teacher turns out the lights, points to the shadows with a flashlight, and asks: "What do you think this has to do with Plato and the analogy of the cave?"

Step two: Objective and purpose   The initial rhetorical question sets the stage. The teacher now moves to tell students what the point of the unit is and why it's important.[13] This is particularly necessary for concrete thinkers, those at low to moderate conceptual levels. Surprising as it may seem, discussions with pupils at the end of a class often reveal rather poignantly that they completely missed the point of the lesson. Presenting the objective is no guarantee of comprehension. Hunter says, however, that you will increase the probability by being quite explicit in spelling out the goals. Thus, the teacher who raised the American Indian question might then explain, "The goal is to help you understand how differently a group of people in a country may interpret the meaning of a historical event. Most of us have been brought up to understand that Thanksgiving is a national holiday celebrating. . . ."

In the case of our other examples, similar goal statements would be made to give students an idea of where the class is headed. After all, almost any material can be introduced with a wide variety of possible outcomes. Students are not particularly adept in reading your mind. Hunter says you can reduce the ambiguity by describing the goals.

Step three: Input   Essentially, this is where you select and apply your specific teaching strategy. It could be a lecture (Model One), a small-group discovery (Model Two), an inter-personal discussion (Model Three), or a blend of direct and indirect methods. Teachers have often misinterpreted Hunter on this point and felt that they must use a direct model. Such is not the case. In fact, you need to decide (your best guess) which of a variety of models best suits the particular day, the material, and other available resources, including student presentations of information, filmstrips, video material, overheads, and even the blackboard. The idea is to select an input method that is keyed to the outcomes noted in step two. Thus, if your goal is to help students understand historical events from the Indians' point of view, you would not have them memorize long lists of tribes.

Once again it may seem obvious, but Hunter did find that one of the most common errors in teaching was the failure to link input with teaching objectives. In fact, you may experience exactly this problem in some college classes. The lectures and readings cover material not related to the examination questions. Such an approach makes learning difficult, no matter at what conceptual level you may be.

Step four: Modeling   This is a most easily misunderstood term. Modeling means more than just going through the motions. Years ago a famous baseball player tried to "model" batting by standing in front of children and swinging his bat. He had spent some five years practicing (before a mirror), carefully adjusting his swing, coordinating eyes, arms, hands, wrists, hips, feet, body, balance, stance—probably over fifty separate variables. He modeled the final product, a poetic *Gestalt*. The children, of course, hadn't a clue as to the process. Some saw his head, others his feet, still others his fingers, and some were just in awe of the uniform itself. Such demonstrations are not what Hunter means by modeling. Instead, think of modeling as a demonstration accompanied by verbal description of what you want the students to do. Sometimes, for example, if the students are to work in small groups, you set a small group up in a "fish bowl" for a brief demonstration. If you want students to look up Latin roots in a dictionary, you might put a dictionary entry on an overhead and talk through the process. The point of modeling is

CONTEMPORARY ISSUE

Testing the Teachers: Fact or Fantasy?

Supposedly the great Russian purge during the Stalin era finally ended when the head of the secret police was accused of disloyalty. At that point it seemed to all that the movement to cleanse the bureaucracy had gone too far. Are we reaching the same point in regard to the massive national interest in improving the quality of classroom instruction by administering standardized testing to the teachers themselves? Will standardized test scores, which are commonly used to sort pupils into acceptable and unacceptable admission categories, now become a criterion for the teachers?

The movement to "test the teachers" seems to be in full swing. Many states are enacting legislation setting cut-off scores for those seeking entry into the teaching profession. No longer are grades in college and successful performance in student teaching sufficient. Nor does the push for testing stop with induction. Another movement seeks to require even experienced teachers to pass

standardized tests. Thus, a teacher may have a master's degree in education and a number of years of successful teaching, including perhaps numerous citations as teacher of the year and accolades from pupils, parents, colleagues, and principals; even that teacher would be required to pass a standard exam. In fact, one state, Texas, has already passed such a law. All teachers, regardless of credentials, had to take and pass an exam in order to continue in the teaching profession. Is this a misuse of testing? Will such tests identify the incompetent? Will the profession be cleansed? Will the children benefit? The current interest in testing teachers raises these fundamental questions.

James D. Raths and his colleague Marlean Pugach at the Center for Instructional Research and Curriculum Evaluation at the University of Illinois, Urbana, have examined the testing issues very carefully and have come to some startling conclusions.[a] Their review raises major doubts about

the validity of the tests themselves. As surprising as it may seem, they fault the tests on a series of fundamental theoretical and empirical grounds:

1. The standardized teacher tests do not measure teaching effectiveness. There is no evidence that higher scores predict high levels of performance.
2. There is no evidence that the cut-off scores actually separate those who can teach effectively from those who cannot. The cut-off score is an arbitrary criterion.

We have, then, a basic challenge to the idea of testing as a method of raising standards. Nationally standardized exams do not predict actual teacher competency in the classroom. Nor should such an outcome be surprising. Effective teaching, as we have shown, is a highly complex set of interactions among four interrelated domains—teacher,

---

to ensure that the students employ the process in a manner that facilitates their understanding of the input.

Step five: Checking for understanding Hunter makes it clear that effective planning of lessons is interactive. Thus, some time should be set aside for questions to check student understanding. Every once in a while a teacher is absolutely floored when the questions reveal how far off-task a particular student is. Charles Schulz in the Peanuts strip has almost turned Peppermint Patty into a folk heroine in how to misunderstand a teacher's lesson. On a more serious note, not all students are as brave as

Peppermint Patty. Most will not ask what may appear to be a "dumb" question. Your role is to maintain a class atmosphere supportive enough to encourage students who aren't sure to ask for help.

Step six: Guided practice   By this Hunter means that the students "do" the activity under your direct supervision. Guided practice precedes the last step, independent practice. Before you move to independent practice, either in class or as homework assignments, you should have the students perform some of the task and show you their products. Suppose, for example, you are teaching a grammar unit on the period.

pupils, methods, and content. Answering multiple choice questions *about* teaching is clearly a light year away from knowing *how to* teach. It would be the same as assuming that knowledge about baseball would predict effectiveness at the plate or on the mound, that knowing about art would lead to great paintings, that understanding music would ensure success as a composer. If we go back to Bloom's taxonomy, we will have a further understanding of the problem. Effective teaching requires at least level three and higher, while the standardized tests measure only level one or two at best. Thus, such tests cannot possibly measure the ability to interact effectively with pupils, to "read and flex," to match and mismatch, and to select the appropriate model during the process.

Probably the most unfortunate outcome, according to Raths and Pugach, is that the test score is interpreted as if it were a valid indicator. Thus, the public believes the myth, as do state legislators. Such groups believe that if we set a high standard for the test score, we will cleanse the profession and the pupils will be protected. Instead, all we may do is drive out potentially effective teachers during the induction phase and terminate the careers of teachers already practicing.[b]

This is not to say, however, that Raths and Pugach favor an open-entry, a social-promotion, or a laissez-faire approach to teacher education. Instead, they propose a strengthening of genuine admission standards, careful monitoring of performance in college, rigorous supervision of student teaching, and an enhanced method of on-the-job selection and evaluation of actual performance. They are pointed in their criticism of some schools of education that do not enforce such rigorous standards. They note that too often teachers in training may be passed through the system. In one study 97 percent of student teachers in thirty-four programs received either A's or B's in student teaching. In another study 995 of 1,000 provisionally certified teachers were approved for full certification. Such rates do raise questions in the minds of all those concerned about the quality of teacher education. The real solution in their view is to adopt rigorous ongoing evaluation throughout the phases of teacher training. Raising test scores may seem like a solution, but it will help neither the quality of the teaching profession nor the pupils. The profession, however, must clean up its own act or the testing movement will gain further momentum and an excessive purge will be underway.

[a] Pugach, M. C., and Raths, J. D. (1983). Testing teachers: Analysis and recommendations. *Journal of Teacher Education, 34*(1), 37–43.
[b] See also Darling-Hammond, L. (1984). *Beyond the commission reports: The Rand Corporation Report #R-3177RC.* The author makes the point that standardized testing leads to standardized teaching, reducing teaching to a robotlike activity, enforcing procedural conformity, and elevating aspects of teaching that are most easily measured and (presumably) most superficial. The result is that standardized practice becomes professional malpractice.

Have the students practice writing a paragraph and then compare their work to an overhead with the correct punctuation. The idea is simply to prevent too many errors from occurring before you set them free to work on their own. It is clearly easier to correct errors early than to allow a student to do an entire assignment incorrectly. Unlearning bad habits is always more difficult than learning the correct procedure at the outset.

Step seven: Independent practice   The final step, either as seatwork or homework, occurs when students work on the material alone or in small groups without your direct supervision. This is basically a test of the first six steps. If the process has been successful, then you will see evidence from the student products that they have learned the material. Remember that the outcome of this independent practice can be keyed to any level on the taxonomy from basic knowledge to synthesis and/or evaluation. You start by keying the outcomes of independent practice to students' current level of functioning, then gradually increase the level of complexity. Such building on success encourages and motivates students each step of the way.

A final point on Hunter: The seven steps are the fundamentals. She says you need to think about each as you develop your plan. This does not mean every unit must follow every step every time. After reflection you may decide to skip or combine or modify. The plan is a guide, not an invariant routine. However, as you vary the elements, keep in mind the need to assess the quality of the independent practice and the level of your objectives. If all or even some students do not seem to learn, then revise the plan. Do not leap to the conclusion that the students are at fault. More likely the fault lies in how the plan has been implemented. In fact, Hunter estimates that only 50 percent of the children in an ordinary classroom can follow through on assignments without the steps of checking and guided practice.

As in other aspects of teaching, there are basic principles to follow as well as times to be flexible and depart from a plan. Watch the outcomes carefully as a basis for recycling or even adding to any of the steps you may have disregarded. Then the plan will become a more adequate teaching vehicle to achieve your objectives. Flexibility in implementing a lesson plan does not mean flying by the seat of one's pants, despite its intuitive appeal to our sense of creativity. Nor does a lesson plan have to become the opposite, a deadly, routine, "paint by numbers" approach. Our view is that learning outcomes and educational objectives can be achieved through the use of a modifiable sequence of lesson-planning steps.

In the previous chapter we outlined much of the recent research on specific teaching strategies that help increase academic learning time. The lesson-planning approach combined with information on pupils' conceptual level add further components that can help reach this goal. Time on task just does not happen automatically. Nor is the subject matter itself, no matter how intrinsically interesting, enough to maintain on-task behavior. You must guide the process each step of the way. Since the overall goal is to increase the student's independence as a learner, lesson planning is a means toward the goal of helping students learn to think for themselves. Such planning, then, helps liberate pupils rather than enhancing their dependence.

SUMMARY

Objectives remain a topic of interest to educational psychologists. The spoof *The Saber-Tooth Curriculum* continues the debate about general education versus skill-based education that has been with us for centuries. Focusing on Bloom's taxonomy, we attempted to show how his classification system could be most useful in the selection of educational goals at different levels.

Hunt's scheme illustrates the different levels and modes of thinking that school students typically employ. Through his framework of ATI, Hunt tries to bridge the gap between teaching strategies you may use and the preferred learning strategies (CL stages) that the pupils employ. By attributes Hunt means the characteristic learning style of the pupil. By treatment he means the instructional method. Whether learning really takes place will depend on the interaction between the two. He further specifies that such interaction can follow a mode of "matching"—a strategy that fits the learner's current mode—followed by graduated "mismatching"—teaching at a level just beyond the current mode. There are some important qualifications, however, for using a highly structured strategy even for students who generally function at higher conceptual levels.

Besides paying attention to the interaction between teaching style and student modes of learning, teachers must learn how to effectively organize their material through lesson planning. Hunter has suggested a system for lesson planning that can and should be keyed to learning outcomes. By following the steps she outlines, teachers can reduce the likelihood that students will misunderstand either the point of the unit or the learning activities expected of them. By preventing students from going down the wrong road, they can thus increase the amount of academic or on-task learning time.

KEY TERMS AND NAMES

saber-tooth curriculum
David Hunt
   conceptual level
   attribute-treatment interaction (ATI)
Penelope Peterson

Alan Miller
matching and mismatching
preferred style of learning
Madeline Hunter

REFERENCES

1. Peddiwell, J. A. (1939). *The saber-tooth curriculum.* New York: McGraw-Hill.

2. Tyler, R. (1933). Permanence of learning. *Journal of Higher Education, 4,* 203–204.

3. Bloom, B. (Ed.). (1956). *Taxonomy of educational objectives, Handbook 1: Cognitive domain.* New York: McKay.

4. Hunt, D. E. (1974). *Matching models in education.* Toronto: Ontario Institute for Studies in Education.

5. Hunt, *Matching models,* p. 46.

6. Hunt, D. E. (1981). Teachers' adaptation: Reading and flexing to students. In B. Joyce, C. Brown, and L. Peck (Eds.), *Flexibility in teaching* (pp. 59–71). New York: Longman.

7. Cronbach, L., and Snow, R. (1977). *Aptitudes and instructional methods.* New York: Irvington Press.

8. Peterson, P., Janicki, T., and Swing, S. (1980). Aptitude-treatment interaction effects of three social studies teaching approaches. *American Educational Research Journal, 17*(3), 339–360. See also Levin, J., and Peterson, P. (1984). Classroom aptitude by treatment interactions: An alternate analysis strategy. *Educational Psychologist, 19*(1), 43–47.

9. Miller, A. (1981). Conceptual matching models and interactional research in education. *Review of Education Research, 51*(1), 33–85.

10. See also Widick, C., and Simpson, D. (1978). Developmental concepts in college instruction. In C. Parker (Ed.), *Encouraging development in college students.* Minneapolis: University of Minnesota Press. At the college level Widick and Simpson demonstrated the importance of varying the structure according to cognitive-developmental level. Concrete "dualist" college students required all the elements outlined in the chart. Students operating on a more abstract level benefited from open-ended inquiry.

11. Hunter, M. (1984). Knowing, teaching and supervising. In P. L. Hosford (Ed.), *Using what we know about teaching* (p. 175). Alexandria, Va.: Association of Supervision and Curriculum Development.

12. Hunter, Knowing, teaching and supervising (pp. 162–192).

13. See also Gronlund, N. (1985). *Stating objectives for classroom instruction.* New York: Macmillan. This is an excellent approach to the problem of how to state objectives.

14

TEACHING: THE PERSONAL DIMENSION

Thus far in our discussion of teaching effectiveness, we have focused on teaching from the standpoint of strategies, objectives, characteristics of students, and planning. We now shift to the teacher as a person. How do you as an individual understand yourself in the teaching role? That is the basic question—a quite broad one, encompassing your attitudes toward yourself, the subject matter you are teaching, and finally your students. These three dimensions of knowing yourself make up the core material in this chapter. Without question, the person of the teacher exerts a telling influence on the classroom. You make the rules, you translate the material, you organize the schedules—in short, you orchestrate the class. One writer put it rather starkly: The teacher is boss, never the student. Such an observation is clear from the first day. Even a first-grade student recognizes that "an absent teacher requires a substitute, an absent student doesn't."[1]

Whether the teacher's influence is positive or negative in orchestrating the class is the topic of significance. Quite obviously, how you think and feel about teaching, the material, and the pupils sets an atmosphere or climate. Since your attitudes and perceptions do exert considerable influence, even though it may be subtle, it is important to examine them. The early Greek philosophers knew the significance of self-knowledge. To know oneself as a teacher, then, represents a key sensitivity and necessary awareness.

THE TEACHER AS A PERSON: THE ELUSIVE QUESTION

One of the most elusive questions in education is what human qualities make an effective teacher. One longstanding myth is that teachers should manifest all the noble virtues and have no human frailties. Like Caesar's wife the teacher should be beyond reproach. For example, a teacher's contract in North Carolina in the 1930s specified the following personal requirements:

I promise to abstain from all dancing, immodest dressing, and any other conduct unbecoming a teacher and a lady.

335

I promise not to go out with any young man except insofar as it may be necessary to stimulate Sunday School work.

I promise not to fall in love, to become engaged or secretly married.

I promise to remain in the dormitory or on the school grounds when not actively engaged in school or church work elsewhere.[2]

Sounds a bit like an acceptance speech at a national political convention. The problem is that no human can possibly live up to the myth. Even worse, teachers soon realize the impossibility of such a goal but have to keep busy preventing other people from finding out. A more realistic perception of the teacher would dispense with both the myth of human virtues (all teachers love all children all of the time) and the assumption that teachers are not responsible for the failure of children to learn.

What Is Teaching Really Like?

A number of popular accounts have recently presented both the humorous and the tragic aspects of what it is really like to teach. Bel Kaufman's *Up the Down Staircase*,[3] Jonathan Kozol's *Death at an Early Age*,[4] and Kevin Ryan's

Don't Smile 'til Christmas[5] and *Biting the Apple*[6] are some first-person accounts that reveal the disparity between the myth and the reality of school, depicting harried teachers trying to live up to some idealized version of patience, love, and total responsiveness, all of the time, every day. Such teachers are like overpermissive parents who try to fulfill the perfect mother or father ideal by withholding all genuine feelings ("Don't smile 'til Christmas!") and finally "boil over," screaming out and hitting their children. Teachers are no better than parents at holding in their genuine feelings. Some incident inevitably opens the floodgate, and all the pent-up anger and personal disappointment break loose. The class learns just what it had suspected all along and may, in fact, have been testing: The teacher was putting on an act of always being "nice."

Unfortunately, the teacher usually feels guilty about having lost control and therefore never realizes the true nature of the problem: It is the impossibility of living up to the myth that sets the entire process in motion. Instead of developing more realistic perceptions of teaching and learning, teachers who have tried and failed often adopt a set of attitudes that justify and rationalize their failures. "Pearls before swine" becomes their bitter motto.

The teacher: A model of perfection or a human being?

TEACHER ATTITUDES AND TEACHING

The Hidden Agenda

One of the most important—and discouraging—findings from recent research is the extent to which teachers' true feelngs about children (as opposed to their idealized version) affect their ability to be effective educators.

We need to realize that our attitudes are not always clearly known to us. Because we develop our attitudes slowly over a long period of time, we are often not conscious of what they are nor of how our attitudes and expectations influence our behavior. This is why we can say one thing and do another. We may pay lip service to one set of goals, yet a careful examination of how we act may reveal a completely different set. This discrepancy has been called the hidden agenda or the implicit curriculum of teaching.

The hidden agenda has special significance for the teacher. We have to be honest with ourselves in determining how much we act without consciousness. As teachers, our own attitudes toward learning will determine the conditions we create for learning in the classroom. For example, if we feel that learning requires that there be no ambiguity, that the "right" answers be presented, and that the pupils know exactly what to say, you can imagine what sort of classroom environment we would provide. Our attitude would affect the way the desks would be arranged, the books and readings we would use, and the way we would manage the discussion time. And this environment would have a very definite influence on the pupils' learning "set." In other words, we affect the attitudes the pupils themselves develop toward learning. There is truth to the old saying "Actions speak louder than words"; our attitudes, motives, and perceptions influence the way we act, and they are transmitted to our pupils through our actions, thereby affecting their attitudinal development.

The Medium and the Message

Marshall McLuhan has suggested one of the ways our attitudes influence our communications.[7] McLuhan's famous phrase "the medium

"Oh, my teacher and I communicate, all right . . . she looks at me in a certain way and I understand what I'd better do!"

is the message" expresses the idea that the verbal content of a message is interpreted, or given its true meaning, by the way it is delivered.

Our view is less extreme: Content is important, yet we do wish to emphasize the importance of the way messages are transmitted. We have all had the experience of being put down by someone. It isn't so much what that other person says but the way it is said (the medium). The real message lies in the person's tone, inflection, facial expression, demeanor. It is the nonverbal visual and auditory cues that deliver the real message. A poor attitude in the classroom is reflected in a bad medium, which in turn creates an atmosphere in which learning and growth cannot take place.

Teachers' attitudes can be grouped into three related categories: attitudes toward teaching and learning, attitudes toward pupils, and attitudes toward self.

ATTITUDES TOWARD TEACHING AND LEARNING

We have often mentioned that the way teachers perceive teaching and learning is crucial. Is "knowledge" a finite list of facts for students to memorize? Do we tend to encourage "correct answers" and focus on outcome, or do we consider the process of learning important? Do we consider teaching to be more like training, so that we "tell" pupils what to do? There are widely divergent assumptions about teaching and learning, and our own attitudes and the way we actually behave in class are molded by those assumptions.

If we had to single out one major attitude that pervades schools, it would be the cherished belief that knowledge equals truth. Teachers and pupils tend to believe that there is an answer for every question, that the truth is known, and that the teacher's voice is like the voice of God. In Chapter 1 we discussed classroom trivia, a form of rapid-fire question-and-answer interaction. Obviously, this kind of teaching reinforces the concept of knowledge as truth and puts the teacher in charge of deciding whether the pupil is "right." The teacher is the center of the classroom, the decision maker. "That's absolutely correct" means a bull's-eye. "That's almost right" means a near-miss. A scowl ("teachers' dirty looks") means the student was completely and absolutely wrong.

This view of knowledge as truth also has unfortunate consequences from a developmental standpoint. During elementary school, chil-

dren move into Jean Piaget's stage of concrete operations (see Chapter 5) and are extremely literal-minded. They also, at this age, tend to divide the world into two camps, the "good guys" and the "bad guys" (see Chapter 7). In other words, children already have a built-in personal and cognitive bias in favor of "truth." If we then consider the special influence of initial learning experiences—recall how strongly we are affected the first time we experience something (see Chapter 4)—we begin to realize how easy it is for the pupils to accept the notion that there is only one answer. The main problem for teachers is the temptation to exploit this situation. It's very easy for them to become the fountainhead of all knowledge, the master who knows the truth and then decides how close or far away the pupils' answers come. In fact, pupils actually encourage such behavior by the teacher. And teachers may enjoy their presumed omniscience.

In this way the teacher's authority can easily become authoritarianism. The confusion of authority and authoritarianism is perhaps the basic dilemma teachers face. This is partly our own fault, especially if we are guilty of confirming the pupils' view of knowledge as fixed and

The teacher should avoid the "knowledge as truth" syndrome and should discourage black-and-white thinking.

unchanging. Many poignant examples come to mind. Think of the number of times students of all ages ask questions like "What are you going to cover on the next exam?" "How much will this count toward the final grade?" "Do we have to read all the assigned pages?" If you listen closely, you will hear exactly what such students have learned: To please the teacher, you only have to mouth the "right answer."

These attitudes have been learned for the most part in school. Don't blame the students if they are expert apple polishers. That is the behavior that has received the most positive reinforcement throughout their school life.

Conceptual Levels of Teachers

We pointed out in Chapter 13 that how a student understands knowledge is related to his or her conceptual level. The research and theory

TABLE 14.1 TEACHER ATTITUDES TOWARD LEARNING AND TEACHING (BASED ON HUNT'S CONCEPTUAL LEVEL MODEL)

STAGE A
Shows strong evidence of concrete thinking
Sees knowledge as fixed
Employs a single "tried and true" method
Exhibits compliance as a learner and expects the same from pupils
Is low on self-direction and initiative; needs detailed instructions
Doesn't distinguish between theory and facts
Relies almost exclusively on advance organizers
Believes teaching is "filling the students up" with facts
Stays at Bloom's level one and two regardless of student level
Enjoys highly structured activities for self and for pupils
Is very uncomfortable with ambiguous assignments
Does not question authority
Follows a curriculum guide as if it were "carved in stone"
Verbalizes feelings at a limited level. Has difficulty recognizing feelings in pupils
Is reluctant to talk about own inadequacies; blames pupils exclusively

STAGE B
Shows growing awareness of difference between concrete versus abstract thinking
Separates facts, opinions, and theories about teaching and learning
Employs some different teaching models in accord with student differences
Gives evidence of teaching for generalization as well as skills
Shows some evidence of systematic "matching and mismatching"; can vary structure
Is open to innovations and can make some appropriate adaptations
Shows sensitivity to pupils' emotional needs
Enjoys some level of autonomy and self-directed learning as a goal for self and for the pupils
Employs Bloom's levels one through four when appropriate
Uses evaluations that are appropriate to assignments

STAGE C
Understands knowledge as a process of successive approximations
Recognizes that today's theories may be tomorrow's anachronisms
Shows evidence of originality in adapting innovations to the classroom
Is comfortable in applying all appropriate teaching models
Is most articulate in analyzing his or her own teaching in both content and feeling
Has high tolerance for ambiguity and frustration; can stay on task in spite of major distractions
Does not automatically comply with directions—asks examiner's reasons
Fosters an intensive questioning approach with students
Can use all six of Bloom's levels when appropriate
Responds appropriately to the emotional needs of all pupils
Can "match and mismatch" with expert flexibility
Exhibits careful evaluations based on objective criteria according to level of assignment

of David Hunt detailed how pupils at lower levels of conceptual development would prefer concrete to abstract concepts, high rather than low structure, immediate and concrete rather than delayed and intrinsic feedback and rewards. We discussed this as the ATI approach. Now if that was true for students as persons, what are the implications for teachers as persons and their attitudes toward learning? David Hunt has examined just that. He has applied his research method to teachers themselves. Through the use of a test that assesses an individual's conceptual level (CL), he has found that teachers, like students, also have different conceptual systems in regard to teaching and learning. We've asked you to look and listen carefully to your students in order to understand how they understand the process. Hunt's work also suggests that with regard to yourself you look and listen just as carefully.

Hunt's research has indicated that teacher attitudes toward teaching and learning can be clustered into one of three stages.[8] Table 14.1 outlines the three stages.

As an example, a study examined the natural, uncoached teaching style of student teachers according to their stage of development on conceptual level. Using the Flanders index of direct versus indirect teaching modes, researchers found a significant difference between the high CL and low CL student teachers, even though no difference showed up in grade-point achievement.

As Table 14.2 shows, the high CL student teachers used all seven teacher strategies with a ratio of direct to indirect modes of close to 50 percent. The low CLs, on the other hand, were much less flexible and used the indirect categories much less frequently, less than 33 percent of the time. This study is highly similar in outcome to numerous other contemporaneous investigations. The higher-stage teacher is less dependent, more flexible, and essentially more competent as a teacher.

Does Conceptual Level Make a Difference?

Naturally a most important question is the empirical one: What is the relation between the teacher's conceptual level and actual teaching behavior? Is this just another case of an inter-

TABLE 14.2 CONCEPTUAL LEVEL OF STUDENT TEACHERS AND CLASSROOM INTERACTION

	FLANDERS RATIO 1, 2, 3, 4 1–7
High CL (N = 16) GPA = 3.1	45% indirect modes
Low CL (N = 13) GPA = 3.0	31% indirect modes

Based on over 6,000 teacher-pupil interactions.
N = number of student teachers.
GPA = grade-point average.

Data from L. Thies-Sprinthall, "Supervision: An Educative or Miseducative Process?" Journal of Teacher Education, 31(2) (1980): 17–30.

esting and perhaps elegant set of ideas that doesn't translate to the real world of the classroom? In fact, a definite relationship has been found between the CL stage and teacher behavior. At stage C teachers exhibit the following:

Allow constructive student expression

Allow students to raise questions

Allow students to hypothesize

View the student as a participant in learning

View knowledge as an open-ended process

Vary the structure and pace according to learner need

Use a variety of teaching models

Exhibit empathy toward nearly all students

"Read and flex" with the students[9]

In other words the stage C teachers can manage group instruction and respond to individual and small-group differences. The results indicated that academic performance in such classrooms was higher than in the other classrooms. The key seems to be the concept of "reading and flexing." By that, Hunt means the ability of the teacher to be affected by the pupils. We all know how pupils are affected by teachers. Hunt says the same is true for effective teachers. Thus, some students need high structure, others less. The stage C teacher modifies the approach. Such flexibility in teaching is not random. Instead the teacher systematically selects different approaches in the best sense of matching and mismatching as described in the previous chapter.

The stage A teachers, on the other hand, hold quite strongly to the view that there is only one correct way to teach. Their concept of subject matter is just as singular. All material has to be boiled down to a group of facts that the students memorize. They give out large amounts of information almost exclusively in a directive fashion. The students are not allowed to raise questions. Rather they are asked a succession of precise factual questions, resembling our metaphor of classroom trivia. Such teachers also draw nearly all the conclusions for the students, regardless of the students' levels of development.[10] In other words, everyone "gets" the same method whether they need it or not. In contrast, the stage C teachers also use a highly managed approach with some, but they use an interdependent approach with students who are ready to exercise more self-direction and autonomy in learning.

In philosophical terms Hunt's framework reminds us of the importance of understanding our own assumptions and beliefs about the purpose of teaching. At one level of complexity, students are grouped together as basically the same, as passive receptors of knowledge. The teaching methods are few, largely "tried and true." The outcomes indicate that students don't learn much, except that teaching and learning involve mostly passive memorization. On the other hand, teachers who understand the process of teaching and learning at a more complex level, who essentially can apply all levels of Benjamin Bloom's taxonomy to *their own teaching*, are more likely to have a positive impact on a much broader cross-section of pupils.

ATTITUDES TOWARD PUPILS

Teachers' attitudes toward the pupil are also important in determining the classroom atmosphere. Learning climates are subjective, and we were all adept as children in determining whether a teacher "likes kids." The feeling is readily apparent. Does the teacher feel we are competent? Does he or she expect us to do well?

Do we feel that the teacher really wants us to be successful?

Teacher Expectations

The importance of teacher expectations, attitudes, and feelings about children has been demonstrated dramatically in a series of studies by Robert Rosenthal, a social psychologist.[11] He has shown that the teacher's expectations determine to a considerable extent how much pupils, or for that matter almost any animal, will learn. His studies have demonstrated, for example, that if experimental psychologists are told that the rats in their study are especially bred for intelligence, these rats will learn the mazes quicker than the "control" rats, even though no such special breeding was carried out. In other words, Rosenthal has shown that when experimenters expect their rats to do well, those rats outperform their rivals. If they expect a good performance, experimenters encourage their breed, handle them more carefully, pat them frequently, root for them—in short, they treat them with concern and great care because they expect them to do well. If that is so for rats, what about pupils?

In the now famous Oak-Hall School experiment, Rosenthal and coworker Lenore Jacobsen told a group of schoolteachers at the beginning of the school year that particular pupils would have a "growth spurt" during the coming term. In order to lend credence to this prophecy, the researchers said that a special test, "The Harvard Test of Inflicted Acquisition," had been administered to all of the children in the elementary school. The results of the test became the basis for their alleged prediction. They identified some pupils as "growth spurters" even though their selection had been random: The identified pupils as a group were not any "smarter" than the remaining pupils.

At the end of the school term, the results showed that the pupils originally identified as in the growth-spurt group did much better on a series of tests than the other pupils. Their academic performances had improved and, especially in the early grades, their measured IQs were significantly higher than the other pupils'. Also, all the designated children received glowing comments from their teachers. Thus, a major research study has substantiated the effect

ROBERT ROSENTHAL

Born in 1933, Robert Rosenthal dashed over the academic hurdles in record time. He received his B.A. at twenty years of age and his Ph.D. by the time he was twenty-three, both at the University of California at Los Angeles. He then spent brief periods at UCLA, Ohio State, and the University of North Dakota. His work attracted increasing notice throughout the professional world. The idea of the self-fulfilling prophecy was not new to psychology. What was new, however, was Rosenthal's ability to demonstrate how often this phenomenon was affecting the work of the psychologists themselves. His findings were almost immediately controversial. And, as if to create more controversy among psychologists, since his early work had not then been replicated, the department of social relations at Harvard University reached halfway across the country to North Dakota and offered Rosenthal a Harvard professorship, all by the time he was twenty-nine years old.

With the move to the East and more time for research, Rosenthal shifted into high gear. He not only replicated his original findings but began to produce studies on his important concept in a wide variety of areas. As noted in the text, each time one of his studies is criticized, he has been able to answer the critics not with rhetoric but rather with more research data to validate his position. The controversy itself, of course, continues. The major outcome has been to produce more evidence, more sophisticated research designs, and thus more comprehensive information for educational psychology. In addition, he has now established the importance of nonverbal channels as the meaning of communicating expectations to others.

of the self-fulfilling prophecy. When teachers expected some pupils to experience a growth spurt, the pupils improved in academic performance and intelligence.

A second major finding of this study—and one that is rarely reported—concerns the teachers' attitudes toward the other children. Rosenthal selected a subgroup of pupils in his control group, a group of children who showed intellectual gains during the term but who hadn't been identified ahead of time to the teachers. He found that the teachers regarded these children as less well-adjusted, less interesting, and less affectionate than the others. In other words, the pupils who made it on their own, who gained intellectually in spite of the prediction, were perceived negatively by the teacher.

Thus, the Rosenthal effect is threefold: (1) Pupils who are expected to do well tend to show gains; (2) pupils who are not expected to do well tend to do less well than the first group;

and (3) pupils who make gains despite expectations to the contrary are regarded negatively by the teacher. What the effect of those negative expectations may be on such pupils the next time around has not been determined. We can guess, however, what negative expectations in general produce. Rosenthal quotes Eliza Doolittle from George Bernard Shaw's famous play *Pygmalion:*

> You see, really and truly, . . . the difference between a lady and a flower girl is not how she behaves, but how she's treated. I shall always be a flower girl to Professor Higgins, because he . . . treats me as a flower girl, . . . but I know I can be a lady to you, because you always treat me as a lady, and always will.[12]

At the time of the original study, serious objections were raised concerning technical aspects of the research design. Very rarely can a researcher design a single study that is "failsafe." Rosenthal's response to the criticisms has been instructive. Rather than engage in an endless debate on details, he has instead sponsored a large number of continuing studies. In fact, by 1978, some ten years after the Oak-Hall School experiment, he had reviewed some additional 345 studies on the topic. He was able to show the cumulative significance of how our expectations unintentionally affect the outcomes of our studies.[13] It is important to underscore the unintentional nature of the influence. The adult (teacher, researcher, professor) does not consciously seek to affect the outcome, yet nonetheless our attitudes and perceptions shape how we interact. Perhaps the best summary of the current state of the art with regard to the validity of teacher expectations comes from an independent source. In their evaluation Jere Brophy and Thomas Good avoided too close an identification with either the original Rosenthal work or with the host of critics. Their somewhat dispassionate summary concludes:

> Regardless of where one stands concerning the original data, work by a large number of investigators using a variety of methods over the past several years has established unequivocally that teacher's expectations can and do function as self-fulfilling prophecies.[14]

Perhaps we should recall that the whole question of the self-fulfilling prophecy first came to light some seventy years ago. A horse in Germany who came to be known as "Clever Hans" gained notoriety for his ability to add, subtract, multiply, and divide by tapping his foot. A psychologist named Pfungst, after long study, finally figured out that the questioners were unintentionally cueing the horse by lifting their heads up just before the horse reached the correct number of taps. He found that most humans who questioned Hans gave some cue without meaning to—raising their heads, lifting an eyebrow, or even dilating their nostrils. Pfungst concluded that he had spent far too much time "looking for, in the horse, what should have been sought in the man."

How are expectancy messages transmitted? Since teacher expectations are not for the most part conscious intentions, how are the messages conveyed? So far it seems as if the nonverbal communication channels are a main mode for transmission. Charles Galloway's work, cited in Chapter 12, pointed out the importance of nonverbal behavior. Rosenthal, following this lead, has now provided a creative series of studies detailing just how the expectations are communicated.[15] He masks the verbal content of a statement so that those tested can't quite make out the words. Then he asks them to guess the meaning of the statement. The test, called Profile of Nonverbal Sensitivity (PONS) assesses the ability to read between the lines, so to speak, and understand quite accurately what the person really means, even with the exact content obscured.

Rosenthal's work clearly indicates that you can't really hide your true attitudes. Perhaps highly skilled actors, after disciplined practice, can successfully cover their real feelings, but for most of us, students can read us almost like a book. Tone of voice, facial expression, body stance, eye contact, and similar aspects of body language act as channels, sounding clear messages about our real expectations. From research findings we know, first, that our expectations represent a self-fulfilling prophecy, and second, that our body language sends the message, either in a positive or negative mode. Thus, the findings help us to understand how the process works. One highly surprising finding, however, is most important to note. Especially in Rosenthal's U.S. samples, adults were highly inaccurate in judging their own nonverbal behavior. The correlations were close to zero on the self-ratings. This should remind us of Robert Burns's famous line "To see ourselves as others see us." The research lends further credence to the notion that our expectations as well as how they are communicated are unintentional. Rosenthal's findings suggest that we ask *not* ourselves but rather those with whom we are working.

Student Characteristics that Affect Expectations

The next question concerning teacher expectations shifts the focus to student characteristics. Is there any pattern or cluster of student characteristics that may be associated with positive or negative expectations? Rosenthal, remember, looked only at one variable in his original study, student ability, as "readiness for a growth spurt." But, as it turns out, other student characteristics do have an impact on teacher expectations.

Social class   Howard Becker, a sociologist, demonstrated the importance of the social class of the pupil a number of years ago in a now classic study. He found that most teachers in the large urban school system he examined could be grouped as lower-middle class on a socioeconomic scale.[16] In general, these teachers valued conformity, obedience, neatness, cleanliness, punctuality, hard work—highly conventional values. He then interviewed over sixty such teachers to find out how they perceived their pupils. He found three sets of perceptions that closely followed class lines. These teachers perceived children from their own class (lower-middle class and blue-collar working class) as the "best" pupils. They were neat, orderly, clean, and followed directions.

Teachers felt that pupils from lower-class backgrounds (essentially poor blacks) were, in general, morally unacceptable: "They don't wash." "They never use a toothbrush." "They will steal anything movable." "One girl in my class now makes money as a prostitute." These teachers reported being shocked by the "awful" language and upset because "they" (the lower-class students) don't really value education or wish to improve themselves. It is not difficult to imagine how such attitudes affected the teachers' expectations regarding the pupils they described in these terms.

Finally, the teachers had a third set of attitudes toward children from upper-class, well-to-do homes. They found these children to be very fine students, bright, clever, quick—but very difficult to teach: "They are too unruly—have no manners—interrupt me—are quick to correct my mistakes," noted one teacher. Another said, "They all have maids and servants at home. They won't pick things up that they drop. One student said to me 'If I picked that up, there wouldn't be any work for the janitor to do.'"

The teachers also tended to be fearful of reprisal from the parents of the third group. Although the children from the ghetto could be dealt with severely if necessary (including being subjected to corporal punishment), the children from well-to-do backgrounds were immune from direct punishment. The teachers were obviously worried about "influential" parents calling the school board or going directly to the superintendent with complaints about the teachers' actions toward their children.

More recent and psychologically oriented research has validated Becker's work on the importance of social class. Where the social class of the teacher and the pupils differ, especially if the pupils come from a lower socioeconomic class than the teacher, then there is a real possibility that the teacher systematically expects less from and does less effective teaching with such children.[17]

Ethnic background: Race   The first major study detailing the achievement outcomes of students whose racial or ethnic background was different from the teacher's was done by Eleanor Leacock and her associates from the Bank Street School in New York[18] Leacock's researchers, unlike Rosenthal or Becker, actually went into the classroom. They observed the teacher's behavior and checked student achievement. As a result, they found a fairly systematic pattern of negative attitudes and expectations toward most lower-class ghetto blacks. Teachers universally expected less of those pupils, even in the very first years of elementary school, than they did of other children. In addition, their expectations declined the longer the pupils were in school. Fifth-graders were seen as less capable and less competent than second-graders in the same school. Leacock found that the schools in the areas where poor blacks lived were neither in continual rebellion nor were they a "blackboard jungle." Rather, the schools were populated by overworked, ineffective, and frustrated teachers and bored, uninterested and withdrawn children. There were one or two "trouble makers" in each class, but the majority of pupils were quiet, dull, and listless. Leacock also compared teacher-pupil interaction in the lower-class black schools with that in middle-class schools (with both black and white children) and found less than half as much interaction in the lower-class school. This low rate of interaction means that the "poor" children are being ignored, that most of the time they spend in class is passed in quiet boredom, and that their teachers display a genuine lack of interest. Also, the interaction that did take place tended to be twice as negative as that in the middle-class schools; teachers tended to undermine the children, were very derogatory toward their work, and were supercritical of their attempts to read, do math problems, and do blackboard work.

Another classroom observation study by Brophy and Good gave a detailed account of the different teacher behaviors according to the ethnic background of the children.[19] They watched for teacher eye contact and the frequency of goal-setting behavior by teachers and pupils. The results are summarized in Table 14.3.

The message is clear as far as children from different ethnic backgrounds are concerned: They are either ignored, criticized, or undermined in their attempts to learn. This suggests that teachers in ghetto schools are teaching their children not to learn. It therefore comes as no surprise to find that pupil achievement in such schools is significantly lower than in ethnically similar schools. The teachers' unfortunate attitudes toward their pupils pervade some schools and doom these children to failure. Other research has indicated that such children end up not only with lowered academic achievement but also with a negative concept of themselves as learners. They have lower self-confidence in problem-solving situations. For such children, "formal" education in school may be worse than no education at all.

Family background: Single parents   A third factor that affects teacher expectations and also is beyond the control of the individual pupil, is

family composition. Whether the pupil comes from a two-parent or a single-parent home makes a significant difference in teacher predictions. Diane Scott-Jones completed a most extensive review of the literature.[20] Studies indicated that even when teachers viewed videotapes of children demonstrating precisely the same behaviors, their predictions differed. For children denoted as from one-parent homes, the teachers expected *both* a lowered academic performance and greater psychological problems. When children were said to be from intact homes, the attitude changed markedly despite the behavioral similarity. Further (almost to prove Rosenthal's point), another study indicated that both single and dual parents were accurate in their predictions of the different teacher expectations. In other words, the message did get through that teachers had different expectations, just on the basis of family make-up.

Scott-Jones also noted that when social class is controlled as a variable, research studies indicated no difference in either intelligence or academic achievement between children from single-parent and intact homes. Since the number of single-parent homes has grown dramatically in the last decade, she was concerned about this teacher bias, with good cause. According to some estimates, as many as 60 percent of all children may at one time or another live in a single-parent family. Such estimates do vary with both ethnic background and family income. Unfortunately, the likelihood of living in a single-parent home is much greater among economically poor and ethnically different children; such children may be doubly impaired as learners from negative expectancies.

Student temperament and sex differences The fourth area of significance is represented by the students' basic personality temperament: At the broadest level, research has shown that teachers can be affected by the general social skills of children. Pupils with "easy" temperaments (that is, likable personalities) who were quick to adapt to the teacher's requests and were pleasant to be around were consistently overrated as to their actual abilities. "Slow to warm up" children, who were not as likable, moodier, less quick to adapt, and more "emotional," were rated lower on the same estimates.

TABLE 14.3   TEACHER RESPONSES ACCORDING TO PUPILS' ETHNIC BACKGROUND

EYE CONTACT	TEACHER RESPONSE RATE
Initiated by white pupils	57% (14 to 8)
Initiated by black pupils	11% (35 to 4)
TEACHER GOAL SETTING WITH PUPILS*	
White middle-class school A	43 (12.3 instances/hour)
White middle-class school B	46 (15.3 instances/hour)
White lower-class school	18 (6 instances/hour)
Black lower-class school	15 (5 instances/hour)

* Based on three-hour-long observations.

CONTEMPORARY ISSUE

Cultural Differences and School Learning: How Different?

Shortly after the process of desegregating the public schools began in 1954, with "deliberate speed" akin to that of a glacier, a few minority children began appearing in the classrooms of previously segregated white schools. Often the transition was marked by riots, federal marshalls, bomb threats, stonings, and the use of electric cattle prods. These were the outward and visible signs of massive resistance. With a few exceptions, that era has ended. The public schools are increasingly integrated.

The resistance to cultural pluralism, however, did not officially end with the removal of the last police dog, the break-up of the final gathering of white supremacists at the curbstone of the school, or the mapping out of new bus routes. The legal guarantees ended physical resistance. As the reality changed and increasing numbers of blacks, American Indians, and Chicanos actually sat at the desks, a new set of barriers was erected. As we shall see in the chapter on intelligence, a new series of studies attempted to show just how inferior black children were because of an inadequate pool of inherited genes. (Shades of the "good" and "bad" Kallikaks!) The implication was direct: Desegregation would fill the schools with inferior humans of limited potential. Teaching procedures would have to be adjusted—downward.

Because the inferior gene pool theory could not be supported scientifically, a second theory was proposed: The problem was not poor genes; it was that most minority children came from psychologically deprived environments,

for example, "the Negro family." The result was still the same, but the cause was different. Minority children entering school were still viewed as significantly less competent. As was the case with the genetic theory, careful reexamination of the so-called family deficit theory has shown that such a conclusion was a dangerous oversimplification. Certainly, some minority children do experience an inadequate home environment and comes from economically weak families with parents who are incompetent and/or violent. Such families, however, are the exception, not the rule. Malnutrition, crowding, excessive noise, premature autonomy, and similar environmental problems will impair any student from any background. Yet to claim that all or nearly all minority children live in such disorganized families creates an unwarranted stereotype. Rather than attributing the difficulty to the minority status of the parents, it would be far more accurate to link such environments to economic poverty rather than ethnicity.

Thus, we have evidence that indicates that minority children do not inherit from an inferior gene pool, nor are minority families deficient as home environments. What about learning styles such as impulsivity or concrete versus abstract thinking? A recent massive review of such learning style differences concluded in no uncertain language: "As the research evidence indicates, cognitive styles vary as much within ethnic, racial, socioeconomic status and language groups as they do between groups."[a]

Two major factors, however, do

distinguish minority and nonminority children in a school situation. The differences are not explained by genes, by home environments, or by learning styles, but rather by psychological variables—attitudes. As noted in the text, minority children are systematically treated differently— namely, as less competent, with lowered achievement goals—and receive less adequate teaching strategies. Thus, one major factor is the difference in educational treatment, not in the children themselves. Minority children tend to receive less. While as a group they may enter the first grade slightly behind majority students, the longer they remain in school, the further behind they fall. In other words the school experience itself does not produce growth.

A second factor, which is even broader, has to do with the general social and economic goals available to all students. Harshly put, minority students ask, "What's the use of studying in school?" Not only is the daily experience more often negative than positive, but in the long run there may also be few opportunities for advancement. John Ogbu, a cultural anthropologist, has done a careful study of the origins of human competence in different countries.[b] Each country had easily identified minority members regarded as "outcasts." These outcasts for a number of generations, indeed centuries, were systematically denied full participation in society. They were taught, often through violent means (beatings and murder), to remain in their "place." After so many years of harsh repression, such outcast minorities did learn their lesson. No matter how hard they worked in school, their future opportunity was extremely limited.[c] Each new generation had ample evidence as to what happened to the previous generation.

Ogbu's point is that the apparent "failure" of black, Chicano, and other minority students to complete their schooling (e.g., the high-school dropout rate for American Indians is over 90 percent) has been a functional adaptation to reality. Until recently, the virtual exclusion of black, Chicano, and Indian workers from any high-status and highly paid employment that required a formal education sent a strong message. If you want to get ahead in this society, don't waste your time studying. There has been, in Ogbu's words, a "job ceiling." Most of the adults whom minority youth knew were in low-wage, low-skill jobs for which a high-school diploma was hardly a ticket to upward mobility. This has resulted in a situation that might be called a combination of fantasy and reality. A minority youth may say on one hand, "Yes I'd like to be a doctor or a lawyer," then turn around and take whatever low-paying job he or she can get.

What this means is that any differences between minority students and majority students in school performance are most likely *not* due to specific (or inborn) cultural differences. Characteristics that minority students are supposed to possess, such as short attention span, hyperactivity, verbal deficits, and so on, are simply stereotypes. There is no major evidence that identifies a unique cultural trait that either promotes or prevents learning. Instead, the differences you may observe are most likely a result of social conditions such as direct prior experience in negative schooling or a deep-seated feeling rooted in history that school achievement is not a pathway to a better life. Of course, since the enactment of civil rights legislation and the slow integration of schools, the atmosphere is changing. It may be years, however, before the majority culture can honestly and genuinely convince previously oppressed minorities of a real change in educational opportunity. Each time a teacher, even unintentionally, negatively reinforces a minority student, employs less eye contact, praises majority students more frequently, or uses different cues, that teacher reconfirms the suspicion in the minority student's mind and heart of unequal and unfair treatment. Each time the society as a whole uses what is called "systemic discrimination" to prevent access to better-paying occupations, higher education, and to professions, the job ceiling effect is reawakened.

The only meaningful difference, then, between minority and majority students in school situations is in motivational patterns. The motivation to learn has been redirected for many minority students. In the past such children received a strong message in the school itself as well as from the larger society. Their "place" was not with books and learning and upward economic mobility. Instead their place was with physically demanding, back-breaking, low-wage, and low-status roles. Educationally related career achievement was the road to nowhere.[d]

These findings have two implications. If you are from a majority background, as a teacher you will need to become particularly sensitive to the motivation issue. In fact you may have to go "the extra mile," at least in the beginning, to convince minority students that you will treat them in the same respectful manner and with the same effective methods as the other children. Remember such children and adolescents have every right to be suspicious and guarded. Too many prior generations have suffered at the hands of so-called white benefactors. Do not expect immediate acceptance, and do not push too hard. Gushing over a student's half-hearted and first product will be viewed as a phony performance. Also do not attempt to "buddy up" by quickly adopting any form of minority verbal expressions or vernacular. That too will be seen as false. Expect a period of legitimate testing to clear the air. Minority students like all others are fair and generous interpersonally, after you show them fairness and generosity in concrete ways. It's the actions they will look for, not the words.

How about the case of the minority member as teacher? If you are in that category, should you expect "instant rapport"? Yes and no. Obviously it will be easier for you to understand the legitimate emotional and motivational needs of minority students. Most likely such issues are close to you, personally. This doesn't mean, however, that you will have an automatic acceptance level with those minority students whose background may be different from your own. Thus, you will need to exercise some care if you begin to notice some mistrust. Also, and especially with adolescents, you may notice some hints or subtle feelings that your own educational

Contemporary Issue continued

attainment is only a case of "to-kenism" and that you "sold out" to the white establishment. Such doubt on their part, while genu-ine, is apt to disappear quite rap-idly as your humanity and care become more evident. So, on one hand, you will start with minority students in a far stronger position that teachers from majority back-grounds. That's a real plus. But you will have another set of very difficult problems. Quite unfortu-nately, as the expectancy research shows, almost half of all teachers (your colleagues) do not accept their pupils on an equal basis. These are some of the teachers who believe the stereotype that any difficulty in classroom learn-ing is caused by the skin color of the child. Failure is laid at the doorstep of the student. This can be a highly distressing situation for you. Such teachers, thought-lessly, may start a practice of ask-ing you to give those students "a good talking to," or they may make a series of increasingly dis-

paraging comments in front of you about some of their minority students. In pointing a finger at such students, they are often una-ware that they may be pointing the remaining three fingers at themselves. In any case there are certainly no quick solutions to the problems of prejudice and racism. You can remind such teachers that their attitude can become a self-fulfilling prophecy and that no re-lationship exists between ability and ethnicity. It will also serve as yet another reminder of just how far we still have to go on the road to equity and full participation for all students.

[a]   Shipman, S., and Shipman, V. (1985). "Cognitive styles: Some con-ceptual, methodological and applied issues." In E. W. Gordon (Ed.), *Review of Education Research*, Vol. 12. Washing-ton, D.C.: American Educational Re-search Association.
[b]   Ogbu, J. (1978). *Minority education and caste: The American system in cross-cultural perspective*. New York: Aca-demic Press.
[c]   A good example is the famous Su-

preme Court case, *Griggs*. v. *Duke Power*. Blacks working as laborers in a coal mine were barred from becoming miners unless they made a certain score on an IQ test. Those new rules virtually prevented promotion of any black laborers. Since the test score had no relationship to actual job perfor-mance, the Court ruled against Duke Power. The selection procedure was systemic discrimination—in the words of the Court, "Build-in headwinds for minority groups." The system ensured that a disproportionate number of mi-norities would be excluded.
[d]   The recent publicity concerning a successful New York businessman, Eu-gene Lang, seems to prove Ogbu's point quite dramatically. In 1980 he visited his old elementary school (PS 121). Instead of giving the usual Hora-tio Alger sermon to the ghetto sixth-graders, he promised the sixty-one students free college tuition. As we go to press fifty-two who still live in the area are completing their junior year in high school (versus a historical drop-out rate of 40 percent) Lang and his assistant have maintained contact. Of course, not all will go to college since some wish to enter skilled trades. However, all are still working hard in school as a stepping stone toward their own career development. The ceiling, in this case, has been raised.

In fact, one study suggested that such temper-amental differences were more significant than IQ or socioeconomic status as factors influenc-ing teacher expectations. There is insufficient evidence to back up such a claim. In any case pupil temperament does have an influence.[21] Teachers are unintentionally more positive to likable children and less positive to the "slow to warm up" ones. As in the case of Brophy and Good's research, the teacher expectations were assessed at a nonverbal level. Their tone of voice was different and they maintained less eye contact with those they considered difficult to teach.

As to the influence of sex differences, the evidence can be misleading. Years ago, the stan-dard view was that sex differences, particularly in elementary school, favored girls. Boys tended

to be more hyperactive, noisier, shorter on at-tention span, and less "academic" than girls. As a result it seemed natural to conclude that the teachers favored girls as more docile, easier to teach, and quicker to learn how to behave like a good pupil.[22] Now, however, the evidence isn't nearly as clear-cut. In fact, a case can be made for the converse. In the 1970s, for exam-ple, based on careful classroom observations in preschool, it appeared as if the teachers were responding to the sexes differently and to the disadvantage of girls.[23] Teachers encouraged as-sertiveness, autonomous problem solving, and independence on the part of boys. They were more likely to devalue the very same behavior in girls. The girls were getting a different mes-sage—less activity and more docility in learn-ing.

In addition to the work at the preschool level, studies of science and math teaching at the secondary level indicated similar differences.[24] Boys were encouraged and girls discouraged, or "cooled out," even though no major differences in ability were evident. Thus, there seems to be reasonable evidence that the gradual decline in science and mathematical achievement by females, which doesn't start until adolescence, is in part brought on by lowered teacher expectations.[25] As a somewhat cynical commentator might put it, "It's a good thing that Madame Curie didn't believe that females couldn't think scientifically."

One reason for such an apparent shift in teacher expectations may come from the change in learning outcomes over the past thirty years. With today's greater emphasis on educational equity stressing factors such as independence and self-direction as opposed to conformity and docility, especially for women, some teachers may not have accommodated their expectations to such objectives. Some may still view the girls as slightly less intellectually competent than boys, especially during adolescence. The main point here, however, is that temperament and gender can result in different expectations.

Academic achievement   Certainly of all the areas where we might anticipate teacher expectation to have an impact, academic performance is the most obvious. This is also an area where most of the school-based research has been done. Table 14.4 summarizes the results of one study in the area. In nine elementary classrooms that were observed, the teaching behaviors systematically varied with the student groupings. Students identified as having high potential received "appropriate" teaching. Herbert Walberg's research, cited in Chapter 12, had demonstrated the importance of positive reinforcement, use of cues, and the avoidance of criticism. The highs received such treatment. Conversely, those seen as having low potential were criticized *three* times more often for wrong answers than the highs, who also gave wrong answers. Positive cueing, that is, encouraging a pupil who isn't sure, also favored the highs by almost two to one. Finally, lack of feedback to pupils was almost five times more frequent with the lows than with the highs.

TABLE 14.4   TEACHER VERBAL INTERACTION WITH PUPILS RANKED AS HIGH VS. LOW POTENTIAL*

	HIGH POTENTIAL	LOW POTENTIAL
Correct answer followed by praise	12.8	5.8
Wrong answer followed by criticism	6.4	18.7
Positive cueing by teacher	67.1	38.4
No feedback to pupils' answers	3.3	14.7

* Based on nine elementary classrooms, forty-eight pupils. From *Teacher-Student Relationships: Causes and Consequences*, by J. E. Brophy & T. L. Good. Copyright © 1974 by Holt, Rinehart & Winston. Used by permission of CBS College Publishing.

The researchers identified four typical teacher responses to those children perceived as slow learners:

1. Waiting less time for the pupil to answer

2. Not following up when a pupil answered incorrectly

3. Rewarding inappropriate behavior (such as praising failure)

4. Not providing feedback to such pupils

How Widespread Are Negative Expectations?

Having established the importance of teacher expectations, how they are communicated, and the different forms they take, we come to the final point. How broad is the phenomenon? Does it happen only infrequently and then only to a small proportion of pupils? Naturally, it is difficult to derive a firm index. One group of researchers estimates that as many as 33 percent of all teachers show highly differentiated teaching behaviors toward children perceived differently according to academic potential.[26] This is a highly conservative estimate for two reasons: First, only teachers who were clearly (indeed almost blatantly) highly different were included. Second, the expectations were based on only *one* student characteristic, learning potential. If we add in the other findings indicating a

On Learning Shame

Dick Gregory

I never learned hate at home, or shame. I had to go to school for that. I was about seven years old when I got my first big lesson. I was in love with a little girl named Helen Tucker, a light-complected little girl with pigtails and nice manners. She was always clean and she was smart in school. I think I went to school mostly to look at her. I brushed my hair and even got me a little old handkerchief. It was a lady's handkerchief, but I didn't want Helen to see me wipe my nose on my hand. The pipes were frozen again, there was no water in the house, but I washed my socks and shirt every night. I'd get a pot, and go over to Mister Ben's grocery store, and stick my pot down into his soda machine. Scoop out some chopped ice. By evening the ice melted to water for washing. I got sick a lot that winter because the fire would go out at night before the clothes were dry. In the morning I'd put them on, wet or dry, because they were the only clothes I had.

It was on a Thursday, I was sitting in the back of the room, in a seat with a chalk circle drawn around it. The idiot's seat, the troublemaker's seat.

The teacher thought I was stupid. Couldn't spell, couldn't read, couldn't do arithmetic. Just stupid. Teachers were never interested in finding out that you couldn't concentrate because you were so hungry, because you hadn't had any breakfast. All you could think about was noontime, would it ever come? Maybe you could sneak into the cloakroom and steal a bite of some kid's lunch out of a coat pocket. A bite of something. Paste. You can't really make a meal of paste, or put it on bread for a sandwich, but sometimes I'd scoop a few spoonfuls out of the paste jar in the back of the room. Pregnant people get strange tastes. I was pregnant with poverty. Pregnant with dirt and pregnant with smells that made people turn away, pregnant with cold and pregnant with shoes that were never bought for me, pregnant with five other people in my bed and no Daddy in the next room, and pregnant with hunger. Paste doesn't taste too bad when you're hungry.

The teacher thought I was a troublemaker. All she saw from the front of the room was a little black boy who squirmed in his idiot's seat and made noises and poked the kids around him. I guess she couldn't see a kid who made noises because he wanted someone to know he was there.

It was on a Thursday, the day before the Negro payday. The eagle always flew on Friday. The teacher was asking each student how much his father would give to the Community Chest. On Friday night, each kid would get the money from his father, and on Monday he would bring it to the school. I decided I was going to buy me a Daddy right then. I had money in my pocket from shining shoes and selling papers, and whatever Helen Tucker pledged for her Daddy I was going to top it. And I'd hand the money right in. I wasn't going to wait until Monday to buy me a Daddy.

I was shaking, scared to death. The teacher

bias due to social class, race/ethnicity, single-parent status, temperament, and sex, we would have to conclude that negative expectations are probably operating in over one-half of all the classrooms in the country.

It is clear that for all who plan to teach, systematic awareness of expectations represents a crucial learning. The ability to relate in a positive and constructive manner to all children is not easily achieved; however, it can be developed. It is critical. Perhaps the clearest way to put it is to review the long list of variables known to bias teachers. How many of those factors are within the student's current power to change—ability, social class, race, tempera-ment, intact families, prior academic achieve-ment? Should such unchangeable elements influence over half of those currently in teaching? As you review this material, try not to view it as just a litany of complaints about teachers. Instead consider it an important agenda for change so that pupils may have a better chance to learn.[27]

ATTITUDES TOWARD SELF

We humans have known about the importance of self-knowledge for a long time. Socrates said that the unexamined life was not worth living.

opened her book and started calling out names alphabetically.

"Helen Tucker?"

"My Daddy said he'd give two dollars and fifty cents."

"That's very nice, Helen. Very, very nice indeed."

That made me feel pretty good. It wouldn't take too much to top that. I had almost three dollars in dimes and quarters in my pocket and held onto the money, waiting for her to call my name. But the teacher closed her book after she called everybody else in the class.

I stood up and raised my hand.

"What is it now?"

"You forgot me."

She turned toward the blackboard. "I don't have time to be playing with you, Richard."

"What is it now?"

"My Daddy said he's . . ."

"Sit down, Richard, you're disturbing the class."

"My Daddy said he'd give . . . fifteen dollars."

She turned around and looked mad. "We are collecting this money for you and your kind, Richard Gregory. If your Daddy can give fifteen dollars you have no business being on relief."

"I got it right now, I got it right now, my Daddy gave it to me to turn in today, my Daddy said . . ."

"And furthermore," she said, looking right at me, her nostrils getting big and her lips getting thin and her eyes opening wide, "we know you don't have a Daddy."

Helen Tucker turned around, her eyes full of tears. She felt sorry for me. Then I couldn't see her too well because I was crying too.

"Sit down, Richard."

And I always thought the teacher kind of liked me.

From *Nigger: An Autobiography* by Dick Gregory with Robert Lipsyte. Copyright © 1964 by Dick Gregory Enterprises, Inc. Reprinted by permission of the publisher, E. P. Dutton, a division of New American Library.

It is obvious that the way teachers perceive and feel about themselves is a major determinant of classroom atmosphere and student performance. Self-confidence, poise, self-control, an eagerness to lead a class of children will obviously set the tone for cooperation and learning in the class. Similarly, a superanxious, trembling, insecure teacher will set the opposite tone.

As David Powlett-Jones makes clear in his discussion of the first day of teaching (see the box), a teacher with an insecure self-concept can invite trouble in the classroom. How we see ourselves is a most important component in determining classroom atmosphere.

Seven Self-Image Models

Herbert Thelen from the University of Chicago has catalogued some of the common views teachers have of themselves and of their roles as teachers.[28] He uses some interesting metaphors.

Model one: Socrates The teacher sees himself or herself much like the wise old tutor of antiquity, with a reputation based on love of argument, debate, and deliberately provocative statements. He or she often takes the role of devil's advocate, arguing for unpopular views. The self-image is of a person constantly searching, asking questions, and rarely, if ever, coming to a conclusion. Finality is rarely appropriate. Rather, the teacher strolls around the classroom asking new questions when the old ones have been fully debated. The style is highly individualistic and unsystematic.

Every once in a while, when professional agencies mention teacher certification, someone is bound to hold Socrates up as an example of an excellent teacher who would not meet the usual standards. His or her lesson plan consists of relentless questioning. Through constant confrontation, much like a cross-examination in a trial, pupils are forced to defend their own conclusions, or more likely, to end up agreeing with the cross-examiner.

Model two: The town-meeting manager   This teacher is always seeking consensus and cooperation among members of the class. Educators who speak of the importance of community fall into this category: They view their classes as communities of interdependent and equal human beings. Thelen notes that the town-meeting manager is more of a moderator than an expert. As moderator, the teacher encourages members to participate and contribute to the group. Thus, he or she views the process of seeking this democratic consensus as more important that the specific outcome.

Educators have just begun to take a closer look at the idea of community as an educational force for the classroom. Should this idea continue to take hold, teachers may have to view themselves more and more as moderators seeking consensus and group participation.

This model should not be confused with the idea of direct involvement in the school by people who live in the community, by community residents as teachers and as policy makers in the school program. The classroom as a community does not include such "outsiders." Instead, it includes only the teacher and the pupils working together as a group. Direct participatory democracy is the major educational objective when the teacher perceives himself or herself as a town-meeting manager.

Model three: The master/apprentice   This teacher perceives himself or herself as a genuine model for students. (We are using the word model in its literal sense, as something to be emulated.) The teacher is like an old-fashioned preceptor, and the pupil is the apprentice. This teacher is concerned with far more than academic performance; he or she is concerned with how the student learns to live. Consequently, the teacher plays multiple roles, as teacher, father, mother, friend, colleague, and boss. The pupil becomes a miniature version of the master. Perhaps we should rename this model the Father or Mother Goose image. The teacher gathers the flock around and the class becomes a "gaggle," waiting to be imprinted.

Model four: The general   This teacher adopts pretty much of an "old blood and guts image." He or she lays down the law and expects and demands obedience. There is no room for any sort of ambiguity, and the teacher has the power to reward or punish as he or she sees fit. Thelen reminds us that this teacher doesn't necessarily use severe punishment. In fact, the teacher can be kind and gentle as long as the pupils remain dependent and subordinate. The self-image obviously has to do with the teacher knowing best and the pupil following orders. Like an army recruit, the pupil must do exactly what he or

she is told. When you have a general for a teacher, it's true to say: "I'm free to do as I please as long as I do as I'm told." Thelen notes that this model is more prevalent than all the others combined.

Model five: The business executive   This teacher functions as a business executive, operating a company (the classroom) and working out business deals with the employees (the pupils). The pupils write contracts specifying what tasks they will take on during the contract period. The business executive then consults with each employee during the task, to exert a kind of quality control, and inspects the final product. An air of efficiency and crispness goes along with this image. Detailed "production charts" may line the walls of the classroom, and the chief executive can usually be identified by a very tidy desk. This corporate image has become "official" in some of the newest classrooms, where thick wall-to-wall carpeting is now standard equipment.

Model six: The coach   This teacher is worlds apart from the business executive. The atmosphere now resembles that of a locker room. Pupils are like members of a team; each one is insignificant as a individual, but as a group the students can move mountains. The teacher

views his or her role as inspirational—desire, dedication, and devotion are the hallmark of team talks. "Go get this one for the Old Gipper" or words to that effect echo down the corridors, and the pupils can be heard responding in unison precise phrases learned by heart. The coach is totally devoted to the task. The only measure of effectiveness is the outcome, the final score. "Nice guys" come in last when the name of the game is WIN. To the coach, "Winning isn't everything, it's the only thing."

Model seven: The tour guide   This teacher bears an unmistakable resemblance to a professional guide. He or she clearly knows the way around, all the facts, all the time—indeed, the teacher seems to be a walking encyclopedia. He or she also tends to be somewhat reserved, disinterested, and laconic. After all, the guide's been over this route many times before and has heard every possible question hundreds of times. The answers are comprehensive and soundly programed. Technically perfect, the guide shows only a hint of boredom. He or she could be conducting a tour of the Washington Monument, the Empire State Building, the Mayflower, Yosemite, Sutter's Creek. We have all met this type before; we will meet the type again, and not only in class. It is, after all, a relatively safe, impersonal role.

Teacher Attitudes Toward Self: A Shaky Start That Came Close to Disaster

In R. F. Delderfield's award-winning novel *To Serve Them All My Days*,[a] David Powlett-Jones, the hero, has just returned to civilian life after a series of injuries at the close of World War I. He finds himself in front of his first classroom, a group of unruly fifteen-year-olds in an English prep school. He's had no real teaching experience and felt subtly pressured into accepting the position as a result of a very persuasive and charismatic headmaster. In addition, his physical recovery from his injuries has been quite slow, leaving him with an obvious case of tremors both in his hands and voice. In fact, he had originally looked forward to attending a major university but in his current condition that seems impossible, almost as unlikely as teaching school. He muses, "What headmaster in his senses would engage a wreck like me, who jumps a foot in the air every time a door bangs?"

The boys, of course, are quick to sense the whole picture. A partially shell-shocked veteran, unsure about his role, inexperienced, shaky, and desiring to retreat to the hills of his native Wales— the invitation to mischief is unmistakable. Quietly the boys go to work. Eyes dart. Hand signals are passed. The air is electric. The staged melodrama is ready. On cue one of the boys goes into a paroxysm. His distress looks real. He writhes on the floor. His companions run about—one to the window, one to the door, another to Mr. Powlett-Jones. "Don't worry, sir! Only one of Boyer's fits, sir!" The class waits in anticipation. Surely the teacher is on the verge of falling for the whole stunt. What a laugh the boys will have afterward. To defeat the newcomer on the first day will go down in the annals of Bamfylde. Little do they really care about this shaking, nervous teacher in front of them.

It is not to be. In spite of his inner feelings, Powlett-Jones is able to draw on his dwindling inner resources. Something about Boyer gives him a clue. The game is overplayed just enough to cast some doubt. Just on instinct he takes a chance. He steps back and, using his best military voice, calls, "Silence! Places!" The well-rehearsed trick has been uncovered. Boyer's face is now drained of color for real. The confederates are marched up in front of the class while the teacher now calmly dresses them down. "Quite a performance! But it needs working on Boyer! You're not bad, but your partner is a terrible ham."

He quickly reestablishes order, having gained an entirely different attitude toward himself. He is a teacher after all.

---

[a] Delderfield, R. F. (1972). *To serve them all my days.* New York: Simon & Schuster.

Adult-Centered Versus Child-Centered Self-Images

It is important to remember that these models are all derived from the needs of the teachers, not from the requirements of the pupils. Each one is, at best, an extremely truncated version of what an educator should be. When critics speak of adult-centered rather than child-centered classrooms, it is with reference to these images. We must have an unusual self-image to be able to set aside our own needs and really serve those of the children in our charge. The model that is conspicuously absent from Thelen's catalogue is that of an educator of children.

At this point, you may be wondering whether there is any way out of this value dilemma. We know that attitudes, expectations, and images toward learning, pupils, and self are of critical importance in the classroom. We also realize that in many cases teachers become trapped by their own values. Recall the studies showing that teachers reward only those children whose background is similar to their own. Recall Thelen's observation about how teachers' self-images fill their own needs in the classroom. Are we doomed to teach only for our own benefit or only for those few children who are just like us? Isn't education supposed to be for all children? Sooner or later we must confront these questions head on.

VALUES AND TEACHING

A number of attempts have been made to resolve the above-mentioned dilemma. One very common approach has been to say that teaching is like indoctrination. "Face it, teaching is a form of brainwashing," or so this view proclaims. Since adults know more than kids, it is right and just for the adults to induct each new generation of children into the ways of the adult world. There is no need to be upset by this indoctrination; it's simply the way things are— a natural law. This is something like saying, "Well, so what's wrong with teaching middle-class values; after all, that's the majority view. And most everybody would like to be middle class anyway!" The fact that such rhetoric makes the shabby rationalizations seem palatable to some raises more questions than it answers.

Another, more elegant, solution to the value dilemma has been to suggest that teaching should be value-free—that is, teachers really should express no genuine personal values. They should present all sides of any question fairly and impartially. Like anthropologists studying another culture, teachers would be trained for neutrality. Their only values would be plurality and relativism: All views would

have merit and receive equal treatment. Not only would there be freedom for all views, but teachers would also be expected to pursue and embody all views with equal vigor.

Perhaps the most adequate means of conveying the impossibility of value neutrality in teaching is to offer a brief example. A social studies teacher who was supervising a group of teacher trainees had become embroiled in this very controversy. His trainees insisted that the pupils were to be "free." They, as future teachers, had no right to impose their views on the children. The social studies master teacher at this point gave up on the dialogue and invited the teachers-in-training to observe his next class. To make his point as dramatically as he knew how, he decided to teach his pupils about the disadvantages and the advantages of the concentration camps of World War II. After listing the obvious disadvantages, he proceeded "objectively" to list the advantages—the creation of jobs (guards, dog trainers, searchlight makers), the uncrowding of cites, the increase in availability of housing, and even the production of certain goods almost too grisly to mention. The horrified practice teachers immediately protested that the master teacher was being unfair. How was it possible to even consider a concentration camp as an advantage to anyone? The master teacher had reduced the idea of value-free teaching to an absurdity. To say that he was merely presenting evidence from a "different point of view" was simply a means of begging the question of values.*

TEACHING GOALS AND STRATEGIES: A DEVELOPMENTAL MODEL

It is apparent that teaching can hardly be considered as brainwashing and that relativism just as obviously leads in a circle. We need to return to the ideas from prior chapters on strategies and goals as a framework for our role concepts. The attitudes we hold toward the role of the teacher bear a direct relationship to the strate-

---

* This case example was provided by Dr. Bernard Seiderman of the Great Neck, Long Island, school system.

gies we employ and the goals we seek to achieve. If we examine the question from the student's point of view as well as from the view of the goals of a democratic society, we can begin to formulate an answer.

We have shown, especially in the first sections of this book, that all children enter school with potential for development. Such development takes place in the cognitive, personal, and value domains. By viewing students developmentally, we gain a picture of how pupils presently function *and* their potential for developing increasingly more complex systems of thinking, self-development, and value judgment. Whether or not such growth takes place depends on an appropriate match between where the learner is and what level he or she is moving toward. The teacher's role is to arrange the learning environment in all subject areas to stimulate the natural process of development. Each child brings to us a natural desire to learn, an innate urge to grow. Of course, as a result of past experience, this desire may not be as obvious with some pupils as it is with other, more openly eager learners. Yet all have the potential. We've called this the process of accommodation, the need to learn more about the world and find better ways to solve problems.

On one side of the teacher, then, we have a group of youngsters whose developmental needs are ready to be met in the service of their own growth. But consider a different perspective—the teacher as an agent for the democratic goals of the adult society. Without going into the deep philosophical questions, it is clear that the goals of a democracy absolutely demand effective education for its young people. The purpose of education in its broadest sense is to teach them how to think, especially about democratic principles. For adults to function successfully as citizens they must know not only how to work and contribute to the general welfare but also how to weigh questions, vote intelligently, and understand equity and the generic meaning of democratic freedom and responsibility. For that to happen, for such broad societal goals to be achieved, the schools' role is critical. An informed public is the keystone to anyone's definition of democracy. Without development, our children will remain in prejudice, ignorance, and self-centeredness. Thomas Jefferson stated the issue most suc-

cinctly: "If a nation expects to be ignorant and free, in a state of civilization, it expects what never was and never will be."

The daily activity of the classroom can be a vehicle to accomplish this admittedly lofty goal. Mouthing great phrases and calling on eternal virtues will not do it. In fact, we have shown through Lawrence Kohlberg's research that talk and moral behavior do not go hand in hand. Thus the day-to-day process of gradual development in the classroom is very significant. We can't hurry the process; acceleration too often leads to low-level memorization. Thus, the goals and strategies of teaching aim to promote the developing potential of each child through a sequence from less complex to higher-order, more complex thinking, self-development, and value judgment.

Since this chapter has focused on the person of the teacher, where does that person come into this picture? Learning more intensively about children outlines their potentials for growth. Learning more about your own attitudes and stages outlines your potential. So we can hold up the same mirror. Your own growth as a professional teacher is a central consideration. As the orchestrator of the classroom, you determine much of what transpires. We have shown how negative teacher expectancies adversely affect student growth. We have also shown how a limited range of strategies has similarly negative outcomes. Only the teacher who gradually develops to higher levels of complexity as an individual can also increasingly master the art of teaching. Matching and mismatching requires a substantial ability to engage in what Arthur Cruickshank calls "reflective teaching."[29] Teaching cannot be reduced to a series of robot moves. Reflective teaching means the ability to analyze the process of what you are doing and have an impact on children simultaneously. Sometimes this is called on-the-spot decision making.

Research has shown that even experienced teachers are not particularly adept at considering alternatives while teaching.[30] Instead, the norm seems to be quick closure even though the research also indicates that such a limited ability to choose and select reduces student learning. The reason we point this out is that a strong tendency exists in all of us when we become aware of the developmental approach to expect that we can quickly go through a "growth spurt." In other words, we can accept the idea of gradual development, of slow but sure growth in others, but not in ourselves. We can take the "fast-track" and get on with the process. The developmental method is for others. Bill Perry's wise father makes the point in the box that closes this chapter: It is all right to "be" where you are right now, yet still understand that you can grow slowly.

Research has demonstrated that teachers who try out their current methods, master those, and systematically increase their repertoire of strategies show definite evidence of developmental growth.[31] An important component is cognitive reflection, that is, the ability to analyze your own teaching.[32] The two go hand in hand. You try a new approach and then review and analyze the results, make changes, and try again. To act without reflection leads to unguided fads. To reflect only leads to excessive introspection and no action.

SUMMARY

The personal side of teaching involves teacher attitudes in three general areas: (1) attitudes about teaching and learning, (2) attitudes toward pupils, and (3) attitudes toward self.

Teachers' attitudes toward learning sometimes harden into the belief that knowledge is truth; with this belief teachers expect pupils to look for the single correct answer to the problems posed in the classroom. Hunt has found that teachers' conceptual level influences how they teach. Teachers at a low conceptual level tend to be more authoritarian than teachers at higher levels and they use a single method of teaching with all students.

Teacher attitudes toward students also influence teaching style. The early and now classic study of the importance of a self-fulfilling prophecy by Rosenthal and Jacobson illustrates the importance of such attitudes. A review of recent research documents the wide variety of student characteristics that "cause" teachers to treat some pupils negatively, reducing the possibility of academic achievement. Student social class, race, rearing in a single-parent family, temperament, gender, and academic achievement are among the important factors that influence teacher attitudes.

The attitudes toward self of teachers are also important. Thelen catalogued seven views teachers have of themselves and their role that affect their classroom behavior.

Teachers cannot be value-free in their interactions with students. They must strive to incorporate in their teaching a genuine developmental model designed to promote pupil growth both in subject matter competency and in the values needed for future citizenship in a democratic society. By nurturing their own capacity for reflective teaching, teachers can play a major role in pupil growth.

KEY TERMS AND NAMES

hidden agenda
Rosenthal effect
Profile of Nonverbal Sensitivity (PONS)
Howard Becker

teacher expectations
Thelen's seven teacher images
developmental model

REFERENCES

1. Cuban, L. (1984). Policy and research dilemmas in the teaching of reasoning: Unplanned designs. *Review of Educational Research*, 54(4), 659.

2. Smiley, M. B., and Diekhoff, J. S. (1959). *Prologue to teaching* (p. 32). New York: Oxford University Press.

3. Kaufman, B. (1964). *Up the down staircase.* Englewood Cliffs, N.J.: Prentice-Hall.

4. Kozol, J. (1967). *Death at an early age.* Boston: Houghton Mifflin.

5. Ryan, K. (1970). *Don't smile 'til Christmas.* Chicago: University of Chicago Press.

6. Ryan, K., Newman, G., Mager, J., Applegate, J., Lasley, T., Flora, R., and Johnston, J. (1979). *Biting the apple: Accounts of first year teachers.* New York: Longman.

7. McLuhan, M. H. (1964). *Understanding media.* New York: McGraw-Hill.

8. See Joyce, B., Brown, C., and Peck, L. (1981). *Flexibility in teaching.* New York: Longman. This work provides an extended discussion and detailed examples of Hunt's research.

9. This research has been summarized by Miller, A. (1981). Conceptual matching models and interactional research in education. *Review of Educational Research, 51*(1l), 33–85.

10. Miller, Conceptual Matching Models, 63.

11. Rosenthal, R., and Jacobson, L. (1968). *Pygmalion in the classroom.* New York: Holt, Rinehart & Winston.

12. Quoted in Rosenthal and Jacobson, *Pygmalion in the classroom* (p. 183).

13. Rosenthal, R., and Rubin, D. (1978). Interpersonal expectancy effects: The first 345 studies. *The Behavioral and Brain Sciences, 3,* 377–415.

14. Brophy, J. E., and Good, T. L. (1974). *Teacher-student relationships: Causes and consequences* (p. 32). New York: Holt, Rinehart & Winston. This work summarizes a wide variety of studies.

15. Rosenthal, R. (1979). *Sensitivity to nonverbal communication: The PONS test.* Baltimore: Johns Hopkins Press.

16. Becker, H. (1969). Social class variation in the teacher-pupil relationship. In R. C. Sprinthall and N. A. Sprinthall (Eds.), *Educational psychology: Selected readings* (pp. 300–308). New York: Van Nostrand-Reinhold.

17. Good, T. (1983). Recent classroom research: Implications for teacher education. In D. C. Smith (Ed.), *Essential knowledge for beginning educators.* Washington, D.C.: American Association of Colleges of Teacher Education.

18. Leacock, E. (1969). *Teaching and learning in city schools.* New York: Basic Books.

19. Brophy and Good, *Teacher-student relationships* (p. 98).

20. Scott-Jones, D. (1984). Family influences on cognitive developmental and school achievement. In E. W. Gordon (Ed.), *Review of research in education* (pp. 259–306). Washington, D.C.: American Education Research Association.

21. Woolfolk, A. E., and Brooks, D. M. (1983). Nonverbal communication in teaching. *Review of research in education, 10,* 103–150.

22. Meyer, W. J., and Thompson, G. C. (1969). Sex differences in the distribution of teacher approval and disapproval among sixth grade children. In R. C. Sprinthall and N. A. Sprinthall (Eds.), *Educational psychology: Selected readings* (pp. 308–314). New York: Van Nostrand-Reinhold.

23. Maccoby, E., and Jacklin, C. (1974). *The psychology of sex differences.* Stanford, Calif.: Stanford University Press.

24. Wolleat, P. (1980). Sex differences in high school students' causal attribution of performance in mathematics. *Journal of Research in Mathematics Education, 11,* 356–366.

25. Hyde, J. S. (1981). How large are cognitive gender differences? *American Psychologist, 38*(8), 892–901.

26. Good, Recent classroom research. See also, Good, T., and Brophy, J. (1984). *Looking in classrooms,* 3rd ed. New York: Harper & Row.

27. See Martorella, P. H. (1986). *Classroom teaching skills.* Lexington, Mass.: D. C. Heath. This point as well as other insightful comments can be found in this work.

28. Thelen, H. (1954). *Dynamics of groups at work* (pp. 36–41). Chicago: University of Chicago Press.

29. Cruickshank, A. (1985). Applying research on teacher clarity. *Journal of Teacher Education, 36*(2), 44–48.

30. Shavelson, R. J., and Stern, P. (1981). Research on teachers' pedagogical thoughts, judgments, decisions, and behavior. *Review of Educational Research, 51*(4), 455–498.

31. Thies-Sprinthall, L. (1984). Promoting the developmental growth of supervising teachers: Theory, research, programs, and implications. *Journal of Teacher Education, 35*(3), 53–60.

32. Glassberg, S., and Sprinthall, N. A. (1980). Student teaching: A developmental approach. *Journal of Teacher Education, 31*, 31–38.

Before Going On: Bill Perry's Wise Father

So far in this volume we have been stressing a set of assumptions that represents a system of values, attitudes, and perceptions we prize. We feel, for example, that the idea of stages of growth and development allows us to view the problems of education from the point of view of our children's needs. When L. K. Frank (see Chapter 6) spoke of the fundamental psychological needs of children as opposed to those of adults, he provided us with a basic framework for examining our values as educators. If children grow and develop at different rates and proceed through different stages, we as educators have the opportunity to facilitate and nurture that growth. We noted that certain sensitive periods provide us with an opportunity to nurture particular kinds of growth. We also outlined in greater detail the stages of cognitive, personal, and moral development. Equipped with this understanding, the teacher can draw up a self-definition as an educator that can include the objectives of promoting maximal growth and development within each stage and across all stages. Then we stressed the problems of intervention, both from a theoretical and from a practical point of view. These chapters should allow you to put theory to practice.

When we noted the problems confronting educational psychology in Chapter 1, we emphasized the troublesome dichotomy between thinking about educational problems and doing something about them. The teacher's self-image is clearly a key element in resolving this separation. If the self-image is that of someone who arranges practice and creates the conditions for maximal

learning matched to the pupils' developmental stages, then the dichotomy disappears. By valuing the growth and development of each child and by knowing what the effective teaching techniques are, the educator comes close to the original definition of an educator. To educate, in its root sense, means to draw out, to elicit, to develop. We need to clear away the psychological blind spots imposed by social-class distinction, our own stereotyped perceptions, and the narrow and confining sets of attitudes we have toward knowledge, children, and ourselves. By putting on a new set of personal "lenses" we may come to see both ourselves and children in significantly different ways.

In closing this section, one final, very significant point should be made. Developmentally oriented teachers and professors are generally so convinced of the basic value of growth and development that they at times become overly zealous and ideological. If we are convinced that it is important for children and teen-agers to learn to think more logically, systematically, divergently, and convergently, as well as to develop empathy, compassion, and their own humanness, then it is all too easy to become a single-minded "pusher" of our own pet goals. If we are convinced that growth is good, we may find ourselves constantly pulling, exhorting, cajoling, shoving, engendering perpetual dissonance, always "jamming," always saying to pupils in so many words, "Well, that's O.K., but not quite good enough. Let's move on!"

This creates a double bind for the pupil. If new growth requires constant agitation, we will soon opt out. We all get sick of being constantly prodded, nagged, or exhorted to excel. Thus, the educator needs a special blend of competence to create a learning atmosphere that helps pupils grow *and* affirms the acceptability of their current status.

Robert White has used the metaphor of the horticulturist as a way to sum up the paradox of human teaching and human learning:

The nurturing of growth requires the patience of the gardener rather than the hasty intervention of the mechanic. It requires waiting for impulse to declare itself, for interest to appear, for initiative to come forth. . . . When the fast technological march of our civilization is encouraging us all to think like mechanics it is particularly important to preserve where it is still needed the long patience of the husbandman.[a]

William Perry presents the process and the paradox in more personal terms. He recently described an incident in his own life as an illustration. He was introducing his wife, Mary, to his aging father; only later did he learn his father was terminally ill at the time and this was to be the last meeting of Bill, his wife, and his father. At one point in the conversation, the father looked carefully at Mary and asked her if she was progressing. When she nodded in the affirmative, he then went on: "Well that's just fine, Mary, I'm glad that you're progressing. It's always important to grow, to improve yourself, to move ahead." At this point there was a moment of silence. Then the aging man leaned forward and, looking very directly at Mary, said: "But, remember, it's also important to be okay where you are right now!"

[a]   White, R. W. (1966). *Lives in progress,* 2nd ed. (pp. 509–510). New York: Holt, Rinehart & Winston.

INDIVIDUAL DIFFERENCES: MEASUREMENT AND RESEARCH

15

MEASUREMENT AND INDIVIDUAL DIFFERENCES

The material presented in this chapter is aimed at giving you a general introduction to some of the techniques employed by statisticians and educational researchers. Though as a working teacher you may never have to compute the reliability or the validity of a measuring instrument, your understanding of these vital concepts will be greatly enhanced if you roll up your sleeves and "dirty your hands with the data." If you can calculate the standard deviation and Pearson r, you will not necessarily be a master statistician, but you will be better able to evaluate the statistical analyses of researchers in the field. In the next chapter you will see how researchers use some of these techniques to achieve a better understanding of the facts and theories of educational psychology. As a professional teacher you will be expected to read and understand the literature of the field. A basic introduction to statistical procedures will enhance your ability to understand this literature.

MEASUREMENT

As you look within yourself and at the people around you, you realize that you are a very special and unique being. Nobody else in the world is quite like you. Nobody else in the world has the same physiological equipment, the same genetic endowment (unless, of course, you are an identical twin), or has experienced the same sequence of life situations. Nobody else uses the identical blend of defense mechanisms that you use when encountering stress, and nobody else is guided by the exact mixture of motives, attitudes, and feelings. Thus, one of the basic themes of psychology is that of individual differences: No one is exactly like anyone else.

It is, however, impossible to avoid drawing comparisons as you look at the people around you. Perhaps you notice many similarities. You have a friend who seems to enjoy the same things you do. You play chess with someone who beats you just about as often as you beat her. You and your best friend spend about the same amount of time studying for an exam, and you make similar grades on that exam. Perhaps you have been pleasantly surprised to discover, during a conversation with someone you have just met, how similar your abilities, goals, tastes, and feelings really are. In many ways you are surprisingly like many other people. In some ways you are just like all other people; that is, you eat, drink, breathe, sleep, exercise, and have the same physiological needs. Therefore, it can be said that in some ways all people are exactly alike.

In order to assess how much you resemble and how much you differ from other people, you must in some way be measured. Meaningful comparisons cannot be made without meaningful measurements. Measurement is the assignment of a number to an object or event according to rules. This may represent something physical, as when you step on the scales and note, with dismay or pleasure, the number that indicates your weight. Or it may be more subtle, as when you take a vocational aptitude test and receive your score in mechanical aptitude. You have, in fact, been measured hun-

dreds of times in hundreds of areas. In order to buy new clothes you must know your size. When you visit a physician, your temperature and blood pressure are taken. Before entering college, you probably took an aptitude test. Hundreds of numbers have been assigned to you, from shoe size to that first quiz grade you received in elementary school.

Reliability and Validity

In order to draw meaningful comparisons, measurements must be meaningful. In order to have meaning, all measurements must satisfy two basic criteria: They must be reliable and they must be valid.

Reliability   Reliability is an indication of the consistency of a measurement; that is, if we measure something that is not itself changing dramatically, we should assign roughly the same number to it over repeated measure-

Measurement of progress is important in the classroom.

ments. If you stepped on the scales and read 140 pounds one day, 240 pounds the next day, and 40 pounds the day after that, your faith in the precision of the scale would be severely shaken. The numbers would be meaningless. The same is true of psychological tests. If you took an IQ test one day and received a score of 140, and then you took the same test the next day and received a score of 50, you would undoubtedly feel bewildered. In order to have any meaning, our measurements must be consistent over repeated measurements—that is, reliable.

On the other hand, a test cannot be so consistent as to be rigid and misleading. It was mentioned that a good test yields roughly the same scores over repeated measurements as long as that which is being measured does not change dramatically. Suppose, however, you went on a crash diet, and every day your friends commented on how much weight you had lost, and after a few weeks you found your clothes no longer fit. If, in this instance, you still found the scales were reading the same weight, it would be obvious that the measurements were too consistent to be an adequate reflection of reality.

Validity   Measurements must also be valid. Validity is an indication of the extent to which a test measures what it is supposed to measure. When you step on the scales you want to know your weight, not your IQ or mechanical aptitude or some unknown quality. To assess validity we compare test scores against some separate or independent observation of the thing being measured. For example, if we were trying to establish whether or not a certain test of flying ability is valid, we might give the test to a large group of student pilots and then compare their test scores with the flight instructor's ratings of each person's actual ability to fly a plane. If those with the highest test scores also turn out to be the best pilots, the test is considered valid. The validity of such a test is important, because it allows us to predict on the basis of a person's test score whether or not that person will profit from flying lessons. Similarly, a valid test of college aptitude would predict whether an individual will be able to profit from the college experience. Thus, measurements must be an accurate reflection of what they are intended to measure—that is, valid.

Correlation: A tool for judging reliability and validity   In order to give precise statements about reliability and validity, a statistical technique called correlation is utilized. Although correlation does not allow for direct cause-and-effect statements, it does allow the scientist to make predictions.

Correlation is a statement about the strength of the association between two (or possibly more) variables. If the correlation between two variables is high, the variables will tend to vary together; that is, wherever one of the traits is found, chances are good that the other trait will also be found. If we observed that people with blond hair usually have blue eyes, then we would say that there is a correlation between the variables hair color and eye color. This is not to say that having blond hair causes one to have blue eyes, but it does allow us to predict, whenever we know that certain individuals have blonde hair, that they are also likely to have blue eyes.

Correlation is one way to assess reliability. If a certain test is given to a large group of subjects on two separate occasions, and if those individuals who score high on the test the first time also score high the second time and those who score low the first time also score low the second time, the two sets of measurements are said to correlate and the test is considered reliable. A high correlation between the two sets of scores indicates reliability because it demonstrates that the test is yielding consistent scores. The two variables, that is, the scores on the first administration of the test and the scores on the second, are in fact occurring together, or correlating.

Correlation can also establish validity. To establish validity we would give a test measuring some ability or trait to a group of individuals and then correlate their scores with actual performances by these same individuals on the ability or trait being measured. For example, we might compare scores on a sales aptitude test with actual performance in selling a certain product. If, in fact, there is a correlation between the two variables (the test scores and the number of sales achieved), the test has been shown to be valid—it is indeed measuring what it is intended to measure.

Reliability and validity are only two ways to apply this extremely useful technique. Later in

CONTEMPORARY ISSUE

Culture-Fair Testing: A Question of Validity

Intelligence tests, to be useful, must predict something—academic performance, success in life, something. For white middle- and upper-class Americans, intelligence tests have had a fairly good record, with higher validity coefficients than for any other type of psychological testing. But what about minority children? There are biases built into most of the well-known individual and group measures of intelligence. Minority populations have pointed out that many tests are not culture-free and that they therefore discriminate against them. This issue is not a new one in this country. During the early 1900s, immigrants arriving at New York's Ellis Island were tested by means of the methods available at the time. Henry Goddard, of Kallikak fame, used his own version of the Binet-Simon test, in pantomime, for the assessment of the non-English-speaking groups. His published results proclaimed that many immigrants from southern and eastern Europe were profoundly and innately retarded—79 percent of the Italians, 80 percent of the Austro-Hungarians, and 87 percent of the Russians.

Similarly, during World War I, the first group intelligence tests, the Army Alpha and Beta, were administered to large groups of non-English-speaking inductees. The groups were graded by four categories, A through D. The latter category was an indication of feeble-mindedness. The results also proclaimed that well over one-half the inductees from Poland, Italy, and Russia were retarded, while (astonishingly) those from England, Scotland, Holland,

and Denmark had very low rates of retardation. Similar conclusions were later reached for native minority groups. In the words of Lewis Terman, using the Stanford-Binet, the results indicated that mental retardation "is very, very common among Spanish-Indian and Mexican families of the Southwest and also among Negroes. Their dullness seems to be racial, or at least inherent in the family stocks from which they come."[a]

Apparently, it was never clear to some of the early giants of testing in this country (especially Goddard) that the intelligence tests they employed could not assess innate ability. If a youthful Albert Einstein, tested on the Army Alpha, did not know what the Brooklyn Nationals were called or what company in this country made revolvers, he might have been on his way to a Grade D designation of a feeble-minded immigrant. If an American Indian on a reservation had difficulty with such Stanford-Binet questions as the meaning of a birthday cake and candles or identifying an umbrella or knowing how a ship and auto are the same or different, then such a person would also be on the way to the retarded class.

Thus, the critics of IQ testing point out that such tests are first, culturally biased, and second, inadmissible as evidence of genetic racial differences. In fact, as Leon Kamin points out, Alfred Binet never believed that a test such as his could be used as an indicator of innate ability. The problem with these early tests, then, was not in the people being tested but in the

method of assessment. The techniques stacked the deck, so to speak, against anyone not from the standard American middle-class background.

Following the same logic, Jane Mercer, a sociologist, finds that current minority populations such as blacks, Puerto Ricans, Spanish-Americans, Native Americans, and rural children in general are unfairly classified, since the IQ tests are not valid for these children. The current intelligence measures do not adequately sample the abilities of groups like these. For example, in one study it was shown that a black urban child was sixteen times more likely than a white urban child to be assessed as retarded, even though further assessment indicated the actual rates were not that disparate.

To readjust our assessment procedures, particularly the heavy reliance on IQ tests, Mercer suggests a method to broaden the behavior sample.[b] Mercer indicates that scores should be "adjusted" upward for minority children. And instead of using only an individual IQ test, she tests in four additional areas: (1) the family, (2) the neighborhood, (3) the school, and (4) the community. Her questions are designed to tap the child's behavior in performing a variety of roles in these domains. How much independence and self-direction does the child exhibit in these areas? How much activity must be monitored and supervised? How complex are the tasks that the child performs? These three themes form the basis for assessment—self-direction, internal control, and complexity.

She then proposes that educators use this information systematically to change the IQ test score. Each minority child in her system would receive an "Adjusted Intelligence Quotient." Essentially, this means that the test score is changed on the basis of additional ratings of the child's competence. If, for example a seven-year-old Spanish child from the Los Angeles "barrios" tested out at 80 on the Weschler scales, the score would be adjusted upward if further study showed that she could find her way around the neighborhood, shop in stores, responsibly take care of younger siblings, or take on similar kinds of social roles. The SOMPA (System of Multicultural Pluralistic Assessment) method provides a calibrated system of adjusting IQ scores on the basis of such additional behavioral information on each child.

The controversy over testing, however, is not stilled by Mercer's work. In fact, one could almost say that critics on either side of the issue agree on only one thing, namely, that SOMPA may be a bad compromise. The conservative test constructionists are quick to point out some new gaps in both reliability and validity. How reliable are the questions of social competence? Don't questions like these become highly subjective? The ability to roam the neighborhood can be viewed positively or negatively. Also, the validity question arises: How do social skills relate to school performance? Just because a child may possess advanced interpersonal "cleverness" is no guarantee of a quick, inquiring mind. Thus, the more empirically bound test makers find much to criticize on the items, the norms, and the predictive power of the "adjusted" IQ.

On the other side, the critics of the "old" standardized tests are not really much happier with the new version. Making a small adjustment with a "bad system" does not solve anything, according to this view. If IQ tests are not culture-free, then toss out the tests. There is only one thing to do about such testing: Stop it! Raising a child's score a few points doesn't really change the injustice of subjecting that child to an entire battery of biased and prejudiced items. SOMPA may be only the newest version of the old white-liberal game—the appearance of sensitivity to the needs of minority children but "business as usual" underneath the façade. Why develop an IQ test whose norms are based primarily on white American children and then propose some adjustments only for minority children?

The answers are hard. The questions are easy. Do we adopt one standard or many? Do we choose cultural universalism or cultural relativity? Do we continue possibly to misclassify children on intelligence tests or do we continue to grope for more adequate measures? Is SOMPA a step forward or a step sideways? Has SOMPA increased the validity or simply dodged the question?

[a] Kamin, L. J. (1974). *The science and politics of I.Q.* Potomac, Md.: Erlbaum.
[b] Mercer, J. and Lewis, J. (1978). *System of multicultural pluralistic assessment.* New York: Psychological Corp.

this chapter we will cite other applications of correlation in educational psychology, and we will present a simple mathematical procedure for computing correlation.

Distributions

To create meaning out of the apparent chaos of raw data, the researcher begins by putting his measurements into an order. The first step is to form a distribution. Distribution simply means the arrangement of any set of scores in order of magnitude. Table 15.1 is a set of IQ scores.

Arranging these scores into a distribution means listing them sequentially from high to low. Table 15.2 is a distribution of the IQ scores from Table 15.1.

A distribution allows the observer to see general trends more readily than the unordered set of raw scores does. To further simplify our inspection of the data, they can be presented as a frequency distribution. A frequency distribution is a listing of each score achieved, together with the number of individuals receiving that score. Table 15.3 is a frequency distribution of our IQ scores.

TABLE 15.1 UNORDERED IQ SCORES
75
100
105
95
120
130
95
90
115
85
115
100
110
100
110

TABLE 15.2 DISTRIBUTION OF IQ SCORES
130
120
115
115
110
110
105
100
100
100
95
95
90
85
75

TABLE 15.3   IQ SCORES PRESENTED AS A FREQUENCY DISTRIBUTION

X (RAW SCORE)	f (FREQUENCY OF OCCURRENCE)
130	1
120	1
115	2
110	2
105	1
100	3
95	2
90	1
85	1
75	1

The X at the top of the first column stands for raw scores (in this case, IQ) and the f over the second column stands for frequency of occurrence. As can be seen, of the fifteen people taking the test, two received scores of 115, two received 110, three scored 100, two scored 95, and everyone else made a unique score.

In addition to presenting frequency distributions in table form, statisticians often present their data in graph form. A graph has the advantage of being a kind of "picture" of the data. It is customary to indicate the raw scores, or actual values of the variable, on the horizontal, X axis, called the "abscissa." The frequency of occurrence is presented on the vertical, or Y axis, called the "ordinate."

Figure 15.1 shows the data previously pre-

sented in tabular form arranged in a graphic form called a histogram, or bar graph. To construct a histogram, or bar graph, a rectangle is drawn over each raw score. The height of the rectangle indicates the frequency of occurrence for each score. Much of the data in educational psychology is presented in this way.

Figure 15.2 shows the same data arranged in another commonly used graphic form, called a "frequency polygon." To construct a frequency polygon, the IQ scores are again shown on the X axis and the frequency of occurrence on the Y axis. However, instead of rectangles, we use a single point to designate the frequency of each score. These points are then connected by a series of straight lines.

In both the histogram and the frequency polygon, it is essential that the base of the ordinate represent a frequency of zero—if not, the graph may tell a very misleading story. For example, suppose we are graphing data from a learning study that shows how increasing the number of learning trials increases the amount learned.

Let us plot the number of trials on the abscissa and the frequency of correct responses on the ordinate (Figure 15.3). Our graph shows that by trial four the subject made eight correct responses and that by trial ten the subject made twelve correct choices. These data are typical of the results obtained in learning studies; that is, a great deal of learning usually occurs during the first few trials, but, as the number of trials increases, further increase in learning lessens.

Suppose, however, the statistician wished to give a false interpretation of the data. He or she could simply focus on one small area of the graph (see Figure 15.4). Now the same data tell a very different story about how learning takes place. It looks like no learning took place before trial four and that the great bulk of learning took place between trials four and ten. We know from the previous graph that this is incorrect. In fact, most of the learning took place during the first four or five trials, and between trials four and ten, the learning was actually beginning to top out or level off. This is one instance of how statistics can be used to distort data—if the audience is naive about statistical techniques. Whenever a graph is presented in which the base of the ordinate is not set at zero, be on the alert. The stage has been set for a possible sleight-of-hand trick.

FIGURE 15.1 A histogram, or bar graph, of IQ scores.

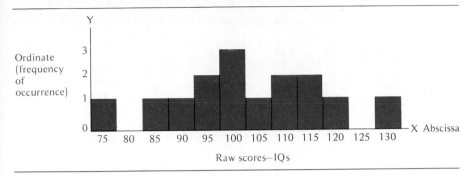

FIGURE 15.2 A frequency polygram.

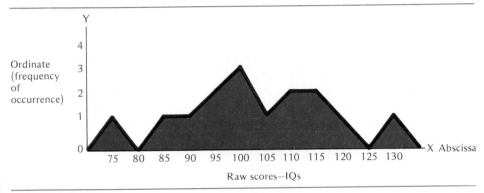

FIGURE 15.3 Data that is correctly plotted.

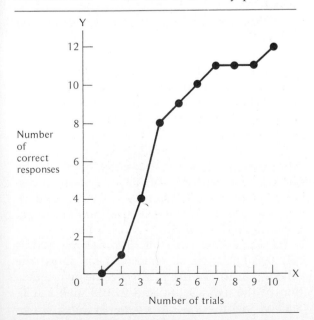

FIGURE 15.4 Here, the base of the ordinate in not set at zero. Be wary of such graphs, since they can easily lead to a false interpretation of data.

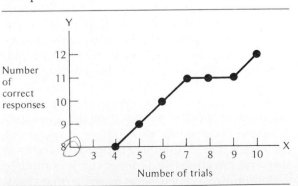

Measures of Central Tendency

To help us understand how individuals differ and how they are alike, we have some useful techniques for finding the "average," or typical score, in a distribution. Knowing the average IQ for a certain class may help us plan the curriculum, decide how extensively certain topics should be covered in class, or choose books for the library. Information about the typical score in a distribution allows us to interpret more meaningfully all the scores in the distribution.

Statisticians have three methods for obtaining the average, and each is designed, when used appropriately, to give us the most accurate picture possible of the distribution. The averages are called "measures of central tendency," because they describe the typical, middle, or central score in a distribution; they tell us about our average or typical person's score. Choosing the appropriate method can be tricky because the interpretation of the data may vary widely, depending on how the average has been obtained.

The mean If you were given a set of IQ scores and asked to find the average score, you would most likely compute the mean. That is, you would add all the IQ scores together and divide by the total number of scores. The mean is thus the arithmetic average; it is certainly the most commonly used measure of central tendency.

Statisticians use the symbol $\overline{X}$ to denote the mean. The equation for computing the mean is:

$$\overline{X} = \frac{\Sigma X}{N}$$

The Greek letter Σ (sigma) is a symbol that tells us to add; it is read as "summation of." N stands for the number of cases. Thus, the equation tells us that the mean ($\overline{X}$) is equal to the summation (Σ) of the raw scores (X) divided by the number of cases (N). The mean of our distribution of IQ scores would be computed as in Table 15.4.

As it happens, the mean is an appropriate measure of central tendency in the preceding example because the distribution is fairly well balanced; that is, there are no extreme scores in any one direction. Since the mean is computed by adding together all the scores in the distri-

TABLE 15.4 CALCULATION OF THE MEAN FROM A DISTRIBUTION OF RAW SCORES

X	CALCULATION
130	
120	
115	
115	
110	
110	
105	
100	
100	
100	
95	
95	
90	
85	$\overline{X} = \frac{\Sigma X}{N} = \frac{1545}{15}$
75	
1,545	$\overline{X} = 103$

bution it is not easily influenced by extreme scores, unless the extreme scores are all in one direction. The mean is typically a stable measure of central tendency.

Interpreting the mean can sometimes be very deceptive, especially in groups where the population itself or the size of the population changes. For example, the mean IQ of the typical freshman class in a college is usually about five points lower than the mean of the same class when the students later become seniors. Does this indicate that students increase their IQs as they proceed through college? No, because since the size of the senior class is almost always smaller than the size of the freshman class, the two populations are no longer the same. Those with the lowest IQs in the freshman class are apt to leave college and never become seniors.

The median In some situations, however, the use of the mean can lead to an extremely distorted picture of the "average" in a distribution. For example, look at the distribution of annual incomes in Table 15.5.

In Table 15.5 one of the income scores ($10,000,000.00) is so extremely far above the others that to use the mean income as a reflection of the average income would give a misleading picture of high prosperity for this distribution. A distribution that is unbalanced due to a few extreme scores in one direction is said to be "skewed."

A much more accurate representation of central tendency for a skewed distribution is the median, or middle-most score in a distribution. Whereas the mean income in Table 15.5 was found to be $788,338.46, the median would be $19,400.00, a far more accurate reflection of the typical income for the distribution. Since income distributions are usually skewed, you should be on the alert for an inflated figure whenever the mean income is reported. The median is generally a more appropriate value when reporting incomes. To calculate the median, be sure the scores are in distribution form, that is, arranged in order of magnitude. Then count down through one-half of the scores. For example, in Table 15.5 there are thirteen income scores in the distribution. We therefore count down six scores, and the seventh score is the median. (There will be the same number of scores above the seventh score as there are below it.) If there are an even number of scores in a distribution (see Table 15.6), the median is found by determining the score that lies halfway between the two middle scores or, in this case, 114.5. Unlike the mean, the median is not affected by an extreme score in one direction. In Table 15.6, for example, the median would still be 114.5 even if the low score were 6 instead of 112, whereas the mean would be an unrepresentative 97.83 (see Table 15.7).

TABLE 15.5   DISTRIBUTION OF INCOME SCORES SKEWED TO THE RIGHT

$10,000,000.00
30,000.00
30,000.00
19,600.00
19,500.00
19,500.00
19,400.00—Median
19,300.00
19,000.00
18,500.00
18,000.00
18,000.00
17,600.00
$10,248,400.00
$\overline{X}$ = $788,338.46

TABLE 15.6   CALCULATION OF THE MEDIAN WITH AN EVEN NUMBER OF SCORES

120
118
115
114 —114.5 Median
114
112
693

$\overline{X}$ = 115.50 Mean

Figure 15.5 shows what skewed distributions look like in graphic form. In the positively skewed distribution, most of the scores are found at the low end of the distribution, whereas in the negatively skewed distribution, most of the scores are at the high end. We label this according to the direction of the tail. When the tail goes to the right, we call the curve positively skewed; when it goes to the left, it is negatively skewed.

The mode   The third measure of central tendency is called the mode. The mode is the score that occurs most frequently in a distribution. In a frequency polygon the mode is located where the curve is at its highest point; in a histogram it is located at the tallest bar. Some distributions, called "bimodal," have two modes (see Figure 15.6). Distributions of this type occur where scores are clustered in two separate places, or where the group being measured probably breaks down into two subgroups.

Assume that the distribution in Figure 15.6 represents the running speed (in seconds) in

TABLE 15.7   CALCULATION OF THE MEDIAN WITH AN EVEN NUMBER OF SCORES AND A SKEWED DISTRIBUTION

120
118
115
114 —114.5 Median
114
6
587

$\overline{X}$ = 97.83 Mean

FIGURE 15.5   A graphic presentation of skewed distributions: (a) negatively skewed; (b) positively skewed.

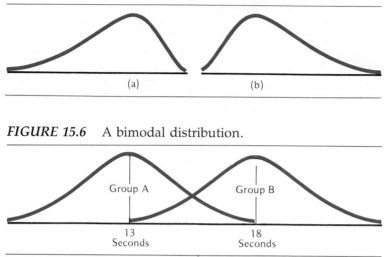

(a)   (b)

FIGURE 15.6   A bimodal distribution.

Group A   Group B

13
Seconds

18
Seconds

the seventy-yard dash for a large group of seventh-graders. There are two modes: one at thirteen seconds and the other at eighteen seconds. Since there are two scores sharing the same high frequency, it is probable that two subgroups are being portrayed. For example, the running speeds for boys may be clustering around one mode while the speeds for girls are clustering around the other.

VARIABILITY: THE NAME OF THE GAME IN EDUCATIONAL PSYCHOLOGY

Just as the measures of central tendency give us information about the similarity among measurements, measures of variability give us information about how scores differ or vary. Measures of variability are crucial in education since they give us vital information about one of psychology's basic themes—individual differences.

The Range

One way to describe variability in any distribution of scores is to compute the range (R). The range is the difference between the highest and lowest scores, and it is a measure of the width of the total distribution. The range is

given as a single value. For example, if the highest score in an IQ distribution is 140 and the lowest score is 60, then R would equal 80.

The Standard Deviation

The standard deviation (S.D.) is the absolute heart and soul of the variability concept. Although the range is important in giving some meaning to a set of scores, it does have one fairly significant limitation: It is based on only two scores, the highest and the lowest. The standard deviation, on the other hand, takes into account *every single* score in the entire distribution. The standard deviation, therefore, is a measure of variability that indicates how far *all* the scores in a distribution deviate from the mean. The higher the numerical value of the S.D., the more the scores vary around the mean, or the more the scores spread out around the mean. The smaller the value of the S.D., the less the scores spread from the mean—in fact, the more tightly they cluster around the mean. A distribution with a small standard deviation tells us that the group being measured in homogeneous, whereas a distribution with a large standard deviation describes a heterogeneous group of scores. This standard or typical deviation is always expressed as a single value.

In calculating the S.D., the following steps are needed (see Table 15.8):

TABLE 15.8   CALCULATION OF THE STANDARD DEVIATION FROM A DISTRIBUTION OF RAW SCORES

X	X²	CALCULATIONS
15	225	$\bar{X} = \dfrac{\Sigma X}{N} = \dfrac{72}{8} = 9.00$
12	144	
10	100	
9	81	$\text{S.D.} = \sqrt{\dfrac{\Sigma X^2}{N} - \bar{X}^2} = \sqrt{\dfrac{748}{8} - 9.00^2}$
9	81	
8	64	$= \sqrt{93.50 - 81.00} = \sqrt{12.50}$
7	49	
2	4	$\text{S.D.} = 3.535 = 3.54$
72	748	

1. Add the X's to obtain $\Sigma\ X$.

2. Divide by N to obtain $\bar{X}$.

3. Square each X to obtain X^2.

4. Add these squares to obtain $\Sigma\ X^2$.

5. Divide the ΣX^2 value by N and subtract the squared mean, $\bar{X}^{\,2}$.

6. Take the square root to obtain the S.D.

In Figure 15.7 we see a representation of two IQ distributions, both of which have the same range (60) and the same mean (100). The distributions are different because they have different standard deviations. Distribution (b) has a relatively large standard deviation, indicating that the scores deviate widely from the mean. Distribution (a), with a smaller standard deviation, indicates that the variability is much less, that most of the scores are clustering rather tightly around the mean.

FIGURE 15.8   The normal curve is a frequency-distribution curve with scores plotted on the x axis and frequency of occurrence on the y axis.

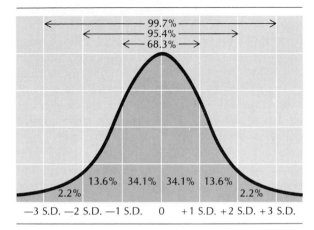

The Normal Curve

Many behavioral measures in educational psychology conform to what statisticians call the "normal curve" (see Figure 15.8). The normal curve is actually a theoretical distribution, but so many measurements come so close to this ideal that it is of utmost importance. The normal curve is a frequency-distribution curve with scores plotted on the x axis and frequency of occurrence on the y axis. However, it has a number of interesting features that set it apart from other frequency-distribution curves. First, in a normal curve most of the scores cluster around the center of the distribution, and as we move away from the center in either direction, there are fewer and fewer scores. Second, it is symmetrical; that is, the two halves of the curve are identical. It is in perfect balance. Third, the

FIGURE 15.7   Two IQ distributions with different standard deviations.

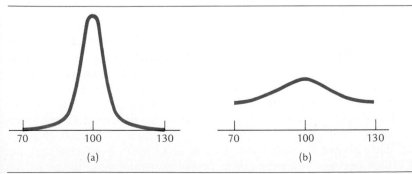

mean, median, and mode all fall at the same point, the midpoint of the distribution. Finally, the normal curve has some constant characteristics with regard to the standard deviation.

The mean divides the normal curve into two equal halves, with 50 percent of the scores falling above the mean and 50 percent falling below it. (Note that the mean and mode are at exactly the same point as the median in the normal curve.) The area between the mean and a point one standard deviation above the mean includes 34 percent of the scores. Since the normal curve is symmetrical, 34 percent of the cases also fall between the mean and a point one standard deviation below the mean. Thus, between the two points that are one standard deviation away from the mean, that is, ± 1 S.D., there are 68 percent (just twice 34 percent) of all the cases. As we go away from the mean another full standard deviation, 13.5 percent of the distribution is added to each side. Thus, approximately 95 percent of the cases fall between ± 2 S.D. units. Similarly, since going out a third S.D. from the mean adds 2.5 percent in each side, 99 percent, or virtually all the cases, fall between ± 3 S.D. units. Less than 1 percent of the scores lie beyond ± 3 S.D. units.

These facts relating percentage of cases to units of the standard deviation are constants; that is, the facts are true regardless of the size of the standard deviation. These constants hold as long as the curve is normal.

Standard Scores

It is difficult to compare scores on different tests without knowing the mean and the standard deviation for each test. For example, if you were to get a score of 72 on a certain math test and 64 on an English test, you wouldn't know on which test your performance was higher. The mean on the math test might have been 85, and the mean on the English test might have been 50, in which case you scored higher on the English test even though your raw score was lower. The point is that information about the distribution of scores must be obtained in order that raw scores can be interpreted. For this reason, we use z scores, or standard scores, which take the distribution into account. This allows us to understand an individual's test performance relative to others taking the same test.

The z score is equal to the difference between the raw score and the mean, divided by the standard deviation.

$$z = \frac{X - \bar{X}}{\text{S.D.}}$$

The z score indicates, in units of standard deviation, how far above or below the mean a certain score lies. If the mean of the math distribution (85) were subtracted from your math score (72) and divided by the S.D. (10), your z score would be -1.3.

$$z = \frac{72 - 85}{10} = \frac{-13}{10} = -1.3$$

Thus, on the math test you fell 1.3 S.D. units below the mean. A negative z score always indicates the score is below the mean, while a positive z score shows the score is above the mean. A score of 64 on the English test minus the mean of 50, and divided by a standard deviation, again of 10, yields a z score of 1.4.

$$z = \frac{64 - 50}{10} = \frac{14}{10} = 1.4$$

Since the sign in this case is positive, your score on the English test falls 1.4 S.D. units above the mean. Though your raw score on the English test is lower than your raw score on the math test, your actual performance on the English test, compared to all other performances on the same test, is considerably higher. Thus, by converting raw scores into z scores, comparisons can be made between an individual's performance on different distributions, with different means and standard deviations.

Percentiles

A raw score can be described very precisely by converting it into a percentile. A percentile is that point in a distribution at or below which a given percentage of scores fall. For example, a score at the 95th percentile means that 95 percent of the scores in the distribution are at or below that point, whereas a score at the 5th percentile means that only 5 percent of the scores fall at or below that point. By knowing the percentage of cases falling between various

S.D. units on the normal curve, one's percentile may be calculated. In the distribution for the normal curve (Figure 15.8), for example, 34 percent of the cases fall between the mean and −1 S.D. Since 50 percent of the cases fall below the mean, and since 34 percent of these cases fall between the mean and −1 S.D., we can see that 16 percent of the cases must fall below −1 S.D. A z score of −1, meaning a raw score one full S.D. below the mean, would yield a percentile score of 16. Or, a z score of +1, indicating a raw score of one full S.D. above the mean, would mean a percentile score of 84 (the 34 percent falling between the mean and 1 S.D. plus the 50 percent falling below the mean).

Statisticians can determine the percentile for any z score, not just those for whole numbers. For example, a z score of 1.52 shows that about 44 percent of the cases fall between the mean and 1.52 S.D. units. Thus, the percentile for that z score would be 94 (the 44 percent falling between the z score and the mean plus the 50 percent lying below the mean). Statistical tables are available that indicate the exact percentage of cases lying between the mean and any z score.[1]

Assume that we are working with an IQ distribution whose mean is 100 and whose S.D. is 15. A student with an IQ of 122 would have a z score of 122 − 100, divided by the S.D. of 15, or 1.47. The student with an IQ of 122 would fall 1.47 S.D. units above the mean. A z score table indicates that 43 percent of the cases fall between a z of 1.47 and the mean. Adding that to the 50 percent below the mean, we now know that the student with an IQ of 122 is at the 93rd percentile.

Norm-Referenced and Criterion-Referenced Testing

The various tests used in psychology and education use either norm-referenced or criterion-referenced scoring systems. The difference is fundamental. In a norm-referenced test an individual's performance is *compared* to the average performance of the entire test-taking population. For example, for an IQ test, an individual's score is not reported in terms of the absolute number of correct answers given but instead on the basis of a comparison between the individual's absolute performance and the average performance of all the individuals of the same age who have taken the test. This procedure, in fact, was precisely the same as that used way back at the turn of the century by that giant in the field of intelligence testing, Alfred Binet. Binet used the term *mental age* to describe his scoring technique, and this early system is an example of norm-referenced scoring. In order to establish a student's mental age, Binet would give his intelligence test to large numbers of children of various ages. The average performance for a given age became the benchmark for evaluating a given student's performance. For example, he discovered how many items the average eight-year-old (having tested thousands of eight-year-olds) could answer correctly, and then a child *of any age* who answered the same number of items was assigned a mental age of eight. The mental-age technique, as with all norm-referenced scoring systems, thus provides information regarding a person's relative standing. Most of the mass-produced tests used in psychology and education today are of this type. Intelligence tests, achievement tests, aptitude tests, and so on are accompanied by national norms with which an individual's performance can be compared.

The criterion-referenced test, however, is not based on relative performance but on *absolute performance*. The focus is on what absolute fraction of the material covered on the test the student has mastered. For example, the Federal Aviation Administration gives a test to each prospective pilot before that pilot is allowed to solo. The applicant must get at least 70 percent of the questions correct before taking to the air without the instructor. Thus, the FAA demands that the pilot know the vast majority of the material on the test, regardless of how others have performed. The FAA reasons that it's not enough to have a high relative standing on the test, since it's possible that the majority of those taking the test are so ignorant of flying techniques and procedures that they would probably all kill themselves.

In point of fact, most teacher-made tests (and these, after all, account for most of the educational tests given each day throughout the country) are criterion-referenced. The teacher makes up a history test and scores it on the basis of the absolute percentage of a student's correct answers, not on the basis of what percentage of the class did worse than that student. The algebra teacher who wants to know how a given student is doing with reference to *instructional objectives* in a particular classroom is going to use a criterion-referenced test.

Test specialists Arthur Bertrand and Joseph Cebula have identified three crucial components of good criterion-referenced testing.

1. Learning behaviors to be demonstrated by students must be clearly stated prior to the learning experience (e.g., the child will be able to punctuate a four-sentence paragraph).

2. Acceptable levels of success must be stated explicitly (e.g., punctuation must be done with 80 percent accuracy).

3. Test situations or conditions must be made available in order that the students can demonstrate whether or not they have met the criteria.[2]

Finally, according to Lorrie Shephard, norm-referenced tests should be used for monitoring pupil (and program) progress over the long run, from fall to spring or from year to year. Criterion-referenced tests, however, are preferred for day-to-day testing in the classroom. These tests are more easily keyed to current instructional objectives.[3]

Teachers typically prefer not to use standardized, norm-referenced tests, usually saying that their particular instructional activities should not be narrowed to those areas sampled by the norm-referenced tests. In fact, research shows that teachers usually don't use the results of norm-referenced tests in their academic decision making.[4]

CORRELATION: A USEFUL TOOL FOR MAKING PREDICTIONS

Although correlation does not imply causation, it is a useful tool for making predictions. A correlation is a statement about the relationship between two variables; it tells us the extent to which the two variables are associated, or the extent to which they occur together. There is, for example, a correlation between College Board scores and college grades. This means that the two variables, College Board scores and college grades, tend to occur together: People with high College Board scores tend to have higher college grade-point averages than do people with low College Board scores.

The Sign of the Correlation

Correlations come in three general forms: positive, negative, and zero. Positive correlations are produced when individuals who score high on the first variable also score high on the second, and those who score low on the first variable also score low on the second. For example, a positive correlation between height and weight means that those individuals who are above average in height are also above average in weight, and those who are below average in height are correspondingly below average in weight. Negative correlations are produced when individuals who score high on the first variable tend to score low on the second, and those who score low on the first, score high on the second. A negative correlation between college grades and number of absences means that those who are above average in college grades tend to have fewer absences, whereas those who are below average in college grades tend to have more than the average number of absences. Finally, zero correlations are produced when individuals who score high on the first variable are as likely to score high on the second variable as they are to score low; or, when individuals who score low on the first variable are as likely to score low on the second variable as they are to score high.

Correlation Values

In order to express the degree to which two variables are associated, or correlated, a single number is used. This number may vary from +1 through 0 to −1. A value of +1 indicates a maximum positive correlation. A maximum relationship is obtained when two measures of a group of individuals, for example, height and weight, associate perfectly. There can be no exceptions when the correlation is +1. Thus, every single individual in the group who is higher than another in height is also higher in weight. A value of 0 indicates no relationship at all, or a zero correlation. A value of −1 indicates a maximum negative correlation. A correlation of -1 between college grades and number of absences would mean that every single individual in the group who is higher than another in college grades is also lower than that other in number of absences. Most correlations found in the literature fall somewhere between these perfect correlations of $+1$ and -1. The closer the correlation is to ± 1, however, the more accurate the resulting prediction; and prediction, after all, is the major goal of correlation research. For example, if the correlation between height and weight were $+.65$, we could more accurately predict a given individual's weight, knowing his height, than if the correlation were only $+.25$.

Scatterplot Diagrams

In order to get a visual representation of how two variables might correlate, statisticians use a graphic device known as a scatterplot diagram. A scatterplot diagram is a correlation graph in which each dot represents a pair of scores: one for the distribution of one set of scores and the other for the distribution of the other set of scores. Figure 15.9 shows the three kinds of relationships that can exist between two variables. The scatterplot diagram on the left portrays a positive correlation: The array of dots goes from lower left to upper right, telling us that as one variable increases, so too does the other. The scatterplot diagram in the middle portrays a negative correlation: The array of dots goes from upper left to lower right, telling us that as one variable increases, the other decreases. Finally, the scatterplot diagram on the right portrays a zero correlation, or no relationship at all: As one variable changes, there is no related change in the other.

Karl Pearson, a student of Sir Francis Galton, devised the Pearson product moment correlation, the Pearson r, which indicates the strength of the possible association between two variables.

The Pearson r

One of the most frequently used correlation coefficients is the Pearson product moment correlation or, more simply, the Pearson r. This measure was developed by Karl Pearson, a student of Sir Francis Galton.

The Pearson r is the mean of the z-score products of the X and Y variables:

$$r = \frac{\Sigma z_x z_y}{N}$$

To compute the Pearson r, each raw score is converted into a z score. The z scores for each variable are then multiplied, and these products

FIGURE 15.9 Scatterplot diagrams showing three kinds of relationships existing between two variables.

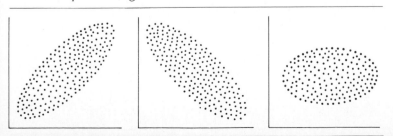

are added. The sum of the products is then divided by the number of products to get the mean product, which is the correlation coefficient. This is obviously a long and laborious process. Statisticians have therefore derived a simpler equation, one with fewer mathematical manipulations. If you have learned to calculate a standard deviation, computing a Pearson r will be fairly easy. Assume that we are interested in testing the hypothesis that there is some relationship or correlation between math ability and spelling ability among fifth-grade students. We administer a twelve-item math quiz and a twelve-item spelling quiz to a group of fifth-graders. Let the math scores be represented on the X distribution and the spelling scores on the Y distribution. Then the Pearson r is calculated as follows:

1. Calculate the mean for each distribution. In Table 15.9, ΣX (or 65) divided by N (or 10) equals 6.5. Similarly, ΣY (or 70) divided by 10 equals 7.

2. Compute the standard deviation for each distribution. Square each score and add the squares. Thus, for the X distribution, the first score, 4, when squared equals 16. Next, the score of 12 is squared, yielding 144, and so on. These squared scores are then added, yielding 527 for the X distribution. The Y distribution is treated in exactly the same way: Square the first score, 6, and get 36. Add all the squares and get 576. Each of these values is used to obtain the standard deviation for each distribution. For X, divide ΣX^2 (527) by N (10) and get 52.70. From that,

TABLE 15.9   CALCULATION OF THE PEARSON r

Student No.	MATH SCORE X	MATH SCORE X²	SPELLING SCORE Y	SPELLING SCORE Y²	XY
1	4	16	6	36	24
2	12	144	10	100	120
3	2	4	3	9	6
4	5	25	4	16	20
5	9	81	5	25	45
6	6	36	10	100	60
7	2	4	3	9	6
8	10	100	10	100	100
9	6	36	9	81	54
10	9	81	10	100	90
	10)65	527	10)70	576	525

$\bar{X} = 6.50$ $\bar{Y} = 7.00$

$$\text{S.D.}_x = \sqrt{\frac{\Sigma X^2}{N} - \bar{X}^2} \qquad\qquad \text{S.D.}_y = \sqrt{\frac{\Sigma Y^2}{N} - \bar{Y}^2}$$

$$= \sqrt{\frac{527}{10} - 6.50^2} = \sqrt{52.70 - 42.25} \qquad = \sqrt{\frac{576}{10} - 7.00^2} = \sqrt{57.60 - 49.00}$$

$$= \sqrt{10.45} \qquad\qquad\qquad\qquad = \sqrt{8.60}$$

$$\text{S.D.}_x = 3.23 \qquad\qquad\qquad \text{S.D.}_y = 2.93$$

$$r = \frac{\Sigma XY/N - \bar{X} \times \bar{Y}}{(\text{S.D.}_x)(\text{S.D.}_Y)} = \frac{525/10 - 6.5 \times 7}{3.23 \times 2.93} = \frac{52.50 - 45.50}{9.46}$$

$$r = \frac{7}{9.46}$$

$r = .739$, which is rounded to
$r = .74$

subtract the square of the mean (52.70 − 42.25). For the resulting value, 10.45, extract the square root, 3.23, which is the standard deviation. For the *Y* distribution, divide 576 by 10, which equals 57.60. Subtract the square of the mean (57.60 − 49.00) and get 8.60. Extract the square root, 2.93, to obtain the standard deviation.

3. Multiply each raw score in the *X* distribution by its corresponding score in the *Y* distribution. Thus 4 times 6 equals 24; 12 times 10 equals 120; 2 times 3 equals 6, and so on. These *XY* values are then added, yielding a total Σ*XY* of 525.

4. Divide the Σ*XY* by *N*, and then subtract the product of the means. Thus 525/10 minus the product of 6.50 times 7 equals 7.

5. This value is then divided by the product of the standard deviations of *X* and *Y*. Thus 3.23 times 2.93 equals 9.46. Dividing 7 by 9.46 gives us a Pearson *r* of .739, which is rounded to .74.

Interpretation of *r*   Since the highest possible correlation is 1.00, which is a perfect positive correlation, the Pearson *r* of .74 indicates a fairly strong association between the two variables, math scores and spelling scores. Thus, our sample of fifth-graders provides data that tell us that students who perform well on the math quiz are also likely to perform well on the spelling quiz. Since the correlation is not 1.00, we cannot say that every student who is high in math ability is also high in spelling ability. Our correlation of .74 indicates that there will be some exceptions but that in general the relationship will be dependable. Thus, knowing a student's math score allows us to predict his or her spelling score, and because the correlation is fairly strong, we will be right in our predictions far more often than we will be wrong. Although correlation does not imply causation, it does allow for accurate predictions. We can't say that an individual is a good speller because he or she has high math ability, but we can say that, given information about the pupil's math ability, we can predict fairly accurately how well he or she will spell.

SAMPLING: GENERALIZING FROM THE FEW TO THE MANY

Perhaps you have been told never to generalize, never to leap to conclusions on the basis of a few observations. An old proverb states that one swallow does not make a summer. Statisticians say, "Never generalize from an *N* of one." Someone once said that no generalization is absolutely true, even that one.

This is certainly all good advice. It prevents us from committing the inductive fallacy—that is, automatically assuming that all members of a class have a certain characteristic because one member of that class has it. It would be fallacious to say, "I once met a Mongolian who was a liar; therefore, all Mongolians are liars."

However, under certain prescribed conditions—that is, using certain strategies or rules of the game—it can be appropriate to generalize on the basis of a limited number of observations. Certain statistical techniques exist that allow us to generalize to a whole group after observing some part of that group. The key to these techniques is that the small groups must be representative of the entire group; they must reflect the traits and characteristics of the entire group. If we want to predict political attitudes of Americans in general, we cannot interview just men, or just women, or just Democrats, or just people who are receiving social security. We must interview a group that represents all these traits and many more.

The entire group, or the total number of people, things, or events having at least one trait in common is called a "population." Any group selected from the population is called a "sample." In order to ensure that the sample is representative of the population, statisticians usually use the technique of random sampling. Random sampling gives every single member of the entire population an equal chance of being selected for the sample. If you wanted to select a random sample of the population of students at your college, you could not do it by selecting every third person in the college cafeteria. Perhaps some students never eat in the cafeteria, and they would not be represented in the sample. Nor could you choose a random sample by selecting every *n*th person who enters the library. Again, some students avoid the library and would not be represented in the

ANNE ANASTASI

Anne Anastasi was born in 1909 and brought up in New York City. She attended Public School 33, where she was awarded a gold medal for general excellence. She then entered public high school, but after two frustrating months she dropped out. Although she had found her stay at P.S. 33 to be happy and productive, she found high school to be a total waste of time. Her high school was overcrowded, and she resented both the fifteen-minute trolley-car ride and also the fact that her teachers were remote and impersonal.

During her drop-out phase, there were many family discussions about her academic future. Finally, a friend suggested that she should simply skip high school completely and go to college. Thus in 1924, at the precocious age of 15, Anne Anastasi became a freshman math major at Barnard College. As a freshman, she took an introductory psychology course, and although she found the course interesting, it was not until her sophomore year, when she took a course in developmental psychology, that she decided psychology was to be her life work. Psychology gave her the opportunity to have the best of two worlds. She could satisfy her interest in mathematics through the study of psychological statistics and also her emerging interest in human development and behavior.

She graduated from Barnard at nineteen and immediately entered the Ph.D. program in psychology at Columbia University. She received her doctorate two years later. The high point of her short tenure as a graduate student came during the summer of 1929. She began that memorable summer as a research assistant to the famous American geneticist Charles B. Davenport. Next she took a six-week course with the illustrious learning theorist Clark Hull. Finally, as the summer ended, she enjoyed the "heady privilege" of attending the International Congress of Psychology at Yale University. There she saw and heard great psychologists from all over the world, including Ivan Pavlov, Charles Spearman, and William McDougall.

sample. To be sure to have a random sample, to be sure that every student in the college has an equal chance of being chosen, you would take the names of every student enrolled in the college, drop the names in a barrel, and, blindfolded, select out, say, fifty or a hundred names. In this way the group selected would be truly random, and because the group was selected on a chance basis, it would likely be representative of the entire population. Random sampling allows the statistician to legitimately generalize to the population.

In 1930 Anastasi joined the faculty at Barnard College, where she remained until 1939. She then went to Queens College in New York as chairman of the psychology department, and in 1947 she joined the faculty at Fordham University.

Anastasi considers herself to be a "generalist" in the field of psychology. Her interests range widely, and she has published in such diverse areas as the psychology of art, memory, personality, intelligence, emotion, statistics, language development, test construction, cultural differences, creativity, male and female differences, and the nature-nurture controversy. The bibliography of Anastasi's papers and books reads like a compendium of the whole field of psychology. There are few areas in psychology to which this talented woman has not devoted some of her time and energy.

In 1971 Anastasi was honored by her professional colleagues by being chosen as the president of the American Psychological Association, a group at that time of over 31,000 members.

Anastasi is a firm believer in the influence of early experience on intellectual growth and development. She urges a program of concentrated effort on improving environmental conditions at early life stages, especially for disadvantaged groups. She feels that early in life the cumulative effects of an impoverished environment can be minimized. She is also a firm believer in intelligence testing, when the tests are administered properly and evaluated fairly. She feels that IQ tests should not be discontinued just because some children receive lower scores than others. This would be like asking a physician to throw away his thermometer just because children who are ill register an undesirable deviation from the norm. Measuring instruments don't produce social discrimination; only people do.

In 1958, in her paper "Heredity, Environment and The Question 'How?' " Anastasi argued that people should stop asking the question about which component, heredity or environment, is more important in determining individual differences. A better question is "how" heredity and environment interact in the development of behavioral differences. The focus should be on the mechanism of the interaction, because behavior is the result of the interaction. Anne Anastasi, the generalist, specifically recommends here that we take a new look at one of psychology's oldest and most often debated problems.

SUMMARY

Measurement is the assigning of a number to an object or event according to rules. To give meaning to these numbers, all measurements must satisfy two basic criteria. They must be reliable, and they must be valid. Reliability indicates the consistency of a measurement, while validity is the extent to which a test measures what it is intended to measure.

To make meaning out of the chaos of the raw data from a study, the statistician arranges his or her scores in order of magnitude, called a "distribution of scores." When the scores are listed beside another column giving the frequency of occurrence for each score, a frequency distribution is created. Statisticians also use graphs to present their data in more meaningful form. The actual scores are indicated on the horizontal axis, or the abscissa, and the frequency of occurrence is presented on the vertical axis, or the ordinate.

In order to aid in our understanding of both the ways in which individuals differ and also the ways in which they are alike, techniques are employed for finding the average or typical score in a distribution. These techniques are called "measures of central tendency," and include the mean, which is the actual arithmetic average; the median, which is the middle-most score in a distribution; and the mode, which is the most frequently occurring score in a distribution.

Just as the measures of central tendency give us information with regard to similarity among measurements, measures of variability give us information regarding how scores differ or vary. Two measures of variability are the range, which is the difference between the highest and lowest scores in a distribution, and the standard deviation, which is a measure of how much each of the raw scores varies or deviates from the mean. In addition, many behavioral measures in psychology conform to what is called the "normal curve," a theoretical distribution of scores that in general shows the majority of scores falling in the center of the distribution. As we move away from this center, in either direction, we find fewer and fewer scores. A standard score, or z score, is a translation of a raw score into units of standard deviation. A percentile is that point in the distribution at or below which a given percentage of cases fall.

Tests can be scored by being (1) criterion referenced or (2) norm referenced. Criterion-referenced tests are those that evaluate individual performance on the basis of a comparison with some arbitrarily fixed standard. Norm-referenced tests judge the individual's performance on the basis of a comparison with the average performance of all the individuals who took the test.

Correlation is a statement as to the strength of the association between two (or possibly more) variables. Though correlational statements do not imply causation, they can be used to make better-than-chance predictions.

By using proper sampling techniques, such as random sampling, the scientist can legitimately generalize the results of his or her measurements of a small group to an entire group. Thus, the scientist may measure only a sample and yet generalize to a population. The key issue in this procedure is that the sample must be representative of the population.

KEY TERMS AND NAMES

individual differences
measurement
reliability
validity
correlation
distribution
measures of central tendency
   mean
   median
   mode
variability measure
   range (R)

standard deviation (S.D.)
normal curve
z score (standard score)
percentile
norm-referenced test
criterion-referenced test
Pearson product moment correlation
   (Pearson r)
inductive fallacy
random sample
Anne Anastasi

REFERENCES

1. Sprinthall, R. C. (1987). *Basic statistical analysis*, 2nd ed. Englewood Cliffs, N.J.: Prentice-Hall.

2. Bertrand, A., and Cebula, J. (1980). *Tests, measurement and evaluation: A developmental process*. Reading, Mass.: Addison-Wesley.

3. Shephard, L. (1979). Norm-referenced vs. criterion-referenced tests. *Educational Horizons, 68*(1), 26–35.

4. Salmon-Cox, L. (1981). Teachers and standardized achievement tests. *Phi Delta Kappan* (May), pp. 631–634.

16

INTELLIGENCE: CONCEPTS AND MEASURES

Among the lay public, the term *intelligence* is probably the most widely used psychological concept of them all. The media constantly bombard us with stories of new theories and studies, often anecdotal, on the topic of intelligence. Historians estimate the IQs of important persons from the past. People talk about whether they or others are intelligent enough for this job or that college or to marry this or that person. Politicians have even legislated immigration quotas on the basis of their versions of intelligence. Hardly a day goes by without your hearing the term mentioned at least once, but what does it mean? What is intelligence? Does it even exist, and if it does, is it displayed differently among different people engaged in different tasks?

WHAT IS INTELLIGENCE?

If you could step back in time and observe those first humans living among large and ferocious beasts, you probably wouldn't have given those weak, skinny, hairless creatures much chance for survival, never mind even an outside chance of taking over the planet. In an eagle-and-claw world, the human being would not have appeared as "fit" enough to survive. But we humans did survive and did take charge of our world. Why? Undoubtedly because of our wits. Our ability to size up new situations, learn from past mistakes, and create new patterns of thought all contributed heavily to our overall capacity to *adapt to new situations* and then *transmit our learning to new generations.* Intelligence had and continues to have survival value. Sandra Scarr has said that from the point of view of biology, intelligence has evolved as a primary adaptive mechanism and as such shows typical patterns of individual variability.[1]

During the early years, many psychologists had assumed that intelligence was a unitary trait or an absolute like height or weight. Some theorists, however, began taking a far less simplistic view. For example, just after the turn of the century, Charles Spearman theorized that intelligence was made up of two factors, an underlying general factor (g), and a series of very specific factors (s's). According to Spearman, the g factor acted as a driving force that would power a set of special skills unique to specific situations, such as verbal ability, math ability, and even musical ability. The *g* factor, however, provided the main thrust for activating the *s* factors. According to Spearman's model, *g* was a form of dynamic brain energy that would set in motion the "specific engines" of ability. Spearman also believed that *g* was largely inherited.

L. L. Thurstone, from the 1920s through the 1940s, worked diligently on an attempt to refine Spearman's factors but could find no substantive evidence to support the *g* concept. Thurstone suggested, instead, that intelligence was always a composite of special factors, each peculiar to a specific task. He identified seven different "vectors of the mind," or major components of intelligence: verbal comprehension, word fluency, numerical ability, spatial visualizations, associative memory, perceptual speed, and reasoning. Since then, J. P. Guilford's factor approach has pointed to the possibility of intelligence being composed of up to 120 separately identifiable traits.[2] More recently, in a fashion very similar to Thurstone, Howard Gardner has identified seven kinds of intelligence: (1) linguistic, (2) logico-mathematical, (3) spatial, (4) musical, (5) bodily-kinesthetic, (6) interpersonal (knowing how to deal with others), and (7) intrapersonal (knowledge of one's self). The problem, according to Gardner, is that traditional tests of intelligence measure only the first two. Gardner has even gone so far as to suggest getting rid of traditional IQ tests, even though he admits they are good predictors of school success. His argument is that despite their predictive accuracy, IQ tests have too often had destructive social consequences.[3]

In his triarchic theory of intelligence, Robert Sternberg (who as we saw in Chapter 11 views intelligence from an information-processing perspective) has found intelligence to be made up of three major components: (1) metacomponents, (2) performance components, and (3) knowledge-acquisition components. Says Sternberg:

> Metacomponents are higher-order executive processes used in planning, monitoring and decision making. Performance components are processes used in the execution of a task.

Knowledge-acquisition components are processes used in learning new information.[4]

Sternberg further breaks down these three major components of intelligence into subcomponents. For example, knowledge-acquisition has three basic subcomponents: (1) selective encoding, (2) selective combination, and (3) selective comparison. It is interesting to note here that Sternberg uses one of his major components, the metacomponent, to explain Spearman's long-sought *g* factor.

In a famous statement, P. E. Vernon suggested three basic meanings of the concept of intelligence.

1. *Intelligence as genetic capacity.* This assumes that intelligence is completely inherited, that intelligence is simply part of one's genetic equipment. Donald O. Hebb refers to this as Intelligence A, the genotypic form of intelligence (see Chapter 4).

2. *Intelligence as observed behavior.* This second meaning, referred to by Hebb as Intelligence B, is based on an observation of what the individual does. This is the phenotypic form of intelligence and is a result of the interaction of genes and the environment. In this sense intelligence becomes an adverb, and we define it on the basis of whether or not the individual acts *intelligently.*

3. *Intelligence as a test score.* The third meaning of intelligence, Intelligence C, is based on a strict operational definition of the concept. Intelligence is what the intelligence test measures. Though this seems to be a straightforward, no-frills definition, it creates a meaning of intelligence that can differ from what the majority of individuals would regard as intelligent behavior.[5]

According to Jerome Sattler, an expert in the assessment of children's intelligence, there are a number of problems associated with Intelligence C.

> A number of extrinsic handicaps, especially found among disadvantaged children and among those from underdeveloped nations, can serve to lower test performance, including

(a) the examinee's unfamiliarity with the test situation and his lack of motivation; (b) difficulties associated with the item format and testing conditions; (c) mistrust of the examiner, and anxiety and excitement; and (d) difficulties in understanding the instructions or in communicating the responses.[6]

Despite these problems, however, neither Sattler nor Vernon advocates the abandonment of intelligence tests. Vernon believes that since Intelligence B is based on observed behavior, a good IQ test is one way through which that behavior can be observed—that is, both the Stanford-Binet and the Wechsler Intelligence Scale for Children (WISC), in the hands of skilled examiners, thoroughly sample Intelligence B (at least among Western children). Sattler says that despite the limitations inherent in intelligence testing, the tests have made valuable contributions to the decision-making processes in schools and clinics.

IN THE BEGINNING: THE HISTORY OF IQ TESTING

Over a century ago, an Englishman named Sir Francis Galton began speculating on a subject that has very recently become one of the most explosive in all of educational psychology. Galton, who was Charles Darwin's younger cousin, attempted to relate Darwin's theory of evolution to human intellect. Believing that intelligence was a result of one's sensory equipment, and that one's sensory equipment was a result of heredity (since keen sensory powers would seem to have survival value), Galton tried to measure these sensory powers, and thus, intelligence. In 1882 he set up a testing booth in a London museum and charged people a fee to have their hearing, vision, reaction time, and other sensorimotor equipment measured. It is certainly an indication of Galton's own genius that he could devise a way to turn a profit while collecting his data. Perhaps the most significant fact to emerge from his data was the concept of individual differences: Galton found that people varied widely in their abilities to perform on simple sensorimotor tests. Despite their seem-

ing simplicity, one thing is certain about Galton's tests—they were definitely not culturally biased.

Galton firmly believed that intelligence was inherited. He may have felt this way partly because he had some extremely bright relatives, including Charles Darwin. But he also felt he had objective evidence. He collected data on assumed intellectual relationships between pairs of twins. As we will see, virtually all later studies of intelligence are based on Galton's idea of studying relationships in the context of individual differences. As we saw in the last chapter, one of Galton's students, a mathematician named Karl Pearson, actually worked out the basic equation for the correlation coefficient, and thus furnished the statistical groundwork for the data analysis that has proved so useful in the study of intelligence.

Individual Differences and Correlation

Galton and Pearson were impressed by the fact that individuals varied so greatly in such characteristics as height, weight, and intellect. Because of this variety, the measurements of these characteristics would be more useful if they reflected the frequency with which they could be expected to occur in the population, on the basis of chance, rather than their own absolute units of measurement, such as feet or pounds. The idea of relative standing is of great importance in psychology. It is more important to know that a man's height places him in the relative position of exceeding 50 percent of the adult male population than to know that he stands five feet, eight inches tall.

The concept of individual differences also makes it possible to find a common ground of comparison between different kinds of measurements. Even though height and weight cannot be compared directly because different units of measurement are used, they can be compared in terms of how much they vary from eacn of their own average. In effect, this means that apples and oranges can be compared on the basis of whether, say, a given orange and a given apple are both larger or smaller, or juicier or riper, than the average orange and apple. Thus, the relationships between two measure-

SIR FRANCIS GALTON

Francis Galton was born near Birmingham, England, in 1822. His family was wealthy and highly educated. Among his relatives were many of England's most accomplished and gifted citizens, including Charles Darwin, who introduced the modern theory of evolution, and Arthur Hallam, the subject of Tennyson's "In Memoriam." Galton even published a list of his wife's "connections," indicating that her father had been headmaster of Harrow.

In 1838 Galton took up the study of medicine at Birmingham General Hospital and later at King's College in London. In 1840 he shifted his

career plans and transferred to Trinity College, where he majored in mathematics.

Following college, Galton went on several trips to Africa, exploring some areas of that continent for the first time. For his African explorations, Galton received the Royal Geographical Society's gold medal in 1854. After his marriage in 1853, Galton turned to writing. His first book, *The Art of Travel*, was a practical guide for the explorer, and his second book, on meteorology, was one of the first attempts to set forth precise techniques for predicting the weather.

During the 1860s Galton became

impressed with his cousin Charles Darwin's book on evolution, *On the Origin of Species*. He was fascinated with Darwin's notion of the survival of the fittest, and he attempted to apply this concept to human beings, thus founding the field of eugenics, or the study of how the principles of heredity could be used to improve the human race.

In 1869 Galton published his first major work, *Hereditary Genius*, in which he postulated the enormous importance of heredity in determining intellectual eminence. He felt that "genius" ran in families, and he was able to point to his own family as "exhibit A." He also became impressed with the wide range of individual differences that he found for virtually all human traits, physical as well as psychological. Assuming that intelligence was a function of a person's sensory apparatus, he devised a series of tests of reaction time and tests of sensory acuity to measure intellectual ability. He is considered, therefore, to be the father of intelligence testing. Although Galton's tests seem naive by modern standards, his emphasis on the relationship between sensory ability and intellect foreshadows much of today's research on the importance of sensory stimulation in determining cognitive growth. Galton also invented what he termed the "index of co-relation" in order to analyze the test data that he was collecting. It was left to one of his students, Karl Pearson, however, to work out the mathematical equation for this index, which is now known as the Pearson *r*, or product moment correlation.

Following the publication of *Hereditary Genius*, Galton wrote other major works, including *English Men* of *Science, Natural Inheritance,* and *Inquiries into Human Faculty.* His range of interests in psychology was extremely wide, delving into such topics as imagery, free and controlled associations, personality testing, and, of course, the assessment of intellect. Certainly Galton takes his place in history as a hereditarian. He did not overlook environment completely, however. To gain understanding of the possible differential effects of heredity and environment, Galton performed psychology's first research studies on twins.

In 1909, just two years before his death, Galton was knighted. Galton's place in the history of psychology is ensured. More than any other person, he set psychology on the road to quantifying its data, and, of course, the whole testing movement in educational psychology owes a major debt to Galton's early work.

Perhaps the most significant fact to emerge from Galton's study was the concept of individual differences. The concept allows for a comparison of unlike traits.

ments can be expressed in quantitative terms, and this value is called the correlation coefficient. As we saw in Chapter 15, correlations range in value from +1 through zero to −1. The stronger the relationship, the greater the deviation from zero.

Alfred Binet and Mental Age

In 1904, the Minister of Public Instruction in Paris, France, appointed Alfred Binet to a special commission that was to study the problem of educating mentally retarded children. The

ANTHROPOMETRIC
LABORATORY

For the measurement in various ways of Human Form and Faculty.

Entered from the Science Collection of the S. Kensington Museum.

This laboratory is established by Mr. Francis Galton for the following purposes:—

1.   For the use of those who desire to be accurately measured in many ways, either to obtain timely warning of remediable faults in development, or to learn their powers.

2.   For keeping a methodical register of the principal measurements of each person, of which he may at any future time obtain a copy under reasonable restrictions.   His initials and date of birth will be entered in the register, but not his name.   The names are indexed in a separate book.

3.   For supplying information on the methods, practice, and uses of human measurement.

4.   For anthropometric experiment and research, and for obtaining data for statistical discussion.

Charges for making the principal measurements:
THREEPENCE each, to those who are already on the Register.
FOURPENCE each, to those who are not:— one page of the Register will thenceforward be assigned to them, and a few extra measurements will be made, chiefly for future identification.

The Superintendent is charged with the control of the laboratory and with determining in each case, which, if any, of the extra measurements may be made, and under what conditions.

H & W. Brown, Printers, 20 Fulham Road, S.W.

commission concluded that separate schools should be established to educate those children who could not profit from the regular classroom situation. Binet and his colleague, Theodore Simon, developed the first real intelligence test for the express purpose of identifying these children. Binet discarded Galton's notion of measuring intelligence through the use of sensori-motor tasks and assembled instead a series of intellectual tasks. It was Binet's belief that intelligence was the ability to make sound judgments. The various tasks were arranged in order of difficulty and presented to a group of French children. Binet later used the concept of mental age to score the test. He discovered, for example, how many of the tasks the average six-year-old could pass, and then any other children who passed the same number of tests were assigned a mental age of six years. Thus, Binet defined mental age in terms of the age at which a given number of test items are passed by an average child. This means that from the very beginning the measurement of intelligence has been a relative measure of mental growth. Binet's intelligence scores were not absolute for they were based on how well a given child does compared to the average child of the same age. As we saw in Chapter 15, this is a clear example of a norm-referenced system. Binet's scores were assigned relative to the performance shown by children of the *same age*, taking the *same test*.

Binet tried to define intelligence in terms of an individual's ability to make sound judgments. "To judge well, to comprehend well, to reason well, these are the essentials of intelligence. A person may be a moron or an imbecile if he lacks judgment, but with good judgments he could not be either."[7] But, unlike many of the theoreticians who followed, Binet spent little time fretting over the intricacies and possible embellishments of his definition. Binet's goal was to measure intelligence, not merely to talk about it. He understood intelligence by what it enabled children to do, in much the same way an electrician understands electricity. The point is, Binet's test worked. With it, he could predict reasonably well which children would do well in school and which ones would have difficulties. Of course, there were exceptions, but these

were fewer and fewer as the test improved. Sometimes a bright but disobedient child would do worse in school than his intelligence test score would predict, and sometimes a dull but docile child would do better. This, however, may have been due as much to faulty teacher evaluation as to inaccurate test scores. Binet's test was an individual test of intelligence; that is, the test was given to one child at a time and administered by a trained examiner.

The Early Stanford-Binet

Binet continued working on his 1905 scale, creating new items to improve the test. He revised the whole test twice, in 1908 and in 1911. In 1916, an American psychologist, Lewis M. Terman of Stanford University, published an American revision of the Binet test. Terman's test was standardized on American children and introduced so many new items that it was virtually a new test. He called it the Stanford-Binet, and this test soon became immensely popular in this country. In scoring the test, Terman introduced to America the concept of the intelligence quotient, or IQ.* IQ was determined by dividing mental age by chronological age and multiplying by 100 to get rid of the decimals. Thus, IQ = MA/CA × 100. A six-year-old child scoring a mental age of nine years would have an IQ of 9/6 × 100, or 1.5 × 100, or 150. On the other hand, a six-year-old child scoring a mental age of five years would have an IQ of 5/6 × 100, or .833 × 100, or 83. Since the test was standardized in such a way that the mental age was determined by how well the average child in a given age group did on the test, the average IQ for each age group had to be 100. That is, a six-year-old child scoring a mental age of six years (as the average six-year-old had done), would have an IQ of 6/6 × 100, or 100. Since the IQ expresses a child's rate of mental growth, the child whose IQ is 100 is progressing at an average rate.

---

* Terman borrowed the term IQ from a German psychologist, William Stern, who published a paper describing its use in 1913.

ALFRED BINET

Alfred Binet was born in Nice, France, in 1857. He later went to school in Paris and received a law degree in 1878. Practicing law did not appeal to Binet, and he soon decided to go back to school. In 1890 he received a degree in the natural sciences, and in 1894 he earned his Ph.D. in science. His doctoral thesis was on the nervous system of insects. During the time he was working on his doctorate, Binet became deeply interested in hypnosis, and in 1886 he published a book on the subject, showing the effect of different suggestions on subjects in both the hypnotic and waking states. He published another book in 1886 on the general topic of reasoning and intelligence. Later he would devote all his time to the pursuit of knowledge in this field.

In 1902 Binet wrote another book on intelligence, using as his basic data the thinking processes displayed by his two teen-aged daughters. He would give a reasoning problem to his daughters and analyze the steps they took to reach a solution. Though he found that they attacked and solved some problems in the same way, he noted marked differences in their approach to other problems. In his own immediate family, Binet thus observed the pervasiveness and importance of individual differences.

When in 1904 the French minister of public instruction announced his wish to identify and place in special schools those children who were mentally retarded, it was no wonder that Binet took on the challenge. This was a situation made to order for a student of individual differences. He asked for and was granted an appointment to the special committee being set up for this purpose. If children who could not seem to profit from reg-

IQ TESTS TODAY

The Current Stanford-Binet

The Stanford-Binet test was revised in 1937 and again in 1960. The 1960 revision used a different method of computing IQ, a method previously used by David Wechsler and called the "deviation IQ." The problem with the original method of calculating IQ was that by about age thirteen the ratio began to break down. Teen-agers no longer continue to increase their mental age as they did when younger. Nor do adults add to their mental age from year to year. Thus, the ratio of mental-to-chronological age could be used only with fairly young children, unless statistical corrections were added in. The deviation IQ avoids this problem by using the percentage of cases in each age group achieving a given score. Thus, a seventeen-year-old scoring at the eighty-fourth percentile for that age group (that is, equaling or exceeding 84 percent

ular schooling were to be placed in special classes, a device or technique had to be developed to identify these children. Binet argued that the diagnostic technique should be intellectual, not medical. It had been the practice in France to use physicians to diagnose mental retardation, since retardation was believed to be a physical condition. Binet pointed to the errors and inconsistencies that occurred in these medical diagnoses. If a child was seen by three different physicians on three successive days, three completely different medical diagnoses would result from these examinations.

Thus, in 1905 Binet, with a collaborator named Theodore Simon, published the first real intelligence scale. For their test, Binet and Simon assembled a series of intellectual tasks, rather than the sensorimotor tasks that Galton had used.

Binet felt that intelligence was displayed in one's ability to make sound judgments rather than in one's ability to react quickly to a physical stimulus. Binet thus took intelligence out of the medical-physiological realm and placed it in the intellectual-psychological area.

In 1908 Binet revised his original test, retaining the best items from the 1905 scale and adding a number of new tasks. In scoring this 1908 test, Binet utilized a new phrase, *mental age*. The test would not be scored simply on the basis of the number of items a child passed but rather in reference to age standards. Binet's scoring technique thus defined intelligence as a *developmental* rather than a *static* concept.

In 1911, shortly before Binet's untimely passing, a second and final revision of the Binet-Simon test was published. This test was a fur-

ther refinement of the original scale, again substituting new items for previous items that had failed to predict which children would profit from the school experience.

Binet's death in 1911 shortened a career just reaching full bloom. It is certain that many of the controversies that erupted in the field of intelligence would have been lessened had Binet lived long enough to complete his work. For example, Binet believed that intelligence was not just a fixed, immutable individual trait, but rather a developing, trainable, dynamic cluster of abilities that could be nourished or stifled as a result of environmental inputs.

Binet's contribution to educational psychology was enormous. If a man's work can be measured by the amount of research his work has generated, Binet must stand near the very top in psychology.

---

of all seventeen-year-olds taking the test) would have a Stanford-Binet IQ of 116. This is because the Stanford-Binet has a standard deviation of 16 IQ points. Statistical tables are used to find what percentages of cases fall below the various standard deviation unit points.

In 1972 the Stanford-Binet test was restandardized on a representative sample of 2,100 children. The new norms again produced a mean IQ of 100 and a standard deviation of 16. The 1972 standardizing group, unlike the one used in 1960, did include some black children and other nonwhites with Spanish surnames. The test itself, however, is almost identical with the 1960 revision, both in content and in scoring procedures.

The Wechsler Tests

David Wechsler has produced a number of individual intelligence tests. Like the Stanford-Binet, these tests are administered individually by trained examiners and take about an hour. Wechsler introduced his first test, then called the "Wechsler-Bellevue," in 1939. This was an adult test, standardized on an adult sample group. In 1955 he revised his adult test, calling it the Wechsler Adult Intelligence Scale (WAIS). The adult test has since been revised yet again, in 1981, and is now called the WAIS-R (the R for "revised").

In 1949 Wechsler published the Wechsler Intelligence Scale for Children (WISC). In 1963 he published the Wechsler Preschool and Primary Scale of Intelligence (WPPSI), which was designed for children from four through six-and-one-half years of age. In 1974 Wechsler introduced a new version of the WISC, calling this test the WISC-R.

The WISC-R was standardized on a group of 2,200 children, and this sample included both whites and nonwhites (blacks, Puerto Ricans, Mexican-Americans, American Indians, and Orientals) in somewhat the same proportions as

Binet defined mental age in terms of the age at which a given number of test items are passed by an average child. In 1916 Lewis Terman of Stanford University introduced the Stanford-Binet test. The latest version of the test, last revised in 1960, uses a different method of computing IQ. The method is particularly important in measuring the IQs of individuals.

they are represented in the population. About 28 percent of the test items in the WISC-R did not appear in the original test. Also, the age range is slightly different in the revision, the WISC having covered ages five to fifteen whereas the WISC-R covers ages six to sixteen. Like its predecessor, the mean IQ on the WISC-R is still 100, and the standard deviation is 15. The IQ range on the WISC-R is 40 to 160. Anyone familiar with the WISC should read the WISC-R manual carefully before administering this test. Administration of the WISC-R demands far more probing in order to determine whether or not the child really knows the answers.

The Wechsler tests mark a rather significant departure from the tradition of the Binet tests. Wechsler believed that the Binet tests were too heavily loaded with verbal items. According to Wechsler, "Intelligence . . . is the aggregate or global capacity of the individual to act purposefully, to think rationally, and to deal effectively with his environment."[8] Thus, not only is the poet with high verbal facility able to score well on the WAIS-R, but so too is the garage mechanic who can expertly reassemble a four-barrel carburetor, even if he or she cannot quote long passages from Shakespeare. The Wechsler tests, which use a deviation IQ, produce three IQ scores: a verbal IQ, a performance IQ, and a full-scale IQ score. Thus, the garage mechanic may receive a verbal IQ of only 105, but with a performance IQ of 126 he would achieve a full-scale IQ of 115, which is at the eighty-fourth percentile.

The verbal subtests   On the WAIS-R, the verbal IQ is calculated on the basis of six subtests:

1. *Information.* Twenty-nine items that test the subject's general storehouse of information about the world.

2. *Comprehension.* Fourteen questions that evaluate the individual's level of practical information and general ability to utilize past experience.

3. *Arithmetic.* Fourteen questions that test the individual's powers of arithmetical reasoning. The skills needed for this subtest don't go beyond those taught in grade school.

4. *Digit span.* A test of short-term memory in which the examiner reads a series of digits and asks the subject to repeat them.

5. *Similarities.* Thirteen items in which the subject attempts to discover in what way two things are alike. This test appears to measure an individual's ability to think in abstract terms.

6. *Vocabulary.* Forty words that attempt to predict the size of a person's vocabulary.

The performance subtests   The performance IQ is computed on the basis of five subtests:

1. *Picture arrangement.* Seven pictures that, when arranged properly, tell a logical story. This is an attempt to measure an individual's ability to size up and understand a total situation.

2. *Picture completion.* The subject is shown a set of incomplete pictures and is asked to name the missing part. This is a test of visual recognition.

3. *Block design.* The subject is given a number of small wooden blocks that must be put together to form a number of patterns. This is a test of perceptual analysis and visual-motor coordination.

4. *Digit symbol.* The subject must associate certain symbols with certain digits and then be able to write the appropriate symbol in squares containing the associated digit. This is a test of speed of movement and memory.

5. *Object assembly.* The subject must arrange various puzzle parts to form a certain object. This is a test of manual dexterity and powers of recognition.

In addition to being important instruments for measuring intelligence, the Wechsler tests have useful diagnostic capabilities that enable a skilled examiner to evaluate such personality characteristics as defense mechanisms, the ability to cope with stress, and the general mode

DAVID WECHSLER

thousands of recruits on the Army Individual Performance Scales, the Yerkes Point Scale, and the Stanford-Binet IQ test.

During this time, Wechsler became increasingly impressed by the disparity often shown between a man's tested intelligence and the quality of his previous work record. Often a man would test at a very low level on the various assessment devices, yet his past history indicated that he had been quite successful on his civilian job. The same man often proved later to be extremely competent in performing his military duties. Wechsler began to question the validity of the tests, especially the Stanford-Binet with its high verbal content. Perhaps the Binet test did predict success or failure in school, but it was proving to be less effective in predicting performance in the military. Wechsler concluded that perhaps by emphasizing the intellectual component, the Stanford-Binet was missing other aspects of a person's makeup that may contribute to one's overall intelligent behavior. These ideas, however, were not fully solidified, nor did they result in public expression until 1939, with the publication of Wechsler's own intelligence test.

In 1919 the Army sent Wechsler to France and later to England, where, at the University of London, he had the rare opportunity of working with both Spearman and Pearson. From Spearman, Wechsler learned of the two-factor theory of intelligence, g and s, and from Pearson he was schooled in statistical techniques, especially the techniques of correlation.

Wechsler was discharged from the army in August 1919 and then applied for and won a fellowship for study in France. From 1920 to 1922, he studied at the University

David Wechsler was born in Lespedi, Rumania, in 1896, one of seven children. His family moved to New York City when David was six years old. He attended the New York public schools and in 1916 graduated from the College of the City of New York. Following college, he immediately enrolled in the graduate psychology program at Columbia, doing his M.A. thesis under R. S. Woodworth in 1917. With America's entry into World War I, Wechsler was drafted into the army. While awaiting his induction, he joined the great Harvard psychologist E. G. Boring at Camp Yaphank on Long Island and helped to administer and score the recently developed Army Alpha intelligence test. Because of his training in psychology, and especially because of his work with Boring on the Alpha test, Wechsler, after his own induction, was sent by the army for basic training at the School of Military Psychology at Camp Greenleaf in Georgia. He was then assigned to Fort Logan, Texas, where his duties included testing

of Paris and at the Laboratory of Psychology at the Sorbonne. During this time he met both Theodore Simon and Pierre Janet.

In 1922 Wechsler returned to the United States, where he became both a part-time graduate student in psychology at Columbia and a staff psychologist at the Bureau of Child Guidance. In 1925 he received his Ph.D. from Columbia.

From 1925 to 1932 Wechsler worked in private practice as a psychologist. During this period he also worked part-time for the Psychological Corporation, the company that was later to publish the tests that bear his name.

In 1932 he became chief psychologist at New York's Bellevue Psychiatric Hospital, and in 1933 he also joined the faculty at New York University's College of Medicine. From this point on, Wechsler devoted much of his energy to the creation of a new intelligence test, a test that would be suitable for adults (the Stanford-Binet wasn't), and a test that would tap performance as well as verbal factors. After trying out many items from previous tests, and also creating new items of his own, Wechsler produced in 1939 the now famous Wechsler-Bellevue Intelligence Scale. Concurrently, he published *The Measurement of Adult Intelligence,* a book in which he brought together all his ideas on the question of intelligence and how it should be measured. He defined intelligence as "the global capacity of an individual to think rationally, to act purposefully, and to deal effectively with his environment." He saw intelligence, thus, not as a narrow capacity but as a global capacity that includes emotional and motivational as well as intellectual components. Wechsler did not separate intelligence from other personality factors.

Wechsler's name has become synonymous with intelligence testing in America. He is truly one of the great psychologists of our time, and up to the year of his death, 1981, he continued his contributions to our understanding of intelligence and its measurement.

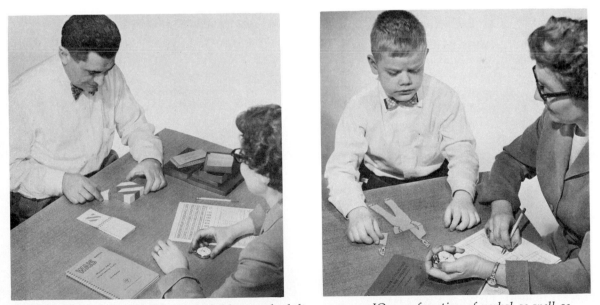

The Wechsler tests—those for both children and adults—measure IQ as a function of verbal as well as performance abilities. Wechsler's tests also perform another valuable function, that of personality evaluation.

of handling life's situations. Thus, a Wechsler test gives a three-dimensional picture of the subject, and can often tell us not only that a given child lacks motivation, but also why.[9]

Group Tests of Intelligence

Though the Stanford-Binet and Wechsler tests have made an extremely important contribution to the field of intelligence testing, the fact that they are individual tests means that they are time-consuming and therefore rather expensive to administer. During World War I there was suddenly an urgent need to test huge groups of men quickly, and a new approach to testing was introduced. Two group tests of intelligence were devised in 1917, the Army Alpha Test for the men who could read, and the Army Beta Test, a nonverbal test for illiterates. Though the Beta test, the nonverbal test, proved to be less effective than the Alpha, the success of the Alpha led to the development of a great number of group tests.

The most widely used group tests in the schools today are: the California Test of Mental Maturity (McGraw-Hill), the School and College Ability Tests (SCAT, Educational Testing Service), the Tests of General Ability (TOGA, Science Research Associates), the Otis-Lennon Mental Ability Tests (Harcourt Brace Jovanovich), the Kuhlmann-Anderson Intelligence Test (Personal Press), and the Lorge-Thorndike Intelligence Test and the Henmon-Nelson Test of Mental Ability (Houghton-Mifflin). These group tests are also referred to as paper-and-pencil tests, and they usually consist of a series of multiple-choice items. They must be administered and timed precisely as stated in the directions.

Hebb has suggested the possibility of banning the group tests of intelligence. Hebb feels that group tests are simply not accurate enough to be used in the determination of a child's fate. He feels, rather, that "competent determination (of IQ) means individual testing."[10] Further, Hebb suggests that those giving the IQ tests should be rigorously schooled and strictly licensed, just as physicians are. IQ tests placed in the wrong hands can have tragic consequences.

WHAT DO IQ TESTS PREDICT?

Academic Achievement

During our earlier discussion of Alfred Binet and the first intelligence test, we said that Binet's test was effective in predicting which children would do well in school. The evidence gained since then is generally consistent with Binet's early results. Over seventy years and hundreds of studies later, it is now clear that IQ tests do predict scholastic success. The correlation between IQ and grades in school runs better than +.50. Since the highest possible correlation is 1.00, IQ scores are not infallible predictors in every case. There are children whose IQ scores are lower than other children's but whose grades are higher, because a number of nonintellectual factors also influence scholastic success. Physical illness, emotional upset, and lack of motivation, for example, all can interfere with success. Recent research suggests that lack of ego strength is another related factor. Academic achievement has been shown to be largely a result of a student's reality orientation, or ego strength. That is, successful students possess strong egos, are willing to postpone pleasure, are not so easily distracted, and are generally more able to pursue tasks in an organized fashion. Underachievers, on the

IQ scores are not infallible predictors of school achievement. Among other factors influencing academic success is ego strength, that is, how a student perceives himself or herself. Successful students possess strong egos.

other hand, have low ego strength, are less able to control their impulses, and are especially unable to postpone gratification.[11]

Success in Life

Although it is true that IQ tests do predict academic achievement with some degree of accuracy, this fact in and of itself may not seem all that important. After all, IQ is measured by means of tests, and grades are determined exactly the same way, by performances on tests. Perhaps all this proves is that children who do well on one test also do well on other tests. How well does an IQ score predict success or failure in other areas of one's life? Do children with high IQs and high-school grades also succeed in later life, financially and emotionally?

To help answer these questions, Terman began a monumental study of hundreds of California schoolchildren in the 1920s.[12] All of the children had performed exceptionally well on IQ tests (i.e., they all had tested IQs of 140 or more). Terman followed the lives of these subjects for the next twenty-five years in order to find out whether there were any significant adult correlates of a high IQ in childhood (and many of these subjects are still being followed today by some of Terman's later coworkers).

First, Terman dispelled the myth that very bright children are physically fragile and undersized. Terman's subjects were above average on many physical characteristics, including height, weight, physical development, and general health. Also, the gifted children tended to be heavier at birth, cut their first tooth two months earlier than average, walked and talked two months earlier than average, and reached adolescence earlier than the average child.

While in school the gifted children received significantly higher marks than their classmates and were more likely to be skipped ahead to a higher grade. In fact, by the end of elementary school Terman's entire group of 1,500 children had averaged a skip of one full grade. Perhaps this is how the myth of the undersized and puny genius originated. Since children with high IQs do tend to skip frequently, they are likely to end up in classrooms with children who are larger because they are older.

On tests of emotional adjustment the gifted children were found to be better adjusted than

Terman's study of gifted children suggested that high-IQ children are healthier and stronger than average children, are better adjusted emotionally, and tend to be leaders among their peers.

the average child. They were also more socially adaptable and more likely to be leaders among their peers.

As adults, Terman's group continued to be successful. They earned more money, had more managerial jobs, and made far more literary and scientific contributions than the average adult. When checked in 1959, the group had published over 2,000 scientific papers and 33 novels and had taken out 230 patents. A great number of them were listed in *Who's Who* and in *American Men and Women of Science.*

Finally, they had fewer divorces than the average adult, and criminal convictions and alcoholism were rare. Even the death rate was about 33 percent lower than that for the general population.

In a more recent study it was found that IQ has a significant correlation with income. As a matter of fact, IQ predicted a person's income better than such other measures as parents' education or parents' income.[13]

It is obvious that the IQ test predicts more than just elementary-school grades. It must be pointed out, though, that not all of Terman's subjects attained that great success of the majority. It is also true that many highly successful people in this world do not have IQs of 140 or more. High IQs are associated with a wide range of achievement in a wide variety of areas, but high IQs do not tell the whole story. Per-

According to the Wechsler Adult Intelligence Scale, 2.2 percent of Americans have an IQ over 130, and a corresponding 2.2 percent are mentally retarded. Of course, the majority are in the middle range, with IQs between 90 and 109.

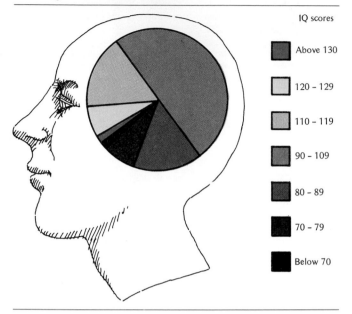

IQ scores

- Above 130
- 120 – 129
- 110 – 119
- 90 – 109
- 80 – 89
- 70 – 79
- Below 70

sonality variables such as ego strength and motivation, and physical variables such as health or accidents, also play a vital role in determining one's ability to live effectively and achieve success.

HEREDITY, ENVIRONMENT, AND TIME

In earlier chapters of this book, especially in Chapter 3, we pointed out that all human behavior, including intelligent behavior, is a product of heredity interacting with environment interacting with time. This is one of psychology's basic axioms, and nowhere is the validity of this axiom more compelling than in the area of intelligence.

Hereditary Factors

Heredity limits the extent to which intelligence can be influenced by environment and time. It is now fairly certain that intelligence has a genetic component. The genetic component sets

the limits as to how any given trait will respond to environmental stimulation. This genetically constrained range is the reaction range[14] and can be most clearly shown in the case of human height. Despite the fact that one's height, a polygenic trait, can be greatly influenced by environmental factors such as nutrition, there are some pygmy groups in Africa whose height could never approach that of the average American, regardless of environmental influences.[15]

As long ago as 1937, it was demonstrated that the closer two people are genetically related, the more similar their IQs will be.[16] This study showed that identical twins reared apart had positive IQ correlations of .79. In other words, even though these genetically identical individuals had been raised in different environments, they still had fairly similar IQs. A fairly exhaustive review of the literature revealed the IQ correlations shown in Table 16.1.[17]

These data make it clear that genetic factors are indeed involved in determining IQ. The closer the genetic relationship, the higher the reported IQ correlations.

A study conducted at the University of Minnesota in 1980 showed that identical twins reared apart displayed marked similarities on such measures as intelligence, achievement, and a number of personality factors. Even the

TABLE 16.1 IQ CORRELATIONS

RELATIONSHIP	NUMBER OF STUDIES	AVERAGE CORRELATION
Unrelated children reared apart	4	−.01
Foster parent and child	3	+.20
Unrelated children reared together	5	+.24
Siblings reared apart	33	+.47
Siblings reared together	36	+.55
Identical twins reared apart	4	+.75
Identical twins reared together	14	+.87
Grandparent and grandchild	3	+.27
Parent and child	13	+.50

brain-wave tracings of these monozygotic (MZ) twins showed an extremely high degree of resemblance. The genetic prewiring for MZ twins appears to be significantly more similar than could be accounted for on the basis of a straight environmental explanation.[18]

Environmental Factors

The IQ correlation chart also shows the importance of environmental factors. For example, when identical twins are reared together in the same environment, their IQs are more similar than when they are raised apart. Note, too, that when unrelated children are reared together, there is a significant correlation between their IQs. In this instance, where there is no genetic linkage at all, similar IQs result from the similar environment. The correlation for unrelated children reared together is almost the same as the correlation for grandparent and grandchild. The correlation of +.20 between foster parents and children is also of great importance. Here again we have an example of genetically unrelated persons whose IQs are too similar to be simply the result of chance.

In another very important study, a correlation of +.43 was obtained between the quality of the home environment and the child's IQ.[19] In this study the homes of 133 children (mostly white and mostly low socioeconomic status) were visited and scored on an instrument called the Home Environment Review. The significant correlation that was obtained indicates that the higher the quality of the home environment, the higher the IQ of the children. The most important of the home factors were the following:

1. The number of books and other learning materials in the home

2. The amount of reward and recognition the children receive from their parents for academic achievement

3. The parents' expectations regarding their children's academic achievement

Specific environmental influences   It's not enough to talk in generalities about environmental influences. Just what are some of the specific environmental inputs that appear to affect intelligence?

Gross nutritional deficiencies can adversely affect IQs and even produce mental retardation. Kwashiorkor, an illness resulting from a protein-deficient diet, has been found to be extremely damaging to intellectual development.[20] If nutritional deficiencies occur in early childhood, the damage to intelligence can be pronounced, even if the protein deficit is less than that needed to produce kwashiorkor. The exact physiological link between nutritional deficiencies and mental retardation is still unknown. However, recent studies have led to some speculation that inadequate protein intake prevents full development of the brain, especially those areas involved in memory storage.[21]

Further, as we pointed out in Chapter 3, Bonnie Kaplan's lively review of the relationship between inadequate dietary intake and mental deficiency presents rather convincing evidence that mental retardation can result from malnutrition. This is especially true if the malnutrition occurs during the nine months of gestation and the first two or three years of the baby's life.[22]

A second important environmental factor in intelligence is stimulus variety, especially in

This child is a victim of protein malnutrition. Nutrition deficiencies occurring in early childhood can result in pronounced damage to intelligence.

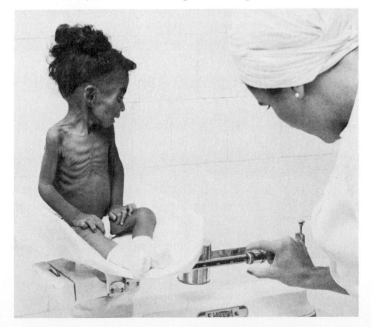

early childhood. As we saw in Chapter 4, important figures in the field of psychology, such as J. McVicker Hunt, Jerome Bruner, Benjamin S. Bloom, and David Krech, feel that stimulus variety is perhaps the most important ingredient in intellectual development. Hunt states that the more we see, hear, and touch in early childhood, the more we will want to see, hear, and touch later on. The key to cognitive growth, according to Hunt, is matching the child's present intellectual ability with just the right amount of stimulus variety to bring out the natural desire to continue learning. Bruner insists that infants must be exposed to a wide variety of stimulus inputs and a shifting environment if normal intellectual growth is to be maintained. Bloom says that an abundant early environment is the key to full development of intelligence. And Krech has shown, at least in animals, that without stimulus heterogeneity, animals are less able to learn, and their brains never develop fully.

Past experience in learning situations is another crucial environmental ingredient in intellectual development. Children who learn to master one problem are able to transfer this knowledge to other problems they may encounter later. The knowledge gained from past experience may begin to snowball and provide the child with a solid base for future understanding. Harry Harlow has shown how this works with monkeys. Monkeys that were trained to solve a certain problem (the oddity problem) were far better at solving complex discrimination problems presented to them at a later time than monkeys that were not so trained. Through training, the monkeys had developed what Harlow called a "learning set." They had, in effect, learned how to learn. As Harlow says, "Learning to learn is no doubt an essential feature of the intellectual development of monkeys, apes, and children growing up in their natural environments."[23]

Finally, Bloom lists three environmental variables that he feels are important in developing a child's intellectual abilities.

1. The amount of stimulation children receive for verbal development

2. The amount of affection and reward children receive for verbal reasoning accomplishments

3. The amount of encouragement children receive for "active interaction with problems, exploration of the environment and the learning of new skills"[24]

Time

We have seen the importance of hereditary and environmental interactions for intellectual development. It is also vital to understand the nature of this interaction from the point of view of time. Chapter 4 was devoted entirely to the importance of early experience on psychological development. Let us now look at some of the highlights.

Most psychologists today are convinced of the profound importance of early experience for proper cognitive growth. Bloom states the case forcefully in saying that environmental effects on intelligence are most pronounced during a child's first few years of life.

The heavy line in Figure 16.1 shows Bloom's famous negatively accelerated curve for intellectual growth. Notice that as age increases, intellectual development increases less and less. By four years of age we have already achieved 50 percent of our adult intelligence, and by eight years of age we have achieved 80 percent. The shaded area surrounding the main curve indicates the potential for changes in intelligence. You will notice that as age increases, there is also less and less potential for changes in intelligence. Therefore, during the first few years, a beneficial environment is most effective in increasing intellectual development, but as time goes on this beneficial environment comes to have less effect. Similarly, a stultifying environment is most damaging during those early, critical years. Bloom feels that the difference between a beneficial and a stultifying environment during these early childhood years can produce IQ differences of twenty points or more. Bloom may be too conservative, however.

Wayne Dennis's study of a Teheran orphanage where the children were kept in a condition of extreme sensory deprivation also showed that stimulus variety at an early age is critical for cognitive growth (see Chapter 4). Almost all of these sensory-deprived children were intellectually retarded.[25] In another study, Dennis described a Lebanese orphanage where environmental conditions were so dismal that men-

Figure 16.1 Bloom's negatively accelerated curve for intellectual growth.

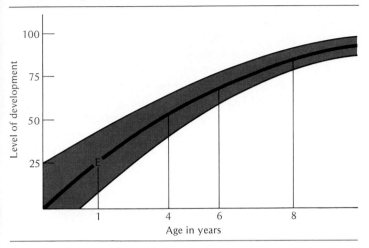

tal retardation was the rule.[26] The average IQ of the 133 children tested was only 53. This is probably the lowest average IQ ever reported for a group of children who were otherwise considered normal. Some of these children were later adopted to middle-class families and in every case dramatically increased their IQ. The more stimulating home environments provided an average gain of twenty-eight IQ points. De-

Environmental effects on intelligence are most pronounced during a child's first few years of life. By four years of age, a child has already achieved 50 percent of his or her adult intelligence.

spite the improvement, the mean IQ of the adopted children was still only 81, again showing that improved environmental conditions at a later age cannot compensate fully for a deprived environment during the first few years of life. As Hebb says, "There are fundamental aspects of a baby's learning that must occur at the proper time if they are to have their full value as the basis of later learning."[27] Thus Hebb is fully endorsing the early-experience position regarding mental growth. In fact, he says that you cannot take even a six-year-old out of the slums and expect to undo the damage already inflicted by that environment. "In a word, the child from a seriously deficient environment is an intellectual *cripple*," and this damage is no longer reparable.[28]

INFANT INTELLIGENCE

Attempts to measure the intellectual potential of infants dates at least as far back as the work of Nancy Bayley (see biography, p. 72). Recently, Marc Bornstein has been conducting studies in which six-month-old babies were measured on the basis of how long it would take them to process information concerning moving stimuli.[29] Bornstein hypothesized that the more intelligent the baby, the sooner he or she would lose interest in the stimuli, since the more intelligent infant would process the information about the stimulus more quickly in the form of an internal stimulus representation. Later, when the child was four years old, he or she was given the WPPSI IQ test. Bornstein found significant correlations ($r = .54$) between how well the subjects scored as babies and how they later scored as four-year-old children.

Bornstein also found a correlation between the child's IQ and the quality of the interactions between mother and child, assessed when the child was one year old. To be sure, the amount and quality of mother-baby interactions can vary with either party in the relationship. Do intelligent and responsive babies induce more parental responses, or are highly responsive parents responsible for the response levels of their offspring? The best guess is that the most important factor is the interaction itself, with both mother and baby playing critical roles in the quality of the interplay.

SEX DIFFERENCES IN IQ

The full-scale IQs of males and females of a given age are almost identical. This is partly due to the averaging out of differences that do occur among various subtest scores. Males typically score higher on spatial, mechanical and numerical tests, whereas females score higher on verbal tests and tests involving quick, manual movements and attention to detail.

The development of IQ also reveals certain sex differences. The mean IQ of males increases slightly after age six, while the female mean tends to go down.[30] This difference may have a cultural explanation. If society demands more achievement from males than females (and this apparently is the case), and if achievement motivation and IQ correlate at all, then perhaps society's emphasis on inculcating the achievement motive more in males accounts for this difference. As social psychologists continually remind us, people tend to behave as others around them expect them to behave.

ARE THERE GENETIC DIFFERENCES IN INTELLIGENCE BETWEEN RACIAL GROUPS?

It has long been known that on standard IQ tests (standardized primarily on white sample groups) the average IQ of white children and the average IQ of black children generally differ. It is also known that the difference favors the white children. The two IQ distributions do overlap, so that despite the difference between the averages, there are still many black children whose IQs are higher than those of many white children. Also, a trend has been identified indicating that the black-white gap on intelligence and academic achievement tests has begun to narrow.[31]

A study of World War I Army Alpha IQ scores found that although the average IQ of black soldiers was lower than that of white soldiers, there were some fairly interesting reversals. For example, the average IQ of black soldiers from several northern states was higher than the average IQ of white soldiers from certain southern states.[32] It has also been found that the more money a state spends on education, the higher the IQs of its schoolchildren, black and white.[33] The correlation between the amount of money a state spends on education and the IQs of the state's children is $+.70$.

Arthur R. Jensen of the University of California at Berkeley has interpreted the difference between the tested IQs of blacks and whites as implying that white children are genetically superior to black children. This argument claims that IQ has an extremely high genetic factor (about 80 percent) and that there must therefore be racial differences in intelligence.[34] Jensen says that differences in intelligence are "predominantly attributable to genetic differences, with environmental factors contributing a minor portion of the variance among individuals in IQ."[35]

This claim must be closely examined. The rules of science demand that in order to establish a cause-and-effect relationship, all the possible input variables must be controlled. If, for example, you wished to determine whether increased noise in a classroom had a depressing effect on reading speed, you wouldn't put all the fast readers in the low-noise group and all the slow readers in the high-noise group. Nor would you have different conditions of illumination in the two groups. Nor would you test one group at 9:00 A.M. and the other at 3:00 A.M. Instead, you would want the two groups to be as equivalent as possible: same age, same average reading speed, same conditions of illumination, same time of testing. If, after controlling for all the variables, the group tested under high-noise conditions reads significantly more slowly than the group tested under low-noise conditions, you could say that noise does, indeed, lower reading speed. This is the cautious way science proceeds before assigning causal factors to observed differences. Perhaps Jensen is correct when he says that the assumption of a genetic difference in intelligence between the races is not an unreasonable hypothesis. But the point is, and this is an important point for the prospective teacher to remember, Jensen's hypothesis has not been proved, nor may it ever be a testable conclusion.

As we have seen, intelligence has three crucial inputs: heredity, environment, and time. In order to determine the extent to which any one of these variables affect intelligence, the other two must be controlled. Large numbers of children, black and white, would have to be raised in identical (or, at the very least, reliably measured) environments. Also, because of the time variable, stimulus variety would have to be increased at precisely the same developmental stage for each child. The enormity and complexity of such a study make it appear improbable that Jensen's hypothesis could ever be adequately tested. All of Jensen's reported twin studies (which were all done on white children, incidentally), and all of his correlations (regardless of whether they're "corrected for unreliability") cannot alter the fact that the average black child is not raised under the same, or under even remotely similar, environmental conditions as the average white child. Does anyone seriously believe that if white children were to be raised in black homes in Harlem's ghettoes they would achieve the same scores on an IQ test as if they had been raised in Scarsdale's suburbs?

IQ comparisons between the races are made even more difficult to evaluate because of the possibility that IQ scores may reflect the race of the examiner. A number of studies have suggested that the IQ scores of black children are underestimated by white examiners, or perhaps overestimated by black examiners. In one experiment a single group of black children was tested by both black and white examiners. By the use of different forms, L and M of the Stanford-Binet, the children were tested in a counterbalanced design, first by an examiner of one race and then by one of the other. The mean IQ score of these black children when tested by the black examiner was 105.7 but dropped to a mean of 101.9 when tested by a white. This difference was statistically significant.[36] Since both black and white examiners were equally trained and equally competent, the difference in IQ scores probably results from either differing expectations on the part of the examiner or differing motivational sets on the part of the children.

It is important to note that the high correlation obtained between the IQs of parents and children overemphasizes the genetic explanation. An improverished home environment has an adverse effect not only on the intellectual development of the children raised in it but also on the way those children eventually raise their own children. The childhood experiences of the second generation are a function of the childhood experiences of the previous generation:

> Such handicaps combine to sustain the very conditions from which they are derived, so the vicious circle tends to be repeated for generation after generation. Clearly the correlations between IQs of parents and children are bound to be high, and give a superficial impression of genetic determination.[37]

One way to eliminate the possibility of a genetic interpretation of the similarity between the IQs of parents and children is to study the mental development of black children who are reared by socially advantaged white parents. Sandra Scarr conducted just such a study.[38] She analyzed 101 white, middle-class families who had adopted 176 children, 130 of whom were black and the rest of whom were Asian and American Indian. The mean IQ of these adopted black children was 106, which is 21 points higher than the national mean for blacks. More important, however, was the fact that the mean IQ for the black children who had been adopted as infants was 110. This latter group, of course, was in the advantaged cultural environment all through the early, critical periods of intellectual growth.[39]

Heritability

Jensen based his argument on the concept of heritability. Heritability (H) is the proportion of the total variability in a population that is due to genetic, as opposed to environmental, factors. Thus, if all the variation in IQ scores in a given population is due to genetic factors, the heritability of IQ would be 1.00. If all the variability is due to environmental factors, then the heritability of IQ would be zero. Since, as we have seen over and over again, IQ is the result of heredity, environment, and time, the heritability value for IQ lies somewhere between 0 and 1.00. Jensen argues that the actual value is around .80. Regardless of Jensen's estimate, however, we must remember that heritability does not apply to any single individual. Behavior geneticist Jerry Hirsch has said that heritability only explains variation "in some particular population at a single generation under one set of conditions."[40] Thus, since heritability applies only to a specific environment, it really matters very little what the estimate of the actual heritability value is in the discussion of a given black child's IQ. "High or low heritability tells us absolutely nothing about how a given individual might have developed under conditions different from those in which he actually did develop."[41]

Jensen appears to accept this definition when he says that heritability is a population statistic that has "no sensible meaning with reference to a measurement or characteristic of an individual. . . . Estimates of *H* are specific to the population sampled, the point in time, how the measurements were made, and the particular test used to obtain the measurements."[42] Despite the clarity and precision of this definition, Jensen then presents a case that goes far beyond the bounds of his own careful restriction. Jensen's estimated *H* value of .80 is generated by a review of identical twin studies done exclusively on white American and English children, and yet he applies this value to both black and white children alike—hardly identical populations. As a matter of fact, in a study of over 1,000 twins of differing economic and racial backgrounds conducted by Scarr, it was found that the heritability of IQ is always higher among economically advantaged than among lower-class children.[43] Thus, it is not an unreasonable hypothesis that the value of *H* increases as a function of an increase in the socioeconomic backgrounds of the populations being studied. As one reviewer stated it: "In other words, 'native talent' may manifest itself conspicuously in people who grow up in favorable environments and remain suppressed in adverse environments."[44] In fact, Scarr argues that this is precisely how the nature-nurture interaction works. "When the environment is good, heredity exerts a strong influence on IQ," stronger than when the environment is improverished.[45]

Jensen also argues that compensatory education has been tried and has failed. He makes two main points on this subject. First, he feels that experiments with early education (such as Head Start) have not lived up to expectations; that, although the Head Start program does produce some short-term IQ gains, these gains are not sustained over the years. Second, he implies that since the IQ disadvantage of blacks is mostly inherited, it is useless to spend money for early-education programs that obviously cannot affect the genes.

With regard to the first point, although Head Start did not at first live up to the hopes of many educators, newer studies suggest that Head Start's death knell may have been tolled too soon. Even though by the time children were enrolled in Head Start programs, they may have already passed through many critical learning periods, recent evidence, such as that supplied by the Perry Project (see Chapter 4), shows that remarkable gains are still achievable. However, just as there are cumulative positive effects on intellectual growth as a result of an improved environment, so, too, there are cumulative negative effects from an impoverished environment. A study of white children from the "hollows" of rural Virginia found the average IQ of six- to eight-year-olds to be only 84, and the average for ten- to twelve-year-olds to be only 53.[46] The point is that with children from impoverished environments, early education intervention would be a marked success if all it accomplished was the prevention of IQ decline.

The Cumulative Deficit in IQ

Studies such as the one on the children from the "hollows" of rural Virginia show that en-

SANDRA SCARR

After graduating with honors from Vassar in 1958, Sandra Scarr worked first as a case aide in a family clinic and then as a research assistant at the National Institutes of Health. It soon became obvious to her that her career pattern could continue in this line, that of serving as a helper and facilitator for other people's work. On the other hand, given her inquiring mind, it also became obvious that alternatives were possible. Youthful women honors graduates of liberal arts colleges did not necessarily have to be content to perform minor, ancillary roles as helpers and assistants. Such persons, just as well as anyone, could aspire to leadership roles. There were very few women of eminence who had chosen to enter the competitive and heretofore male-dominated area of research psychology. With this in mind, she entered Harvard University, completed her M.A. degree in 1963, and entered the Ph.D. program in social relations.

Under that somewhat quaint Harvard tradition, Scarr was assigned to a sponsor, John Whiting, a world-renowned anthropologist, and to a thesis advisor, Irving Gottesman, an equally renowned genetic psychologist. She clearly thrived in the atmosphere of the Harvard program in Social Relations, with its diverse faculty reading like a list of Who's Who in Psychology: Gordon Allport, Jerome Bruner, Robert White, B. F. Skinner, Roger Brown, Thomas Pettigrew, David McClelland, Jerome Kagan, and Eric Erikson. She quickly mastered the fundamentals of such a broadly gauged psychology, and she completed her Ph.D. in just two years with a research thesis titled, "Genetics and Human Motivation."

Graduation was followed by a series of academic and administrative appointments at Bryn Mawr, the University of Maryland, the Carter Foundation for Child Development (as acting director), and the University of Pennsylvania. Her talent was obvious and her scholarship promising. Promotions were rapid. She moved to Minnesota in 1972 as an associate professor in the School Psychology Training Program. Just two years later, she was offered and accepted a full professorship at the University's Institute of Child Development. She was elected a Fellow of the American Psychological Association and a Fellow of the American Association for the Advancement of Science, and she was also received into numerous other scientific and professional organizations.

She left Minnesota in 1977 and became the first woman ever to be named to a full professorship in the Department of Psychology at Yale University. In 1983 she was selected as the Commonwealth Professor of Psychology at the University of Virginia. She also serves as the editor of the American Psychological Association journal *Developmental Psychology* and is on the editorial board of the series *Advances in Psychology*. Her own family consists of four children, her husband (a pediatrician), and two cats.

---

vironmental deprivation tends to accumulate as the child grows older. That is, a child from an impoverished background who is one year below grade level by age six may fall back to two full years below grade level by age twelve. Just as the intellectually rich get richer, so too do the intellectually poor get poorer. Such studies lend dramatic support to the mounting evidence regarding the environment's power in affecting mental growth.

Ironically, the evidence from one of Jensen's more recent studies,[47] goes a long way toward providing perhaps the most damaging evidence yet obtained against the purely genetic interpretation. Jensen studied large groups of children, both black and white, from an area in the rural South. Jensen states that the blacks in this locality are "as severely disadvantaged, educationally and economically, as can be found anywhere in the United States today."[48] Yet what Jensen found was that for black children there was a progressive *decline* in IQ scores. And what caused the decline? The cumulative effects of an impoverished environment.

It was found that blacks (but not whites) showed significant and substantial decrements in both verbal and nonverbal IQs as a linear function of age . . . from about 5 to 16 years of age.[49]

Studies of this type, although not refuting the importance of heredity on intelligence, make it clear that time and environment are extremely important in determining later levels of intellectual functioning. "To overstress the genetic factor is inevitably to assert that the blame belongs on the shoulders of the victim. This whole method of diagnosis and treatment takes us into the theatre of the absurd."[50] Jensen's comment that compensatory education has been tried and has failed may be like that of an observer who, after watching Orville Wright's first flight at Kitty Hawk, said that air travel has been tried and failed.

Sir Cyril Burt and the Taint of Scandal

Some of Jensen's correlational evidence supporting the .80 heritability argument came from the work of the English psychometrician, Sir Cyril Burt. Burt had allegedly conducted a large number of studies in which the IQs of MZ twins reared apart were compared with the IQs of MZ twins reared together. However in 1977, three years after Burt's death, Leon Kamin published his now famous *The Science and Politics of IQ,* in which he demonstrated that much of Burt's data were not only flawed but fraudulent.[51] At least some of the raw IQ data that Burt had used to support his hereditarian view could not be found among his papers. The suspicion grew that Burt had simply created correlations out of nonexistent data.[52] Even Jensen has now acknowledged that Burt must have perpetrated deliberate fraud. Excluding the Burt data, Jensen now estimates the total heritability of IQ to equal .70. Finally, Jensen feels that even if newer studies indicate the true heritability value to be only .50, that would still show the effect of heredity as greater than any environmental variables.[53]

In a very reasoned and objective work on the history and current status of the IQ controversy, Raymond Fancher concludes that both the hereditarians and the environmentalists are right,

though neither are as right as they would pretend. Says Fancher:

It seems fair for a neutral observer of the IQ controversy to conclude that IQ heritability in our time and society is certainly less than .70, and probably less than .50. This still leaves room, of course, for a substantial genetic factor in intelligence. . . . Thus, there is no doubt that environment plays a large role in determining both average levels and individual differences in intelligence within our society. Its influence tends to be exerted gradually and cumulatively, however, through the pervasive effects of home and culture acting over years and decades.[54]

Robert Carkhuff, an expert in the fields of counseling and human relations, makes the point that although the mean IQ of black children is about 86 when they enter first grade, it drops even lower by the time the children reach fifth grade. Carkhuff attributes this drop to environmental forces working on the black child in the school setting. Since teachers and counselors often treat black children as if they were devoid of intellectual resources, the children begin to fulfill this expectation by achieving less and less as the school years go by. Says Carkhuff, "The teachers and counselors respond to black children as if Jensen and Garrett were correct."[55]

To compound the felony, Carkhuff argues, the least competent teachers are assigned to ghetto and predominantly black schools. It can be no wonder, then, that black children often do not achieve beyond the eighth- or ninth-grade level, since it may be that the level of their teacher's own competence does not extend beyond this point. One study found that two-thirds of the teachers tested scored lower than junior-high-school level on tests of proficiency in the teacher's own specialty area.[56] Says Carkhuff of these teachers, "They could not pass their own exams."[57]

THE CONFLUENCE MODEL: THE FAMILY ENVIRONMENT

Robert B. Zajonc (rhymes with "science") has proposed a provocative theory of intellectual development that views the family unit as being

CONTEMPORARY ISSUE

Should IQ Tests Be Abandoned?

The controversy currently raging about whether or not intelligence is racially correlated is not just an esoteric scientific debate, for the lives and futures of our children are at stake. This is not like a group of physicists debating the theory of aperiodic crystals; this is a here-and-now issue. If government officials become convinced that Jensen is correct, funding for urgently needed preschool programs could be siphoned off into other areas. One recent result of this controversy is that some school systems are inclined to do away with IQ testing completely: They feel that if the results of such testing are going to reinforce racist attitudes, then perhaps the best solution is to stop giving the tests, especially to black children. This position certainly has some merit, for IQ testing has at times damaged the lives of some children. Robert Rosenthal and Lenore Jacobson's study discussed in Chapter 14 showed that

children's test scores can be affected by the teacher's belief about the child's intellectual potential.[a] This phenomenon of a self-fulfilling prophecy on test scores is now known in the literature as the Rosenthal effect. Teachers must not be allowed to use low IQ scores as a "cop-out" for not doing their jobs. The use of IQ tests does pose a danger, especially for minority children.

Despite the dangers of misusing and misinterpreting the results of IQ testing, there is perhaps another danger in simply abandoning IQ testing. In the first place, the IQ test, with all its limitations, is still the most reliable and the most valid test in all of psychology. It has had too long a history of success to be casually dismissed. The IQ test, for example, is a very effective instrument for identifying underachievers, students whose academic achievement falls far short of what their IQ scores predict. The case of the

underachiever is often tragic, but without a means of testing children's intellectual potential, we would have no way of identifying the underachiever and, thus, would be unable to intervene to try to correct the problem.

In the second place, abandoning IQ testing might have severe racial overtones. If we stop testing and are no longer able to identify those children who need help, we may begin to believe that there is no problem. This kind of Alice in Wonderland approach could halt any further efforts to erase the differences. It could doom a major segment of the population to failure in our competitive and technological society.

---

[a] Rosenthal, R., and Jacobson, L. (1969). Teachers' expectations and self-fulfilling prophecies. In R. C. Sprinthall and N. A. Sprinthall (Eds.), *Educational psychology: Selected readings*, pp. 295–300. New York: Van Nostrand-Reinhold.

---

the key ingredient in the formation of eventual IQ growth. Although Zajonc interprets his data on the basis of the family's influence as an environmental variable, there may again be a hint, as some critics suggest, of an interaction effect between the family's gene pool and its ability to produce a stimulating intellectual environment. Zajonc has interpreted the relationship between family size and intelligence as a product of general environmental stimulation. The data are as follows:

1. First-born children tend to have higher IQs than their younger siblings.

2. The more children there are in a family, the lower the IQs of all the children.

3. Twins have lower IQs than nontwins.

4. Children in one-parent homes have lower IQs than children from homes where both parents are present. (The younger the child at the time of parental loss, the more severe the resulting IQ deficit.)

5. The only child has a lower IQ than does the first-born in a two- or three-child family.[58]

In his interpretation of these facts, Zajonc uses what he calls the "confluence model," a model that predicts that the intellectual growth of each child is a function of the intellectual levels of all the other family members. A given child's intellectual environment is based on the average of the intellectual levels of all the family members, and since children contribute less than their parents to the absolute level of the family's intellectual environment, the more children there are, the lower the absolute level. However, the more spacing between children, the less the damage to the family's intellectual environment. The data on only children do reveal a discontinuity in this prediction, and Zajonc suggests that a child in some way benefits from having younger siblings. The only child has less opportunity to be a "teacher," to show his other younger brother or sister how to hold a pencil, grip a baseball bat, or tie shoes.

Zajonc has provided an interesting and provocative explanation, also based on his confluence model, of the steady decline in Scholastic Aptitude Test (SAT) scores that had occurred during the 1970s. The decline was simply a reflection of the fact that, following World War II, American parents decided to have large families and to have these children close together. Further, since the size of American families began decreasing in the early 1960s, Zajonc predicted a dramatic upswing in SAT scores during the 1980s. Recent evidence has already shown an increase in average SAT scores over the past few years, a trend that appears to lend further support to the Zajonc model.

However, an alternate explanation exists for the recent rise in SAT scores. Since the population of students who take the test is self-selected, average SAT scores may be a function of the overall strength of the nation's economy. When economic times are good, more students are in a financial position to elect to go to college and therefore take the test. According to this explanation, during the 1981–1983 recession,

the rise in SAT scores may have been due to the fact that fewer students were taking the test, and the very ones who opted not to take the test were most likely to be at the economic margin. Financially disadvantaged students as a group have traditionally not done well on the SAT. According to this theory, then, as the economy improves, SAT scores go down, and as the economy weakens, SAT scores go up.[59]

Regardless of whether Zajonc's model is correct or incorrect with respect to SAT scores, Zajonc believes it can be used to explain another phenomenon: racial IQ differences. Since black families generally have more children (and have them closer together) than do average white families, that fact alone could explain the difference in average IQ scores between the two groups. Add to this the further fact that more black than white families are one-parent families.

Zajonc's conclusions are based on studies conducted on well over 1 million subjects from four different countries: the United States, France, the Netherlands, and Scotland. And, more important, his predictions have held up regardless of nationality, race, social status, or income level.

Critics suggest that since the confluence model has been analyzed using correlational techniques, perhaps Zajonc has overinterpreted the direction of the relationship. Although it may be that Zajonc is correct and that large numbers of children in a family do tend to lower overall average IQ levels (an environmental argument), the reverse might also be true: that parents with lower IQs tend to have more children in the first place (a genetic argument).

SUMMARY

Psychologists have generally used three meanings of the concept intelligence : intelligence as a genetic capacity, intelligence as observed behavior, and intelligence as a test score.

The history of intelligence testing begins with Sir Francis Galton. Galton believed that intelligence was largely an inherited characteristic and attempted to measure intelligence through the use of simple sensorimotor tests. Galton's

test results led him to emphasize what later became the theme of all measurement practitioners—individual differences. Galton's student and colleague, Karl Pearson, analyzed the testing data and, in order to make some meaningful comparisons, introduced a new statistical technique, the correlation coefficient.

Binet discarded Galton's idea of measuring intelligence through the use of sensorimotor tasks and adopted instead the approach of using intellectual tasks. Binet used the concept of mental age in order to assign a numerical value to performance on his test.

In 1916 an American psychologist, Lewis M. Terman, published an American revision of the Binet test. The scoring of this test, the Stanford-Binet test, was based on the concept of the intelligence quotient or IQ.

In 1939 David Wechsler introduced the first of a series of new individual IQ tests. Wechsler felt that the Stanford-Binet test was too heavily laden with verbal items, and so he created a series of performance tasks to be presented along with the more traditional verbal tests.

During World War I, group tests of intelligence were introduced, allowing for the testing of large numbers of people in one sitting. Because of their ease of administration and lack of expense, group tests of intelligence quickly became popular throughout most school systems.

What do tests of intelligence tell us that we couldn't determine before? Studies have shown that IQ tests do predict how well a child will perform in school. Studies also indicate that high IQ scores correlate with success in later life, as measured by such factors as physical health, emotional adjustment, financial income, and literary and scientific contributions.

Intelligence, like all human behavior, is a product of heredity interacting with environment interacting with time.

1. *Heredity.* Studies show that the closer the genetic similarity between people, the higher the resulting IQ correlation.

2. *Environment.* Similar environments also produce similar IQs. The specific environmental parameters studied include home factors (such as number of books in the home and parental attitudes toward schooling), nutrition, stimulus variety, past experience, and parental encouragement.

3. *Time.* The Bloom curve indicates that environmental influences on intelligence are most pronounced during a child's first few years of life.

Bornstein has provided evidence indicating that fairly reliable measures of infant intelligence can be achieved and that these measures correlate both with later IQ measures and with the quality of the interaction displayed between mother and child.

The question of racial differences in intelligence was raised by Jensen. The evidence thus far fails to substantiate any claims of racial superiority or inferiority based on intelligence. Though the average IQs of black and white children do differ, there is no reason to assume that this difference is due more to genetic than environmental factors.

Zajonc's theory, called the "confluence model," predicts that the more children there are in a family, especially if the children are close together in age, the lower the IQs of all the children will be. Birth order is also important since first-borns have the highest IQs, unless there is a wide age spacing between the children. Zajonc's findings have held up regardless of nationality, race, income level, or social status.

KEY TERMS AND NAMES

intelligence
Charles Spearman
J. P. Guilford
L. L. Thurstone
factor approach
Alfred Binet
Lewis M. Terman
mental age
Stanford-Binet test
intelligence quotient (IQ)

deviation IQ
David Wechsler
WAIS (WAIS-R)
performance IQ
group tests of intelligence
Bornstein's Infant Intelligence test
Arthur R. Jensen
heritability
confluence model

REFERENCES

1. Scarr, S. (1981). *Race, social class and individual differences in IQ.* Hillsdale, N.J.: Erlbaum.

2. Guilford, J. P. (1967) *The nature of human intelligence.* New York: McGraw-Hill.

3. Gardner, H. (1985). Human intelligence isn't what we think it is. In F. Linder and J. H. McMillan (Eds.), *Annual editions: Educational psychology* (pp. 85–86). Guilford, Conn.: Dushkin.

4. Sternberg, R. J. (1985). *Beyond IQ: A triarchic theory of human intelligence* (p. 99). New York: Cambridge University Press.

5. Vernon, P. E. (1969). *Intelligence and cultural environment.* London: Methuen.

6. Sattler, J. M. (1974). *Assessment of children's intelligence.* Rev. ed. (pp. 8–9). Philadelphia: Saunders.

7. Binet, A., and Simon, H. (1905). Application des méthodes nouvelles au diagnostic du niveau intellectuel chez des enfants normaux et anormaux d'hospice et d'école primaire. *L'Année Psychologique, 11,* 245–266.

8. Wechsler, D. (1944). *The measurement of adult intelligence.* Baltimore: Williams & Wilkins.

9. Fancher, R. E. (1985). *The intelligence men: Makers of the IQ controversy* (p. 157). New York: Norton.

10. Hebb, D. O. (1978). Open letter: To a friend who thinks the IQ is a social evil. *American psychologist, 33*(12), 1143.

11. Hummel, R., and Sprinthall, N. A. (1965). Under-achievement related to interests, attitudes, and values. *Personnel and Guidance Journal, 44,* 388–395.

12. Terman, L. M. (1925, 1926, 1930, 1947, 1959). *Genetic studies of genius.* Stanford, Calif.: Stanford University Press.

13. Duncan, O. D., Featherman, D. L., and Duncan, B. (1972). *Socioeconomic background and achievement.* New York: Seminar Press.

14. Gottesman, I. I. (1974). Developmental genetics and ontogenetic psychology. *Minnesota Symposea on Child Psychology, 8,* 54–78.

15. Freedman, D. G. (1979). Ethnic differences in babies. *Human nature, 2*(1), 40.

16. Newman, H. H., Freeman, F. N., and Holzinger, K. J. (1937). *Twins: A study of heredity and environment.* Chicago: University of Chicago Press.

17. Erlenmeyer-Kimling, L., and Jarvik, L. F. (1963). Genetics and intelligence: A review. *Science, 142,* 1479.

18. Holden, C. (1980). Identical twins reared apart. *Science, 207,* 1323–1328.

19. Garber, M., and Ware, W. B. (1970). Relationships between measures of home environment and intelligence scores. *American Psychological Association Proceedings, 5,* 647–648.

20. Eickenwald, H. F., and Fry, P. C. (1969). Nutrition and learning. *Science, 163,* 644–648.

21. Harlow, H. F., McGaugh, J. L., and Thompson, R. F. (1971). *Psychology* (p. 354). San Francisco: Albion. See also Krech, D. (1968). The chemistry of learning. *Saturday Review, 20* (January), 48–50.

22. Kaplan, B. J. (1972). Malnutrition and mental deficiency. *Psychology Bulletin, 78,* 321–334.

23. Harlow and others, *Psychology* (p. 353).

24. Bloom, B. S. (1964). *Stability and change in human characteristics* (p. 190). New York: Wiley.

25. Dennis, W. (1960). The mental growth of certain institutional children: Iran. *Journal of Genetic Psychology, 96,* 47–59.

26. Dennis, W. (1969). The mental growth of certain foundlings before and after adoption. Paper delivered at American University of Beirut, Lebanon.

27. Hebb, Open letter, 1143.

28. Hebb, Open letter, 1144.

29. Bornstein, M. (1985). How infant and mother jointly contribute to developing cognitive competence in the child. *Proceedings of the National Academy of Science, 82,* 7470–7473.

30. Haan, N. (1963). Proposed model of ego functioning: Coping and defense mechanisms in relation to IQ change. *Psychological Monographs, 11.*

31. Jones, L. V. (1984). White-black achievement differences. *American Psychologist, 39,* 1207–1213.

32. Yerkes, R. M. (1921). Psychological examining in the U.S. army. *Memoirs of the National Academy of Sciences,* No. 15.

33. Spuhler, J. N. and Lindzey, G. (1967). Racial differences in behavior. In J. Hirsch (Ed.), *Behavior-genetic analysis.* New York: McGraw-Hill.

34. Jensen, A. R. (1969). How much can we boost IQ and scholastic achievement? *Harvard Educational Review, 39,* 1–123.

35. Jensen, How can we boost IQ and scholastic achievement, 4.

36. Forrester, B. J., and Klaus, R. A. (1964). The effect of race of the examiner on intelligence test scores of Negro kindergarten children. *Peabody Papers in Human Development, 2(7),* 1–7.

37. Rose, S., and Weinberg, R. (1976). IQ test performance of black children adopted by white families. *American Psychologist, 31,* 731.

38. Scarr, S., and Weinberg, R. (1976). IQ test performance of black children adopted by white families. *American Psychologist, 31,* 726–739.

39. Scarr, S., and Weinberg, R. (1978). The rights and responsibilities of the social scientist. *American Psychologist, 33,* 955–957.

40. Hirsch, J. (1971). Race, intelligence and IQ: A debate. In N. Chalmer, R. Crawley, and S. P. R. Rose (Eds.), *The biological bases of behavior* (pp. 244–245). London: Open University Press, Harper & Row.

41. Hirsch, Race, intelligence, and IQ (p. 244).

42. Jensen, How much can we boost IQ and scholastic achievement, 42.

43. Scarr, S. (1971). Race, social class and IQ. *Science, 174,* 1285–1295.

44. Piel, G. (1975). The new hereditarians. *The Nation, 19,* 457.

45. Scarr, S., and Weinberg, R. (1978). Attitudes, interests and IQ. *Human Nature, 1,* 33.

46. Sherman, M., and Key, C. B. (1932). The intelligence of isolated mountain children. *Child Development, 3,* 279–290.

47. Jensen, A. R. (1977). Cumulative deficit in IQ of blacks in the rural south. *Developmental Psychology, 13,* 184–191.

48. Jensen, Cumulative deficit in IQ, 185.

49. Jensen, Cumulative deficit in IQ, 184.

50. Daniels, D., and Houghton, V. (1972). Jensen, Eysenck and the eclipse of the Galton paradigm. In Ken Richardson and David Spears (Eds.), *Race and intelligence* (p. 75). Baltimore: Penguin Books.

51. Kamin, L. (1977). *The science and politics of IQ.* Harmondsworth, England: Penguin Books.

52. Eysenck, H. J., and Kamin, L. *The intelligence controversy.* (1981). New York: Wiley.

53. Jensen, A. R. (1981). *Straight talk about mental tests.* New York: Free Press.

54. Fancher, R. E. (1985). *The intelligence men: Makers of the IQ controversy* (pp. 235, 238). New York: Norton.

55. Carkhuff, R. R. (1971). *The development of human resources* (p. 125). New York: Holt, Rinehart & Winston.

56. Brenton, M. (1970). *What's happened to teachers?* New York: Coward.

57. Carkhuff, R. R. (1971). The development of human resources (p. 264). New York: Holt, Rinehart & Winston.

58. Zajonc, R. B. (1976). Family configuration and intelligence. *Science, 192,* 227–236.

59. Wainer, H. (1986). Minority advances in test performance: A response to Jones. *American Psychologist, 41,* 103.

17

READING AND UNDERSTANDING RESEARCH

Every teacher should have a basic understanding of research methods, since the findings of research studies are reported at teachers' meetings and conventions and in educational journals. The results of these studies may often appear bewildering and at times can even be misleading if the teacher is unfamiliar with the general rules of science and statistical analysis. Benjamin Disraeli, Queen Victoria's prime minister, once said that there are three kinds of lies—lies, damned lies, and statistics. Disraeli was concerned over the fact that it often seems that one can prove anything with statistics.

INTERPRETING RESEARCH: FIGURES DON'T LIE, BUT LIARS CAN FIGURE

If it is true that one can prove anything with statistics, then of course there should be a real question regarding the value of statistical analysis. The fact is, however, that the only time one can "prove anything with statistics" is when the audience is totally naive about statistical procedures. To the uninitiated, liars can indeed figure, and these figures can seem plausible. But an audience that has even a little knowledge of statistical techniques will not easily be misled by the statistical artful dodger. Unscrupulous persons will probably always try to make points with faulty statistical interpretations, but by the time you finish this chapter, they will not so easily be able to lie to you.

Pass-Fail: A Research Example

One controversy in higher education revolves around the issue of whether or not to adopt the pass-fail grading system. Proponents of pass-fail claim that students will actually learn more, that they will be more likely to explore different course areas, and that they will feel less anxiety when taking a course without the pressure of regular letter grades. The opponents, on the other hand, argue that students will be less motivated and therefore learn less if they are graded on the less precise pass-fail basis. A large number of studies have been done at a wide variety of educational institutions, and the data are fairly consistent on the following point:

CONTEMPORARY ISSUE

Grading Pupils: Psychological Destruction or Helpful Feedback?

Ever since the first teacher decided to rate the first pupil's performance, the use of grades has been a smoldering controversy. The abolitionists probably win the argument from an emotional view. When a teacher grades a pupil, the pupil experiences a dehumanized process. Humanistic educators such as Sidney Simon as well as behaviorists like B. F. Skinner agree, although for different reasons. They both think that grading pupils through traditional means is miseducative. Simon indicates (rather than says) that grading creates two warring camps, pupils versus teachers, and that this dichotomy promotes distrust, separation, and manipulation through the creation of "a wall as impenetrable as barbed wire, known as a transcript." However, the litany of complaint does not stop there. Grading rewards and overrewards some pupils at the expense of others. And it even has bad effects on those whom it rewards, turning scholars

into grade grubbers. Only "the wastrel reads novels or plays which are not assigned." [a] Finally, it is the impact on the self-worth of all pupils that is the biggest drawback. Students receiving low grades are confirmed in their identity as inadequate. Achievers, however, are not much better off. High grades provide only temporary reassurance, still leaving the pupil fearful and anxious: "Will I be able to pull it off next time or will I be uncovered as a fraud?"

Skinner's opposition is less emotional than Simon's, as you might guess, but still as strong. He says simply that traditional grading essentially places students on an intermittent, yet aversive, reinforcement schedule. The teacher uses grades as a threat to coerce the pupil. The almost universal system of assign-and-test means that the teacher doesn't teach at all but rather holds the pupil exclusively responsible. "The student must read books, study texts, perform experiments,

and attend lectures, and he is responsible for doing so in the sense that, if he does not correctly report what he has seen, heard or read, he will suffer aversive consequences."[b] When professors read papers, they "correct" them. Exams are usually designed to show what the pupil doesn't know. If the exam doesn't do that, the teacher makes it harder.

The proponents of grading, on the other hand, agree that the present system often contains excesses. In some schools and some colleges, the student drive for grades has gone out of control. Such excesses, however, are the result of inadequate application of grading rather than the practice itself. After all, the proponents say, look at what happened in those few schools and colleges that adopted narrative transcripts. Instead of grades with their standard of comparison upon which to judge students for admission, the transcripts contain long, subjective paragraphs that create confusion

When students who are taking a course for regular grades are compared with students who are taking the same course on a pass-fail basis, the graded students achieve higher grades.[1] The comparison is made possible by not telling the instructor which students are taking the course on the pass-fail basis and having him or her assign letter grades to all students. The registrar converts these to pass-fail for those students who had previously elected this option. This provision is included to protect the pass-fail students from possible instructor bias.

The data clearly show that there is a difference in grades between the two groups of stu-

dents in the same class, those electing to take the course for pass-fail and those taking the course for regular letter grades. The interpretations of this difference, however, vary widely. Some claim that this difference proves that pass-fail students simply don't work as hard or take the course as seriously as students taking the course for letter grades. Others claim that this difference proves that only the less competent students elect the pass-fail option. Others claim that this difference proves that students only take their most difficult (for them) courses under the pass-fail option and therefore are exploring areas they might otherwise attempt to

in the mind of a reader. How can anybody decide what the difference is between a pupil who produces "good solid work" and one who is "most interesting and provocative to have in the classroom"? The narratives are seen more as individual case studies than as a basis for evaluation or selection. Grades, in spite of some drawbacks, do provide a system of comparative analysis. "I know," a proponent might say, "that an A is better than a C. I do not know if solid work is better or worse than an interesting and provocative performance."

Similarly, the proponents point out that the shift from grading to a pass-fail system certainly did not yield clear-cut, unequivocal results in favor of pass-fail. Instead, it is highly debatable whether replacing the traditional four categories, A through D, by two new categories, Pass or No Pass, accomplished anything at all.

Proponents further suggest that if grades are looked at in an even-handed way without emotional rhetoric, they emerge as simply a means of providing pupils with needed evaluation. There are qualitative differences in performance in almost all areas of human activity. Some baseball teams win more games than others; some dancers are more skilled than others; some cooks produce better products. So, too, in learning: Some students write better papers, comprehend more information, or synthesize ideas more easily than others. As a result, they should be rewarded and given some kind of feedback. Similarly, students who, for whatever reason, may not perform well on a particular test need to know where they stand. The proponents argue that probably the greatest need is to help pupils use and understand the positive educative aspects of grading. Certainly Ellis Page's classic study indicated that grades plus written teacher comments provided pupils with effective feedback and stimulated their actual achievement.[c] Thus, the proponents hold that the system is not intrinsically evil nor necessarily destructive. We don't need to continually throw out the baby with the bath water and junk grading.

Or do we? Must we compare pupils to their peers? Could we individualize the process so that each pupil competes only with himself or herself? Could we, like the Soviets, award team grades to groups of students? Or is it fundamentally important for us to be able to compare all students' work on the same standard for their own benefit as well as a means to preserve the system?

[a]   Simon, S. (1970). Grades must go. *School Review, 78,* 398.
[b]   Skinner, B. F. (1969). Why teachers fail. In R. C. Sprinthall and N. A. Sprinthall, *Educational psychology: Selected readings,* p. 166. New York: Van Nostrand-Reinhold.
[c]   Page, E. B. (1959). Teacher comments and students performance. *Journal of Educational Psychology, 49,* 173–181.

avoid. Others claim that this difference proves that students use the pass-fail option only in courses where the teacher is so personally uninspiring as to need the threat of letter grades in order to goad the students into studying.

What, in fact, do the data really prove? Nothing, other than that a difference in grades does indeed exist between the two groups. All the previously mentioned explanations are only hypotheses, that is, guesses about the possible reason for the difference. One or even several of these hypotheses might eventually be proved valid, but at present none of the studies really proves any of the hypotheses. Yet, in the hands of a statistical charlatan, the data may seem to an unsophisticated audience to prove whatever he or she says they prove.

Isolating the Elusive Causal Factor

The most common error in reading and interpreting research studies is assuming that a causal factor has been isolated when, in fact, it has not. As will be seen, most studies in the field of educational psychology do not allow for a cause-and-effect interpretation, and yet it is extremely tempting to interpret them as though they did. This is probably the major booby trap awaiting the unwary student. Just because two variables are associated doesn't necessarily mean that one is the cause of the other.

A study was done to discover if there was a relationship between the amount of time teachers spend smiling and the achievement level of their students.[2] Observers noted the various lengths of time that a group of teachers spent smiling and compared this with the grades their respective students received. It was found that the more the teacher smiled, the higher the students' grades were. The reader of this study should not assume that smiling teachers cause students to achieve more. It is just as likely that the reverse is true, that is, that the high level of student achievement causes the teacher to smile, apparently basking in reflected glory. Or it might be that the teacher who smiles a great deal is a happy optimist who sees only the best in everyone and therefore likes to award higher grades. The point is that although all these explanations are possible, none of them was proven by the study.

When a cause-and-effect relationship is indeed discovered, it must be unidirectional; that is, there must be a one-way relationship between the variables. When you flip the light switch and the lamp goes on, you have established a unidirectional relationship because the reverse relationship is not present in this case; although flipping the switch lights the bulb, unscrewing the bulb does not move the switch.

THE TWO BASIC TYPES OF RESEARCH

In general, people conduct two basic types of research: experimental (EXP) and post-facto (P/F). With the experimental method the researcher manipulates a stimulus or input variable, to see if it produces response changes on the part of a group of subjects. The experimental method, therefore, does allow for cause-and-effect statements. In post-facto research, on the other hand, the researcher does not manipulate a stimulus. Rather, the responses of a group of subjects are measured on one variable and then compared with their measured responses on a second variable. Post-facto research does not allow for direct cause-and-effect inferences. In the social sciences, experimental research is sometimes called "S/R research," since the researcher manipulates a stimulus (S), or stimuli, in order to establish whether this produces a change in a certain response (R), or responses. Post-facto research is often called "R/R research," since changes in one set of responses

(R) are compared with possible changes in another dimension of responses (R).

EXPERIMENTAL RESEARCH: THE CASE OF CAUSE AND EFFECT

The experimental method requires careful controls on the part of the experimenter. It also requires the experimenter to actively manipulate the stimulus variable. This actively manipulated stimulus variable is called the "independent variable." In educational psychology the independent variable is all of the following:

1. Some form of stimulus that is presented to the subjects

2. The presumed causal half of the cause-and-effect relationship

3. Always under the full, active control of the experimenter

After presenting the subjects with the stimulus variable, the experimenter seeks to determine whether any response changes in the subjects result. The measurement of the subject's response is called the "dependent variable," for it depends on whether or not the stimulus was previously presented. The dependent variable is:

1. A measure of the response made by the subject

2. The presumed effect half of the cause-and-effect relationship

For example, suppose a researcher wishes to test the hypothesis that a certain drug will increase IQ scores. She selects two groups of subjects, groups that are as equivalent as it is humanly possible to make them. Once the two groups are formed, the experimenter treats them exactly alike, except that one group gets the drug and the other does not. The group that receives the drug is the experimental group, and the group that does not is the control group.

The subjects should not know which group they are in, for it is possible that if subjects know they are in the experimental group, they might somehow be affected, perhaps be more motivated. For this reason, when the members of the experimental group are given a capsule containing the drug, the subjects in the control group are given a placebo. In this case the placebo would be an identical-appearing capsule that contains an inactive substance. The experimenter should also not know which group is which. Otherwise, she might unconsciously help one group more than another. When neither the subjects nor the experimenters are aware of which group is which, the experiment is said to be a double-blind study. This procedure should be followed wherever possible in carrying out actual experimental research. Obviously, both groups must be given the same IQ test, with the same directions and time limits.

In this example, whether or not the subjects received the drug would be the independent variable and the IQ scores the dependent variable. If, all other things being equal, the subjects who received the drug scored significantly higher on the IQ test than those subjects who did not receive the drug, the claim can legitimately be made that the drug caused an increase in IQ. Notice that the drug was (1) a stimulus, (2) the causal half of the cause-and-effect relationship, and (3) actively manipulated by the experimenter. By active manipulation, we mean that the experimenter, not the subjects, decided which group would receive the drug and which group would not. Notice also that the IQ scores were (1) responses made by subjects on the test, and (2) the effect half of the cause-and-effect relationship.

Significance

In the previous example it was mentioned that in order to validate the hypothesis, the researcher had to show a significant difference in the way the two groups scored on the test. The term *significant* simply means nonchance; a significant difference is one that the researcher feels confident is due not to chance variation but to the manipulation of the independent variable. When reading the research in educational psychology, you should keep this in mind. A significant difference is simply one in which chance has been ruled out; it doesn't mean that

In a double-blind study, neither the experimenter nor the subjects should be aware of which group is receiving the stimulus variable.

the difference is necessarily important, profound, or even very meaningful. A significant difference can be trivial, but at least it is not due to chance. Significance should never be confused with importance, though, of course, important differences must first be significant.

Experimental Designs: Creating Equivalent Groups

There are three basic experimental designs: the after-only, the before-after, and the matched subjects. In each instance the researcher is attempting to create that crucial experimental condition: equivalent groups.

After-only   Here the researcher measures the dependent variable only after having manipulated the independent variable. The problem of equivalent groups is solved through random selection. Subjects are randomly selected and randomly assigned to the experimental or the control group. It is assumed that whatever differences might exist between the two groups will be cancelled through the random selection process. In the previous example—testing the effect of a certain drug on IQ—an after-only design would mean that the researcher would do the following:

1. Select the groups randomly

2. Administer the drug to the experimental group and a placebo to the control group

3. Give all subjects the IQ test

The dependent variable (IQ) is measured only after the introduction of the independent variable (the drug).

Before-after   The before-after design assumes that nobody could be more like you than you, so let's use you twice. The dependent variable is measured both before and after the introduction of the independent variable, and any change in the second measurement is assumed to result from the administration of the independent variable. There are hazards in this technique, however, simply because some amount of time must elapse between measurements. During this period of time the subjects are open to a myriad of possible influencing stimuli. It is essential, therefore, that a control group be used, a group that is given both the before and after tests but is not presented with the independent variable. For example, assume that we wish to test the hypothesis that a speed-reading course improves scores on an English achievement test. One group of subjects is given the achievement test, then the speed-reading course, and then the achievement test again. The control group is given the achievement test twice but is never given the speed-reading course. The researcher can then ferret out the pure effects of the speed-reading course, as opposed to an improvement on the test the second time around due to other factors such as maturation, more schooling, or just simply having taken such a test before. With a control group, the before-after design can be a powerful research tool. Without a control group, it often leads to ambiguous results.

Matched subjects   Another method of forming equivalent groups is to equate or match the members of each group, subject for subject, on the basis of relevant variables. Thus, the researcher interested in assessing the effects of a certain drug on IQ would probably want to equate his or her subjects on the basis of IQ, age, past schooling, and so on. If one group includes a ten-year-old boy with an IQ of 118 and five years of previous school experience, then the researcher must find another boy of similar characteristics for the other group. This method, though certainly effective, is sometimes difficult to follow. It might be very difficult

to find subjects with the necessary characteristics. Often, too, it is not entirely obvious what the relevant matching variables should be.

The Hypothesis of Difference

In all experimental research the hypothesis of difference must be tested; that is, after equivalent groups are formed, they are exposed to different stimulus conditions and then measured to see if response differences can be observed. If these differences are significant (nonchance), then the researcher concludes that they are caused by the differential treatment the subjects received.

POST-FACTO RESEARCH: CAUSATION NEVER PROVED

Large numbers of research studies in educational psychology use the post-facto, or P/F, method. The subjects are measured on one dimension, and these measurements are compared with measurements in other dimensions; that is, responses are compared with other responses. Since there is no active stimulus manipulation, however, P/F research never proves a direct cause-and-effect relationship. However, it does allow the researcher to make predictions, and this is the real goal of P/F research. The fact that the researcher can make predictions gives researchers an extremely valuable research tool. But the researcher who uses this method must be very careful not to be enticed into assuming that a causal factor has been isolated.

To illustrate, suppose a researcher is interested in finding out whether teacher rejection of a student is related to student aggression. Assume that the researcher has developed a reliable and valid scale for measuring teacher rejection; that is, the researcher has a tool for determining a given teacher's acceptance-rejection attitude toward each student. It can thus be shown that the teacher psychologically rejects student 20 more than student 12, student 8 more than student 16, and so on. The researcher then spends a week observing the students and counts the number of aggressive responses each student exhibits during that time. Lo and behold, the researcher finds that a relationship does indeed exist; that is, the more the student is rejected by the teacher, the more aggressively he or she acts.

Now, this would be a very interesting finding, since it would allow for predictions of future behavior. We could predict the amount of each student's aggressiveness on the basis of the teacher's rejection-acceptance attitudes toward them. But has a cause-and-effect relationship been established? In fact, it has not, for without active stimulus manipulation, we cannot determine the direction of the relationship. Let us use the letter A to symbolize teacher rejection, the letter B to symbolize student aggression, and an arrow to indicate cause. (Using letter symbols in analyzing research is usually a good idea, because symbols don't have the added literary overtones that are almost always carried by word descriptions of the variables.) The following hypotheses are then possible:

$$A \rightarrow B$$

It is possible, though not proven by this study, that A (teacher rejection) does cause B (student aggressiveness).

$$B \rightarrow A$$

It is also possible that B (student aggressiveness) caused A (teacher rejection). The teacher may not have warm feelings of acceptance toward a student who is constantly punching other children or throwing chalk at her.

$$X \rightarrow A + B$$

It is further possible that X (some unknown variable) is the real cause of both A (teacher rejection) and B (student aggressiveness). Variable X could be a general atmosphere of frustration and despair that permeates a given school, leading both teacher and pupil to generate basic feelings of hostility.

All three of these situations are possible explanations, but the point is that with the P/F method we don't know which is the real explanation.

Again, it must be emphasized that there is nothing inherently invalid about the use of the P/F technique. It is the misuse of P/F research that is at issue. As we stated previously, P/F research is invaluable in allowing us to make predictions. The problem is that newspapers, magazines, and even a few journal articles have so blatantly ignored the rules of good P/F research that the reader must be alerted to the dangers that lie in wait. For example, a newspaper headline states that our prison population has tripled since women in large numbers have invaded the field of politics, and the article advises women to stay at home. Or, a magazine compares the growth in the number of PTA room mothers to that of small business failures and finds that they tally. Again, women are advised to stay home. In both cases the cardinal sin of implying a cause-and-effect relationship, when indeed there was none, was committed.

A study attempting to determine whether participation in the Boy Scouts led to better community adjustment in later life provides an example from the professional literature.[3] The researcher selected a group of adults and then went back and checked the records to see how much Scout work each adult had once been involved in. He then measured the differences in community adjustment between those who had done several years of Scout work and those who had done little of such work. This is definitely P/F research, and again, it is improper to imply a cause-and-effect relationship. Too many variables other than Boy Scout work could have caused an individual to have good community adjustment later in life. In order to isolate a causal factor, the researcher in this study would have had to select a random sample of young boys and would have had to randomly assign half of them to an experimental group and half to a control group. He would then assign all the boys in the experimental group to the Boy Scouts and prevent any boys from the control group from ever joining the Scouts. Years later, the researcher would check all the subjects in terms of their community adjustment. This would then be an EXP study with active stimulus manipulation; if differences were noted, a cause-and-effect statement could be made.

An EXP study of this nature, however, raises some important ethical questions. Is it ethical to force some boys to join the Scouts and prevent others from joining? Was not the P/F study, in which the boys were free to join or not to join, a far better study from an ethical point of view? These questions indicate another reason for the importance of P/F research. Although the P/F method does not allow the researcher to isolate a causal factor, it does allow him or her to gather evidence in areas that might be too sensitive and possibly harmful to subjects if the method were employed.

As an example, suppose a researcher is interested in testing the possible negative relationship between a certain drug and school achievement. To do this as an EXP study, one would have to randomly select students who had never used the drug, divide them into two groups, and then force one group to take the drug and the control group to take a placebo. Then, if grade-average differences were found between the two groups, the researcher could legitimately claim that the drug was the cause of these differences. But in order to isolate the causal factor, the experimental subjects may have suffered in ways other than just receiving lower grades. Suppose just one of the experimental subjects developed a drug-induced psychosis and had to be hospitalized. Should the researcher be allowed to expose his or her subjects to possible long-term damage merely for the sake of nailing down the causal factor? Of course not; the EXP method should be used only when the risks to the subjects are minute compared to the potential benefit to humankind.

The previously mentioned study on drug effects might have been more ethically handled by the P/F method. For example, the researcher could compare the grades of those students who are already using the drug with the grades of those who aren't. In this case, the subjects themselves choose whether or not to use the drug, and the researcher simply finds out whether a relationship exists between this choice and grade averages. Of course, no cause-and-effect inference is possible, for even if a significant relationship is found, we don't know the direction of the relationship. Perhaps *A* (use of the drug) caused *B* (lower grades). Perhaps *B* (lower grades) caused *A* (drug use). Or perhaps *X* caused both *A* and *B*. In this case *X* might be a depressed state of mind that caused the student to use the drug and also made the

student unable to do the work necessary for academic achievement.

Hypotheses Tested in Post-Facto Research

The post-facto researcher may test two general hypotheses, the hypothesis of difference and/or the hypothesis of association.

The hypothesis of difference   In this case the researcher selects two groups that are clearly different in one measurement and then seeks to find out whether they also differ on some other measurement. Unlike the EXP researcher who selects equivalent groups and then subjects them to differential treatment, the P/F researcher selects different groups and then subjects them to equivalent treatment. For example, a study was done to compare college grade-point averages of those students who had previously attended public schools and those who had attended private schools.[4] This study found significant differences between the two groups, differences consistently favoring the public-school graduates. (When the two groups were compared on the basis of aptitude and motivation, however, most of the differences disappeared.) This is a classic example of P/F research testing the hypothesis of difference. It is P/F research because the students themselves, not the researcher, decided which school they should attend. It tests the hypothesis of difference because the researcher seeks to determine whether these groups differ on their college grade-point averages.

The hypothesis of association   In this case one group of subjects is selected and measured on two or more variables to determine whether there is any correlation between the variables. This is correlational research and, although no cause-and-effect assumptions can be made, valid predictions are possible. For example, a study was done to investigate whether there is a relationship between grade-point average and number of absences.[5] A group of almost 3,000 students was selected and a correlation was computed between their grade-point averages and their number of absences. A significant negative correlation was obtained, showing that the more a student was absent, the lower that student's grades were. Although no cause-and-effect relationship could be (or was) implied, the results allow for a better-than-chance prediction of a student's grades on the basis of that student's attendance record. Another study was done in which length of time spent studying was correlated with grade-point average.[6] The researcher in this case compared the hours of study time reported by the students with the grades they later obtained. The positive correlation was significant, indicating that the more a student studies, the higher the grade point.

Thus, P/F research testing the hypothesis of association attempts to establish associations, or correlations, among various subject response measures. The goal is to seek significant correlations that will allow for better-than-chance predictions.

Path Analysis

Sophisticated correlational procedures have been used in a causal modeling technique called "path analysis." Although path analysis is definitely a correlational technique, it is being used to establish the possibility of cause-and-effect relationships among a series of variables that are logically ordered on the basis of time.[7] Since, logically, a causal variable must precede (in time) a variable it is supposed to influence, a correlational analysis is done to determine the possible interrelationships among a whole series of variables. The attempt is made to find out whether a given variable is being influenced by the variables that precede it, then in turn influencing the variables that follow it. A path diagram is drawn that indicates the direction of the various relationships. Although not as definitive a proof of causation as when the independent variable is experimentally manipulated, path analysis takes us a long step forward from the naive extrapolations of causation that at one time were taken from simple correlations of two variables. An excellent example of the path-analysis model as used in an educational setting can be found in a study directed by Ellis Page.[8] They found that minority student achievement could indeed be improved through attending Catholic, as opposed to public, high schools.

RESEARCH HAZARDS

The Halo Effect

It has long been known in psychology that people who are viewed positively on one trait tend also to be thought to have many other positive traits. If the public recognizes that certain athletes are extremely competent on the playing field, they often attribute to those athletes expertise in many nonathletic areas. This is called the "halo effect," and it explains why advertisers pay huge fees to athletes for endorsing their products. If a football player can score dozens of touchdowns, then "obviously" he is also an expert in the field of selecting razor blades, deodorants, and any number of other products.

The halo effect can be a hazard to both the researcher and the research consumer. The problem is especially apparent in P/F research testing the hypothesis of association. An investigator was interested in determining whether the grades a student receives from a teacher might be influenced by that student's personality.[9] The research was P/F; that is, the students' measurements on one trait were compared to their measurements on other traits. In this case, the researcher had the teacher make personality ratings for each pupil and compared these ratings with the grades the pupil had received from the same teacher. The correlation was high and positive: The more favorable the personality rating, the higher the grades. What the study tells us is that teachers must guard against the halo effect in assigning grades. A poor grade in reading, for example, should reflect the student's poor level of reading achievement, not the teacher's unfavorable impression of the student's personality. If, on the other hand, the study had been designed to test the possibility of an independent relationship between personality and academic achievement, then the personality ratings should have been given by someone other than the person who was doing the grading.

In another study, conducted at the Institute for Child Behavior in San Diego, subjects were asked to rate the ten persons whom they "knew best" on two variables—happiness and selfishness. The results showed an inverse relationship: The more a person was judged to be happy, the less that person was seen as being selfish. The conclusion implied a link between the two variables, or that being unselfish (helping others) tended to create a state of personal happiness in the helper.[10] However, since the same observer evaluated a person's selfishness and happiness, these results might just as easily be explained on the basis of the halo effect. When you like someone, you may easily become convinced that that person abounds in a whole series of positive virtues, even in the face of contrary evidence.

The Hawthorne Effect

Another pitfall awaiting the unwary reader of research is the Hawthorne effect. Many years ago, a research study was conducted at the Hawthorne plant of the Western Electric Company.[11] The object of the study was to determine whether more illumination would increase worker productivity. The researchers went into one of the assembly rooms and measured the rate of worker productivity. Then they increased the illumination and measured productivity again. Just as they had suspected, with more illumination productivity did indeed go up. This is an example of EXP research, before-after design, but with no control group. When the researchers later added a control group—that is, another group of workers whose illumination they only pretended to increase—they found to their dismay that productivity also went up. This again points up the importance of using a control group in the research situation, for it often happens that subjects will improve their behavior merely because someone is paying attention to them. If a control group isn't used, the researcher will never know whether the subject's response improved because of manipulation of the independent variable or because the subject was flattered by the researcher's attention.

The Hawthorne effect has great significance in educational psychology. Researchers must especially be aware of the possible Hawthorne effect in all studies of student change. For example, a researcher may feel that she has discovered a new technique that helps students greatly increase their ability to solve math problems. She designs a study in which she first measures the math ability of a group of students. She then spends two weeks instructing them about how to use this new method, a magic formula she probably calls the "rich, meaningful method," and then she measures their math ability again. The researcher may find that great gains have occurred, that the students have significantly increased their ability to solve math problems. But, can the researcher be certain that it was the new teaching technique that caused the difference? Certainly not! The gain may have been the result of the Hawthorne effect. Perhaps any change in the math curriculum might have produced the gain. The gain might have occurred if the researcher had simply, yet enthusiastically, stood on her head and repeated the multiplication tables eight hours a day.

Ambiguous results due to the Hawthorne effect are most common when the researcher is using the before-after experimental design without an adequate control group. One researcher in the field of learning disabilities has complained that "any idea or finding which is unacceptable to anyone today can be explained away on the basis of the Hawthorne effect."[12] In point of fact, the only time results can be

Any changes in a teacher's behavior may appear to produce student gains. Only by using a control group can we be sure.

"explained away" on the basis of the Hawthorne effect is when the researcher carelessly fails to use a control group. In one sense, the Hawthorne effect is important to the researcher in that it teaches extreme caution in assigning specific causes to observed changes in student behavior.

LONGITUDINAL AND CROSS-SECTIONAL RESEARCH

Researchers often wish to obtain data on possible growth trends, or changes in population characteristics that might occur over the years. For example, we might like to know whether a person's IQ tends to decline after age sixty. One method of obtaining this information would be to conduct longitudinal research, a subject's IQ at age twenty and then again at age sixty-five. This obviously takes a very patient researcher (and a very young one) since it will take forty-five years to answer the question. This is, however, the way longitudinal research proceeds. Subjects are measured, followed through the years, and measured again. The Perry Project's study of Head Start children, cited in Chapter 4, is an example of longitudinal research.[13]

Another method, a shortcut for gathering this type of data, is called "cross-sectional research." Using this method, the researcher would select a sample (or cross-section) of twenty-year-olds and compare their IQs with those obtained from measuring a sample of sixty-five-year-olds. The trouble with this method is that although we may learn that the average sixty-five-year-old has a lower IQ than the average twenty-year-old, we don't know whether the older subjects have actually suffered an IQ decline. It might very well be that those sixty-five-year-old subjects have always been less bright than the present twenty-year-old subjects. Perhaps they had less schooling, less adequate diets, or a host of other variables that affected their generation's ability to score well on an IQ test compared to today's twenty-year-olds. The point is that in order to assess whether or not behavioral changes are due to the aging process, the cross-sectional method just won't do. Whenever we need research answers to problems of growth and development, the longitudinal method should be used.

STATISTICAL TESTS

A bewildering number of statistical tests are used in research studies today. The reader who is new to the literature of educational psychology may be hopelessly confused by the myriad of Greek and English symbols and letters that are woven into almost all research studies. The goal of all these statistical tests, however, is the same: to determine whether or not the findings are due to chance. Assume that a researcher wishes to find out whether watching violence on TV causes aggressive behavior. He does an appropriate EXP study and finds that there are indeed more aggressive responses among the subjects in his experimental group (exposed to TV violence) than in his control group (not so exposed). Just to be certain, he replicates (repeats exactly) the experiment on another group. This time the results are reversed; that is, the control group now exhibits more aggressive behavior. The researcher replicates again, perhaps eight more times, only to find the original result occurring in half the studies and the reverse occurring in the other half. In this instance, it is obvious that the results are probably due only to chance. The probability of his original finding being due to chance, it now becomes apparent, is .50; that is, there are 50 chances out of 100 (or 1 out of 2) that his original finding was correct. As it turns out, instead of doing the study, he might just as well have flipped a coin, for his original finding was apparently a result of chance factors. Through the use of statistical tests, however, he could have determined, after the first study, what the probability was that his result was due to chance. This is not to say that the replication of studies is never needed. Replication is often necessary and is one of the great advantages of the scientific method. But statistical tests make it unnecessary to do a study over and over to estimate the probability that the result was due to chance.

Can Chance Be Ruled Out?

Regardless of the power or elegance of the statistical analysis, chance can never be completely ruled out of any study. The statistical test, however, tells us what the probability is that the result is due to chance; if the probability is .05 (5 chances out of 100) or less, the researcher can be far more confident in his or her result than if the probability of chance had been .50. Research studies never provide ultimate truth for that will not be known until the last fact is in on Judgment Day, but they do tell us how probable it is that the findings are accurate.

Statistical studies typically use two levels of significance: the .05 level and the .01 level. When a result is said to be significant at the .05 level, there are only 5 chances out of 100 that it is due to chance. Similarly, if the result is shown to be significant at the .01 level, there is only 1 chance in 100 that it is still a chance result. (Sometimes differences are found to be so great or associations so strong that a significance level of .001, one chance in a thousand, is reported.) A .05 level of significance is usually considered acceptable by the majority of researchers in educational psychology.[14]

The Four Most Common Tests

Despite the tremendous number of statistical tests used in research studies today, four tests are used so often that they deserve special mention. With a little understanding of each of these four tests, you will be remarkably well equipped to pursue the literature in a more secure fashion.

The t test   The t test, or t ratio, is a method of testing the hypothesis of difference when only two groups are being used. It can be used in either EXP or P/F research and always answers the question as to whether there is a significant difference between *two* groups.

In EXP research the t test is used when the independent variable is manipulated at two levels, one level for the experimental group and a different level (usually zero) for the control group. Thus, to test whether a certain drug increases IQ, the experimental group would receive one level of the drug (say, 25 cubic centimeters) and the control group would receive a placebo, or none of the drug. Both groups would take the IQ test, and the t test would be used to tell us whether the average IQs for the two groups differed significantly.

In P/F research, the t test can be used to establish whether two groups known to be different on one characteristic are also different on a second. For example, to determine whether people raised in the city have higher IQs than people raised in the country, two groups would be selected that differ on the characteristic of where they had been reared. Both groups would then be given IQ tests, and the t test would tell us whether the average IQ of the two groups differed significantly.

The value of the t ratio needed to establish significance depends on the size of the two sample groups. For example, if the two groups were composed of fifty persons each, a t ratio of only 1.98 would be needed to indicate significance at the .05 level. If, however, the groups were composed of five persons each, the t value needed to indicate a .05 significance level would be 2.31. Statistical tables are used to indicate precisely what t values are needed for whatever size groups are being tested.[15]

The F ratio   The F ratio is the statistic resulting from a procedure called "analysis of variance." This is also referred to as ANOVA, from *ANal*ysis *Of VA*riance. The F ratio, like the t ratio, is used to test the hypothesis of difference. Unlike the t ratio, however, the F ratio can establish differences among many groups simultaneously. Whereas we use "t for two," we use F when many groups are being compared.

The F ratio tells us whether the differences that separate the groups are greater than the differences that exist within the groups. For example, an F ratio of 10.00 would tell us that the differences separating the groups are ten times greater than the random differences existing within the groups.

Like the t ratio, the F ratio can test the hypothesis of difference in the context of either EXP or P/F research. In the previous example of EXP research, we could test the drug/academic-success hypothesis, but this time we could use more than two groups and test the effects of various amounts of the drug. For example, we could set up a four-group design—three experimental groups and one control group. The control group would receive none of the stimulus variable (the placebo); the second group would receive 25 cubic centimeters of the drug; the third group, 50 cubic centimeters; and the fourth group, 75 cubic centimeters.

In P/F research, we could use the F ratio to test more precisely the relationship between IQ and the area in which the subject was raised. Rather than simply comparing city-raised and country-raised people, as we did with the t test, we could select people from various population-density areas. For example, group I would contain people raised in communities of less than 5,000 people; group II, people raised in communities of 5,000 to 25,000; group III, people raised in communities of 25,000 to 50,000; and so on. Then we give all the groups IQ tests and use the F ratio to establish whether or not there are significant IQ differences among the groups.

The Pearson r   The Pearson r, or product moment correlation, is a statistical test used to test the hypothesis of association. Used in P/F research and path analysis, it tells us whether or not there is a relationship between two sets of measurements. If there is a significant relationship, the Pearson r also tells us the strength of that relationship. The value of r ranges from $+1.00$, down through zero, to -1.00. The farther the r is from zero, whether in a positive or negative direction, the stronger the relationship. The Pearson r is used ultimately to make predictions, and can never be used directly to ferret out a causal factor. A researcher may wish to discover whether there is a relationship between reading speed and academic grades. She selects a large number of students and compares their reading-speed scores with their grade average (P/F research). Assume she obtains a significant r of $+.70$, meaning that most of the subjects who scored high on the reading-speed test also had high grade averages, and those who scored low had low grade averages. From this, she can now make a better-than-chance prediction of a given student's grade average by knowing how that student performed on the reading-speed test. This research, however, offers no proof that taking a speed-reading course causes a student to have higher grades. It may be that A (reading speed) causes B (high grades). Or, it may be that B (high grades) causes A (high reading speed). Or, it may be that some X (perhaps a high IQ) causes both A (high reading speed) and B (high grades).

Chi square χ^2   Chi square, symbolized χ^2, is the real work-horse test in educational psychology. It is used in virtually every type of research situation, to test both the hypothesis of difference and the hypothesis of association. Chi square is useful whenever research data are in the form of classified frequencies, that is, whenever the researcher is interested in the actual number of cases that fall into two or more discrete categories. When results are recorded in this way, they are called "nominal data." They reflect the frequency of occurrence within discrete categories rather than the exact or relative performance of any individual. For example, subjects might be categorized according to their college major and then compared with regard to whether or not they went on to graduate school. In both cases the data are in the form of frequencies of occurrence within categories: When we categorize our subjects on the basis of college major, we know exactly how many students majored in each subject. When we then compare these frequencies with the on-to-graduate-school variable, we again know exactly how many persons went to graduate school and how many did not. This is the kind of situation in which chi square is the ideal statistical test. With the t, F, and r statistical tests, the actual measurements of the subjects are used. That is, with t, F, and r, we know exactly how each subject scored in a given area, such as IQ, grade-point average, height, weight, correct responses on a learning task, whatever. With chi square, we know only how many subjects fall into certain discrete categories: how many took a college-prep course as opposed to how many did not; how many subjects live on campus as opposed to how many do not; how many children in a given school district eat hot lunch as opposed to how many do not, and so on.

Chi square is extremely versatile, since even when the researcher has actual measurements of his or her subjects, these measurements can always be converted into frequency data. For example, if we know the actual IQ scores of our subjects we can, if we want to, categorize these measurements according to how many subjects scored above 100 and how many scored below. Or, if we know the actual grade-point averages of a group of students, we can (if we want to) categorize them on a pass-fail basis.

A TEACHER'S OBLIGATION

A knowledge of the rudiments of research methodology is essential to any student or teacher who hopes to profit from the literature in the field of educational psychology. Although this chapter has only skimmed the surface of the subject, a thorough reading and analysis of the material it contains should pay rich dividends in future understanding. The student who is serious about becoming a professional teacher is urged to follow this up with at least a one-semester course in statistics and research design. The field of educational psychology is constantly changing. New theories are being offered and new supporting data are being introduced. The dedicated teacher, in whose hands the lives of our children are placed, has an obligation to stay on top of the research literature.

SUMMARY

The most common error in interpreting research studies is the assumption that a cause-and-effect relationship has been established when in fact it has not.

Two general types of research are used in educational psychology: experimental (EXP) and post-facto (P/F). EXP research involves active stimulus manipulation on the part of the experimenter and attempts to specify whether the manipulated stimulus *causes* a response difference. P/F research involves comparing measured responses on one dimension with different measured responses on another dimension. This method does not allow for direct cause-and-effect inferences.

The term *significance* as used in research simply means nonchance. A significant difference or a significant correlation indicates only that chance has been minimized; it does not refer to the importance or even meaningfulness of the result.

There are three basic experimental designs, all aimed at creating equivalent groups when EXP research is used:

1. After-only, where random selection and random assignment of subjects to two or more groups is used to create equivalence

2. Before-after, where a group is measured before and after the introduction of the manipulated variable, and equivalence is maintained by the use of the same subjects in each condition

3. Matched subjects, where subjects are selected for the various groups on the basis of a matching process

EXP research always tests the hypothesis of difference—that is, the hypothesis that the measured responses of the subjects are in some way different as a result of the previously manipulated stimulus. P/F research may test either the hypothesis of difference (though not directly implying a cause-and-effect relationship) or the hypothesis of association. In the latter case, the researcher attempts to discover whether two or more response measures of the same subjects are significantly related.

Path analysis is a type of correlational technique that determines possible causal relationships among a number of variables.

Two major research pitfalls are the halo effect and the Hawthorne effect. The halo effect occurs when a researcher measures a subject on one variable and is then influenced by that measurement (either positively or negatively) when evaluating the subject in a different area. This problem can be eliminated by using independent observers when measuring subjects on more than one trait. The Hawthorne effect occurs when the researcher, using a before-after experimental design, assumes that a given response difference is the result of the stated stimulus variable, when in fact the result may be due to the attention the researcher paid to the subjects. The judicious use of extra control groups can help to eliminate this problem.

The longitudinal research method, in which the *same* subjects are measured at different ages throughout life, is preferred over the cross-sectional method, in which different subjects of different ages are measured. This preference is especially apparent whenever the research is concerned with growth and development.

Though a number of statistical tests are used in research studies today, the prospective teacher can become reasonably adept at reading these studies if the four most common tests are understood:

1. The *t* test: for testing the hypothesis of difference when no more than two groups are being compared.

2. The *F* ratio for testing the hypothesis of difference when many groups are being compared.

3. The Pearson *r* for testing the hypothesis of association.

4. The chi square for use in research studies in which frequencies of occurrence are compared within various categories. This is an important test when we don't have the subject's actual measured score.

KEY TERMS AND NAMES

experimental research (EXP)
post-facto research (P/F)
variable
   independent variable
   dependent variable
experimental group
control group
double-blind study
significance
after-only experimental design
before-after experimental design

matched subjects experimental design
hypothesis of difference
hypothesis of association
path analysis
halo effect
Hawthorne effect
longitudinal research
cross-sectional research
t test
F ratio (ANOVA)
chi square (χ^2)

REFERENCES

1. Stallings, W. M., and Smock, H. R. (1971). The pass-fail grading option at a state university. *Journal of Educational Measurement, 8,* 153–160.

2. Harrington, G. M. (1955). Smiling as a measure of teacher effectiveness. *Journal of Educational Research, 49,* 715–717.

3. Chapin, F. S. (1947). *Experimental design in sociological research.* New York: Harper.

4. Finger, J. A., and Schlesser, G. E. (1963). Academic performance of public and private school students. *Journal of Educational Psychology, 54,* 118–122.

5. Anikeef, A. M. (1954). The relationship between class absences and college grades. *Journal of Educational Psychology, 45,* 244–249.

6. Carver, R. (1970). A test of an hypothesized relationship between learning time and amount learned in school learning. *Journal of Educational Research, 64,* 57–58.

7. Yarenko, R. M., Harari, H., Harrison, R. C., & Lynn, E. (1982). *Reference handbook of research and statistical methods in psychology* (p. 172). New York: Harper & Row.

8. Keith, T. Z., and Page, E. B. (1985). Do Catholic high schools improve minority student achievement? *American Educational Research Journal, 22,* 337–349.

9. Russell, J. L., and Thalman, W. A. (1955). Personality: Does it influence teachers' marks? *Journal of Educational Research, 64,* 561–564.

10. Rimland, B. (1982). The altruism paradox. *Psychological Reports, 51*, 521–522.

11. Roethlisberger, F. J., and Dickson, W. J. (1939). *Management and the worker.* Cambridge, Mass.: Harvard University Press.

12. Kephart, N. C. (1971). On the value of empirical data in learning disability. *Journal of Learning Disabilities, 4*, 393.

13. Berrueta-Clement, J. R., Schweinhart, L. J., Barnett, W. S., Epstein, A. S., and Weikart, D. P. (1984). *Changed lives: The effects of the Perry Preschool Program on youths through age 19.* Ypsilanti, Mich.: High/Scope Press.

14. Cowles, M., and Davis, C. (1982). On the origin of the .05 level of significance. *American Psychologist, 37*, 553–558.

15. Sprinthall, R. C. (1987). *Basic statistical analysis,* 2nd ed. Englewood Cliffs, N.J.: Prentice-Hall.

UNIT 5

MANAGING STUDENTS IN GROUPS

18

THE CLASS AS A SOCIAL UNIT

Every classroom is a distinct social unit with its own set of norms, its own psychological atmosphere, its own set of role relationships, its own special blend of behavioral expectancies. Every classroom has a social climate unlike that of any other classroom. An observer walking from room to room in a typical elementary school finds one room charged with excitement and enthusiasm; another, tense, with submissive pupils going through the motions; and still another, bordering on anarchy.

The psychology of the classroom does not operate in a vacuum, for every classroom is part of the larger social unit, the school itself. Again, the observer traveling from school to school can sense differences in social climate among the various schools. The differences among schools may not be as blatant as the differences among classrooms, but they are there, and they do have an effect.

What causes these differences among rooms, among schools, among any different number of groups? The quick and easy answer is the personality of the teacher or principal. This, however, is only part of the answer. Just as the principal's behavior helps shape the teachers', so the teachers' behavior shapes the principal's actions. And just as the teacher's behavior influences the pupil's behavior, so the pupils' behavior has a profound effect on the teacher. Teachers may firmly believe that their classrooms have the same social climate year in and year out, despite the shifting student population, but these same teachers will stare in shocked disbelief at a videotape showing one of their classes two or three years ago, or even last year. The shifting student population creates a shifting social climate. Sometimes the shift is subtle, but often it is dramatic. Many teachers freely confess that with one particular class they barely weathered the year, or the opposite: "For the first time in my life my class this year was an absolute dream." This chapter takes a look at some of the findings of social psychology, which, we hope, will increase your understanding of the classroom as a social unit.

SOCIAL PSYCHOLOGY DEFINED

Social psychology attempts to understand human behavior in the context of the social situa-

Different schools have different social climates.

tion. Social psychologists study the ways people affect and are affected by other people. As a subfield of psychology, social psychology still uses the behavior of the individual as its unit of analysis, the individual's behavior in the social context. The social psychologist would probably not be interested in the lonely figure of Hermann Ebbinghaus going about the business of memorizing long lists of nonsense syllables, but would be very much interested in how Ebbinghaus's performance might have been affected by the presence of other people. The very first studies in the field of social psychology were concerned with the effect of a group situation on a person's behavior.

SOCIAL FACILITATION

Even before the turn of the century, studies indicated that on certain tasks a person's performance would improve when others were around.[1] This phenomenon later became known as social facilitation. It was also found that this was not a universal phenomenon. So-

cial facilitation was most pronounced in the case of fairly simple mechanical tasks. The more difficult and the more intellectual the task, the less the effect of social facilitation. Later studies have revealed the operation of social inhibition; that is, on some tasks, a person's performance suffers when there are others around. In one study students were given a word-learning task, either alone or in the company of other students. Some of the tasks were designed to be easy; others were much more difficult. On the easy tasks the students did better when in the presence of others (social facilitation), but on the difficult tasks they did much worse when in the presence of others (social inhibition).[2] Still other studies have shown that when a person is first attempting to learn something new, the presence of other people is detrimental. Thus, in preparing for a final exam, when the material has already been learned well, reviewing the course in a small-group situation would probably be facilitative. When the material is new, however, spending the night before the exam in absolute solitude would be more productive.

The Risky Shift

When people get together in group situations, one effect that has been demonstrated in several experiments is the risky shift.[3] The group situation apparently produces an environment in which individuals become far less cautious than they would be if they were alone; consequently, an attitude shift in the direction of "throwing caution to the wind" occurs. Individuals are suddenly willing to take greater risks regarding their attitudes and behavior. They become less conservative and more willing to gamble. One explanation of this phenomenon is that individuals who are basically risk takers to begin with also happen to be more persuasive and better able to have their opinions prevail in the group setting. These high-risk people become opinion leaders when interacting in the group. Another explanation is that in our culture the daredevil is more revered than is the individual who prudently and cautiously weighs all the outcomes before acting. We are more apt to honor an Evel Knievel than a stodgy, trust-department banker. Thus, many individuals would prefer to have the group see them as risk takers. They prefer the public image of being a "gutsy gambler" and therefore shift in the culturally approved risky direction when in a group situation.

Whatever the explanation, the risky shift is an empirical fact. The teacher who is aware of this is less apt to be overconcerned when some budding daredevil disrupts the class with an image-building display of bravado. Perhaps a short session alone with the student will be sufficient to restore the equilibrium and integrity of the classroom.

Brainstorming

The concept of social facilitation has also been used to promote a technique called "brainstorming," in which individuals get together in an attempt to solve problems in new and creative ways. The idea is that because of the mutual stimulation of a brainstorming session, each participant will individually produce more creative solutions than when in isolation. Individuals in a brainstorming session are urged to interact freely, to call out any ideas no matter how bizarre, and to hold nothing back. The technique is used in many businesses, especially in areas where creativity is crucial, as in an advertising agency mapping out a new campaign. Actual research in this area, however, casts some doubt on the real benefits of this technique. The most famous study on brainstorming had subjects assigned either to a five-person group situation or to an isolated situation.[4] In both situations, the subjects were given five problems to work on and a time limit of twelve minutes. One problem, for example, asked the subjects to suggest methods for increasing the number of European tourists visiting the United States. Subjects were told that they should come up with as many ideas as possible and that they should be as creative as possible. They were also told the following:

1. Criticism is ruled out. Adverse judgment of ideas must be withheld until later.

2. Freewheeling is welcomed. The wilder an idea, the better. It is easier to tame down than to perk up.

3. Quantity is wanted. The more ideas there are, the more winners there are likely to be.

4. Combination and improvement are sought. In addition to contributing ideas of your own, you should suggest how others' ideas can be improved or how two or more ideas can be put together into an even better one.[5]

The results of this study startled many social psychologists. Subjects who were isolated produced almost twice as many different ideas as the subjects who were working in groups. Also, the subjects working alone produced twice as many ideas judged to be unique and creative.

Differential Effects on Behavior

Research in the area of social facilitation thus suggests that people do behave differently when in the group situation. The seemingly contradictory results of the studies (groups sometimes enhance performance and sometimes inhibit it) show that the group has differential effects on behavior.

Working in a group situation has two main effects: It increases feelings of competition and motivation on the one hand, and it increases

feelings of anxiety and provides distractions on the other. The presence of other people explicitly or implicitly creates a competitive situation. However, the research studies in this area may be slightly artificial for it has been found that in these studies the subjects tend to become somewhat self-conscious. The subjects assume that the researcher may be making comparisons among them and/or they hope to impress other members of the group.

Cohesiveness

When individuals interact in a group situation, one possible by-product is the spread of a group phenomenon that social psychologists call "cohesiveness." When cohesiveness develops, group members tend to stick together more and have more of a sense of "we-ness" than "I-ness." Some teachers have been known to feel threatened by this turn of events.

Cohesiveness is one of the few truly group concepts in social psychology. It is the cement that binds the group together, or the attraction of the group for its members. Groups can range from collections of unrelated individuals (strangers waiting together at a bus station) to highly cohesive groups, in which norms are shared and status and role relationships are highly structured. When students and teachers

meet in the classroom for the first time in September, they resemble a collection of individuals more than they do a cohesive group. As the weeks go by, however, the social situation may change dramatically as the loosely knit collection of individuals becomes more cohesive. Cohesiveness may be enhanced by the following:

1. *Friendly interaction.* Interaction per se is not the crucial ingredient; a husband and wife fighting it out in divorce court are interacting. The interaction must be on friendly terms.

2. *Cooperation.* The more the group works together to achieve superordinate goals, the more cohesiveness is allowed to develop.

3. *Group status.* High-status groups tend to be more cohesive than low-status groups. If a classroom is broken down into various reading groups, for example, and if it is obvious to every child that the groups have been rank-ordered on the basis of ability, the top group will feel more cohesive than the bottom group. A teacher may also increase the status of the entire classroom by pointing out that they are in some way a special group and will have special privileges.

4. *An outside threat.* A group's cohesiveness may be dramatically increased by the pres-

ence of an outside threat. This is true of large and small groups. In wartime, when a country's very existence is threatened by an outside force, a country's morale and cohesiveness are often at their highest level. In a classroom this same kind of situation may inadvertently occur when a coercive teacher is perceived by the class as overly threatening. The class may band together and form a highly cohesive group—a group, incidentally, that does not include the teacher.

5. *Style of leadership.*   We will look at this phenomenon in more detail in a later section. Suffice it to say here that groups in which the leadership is based on democratic factors are usually more likely to be cohesive than are groups in which more authoritarian leadership techniques are employed.

Cohesiveness and productivity   Research indicates that there is no simple one-to-one relationship between cohesiveness and productivity. A cohesive group is one in which the members stick together, but this doesn't necessarily mean that the group is more productive. For example, a highly cohesive labor union is more likely to be able to call a strike, during which production on the job goes down to zero, than is a union whose members are not so attracted to one another. Highly cohesive groups may be more productive than less cohesive groups when the motivation of the members is positive, yet when the motivation is negative, the more cohesive group will be even less productive than the less cohesive group.[6]

Cohesiveness and conformity   Any group brings a certain amount of pressure to bear on its members to conform to the group's standards and norms. In a highly cohesive group the pressure to conform is greater than in a less cohesive group. This helps explain the previously mentioned relationship between cohesiveness and productivity. When the group norm is for high productivity, the highly cohesive group conforms to that norm; likewise, when the group norm is for low productivity, the highly cohesive group conforms to that norm, especially in matters of consequence to the group (working conditions and salary, for example).

Conformity

One of the most striking facts about life on this planet is that human beings form groups and live out their lives in group situations. Equally striking is the fact that, while in the group situation, people tend to behave in a uniform way. Conformity is a fact of life. Wherever we look we find groups of people, and within each group almost everyone is behaving alike. The behavior of an individual may change from group to group, and the norms of any particular group may shift from time to time, yet the phenomenon of conformity remains. We may like to feel as if we can act with some degree of independence, and yet in truth our freedom of action is severely limited by group pressure.

In a structured situation such as in church, conformity may be most obvious. People stand, sit, and kneel with the precision of a marching band. The pressure to conform, however, can be just as compelling in less structured situations. If, during the give and take of a dormitory "rap" session, someone suddenly stood up and started singing "Onward Christian Soldiers," that person might be referred to the counseling center.

The message from the group is always the same: "Be like us!" The pressure to conform is

Within a group, great pressure exists for conformity, and group pressure to conform is highest when the group is highly cohesive.

virtually irresistible and may come in a variety of forms. It may be physical force, as in the case of a bouncer throwing a rowdy customer out of the local tavern—a customer who has exercised too much individuality. Or, it may be more subtle, as when the hostess at a formal dinner party raises her eyebrow when one of the guests chooses the wrong fork for the salad. Regardless of the form it takes, the pressure on the individual to conform makes itself known. Conformity has been demonstrated experimentally in many studies. The two most famous, however, are the classic studies by Muzafer Sherif and Solomon Asch.

Sherif and the autokinetic effect   A stationary, pinpoint source of light in an otherwise darkened room will appear to move. You may have noticed this phenomenon yourself. You may have been looking up at a certain star, and out of the corner of your eye it appears that another star has suddenly moved. Or you may have been driving on a turnpike when the rear light of the car in front of you suddenly starts to dance crazily before your eyes. Some plane crashes have even been caused by this autokinetic effect. The stationary runway lights suddenly appear to move just before the pilot lands the plane. The effect is even more dramatic if the subject doesn't know how far away the light really is.

Sherif utilized the autokinetic effect to demonstrate conformity.[7] He put his subjects in a darkened room in groups of three, presented them with the pinpoint source of light, and asked them to call aloud their estimates of how far the light moved. The first subject might estimate that the light moved sixteen inches; the second subject, three inches; and the third subject, twenty-four inches. After a few trials, however, all three subjects reported essentially the same distance—a group norm emerged. Repeating this procedure with other groups, Sherif found that conformity occurred in every case. The groups formed different norms, to be sure, but they all created some standard to which every member conformed.

Another interesting result of Sherif's study was that when he later tested many of the subjects individually, they still perceived the light on the basis of the norms created in the group

situation. A member of a "seven-inch" group, for example, when later tested alone, would continue to conform to this seven-inch standard. A member of a "twenty-two inch" group would continue to see the light moving this distance, even when tested individually.

Sherif's study shows us that in a relatively unstructured situation, group norms will be created and that individuals will follow these norms, not only when they are in the group, but even when they are alone.

Asch and group pressure   Sherif had shown that conformity occurs in a fairly unstructured situation (remember that, in fact, the light didn't move at all), and Asch wondered whether the same result would be obtained in a more structured setting.[8] Asch presented his subjects with cards showing four lines: three comparison lines and a standard (see Figure 18.1). The subject was asked to indicate which of the three comparison lines was closest in length to the standard line on the left of the card. As you look at the illustration, you may feel that the task is too easy, that the solution to the problem is too obvious. Yet, when Asch conducted this study, his subjects were in error one out of three times. The difference is that as you look at the lines, you are not being exposed to group pressure, whereas Asch's subjects most certainly were. Asch's subjects sat in a room with what appeared to be eight other subjects. In fact, these other "subjects" were really stooges, told beforehand just what to say and how to respond. Each group contained one naive subject and eight previously rehearsed bo-

Figure 18.1   Asch used a card such as this to study group pressures to conform.

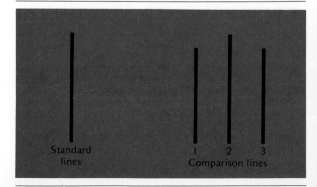

"Well, heck! If all you smart cookies agree, who am I to dissent?"

Drawing by J. B. Handelsman;
© 1972 The New Yorker Magazine, Inc.

gus subjects. The subject was thus in a situation in which his eyes told him one thing, while all the other people in the room made a unanimous judgment that contradicted his own. The stooges were set up in advance so that every once in a while they would all agree on a certain line, even though that line could not possibly be the correct one. It was in this setting that the subjects were incorrect one-third of the time; that is, 3.3 percent of their judgments were errors in the direction of the majority. As we have already said, group pressure is tremendous in its insistence on conformity.

As a matter of fact, the majority does not have to be so large. Asch's later studies revealed that a majority of three-to-one has just as much effect as a larger majority; that is, the naive subject made as many errors with three stooges as with eight. A two-to-one majority caused errors to drop only to about 12 percent, while the influence of only one stooge was negligible.

When the situation was reversed, when there was a naive majority of sixteen against one lone stooge, the errors of the stooge were met with uncontrolled laughter from the rest of the group.

Sherif and Asch have thus demonstrated experimentally the compelling power the group exerts on the individual to conform. Sherif has

been able to produce norms in the laboratory and show how they govern individual behavior, and Asch, though artificially creating the norms, has shown us the force of the group's influence in a relatively structured situation.

Can group pressure be liberating? So far, conformity and group pressure have been shown to be repressive and limiting, generally robbing people of their individuality. Sherif has shown us how a group of people can come to believe that a stationary light is moving a certain distance; Asch has shown that our need to conform to group standards will cause us to distort our perceptions and judgment. In fact, virtually all of the studies done in the area of conformity follow this theme: The noble individual is robbed of human integrity by the insidious pressure of the group.

The experiment by Stanley Milgram that was discussed in Chapter 7 shows the reverse side of the coin.[9] Milgram, in a somewhat frightening experiment, shows us that group pressure can also have a liberating effect. We say "frightening" experiment because Milgram's study also points up the destructive potential of human beings and shows what a thin veneer of socialization we have.

To establish a base line for our potential for hostility, Milgram asked subjects to deliver in-

Asch found, in studying conformity, that some subjects are able to maintain independent judgment throughout. Most, however, are unable to do so and yield to group pressure on at least one trial. (a) The experimenter gives instructions. (b) The critical subject, the sixth from the left, listens to the instructions. (c) He makes his first judgment that disagrees with the consensus. (d) He leans forward as the next set of lines appears. (e) He feels conflict as he listens to new, incorrect peer judgments.

creasing amounts of electric shock to another person. Despite the "victim's" anguished cries and pleas for mercy, the experimenter urged the subject to keep increasing the voltage all the way up to 450 volts. The dial in front of the subject contained 30 voltage levels from 15 to 450 volts and was printed with such warnings as "Danger" and "Severe Shock." The subject had witnessed the "victim" being strapped into the electric chair and could clearly hear the "victim's" cries.

Milgram established his base line. Fully 65 percent of his subjects were willing to admin-

ister the maximum 450 volts; that is, almost two-thirds of the subjects were willing to risk killing a fellow subject.

Who were these subjects? Where and when was this experiment conducted? Were these Gestapo agents being trained in some sadistic Nazi laboratory during the 1930s? In fact, these subjects were ordinary American citizens, from twenty to fifty years of age, from all walks of life, and living in New Haven, Connecticut. The study was done at Yale University during the 1960s. Unknown to the subjects, of course, was the fact that the "victims" did not really get shocked. The wires connecting the control panel to the electric chair did not really carry any electricity, and the victim was really an ally of the experimenter. But the subjects didn't know this and were still willing to deliver the shock as the experimenter instructed.

The second phase of Milgram's study was to see what would happen in a group situation. How would subjects react if they were placed in the same situation with two other subjects who refused to follow the experimenter's commands? The results were dramatic. Under the condition of group pressure, only 10 percent of the subjects still pushed the lever all the way to 450 volts. The majority of the subjects refused to go beyond the half-way point. In this case, then, group pressure liberated the individual from the experimenter's authoritarian control and had a positive effect.

Conformity and group pressure may often be beneficial to the individual. Milgram's study suggests that they may help a person act in a more humane and less destructive manner.

Locus of control   Despite the insistent demands of group pressure, people differ on how readily they yield to the seductive lure of conformity. Psychologists have categorized people on the basis of whether their locus of control is internal or external. Persons who have been identified as having an *internal* locus of control typically view themselves as being personally in control of their actions and in charge of their own destinies. Persons measured as having an *external* locus of control, on the other hand, feel that they are largely at the mercy of environmental circumstances.[10] It follows, then, that the individual who is externally controlled is more easily swayed by group pressures, whereas the internally controlled person is more apt to stand up to the group's demands and be more *flexible under conditions of stress*.[11] Typically, the child who develops a strong sense of internal control has greater ego strength, greater feelings of personal competence, and is less likely to go along with the crowd.

As we have seen, conformity pressures are pervasive in our society, and even the internally controlled person is not totally immune. In fact, the power of the group is enhanced even further when that group is composed of persons we tend to like.[12]

SOCIALIZATION

Conformity is a key issue in social psychology because it is a driving power of socialization. Socialization is the process of learning society's rules and customs and is accomplished through pressures to conform. The newborn infant—at best an innocent little hedonist and at worst a savage bundle of Freudian instincts—is slowly transformed into a conforming member of society. The individual slowly but surely gives up personal independence as socialization continues, learning how and when to eat, where and when to urinate and defecate, how to interact with other people, and so on. Finally, the mature adult emerges who has learned these lessons so well that he or she conforms with the instinctive precision of a homing pigeon.

Are there any nonconformists? There are only a few, and most of them are either in prison or in a psychiatric hospital. For example, you might think that members of a nudist colony are nonconformists, and yet they are all conforming to their own group norm. The only nonconformist in a nudist camp would be the person who is fully dressed. Or, you might assume that members of a commune are nonconformists, and yet they are conforming as rigidly to their norms as middle-aged Rotarians are to theirs.

The so-called generation gap is essentially a difference in group norms. Both the under-thirty and the over-thirty groups are conforming to their own group norms. Each group is marching in unison, but to different drummers.

Who is the drummer in the classroom? Who sets the beat for the in-unison march of classroom members? To a large extent, it is the norms of society at large. After all, most students and teachers have been socialized in a common culture. The way they dress, the ideas they consider important, the way they interact, the way they express feelings are all determined by the core culture. The fact that most students feel a sense of competition is in large part culturally determined and already part of their characters before they ever set foot in the class-

Socialization, the process of learning society's rules and customs, is accomplished through pressures to conform. True nonconformists are rare.

room. The fact that they are in the classroom at all, pursuing an educational goal, is a cultural dictate. But this doesn't explain it all for each classroom has its own distinct set of norms that exists within the larger context of society's norms. The teacher contributes much of the tone, but so does every single member of the class. The crucial ingredient in formation of a norm, and thus conformity, is interaction among group members. Interactions produce group norms, which then set the limits within which further interactions can take place. Status and role relationships begin to emerge, and further demands and expectancies are set for each individual's behavior. Who sets the beat? The classroom, within the context of the larger social situation, sets its own beat, and every single member of the class participates in the process.

Cognitive Dissonance

Another aspect of socialization has been described by Leon Festinger. According to Festinger, people strive to achieve a state of equilibrium among their various attitudes (or learned predispositions to persons, situations, or things) and behaviors.[13] This is because we prefer consistency, or consonance, to inconsistency, or dissonance. Therefore, whenever we have a thought that is not consistent with our behavior, we experience cognitive dissonance and are motivated to restore the equilibrium. To avoid self-contradiction, we can either change our thinking so that it conforms to our behavior or change our behavior so that it conforms to our thought. For example, someone who enjoys smoking and who hears that smoking is a health hazard can either conclude that the evidence linking smoking with disease is flimsy or stop smoking. One smoker, it has been said, became so nervous after reading the evidence linking smoking with cancer that he gave up reading.

The point is that whenever our thoughts and deeds conflict, we are driven to reduce the anxiety-provoking dissonance. Teachers should be alerted to the possible consequences of cognitive dissonance when it occurs in the classroom. The desire for consonance operates within the individual and within the group. The chances against finding a classroom in which all thirty pupils and the teacher have totally compatible interests, attitudes, and values are so great that it is safe to say that dissonance is inevitable. The important thing is the way that dissonance is resolved. If the teacher decides to always "fight and never switch," if the pupils have to do all the changing, then the reduction of dissonance in the classroom will be more apparent than real. We will see in Chapter 20 that the way in which a teacher handles pupil discipline will help define the educational atmosphere of the class. The imposition of too strict a set of sanctions may reduce dissonance, but the resulting compliance is likely to be begrudging at best. Pupil discipline is just one instance of the general problem of the incongruity between the individual and the group.

AGGRESSION

Social psychologists have long been interested in the phenomenon of aggression. Human society is obviously fraught with violence. The United States has the dubious distinction of leading the world in rates of homicide, rape, assault, and robbery. In fact, the homicide rate in the United States is twice that of Finland, which is the second most violent nation on the planet. Over 2,000 children are murdered by their parents or caretakers every year in the United States, and even more common are the tiny broken bodies resulting from the "battered child syndrome." As every football, hockey, and boxing fan knows, violence also has crowd appeal. And "hit 'em again harder" apparently is not reserved for the sports arena. On September 23, 1967, at a large southwestern university, when a depressed student crawled to the edge of a dormitory roof and threatened suicide, thousands of students stood below and chanted in unison, "Jump! Jump! Jump!" As for major conflicts, the world has rarely seen a day since the beginning of recorded history when there wasn't a full-scale war going on somewhere on the globe. These facts seem to argue that aggression is an inevitable by-product of people getting together in groups.[14]

Psychology has generated four basic positions regarding the issue of aggression:

1. *The Freudian.* According to Sigmund Freud, aggression is built into the organism and is as basic to human behavior as sexuality. The urge to violence is a result of pressure from our innate and irrational instinct. The trouble with the Freudian hypothesis is that, by explaining so much, it may in fact not explain anything. To say that people are aggressive because they have a built-in aggres-

sive instinct smacks of circular reasoning. This was referred to in Chapter 2 as the nominal fallacy.

2. *The ethological.* Konrad Lorenz and other ethologists view aggression as a constant potential in virtually all organisms. If the proper releaser occurs, the potential for aggression will quickly be translated into action. For example, the male stickleback fish attacks whenever stimulated by the color red. As for humans, Lorenz feels that aggression actually has survival value for the species. Since population density often outruns available food supplies, aggression acts both to reduce the size of the population and to spread the remaining population over a larger area.[15] Another ethologist, Robert Ardrey, suggests that aggression results from a fundamental territorial need. Ardrey says that all organisms have an innate drive to own, defend, and gain territorial areas.[16] The ethological explanation runs the risk of possibly having ventured beyond the actual observed data. Since Lorenz has based his theory on observations of lower organisms, more research is needed before extrapolation to the human level becomes convincing.

3. *Frustration-aggression.* Led by Neil Miller and John Dollard, a group of Yale psychologists in the late 1930s introduced the now famous frustration-aggression hypothesis.[17] Aggression was explained as the result of being frustrated, or of having one's goals blocked. Said Miller, "The occurrence of aggression always presupposes frustration."[18] In many instances the Miller-Dollard hypothesis is obviously valid. We have all seen people become angry, sometimes to the point of irrationality, over having a goal blocked: An individual, already late for an important appointment, becomes furious when the car won't start; a teen-age boy gets in a fist fight on the way home from school after having been "cut" from the varsity basketball team.

The frustration-aggression hypothesis, however, does have some major drawbacks as an explanatory model. Some people react to frustration not with overt aggression but merely by sitting quietly and seething inwardly. Another person may respond to

"This will teach you not to hit people."

goal blockage by regressing, that is, acting in a less mature fashion. Also, there are countless examples of aggressive behaviors that are not triggered by frustration. Being annoyed or attacked by another person often results in aggression aimed at the source of the annoyance. A student was playing poker in the dorm when, without provocation, another student moved quietly behind his chair and playfully poured beer on his head. Five seconds and two punches later the "playful pourer" was on his back and nursing a bruised eye and jaw.

4. *Social learning or modeling.* As we noted in Chapter 10, Albert Bandura's social learning theory has been used to explain aggressive behavior. Children who watched an adult model punch and kick a large "Bobo" doll also punched and kicked the doll when they later got the chance. In this instance, the children were imitating the adults' aggressive behavior. The children had not been provoked, annoyed, or frustrated, and yet because of modeling they exhibited aggressive responses. It has also been shown that

if children watch a film of an aggressive adult model, they, too, will imitate the aggressive behavior.[19]

Aggression and the Mass Media

One question that has recently become of great concern to social psychologists is whether the portrayal of violence in movies and on TV encourages aggressive acts on the part of the viewer. This question is especially important with regard to TV since most children are avid television viewers. One survey report indicates that the average sixteen-year-old has spent more hours of his or her young life in front of the TV than in class.[20] Some of the studies done in this area have shown a relationship, especially among boys, between watching violence on television and the acting out of aggression. In the typical study a group of boys are asked to indicate which TV shows they watch, and these results are then correlated with the peer group's evaluation of each boy's overt aggressiveness. Significant relationships have been discovered. That is, boys who report watching the most TV violence are also the ones rated most aggressive by their peers.[21] As we pointed out in Chapter 17, studies such as these are difficult to evaluate in terms of the direction of the possible cause-and-effect relationship. Does the violence on TV cause the boys to be aggressive, or does aggressiveness in boys cause them to select violent TV shows? Or are some boys aggressive by nature, and because of this do they act out their aggression more and do they also choose to watch more aggressive TV shows? With post-facto research studies such as these, the direction of the relationship is virtually impossible to interpret.

Milgram attempted an experimental evaluation of this problem by using a large portion of the United States as his laboratory. Milgram talked CBS into creating two versions of a popular program, one version having far more aggressive cues than the other. Milgram was unable to detect any difference in the rates of violence among the cities receiving the aggressive versus nonaggressive programs, even though they were equated for prior levels of violent crimes.[22]

Finally, in an attempt to subject this problem to a controlled, experimental analysis, a study was conducted in which the TV fare was actually manipulated (as an independent variable) by the experimenter.[23] The subjects, again all boys, were enrolled in private boarding schools or state residential schools. By random assignment, the boys were required to watch either violent shows or nonviolent shows. Both before and after six weeks of this controlled-viewing regimen, the boys were measured for both overt and covert aggressiveness. Overt aggressiveness was determined by a supervisor's daily tally of each boy's aggressive incidents. Covert aggressiveness was measured by projective personality testing.

The results showed that the boys who watched the violent TV shows expressed more covert or fantasy aggression as measured by the Thematic Apperception Test. The boys who watched the nonviolent shows, however, exhibited twice as many fist fights and far more overt, verbal aggression. The results suggest that TV violence has a possibly cathartic effect on boys, rechanneling their hostility so as to inhibit overt aggression. The authors of the study caution, however, that watching real-life violence on newscasts may increase rather than decrease the expression of aggressive responses on the part of the viewer. They say that "violence presented in the form of fiction is much less likely to reinforce, stimulate, or elicit aggressive responses than violence in the form of a news event."[24] Thus, whereas TV's coverage of a violent news story may increase viewer aggression, fictitious violence may possibly even inhibit overt viewer aggression. This is obviously a very difficult area to research. As we have seen, the results, and more important, the interpretations of the results in this area, seem to flip-flop back and forth.

Certainly, the amount of televised aggression has not diminished over the years. In one study, in which an index of TV violence was calculated, it was found that although the percentage of programs containing violence had not increased between the years 1967 and 1984, the number of violent acts per program had.[25]

One cannot casually dismiss the possibly profound effects that television has on viewer behavior. The advertisers obviously believe that television affects behavior, and they back up their belief not just with a heartfelt wish but with millions of dollars spent for commercials.

Nature or Nurture?

Like the great intelligence debate, the question of whether aggression is primarily innate or learned has also stirred controversy among psychologists. The nature theorists see humans as instinctively violent, destined by their genes to be aggressive. The nurture position is that humans, being a product of environmental stimulation, can be shaped into peaceful and loving beings. Indeed, the four positions on aggression just outined can be categorized according to this issue. Both the Freudian and ethological positions rest on the assumption that aggression is largely inherited. Both the frustration-aggression and social learning explanations, however, view aggression as basically a product of the environment.

The genetic argument   As pointed out in Chapter 3, white mice have been selectively bred for aggressiveness. In one study, a large group of mice was separated on the basis of the amount of aggressiveness displayed. The most aggressive and least aggressive mice were then selectively bred, and after seven generations two nonoverlapping groups were identified. That is, the least aggressive of the aggressive strain were more aggressive than the most aggressive of the nonaggressive strain.[26]

At the human level, a number of studies have been done comparing MZ (identical) twins with DZ (fraternal) twins on the criterion of aggression. Regarding crimes of violence, it has been found that the concordance rate (the percentage of cotwins having the trait) was significantly higher for MZ than DZ twins.[27] Since MZ twins result from a single fertilized egg, they have identical genetic endowments. DZ twins derive from separate eggs fertilized at the same time and are thus no more alike genetically than other siblings.

The environmental argument   Psychologists holding the environmental view see aggression as resulting from the way society reinforces and punishes its members' attitudes and behavior. The environmentalists state that the attitudes of the majority of people in each society determine whether or not violence will be tolerated. Cultures are cited in which aggression is apparently almost nonexistent, and other cultures have

CONTEMPORARY ISSUE

Children's Television: The Bane of the Bassinet?

Each new technological advance carries with it the possibilities of good or evil. Thus the wheel made it possible for farmers to plow their fields; it also enabled enemy cannons to be pulled into positions of destruction. The world of media is no exception. Advances in communication systems from the humble blackboard to sophisticated printing systems have opened up new vistas. Children's television is one of the most recent.

Given the possibility of transmitting sound and sight messages on a nationwide basis, it was inevitable that educators would eventually attempt to harness such a powerful technique for teaching. In fact, and even before the fact, children were already watching. They devoured reruns, daytime soap operas, and cartoons; they mimicked commercials and copied the latest slang and attire of the western. The proponents of children's television argued that as a country we were wasting a golden opportunity to enlist TV in the service of education. Finally, in the late 1960s, a major project was launched. "Sesame Street" came to the air-

waves under the dynamic leadership of Harvard professor Gerry Lesser.

A careful evaluation of "Sesame Street" indicated quite clearly that not only did children enjoy its format but they also made academic gains as a result of viewing it. Prereading skills, number concepts, visual discrimination, and reasoning all improved as a result of the program. Therefore, it was easy to conclude that the program was an unqualified success.[a]

There is another side to the picture, however. Psychoanalytic (Freudian) theorists have raised the specter of Big Bird as Big Brother in disguise. These theorists argue that during the sensitive years, or the magic years between three and five, a rich fantasy life should be allowed to run its course. Children's imaginations should not be channeled toward the "boob tube." Freewheeling thoughts and feelings should be encouraged instead of a reliance on advertising techniques to trick kids into learning numbers and letters. Activity, rather than passivity, should predominate during these years. Plopping chil-

dren down in front of the TV is indeed the "bane of the bassinet."

The evidence, of course, seems to be on the side of "Sesame Street." The fears may be baseless. Yet there are some lingering worries that "Sesame Street" could unwittingly lead to unselective TV watching. Perhaps the greatest fear is that parents will come to rely not just on "Sesame Street" but on TV in general, that they will leave young children for hours on end in front of mindless reruns, canned laughter, and unnecessary violence. And even with proper control, questions remain. Must "Sesame Street" be so fast-paced? Does such speed actually shorten rather than increase attention span? What really does happen to imagination and creativity with a regimen of televised instruction? And some of the responses also raise questions. Early education *is* important. As the adage suggests, "The hand that rocks the cradle rules the world." Or does it?

---

[a]   Lesser, G. S. (1974). *Children and television: Lessons from* Sesame Street. New York: Random House.

been found in which hostility is a major characteristic. In short, the environmentalists argue that aggression is determined by group norms and the frustrations of day-to-day living.

Is there an answer?   As is the case with so many areas in psychology, all the answers are not yet in on the issue of human aggression. It is known, however, that behavior is caused by many factors, and perhaps the safest prediction is that aggression will be found to result from

heredity interacting with environment interacting with time. The fact that there is a genetic component in aggression seems to be fairly well established. Also, the built-in aggressive tendencies emerge at different times through maturation, depending on individual differences, sex, and species. Just as certainly, since aggression can be expressed in so many ways and in so many different situations, there is obviously a very large learning component to it. Harry Harlow comments:

There is little disagreement among comparative psychologists that aggression is part of the biological heritage of primates. However, some social psychologists who limit their studies to the human animal still believe that aggression is basically a learned behavior, and that the differences which occur between the sexes or among individuals within their sex group are accountable solely on the basis of experience. No doubt the late appearance of aggression in the developmental sequence has led some observers to underestimate its biological basis.[28]

STATUS AND ROLE

If you met someone for the first time and he suddenly put his hand into your mouth, you might be pretty startled. Or, suppose a perfect stranger told you to take off all your clothes. Your reaction might be hard to predict. Yet all of us have been in situations like these and have hardly blinked. When the individual putting his hand into your mouth is a dentist, or the stranger telling you to undress is a physician, the situation has a context in which the behavior is expected.

Social psychologists use the term *status* and *role* to describe expected behavior of this type. Status is the position we occupy in society's prestige hierarchy. Role is the behavior that is expected of us because of the particular status we have. Conformity is essential to status and role because status gives us an obligation to behave (act out the role) in the way society expects (conform to society's expectations). For example, our society expects far different behavior from a used-car salesman than from a college president. People might smile if the used-car salesman created a drunken scene in public, but they would be severely disapproving if the college president did the very same thing. Our behavior is expected to conform to society's norms for our position in life. If it does not conform to these expectations, society has ways of exerting great pressure to bring us back into line.

Because of the complicated nature of our society today, most people find themselves occupying different status positions at the same time. A man may have a job as a clerk in a shop and spend each day quietly taking orders, while at night he issues directives with an authorita-

tive flourish in his capacity as Boy Scout executive. In each case his role conforms to his status. A given status often has multiple roles. A woman may have a number of status positions and roles, as mother, clubwoman, wife, and corporate executive. The variety of roles may create conflict and a feeling of frustration and despair if she feels that she cannot carry out all her roles—that, for example, she can't continue to work and also fulfill the role of a good mother. Yet if she doesn't work, she may feel frustrated and perhaps even guilty over the fact that she isn't living up to her full potential as a woman.

It is crucial to understand role behavior in order to understand human behavior. People tend to behave in the way society (as embodied by the people around them) treats them. One of the contributing factors in adolescent rebellion is the lack of consistency with which society treats this nonchild-nonadult. When adolescents are treated like children, they will tend to respond like children, no matter how many speeches they hear about their failure to assume responsibility or act maturely. The parents' words are often drowned out by the volume of their own contradictory behavior.

The Influence of Expectations

Expectations and "looks": Never judge a book by its cover   It has long been suggested that some individuals tend to "get by" on their looks. That is, the individual's appearance, his or her own physical stimulus value, seems to influence the kinds of expectations and treatment provided by other people. Some evidence suggests that this is indeed the case. In one study attractive individuals were judged to possess more positive personality traits, more prestigious occupations, and more potential for future success than were unattractive people.[29] This stereotype about physical attractiveness apparently begins early in life, at least by the time the child reaches kindergarten.[30] What this means to the teacher is obvious. The attractive and docile child should not be overrewarded with grades and praise—"looks" should not be confused with achievement.

Expectations and older siblings   Teacher expectations of a pupil may also be influenced by the past performance of a pupil's older brother or sister. Although teacher remarks such as "I never had this kind of trouble with your sister" tend to frustrate and burden a child, they can, in fact, work to the child's advantage. One study found that a child received higher grades from teachers who knew and admired an older sibling than from teachers who had no such previous knowledge.[31] This is simply one more example of the Rosenthal effect in the classroom—teacher's judgments are clearly affected by expectations.

A recent summary of the research on the relationship between teacher expectations and student achievement again demonstrates the power of this important phenomenon.[32] Because of its power, efforts have been made to train teachers to guard against this source of bias. The Teacher Expectations and Student Achievement (TESA) program was designed to sensitize teachers to their own, often subtle, negative treatment of those perceived as low-achieving children. The TESA technique appears to have had a positive impact when used as part of the Connecticut School Improvement Program.[33]

Expectations and personality   Even the developing child's basic personality structure is largely shaped by social expectations, especially those of the parents. Much of what a child begins to expect of himself or herself develops from the child's attempts to gain parental approval and to live up to parental expectations. As personality theorists Joseph Perez and Alvin Cohen say, "For the developing self, 'Mom and Dad are me.' "[34]

Expectations and teacher behavior   Just as the teacher's evaluation of a student is often clouded by certain preconceived expectations, so students' ratings of their teachers are influenced in the same manner. If a student has been told that her new teacher "really knows her stuff" or "has her act together," or that "she's a hard marker but you're really going to learn something," then the student will almost certainly perceive that teacher in a positive manner. As the weeks go by, however, the teacher must really earn the positive image that the student brought into the class. Some teachers have the ability to generate positive feelings in students from the very first day, even if the students have not received any information about the teacher's reputation. Research has shown that the teacher's physical appearance is the most important single source of initial student expectations.[35] The teacher who "looks good" is immediately perceived as a person who *is* good—at teaching, counseling, whatever. But again, as the term wears on, the students begin using more substantive measures of effectiveness. A teacher can get by on looks and style for only a limited time. Students, even first-graders, are soon able to spot the phony, the teacher who is really not doing the job. Style without substance is like a book with a pretty cover that is filled with blank pages.

Sex Roles in the School

Just as the school often acts to transmit the traditional values of the larger culture in general, it also transmits society's version of the sex role. Boys are encouraged to be more "masculine" and girls to be "ladylike." One recent analysis indicated that this transmittal is done, often inadvertently, in three ways:

1. Schools encourage sex typing by separating male and female activities and interest areas. Young boys are more apt to be sent to the "block corner," whereas girls are placed in the "housekeeping" and art areas.

2. Teachers project sex-typed expectations and the children live up to these expectations—exactly the kind of situation that role theory would predict. If teachers expect little boys to be less manageable than little girls, the boys pick up these cues and don't let the teachers down.

3. Schools have typically created an ideal "pupil role." The ideal pupil is conforming, docile, dependent, and manageable—that is, the pupil exhibits the very traits that have traditionally defined the female role. By more easily adopting this role, girls learn to be more receptive than active. Boys, on the other hand, have more difficulty in conforming to this ideal-pupil image and thus often find school to be a stressful and alienating experience.[36]

Role and Personality

Although the pressure of group expectancies is a powerful influence on our behavior, our basic personality will determine the way in which our role in the group is interpreted and carried out. The fact that individual behavior is consistent across different roles in different groups shows that we each bring an integrated and coherent behavioral unity to our groups. The way in which role and personality interrelate is reciprocal. The role we play in a group also has a definite impact on our personality. For example, an actor who for years plays the "tough guy" in the movies may slowly incorporate this image into his personality and may begin to believe and act as if he *is* that tough guy.

The therapy technique called "psychodrama" is based on this notion. Neurotic patients are put on the stage and given roles that they typically find uncomfortable to act out. With encouragement, and in the context of a non-threatening situation, they learn the behavior required for certain roles and experience a concomitant personality change. The relationship between role and personality also works the other way. We will consciously or unconsciously select roles that are consistent with our underlying personality. Extroverted personalities usually assume roles that allow them to stay in the limelight, while introverts adopt roles that keep them away from stagefront.

Studies have shown that the majority of college seniors majoring in education prefer to work with people rather than things and describe themselves as "conventional in opinions and values."[37] Teachers also tend to score above average in such personality areas as friendliness, sociability, and personal relations.[38] A summary of the research on teacher personality profiles as determined by the Minnesota Multiphasic Personality Inventory (MMPI) describes teachers as the following:

1. Responsible, conscientious, conforming, and friendly

2. Likely to emphasize control of self and adaptation to the needs and demands of others[39]

Evidence indicates that the personalities of teachers are fairly consistent with the role demands of their job. However, the research in this area is correlational, meaning that the interpretations can go either way. In other words, teachers may have a personality style that causes them to select the role of teacher, or the role demands of the teaching position may shape the personalities of those involved in the teaching profession. The best guess is that both selection and shaping are involved.

LEADERSHIP

The highest position in the status hierarchy of any group is that of leader. The leader has the most influence in shaping the group's norms and expectations. Before relating styles of leadership with group functioning, we must first get some understanding of the concept of leadership itself.

Is leadership something we either have or don't have? Are there people who, regardless of the group, the social setting, the cultural norm, will always rise to the top? Or, is leadership strictly a function of the group norms, the task being performed, or the social context? In other words, is leadership a quality of the individual or a quality of the group?

Theories of Leadership

The great-leader theory The great-leader theory sees leadership as a quality of the individual. In its boldest form the theory states that certain individuals possess just the right blend of looks, personality traits, and intelligence to be almost automatically thrust into leadership positions. These individuals—who are said to have charisma—will always become leaders in any situation or in any group. Charisma is a kind of personal magnetism and hypnotic appeal. When a charismatic person walks into a room, the room is suddenly charged with excitement, and the others in it become submissive and willing to follow the individual anywhere. Some of history's charismatic leaders include Mahatma Gandhi, Joan of Arc, Winston Churchill, Cleopatra, Adolf Hitler, Charles de Gaulle, John F. Kennedy, Martin Luther King, and Pope John Paul II. Each had or has a personal appeal that is spellbinding, almost mystical. People such as these, says the theory, have

to become leaders regardless of the times in which they live.

The group theory　According to the group theory, almost anyone who fulfills some basic need of the group can be a leader. And, since the needs of the group shift, so too does leadership. For example, a group on a camping trip would see leadership constantly changing according to the dictates of the situation. If the group became lost, the individual with the compass would become the leader. If someone became injured, the person with first-aid knowledge and supplies would become the leader.

Even history's great leaders are explained on this basis. Winston Churchill became a leader late in his career, when the times called for someone with his special talents. Hitler would have found no followers and would have probably had to spend his entire life painting portraits in Austria had Germany not been rocked by runaway inflation and crushing depression. The group theory suggests that the unfolding of history is like the opening of a combination lock—only when a certain sequence of events occurs will a certain individual be called upon to lead.

A blending of the theories　The actual evidence regarding leadership now suggests that the best explanation lies somewhere between these two theories. Both theories are needed to account for the data. Certain individual qualities do seem to be more common in leaders than in other group members. For example, leaders tend to be taller but not too much taller, and more intelligent but not too much more intelligent, than other members of the group. Leaders also seem to possess more social skills than followers. For example, leaders are apt to give more information, ask for more information, and make more interpretations about a situation.[40] But it has also become increasingly evident that the demands of the situation are crucial in determining the group's choice of a leader. One study of schoolchildren found that the boy who could spit the farthest was the leader in the first grade. By fourth grade it was the child who "sassed" the teacher the most. In high school the girl who had always stayed in the background in grade school suddenly blossomed into leadership because of her "dating

power."[41] Thus, the demands and values of the group are just as important in determining leadership as are many of the personal qualities listed above. Leadership results when the individual's qualities match the group's demands.

Styles of Leadership

Most of you have been members of many different groups—scout troops, athletic teams, school clubs, whatever. You have thus been exposed to various styles of leadership, and you may have noticed that the efficiency of the group's performance and the satisfaction of the group's members were due in large measure to the style of the group's leadership. You may recall a coach who was so lenient that the team failed to perform to expectations. Or perhaps you remember a scout leader who was so rigid and domineering that most of the members quit and the troop had to fold.

Many years ago Kurt Lewin, who had once been a student of Max Wertheimer, conducted an experiment to assess the ways in which groups respond to different kinds of leadership.[42] One aspect of the study was to compare the effects of authoritarian and democratic styles of leadership on group activity. The subjects were young boys who were placed in "club" groups under the direction of adult leaders. The authoritarian leader was domineering, never asking for suggestions about group activities and controlling every aspect of the group situation. The democratic leader, on the other hand, guided the group gently, constantly asking for suggestions and allowing the group to make decisions. The results of the study indicated that completely different atmospheres were generated in the two groups. The democratic group's members were more satisfied, more cooperative, less hostile, and better able to carry on group activities when the leader was not present. Though the authoritarian group did have a higher rate of production (building model planes), the work of the democratic group was of a higher quality.

In interpreting this study, it is important to recall the discussion of social norms and conformity. This study was done in the United States, where childrearing practices are not as authoritarian as in some other cultures. One of the boys in the study was the son of an army officer and had been raised in a highly rigid and disciplined home. This subject actually responded better in the authoritarian group; he enjoyed that group more and felt less anxiety in the highly structured situation.

Classroom Leadership

Although the teacher is handed the main leadership role in the classroom, other leaders are also present. The broad base of influence from which the teacher operates in large measure shapes the social climate in the classroom. The degree to which the teacher is authoritarian or submissive or coercive or democratic sets the tone for norm formation in the classroom. But, once school has been in session for a few weeks, student leaders begin to emerge. Again, it is the teacher who, to a large extent, may determine which students attain leadership positions. The teacher may encourage and reinforce leadership behavior from one child and withhold reinforcement when the same behavior is exhibited by another child. Yet the teacher can also succumb to reinforcement. One prominent sociologist has said that "influence over others is purchased at the price of allowing one's self to be influenced by others."[43] This sociologist feels that an influential leader must have the esteem of everyone in the group. This means that students can exert considerable pressure on a teacher by giving or withholding their esteem and that they can, by this means, shape their teacher's behavior. It also explains why a given teacher might be a successful leader with one group of students and not so successful with a different group.

Social psychology assumes that leadership ability is a set of behavioral skills that most people can learn. One psychologist says that effective leadership depends on the following.

1. Flexible behavior

2. The ability to know what behaviors are needed at a particular time in order for the group to function most efficiently

3. The ability to behave as required or to get other members of the group to do so

An effective leader must learn to spot what the group needs in a given situation and then be flexible enough "to provide diverse types of behaviors that are required under different conditions."[44] The effective leader must also get the cooperation of various members of the group so that they will help perform the necessary group functions.

GROUP DYNAMICS IN THE CLASSROOM

The classroom is a collection of interdependent individuals. The dynamics of their interrelationships depend on the roles that have been established through interaction. Whenever there is a change in the expected behavior of any group member, the dynamic interrelationships of the entire group must necessarily change. The pressure on role behavior is so great that if a group has certain expectations about an individual's behavior, that individual usually responds in a way consistent with those expectations. The group's expectations become a self-fulfilling prophecy.

In a two-person group, or dyad, the expectations of the superordinate member clearly determine the behavior of the subordinate member. Suppose a mother is convinced that red hair causes a child to have a quick temper. She will then tolerate the temper tantrums of her red-haired child, while at the same time extinguishing these same responses in her blond or brunette children. Or, suppose a high-school student complains that his mother treats him as if he were a child; an objective analysis of the student's behavior may reveal that he indeed doesn't let his mother down—he acts like a child. Or, imagine a husband who complains that his wife is domineering. During the conversation he mentions that he recently dropped one of his wife's plant pots and was thereupon banished to the cellar, where his son later brought him his supper. In each case, the dynamic relationship between the people involved could exist only if both members played their expected roles. If the student who was being treated like a child stopped acting like a child, his mother would have to change her expectations and thus her behavior toward him. The man with the domineering wife must have played the role of a dominated husband to the hilt. Why else would he meekly allow himself

Changing the role of one individual in the group may change the whole group, since the classroom is a collection of interdependent individuals and the dynamics of their interrelationship depend on roles established through interaction.

to be served dinner in the cellar? In the words of a once popular song, "It takes two to tango." There can be no tango, or any other consistent form of interaction, unless both partners play their expected roles.

The same phenomenon can also be observed in larger groups. In an educational psychology course taught by one of the authors, the power of role behavior was demonstrated in the following way:

Two students, selected at random, were chosen as subjects and asked to leave the room and wait in the corridor. During their absence, roles were assigned to them: One student was given the high-status position of a world-famous cultural anthropologist, and the other student was given a low-status position of a college dropout who could not find a job. The class was instructed to discuss a certain topic, keeping firmly in mind the roles that had been assigned to the two naive subjects. The two subjects, unaware of their roles, then rejoined the group. The group consistently treated the high-status student with dignity and respect and the low-status subject with derision and inattention. Within fifteen or twenty minutes the group's expectations began affecting the subjects' be-

havior. The high-status subject began dominating the discussions, even pontificating grandly for minutes at a time. He later explained that he had thoroughly enjoyed himself and would like to take part in more group discussions. The low-status subject, especially during the early stages of the discussion, made repeated attempts to become involved, but as time went by these became more infrequent. His behavior showed general signs of regression; the pitch of his voice even rose perceptibly until it bordered on a preadolescent squeak. During the final five minutes of the discussion he withdrew totally and sat stiffly in tight-lipped silence!

This demonstration of the influence of a group's expectations on individual behavior has been tried a number of times. In each case the results have been generally similar, though not always as dramatic as the case just described: Personality differences cause differences in the ways subjects respond to the group's pressure. The point, however, is that consistent and predictable behavioral effects occur despite the personality differences.

In a classic case reported by learning theorist Edwin R. Guthrie, a group of male college students decided to make an all-out effort to cater extravagantly to a shy, socially inept coed. They made sure she was invited to all the social functions, constantly flattered her with gifts and attention, and in general saw that she was the "belle of the ball." By the end of the college year she had developed an easy, confident manner and had become a popular campus favorite even among those not aware of the original plot. Says Guthrie, "What her college career would have been if the experiment had not been made is impossible to say, but it is fairly certain that she would have resigned all social ambitions and would have found interests compatible with her social ineptitude."[45]

The influence of group expectations on individual behavior can also be seen in the area of racial prejudice. Though prejudice is primarily learned in the home, teachers may also implant prejudice, especially during the first few grades. They may not directly teach hatred, but the message still comes through loud and clear. The teacher's differential treatment of minority races and religions sets the stage for differential student responses. Black children, for example, can hardly be expected to act maturely in the classroom when they are not treated with dignity and respect. The mass media have also helped to communicate this social distortion. Until the last few years movies typically cast blacks in subservient roles, as maids and servants. They also played up stereotypes, often characterizing a black as a wide-eyed, frightened fool. This sort of thing could hardly lend dignity to the black race.

Group expectations can be so powerful that the minority-group members may learn to hold the prejudices and stereotyped attitudes toward their own group that the majority group holds. This can be very destructive to the minority-group member's self-image.[46]

The classroom teacher is obviously a potent reinforcer and through the judicious use of social approval he or she can shape the behavior of the entire class. The teacher must realize, however, that the classroom is a social unit with a dynamically balanced set of role relationships. Any shift in the role of one student necessarily results in a change in the social balance of the entire group. If the teacher clamps down on the class joker, for example, the social climate could shift in a negative direction. The joker may be fulfilling the important role of relieving group tensions in moments of social stress. Removing that function could lead to a far more anxious social climate in which the conditions for learning could deteriorate. By the same token, shutting off the antics of a loud-mouth who is motivated more by compulsive attention seeking than by reducing class tensions could produce better learning conditions for the rest of the class. Some tinkering and adjusting can be attempted, but remember that changing the role of any individual in the group produces changes in the whole group.

OTHER VARIABLES AFFECTING SOCIAL CLIMATE

We have discussed the importance of status-role relationships, leadership, conformity, and cohesiveness in influencing the school's social climate, but these variables do not tell the whole story. We would like to mention briefly three other factors:

1. *Socioeconomic status of the school.* The average socioeconomic status of a high school affects the competitive climate of the school. Working-class students are more likely to go on to college when they attend predominantly middle-class high schools than when they attend working-class high schools. Similarly, middle-class students are less likely to go on to college when they attend predominantly working-class high schools.[47]

2. *School facilities.* Another study found that school facilities, such as the size and quality of the library, the number of science laboratories, or the amount of laboratory equipment, have no significant effect on student achievement.[48] This study shows that academic achievement is influenced far more by socioeconomic background than by school facilities.

3. *Size of the school.* In comparing high schools of various sizes, researchers have found that students participate in extracurricular activities more and assume more leadership roles when they attend smaller high schools.[49]

KENNETH B. CLARK

Kenneth Clark, noted educator and psychologist, was born in the Panama Canal Zone in 1914. Clark's father, Arthur B. Clark, was a passenger agent for the United Fruit Company in Panama. When young Clark was five years old, his mother left Panama for the United States, bringing her children with her. To support the children, Mrs. Clark worked as a seamstress in a New York garment factory, where she also helped organize a union. Clark says his first contact with social issues was listening to his mother tell of her problems in trying to organize a union in her shop.

Clark's education began at Public School 5 in Harlem. Later he attended P.S. 139 and then graduated from George Washington High School. The following year he enrolled at Howard University in Washington, D.C. He received his B.A. degree from Howard in 1935 and his M.A. in 1936, when he was twenty-two years of age. For the next two years Clark taught psychology at Howard, but the following year he enrolled as a Ph.D. candidate in experimental psychology at Columbia University. He was awarded his degree in 1940, and during the academic year 1940–1941 he became an assistant professor of psychology at the Hampton Institute in Virginia. The following year, Clark worked as a social science analyst for the Office of War Information, traveling throughout the country in his study of morale problems in black population centers. In 1942 he joined the psychology department of the College of the City of New York. He became a full professor in 1960.

In 1946 Clark and his wife, Dr. Mamie Clark, established the non-profit Northside Center for Child

Development in New York City. The center is devoted to treating children with emotional problems. In 1950 Clark worked on a report that showed that segregation in the schools is detrimental to the growth and development of white as well as black children. The United States Supreme Court relied on Clark's study when, in 1954, it made its important decision that segregation in public schools is unconstitutional.

Clark has devoted his life to improving school conditions for all children. He has found racial prejudice to be a two-edged sword that harms both the prejudiced as well as the objects of the prejudice. In 1970 Clark received his colleagues' highest honor when he was named president of the American Psychological Association. During his presidency, he established the Board of Social and Ethical Responsibility for Psychology. His many

articles and books include *Desegregation: An Appraisal of the Evidence* (1953), *Prejudice and Your Child* (1955), *Dark Ghetto* (1965), *A Relevant War against Poverty* (1968), and *Pathos of Power* (1974).

Clark is now president of Clark, Phipps, Clark, and Harris, Inc., a consulting firm involved in personnel and race relations and affirmative action programs. In 1978 Clark was selected by the American Psychological Association to receive its "Distinguished Contribution to Psychology in the Public Interest Award."

As an educator and psychologist, Clark ranks at the top of his profession. Although a brilliant theorist, he has not sought refuge in an ivory tower but prefers to remain on the front lines, working, doing, and making things happen. He is without question psychology's most prominent spokesperson for social justice.

However, it has also been found that the size of the school has no significant influence on academic achievement.[50]

All the variables mentioned in this chapter will be operative at one time or another in almost any classroom. The question is: What kind of a group will the classroom become? The teacher as leader can clearly exert a major influence on the definition of the group. We have noted that classes can run the entire gamut from a collection of egocentric individuals "doing their own thing" to a smoothly functioning machine in which each individual may be defined only as a group member. If the teacher does not know about the social variables or chooses not to exert definitional leadership, the students will impose their own definition. This is likely to create a very awkward situation: The teacher's role will be totally defined by the group. The opposite extreme, in which the teacher sets the classroom atmosphere and educational objectives solely in terms of his or her own needs and values, is equally undesirable. Thus, the way in which a teacher uses concepts like social facilitation, conformity, competitiveness, cohesiveness, and group pressure is part of the teaching problem. An equally significant question involves the whole area of social goals and objectives. A knowledge of social psychology can truly help the teacher promote human development through education.

SUMMARY

Social psychology is the study of human behavior in the context of the group situation. Each classroom is a social unit with its own unique set of norms, role relationships, and behavioral expectations. Though the social atmosphere of the classroom is in large part shaped by the teacher, it is also a function of each student's behavior.

Sometimes the influence of the group acts to increase an individual's performance (social facilitation), and sometimes the group's influence decreases an individual's performance (social inhibition). Working in a group situation can increase feelings of competition and anxiety. A student's performance will be facilitated by the group's influence when (1) the student's motivation level is on the low side, and (2) when the task is neither overly difficult nor overly intellectual.

The risky-shift phenomenon occurs in group situations and seems to promote more risk-taking behavior among the group members than they would otherwise display were they alone. The group situation has also been used to foster the growth of creative ideas through a process called "brainstorming," in which individuals are encouraged to call out any ideas they might have on a given subject, no matter how seemingly bizarre.

Cohesiveness is defined as the amount of attraction the group has for its members. Cohesiveness can be increased in a group as a result of (1) an increase in the amount of friendly interaction, (2) an increase in the amount of cooperation, (3) an increase in the group's feeling of status, (4) an outside threat, or (5) a change in the style of leadership.

One result of group life is the overwhelming desire of individuals to conform to the norms of their group. Two major studies indicate the compelling nature of conformity: Sherif's research on the autokinetic effect and Asch's study of group pressure. In each case, the behavior of individuals conformed to the group norm. Though most conformity studies tend to show the power of the group as being repressive to the individual, a study by Milgram showed that the influence of the group may actually allow an individual to act in a more humane and less aggressive fashion.

Despite the pressure to conform exerted by the group, some individuals are less likely to yield than others. Individuals whose locus of control is internal (i.e., who see themselves as being personally in control of their actions and in charge of their destinies) are less likely to conform than individuals whose locus of control is external.

The process of socialization is essentially produced by pressures to conform, whereby the child is literally forced into adopting society's standards. Socialization is necessary to society but produces some loss of personal independence.

Another aspect of socialization is dissonance. When a person feels a lack of consistency between attitudes and deeds, he or she undergoes cognitive dissonance, an uncomfortable feeling of disequilibrium. To reduce the anxiety, the individual attempts to restore consistency by changing actions to conform with attitudes or attitudes to conform with deeds.

Social psychologists are also concerned with aggression. The Freudian and the ethological positions assume that a major portion of aggressiveness is innately determined; the frustration-aggression hypothesis and social learning theory view aggression as a product of the environment. Studies of the effect of violence in the mass media on aggression have had equivocal results: Some indicate that violence on TV has increased aggressive behavior in viewers, while other studies suggest that it may have a cathartic effect.

The behavior of the individual also conforms to the expectations society forms on the basis of one's status and role. Status is one's position or niche in society's prestige hierarchy and role is the behavior expected of a person having a particular status.

Society assigns roles by sex, and schools typically encourage these sex roles. Although society influences behavior by the role playing it encourages, the personality of each individual determines how a role is interpreted and carried out.

Leaders seem to be chosen on the basis of both personal characteristics and the demands of the group. In a study comparing styles of leadership, democratic versus authoritarian, it was shown that democratic leaders (those who gently guided the group, asked for suggestions, allowed for group decisions, etc.) were apt to have groups in which the members were more satisfied, more cooperative, less hostile, and better able to follow through on group projects even when the leader was absent.

Because of the present status and role requirements of the classroom, the teacher automatically holds the leadership position. He or she is not the only leader, however, for student leaders inevitably arise and can influence the behavior of both the teacher and the other students.

The group dynamics of the classroom, or of any group situation, are based on interdependent status and role relationships. When a group has a certain expectation regarding an individual's behavior, the individual usually responds in a way consistent with that expectation. This can be especially damaging to the minority-group child when the group's expectation is based on prejudice and stereotyping.

The social atmosphere of the classroom is influenced also by pressures outside the school. Among those variables affecting group dynamics are: (1) socioeconomic status of the school, (2) school facilities, and (3) the size of the school.

KEY TERMS AND NAMES

social psychology
social facilitation
social inhibition
risky shift
brainstorming
cohesiveness
conformity
autokinetic effect
locus of control
socialization
attitudes

cognitive dissonance
frustration-aggression hypothesis
status
role
great-leader theory
charisma
authoritarian leadership
democratic leadership
group dynamics
Kenneth B. Clark

REFERENCES

1. Triplett, N. (1897). The dynamogenic factors in pacemaking and competition. *American Journal of Psychology, 9,* 507–533.

2. Cottrell, N. B., Rittle, R. H., and Wack, D. L. (1967). Presence of an audience and list type as joint determinants of performance in paired-associates learning. *Journal of Personality, 35,* 217–226.

3. Pruitt, D. G. (1971). Choice shift in group discussion: An introductory review. *Journal of Personality and Social Psychology, 20,* 339–360.

4. Taylor, D. S., Berry, P. C., and Block, C. H. (1958). Does group participation when using brainstorming facilitate or inhibit creative thinking? *Administrative Science Quarterly, 2,* 23–47.

5. Freedman, J. L., Carlsmith, J. M., and Sears, D. O. (1970). *Social psychology* (p. 188). Englewood Cliffs, N.J.: Prentice-Hall.

6. Schachter, S., Ellertson, N., McBride, D., and Gregory, D. (1951). An experimental study of cohesiveness and productivity. *Human Relations, 4,* 229–238.

7. Sherif, M. (1936). *The psychology of group norms.* New York: Harper & Row.

8. Asch, S. E. (1952). *Social psychology.* Englewood Cliffs, N.J.: Prentice-Hall.

9. Milgram, S. (1965). Liberating effect of group pressures. *Journal of Personality and Social Psychology, 1,* 127–134.

10. Kobasa, S. C. (1982). Commitment and coping in stress resistance among lawyers. *Journal of Personality and Social Psychology, 42,* 707–717.

11. Parkes, K. R. (1984). Locus of control, cognitive appraisal, and coping in stressful episodes. *Journal of Personality and Social Psychology, 46,* 19–84.

12. Marks, G., and Miller, N. (1985). The effects of certainty on consensus judgments. *Personality and Social Psychology Bulletin, 11,* 165–177.

13. Festinger, L. (1957). *A theory of cognitive dissonance.* Stanford, Calif.: Stanford University Press.

14. Wrightsman, L. S. (1972). *Social psychology in the seventies* (pp. 157–180). Monterey, Calif.: Brooks-Cole.

15. Lorenz, K. (1966). *On aggression.* New York: Harcourt, Brace & World.

16. Ardrey, R. (1966). *The territorial imperative.* New York: Atheneum.

17. Dollard, J. M., Doob, L. W., Miller, N. E., Mourer, O. H., and Sears, R. R. (1939). *Frustration and aggression.* New Haven: Yale University Press.

18. Miller, N. E. (1941). The frustration-aggression hypothesis. *Psychology Review, 48,* 338.

19. Bandura, A., Ross, D., and Ross, S. (1963). Imitation of film-mediated aggressive models. *Journal of Abnormal and Social Psychology, 66,* 3–11.

20. Siegel, A. E. (1969). Mass media and violence effects on children. *Stanford M. D., 8,* 11–14.

21. Eron, L. D. (1982). Parent-child interaction, television violence, and aggression of children. *American Psychologist, 37,* 197–211.

22. Milgram, S., and Shotland, R. L. (1973). *Television and antisocial behavior.* New York: Academic Press.

23. Feshback, S., and Singer, R. D. (1970). *Television and aggression.* San Francisco: Jossey-Bass.

24. Feshback, S. (1969). Film violence and its effect on children: Some comments on the implications of research for public policy (p. 5). American Psychological Association address, Washington, D.C.

25. Pearl, D. (1984). Violence and aggression. *Society, 21,* 17–22.

26. Lagerspetz, K. (1964). *Studies on the aggressive behavior of mice.* Helsinki: Soumalainen Tiedeakatemia.

27. Rosenthal, D. (1970). *Genetic theory and abnormal behavior.* New York: McGraw-Hill.

28. Harlow, H. F., McGaugh, J. L., and Thompson, R. F. (1971). *Psychology* (p. 114). San Francisco: Albion.

29. Dion, K., Berscheid, E., and Walster, E. (1972). What is beautiful is good? *Journal of Personality and Social Psychology, 24,* 285–290.

30. Berscheid, E., and Walster, E. (1972). Beauty and the best. *Psychology Today, 5*(10), 42–46.

31. Seaver, W. B. (1973). Effects of naturally induced teacher expectancies. *Journal of Personality and Social Psychology, 28,* 333–342.

32. Good, T. (1981). Teacher expectations and student perceptions: A decade of research. *Educational Leadership, 38,* 415–421.

33. Proctor, C. P. (1984). Teacher expectations: A model for school improvement. *Elementary School Journal* (March), pp. 469–481.

34. Perez, J. F., and Cohen, A. I. (1969). *Mom and dad are me* (p. 7). Monterey, Calif.: Brooks-Cole.

35. Hurt, H. T., Scott, M., and McCroskey, J. C. (1978). *Communication in the classroom.* Reading, Mass.: Addison-Wesley.

36. Lee, P. C., and Gropper, N. B. (1975). A cultural analysis of sex role in the school. *Journal of Teacher Education, 26* (4), 335–339.

37. Davis, J. A. (1964). *Great aspirations.* London: Aldine.

38. McLean, M. S., Gowan, M. S., and Gowan, J. C. (1955). A teacher selection and counseling service. *Journal of Educational Research, 48,* 669–677.

39. Johnson, D. W. (1970). *The social psychology of education* (p. 57). New York: Holt, Rinehart & Winston.

40. Cartwright, D., and Zander, A. (1953). *Group dynamics* (p. 536). Evanston, Ill.: Row, Peterson.

41. Cunningham, R. (1948). Leadership and the group. *Group dynamics and education.* Washington, D.C.: National Education Association, Division of Adult Education.

42. Lewin, K., Lippitt, R., and White, R. K. (1939). Patterns of aggressive behavior in experimentally created social climates. *Journal of Social Psychology, 10,* 271–299.

43. Homans, G. C. (1961). *Social behavior: Its elementary forms.* New York: Harcourt, Brace & World.

44. Johnson, *The social psychology of education* (p. 128).

45. Guthrie, E. R. (1938). *The psychology of human conflict* (p. 158). New York: Harper & Row.

46. Sprinthall, R. C., Lambert, M., and Sturm, M. (1971). Anti-Semitism: Some perceptual correlates among Jews and non-Jews. *Journal of Social Psychology, 84,* 57–63.

47. Boyle, R. P. (1965). The effect of the high school on students' aspirations. *American Journal of Sociology, 71,* 628–639.

48. Coleman, J. S., and associates. (1966). *Equality of educational opportunity.* Washington, D.C.: U.S. Office of Health, Education, and Welfare.

49. Barker, R. G., and Gump, P. V. (1964). *Big school, small school: High school size and students behavior.* Stanford, Calif.: Stanford University Press.

50. Altman, R. R. (1959). The effect of rank in class and size of high school on academic achievement. *Journal of Educational Research, 52,* 307–309.

MOTIVATION AND THE LAW OF EFFECT
A Current Appraisal
Motivation Never Acts in a Vacuum

THE MOTIVE AND ITS COMPONENTS
PHYSIOLOGICAL MOTIVES
ACQUIRED MOTIVES
Functional Autonomy
Intrinsic Versus Extrinsic Motivation
Maslow's Need Hierarchy
Acquired Motives and Social Forces
Approval
Achievement

Competence
Curiosity
Cooperation and Competition

UNCONSCIOUS MOTIVATION
Repression
The Zeigarnik Effect

MOTIVATION AND CONFLICT
Sources of Motivational Conflicts
Reactions to Conflict

MOTIVATION AND DEVELOPMENT
THE TEACHER'S ROLE

19

MOTIVATION IN THE CLASSROOM

But practice without zeal—with equal comfort at success and failure—does not make perfect, and the nervous system grows away from the modes in which it is exercised with resulting discomfort. When the law of effect is omitted—when habit formation is reduced to the supposed effect of mere repetition—two results are almost certain. By the resulting theory, little in human behavior can be explained by the law of habit; and by the resulting practice, unproductive or extremely wasteful forms of drill are encouraged.

E. L. Thorndike (1913)

MOTIVATION AND THE LAW OF EFFECT

If you were told that people learn more when they try harder, you would probably stifle a yawn and ask wryly, "So what else is new?" The fact that motivation is a crucial component in learning is so taken for granted that such a thought now seems like a statement of the obvious. Yet it wasn't always so. When Hermann Ebbinghaus spent those dismally boring months in learning long lists of nonsense syllables, his motivation level must have been unbelievably high, and yet he didn't mention it. Perhaps he didn't even notice it. Perhaps his motivation, like the air around him, was so all-pervasive that it was virtually impossible for him to sense it.

It wasn't until early in the twentieth century that anyone experimentally validated the link between learning and motivation. E. L. Thorndike accomplished this task in his famous law of effect. Learning, Thorndike stated, is strengthened when it is followed by a *satisfying state of affairs*—satisfying, of course, to the learner. There it is—the obvious—but what a Pandora's box Thorndike opened with that innocent-sounding truism! Not that there wasn't ever anyone before Thorndike who had articulated such a notion. Several had. But it was Thorndike who provided both the experimental evidence and (because of his own personal prestige) the sounding board for getting the message heard.

Educators throughout the country listened when Thorndike spoke. Other psychologists also listened, but they didn't like what they heard. Thorndike was immediately challenged, first, on the grounds that the law of effect was circular in its logic, and second, on the basis that it was totally illogical to assume that an event (satisfactory state of affairs) can work backward in time to influence a previous event (pairing of stimulus and response).

In answer to the first criticism, Thorndike correctly maintained that the law of effect was *not* circular (see *nominal fallacy* in the glossary) since he had given an independent, operational definition of the satisfying state of affairs. Said Thorndike, "By a satisfying state of affairs is meant one which the animal does nothing to avoid, often doing things which maintain or renew it."[1] In answer to the second objection, Thorndike argued that the intricacies of deductive logic cannot be used to refute an observable, experimentally validated fact. It would be like using a deductive proof to indicate that the moon is in a gaseous state despite the fact that Neil Armstrong brought back rock-hard evidence to the contrary. Though there remained a few diehards like Edwin Guthrie who said that motivation need not be directly involved in learning, Thorndike's answers were powerful enough to silence most of the critics, and by 1920 motivation was a firmly established concept in education and psychology.

A Current Appraisal

In the 1980s virtually all psychologists consider the impact of motivational variables on human behavior. It is little wonder that past students of educational psychology could never fully appreciate the concepts of growth, development, learning, and achievement without taking into account motivation. Teachers have long recognized that these motivational or nonintellectual factors are critical in determining the achievement of their students. Even if we were to develop an absolutely reliable, valid, and culture-fair measure of intelligence, no totally accurate prediction of academic achievement could be made without consideration of the motivational variables.

Implicit in the entire literature on under-achievement and overachievement is the assumption that motivational and emotional variables play a crucial, if not *the* crucial, role in academic success. We have probably all known individuals loaded with IQ points and able to

learn with seemingly little or no effort who nevertheless pathetically flunk more courses than they pass. It is more than just a glib cliché that some students seem to be desperately (though probably unwittingly) trying *not* to achieve academically. The student's veiled smile when the parents are presented with a report card filled with low grades is obvious evidence of a tragically self-defeating yet concerted effort at "striking back." "Show this around the country club" is the hidden message to many a coercive parent.

Although we have stressed throughout this book the extreme importance of early experience on the developing child, we should point out here that the environmental impact does not, of course, cease abruptly at age five or six. From the very first day the child—especially the middle-class child—enters the school situation, society exerts enormous pressure to succeed academically. The young child often comes to see the entire adult world as though joined in an enormous conspiracy to urge, cajole, or threaten him or her into believing that scholastic success is the single most important thing in the world. First-grade teachers, and certainly parents of first-graders, have been known to admonish a child who might be having some difficulty in following the plot of a "see-Puff-jump" epic with the awesome threat, "You'll never get into college!"

The pressures often increase geometrically as the child progresses into high school. Some high-school guidance counselors seem to believe that their very existence depends not on guiding the student toward taking advantage of his or her greatest potential and aptitudes, but on what percentage of the senior class is accepted for college. One counselor proudly boasted that all but three of her graduating seniors had been placed in college, and two of those three would have gone on to college but because of emotional problems they had to be institutionalized. "But as soon as they get out, I'll get them into college," she proclaimed.

Motivation Never Acts in a Vacuum

Although the spotlight in this chapter will be clearly focused on motivation, it must be understood that motivation never acts apart from either learning or perception. Psychology's "big three"—learning, perception, and motivation—are in a constant state of interaction, each affecting and being affected by the other two. Not only does motivation affect learning, but learning also affects motivation. As we shall see, most human motives are learned or acquired. Nobody is born with a built-in motive for acquiring three and a half by six-inch slips of green paper with a picture of George Washington printed on one side and the words "In God We Trust" on the other. Yet dollar bills have certainly been known to motivate people. The entire advertising industry is devoted to training and shaping our motives and, indeed, to supplying us with new ones. We are constantly bombarded by ads warning us that it is somehow immoral or un-American not to *want* certain breakfast cereals, deodorants, cars, laxatives—the list is endless.

Motives also affect perception. We often "see" what we want to see and even fail to see what displeases us. We have probably all had the experience of waiting to meet someone at an airport, train, or bus terminal and then prematurely "seeing" that person—only to find out on closer inspection that we were in error. We "saw" the person we were hoping and wanting to see. The extent of our momentary embarrassment is a direct function of the volume of our greeting and of how dramatically we gave a big wave of the hand.

Many years ago, a psychologist performed an experiment in which he showed people an extremely ambiguous picture, simply a blob of different colors daubed across a piece of cardboard. Interestingly enough, when persons who were hungry looked at this picture they reported seeing steak dinners, French fries, loaves of bread, and so on. The study clearly demonstrated that people tend to see the world from the point of view of their own motivational states.[2] As Shakespeare said in *A Midsummer Night's Dream*:

> Or in the night, imagining some fear
> How easy is a bush supposed a bear!

Another important psychological concept is that of perceptual defense. A number of studies have noted that people tend not to see those things in their environment or in themselves that for some reason they find distasteful.[3] A student with a strong distaste for math may literally not see the next day's assignment, even though the teacher clearly inscribed it at the top of the chalkboard. That same student, however, might have eyes like a Mount Palomar telescope if the announcement on the chalkboard had read, "Half day of school tomorrow."

Thus, perception depends on motivation, motivation depends on perception, and both depend and are dependent on learning.

THE MOTIVE AND ITS COMPONENTS

Psychologists who have analyzed motivation have found that a motive has two identifiable components—a need and a drive. Needs are based on some deficit within the person. The deficit may be physiological or psychological, but in either case the deficit must lie *within* the person. Physiological needs are often obvious, such as needs for water, food, sex, sleep, warmth—and all are based on a physical deficit within the body. Psychological needs, though potentially just as powerful, are often more subtle and less easily identified, such as needs for approval, affection, power, prestige, and so on. Drives, on the other hand, though certainly based on needs, have the added feature of an observable change in behavior. Drives imply motion of some sort. The person is not considered to be in a drive state until the need has goaded that person into action. The term *motive* refers to a drive (an activated need) which is directed toward or away from some sort of goal. Technically, then, the inner deficit (need) pushes the person into action (drive) toward or away from some particular goal (motive). Finally, the individual's ultimate behavior may rest on a series of goals, separately or in combination, and is therefore more often than not multimotivated. Human beings are complex creatures, seldom acting on the basis of a single motive. Real life is not like a Skinner box where the whole thrust of the rat's existence depends on whether or not the lever is pressed.

PHYSIOLOGICAL MOTIVES

As we said, motives may be physiological or psychological. The satisfaction of physiological motives is typically beyond the role of the teacher (although an obviously hungry or improperly clothed child should be reported). However, we should take a brief look at the physiological motives in order to make the whole topic more understandable.

Biological deficits are, of course, regulated within the organism. For example, it is known that the hypothalamus (a part of the brain) plays an important role in regulating the body's need for fat.[4] Physiological motives are therefore based on physiological needs, or tissue deficits, within the body. At this level the motive, governed to some extent by the brain, will be aimed at reducing this deficit and returning the body to its natural state.

Physiologists use the term *homeostasis* to describe this process. Homeostasis is the tendency of the body to maintain a "steady state" or balance among its various physiological components, like the internal organs, the blood, the hormones, and so on. The body does this more or less automatically, but often some overt, motivated behavior is also needed. For example, if one's body becomes too hot, sweating occurs and the automatic evaporation of the skin's moisture helps cool the skin area. However, the person also may *act* in ways designed to cool off the immediate environment, such as removing some clothing, opening windows, or turning on the air conditioner. Similarly, under conditions of extreme cold, the body shivers, and this reaction increases the metabolic rate. Thus, by burning the body's fuels faster, extra heat is generated. However, the individual also adds clothing, goes indoors, and generally seeks goals that will reduce the discomfort.

Therefore, physiological needs can be adjusted to some extent by the internal mechanisms of homeostasis, but goal-directed action may also be involved. Deficits of water and food cannot be compensated for internally, and the individual *must* seek out replacements from the external environment. Complicating matters is the fact that the individual will probably be faced with a host of alternative goals in the environment. If a person is hungry, for example, the choice of which food to select is overlaid with all sorts of learned or *acquired* habits and tastes. In an extremely interesting study, Clara Davis took a group of six- to twelve-month-old infants and allowed them to select their own diets from a menu of natural, unprocessed, and unpurified foods.[5] She found that these infants, not yet brainwashed by adults and various commercials, could be trusted to select a balanced diet if given a series of free choices among wholesome foods. Contrast this with adolescent and adult eating habits, such as taking in too many sweets, eating too little at breakfast, or snacking too much at bedtime. Not only human infants but also young and adult mammals generally have this ability, called "specific hunger." Only human adults seem to lose it, through learning.

ACQUIRED MOTIVES

Earlier, we stated that motivation and learning are in constant interaction in the determination of behavior. We also pointed out that even physiological motives can have a heavy learning component, for example, in choosing *how* to satisfy such basic needs as those for food, warmth, and sex. It seems, however, that there are some motives that are acquired—that is, they are entirely learned; they seem not to be continuously dependent on biological needs.

Functional Autonomy

The famous Harvard personality theorist, Gordon Allport, has proposed a theory of motivation called "functional autonomy."[6] In this theory Allport attempts to account for the myriad of human motives for which no biological needs seem present. Allport tells us that many human motives arise when a *means to an end becomes an end in itself*. That is, the route chosen to search out a goal for satisfying a more primitive need may itself become a goal. We have all read newspaper accounts of some miserly recluse living in squalor, existing on fifty-cent cans of dog food, yet owning stocks and bonds and innumerable bankbooks worth hundreds of thousands of dollars. The original reason for saving the money—perhaps to satisfy the biological needs of food and warm shelter—eventually took over and began to override the original intent. The means (saving money) to the end (food and shelter) became an end (saving money) in itself. Thus the motive of saving money began to function autonomously, or in-

tained by intrinsic motivation than when it is driven by the more transitory push of external reinforcers. Bruner does admit, however, that extrinsic motivation may be necessary to get the learner to initiate certain actions or to get the learning process started and off dead-center. But once going, the sometimes fragile process of learning is better nourished and sustained by intrinsic motives. Bruner's position is similar in many ways to Allport's. Intrinsic motivation may require an external reinforcement to get it under way, but once it comes to function autonomously—that is, independently of the external reward—real learning can become a solid, lifetime pursuit.

One educator has provided parents and teachers with a list of five principles for fostering intrinsic motivation in young children:

1. Provide a novel and varied home environment.

2. Provide experiences in which children may have an effect on their environments.

3. Provide environments that are responsive to a child's actions.

4. Respond positively to children's questions while still encouraging children to seek their own solutions.

5. Reward children often with praise, which gives them a feeling of competence.[7]

Maslow's Need Hierarchy

Abraham Maslow, an important psychologist in the area of motivation theory, has suggested that there is a definite order in which individuals attempt to satisfy their needs. When a person is in a situation where several needs are operating simultaneously, that person strives to accommodate the need that is of the highest order of importance at that particular time. Maslow sees this order of importance as universal among human beings. Furthermore, he maintains that a person will remain at a given need level until those needs are satisfied, then move on to the next level.

At the most basic level are physiological needs. Maslow contends that until these needs are at least partially satisfied, the individual will

dependently. The motive came to have a life of its own and was no longer historically connected to its origin.

Suppose a young boy will practice on his violin only if his mother gives him an ice cream cone. Playing the violin is thus dependent on the primary reinforcer of ice cream. Then, one fine day the boy begins to play not for the ice cream but for the sheer joy of creating beautiful music. The motive for playing the violin comes to function autonomously and is no longer dependent on any earlier goal, or on any *external* goal. Someday perhaps that boy will play his violin on stage at Lincoln Center, and it is certainly fondly hoped that he won't have to go off into the wings between concertos and munch on a Dairy Queen.

Intrinsic Versus Extrinsic Motivation

Intrinsic motives are those that are satisfied by internal reinforcers and are thus not dependent on external goals. Extrinsic motives, on the other hand, depend instead on needs that must be satisfied by external reinforcers. As we discovered in Chapter 9, Jerome Bruner, the great cognitive psychologist, is convinced that learning will be far more long-lasting when it is sus-

not be concerned with the needs of the next level, those of safety and security.

The Maslow need hierarchy is as follows:

1. Physiological needs—food, drink, sex, and shelter

2. Safety needs—security, order, protection, and family stability

3. Love needs—affection, group affiliation, and personal acceptance

4. Esteem needs—self-respect, prestige, reputation, and social status

5. Self-actualization needs—self-fulfillment and achievement of personal goals, ambitions, and talent

Maslow does not mean to imply that every human being achieves full success in satisfying all these needs. For example, not everyone gets to enjoy prestige and social status, let alone the ultimate goal of self-actualization. What he does mean, however, is that we must be alert to the fact that persons cannot even consider some of their more social needs when their basic needs are left unfulfilled. The hungry child, or the child riddled with anxiety due to a traumatic family situation, may not wholeheartedly pursue goals of prestige and self-actualization.[8]

Acquired Motives and Social Forces

Acquired motives, such as competition, power, status, approval, even achievement, are dictated by social rules and pressures—either in origin or in the form in which they are expressed. The cultural anthropologists, who have swarmed over every remote nook and cranny on earth, have been unanimous in telling us of the great variation in human motivation and in *how these motives are expressed*. Before the days of the great field treks by such anthropologists as Margaret Mead and Ruth Benedict, many early Western psychologists took the parochial view that what they observed in their own culture was true the world over. Because it was assumed that all these motives were present among all people everywhere, the term *instinct* was used.

William McDougall, who in 1908 wrote the first book to carry the title *Social Psychology*, felt that group life was an inherent part of our basic nature.[9] Therefore, to McDougall, all social life was a result of our inherited instincts. For example, McDougall stated that people get together in groups because of their gregarious instincts. Furthermore, he said that these instincts carried an emotional quality that made their fulfillment irresistible. McDougall's psychology was bleak indeed for it meant that people were destined to play out the preprogramed instincts that were built into their biological natures.

Because of the logical problems of the instinct approach (see *nominal fallacy* in the glossary), McDougall's version of social motivation finally became discredited and an object of real scorn. To declare that students achieved academically because of an achievement instinct meant that those students who were not so blessed were doomed to a school life of academic frustration, and *nothing could be done to change it*. By the mid-1920s psychology in general had dismissed instinct theory as unscientific and ludicrous. And ludicrous it was. By 1924 it was found that McDougall and other instinct theorists had compiled lists of over 6,000 instincts to explain behavior. Virtually any conceivable bit of behavior that a person was capable of had been "explained" by the simple expedient of calling it instinctive. Everything from an instinct to twiddle one's thumbs to "an instinct to insert the fingers into crannies to dislodge small animals hidden there" was seriously cited as a legitimate instinctive behavior. It is now clear that social motives differ widely among peoples throughout the world because social motives are in fact learned, or acquired.

Approval

In retrospect, it is easy to see how instinct theory got started. Though social motives are learned, people tend to learn these lessons so well that they begin to behave with almost the kind of automatic precision of a homing pigeon. One of the best learned social motives is the motive for social approval. An infant soon learns to associate the sound of mother's voice with his or her own satisfactions. Since the mother is usually the one to provide food and warmth for the infant, her voice, and the various intonations of her voice, come to matter a great deal. The infant eventually learns that the sounds of approval follow some responses, and the sounds of disapproval (and then perhaps punishment) follow other responses. As words are learned, the mother's voice becomes even more potent, and the child usually attempts to modify behavior in accordance with her verbal reactions.

Usually during the second year, the child also begins to learn that many of the things he or she really wants to do, like eating candy before meals or drawing on the wall, are constantly followed by disapproval. That is, the child begins to associate personal satisfaction with the sounds of disapproval. This reaction on the part of the child helps to explain the negativism of the ''terrible twos,'' a dilemma for both parent and child. To make matters worse, the child is also faced with many situations in which the sounds of approval follow behaviors the child does *not* want to do, like helping to rake leaves, washing dishes, or going to bed. It is little wonder that most children are caught in an approval-disapproval conflict situation, the overtones of which can last for a lifetime.

Teachers must be alert to this conflict. Since approval, in the form of good grades, gold stars, a friendly ''well done,'' is the teacher's most powerful ally, it is to the definite advantage of both teacher and student that this motive not be stifled. A teacher may unwittingly reduce the intensity of the child's approval motive by using approval too liberally in situations that the child finds distasteful. Too much self-sacrifice on the part of the child in order to receive approval may create a boomerang effect—even to the point where approval is no longer sought. This may be one facet of the underachievement syndrome. The student has learned that approval can be gained only at a terrible price. Therefore, it simply no longer seems worthwhile to seek it.

Although the approval motive obviously originated in the infant's need for physiological satisfaction, it is one of those many acquired motives that eventually seem to have lives of their own. The approval motive comes to function autonomously—even to the extent of overriding more primitive motives. Persons have been known to go hungry rather than give up the opportunity to hear the sounds of applause.

Peer approval   Though the teacher is in an especially powerful position, as are the parents, to shape a child's behavior through the vehicle of approval, adults are not the only source of this potent reinforcement. Students often play to the applause of their peers—a situation that can be extremely disruptive when the students and teacher have widely different goals. When peer approval becomes more important than the approval of the teacher, the classroom situation may clearly get out of hand. In order to avert too many open confrontations, it is sometimes wise for a teacher to ignore a certain amount of student horseplay. This approach must be handled carefully and judiciously because the teacher should not be perceived as a doddering fool in whose classroom anything goes. The students will most certainly test the limits of the teacher's permissiveness.

Peer approval is closely linked to the need for affiliation. People differ regarding their desire to be with other people. Some children feel compelled to constantly seek out the company of others, while other children need more time to be alone. Students who can't stand being alone often find homework, a lonely activity at best, especially burdensome. Typically, people feel stronger needs to affiliate under conditions of stress. This seems to be especially true when the others with whom we might affiliate appear to be competent and strong.[10]

The ripple effect   Sooner or later, usually sooner, every teacher confronts the situation in which a student, seeking peer approval, acts out in some inappropriate way. Perhaps it begins with a student surreptitiously making animal sounds, groaning, or throwing a paper airplane. Soon another student joins in, then another, and quickly bedlam ensues. This phenomenon, in which one disruptive student triggers disruption by the entire class, is known as the ripple effect.[11] Studies have shown that the ripple effect is far more prevalent in classes where the motivation to learn is low. However, these same studies indicate that in highly motivated classes, the teacher's immediate attempt to restore order is greeted by student approval.

In the studies, students in the highly motivated classes seemed to want an environment conducive to learning, and they stated that the teacher's efforts to scold the instigator made them even more willing to do their work. In the classes with low levels of motivation, students took every student-teacher confrontation as a fresh opportunity for more catcalls and general disruption. The general ability of the teacher to prevent such a ripple effect has been called "with-itness" by one psychologist[12] and "keenees" by another.[13] The teacher who is "with-it" creates the impression that "firm hands are on the wheel," that the situation is under control. The "with-it" teacher doesn't always jump in as soon as a child acts out. However, when the "with-it" teacher does move into the fray, she confronts the instigator one-on-one. On the other hand, the "not-with-it" teacher usually lets the situation run on for too long and thereby allows the ripples to become tidal waves. Then, when she does finally step in, she compounds the felony either by reprimanding *the class as a whole* or by punishing the last child she spots acting up.

Achievement

Perhaps no other acquired motive has been the object of as much discussion and research among educational psychologists as achievement motivation. Although it most probably originates in the service of physiological needs, or at least in association with the need for approval, the achievement motive may itself become autonomous. When it does, the student is in the happy position of possessing an intrinsic motive to achieve, not for gold stars but for the sake of the achievement itself.

The achievement motive is usually aimed at emphasizing a high level of ability and avoiding any display of low ability.[14] One study that appears to support the back-to-basics movement found that children show higher levels of overall achievement when teachers spend larger amounts of time in the *direct* teaching of reading, math, science, and social studies than in music, art, or social awareness.[15]

The now famous Coleman report found that a student's personal feeling of self-directed competence was the most important factor in determining academic achievement. This factor

was discovered to be more important than a whole host of seemingly crucial variables, including social-class differences, race, pupil-teacher ratios, the number of books in the library, and even the educational background of the teachers. Academic achievement depended most heavily on the student's personal conviction of being in charge of his or her own fate. The high achievers did not ascribe their fate to luck or to the vagaries of chance but rather to their own personal decisions and efforts. Society's "losers" are far more apt to see their lot determined by impersonal, fatalistic forces than are the "winners."[16]

Underachievers   Society's "losers," however, need constant study, evaluation, and help, for unless this condition can be reversed, society itself will be the real loser. The problem of the underachieving child is one of the more tragic dilemmas in education. When the student has the ability to learn and profit from the educational experience, it is indeed frustrating to witness, as every teacher has, the wasted talent of the underachiever. It is analogous to an Indianapolis racing car with a high horsepower engine not being able to go more than twenty miles per hour because of some mechanical failure that prevents the driver from depressing the accelerator.

The problem of the underachiever illustrates par excellence the importance of the motivational variables in academic success. In one study the researchers, holding intelligence constant, found that academic achievement was a function of the student's ego strength or reality orientation.[17] The study demonstrated that the underachiever possessed a weak ego and was unwilling to postpone pleasure. Underachievers were more easily distracted and less able to set about tasks in an organized manner. In short, these students were less able to control their own basic impulses and, therefore, their destinies.

Another study, in which achievement motivation was related to whether or not women went on to college, found that achieving women were more in tune with the norms of their peer group or reference group than were nonachieving women. The achieving women were better able to predict how members of their peer group would react in various situations.[18]

Some succeed; others fail.

McClelland and Alschuler   Professors David McClelland and Alan Alschuler have been experimenting for many years on a system for the deliberate teaching of psychological control to teen-agers. Their program is a specially designed sequence of educational interactions aimed at helping teen-agers develop greater control over themselves and their environment.

A unique set of classroom simulations allows students to experience the consequences of their own decision making. Problem-solving and personal decision-making activities help students learn the extent to which they are in control of their environment. The emphasis is on showing them how they presently make decisions and on suggesting new ways to approach problems that will place them in more effective control of themselves and their environment. There is an obvious and direct connection between these learning activities and the objective of personal competence.

One of McClelland and Alschuler's techniques makes use of a ring-toss game. The players may vary their distance from the peg on the floor. The scoring system is set so that a successful toss from a great distance is worth many points, whereas a toss from just a few feet away is worth only a few points (see Table 19.1).

Obviously, the amount of risk and the individual skill of the players determine who the successful scorers are. A sure route to score

TABLE 19.1   *RING-TOSS PAYOFF TABLE*

DISTANCE FROM PEG	POINTS
Less than 5 feet	10
5 feet	30
6 feet	50
7 feet	65
8 feet	85
9 feet	110
10 feet	150
11 feet	300
12 feet	500
13 feet	1,000

Source: A. S. Alschuler and associates, Teaching Achievement Motivation *(Middletown, Conn.: Educational Ventures, 1970).*

The McClelland-Alschuler ring-toss game. The most interesting aspect of their work is the system of intervention that evolved. In short, they can teach pupils to become successful achievers.

would be to stand less than five feet away (perhaps even directly over the peg) and place the ring on the peg for ten points each time. A riskier approach, but one that could yield greater rewards, would be to stand thirteen feet away and "go for broke" every time. The game is thus a means of simulating real-life decision making and risk taking. "But life is not a ring-toss game," you might object at this point. The teacher using this approach must have the skills to help students see the relationships between the way they play the game and the way they approach more important decisions in life. It may surprise you to know that there are often very striking relationships between behavior in such a game and behavior in other situations. McClelland and Alschuler have shown that those who play it excessively safe in the game tend to approach all problem solving in the same way. The same is true for the person who always plays the long shots.

Based on a long series of studies, McClelland and Alschuler have concluded that successful decision makers share certain characteristics: They compete with a standard of excellence in mind; they take moderate risks; and they make good use of concrete feedback. These three characteristics form what the authors term the "achievement syndrome." People who excel in a variety of fields demonstrate these motivational characteristics. The most interesting aspect of McClelland and Alschuler's work, however, is not that their research has uncovered a group of psychological traits that lead to general achievement, but that a system of intervention has evolved from their research. In other words, they can teach pupils (or, for that matter, business executives, teachers, salespersons, or anyone at all) to become successful achievers. They can shape motivational patterns through a series of games and produce the achievement syndrome.

These techniques can put students more in control of their environment by helping them abandon excessive caution or excessive risk taking. These experiences help children learn that success is not just a matter of "fate" but that it is well within their own reach.[19] Thus, achievement motivation has implications which transcend achievement itself. The variables involved address the issue of personality development as well.[20]

Achievement and sex differences   Academically, females definitely outperform males, especially in the earlier school grades. By the time they get to high school and college, however, the males catch up, and in the posteducational world they move ahead of females in virtually every area—arts, professions, sciences, corporate life, and so on.[21] Without doubt, this phenomenon is cultural and not genetic. Men are expected to achieve more; they are given more opportunities to achieve and are rewarded more

for their achievements. Men are constantly reminded that they are going to be the breadwinners in the family and that even the social status of their wives and children depends on their efforts. By the time he reaches high school and college, the average male in our society definitely hears this cultural message and begins to work harder, knowing that not only his own fate but that of his future family rests with his ability to achieve.

Sexism in society   The message of sexism is often subtle, but it seems ever present. One study found that many males used conversational ploys to gain the upper hand in interactions with females.[22] These verbal power ploys were dubbed "conversational politics," in which the men tended to ignore topics that the women raised and the women usually picked up on the subjects raised by men. The men were also more apt to interrupt women, even in midsentence—in the same way that parents interrupt children. In general, cultural pressures are so strong that both males *and females* accept conversational power ploys like these as normal.

THE WALL STREET JOURNAL

"Oh, Helen—I saw the counselor today, and he told me to start paying more attention to you."

From *The Wall Street Journal*, by permission, Cartoon Features Syndicate.

In an interesting attempt to discover whether the women's movement has made any impact on sexism, a number of couples went to various restaurants in order to discover whether the man or woman would get the check. Almost always, the check went to the man. Even when a female executive was taking a male friend to dinner and was clearly in charge—asking for the table, ordering for both, answering all questions—she still received the check only five out of thirty-six times. And waitresses, it turned out, were even less apt to give the woman the check than were waiters.[23]

Sexism in schools   Although it appears that women rarely get the check in restaurants, they certainly often get the "shaft" in most American school systems. One survey showed that 90 percent of the nation's elementary-school teachers are women, whereas only 18 percent of elementary-school principals are women—fewer in fact, than there were ten years ago.[24] It's apparently considered all right for women to teach our children but often not all right if they concern themselves with administering the educational enterprise.

Fear of success   Matina Horner has noted that an important factor in creating lower levels of achievement (and sustaining sexism) is the fear of success.[25] She has also noted that females, because of their cultural brainwashing, are more prone to this condition than males. Many females assume that achievement brings with it many extremely unpleasant side-effects, not the least of which is a "loss of femininity." Women also tend to perceive that competing for success is somehow too aggressive an act to be consistent with their stereotyped self-image of "being a lady."

Horner asked college women and men to complete a series of stories like "after first-term grades are out, Joan (John for the males) finds herself at the top of her class." The vast majority of women wrote stories clearly showing the fear-of-success theme, whereas the men typically wrote stories that implied a positive outlook toward success. The women's fear-of-success stories were of three general types: First, and most common, were stories indicating fears of being socially rejected, unmarriageable, unpopular, lonely, and isolated; second, were stories that showed doubts about femininity and normality; and third, were stories that flatly denied that such success was possible ("It was later discovered that there had been a mistake in the registrar's office, and Joan was really not first").[26]

More recently, a group of junior-high-school girls was tested, and although the majority did show evidence of a fear of success, there was an interesting and important sidelight. The girls whose stories predicted a more positive outlook (admittedly a minority) actually performed better by a margin of six to one on an intellectual task than did the girls whose stories reflected a fear-of-success theme.[27]

Finally, the seventeen-year-old daughter of one of the authors wrote the following. It perhaps indicates that the situation may be improving.

> Joan realizes that she had to work very hard to get where she is, but having done so well, she decides she must keep it up. Joan faces a lot of pressure from her friends, who tell her she should put away the books and go to more parties—that she has already proven herself, so why keep pushing? Though Joan is tempted by her friends, she realizes that she wouldn't really be happy unless she was working up to her potential. One night, while in bed, Joan said to herself, "I want to do my best these next two years because this is the only life I have, and I want to make it a successful one."

Although there is obviously an element of conflict in the story, achievement does win out in the end.

Fear of failure   Fear of failure has also haunted some schoolchildren to the point where they won't take any problem-solving risks. To be judged as having failed is seen as so terrifyingly traumatic that an almost trance-like state sets in, causing the child to cling so tenaciously to "safe" knowledge that curiosity, discovery, creativity, and even cognitive growth itself may become stunted. To prevent this, "schools without failure," such as Summerhill, have been introduced. The theory is that the threat of failure does not motivate students but instead acts as a detriment to a secure and efficient learning environment. For these and other reasons, social promotions, where chil-

MATINA S. HORNER

Born in 1939, Matina Horner has had a career little short of meteoric. After receiving her B.A. degree in 1961 from Bryn Mawr, Horner received her M.A. in 1963 and her Ph.D. in 1968 from the University of Michigan. With honors in psychology and an election to Phi Beta Kappa, she demonstrated substantial early promise. She was appointed a lecturer and then assistant professor at Harvard in 1968–1969 with the department of social relations.

Her research focus gained almost immediate attention, not because of the topic nature of her investigation but because of the careful examination she performed and the significance of the findings themselves. Her work provided a breakthrough in understanding the paradox and the dilemma of female development. For educators, of course, the implications of her work are most far-reaching. Her theory, which indicates how societal expectations shape and mold the motivational systems for females, forces educators to revise practically all their assumptions concerning male and female differences. She has been able to show that such differences in motivational patterns are a result of social conditioning or social inventions. This means that educators need to revise their ideas, practices, and policies concerning young women in schools and colleges. The need is to promote full development for all, regardless of gender. Horner's work forms the important basis for these needed changes.

As if to indicate her own versatility and her willingness to meet today's major educational challenges, Dr. Horner moved in 1972 from an assistant professorship at Harvard to the presidency of Radcliffe College—at the age of thirty-four. A model of achievement motivation, scholarship, and administrative talent, she sets a high standard for others to follow.

---

dren are kept with their age-mates regardless of academic performance, have become increasingly common.

This view has not gone unchallenged. Robert Ebel believes that the removal of the threat of failure has, in fact, removed an important academic incentive.[28]

Competence

Robert White, a personality theorist, has suggested that one of the most fundamental human motives is based on a strong, personal desire to master one's environment. White calls this "competence motivation."[29] Competence motivation is without question an intrinsic motive and one that may even have survival value for the species. To become competent—to achieve a degree of mastery over one's environment—allows the individual to take charge of his or her own life—in fact, to be the author of his or her own fate. There is a real question as to whether the human race could have survived so long on this harsh planet without this strong desire for mastery. If we were, instead, simply passive blobs of protoplasm being buffeted about by an impersonal and seemingly cruel environment, perhaps our species would have died out thousands of years ago.

Competence motivation need not depend on

culturally acquired achievement motivations but may itself have deep biological roots.

A teacher can certainly take advantage of this motive in the classroom. Students are always going to be more interested in what they are good at, and by the same token it is nearly impossible to motivate them in areas in which they have no competence. In a sense, it's like J. McV. Hunt's problem of the match (see Chapter 4) or Piaget's *only* motivational concept, that of equilibration (see Chapter 5). The teacher must attempt to match up the new stimulus inputs with the student's level of competence. The most effective technique is to keep the new material a shade or two above the level at which the student is currently operating, always a little out of reach. Some degree of challenge helps initiate and maintain a student's competence motive.

Curiosity

Closely linked to the competence motive is curiosity motivation. Indeed, the two may be in-separable. There is much recent speculation that the curiosity motive is *not* an acquired motive at all, but is, in fact, based on the physiological functioning of the nervous system. There seems to be mounting evidence that the curiosity motive functions autonomously right from birth, that it never depends on food or drink or on any other biological predecessor. Harry Harlow tells us, for example, that monkeys have been observed taking apart and reassembling a metal lock arrangement. Just like the child who takes a clock apart to see what makes it tick, monkeys will manipulate mechanical puzzles for no reinforcement other than the sheer joy of manipulation. One monkey continued taking a complicated metal lock apart for ten straight hours. "At this point the experiment was terminated because of experimenter fatigue; the monkey was still going strong."[30]

In another study, a monkey was trained to push a certain panel inside the cage, with food as the positive reinforcer. In order to observe the monkey during the learning trials, the experimenter made a small peephole in the screen

Curiosity may be inborn.

Harlow's evidence supports the theory of an innate curiosity drive. One monkey continued to take apart a complicated metal lock for ten straight hours.

that separated him from the monkey. The peephole, however, immediately became an object of great fascination for the monkey, and when the experimenter tried to peer through the hole, all he could see was the eye of the monkey peering back. Monkeys have actually been conditioned to discriminate between stimuli (a blue card and a yellow card) with the only reinforcer being the opportunity to open a small door in the training box and to look out. Thus, the drive to manipulate objects and to explore the world visually "is fundamental and primary in monkeys and man."[31]

D. E. Berlyne has suggested that when a person (or animal) is in a situation where conflicting responses are possible, a curiosity drive is generated and the person (or animal) is motivated to seek further information just to satisfy this drive. This could mean that discovery learning, as Bruner has suggested, is indeed self-reinforcing. Berlyne believes that there is an optimum level of arousal that is physiologically

based. He sees arousal level as a function of brain excitation: If the arousal level is too low, the child may attempt to increase it by taking in new stimuli; if the arousal level is too high, however, the child will attempt to lower it by reducing the stimulus inputs.[32]

Cooperation and Competition

Two other acquired motives that have importance for the teacher are those of cooperation and competition. First, let's dispel the myth that competition is built into the human species as some kind of biologically determined instinct. There is simply no evidence to support such a notion. Actually, anthropologists have found groups of people, for example, the Zuñi Indians, in which competition is nonexistent. For the Zuñis, the act of winning at anything is so frowned on that it brings disgrace and social ostracism. One young teacher who got a job working with Zuñi children attempted to invoke a competitive spirit in order to increase their motivation. She had them all at their desks doing arithmetic problems, and she then asked that the first one to finish proudly stand. Instead, the Zuñi children patiently waited for the last one to finish, and then, in unison, *they all stood*. Imagine being an official at a Zuñi track meet!

The evidence, therefore, suggests that competition is an acquired motive, that our culture chooses to reinforce competitive behavior, often at the expense of cooperation. Actually, Bruner has suggested that a case can be made for cooperativeness being the more fundamental of the two motives. Bruner says that reciprocity, which is a motive for working with others cooperatively, may in fact be built into the human species and that society itself developed as a result of this most basic motive.[33]

Cooperation in the classroom   American schools have traditionally utilized a competitive grading system in evaluating students. This is certainly a major reason why the competitive motive is so strongly ingrained among Americans. That schools reflect the cultural norms of the society as a whole should come as no surprise. Actually, one study shows that the longer a person remains in school, the more competitive he or she becomes.[34] Social psychologists

have been concerned, however, that competitive grading may in fact have several harmful side effects. For example, negative attitudes, both toward the teacher and school in general, may result from too high a competitive level. Competition also engenders a general hostility, which causes many students to be highly critical of each other (perhaps in hopes of building their own images). An important social psychologist, Morton Deutch, found that when comparing students in competitive versus cooperative classrooms, the competitive group atmosphere tended to create the following:

1. Students with higher levels of anxiety

2. Students who think less of themselves and their work

3. Students with less favorable attitudes toward their classmates

4. Students with a lowered feeling of responsibility toward others.[35]

Deutch has been studying these factors for over thirty-five years[36] and his message to teachers is clear: The more cooperative the group tasks students can be involved in, the more positive will be the general classroom atmosphere. He urges that when possible, grades be assigned to group efforts—efforts in which the individual's goal can be achieved only if all the individuals in the entire group reach their goals. The focus should be on interdependence among members of the class and not simply on dog-eat-dog competition. Studies also seem to indicate that cooperative learning approaches lead to higher levels of *intrinsic* motivation, especially among less able children.[37] Says Deutch, "The probability of reward is positively linked so that as one's personal situation improves or worsens so do those of the others. . . . To the extent I win, you win, and to the extent I lose, you lose."[38]

However, there are problems inherent in group-grading practices—a fact that Deutch freely admits. These include

> development of vested interests in one's specialized role in the cooperative system, the growth of in-group favoritism that may lead to discrimination against out-group members, and the evolution of excessive conformity and reluctance to question the majority opinion.[39]

Also, some students simply don't have the needed motivation to cooperate with a real sense of responsibility.

The jigsaw approach   One interesting attempt to utilize both competitive and cooperative motivation is the jigsaw approach.[40] Recognizing the importance of both sets of motives, the authors of this approach suggest setting up classrooms that combine an individual reinforcement structure in which grades are assigned on the basis of individual performance *and* a cooperative structure in which groups of students must share their work in order to carry out assignments. In the latter case interdependence and the cooperation needed to attain a superordinate goal are focal. The group effort literally becomes a jigsaw puzzle in which each member receives a part, but only through interaction can the parts be formed into a whole. For example, a textbook chapter may be cut up into paragraphs, and each group member will receive only one paragraph. To reconstruct the chapter, therefore, a sharing of resources will be demanded. Using the jigsaw technique for at least part of every day helps reduce some of the de-

structive elements inherent in the competitive structure.

Group effects   Groups by their very nature change behavior. Working in a group situation has two main effects: It may increase feelings of competition and motivation on the one hand, and it may increase feelings of anxiety and provide distractions on the other. The presence of other people explicitly or implicitly may create a competitive situation. In research studies the subjects seem to assume that the researcher will be making comparisons and/or they hope to impress other members of the group. If the subject's motivation is high to begin with, increasing it may have a damaging effect. However, if the subject's motivation is low, the competitive atmosphere of the group situation may enhance performance.

The nature of the task is also of great importance. When an individual in a group situation begins feeling simultaneously more competitive and more anxious, his or her performance on simple, nonintellectual tasks is enhanced. As the task becomes more difficult and more intellectual, the effect of working in a group becomes increasingly detrimental to performance. Before using any of the group techniques in a learning situation, the teacher should carefully take into account both the level of the students' motivation and the nature of the task.

The classroom by its very nature is always going to promote some competitive feelings. Students, like the subjects in the previously mentioned research studies, assume that performance comparisons will be made. They will also try to gain the attention of their teacher and peers by various methods of "trying to impress." Despite these facts, the teacher can choose to emphasize competition in certain areas and to deemphasize it in others. Highly motivated students who are working on difficult math problems would probably be better off if left alone at their desks. Less motivated students who are working on simpler rote tasks might do better if the work were done openly, for example, by using flash cards to drill the whole class in multiplication tables.

Competition can probably never be completely ruled out of an American classroom situation. Social psychologists have shown over and over again that even in situations where cooperation is the most efficient route to success, competition continues to dominate. Studies have shown that even when subjects fully realize that the rewards will be greater for cooperative group interaction, they still prefer to compete with one another.[41]

Despite this powerful competitive tendency of American students, the teacher can still set up conditions that reduce competition, if not completely eliminate it. Preparing group projects for which a single grade is assigned helps promote cooperation. Any situation in which the students are working toward a superordinate goal—a goal none of them can attain independently—will help to reduce competitive responses.

Cooperation and cognitive development   Cognitive psychologists like Jerome Bruner and Jean Piaget, although suggesting that motives toward cooperation and reciprocity may have strong biological underpinnings, warn that the strength of these motives may vary with the age of the child. For example, Piaget tells us that young children are limited in their ability to cooperate because of "egocentricity"—the inability to take another person's point of view.[42] As the child grows older, however, and acquires more sophisticated levels of thought, cooperative behavior becomes more possible. Moral principles like "mutual respect" can be acted on only when the child's level of cognitive growth allows for their full incorporation.[43] A great deal of research in this area is obviously needed— research that compares in general the effects of competitive versus cooperative structuring and that also makes particular comparisons at various age levels.[44] The young child who firmly believes that obedience to adults is more important than loyalty to peers will have great difficulty appreciating the group spirit inherent in cooperative structuring.

UNCONSCIOUS MOTIVATION

Sigmund Freud stated that roughly two-thirds of all human motivation lies below the threshold of conscious awareness. That is, Freud estimated that most human behavior is motivated by reasons of which we are totally unaware and

which are therefore largely irrational. It was Freud's contention that the human motivational system was much like a floating iceberg, with only a small fraction of its bulk above the surface. To Freud, and also to many modern psychologists, any effort to understand why people behave as they do must take into account *unconscious motivation*—that is, the irrational needs that lurk beneath the level of conscious awareness.

Although these motives may be unconscious to the person having them, a trained observer can often make sense out of this apparent irrationality. For example, a second-grade-student is totally unaware of the reasons for his or her sudden change in behavior—using baby talk, wetting the bed at night, and not concentrating in class. The school psychologist might ascribe these responses to a general motive to regress— perhaps the young student has recently been presented with a baby brother. Similarly, a ten-year-old student suddenly develops symptoms of a full-blown school phobia: The child becomes a truant, getting to school only when brought in kicking and screaming. Again, the school psychologist might find that the youngster's home situation presents great conflict— perhaps the parents are getting a divorce. The teacher certainly should be alert to any dramatic behavior change on the part of a student and should at least be ready, if it continues, to make the proper referral.

Repression

One form of unconscious motivation may be particularly perplexing to the teacher, as when a child does something—perhaps in full view of the teacher and class—and then later denies any personal memory of the event.

> Fourth-grade student Kenny D. comes from a home where parental standards are exacting and nonpermissive. Kenny is typically quiet and conforming. He is what has been called an "overly steered" child. One day in class, Kenny uncharacteristically has a verbal confrontation with John H., a youngster suffering from cerebral palsy. Suddenly, Kenny knocks away John's crutches, pushes him to the ground, and begins to pummel the crippled child. Both the teacher and the other students quickly pull

Kenny away and accuse him of being evil. Later, in the principal's office, Kenny flatly denies that the event has ever taken place. He cries and says he is being falsely accused and even asks to take a lie-detector test.

In this instance, Freud might say that Kenny has repressed any memory of the guilt-provoking situation. Repression is the exclusion from consciousness of anxiety-producing memories, thoughts, or impulses. Repression differs from ordinary forgetting in two ways: First, with repression the memory loss is total, and second, repression is always triggered by anxiety.

Less dramatic cases of repression abound in the classroom—a student with a distaste for math constantly "forgetting" to do his assignment; a student with a fear of being in front of the class "forgetting" to prepare her oral report (and being genuinely surprised when called on); a student, traumatized by the thought of the physical contact involved in athletics, "forgetting" to bring his sneakers to gym class.

Some of these situations, of course, require the professional intervention of the school psychologist, but in many cases an understanding and compassionate teacher can provide the student with enough insight to minimize the trauma that caused the repression. A caring, nonjudgmental, and accepting teacher can often defuse the student's underlying anxieties.

The Zeigarnik Effect

The other side of the repression coin is a phenomenon called the Zeigarnik effect. In some learning situations, the thought of an unfinished assignment motivates the student in such a way that the memory is actually *enhanced*. Students are better able to recall unfinished assignments than those that have been completed.[45]

Think of the time that you yourself had a term paper to write and tried mightily to put it off and out of your mind. Perhaps you went to a movie but couldn't enjoy it because the nagging thought of the unfinished paper haunted your every waking moment. That's the Zeigarnik effect! To alleviate the tension of the memory, you finally had to "bite the bullet" and start the paper.

To a large extent, therefore, the Zeigarnik effect plays into the hands of the teacher, since memory *enhancement* is obviously more positive than memory destruction or repression. It may at first seem as if the Zeigarnik effect and repression are self-contradictory. It may seem that the thought of an unfinished term paper must itself be so anxiety-provoking that the whole idea of it would be repressed. To some extent this is true. More recent studies have shown that if the unfinished task is so threatening that the individual's entire feeling of self-esteem is at stake, it is possible for the Zeigarnik effect to boomerang. In this situation, the finished tasks will be remembered more than the unfinished ones.

Thus, the teacher who attaches too many dire consequences to an assignment may find the Zeigarnik effect being reversed. When this happens, the assignment is no longer self-motivating through memory enhancement, and it may become repressed into the never-never land of "out of sight, out of mind."

MOTIVATION AND CONFLICT

Human behavior does not result from the simple action of a single motive. People constantly seek a number of goals, often simultaneously. One of these goals may act antagonistically to another, thus creating motivational conflicts.

Sources of Motivational Conflicts

Dependence and independence Every child is faced with the conflict of dependence versus independence—a conflict that seems to reach a roaring crescendo during adolescence. The conflict arises from the need to remain dependent, to have somebody else make one's decisions, to have a shoulder to cry on, and the equally strong drive to be free, to make one's own decisions, and to become self-reliant. From birth on, the child is engaged in the long and painful process of slowly giving up dependence in order to attain independence, and even as an adult, there must be some compromise and balance between these two competing needs.

Sex Another source of motivational conflict occurs in the area of sex. As children advance through puberty, they are confronted with the dilemma of becoming aware of their own sexual needs together with society's demand that these needs not be satisfied. Our society does not yet fully condone any form of premarital sexual release. The conflict is further heightened in today's society, for with advancing technology and the need for more and more education and training to compete successfully, marriage and its privilege of socially sanctioned sexual expression are further delayed.

Aggression　　Aggression is still another source of motivational conflict. When persons occasionally have hostile tendencies (and who doesn't?), society allows very few opportunities for this hostility to be overtly expressed (see Chapter 18). Although overt aggression is acceptable in certain prescribed situations such as contact sports and warfare, it typically results in very serious legal consequences when practiced in day-to-day social interactions.

Achievement and altruism　　The child also faces the cultural paradox of competitive achievement versus the Judeo-Christian ethic of "Love thy neighbor." Our children are urged to compete, to win, to succeed at all costs, and yet they are told that this should not be a dog-eat-dog world and that they should be "good Samaritans."

Reactions to Conflict

In the course of these and many more assorted conflicts, individuals react differently. Some children, and adults too, seem to thrive in time of motivational crisis, while others simply fold up and perhaps develop a whole series of psychological symptoms. As Allport once said, "The same fire that melts the butter hardens the egg."

Teachers must be made aware that the manifestations of emotional symptoms may not always be obvious. The teacher usually devotes much time and attention to the rebellious child. Thus, by "acting out" conflicts, the overtly aggressive child receives the attention and recognition of the teacher. However, a more serious psychological symptom, that of withdrawal, may easily escape the attention of the teacher

(and parent, too). The child who withdraws, perhaps into a make-believe world of fantasy, does not upset the school routine and therefore does not seem to present a problem. Some teachers—at times, perhaps all—actually wish they had more withdrawn children, more "little angels," in their classes. This syndrome, however, can be serious since the withdrawn child who does not get needed attention and recognition may slip into a vicious circle that may result in further withdrawal and even a complete loss of contact with reality.

Procrastination　　Research has shown that a lack of ego strength inevitably leads to that bane of human existence—procrastination. Obviously, virtually everyone procrastinates to some degree, but the student (or teacher) with the weak ego makes an absolute fetish of this self-defeating trap. Psychologist William Knaus has shown that procrastinators typically use one or all of three basic delaying tactics for allowing themselves the apparent luxury of putting things off.[46]

1. *Mañana.*　　In this first case the person is convinced that the unpleasant task will be done—but later. Homework is not done during study-hall time but will be done later, at home. Studying cannot be done at home during the afternoon because a "break" is needed after a long, tiring school day. Studying cannot be done that evening because parents have the TV on and sister is listening to records—"But I'll catch up on the weekend, and if not this weekend, then the next one."

2. *Contingency mañana.*　　This method is used when a person sets up contingent conditions for completing a task ("I can't start my term paper until my room is properly set up for studying"). A whole term can pass before the room conditions become just right—pencil sharpener installed, new lights put in, cross-ventilation worked out, sound-proof doors set up—the contingencies may be endless. "I can't write the paper until I've read all the books in the library on the topic, and I haven't gone to the library yet because I don't understand the card system."

3. *Catch-22.* The two previous methods allowed the person to retain the blissful hope that at least sometime the job would be done—maybe not today, but sometime. Catch-22 typically leads to the feeling that the job will never be done, "but it's not my fault." In this situation, circumstances are perceived as conspiring against the person so that whatever way that person turns, the goal of finishing a task is blocked. "Since the teacher doesn't like me I'll flunk anyway, even if I do my homework." "I can't ask Sally to the dance because my teeth aren't straight, and my family can't afford big dental bills." Says Knaus, "While this view frequently brings on gloomy and depressed moods, the excuse makes it easy to give up, to assume the role of a self-declared martyr, while feeling good because one is so nobly facing impossible conditions."[47] The motive is to fail and yet to enjoy it.

To offset the procrastination syndrome, and as a result to create a stronger ego, Knaus offers a variety of suggestions. Among these are the following:

1. Ask the student to make a list of at least six things currently being put off—term paper, dieting, dating, whatever.

2. Establish an objective, limited as it might at first be, for each of the delayed plans—write at least one paragraph each day; take off one pound each week.

3. Slowly increase the rate and strength of the goals.

4. Ask the student to verbalize aloud several key phrases. "It's just as hard to start tomorrow as today." "If I can take the first step, I can take the second." "Even if I don't yet have the ability to complete the task, I will develop my skills as I go along."

5. Indicate to the student that using cop-outs such as "I'm basically lazy" is itself a diversionary tactic.

6. Finally, convince the student that all the smoke screens and diversions being used are indeed very creative and that these creative powers can be channeled toward solid goals.

MOTIVATION AND DEVELOPMENT

In general we can say that broad types of motivational systems will vary according to both age and stage. This means that with younger children in the preschool and elementary grades, the predominant motivators will be extrinsically determined. Young pupils may become "interested" in learning because the teacher is much bigger and more physically powerful, or because they can win a candy bar, a gold star, a smiling face on a paper, or personal recognition and approval from the teacher or the other children. Such motivators are largely extrinsic or separate from the learning material itself.

This does not mean that intrinsic motivation is impossible at this age. However, to expect that elementary-age children will focus on basic skill learning (the three Rs) solely for intrinsic reasons may be unrealistic. The romantic notion that teachers can constantly reveal the mysteries of academic disciplines so ingeniously that pupils will be filled with a gnawing, devouring compulsion to learn results in frustration for the teacher and puzzlement for the pupil. Thus, the teacher's role at that level is to employ a variety of extrinsic motivators in addition to finding material that is intrinsically interesting. In this way, the likelihood of shaping the attention and "time on task" of the pupils will be increased.

During adolescence, of course, there is a greater likelihood for intrinsic motivation to become a major factor in pupil learning because of the adolescent's ability to perform formal operations. Thus, with the increased ability for self-direction and abstract reasoning, secondary-school pupils can, for greater time periods, enjoy learning for its own sake. On their own, pupils can now seek out new ideas, new sources, and new concepts. Intrinsic motivation then becomes self-reinforcing.

However, this does not mean that the problems of motivation and learning are fully solved as a result of the onset of formal operations. In the first place, as we noted in Chapter 5, the majority of secondary-school pupils do not employ formal operations even though that potential exists. In the second place, pupils may become intrinsically motivated to study material totally unrelated to the required school topics. Thus, there is no guarantee at all that adolescents will be bursting with enthusiasm to find out what the reasons are behind the Triangle of Trade or why the Tigris and Euphrates were so important or how English poetry changed with Wordsworth's "Tintern Abbey" or what the Pythagorean theorem means. Also it is apparent that the "time bomb" effect will not work as a motivational device unless the students are at extremely high levels of intrinsic motivation. If a teacher simply resorts to the plea, "Twenty years from now, class, you'll be glad that you learned about gerunds, the ablative case, and parsing," the class may react with glazed eyes, slouched postures, and puzzled expressions. The nonverbal message back to the teacher will be loud and clear—"Oh yeah? Why?"

Thus, from a developmental point of view, the continuum of motivational factors from extrinsic to intrinsic presents the teacher with an array of strategies to be matched with the pupil's age, stage, and interest level. It is most important to remember both White's and Allport's concepts. A teacher can employ a variety of extrinsic rewards as motivators such as learning to please, to earn "tokens," to earn extra recess time, and so on. Such methods do not necessarily mean that the pupils will always be dependent on these specific external and extrinsic motivators. There can be, as we have seen, an intrinsic drive toward self-directed competence as well as toward functional autonomy. Students may start out learning to please the teacher and to earn material rewards and then find that the means (learning) becomes an end in itself. In the long run, of course, this is what is truly wanted—students capable of the enjoy-ment and stimulation that intrinsic learning experiences provide.

THE TEACHER'S ROLE

The teacher is in an especially advantageous position regarding a child's motivational conflicts, because outside of the parents, perhaps nobody else has the unique opportunity of being able to observe the child for so many hours and in such a variety of situations. The teacher can observe how the child relates to adults, to the peer group, or to frustration, and can detect when these reactions seem at all deviant. This is not to suggest that teachers must all become professional psychologists, but like it or not, we do "psychologize" whenever we make inferences about how or why people behave as they do.

The study of motivation in the classroom, especially as it relates to academic achievement, is indeed fascinating. As persons come to better understand themselves, master themselves, and free themselves, all of humankind will be the beneficiaries. To paraphrase the late Lawrence K. Frank, the fundamental motives of the individual are precisely the same as the fundamental motives of society.[48] Ideally, the school and the learning tasks in school should be organized in such a way as to promote the growth of personal competence and self-mastery. Therefore, important goals of the school should include fostering, nurturing, and facilitating personal growth in a learning context counteracting debilitating effects, and enhancing the full realization of human potential.

SUMMARY

Thorndike was the first psychologist to document experimentally the link between learning and motivation. He called this link the "law of effect." Motivation has since become a firmly established concept in psychology and education. Motivation never acts in a vacuum but is always acting on and being acted on by both learning and perception.

Motives are composed of needs (deficits within the person) and drives (needs that cause the person to act). The whole sequence is called "motivational" when the drive is goal-directed.

Although all people have physiological motives based on physical needs for food, sex, warmth, and so on, of more importance to the educational psychologist are the acquired motives. Allport's concept of functional autonomy suggests one way by which motives are acquired—when a means to an end becomes an end in itself.

A distinction is made between intrinsic and extrinsic motives, or between those motives that can be satisfied from within and those that demand external satisfaction. In addition, Maslow has suggested a universal order in which people try to satisfy their needs—from physiological and safety needs to love, esteem, and self-actualizing needs.

One of the most potent acquired motives is for social approval—from one's parents, one's teachers, and one's peer group. The skilled teacher takes advantage of this need and uses it to help nourish a genuine love of learning in his or her students.

Another important motive is based on the need for achievement. This need may become autonomous and function as an intrinsic drive to succeed. McClelland has conducted a great deal of research in the area of achievement. Sex differences in achievement are seen as culturally determined. Certain studies have shown that some women fail to achieve because they have learned to fear success.

White suggests the importance of competence motivation, an intrinsic drive to master one's environment. This motive is even thought to have had survival value for the human race.

Harlow shows the significance of the curiosity motive, an intrinsic and self-reinforcing motive to discover how things work. Bruner's "discovery learning" takes advantage of this motive.

Cooperative and competitive motives are acquired by the developing child, and these, too, can be brought into action in the classroom. Cooperativeness—especially in the older child—can be manipulated to create a less anxious classroom atmosphere. The competitive motive is not instinctive and is just as culturally determined as is an acquired taste for certain foods.

Freud pointed out the importance of unconscious motivation and insisted that most human behavior is so determined. One example of unconscious motivation is repression—a form of motivated forgetting. The Zeigarnik effect, on the other hand, is a kind of motivated remembering of those tasks that have not yet been completed.

Humans are beset by many motivational conflicts, such as needs for both dependence and independence. The way in which these conflicts are resolved depends on a host of cultural and personality factors. People may react to motivational conflicts by procrastinating—putting off for tomorrow (or forever) whatever produces the conflicts and anxiety.

The school is best organized when it promotes the growth of personal competence and self-mastery. The teacher's role is crucial in this process.

KEY TERMS AND NAMES

motives	achievement motivation
drives	Matina S. Horner
needs	fear of success
physiological motives	Robert White
acquired motives	Harry F. Harlow
functional autonomy	curiosity motivation
intrinsic motives	M. Deutch
extrinsic motives	unconscious motivation
need hierarchy	Zeigarnik effect
approval, need for	motivational conflicts
David McClelland	

REFERENCES

1. Thorndike, E. L. (1913). *Educational psychology: The psychology of learning* (p. 2). New York: Teachers College Press.

2. Sanford, R. N. (1936). The effects of abstinence from food upon imaginal processes. *Journal of Psychology, 2,* 129–136.

3. Postman, L., Bruner, J. S., and McGinnies, E. M. (1948). Personal values as selective factors in perception. *Journal of Abnormal and Social Psychology, 43,* 142–154.

4. Bennett, W., and Gurin, J. (1982). *The dieter's dilemma.* New York: Basic Books.

5. Davis, C. (1967). Results of the self-selection of diets by young children. In J. F. Perez, R. C. Sprinthall, G. S. Grosser, and P. J. Anastasiou (Eds.), *General psychology: Selected readings* (pp. 166–171). New York: D. Van Nostrand.

6. Allport, G. W. (1967). Functional autonomy. In J. F. Perez and others, *General psychology: Selected readings* (pp. 157–159). New York: D. Van Nostrand.

7. Gottfried, A. E. (1983). Intrinsic motivation in young children. *Young Children, 39* (1), 64–73.

8. See Maslow, A. H. (1954). *Motivation and personality.* New York: Harper & Row.

9. McDougall, W. (1908). *Social psychology.* London: Methuen.

10. Rofe, Y. (1984). Stress and affiliation: A utility theory. *Psychological Review, 91,* 235–250.

11. Kounin, J. (1970). *Discipline and group management in classrooms.* New York: Holt, Rinehart & Winston.

12. Kounin, *Discipline.*

13. Cronbach, L. J. (1977). *Educational psychology,* 3rd ed. New York: Harcourt Brace Jovanovich.

14. Nicholls, J. G. (1984). Achievement motivation: Conceptions of ability, subjective experience, task choice, and performance. *Psychological Review, 9,* 328–346.

15. Rosenshine, B. V. (1980). How time is spent in elementary classrooms. In C. Denham and A. Liberman (Eds.), *Time to learn* (pp. 107–126). Washington, D.C.: National Institute of Education.

16. Coleman, J. S., and associates (1966). *Equality of educational opportunity.* Washington, D.C.: U.S. Department of Health, Education, and Welfare.

17. Hummel, R., and Sprinthall, N. (1965). Under-achievement related to interests, attitudes and values. *Personnel and Guidance Journal, 44,* 388–395.

18. Sprinthall, R. C., and Bennett, B. (1978). Conformity and non-conformity among married women: The Reisman typologies. *Psychological Reports, 42,* 1195–1201.

19. See McClelland, D. C. (1965). Toward a theory of motive acquisition. *American Psychologist, 20* (2), 321–333. Also see Alschuler, A. S., and associates (1970). *Teaching achievement motivation.* Middletown, Conn.: Education Ventures.

20. Maehr, M. L., and Kleiber, D. A. (1981). The graying of achievement motivation. *American Psychologist, 36,* 787–793.

21. Maccoby, E., and Jacklin, C. (1974). *The psychology of sex differences.* Stanford, Calif.: Stanford University Press.

22. Parlee, M. B. (1979). Conversational politics. *Psychology Today, 12,* 48–56.

23. Laner, M. R. (1979). Sex and the single check. *Psychology Today, 12,* 45.

24. Hechinger, F. M. (1979). The principal is the secret to better schools. *New York Times* (May 29), p. D34.

25. Horner, M. S. (1968). Women's will to fail. *Psychology Today, 3,* 36–38.

26. Horner, M. S. (1969). Fail: Bright women. *Psychology Today, 3,* 46–48.

27. Harvey, A. L. (1975). Goal setting as compensator for fear of success. *Adolescence, 10,* 137–142.

28. Ebel, R. L. (1980). The failure of schools

without failure. *Phi Delta Kappan* (February), pp. 386–388.

29. White, R. (1959). Motivation reconsidered: The concept of competence. *Psychological Review, 66,* 197–233.

30. Harlow, H. F., McGaugh, J. L., and Thompson, R. F. (1971). *Psychology* (p. 271). San Francisco: Albion.

31. Harlow and others, *Psychology* (p. 272).

32. Berlyne, D. E. (1960). *Conflict, arousal and curiosity.* New York: McGraw-Hill.

33. Bruner, J. S. (1966) *Toward a theory of instruction.* Cambridge, Mass.: Harvard University Press.

34. Nelson, L. and Kagan, S. (1972). Competition: The star-spangled scramble. *Psychology Today, 6,* 53–91.

35. Deutch, M. (1979). Education and distributive justice. *American Psychologist, 34* (5), 391–401.

36. Deutch, M. (1949). The effects of cooperation and competition upon group process. *Human Relations, 2,* 199–231.

37. Knight, C. J. (1982). Cooperative learning: A new approach to an old idea. *Teaching Exceptional Children* (May), pp. 233–238.

38. Deutch, Education and distributive justice, 398.

39. Deutch, Education and distributive justice, 400.

40. Aronson, E., Blaney, N., Stephan, C., Sikes, J., and Snapp, M. (1978). *The jigsaw classroom.* Beverly Hills, Calif.: Sage.

41. Minas, J. S., Scodel, A., Marlowe, D., and Rawson, H. (1960). Some descriptive aspects of two-person non-zero-sum games. *Journal of Conflict Resolution, 4,* 193–197.

42. Piaget, J. (1932). *The moral judgment of the child.* New York: Harcourt Brace.

43. Krebs, D. (1979). Reconsiderations. *Human Nature, 2* (1), 93–95.

44. Nelson, S., and Dweck, C. (1977). Motivation, competence, and reward allocation. *Developmental Psychology, 13* (3), 192–197.

45. Zeigarnik, B. (1927). Uber das behalten von erledigten und unerledigten handlugen. *Psychologische Forschung, 9,* 1–85.

46. Knaus, W. J. (1979). *Do it now.* Englewood Cliffs, N.J.: Prentice-Hall.

47. Knaus, *Do it now* (p. 28).

48. Frank, L. K. (1969). The fundamental needs of the child. In R. C. Sprinthall and N. A. Sprinthall (Eds.), *Educational psychology: Selected readings* (pp. 70–74). New York: Van Nostrand-Reinhold.

20

STUDENT DISCIPLINE: A DEVELOP-MENTAL MODEL

Ask almost any teacher or adult to identify the most difficult problem of education and child-rearing and he or she will usually mention discipline. In this chapter, we provide some historical background, showing the timeless nature of the problem and looking at some of the old theories and beliefs about character formation. We then outline the developmental approach to discipline, largely based on Lawrence Kohlberg's theory and illustrated with positive and negative modes of discipline at each stage. A chart outlines the answers to four related discipline questions: Who makes the rules, who keeps them, how are the rules enforced, and why do the students obey? The chapter concludes with some case studies illustrating different methods of humane control according to developmental level.

HISTORICAL BACKGROUND

An archaeologist reportedly found evidence of the antiquity of the problem of discipline in the ruins of ancient Sumeria. He is supposed to have dug up some clay tablets recording a conversation between an adult and a teen-ager. According to the archaeologist's translation, the adult harangued the teen-ager as follows, "Grow up. Stop hanging around the public square and wandering up and down the street. Go to school. Night and day you torture me. Night and day you waste your time having fun."[1]

These words were spoken some 4,000 years ago; the problem—lack of discipline, unruliness, wasting time. The more recently discovered memoirs of President Everett of Harvard suggest that he spent the most miserable three years of his life (1846–1849) dealing with problems of student discipline. As a scholar, Everett was regarded as equal to "Pericles in Athens," yet he complained bitterly about his students:

> Hateful duties in the morning to question three students about beckoning to loose women in the College Yard on Sunday afternoon; to two others about whistling in the passage; to another about smoking in the College Yard. Is this all I am fit for? . . . The life I am now leading must end, or it will end me.
> . . . My time taken up all day with the most

disgusting details of discipline, such as make the heart perfectly sick—fraud, deception, falsehood, unhandsome conduct, parents and friends harassing me all the time and foolishly believing the lies their children tell them.[2]

If we turn to fiction we find similar sentiments. The tragic figure of the father in John Updike's novel, *The Centaur*, is likewise upset and in despair concerning student behavior and discipline. Mr. Caldwell, perhaps overstating the problem for effect, turned to a particularly "slow-witted" pupil, Deifendorf:

"The Founding Fathers," he explained, "in their wisdom decided that children were all an unnatural strain on parents. So they provided jails called schools, equipped with tortures called an education. . . . I am a paid keeper of society's unusables—the lame, the halt, the insane and the ignorant. The only incentive I can give you, kid, to behave yourself is this: if you don't buckle down and learn something, you'll be as dumb as I am and you'll have to teach school to earn a living."[3]

It seems safe to conclude that problems of student behavior and discipline have been with us for a long time and will probably be with us for a long time to come. Studies of teachers' attitudes toward children's behavior have revealed concerns exactly like those revealed by the ruins of ancient Sumeria, by President Everett of Harvard, and by Updike's Mr. Caldwell. In 1928, for example, a study found that the greatest concern of most teachers was acting-out, loud, disruptive children.[4] Some thirty years later, in a replication, another researcher came to very much the same conclusion.[5] A particularly tragic effect of this preoccupation is that teachers may fail to recognize one of the most common mental-health problems—excessive inhibition—because their attention is diverted by the noisy, aggressive pupils. Even though educational psychologists have been trying to convince teachers to look beyond the obvious and recognize that withdrawn children may be a more serious problem than loud, active children, there is still a very strong tendency to equate activity and noise with a discipline problem and to ignore passivity.

STUDENT DISCIPLINE AND THE FALLACY OF CHARACTER EDUCATION

A general assumption we all tend to make about discipline is that pupils learn best when they are quiet. When we say, "Learn with your eyes and ears but not with your mouth," we are assuming that we can't learn anything if we are talking, making noise, or moving around. When all the students are sitting quietly, listening in rapt attention to the teacher, it does look as if they are learning. However, as we have already noted, appearances are deceiving.

If we accept the idea that a quiet atmosphere promotes learning, it follows that any breach of that atmosphere is not to be tolerated. In fact, to carry this logic a step further, it becomes the teacher's moral duty to keep peace in the classroom, because it is by this means that pupils develop the proper moral character. Thus, the teacher's role is seen in terms of simple-minded character training, or moral education.

Because of the seriousness with which moral education is viewed, no latitude or flexibility can be allowed. Student behavior is an indication of character, so teachers may react strongly to noncompliant behavior: There is no room for give-and-take when we are dealing with issues of character.

Finally, to make matters even worse, this view assumes that by forcing obedience and conformity on children in school, self-directing and self-controlled adults will result. To many of us, however, it seems strangely paradoxical to teach self-control, personal independence, and responsibility by forcing students to be dependent and controlled. The discontinuity between demanding one set of behaviors when people are young and expecting a completely opposite set when they are older strikes us as counterproductive. Education will simply not promote personal independence if we insist on dependence and conformity during the formative years. We noted earlier in this volume the almost indelible effect of early experience on later behavior. Teaching dependence and conformity will tend to enhance those behaviors rather than promote independence, inquiry, and self-direction. Or, as Horace Mann, an eminent educator of the nineteenth century, put it,

Teachers often assume that silent attention is a sign of learning and that orderly obedience is a sign of character building. The teacher must face the conflict between the need for classroom control and the encouragement of self-reliance and responsibility.

"We cannot educate for freedom with the methods of slavery."

DISCIPLINE: A DEVELOPMENTAL METHOD

Although the problems of classroom discipline have been with us from the beginning of formal instruction, solutions have been elusive. Generally, most approaches to classroom discipline have been too singular. Each school of thought, so to speak, recommends a single procedure almost regardless of the age of the pupil or the situation. It's like writing a single prescription to be used in any emergency situation. For example, it is common to find a particular dictum or discipline law promoted as *the* answer. There is a view that strongly suggests that a teacher can never permit any departure from a policy of strict obedience. Even the most minor breach of classroom peace is to be met with instant

punishment. There is no room for variation or negotiation, regardless of circumstances. The dictum states, "Lay down the rules." In other words, permit no deviation, or chaos and anarchy will reign. Such a single variable solution to interactions as complex as teaching inevitably fails. Either the teacher gets so caught up with enforcement that there is little time for teaching, or the pupils get so caught up with the game that their energy is spent in constantly testing the limits.

As if in reaction to the absolute obedience approach, an opposite extreme is often employed. Again, a single solution is proposed, only in this case the recommendation is to ignore misbehavior. We have all had teachers who seemed studiously indifferent to our antics. They seemed to be busy organizing activities and were literally unaware of the noise, confusion, spitballs, and paper airplanes all about. This permissive, laissez-faire approach somehow assumes that a classroom group on its own will always be so interested in the learning activities that teacher sanctions and reminders are unnecessary. In either case, however, whether the recommendation is for strict obedience or the permissive approach, the solutions are really bound to fail. The assumption is that one method is best since consistency is important.

A developmental approach to discipline in the classroom rests on a different set of assumptions. As we have stressed throughout this work, pupils process and make meaning from their own experiences in qualitatively different methods. We have stressed the importance of tailoring or matching curriculum materials and teaching strategies to the developmental levels of the pupils. Thus, it will certainly come as no surprise to find that we recommend a similar approach to pupil discipline.

Stages of Development and Discipline

In order to avoid the trap of single prescriptions, the developmental system requires that we view the problem from a complex perspective. We have made the point that the way in which pupils understand intellectual/academic material (Piaget), value questions (Kohlberg), and personal issues (Erikson) depends on their stage. The same is true for discipline. Therefore, if we apply Kohlberg's framework of general value judgment to the question of how pupils understand rules and order, we'll have a more appropriate scheme for discipline. Essentially, the question becomes: Which sanctions should I use as a teacher? What procedures may be more effective with which children? What is the repertoire of methods as opposed to an exclusive reliance on any single type?

Table 20.1 outlines stages of moral development in relation to discipline methods. Most important, the table includes examples of what can be considered positive versus negative methods within each stage. For example, at Stage I, the basic approach involves superior physical force. This can be manifested as brutality in such forms as whipping, breaking bones, bludgeoning, or maiming. A gym teacher instructing a class in sit-ups places his foot on the back of an overweight pupil and pushes his neck hard enough to force the boys'

chin to his knee, all the while making the sarcastic comment, "Gee kid, you bend easy!"

Compare that approach to the technique used by the teacher in the movie, *The Miracle Worker.* Anne Bancroft portrayed Annie Sullivan, a young Irish teacher-companion to Helen Keller. Helen, stricken with several physical handicaps, had been raised from birth with almost no limits set on her behavior. During the initial phase of the relationship, Miss Sullivan literally had to use physical force to restrain Helen. She would not allow Helen to hit her and ended up in exhausting wrestling matches, holding Helen's arms until finally her reluctant pupil was willing to start the process of growth and self-development.

In the life of any teacher, there may be times when physical force is the only appropriate solution. A young child in a temper tantrum, beating up a peer, may need to be physically removed, gently yet firmly, and placed in a time-out room. A teen-ager, out of control on drugs, may have to be physically restrained from doing damage to himself or herself as well as to others.

Thus, the old adage "Spare the rod and spoil the child" does not ring true. In fact, the use of aversive physical force does not achieve positive results, even with highly motivated persons. A series of studies reviewed by Roger Brown and Richard Herrnstien indicated that even with a variety of novel techniques (a cigarette case that electrically shocks the would-be smoker; a remotely controlled "bug in the ear" device by which an out-of-sight therapist could shock a patient up to 300 feet away), the outcomes were not positive.[6] As soon as the aversive stimulus was removed, the individuals reverted to their normal behavior patterns. Physical punishment produced no long-lasting changes. Thus, when the Old Woman who lived in the shoe soundly whipped her too many children, it had no positive impact on the children. The more up-to-date recommendations suggesting that teachers use physical punishment[7] have no supportive research base.

Rather, in particular situations there may be little choice except the application of physical force. The key is the choice between brutality and humane control. There are basically two questions to answer. First, is Stage I the appropriate level on which to base the sanction? Second, is the pupil in such a state that more complex methods will not work? For a variety of psychological reasons there are times when a child may be, literally, out of control. If that seems to be the case, then the second choice is most important, that is, between negative and positive applications of physical force. The amount of physical force employed should be just enough to restore control to the child or to the teen-ager. There is no point in massive retaliation. Also, it is important to remember that such physical control is effective only in the short run and in the immediate situation. Naturally, the educator's goal is to employ more complex methods that will aid the pupil in the development of self-control. Reaching such a goal, however, is a gradual process; it is not achievable overnight.

At the second stage, positive discipline involves the use of extrinsic or materialistic rewards to aid in the shaping of pupil behavior. Pupils at Stage II are still egocentric in the sense of "What's in it for me?" The great variety of so-called Skinnerian techniques fit here. Since we have described these in more detail in Chapter 10, we will not repeat. The key is to use

Annie Sullivan used humane physical constraints to start Helen Keller's learning process.

generally positive reinforcers such as extra recess time, special trips, or treats as rewards. Point systems and token economies are further extensions of that same approach.

Skinner is convinced that his operant conditioning works most effectively when the teacher uses rewards rather than relying exclusively on aversive conditioning. For example, studies of teacher-pupil verbal interaction show ratios as high as eight negative teacher comments for every positive one. A balance of teacher comments, in which the positive exceeds or at least equals the negative-critical, would improve classroom control. This recommendation does not mean, however, that the teacher should never make negative evaluative comments. To praise uncritically every activity of every child does not improve learning outcomes. However, a balance is clearly appropriate.

TABLE 20.1   STAGES OF DEVELOPMENT: PUPIL DISCIPLINE

STAGE I	POSITIVE	NEGATIVE
Use of physical means to require compliance. Obedience because of unequal power. Generally effective only in short-term.	Helen Keller's teacher in *The Miracle Worker*. Placing an out-of-control child in a time-out room. Holding the arms of a child in the middle of a temper tantrum. Walking up to a child, standing over him or her. Making eye contact. Nonverbally indicating that the behavior is unacceptable.	Punching, kicking, breaking bones to teach the child a lesson. Locking a child in a dark closet. Punching the child with fists.

STAGE II	POSITIVE	NEGATIVE
Use of materialistic consequences such as rewards or withdrawal of privileges for acceptable or unacceptable behavior. Generally effective in the short run while the reinforcers are in effect (either positive or negative).	The Premack principle (see Chapter 10). Use of Skinnerian positive reinforcers such as a token economy. A balance between positive reinforcers and negative reinforcers (withdrawing privileges). Selective positive reinforcers. Positive teacher comments exceeding negative by 2:1. Positive reminders and cues on classroom rules.	Exclusive use of aversive conditioning. Exclusive use of negative reinforcers (withholding food or restricting rations, e.g., bread and water; use of criticism, sarcasm). Predominant use of negative verbal statements.

STAGE III	POSITIVE	NEGATIVE
Use of social group (peer and adult pressure) to promote individual conformity to group norms and classroom rules. Concern for feelings of the group. Can be highly effective for significant time periods as long as the individual remains in the group.	Setting classroom rules with group participation. Running classroom meetings to discuss general effects of misbehavior. Use of positive peer pressure. Rewarding the group as a whole to promote cooperative learning. Promoting group cohesiveness: "Our class—our team—our group." Cooperative learning materials. Using I-messages.	Turning the class members into a collective to scapegoat an individual child. Using the group to shame or shun a pupil publicly. Using a group to make individual pupils feel like outcasts (making a pupil sit in a "dunce chair"; standing the child in the wastebasket and having others throw trash in, etc.).

Thus, in selecting goals for reinforcement, choose the positive. If you set up a token economy (so many points for handing in homework on time, for doing seatwork, for listening to directions, etc.), the goal could be special reading time or it could be avoiding detention. The more that teachers and principals use the latter category, the more schools become like prisons. As Skinner says, aversive measures and goals teach the child to seek a psychological escape, to learn not to learn.

It is clear that the Stage II positive approach

Table 20.1   (cont.)

STAGE IV	POSITIVE	NEGATIVE
Governance and sanctions according to legal standards.	Careful observance by both adults and other pupils of each person's individual rights.	Excessive reliance on individual competition for grades.
Individual responsibility and choice are stressed.	Clear understanding of reasons for school laws.	Exclusive stress on individual achievement.
Inner direction and individual decision making toward rules and laws.	A point and contract system for grading.	Narrow interpretation of laws and rules without regard to principles behind them.
Can be highly effective over long time periods.	Understandable and reasonable consequences known to all for misbehavior.	
	Teaching children self-management skills, such as self-directed behavior modification.	
	Assertiveness training.	

STAGE V		
Governance and sanctions based on general democratic principles: fairness, equity, toleration, freedom of thought, and the like.	Rules and laws developed democratically by open participation of adults and pupils. Sanctions imposed by student and teacher councils. Due process followed. Town meeting procedures; each person has one vote. Individual autonomy *and* responsibility to the group stressed. Interdependence a focus. Only appropriate for secondary-age or older students.	

Note: In applying sanctions, the same developmental rules apply. Usually it is most appropriate to use methods that are one stage *up* from the learner.

is more effective as well as easier on both teacher and pupil than Stage I. Using behavioral principles to reinforce positive behavior is a powerful educational strategy. However, it does require extreme consistency on the part of the teacher. Therein lies the weakness, namely, that the teacher must remain absolutely consistent in providing immediate reinforcement for positive behavior. He or she must never (even inadvertently) reinforce negative behavior. For example, if a teacher mistakenly yells at loud, noisy children, the yelling reinforces the children's noise rather than achieving the opposite effect. Thus, for the system to work, the teacher has to monitor reinforcers with vigilance.

As in Stage I, the major responsibility for control is still with the adult. The system will work as long as the adult applies the contingencies with humane goals. Naturally, the system can be employed in the service of out-and-out demeaning manipulation. A most graphic example is found in the movie (and novel) *One Flew Over the Cuckoo's Nest*. Nurse Rachett, stunningly played by Louise Fletcher, expertly manipulates the patients. She controls all of the activities of the ward, allowing no individuality or choice. Like an absolute despot, she employs behavioral principles to prevent human growth. The importance for teaching is obvious. The choice of goals is critical. The means, disciplinary strategies, should be consistent with educative and growth goals.

At the Stage III level, the overall objective is to begin sharing the responsibility for control

CONTEMPORARY ISSUE

Schools: Are Public or Private Schools Better?

Given a recent resurgence of interest in private-school education in the country, it is natural to question the effectiveness of public versus private schools. Tuition tax credits and/or a voucher plan are not new ideas, yet they are now receiving much greater consideration than at any time in the past quarter of a century. Their purpose is to provide public tax incentives so parents can send their children to private schools at some reduction in costs. The proponents suggest that both parents and children will benefit from such choice. Of course, the other side of the argument is that public schools belong to the public, with the expenses to be born by all. Private schools by definition are not public and therefore are not entitled to direct subsidy (a governmental voucher) or a special tax credit.

The question at hand, however, is not public versus private funding but are private schools better? And, if so, in what way? Certainly one of the possible implications or unstated assumptions is that

private schools are better because they have stricter standards of discipline. In military terms, this is referred to as "running a tighter ship." In the mind of the general public, there is a sense that the private and/or parochial schools have firm rules and are better because they are more orderly. Also, the private schools can preselect their students and can suspend unruly students without the lengthy due-process hearings in public schools. Furthermore, the private schools by definition are exempted from court-ordered busing or racial quotas. Finally, such schools do not have to either accept or retain children with low tested aptitude or any kind of handicapping conditions. Thus, the range of differences in ability, race, and social and economic class is ordinarily much smaller in private schools than in public schools. It would seem, then, that from the standpoint of both school discipline and school achievement the private schools would fare much better than the public schools.

In fact, a major study by James Coleman has suggested just that, namely, that private schools in general seem to outperform public schools. That report, based on the initial data from a study entitled "The High School and Beyond," suggested, for example, that Catholic high schools were about 20 percent of a standard deviation higher than public schools in reading, vocabulary, and math achievement.[a] The results announced in 1981 caused a substantial reaction within the research community. Somewhat ironically, some felt skeptical. After all, this was the same James Coleman who had proclaimed, on the basis of the now classic Coleman report, that high schools in general had no appreciable effect on student learning.[b] Now his results seemed to point in the opposite direction. Schools and teachers do have an effect, and it favors private schools. "Will the real Jim Coleman stand up," one of the critics was heard to say.

Of course, there are better ways to examine the findings than

and discipline with the children as a group. The power of the social group as a community can be an extremely strong influence on class effort and behavior. The ability to experience how the group feels about individuals and vice versa means that control and direction no longer need to be exclusively determined by the adult. The group can participate in setting classroom norms and rules. Classroom meetings, in William Glasser's sense, are now possible for discussions on content as well as on feelings about appropriate and inappropriate behavior. The procedures recommended by Glasser are useful at this level.[8] Also, the use of so-called I-messages by the teacher can now be effective. When

children have the ability to understand their own emotions as well as the feelings of adults, the system of I-messages developed by Thomas Gordon becomes an important technique.[9] There are three components of I-messages:

1. A nonjudgmental, precise, objective statement of the pupil's behavior: "When you interrupt Nancy . . ."–*not* "When you rudely/inconsiderately/thoughtlessly blurt out/shout out/scream out at the answers Nancy is giving. . . ."

2. A statement explaining why the behavior is troublesome: "The class can't hear what Nancy is trying to say . . ."—*not* "I cannot

through quips and/or rhetorical questions. Recently J. Douglas Willms, an affiliated researcher at Stanford, took such a better approach. He reexamined the original cross-sectional data base and expanded the time to include a two-year longitudinal analysis as well. His sample size was over 20,000. He also controlled for the effects of prior academic ability as well as social class. In other words, he needed to separate out the effects of preselection criteria. We can't say a coach of an Olympic volleyball team is a better educator than the local junior-high coach because the Olympic team can outscore the junior-high team. We would have to measure the amount of growth on each team without the initial advantages due to selective admission. With such necessary controls and the expanded time and sample size, the reanalysis has shown that Coleman overestimated the private-school effect. In academic achievement Willms found only one of four possible effects favoring the private schools and that was in writing at about a 5 percent level (or a .05 standard deviation separating the two groups). This is such a small difference (generally effect sizes less than .10 of a standard deviation are considered meaningless) that it was safe to conclude, in his words, "The evidence suggests there is no private schooling advantage in academic achievement.[c]

This finding, of course, will not end the debate on private versus public schools. The most important outcome is that Willms's study clearly shows no advantage in academic performance. The argument either in favor of or against private schools will have to shift to other considerations.

[a]   Coleman, J. S. (1981). "Private schools, public schools, and the public interest." *The Public Interest, 64,* 19–31.
[b]   We have already shown in reference to Herbert Walberg's work that schools and teaching do have a measurable effect on student learning. The findings from the first Coleman study have largely been forgotten in the wake of the teacher effectiveness research.
[c]   Willms, J. D. (1984). "Public and private school outcomes: Results from the High School and Beyond Follow-Up Study." Program Report No. 84-134, Institute for Research on Educational Finance and Governance, Stanford University, Palo Alto, Calif.

let you steamroller your classmates/cut people off/have your own way/be so self-centered. . . ."

3. A statement of how you feel: "I feel frustrated trying to listen to two people at once . . ."—*not* "I feel ashamed to have such an unproductive student in my class who casts such a terrible reflection on the rest of us. How do you ever expect not to end up on welfare when you grow up?"

Thus an I-message has three parts—an objective description of troublesome behavior, an explanation of consequences to the teacher and the rest of the class, and a personal statement of the teacher's feelings. It may sound very awkward as a procedure, especially since it may appear that you are leading with your chin, so to speak. To be sure, an I-message will not always work, but teachers trained in Gordon's method report that it has a very substantial probability of success, especially if the teacher pauses and waits through the silence that usually follows.

In addition to classroom meetings and I-messages, the use of cooperative groups is a third important procedure at this level. Students can be taught to think and act in accordance with the welfare of the group as a whole. The decline in egocentric materialism of Stage II means that pupils can be enlisted as peer-teachers and that they can benefit from small group-learning activities. Rewards such as grades or treats can be granted to groups rather than to individuals. Loyalty and cooperation to one's own class or small group act as powerful motivators.

Procedures outlined by David and Roger Johnson are most appropriate for setting up small groups to enhance such cooperative learning.[10] Under such conditions, children can monitor the members of their group who may not be positive contributors. "Come on, Henry and Althea, help the rest of us finish the project so we can all go on the museum trip!" Or, "You know you're leaving us holding the bag because you haven't learned your part yet for the play." The approval as well as the disapproval of the group are powerful conditioners of individual behavior. Also, it is obvious that the direction is more shared than at Stage I or II. The cohesiveness and group togetherness act as a bond. Children are no longer completely at one end of the classroom with the teacher at the other. There is more interaction, more colleagueship, and more mutual decision making. Classroom norms, written on the blackboard, are derived with student input and participation.

There is, however, a negative aspect of the general Stage III approach. It is relatively easy for a teacher, if he or she desires, to use the system as a kind of totalitarian approach. With manipulation, a teacher can use the class group to squelch any kind of individuality. In the Soviet Union's educational system, of course, the purpose is exactly that—to promote loyalty to the state at the expense of individuality. It is possible in any classroom to use group process toward such ends. Any pupil deviation or individual initiative (even relatively mild acting up) can be subject to public shaming. Group punishment for individual misdeeds is another way to turn members of a group against one of their colleagues. In the novel and movie, *Lord of the Flies*, there was a dramatic example of how far a group of children can go to enforce absolute conformity. Adults can mastermind such activities through scapegoating and forcing individual confessions in kangaroo-court atmospheres.

Thus, as is the case at the two earlier stages, the procedures for discipline at Stage III are not "fail-safe." The overall goals and learning activities as well as the methods help to determine if the techniques are educationally sound. However, at Stage III the effects can be longer lasting than at either Stage I or II. The system is no longer exclusively directed by a single adult. The group is more pervasive and more powerful.

At Stage IV, the overall goal is to move the major responsibility for discipline from the group to the individual. This goal is clearly a democratic ethic. Self-governance and direction provide scope for individuality and autonomy. The shift is from social conformity and other directedness to individual conscience and inner direction. The laws that govern behavior are applied equally to teachers and pupils. There is clear public knowledge and acceptance of consequences.

At this level, the teacher may instruct pupils in so-called self-management techniques. There is a difference between this instruction and the control exercised by the teacher at Stage II. At the lower level the teacher regulated the reinforcers. At this higher level the teacher essentially "gives the psychology of behavior modification" away to the pupils. They are helped in setting up their own schedules of reinforcement in certain problem areas, in monitoring the outcomes, and in setting their own rewards. Thus, rather than punishing a pupil for not handing in a term paper, the teacher and pupil (together) could work out a schedule, keep track of study time, and provide short-term and longer-term positive reinforcers.[11] Ultimately, only the pupil can learn how to apply behavioral principles to his or her own problem areas.

A second approach involves what is called "assertiveness training." Individuals are taught to speak up for themselves, to exercise their right of choice, and most important, to negotiate solutions to conflict situations. There is an important distinction here between assertiveness and aggression. These procedures are not designed to encourage a kind of Stage II egocentric aggressiveness. Rather, pupils are helped to develop the ability to speak up for themselves, quietly yet firmly.

With these abilities in the hands of the students, the overall teaching role naturally shifts more to that of a manager and consultant. Instruction and projects can be highly individualized. Learning contracts between teacher and pupil can be negotiated *and* renegotiated. In fact, at this level even the choice of consequences can be mutually determined. Goal setting can vary in accordance with the pupil's differential abilities. Thus, for a particular pupil in a physical education class, improving from five to fifteen push-ups may be just as valued as a Mary Lou Retton-type performance by the star female gymnast in the class. Joint decision making and monitoring increase the likelihood of individual commitment and motivation.

Naturally there is another side to Stage IV. Essentially, the possible difficulty of this system is that it can lead to excessive individualism. Any particular pupil can become so achievement-oriented that there is almost no concern for anyone else. Unmoderated competition can become so intense, the rugged individualism so rugged, that pupils may drive themselves to the brink of psychological breakdown. The achiever may become the overachiever. A pupil's life can become organized in the exclusive pursuit of grades or test scores. Highly "competitive" high schools with public class ranking, published college admission results, and posted SAT score profiles can create personal nightmares for those pupils who are already highly achievement-oriented. The same is true at the college and graduate levels. The signs are all too familiar, such as cheating, bribing, hiding assigned library books or tearing out critical passages from them.

When the individual loses sight of the overall purposes of education and confuses grades as an end in itself rather than as a means, then negative consequences follow. Part of the challenge for the teacher is that much of this problem may remain hidden. The student who is overly achievement-oriented is hardly a discipline problem in the usual sense. Thus, it is important to monitor the level of individual competition in the classroom and to keep in mind that the goal of Stage IV is to promote self-management and self-direction and not rampant self-aggrandizement.

One further point at this level: Since law becomes a reference point for decisions, it is possible to stick too closely to literal interpretations. Schools and state Departments of Education publish the legal aspects of students' rights, which call for highly detailed procedures. Access to file information (the so-called Buckley amendment); the steps that must be followed before searching student lockers; liberalized court rulings on matters of suspension, hair length, dress codes, and legitimate student protests—all these areas are now regulated at the Stage IV due-process level. Such legal codes provide for more stability and equality in how schools and teachers may apply sanctions. Before these changes, children and teen-agers could literally be pushed out, more on the basis of their social class or ethnic background than on anything else.

There is, however, a possible danger in reliance on legalism. It can lead to a narrow interpretation of law. In this view, the rules must always be obeyed. Under no circumstances can a teacher, principal, or pupil change or adjust the rule. The reasons for the laws can be forgotten almost too easily. Stage IV has its limits, particularly because in exceptional cases the principles and reasons for the law may be ignored. Thus, there may be unique and admittedly rare occasions when exact recourse to the letter of the law is not appropriate. For example, a school nurse noticing an incoherent pupil in the midst of an extremely "bad" drug trip may need to know what drug has been taken in order to make a decision on an antidote. Obviously, examining the contents of the locker may be crucial for speedy action. In this case, as in some others, strict adherence to the letter of the law may have to be set aside.

At the Stage V level, the teachers, administrators, and pupils essentially form a democratic community. Each person participates in the creation of sanctions, laws, and rules that include all aspects of schooling. The organization that is set up is much like the town meeting; there is literally no difference between adults and pupils. Through parliamentary-style debate, rules are established and enforced across the board—honor codes, homework assignments, grading practices, attendance requirements, social-service obligations, and so on. Governance by students and teachers is according to majority rule. Arbitrary decisions by either teachers or students are not permitted. All issues are debatable and all consequences carefully examined. The overall concept is that of a community of teachers and pupils based on democratic principles of justice and equality—a kind of Jeffersonian, grass-roots, direct democracy.

The Stage V level of discipline does sound somewhat idealized as a goal and is perhaps unattainable. A basic assumption is that all members of any such community are far enough along developmentally to process at a Stage V level. In other words, such a plan simply will not work unless the participants are capable of understanding issues at a level of principled thought.

There are a few examples of such procedures actually working at the eleventh- and twelfth-grade level in public schools as well as at the college level. Such experiments suggest that this level of discipline may be possible but that it is also extremely difficult to achieve. The system demands a very high level of commitment on the part of teachers and pupils, huge amounts of good will, and high levels of cognitive ability.

Genuine democracy is an extraordinarily fragile commodity. It is well to bear this in mind. Such procedures should be applied only after the most careful examination of the assumptions and required procedures. Ralph Mosher, this country's leading innovator in democratic high-school organization, wryly sums up four years of experience with a quote from a democratic theorist, D. W. Brogan: ''Non-democratic government is like a splendid ship, with all its sails set; it moves majestically on, then it hits a rock and sinks forever. Democracy is like a raft. It never sinks, but damn it, your feet are always in the water.''[12]

Matching Discipline Levels and Pupils

With this five-stage scheme in mind, we can now turn to the question of specific application. We haven't outlined a Stage VI approach for two reasons—one theoretical and one practical. At the theoretical level, Stage VI persons would always follow universal principles; therefore, any system would be unnecessary and clearly redundant. At the practical level, so few persons operate at Stage VI that the school itself might be the size of a phone booth.

As we noted at the outset, the role of the teacher in discipline is to discern in a general way the approximate range of levels within the class. Table 20.2 presents the overall trends by school grades (obviously a very general framework).

The table provides a guideline for choice and

TABLE 20.2   STAGE OF REASONING ABOUT DISCIPLINE AND GENERAL AGE LEVELS

AGE	PREDOMINANT REASONING LEVEL	NEXT MODAL STAGE UP
Preschool (3–4 years)	I	I (II)
Kindergarten to grade 3	I (II)	II
Elementary grades 4 to 8	II (III)	III
Grades 9 through 12	III (IV)	IV–V*

* Under special circumstances.

expectation. Remember, there is individual variation within any class, yet in general the class as a group will function at these levels. Also remember that even though the children cluster at a particular level, there is the plus-one concept. They are capable of understanding and being attracted to a slightly more complex level of discipline. Thus, even if you find yourself confronted with a prekindergarten class with everyone at the collective-monologue stage, you can still use some Stage II rewards and treats. In other words, the matching of discipline to stage can be a slight mismatch in which you try to use some techniques and strategies from the next level up. If there are occasions when that does not work, then you can still employ the humane or positive strategies precisely at the level of the pupils. The overall choice is to select the least restrictive alternative, given the age and stage of the pupils.

In addition to the plus-one idea, a second aspect of the discipline system is important to remember. Each stage is slightly more complex and more effective than the prior level. At the higher levels, more of the responsibility is shared with the pupils. They require less monitoring by you. Thus, the overall goal of discipline is not simply to keep the peace so that children will all sit still and listen. Essentially, the old approaches to discipline aimed at just that—a negative goal—with teachers applying power to control recalcitrant pupils. The developmental approach employs sanctions in the service of general growth. Pupils can gradually take over some of the responsibility and learn the process of self-management. In other words, it's like a creative abdication. The teacher gradually shifts some power, control, and responsibility to the pupils in accordance with their stage of development and readiness.

Certainly, the major procedure to avoid is gross mismatching either way by the teacher. Using procedures way over the heads of the pupils will simply confuse them and frustrate you. To expect second- or third-graders, for example, to understand the principles of participatory democracy is obviously unrealistic. Similarly, to expect pupils at straight Stage II levels to understand and to behave in accordance with a Stage IV ''honor code'' is to invite noncompliance. Finally (and perhaps this need not be mentioned), the teacher should not use methods substantially below the stage levels of the pupils. It would be clearly unnecessary and humiliating for a teacher consistently to employ initial-stage sanctions on children already capable of processing at higher levels. Such a procedure would clearly be regressive.

DISCIPLINE LEVELS: FOUR QUESTIONS

With the stage characteristics in mind, it is possible to organize classroom strategies based on the following four questions:

1. Who makes the rules?

2. Who keeps the rules?

3. How are the rules enforced?

4. Why do students obey the rules?

Strategies at Stage I

At Stage I, the teacher sets the rules—"During seatwork time students are expected to remain at their desks," or "Please raise your hands if you know the correct answer," or "In this class we will all line up by twos before we go out to recess." The teacher has carefully selected a minimum yet essential basic number of rules to preserve the classroom as an orderly, humane workplace for children. Understanding the developmental stage of the pupils means that the teacher does not expect the pupils to figure out what kind of learning environment is most appropriate to their needs. Thus, the answer to the first question is that the teacher makes the rules.

For similar reasons the teacher also monitors compliance. This means keeping careful track of pupil behavior. If a rule is broken a number of times without a response by the teacher, such silence actually encourages further testing of the limits. At the same time it is important to remember that positive monitoring is more effective than negative and/or aversive control. So praise for those who remain seated not only increases their obedience but also is a message quickly heard by the others. In addition, positive, nonverbal body language such as smiles, pats on the back, and nods of the head are other means of humane physical control. At this level,

then, in answer to the question, who keeps the rules, the answer is that it is mostly the teacher and through a positive mode.

For the third question of how the rules are enforced, it is important to remember the system of judgment that the child uses. For those still reasoning at Stage I, what makes the rules effective is the physical presence of the teacher. Children during preschool and early elementary grades vary quite substantially in their ability to monitor their own behavior without an adult actually visible, or at least within earshot. Research has indicated that some (a few) preschool children can monitor their own behavior and delay gratification even without an adult present and with a tempting choice at hand.[13] While it is certainly a positive sign that children even at this early age possess some internal self-control, the researchers also found that young children make life most difficult for themselves in such temptation situations. They focus on what they cannot have, making the "forbidden fruit" even more attractive.

By the third grade, however, most children are fully capable of resisting temptation without an adult monitor. This means that the idea of a positive reward is strong enough in the student's mind that the pupil can postpone the immediate temptation. Yet even in this instance, remember that the findings come from studies of children one at a time and thus indicate a potential. Placing children in group situations, such as a classroom, can lower the ability to resist temptations. As we pointed out both in Chapter 7 and Chapter 18, children like adults (unfortunately) can be swayed quite substantially by pressure to conform to the peer group. Thus, the teacher in preschool and the early elementary grades needs to proceed slowly toward a more complex and humane system at Stage II. This means that outside physical force is still a strong "reason" why children this age will keep the rules. Desire for physical approval or fear of punishment is the answer to the fourth question in our scheme.

One final point: Remember that children can process reasons at different levels. Some children, especially those reared by parents who follow the model of effective parenting outlined in Chapter 6, will show an ability to verbalize and exhibit a higher level of self-control.[14] Not so with other children: If parents of kindergarten children regularly use negative physical force (severe corporal punishment), then children will most likely show very little capacity for self-control without an adult close at hand. In this case much patience and support is needed to prepare the child for discipline based on material rewards rather than physical presence.

Strategies at Stage II

At Stage II during the first part of elementary school the teacher still makes the rules and keeps the rules. The big change, however, occurs with the pupil's ability to delay gratification and to work for concrete rewards instead. This means that the answers are the same for the first two questions but different for the last two.

Rules can be enforced through material rewards simply because that means fits the reasoning level of the children. This does not mean that the children are not capable of working and learning for intrinsic reasons. As we pointed out in Chapter 5, there is an innate drive to learn, a motivation for competence. However, new learning is not universally pleasant. We as educators have sometimes painted a picture of each child just dying to know whatever we are about to teach them—a classroom filled to the brim with eager learners, all waiting breathlessly for the next great moment of insight.

We know that such a view is both romantic and unrealistic. Instead, a part of each person's learning and processing stage likes the present "just fine, thank you." We all have a way of thinking and behaving that is comfortable and habitual. As William James's son noted, the pupils are in part "old fogeys," conservatives who like to keep in touch with the past. Certainly, if students have difficulty learning new material (and we all do at some point), then discouragement can set in and "out-of-seat behavior" increase. Thus, especially with elementary-age children, the teacher who does not use a systematic approach in dispensing concrete rewards is giving up a powerful ally. Discipline problems and pupil anxieties can be addressed simultaneously through a careful sequence of positive reinforcers. It is not manipulative if, in a humane way, you help children give up a reliance on outside physical control and replace it with reliance on point systems, a token economy, gold stars, "smiling faces," special time to work on puzzles and games, and the like. You are then aiding the children in the process of growth toward self-control. The Stage II methods help students gain a level of self-control and as a result facilitate the process of learning new and difficult material.

Strategies at Stage III

Not until the pupils begin to reason at a Stage III level can further shifts be made toward

At the elementary level, using systematic rewards reduces discipline problems.

greater student participation. There is some potential for discipline in this mode by the late elementary- and middle-school years. Interaction in both rule making and rule keeping can increase. The teacher can use much more discussion in formulating rules and deciding on appropriately positive group sanctions. The reason that both making and monitoring rules needs to be "managed" by the teacher is that Stage III reasoning can be overscrupulous. We noted a concern about scapegoating. Other research has shown that junior-high students can be little short of Draconian in their ideas of fair punishment.[15] The Greek despot Draco set up a system of excessively harsh and downright cruel sanctions. Students at this age apparently quite easily suggest similarly fearful punishments for even minor misdeeds. As they emerge from childhood, it's almost as if they immediately identify with adults as authoritarians rather than as authorities. Thus, teacher monitoring is needed to ensure that "mercy" is mixed with their conception of justice.

As we have pointed out elsewhere in detail, junior-high students often exhibit open streaks of racism and sexism. This is part of the Stage III social conformist mode. Students show little tolerance, often outright intolerance, toward anyone obviously "different" in ethnic background or social class.

Strategies at Stage IV

At the high-school level students are developmentally ready to participate more fully in making, keeping, and participating in the sanctions when the rules are broken. They have reached the point of initial individuality and identity as an autonomous person. To be sure, there are still strong aspects of social conformity, but reasoning for and by oneself is now a real potential.

Perhaps the most important aspect of this stage is the rational or abstract understanding of what are sometimes called "natural consequences." It is true that younger children can learn about concrete consequences. Yet by high school, students have a greater depth of understanding. Thus, in setting up a learning contract for, say, a term paper, the student can learn the importance of doing each step in sequence and, most of all, that he or she can't wait until the

Using a contract approach sets clear guidelines for student projects.

night before it's due to start on the project. The wise teacher sets up the contract with a series of check points. "After two weeks, list the references used and the key points of each reference. . . . After four weeks prepare the first draft in outline form." By dividing a large task into manageable pieces, developed with the student, there is a much greater chance for compliance. Similarly, in contracting for homework assignments, students can discuss how many points toward their final grade each assignment is worth, whether make-up homework counts, and if so, how much.

In preparing for and taking "chapter" tests, students and teacher can work out a comparable system of points. Then comes the most important part of the contract approach: failure. You must be firm but not harsh in dealing with failure. Students (and parents) need to know quite clearly that failure to study, to submit homework, and to prepare long-term assignments does have consequences such as not passing the course. At this point each classroom teacher needs the support of the school administration so that failing one or a number of required courses has a real consequence—to repeat the class, to attend summer school, to be ineligible for extracurricular activities, or even to receive in-school suspensions. Such negative sanctions are sometimes necessary even though, as with the other stages, the positive aspects of the contract system yield better and more cooperative results. For the slow or handicapped learner, the contract specifies a reachable level of improvement through an individualized education plan (to be discussed in more detail in Chapter 21).

Strategies at Stage V

Finally, with some high-school students, some teachers, and some administrators it may be possible to go to the last step.[16] The community as a whole handles all three aspects of rules (who makes them, who keeps them, and how they are kept), and the group can reason through discipline dilemmas on the basis of principles of justice. There are some ongoing school-within-a-school programs where this process is actually followed. A town meeting format is employed, and all major discipline decisions are made after full debate. Careful examination is made of alternatives, and consensus is achieved through voting. Such a program cannot work overnight, however. Democratic governance needs to be cultivated slowly. Otherwise, as soon as the first real crisis comes along, students will move quickly to their prior levels and either become excessive sticklers for the letter of the law or conform to their friendship groups. On the other hand, as the "Just Community" discussion indicates, it is possible for students at this age to act responsibly. Decision making can be based on Stage V principles.

At the college level similar approaches to this democratic community milieu have been successfully implemented. The management of college dormitory rules and regulations can be turned over to the students and staff as a community.[17] Such a process promotes the development of greater maturity and responsibility. Just think what life would have been like for President Everett if such a method had been tried earlier.

Table 20.3 summarizes the answers to the four questions as an approach to discipline at the various stages.

At Stage V, a democratic approach to school discipline is a workable option.

TABLE 20.3   PREDOMINANT STAGE OF PUPILS' REASONING AND APPROACHES TO DISCIPLINE

	STAGE I	*STAGE II*	*STAGE III*	*STAGE IV*	*STAGE V*
1. Who makes the rules?	Teacher	Teacher	Teacher and pupils	Teacher and pupils	Pupils and teacher
2. Who keeps the rules?	Teacher	Teacher	Teacher and pupils	Pupils and teacher	Pupils and teacher
3. How are the rules enforced?	Physical methods	Concrete rewards	Group discussions and class meetings	Pupils monitor own "contracts"	Town meetings and student-controlled discipline committees
4. Why do students obey the rules?	Out of fear of punishment or to seek physical approval	To gain some materialistic rewards or to avoid losing rewards	To belong to the class as a group (social conformity) or to avoid being isolated	To develop individual responsibility or to avoid an identity only as a member of a group	Out of an understanding of principles of justice and the meaning of a democratic community of rights and responsibilities

DISCIPLINE STAGE AND VARIABILITY

There is an important reminder concerning the stage approach. We noted in Chapter 7 that reasoning levels vary. Here we have focused on the modes of reasoning—that is, the most common systems—in discipline situations. The point to remember is that these modes represent the reasoning process at *difficult* and *stressful* times. Thus, the modes are what you will hear and see in classrooms during controversial and/or unusually tempting situations. On an everyday basis without unusual stress or upset, the students can and do behave and reason at a higher level than the modes. You might think of these modes as the lowest common denominator, or the worst-case scenario. Where a lot may be at stake for the children, these modes will be evident. Fortunately, most of the time the children will act and think at more mature levels.

A related issue is that the more you discuss reasons for rules of discipline and engage students in these discussions, the greater the likelihood of improvement in their level of understanding. In fact, one study has shown that the discussion approach helped even first-graders become somewhat more reflective and less impulsive in classroom behavior.[18] There was a reduction in Stage I, kids hitting other kids and other acts of physical violence. The teacher, of course, still set the rules and monitored compliance. Discussions about the reasons for rules, conducted at the child's level of understanding, can aid in promoting growth. In addition, you should not accept the current level of stage-linked reasoning about discipline problems as a permanent classification. Instead, always be on the watch for evidence of higher and more complex reasoning as you provide the opportunity for classroom discussion about rules and reasons.

The final and most positive point to remember is that students do have potential for developmental growth even in the "worst-case" discipline situations. They may behave at times in a manner approaching the level of Mr. Caldwell's students or the children in the movie *Lord of the Flies*. There still is some part of each student, as the assimilation-accommodation balance makes clear, that is attracted to a more

CONTEMPORARY ISSUE

A "Just Community" Deals with Truancy

In the "Just Community" approach to discipline, high-school students and staff meet regularly to deal with student problems such as cheating, truancy, stealing, and similar difficulties. Beverly Noia, chair of the English Department of the Garland Country Day School in Denver, visited such a school in Scarsdale, New York, and describes the process below.[a] A student called Martha cut classes regularly, was rude, exhibited temper tantrums when corrected, and rarely did her academic work. The "usual" approaches, such as detention, conferences with the parents, warnings, and the like, had failed. Instead of a faculty decision to expel her (in-school suspension), however, the community as a whole deliberated on what would be best for the school and for Martha. Noia's account of the meeting follows:

The student moderators called the community meeting to order, and Martha's advisor, a teacher, presented the facts to the community. It was made clear that while there were some bright moments in Martha's time at the A-school, they did not offset the fact that she seemed intransigent, or perhaps unable to improve. The faculty consensus that Martha should be expelled was announced. Martha was asked to present her "defense": she had very little to say. Her main point was that although she recognized that she cut classes too often, still she felt that she had made some improvement since coming to the A-School, for in fact the previous year she had been in full attendance at

her school for only six days. She expressed a desire to stay at the A-School, and a willingness to try harder to meet her responsibilities.

Perhaps if they had lowered the boom earlier, I thought to myself, she would have seen the seriousness of the matter sooner, and have taken herself in hand with much less suffering all around. This—the facing of expulsion—seemed to be the first time she had been forced to do some deep thinking and make some hard decisions and commitments. Would it have been less helpful, for her moral development, to have acted sooner?

The members of the community, students and teachers alike, began to ask Martha questions, seeking to understand why she had behaved as she had. It became clear that Martha saw that what she had been doing was not good for the community, and that it was hurting her as well. She seemed genuinely to want to change, but also to recognize that she had what she called "sort of an addiction." The more she cut classes, the less she could do the work; and the less she could work successfully, the more she cut classes. But she was convinced that she had the capability of doing the academic work expected of her, if she could only break that vicious cycle. How might she? She had tried before, and failed. What was there to suggest that another chance to try would end any differently? "I've never been so scared before," she answered. "Now I know I have to do it."

Again I wondered whether this child had been done a disservice by

being given too much freedom—too much rope, to hang herself, some would put it. The primary motivations seemed to be fear *(of being sent back to her former school—where she would have been freer to do the things she was now in trouble for doing!) and* desire *(to remain at the A-School—even though it asked of her behavior she found so difficult). Shouldn't these motivations have been brought to bear earlier, and have spared the child, the faculty, and the whole community much stress and this current distress?*

As the discussion continued, something I had not anticipated began to occur: the community drew together seeking not simply justice (which would have been served had the student been expelled) but something else: the good of the student and of the wider community. One student suggested that interested students might volunteer to be a "support group" for Martha: call her at home in the evenings to see if she'd done her homework, and offer to help if she needed that; say, "Hey, you coming to class?" when they might see her lounging outside just before class; or simply be around to offer encouragement and appreciation. There was enthusiasm evident among Martha's peers as they realized they might be able to help her, and she herself seemed somewhat surprised at their caring, and grateful to accept their involvement. She wisely, though, would not pretend that her fate would be in their hands. "I've got to do this myself," she said repeatedly. She also knew that her tendency to flare up at adults when they "nagged" her might also apply to her peers, and she asked that the support group "not be on my back all the time."

What I was witnessing here was, to me, something both remarkable and beautiful: some sort of transformation was happening, not only for the student but for the whole community. The metaphor of antibodies rushing to a wound to help both cure it and restore the health of the whole organism seemed somehow appropriate. In my prejudice, I had anticipated some sort of "Crucify her!" scene; but I had underestimated the degree of caring, of maturity, and of willingness to share responsibility that existed in this group of adolescents.

The time came for making a decision. Four alternatives were proposed. (1) Martha could stay on, with no conditions. (2) She could stay at the A-School but on probation, with realistic terms to be set by a group including herself, the school director, and her advisor. (3) She could be sent back to her original school; and if her behavior improved there, she could return to the A-School the next fall. (4) Or, she could simply be expelled, with no opportunity to return. Martha asked permission to leave while the vote was taken, but the director convinced her to remain.

Should a fragile youngster be asked to stay while her fate is decided?

Should adolescents be asked to vote on the fate of a peer, in her presence? The secret ballot is a long-standing tradition—why submit this girl to further suffering, or her classmates and teachers to the pressure of showing her exactly how they judged her? I was most uneasy.

The vote was taken: No one voted that she stay at the A-School unconditionally. No one voted that she be expelled with no chance to return. Roughly 95 percent of the community (including the *entire faculty*) voted that she be permitted to remain on probation. A few hands were raised for the expulsion-on-probation option. The mood was immediately one of rejoicing—faculty and students alike seemed to share some sense that goodness had been done: they hadn't given up on one of their community members, nor had they ignored inappropriate behavior, and most of all everyone had come together to find a way to make things good.

I was glad Martha had seen the vote; it had to say something very important to her about the community's caring for her, and that in itself might be the key to her finally freeing herself from her "addiction." The overwhelming statement of support from her community was surely as important as the actual outcome (not being expelled), both for her development and for theirs.

Were the qualities of care,

responsibility and general moral maturity in this community higher than they would have been in a school not run on the "Just Community" model? I do not feel qualified to judge that, but I do believe that their experience in expressing their values and judgments and their opportunity to make decisions that mattered, played a vital role in their capacity to handle this issue of truancy and potential expulsion with such moral maturity.[b]

---

[a] Noia, B. (1983). Cheating and truancy: Discipline and locus of control in a "Just Community." *Moral Education Forum* 8(3), 8–10. Reprinted by permission.
[b] For more research on the "Just Community," see Kohlberg, L. Lieberman, M. Powers, C, Higgins, A, & Codding, J. (1981). Evaluating Scarsdale's "Just Community School" and its curriculum. *Moral Education Forum*, 6(4), 31–42. The "Just Community" approach has been evaluated from an experimental view in three different high schools: the Cambridge, Massachusetts, "Cluster School"; the Brookline, Massachusetts, "School Within-a-School"; and the Scarsdale, New York, Alternative School. In all three cases, it really took a year or two for the process to work. In each case, however, the results were most positive: Stealing was eliminated. There was a major reduction in coming to school high on drugs. Cheating was reduced. At the same time, students exhibited more humane concern for each other and a higher level of value reasoning. The teachers were, of course, most pleased with these results.

---

complex and more humane system of controls. The advantage to you as a teacher is obvious. The greater the growth, the less time you must spend setting, keeping, and monitoring the rules. Then there is more time for learning.

CASE STUDY: ELEMENTARY SCHOOL

You are a third-grade teacher. Your pupils are just beginning their year with you. You notice, in the lunch room and playground, that the boys and girls are beginning to square off at each other. The amount of shoving, pushing, and name calling is on the increase. Also, during class itself, you begin to spot "little" incidents—a girl accidently shoves her spelling book into the ribs of a boy nearby; a boy just happens to slip his foot into the aisle and trips a girl on her way to your desk. What are possible solutions within a stage framework?

As you read the four suggestions that follow, try to assess the approximate developmental level of the strategy, whether it seems humane, and whether it would be appropriate to the level of development of third-graders, who are probably mostly Stage II with some mix of Stage III. Which would seem most effective and which least effective as discipline strategies?

1. "I'd set an example so that they would know how such abuse physically feels. Every time I'd catch a culprit, I'd make the kid take punishment in kind. For example, I'd take the book and shove it into the ribs, not hard enough to leave a mark, but enough so she'd remember what it feels like! I'd teach her a lesson—it's called 'an eye for an eye.' "

2. "I'd approach it through the use of positive reinforcement. I'd explain that there is too much fighting at recess, in the lunch room, and in class. As a class we would discuss some rewards for not fighting—a class field trip, a special movie, extra time for special projects, or things like that. Then we'd set up a chart to keep track of the amount of fighting, shoving, pulling hair, etc. I would show them the chart I kept on them last week. Then we would keep track of misbehaviors next week and compare.

3. "I'd try using some classroom discussions and some of the semistructured materials like Robert Selman's film strips on interpersonal problem solving and Henry DuPont's units on affective development. These materials are like case studies showing difficulties that children have in getting along with each other. We'd also have a chance to talk about alternative methods besides hitting back. Then I'd stress the importance of understanding each other's feelings and that as a class we will have to learn to work to-

gether. If this began to help, then I'd put in a few small-group cooperative learning games."

4. "I'd talk to the class as a whole. I'd explain that they were acting like different countries in the world—fighting all the time. I would show them the need for a United Nations as a means of governance. Each person, like each country in the world, would have to learn that we are interdependent. I would demonstrate that our classroom is like our planet and that we are all on the same spaceship as a unit. In order to survive we all must pull together. I would show them a brief film on Eric Toffler's *Future Shock* and have them read about the Mayflower Compact and then the U.N. Charter."

CASE STUDY: SECONDARY SCHOOL

You are a ninth-grade English and social studies teacher who also heads a guidance "bloc." You notice that most of your students seem to be social outcasts. There is a small group of ten or so (out of thirty-five) who form a clique. They dominate the discussion sessions in class, deliberately exclude most of their classmates from extracurricular activities, and even determine the mode of dress. Recently, the clique (about half boys and half girls) decided to wear good clothes to school—boys in suits and ties, girls in dresses and stockings. Pretty soon the others did the same. Then the "leading crowd" reverted to jeans and laughed among themselves at the "sheep." The clique tends to do well on exams, but there is a strong trend toward "white superiority" in their comments. They also put down the kids who have to work after class as know-nothing "hard hats." Tension in the class is increasing. You overhear some of the working kids and a few of the blacks talking about getting even.

1. "I would get the class together and talk about the need for brotherhood and sisterhood. I'd explain that the world is full of hatred and prejudice. I would point out that it is up to each of us to live according to the "Golden Rule." Then I'd show excerpts from

the film *Brian's Song* and have each student write an essay on Donne's poem 'No Man Is an Island.' "

2. "I would excuse the clique early one day and talk to the rest of the class. I would indicate that I heard rumors of a possible fight. I would point out that fighting was against the school rules and that anyone caught would be put on detention or suspended, with the assistant principal's approval. I would make sure that they all knew that fighting, for whatever reason, was wrong and that we would not tolerate that kind of behavior."

3. "I would develop a unit on cross-age teaching and counseling. This would involve classroom practice units in listening to feelings (communication exercises), sending I-messages, and learning to lead open-ended value-dilemma discussions. The values-clarification material, some Kohlberg-type dilemmas, and similar units would lead to an overall focus on values and relationships. We would include some material on the nature of prejudice, including some role-taking exercises. When the students, as teams, started teaching in the fifth- and sixth-grade classes, I'd be sure to assign team membership to prevent the clique from remaining together."

4. "I would simply ignore the whole thing. My job as teacher is to teach the standard curriculum. We cover the material that the school board requires. If fighting occurs during class, I'd punish the class as a whole. All students would stay after school. If that didn't work, then I'd cancel the field trips and so forth."

Try rating the strategies outlined above for stage level and for positive versus negative orientation. Then turn to the notes that follow for explanations.

Notes

The elementary-school strategies are quite straightforward. Suggestion 1 represents Stage I/negative, the use of force to teach a lesson. Suggestion 2 illustrates the use of reinforcement principles (Stage II/positive) to create a significant positive reward for "attending behavior." Suggestion 3 demonstrates a Stage III/positive method of helping the children begin to experience and to reflect on issues of relationships and feelings. Suggestion 4 is essentially a Stage V approach and would be far too abstract and ideal for elementary-school students to understand. One teacher, in fact, tried the "UN Day" method and the fighting on the playground increased. "Don't countries go to war all the time?" was the children's comment. The most appropriate methods, given the stage of the children, would probably be either Suggestion 2 or Suggestion 3, or maybe both in combination.

At the secondary level, Suggestion 1, outlining a Stage V strategy, would probably go almost totally over the heads of most of the junior-high adolescents. Suggestion 2 represents a Stage IV/negative method, since the solution, although legally correct, in essence misses the point of the problem. Suggestion 3 details the most complicated response since, in order to be effective, the unit would require considerable time. In the long run, however, this would be the most effective approach. The actual role-taking experiences of "helping" others in small groups would help to break down some of the barriers. This solution is essentially a combination of Stage III/positive and Stage IV/positive. The pupils learn to identify feelings in themselves and others (III), to send I-messages (III), and to speak up for themselves (IV). Suggestion 4 is a combination of Stage IV/negative (a narrow legal definition of teaching) and Stage II/negative (the use of aversive techniques to control behavior).

SUMMARY

One of the most potentially stressful aspects of teaching involves student discipline. Policing, monitoring, and keeping the peace often seem like the most unpleasant aspects of the role of the teacher. Individuals who choose teaching generally are not authoritarian personalities who enjoy and seek power and control over others.

Too often the most common approach has been to enforce a kind of "might-makes-right" dictum. Teachers are expected to enforce obedience and mold character almost at any cost. Failing that, teachers can be expected to rely on a series of tricks and games to bring about order. These may range from studied indifference (the head in the sand) to constant classroom entertainment (the teacher as Mary Poppins). There is no particular theory to guide the choice of discipline techniques. An alternative, however, is the developmental model. In using this framework, teachers must ask: (1) Who makes the rules; (2) who keeps the rules; (3) how the rules are enforced; and (4) why students obey. Answering these questions requires an application of stage theory: The choice of technique depends on the stage of reasoning of students. Very young pupils at Stage I may require the human use of physical constraint. In the early elementary grades, pupils at Stage II may respond best to extrinsic behavior modification; in the later elementary grades, pupils at Stage III can be disciplined by peer pressure. In junior high and beyond, students (at Stages IV and V) are ready for more self-governance. Contract systems can be effective in these years.

There are humane and inhumane applications of methods within each stage, which involve carrying the approach too far or using it too literally. For example, harsh physical punishment versus firm physical constraint for an out-of-control child represent the wrong and right ways to approach discipline at Stage I. Excessively zealous application of stage-appropriate methods is a problem at all stages.

At the most complex level, teachers and pupils can form a democratic community along the lines of the old New England town meeting. This form of democratic citizenship training, while rare, can nonetheless serve as an ideal goal for student discipline.

It is important to remember that certain factors, such as the level of difficulty of the discipline problem and the amount of personal stress generated by an issue, may change the "usual" level of stage reasoning. In such worst-case scenarios, teachers may need to shift to greater control. In general, though, whatever the discipline problem, the stage of development of the student must be kept clearly in mind.

KEY TERMS AND NAMES

character education
developmental method of discipline
positive discipline techniques

negative discipline techniques
time-out room
Just Community

REFERENCES

1. Quoted from *Everyday life in Bible times* (1968). Washington, D.C.: National Geographic Society.

2. Quoted in *Harvard Alumni Bulletin* (p. 583), May 1, 1965.

3. Updike, J. (1963). *The centaur* (pp. 80–81). New York: Knopf.

4. Wickman, E. K. (1928). *Children's behavior and teachers' attitudes*. New York: Commonwealth Fund.

5. Beilin, H. (1959). Teachers' and clinicians' attitudes toward the behavior problems of children: A reappraisal. *Child Development, 30*, 9–25.

6. Brown, R., and Herrnstien, R. (1974). *Psychology* (p. 608). Boston: Little, Brown.

7. See Dobson, J. (1970). *Dare to discipline.* Wheaton: Tyndale. See also Rafferty, M. (1970). *Classroom countdown.* New York: Hawthorn. Both are advocates of physical punishment. Dobson recommends squeezing the trapezius (shoulder) muscle since this action doesn't leave bruise marks. Rafferty says, more simply, "Spank."

8. Glasser, W. (1975). *Schools without failure.* New York: Perennial Library. Glasser's method of classroom meetings allows the teacher and the students to develop group rules and norms for appropriate behavior.

9. Gordon, T. (1974). *Teacher effectiveness training.* New York: Wyden.

10. Johnson, D. W., and Johnson, R. T. (1975). *Learning together and alone.* Englewood Cliffs, N.J.: Prentice-Hall.

11. Homme, L. (1970). *How to use contingency contracting in the classroom.* Champaign, Ill.: Research Press. See also Deno, S., and Mirkin, P. (1977). *Data-based program modification.* Reston, Va.: Council for Exceptional Children.

12. Mosher, R. L. (1979). *Adolescents' development and education* (p. 497). Berkeley, Calif.: McCutchan.

13. Mischel, W., and Peake, P. (1982). Beyond "deja vu" in the search for cross-situational consistency. *Psychological Review, 89,* 730–755.

14. Lickona, T. (1983). *Raising good children.* New York: Bantam.

15. Sprinthall, N. A. (1985). Early adolescence and opportunities for growth in the 1980s: Ships passing in the night, again. *Journal of Early Adolescence, 5*(4), 533–547.

16. Wheaton, W. (1984). An interview and coding instrument for measuring teacher attitudes about educational issues. *Moral Education Forum, 9*(1), 2–10.

17. Whiteley, J. (1982). *Character development in college students.* Falls Church, Va.: American Association of Counseling and Development.

18. Enright, R. D. (1981). A classroom discipline model for promoting social cognitive development in early childhood. *Journal of Moral Education, 11*(1), 47–60.

21

MAINSTREAM-ING: STUDENTS WITH SPECIAL NEEDS

As a result of both a gradual revision of educational theory and a series of milestone legal decisions, special education for so-called atypical and exceptional children is undergoing a period of major formulation. Traditionally, societies have followed one of three practices with regard to children and teen-agers labeled handicapped or difficult: (1) remolding, (2) exclusion, or (3) deviate-status placement (segregation). Different civilizations, and the same societies at different times, have naturally used a variety of methods to achieve each policy goal. In this chapter we describe these methods and discuss their shortcomings in view of both our current psychological understanding of such children and the emergence of a series of new "right to education" laws. We follow this with a discussion of current policy in special education, called "mainstreaming," and its implications for classroom teachers.

TRADITIONAL PRACTICES REGARDING PLACEMENT

Remolding

As noted in Chapter 6 practically all societies have practiced remolding and reshaping their children during the early formative years, utilizing methods that vary from the somewhat benign to the most grotesque. For example, one old wives' tale suggests that it is important to play soft music to very young children to soothe the beast within their breasts; at the other extreme might be the medieval practice of exorcism, popularized in a movie.

The objective of all remolding methods is essentially to fit the child to the society. This means that, at least to some degree, the process of socialization was and is designed to eliminate individual variation or difference. Remolding can take the form of physically reshaping a child (binding the feet, elongating the neck, etc.), alteration of the physiological characteristics (such as conditioning feeding patterns—recall the old debate of demand versus scheduled eating), or psychological reshaping (for example, brainwashing). Thus, societies have attempted through physical, physiological, and psychological means to remake children.

Of course, not every society seeks to rebuild

each child completely in its own adult image. It is clear, however, that a major goal of the practice is to eliminate some real or imagined negative attributes in children. Thus, in general, we should take a careful look at some of the procedures in early education to ensure that the programs are in the child's best interests and reflect effective methods toward promoting individual development. We have certainly stressed this view throughout this volume: Children are not miniature adults. For our purpose here, however, the critical question is: What happens when children do not fit, when the procedures for remolding and reshaping do not work? What policies have societies followed when some children remain different? One policy is obvious—simply exclude such children from the rest of society.

Exclusion

The implementation of exclusion policies can vary from an extreme—for example, murder—to psychological avoidance and exile. Ancient Sparta placed physically handicapped children on a mountainside; in seventeenth-century Salem, Massachusetts, teen-aged girls and boys were put to death because they were thought to be witches. David Bakan has provided a detailed account of such bloodcurdling procedures in his appropriately titled work, *The Slaughter of the Innocents.*[1]

Of course not all exclusion policies necessarily result in death. In some instances a society simply pretends that the atypical or different child doesn't really exist. Thus, it is not unusual to find children who are labeled as retarded living a marginal existence, hidden from view most of the time or, even if they do appear in public, generally not acknowledged. Such "different" children are spoken of only in hushed voices, in the hope that they will soon return to attic rooms, cellars, or garages. Every so often newspaper stories announce the "discovery" of such children in a headline story; the famous case of the "wild boy" of Aveyron may be an instance of this exclusion.* It goes without saying that such children have literally no chance to grow and develop, they suffer either actual physical or, perhaps even worse, psychological death at an early age.

Segregation

Deviate-status placement   A more common policy, at least recently, has been the system of categorizing some children as deviant and placing children so designated in segregated environments. Various societies employ literally hundreds of different methods of classification—physical handicaps, racial characteristics, ancestry, intelligence testing, degrees of skin color, and so on. Naturally, a critical question here is the validity of the assessment procedures so employed, and we will discuss this issue more fully in a later section. At this point, we wish to emphasize that the effect of the overall policy is to exclude, separate out, and segregate such children from the mainstream of society.

Sometimes the segregation policy is referred to as "warehousing": States and nations build human warehouses, usually in remote areas, and place designated children within those walls for safekeeping. This policy is, of course, almost the same as deportation. So-called undesirables are literally shipped out and thus are effectively removed from citizenship roles in a manner similar to sending the French Emperor Napoleon to the island of St. Helena. The obvious natural tendency is for a society then to feel it has solved the problem; the education and growth of such children are now taken care of and we can all turn our attention to other concerns. The exclusion policy eliminates designated children from society while the deviate-status-placement procedure segregates. "Out of sight, out of mind" is the hoped-for result.

To show that such a segregated approach has not totally disappeared, we need only recall a recent study of multihandicapped adolescents. The teen-agers were placed in a rural residential facility. Besides the professional staff, they had contact with persons from the "outside" world on an average of less than one visitor per month. The isolation was so substantial that the teen-agers' psychological development ap-

---

* An eleven-year-old boy was found living like an animal in the woods in southern France in 1799. He had been left there some years earlier. He was subsequently cared for and educated by a famous French special educator, Jean Marc Gaspard Itard.

peared halted.[2] In such a barren interpersonal environment, those adolescents would hardly have had a chance to develop any kind of identity in the Eriksonian sense. Without interaction, growth will not occur. Today fewer handicapped children are kept in such isolated residential units, but there are some. To be sure, such children may require medical assistance, yet they also have genuine interpersonal needs.

Segregation policies: A mockingbird   One scene in the Pulitzer Prize–winning novel *To Kill a Mockingbird* depicts the first day of school for a new second-grade teacher, Miss Caroline Fisher, in a small rural southern community. In the middle of a lesson a small "cootie" jumps out of Burris Ewell's hair, scaring Miss Caroline half to death. In the process of examining the youngster more closely, Miss Caroline concludes that he should be sent home to wash his hair with lye soap and the rest of himself with soap and water. As the novel's little-girl heroine "Scout" remarks, Burris "was the filthiest human I had ever seen. His neck was dark grey, the back of his hands were rusty and his fingernails were black deep into the quick. He peered at Miss Caroline from a fist-sized clean space on his face." Miss Caroline emphatically comments then that Burris is to go home immediately and return "tomorrow" for the second day of school, clean as a whistle and ready to learn. But the boy balks:

> The boy laughed rudely. "You ain't sendin' me home, Missus. I was on the verge of leaving. I done done my time for this year."
>
> Miss Caroline looked puzzled. "What do you mean by that?"
>
> The boy did not answer. He gave a short contemptuous snort.
>
> One of the elderly members of the class answered her. "He's one of the Ewells, Ma'am— Whole school's full of 'em. They come the first day every year and then leave. The truant lady gets 'em here cause she threatens 'em with the sheriff, but she gives up trying to hold 'em. She reckons she's carried out the law just gettin' their names on the roll and running 'em here the first day. You're supposed to mark 'em absent the rest of the year."[3]

The Ewell children, then, were deviates and segregated from the other pupils. The letter of

the law in this case was honored, but the educational future of the children was ignored. The school itself could then avoid having to cope with the special problems of the Ewell children, cooties and all. In a less humorous vein, unfortunately, many of the segregated special-class placements for children have had the same effect. For the past forty years or so, the common educational policy has been to place children classified as mild to moderately educationally handicapped (IQ scores roughly in the 50 to 70 range) in special classes, separated from the other school children. This practice has continued until recently, even though a long series of studies beginning in the 1930s has consistently indicated that such special-class placements are not superior to regular-class placements. In fact, no research evidence supports such special-class placements for "mild to moderately" retarded children; there are no academic gains for children placed in these classes and equivocal social gains.[4] A comprehensive review suggests that the pupils placed in segregated classes suffer negative psychological consequences— namely, a lowered self-concept—as a result of separation.[5]

A NEW POLICY: MAINSTREAMING

An alternative policy for children and teenagers classified as exceptional and/or mentally retarded is called mainstreaming. Essentially, the goal here is to expand the boundaries and reduce the barriers that have segregated such children from the mainstream of society. For many centuries this country legally sanctioned a segregated public-school system that prevented black children from attending our society's mainstream white schools. The famous *Brown* v. *Board of Education* decision by the Supreme Court in 1954 ruled that separate facilities were inherently *not* equal. Thus, even if black children attended schools in new buildings filled with books, new carpets, and well-trained teachers, their schooling experience would still not be equal to that of mainstream white children. "Segregation equals second-class citizenship" was the dictum of the court. At a philosophical and psychological level, equal educational opportunity means that each child

CONTEMPORARY ISSUE

Mainstreaming: Whose Problem Is It?

With the onset of classroom mainstreaming, it has generally been assumed that previously designated special-education students would evaluate themselves less positively than would their regular classroom peers. However, recent studied by Thomas Parish and his associates at Kansas State University have cast doubt on this negative self-concept hypothesis.[a]

In one study with over 200 pupils attending mainstreamed classes, there were no differences in the positive self-concepts among (1) regular children, (2) the physically handicapped, (3) the learning-disabled, and (4) the emotionally disturbed. This finding suggests that the degree of positive self-regard was independent on the previously designated special-education handicap, at least in mainstreamed classes—a quite surprising discovery.

An even more surprising discovery was the comparison between the pupils' own self-evaluations and the teachers'

predictions. The teachers were asked to estimate how the four groups of children would rate themselves. The results of this second analysis indicated that the "teachers . . . thought the mainstreamed children would evaluate themselves more negatively than normal children. . . . These findings suggest that, while teachers possessed negative stereotypes regarding how handicapped children should perceive themselves, these attitudes apparently were not characteristic of the children."[b]

Given what we know about the importance of teacher attitudes and expectations, these major differences could have important effects on recently mainstreamed children. If teachers automatically assume that handicapped children have negative self-concepts, a series of self-fulfilling prophecies could be started. Parish's studies at the elementary- and middle-school levels indicate a major discrepancy between the two sets of self-concepts: The children view

themselves in a positive manner, while the teachers expect the mainstreamed children to evaluate themselves in a much more negative light.

Although Parish's studies were not longitudinal, other researchers have shown that during secondary school, handicapped students begin to evaluate themselves more negatively than do their regular class peers.[c] Partly because of the nature of adolescence as a stage and perhaps partly because they can accurately read how others perceive their own self-concepts, handicapped children may begin to "get the message" and, worst of all, may begin to believe it.

---

[a]   Parish, T. S., and Copeland, T. F. (1978). Teachers' and students' attitudes in mainstreamed classrooms. *Psychological Reports 43*, 54.
[b]   Parish and Copeland, Teachers' and students' attitudes.
[c]   Dupont, H. S. (1979). Meeting the emotional-social needs of students in a mainstreamed environment. *Counseling and Human Development 10*(9), I–II.

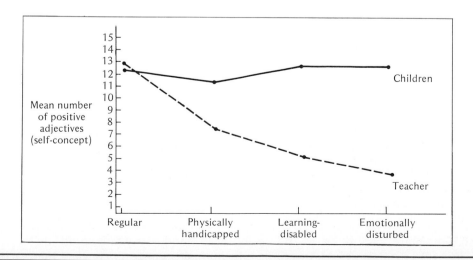

should have access to the same educational experience. To rule otherwise is a logical absurdity. A public school is for the public's children.* Segregation is inherently separate and *not* equal.

In a manner similar to the 1954 *Brown* decision, a number of legal rulings have struck down the segregation of so-called retarded children. Following the reasoning of the Supreme Court decision of 1954, legislation such as the Pennsylvania Right to Education Law (1971) clearly commits educational policy to a goal of integrated education. The schools in Pennsylvania as well as other states are to provide public education for all children, regardless of the "label," "condition," "potential," or any other characteristic of the child.

Public Law 94-142

In 1975 a landmark federal law was enacted—Public Law 94-142, The Education for All Handicapped Children Act—which requires that all public school systems in all states meet the following regulations:

1. Identification of all handicapped children, age four to twenty-one

2. Assessment of their educational needs

3. Individualized program planning

4. Procedural (due-process) safeguards for students and their parents

5. Education in the least restrictive alternative that meets the child's needs

6. Nondiscrimination

Public law 94-142 has been referred to as an educational Magna Carta for all those children who have been excluded from regular classes by reasons of any handicapping condition. Thus, the definition of the law is broad. Included are children and adolescents who may be classified in one or more of the following categories:

For many years this country legally sanctioned segregated public schools that prevented black children from attending the schools of mainstream white children.

1. Deaf or hearing-impaired

2. Blind or partially sighted

3. Crippled

4. Speech defects

5. Physically impaired

6. Educable or trainable mentally retarded

7. Emotionally disturbed

8. Specific learning disabilities

9. Special behavior problems

These nine types of handicapping conditions are deliberately broad so as to include practically all exceptional children and teen-agers. It

---

* We are emphasizing the legal grounds on which the segregation laws were changed. This still doesn't touch the issue of so-called de facto segregation—a system of housing patterns, school-district lines, and the like—that produces a separate, segregated educational system in spite of the legal sanctions.

is no longer optional for schools to educate or not. The law is clear. Provision must be made from age four until graduation from high school (or its equivalent) or to the age of twenty-one.

The "least restrictive" dictum   The most far-reaching and controversial aspect of the legislation is the phrase "least restrictive alternative." This means that each pupil must be educated in an environment that is as normal as possible. The intention of the law is clear. Schools must include rather than exclude. Regular classroom environments must be expanded both physically and psychologically so that exceptional children can function in the mainstream. This aspect of the law may translate into such changes as barrier-free classrooms for wheelchairs and special apparatus for the hearing- and sight-impaired as well as a greater variety of curriculum materials.

The controversy arises from the so-called due-process provision. Before the school system can move a child out of the mainstream, it must prove its case. If parents disagree with the school's plan to place a child out of the regular class, they have the right to a hearing, representation by a lawyer, and access to all of the assessment information. Finally, they have the right to appeal the decision. In everyday language, this means that the burden of proof is on the school for every decision to exclude handicapped children from regular classes. It does not mean, however, that all children, including those with major and multiple-handicapping conditions, must be in regular classrooms all the time. When special services, and even special residential schools, may be required, the school needs to be able to demonstrate that such a facility is indeed the least restrictive alternative for that particular child. However, the boundary line is much broader. As a result of the legislation, literally thousands of segregated special classes have been closed, special-school enrollments have declined sharply, and special residential schools have dramatically reduced their populations.

Even the casual observer in almost any public school will be struck immediately by the increased number of so-called special-ed pupils now attending regular classes. Schools, classrooms, teachers, principals, parents, and children will never be the same in the wake of such massive social and legal change. New approaches to diagnosis and educational programming are now foremost in the minds of educators. The range of individual differences has been increased. The problem facing educators now is how best to respond.

THE DIAGNOSTIC PROBLEM

Assessment: Is It Valid?

The traditional system of classifying children or teen-agers as retarded or deviant has been criticized on at least two grounds: (1) The system of assessment is too narrowly based, and (2) the labels become permanent. The traditional method was based on an attempt to group children by degree of retardation, using an IQ test as the major assessment procedure. This resulted in three major categories:

1. *Educable Mentally Retarded* (EMR).   IQ score is generally between 50 and 80 on standard tests. The child is usually classed as a slow learner and a "concrete" thinker but can be successfully employed later in life.

2. *Trainable Mentally Retarded* (TMR).   IQ score is generally between 25 and 50 on standard tests. The child is considered not capable of "ordinary" academic learning but can learn self-care and safety rules. "Sheltered" workshops can provide an employment environment. The child can learn social adjustment.

3. *Profoundly Retarded*.   IQ score is between 0 and 25. The child requires constant supervision. Many children are bedridden.

As you can immediately see, the IQ score becomes extraordinarily important in deciding on the assignment of children to the EMR, TMR, or Profoundly Retarded groupings.* Also, you may notice that these three labels can easily

---

* The American Association for Mental Deficiency has reclassified this system to four categories—Mild (69–55), Moderate (54–40), Severe (39–25), Profound (24–0)—in an attempt to provide for more accurate differential diagnosis. It is questionable whether creating a distinction between Severe and Profound based on IQ will be an educational advance.

become euphemisms, or "softer" words replacing the older categories of moron, idiot, and imbecile. The primary difficulty, of course, is the effect of such a global classification based on a somewhat singular method of assessment. The major criticism is that we are overgeneralizing from a limited evaluation system. Maynard Reynolds has provided an incisive critique of this issue. He notes the following:

1. There is no sharp discontinuity in mental ability between people with IQs of 79 and 81, or 49 and 51, yet the tests can lend themselves to such absurd assumptions.

2. The test scores are also subject to the limitations of examiner influence and culture bias. Examiners either consciously or unconsciously do influence the scores achieved by their pupils. Also, few if any tests can claim to be completely culturally fair.

3. The tests themselves are not assessing the complete range of the child's functioning. For example, a "blind" child is usually not completely blind, nor is he or she necessarily incapable of functioning well in other areas. In the same way, a low-tested-IQ child is not necessarily without school achievement potential, nor is he or she necessarily incapable of functioning well in other areas.

4. The tests themselves are virtually useless for making educational decisions with regard to placement. Educational classifications for special education only make sense when the classification is related to programs.

5. We should spend far less time in predicting how children with special needs may perform in "traditional" classrooms as a result of an IQ score. Instead, we should develop more effective instructional procedures that will reach more children—that is, increase the educational potential of each classroom to teach almost all children.

6. Special education should talk less about dysfunction, low IQs, deficits, impairments, and disabilities. Instead, school offerings should be differentiated sufficiently so that all children receive the help they need to develop maximally.[6]

The most trenchant examination of the failures of diagnostic testing for special education pupils has been provided by John Salvia of Pennsylvania State University and James Ysseldyke of the University of Minnesota. Their recent work clearly details how most common normative tests discriminate against such children.[7] Essentially, they literally indict almost all tests as having entirely inadequate norm groups. They point out that the test items themselves have been selected, in most cases, after excluding all so-called retarded pupils. In a sense, this is the same argument that was used against the early forms of intelligence tests, which systematically excluded black children from the norm groups and then used the unrepresentative norm-group scores to classify black children.

Salvia and Ysseldyke also note that most national tests of academic ability such as those for reading, arithmetic, and other primary mental abilities *do not* provide local schools or particular classroom teachers with any useful information on which to base an educational program. Thus, they appeal for great caution in the continued use of most of the common national assessment tests of ability. Those procedures too often misclassify and misdiagnose, to the detriment of pupils from special-education backgrounds.

Classification: What Is the Purpose?

In addition to the assessment problem, which suggests that an IQ test itself is too narrow, there is a larger yet related question: What is the purpose of the classification? Is there a distinct body of literature as to teaching effectiveness that carefully distinguishes between the type of handicap and a special teaching method? In our discussion of teaching effectiveness (Chapter 13), we mentioned the concept of ATI: Set up special methods designed to match the pupil's current level of intellectual/cognitive stage and then create a mismatch. With special-education children, have teaching techniques been discovered that would allow such a matching-mismatching process? Clearly, it would do little good for a teacher to know that a mainstreamed pupil is an *X* unless some special procedures for instructing such *X*s that are different from the methods used with other regular children existed. It would be similar to categorizing

Teachers Don't Want to Be Labeled

Harry W. Forgan*

When teaching a course on tests and measurements at Kent State University recently, I decided to administer an adult group intelligence test to the class. I wanted the students to "feel" what it was like to take such a test and realize what items we use to measure intelligence. I also thought they might be more aware of the short time it takes to obtain a number which is regarded as very important by many educators.

The students were told not to write their names on the test papers, but rather to use a code such as their house number, physical measurements, or any less obvious symbol. I explained that I really didn't have faith in IQ scores; therefore, I didn't want to know their IQs.

The administration of the test required only 50 minutes. The students seemed to enjoy taking it and chuckled at some of the tasks they were expected to perform. I had to laugh myself when I saw some of them looking at their hands and feet when responding to items concerning right and left.

Upon scoring the test I found that the lowest IQ was 87 and the highest 143. The mean IQ for the 48 students was 117. I was not astonished by the 87, even though all of the students had successfully completed the general education courses and student teaching at Kent State and were ready to graduate by the end of the term. After all, IQ tests have many limitations.

Then I got an idea. I decided to prepare a report for each student, writing his code on the outside and "IQ 87" on the inside of each. I folded and stapled each paper—after all, an IQ is confidential information!

At the next class period I arranged all of the folded papers on a table at the front of the room. I wrote the range and the average IQ on the chalkboard. Many students snickered at the thought of somebody getting an 87. The students were eager and afraid as I began by explaining the procedures for picking up their papers. I made a point of telling them not to tell others their IQ score, because this would make the other person feel as if he too had to divulge this "total endowment." The students were then directed to come up to the table, row by row, to find their coded paper. I stood sheepishly—ready to laugh out loud as I watched the students carefully open their papers and see "IQ 87." Many opened their mouths with astonishment and then smiled at their friends to indicate they were extremely happy with their scores.

There was dead silence when I began to discuss the implications of the IQ scores. I explained that in some states a person who scores below 90 on an IQ test is classified as a slow learner. The fact that group intelligence tests should not be used to make such a classification was stressed. I also emphasized the fact that *someone* in this class could have been classified as a slow learner and placed in a special class on the basis of this test.

I told how many guidance counselors would discourage a child with an 87 IQ from attending college. Again I emphasized the fact that one person in this room was ready to graduate from college having passed several courses in history, biology, English, and many other areas.

I then went on to explain that the majority of elementary and secondary school teachers believe

children by hair length, eye color, or body size without supportive reasons as to why such children are different *as learners*. So the question turns on the predictive validity of the classification system for classroom learning. Most systems meet their greatest difficulty here.

Although Public Law 94-142 has specified nine types of handicap, the first thing you need to know as a teacher is the likelihood of finding a given type of handicapped student in your class.[8] Recent figures are summarized in Table 21.1. The table shows that over 90 percent of the children classified as handicapped are clus-

tered in just four categories. Then, we must ask, how accurate are these "high-incidence" groupings? We already noted a problem in the Mentally Retarded (MR) category: IQ testing was too narrow and didn't sample learning potential over a broad enough span. In fact, one research has claimed that only 25 percent of the time was the label "mental retardation" accurate.[9]

Recent studies have shown even greater problems with the Learning Disabled (LD) and Emotionally Disturbed (ED) categories. One group of researchers found that the method for determining presence or absence of emotional

in ability grouping. This is usually done on the basis of intelligence tests, so I explained that I would like to try ability grouping with this class—again to see "how it feels." Some students objected right away, saying that "I did not want to know their IQ scores." I calmed them by saying it would be a worthwhile learning experience and assured them that I really didn't believe in IQ scores.

I told the students not to move at this time, but I would like all of those with an IQ below 90 to come to the front so they could sit nearer to me for individual help. I told the students who had an average IQ (between 90–109) to go to the back of the room and then take the seats in the middle of the class. The students with an above average IQ were asked to go to the side of the room and take the seats in the back because they really didn't need much more extra help.

"O.K., all those who got an IQ below 90 come to the front of the room." The students looked around to find those who scored below 90. I said that I knew there was an 87 and maybe a couple of 89's. Again, there was dead silence.

"O.K., all those students whose IQ is between 90–109 go to the back of the room." Immediately, to my amazement, 8 or 10 students picked up their books and headed for the back of the room. Before they could get there I said, "Wait a minute! Sitdown! I don't want to embarrass you, but you would lie and cheat—the same way we make our students lie and cheat—because you don't want to be classified as 'slow.' I wrote 'IQ 87' on every paper!"

The class erupted. It was in an uproar for about five minutes. Some of the women cried. Some indicated that they needed to use the restroom. All agreed it was a horrifying and yet valuable experience.

I asked them to do one thing for me: Please don't label kids. Because we are all "gifted," "average," and "slow," depending on the task at hand. They promised.

---

* Phi Delta Kappan, September 1973. Reprinted by permission.

TABLE 21.1   FREQUENCY OF HANDICAPPING CONDITIONS IN SCHOOL-AGE POPULATIONS*

HIGH INCIDENCE	PERCENTAGE	
Learning Disabled	37	
Speech Handicapped	30	Total High Incidence = 93%
Mentally Retarded	18	
Emotionally Disturbed	8	

LOW INCIDENCE	PERCENTAGE	
Multihandicapped	1	
Orthopedically Impaired	1	
Deaf	1	Total Low Incidence = 6$^+$%
Visually handicapped	0.5	
Deaf-Blind	0.05	
Other	3	

* About 4 million children are handicapped.

disturbance was so arbitrary as to be meaningless. "We are deceived if we think we know about whom it is that most authors of research reports are writing."[10] In the case of LD children, the same conclusion has been reached.

The current methods of classifying a student as LD are basically the same as the methods used to identify low achievers. The problem is that an LD student is supposed to be different from a low achiever. An LD student, by definition, is

Dyslexia: A Case Study in Special Education

A lengthy debate has been waged over the question of word blindness in children and teen-agers. Although given various labels such as "dyslexia" (word disability), "strephosymbolia" (twisting symbols), and "minimal brain dysfunction," the symptoms of the syndrome are all the same. Essentially, children and teen-agers afflicted with this disability reverse words and numbers and have enormous difficulty in spelling, remembering telephone numbers, looking up words in a dictionary, keeping number columns straight, and learning a foreign language—to name just a few of the most common symbolic processing areas.

The syndrome has a long history and has afflicted many famous people. Public figures such as Albert Einstein, General George Patton, Woodrow Wilson, and Nelson Rockefeller have all described in the most poignant way what it was really like during these most difficult school days. They were being asked to perform activities that they literally could not understand. In math, for example, a child might be asked to add 783 and 227, but might actually read these numbers as 873

and 272 without realizing the reversal. Thus, when the answer was marked wrong, the reason for the failure would remain a mystery. Similarly, in writing, *no* might become *on*, *god* might be seen as *dog*, and so on (or so no!).

In spite of the long history of personal accounts, systematic research studies, and a wide variety of documentation, there continues to be substantial opposition within educational circles to acknowledging the existence of the disability. Estimates run as high as one of seven pupils afflicted, with a large preponderance of males over females. There remains, however, on the part of too many teachers, a resistance to admitting that some pupils actually suffer from the disability. At an intuitive level, the common view is that it is just a question of willfulness and motivation; somehow the dyslexic child isn't really working hard enough.

A second common misperception is that, if dyslexia isn't a fancy psychological label for laziness, it's just a cover-up for mental retardation. The reason that Johnny can't read, or add, or spell, is simple—he's stupid. Even though studies have

Dyslexia has afflicted many famous and successful people. Public figures such as Thomas Edison and Woodrow Wilson have described the frustrations they suffered during their difficult school days.

shown that individually administered IQ scores do not correlate with dyslexia, this second myth continues.

If teachers have experienced difficulty in accepting the reality of dyslexia, psychologists and researchers have had difficulty in documenting the causes. In fact, for too long researchers have attempted to discover the single crucial factor. Some feel the problem is basically a physical-coordination deficiency. Others suggest a chemical basis from artificial food coloring or a hyperactivity due to a drug imbalance. Still others think of it as a psychoanalytic problem from anal fixation, a lack of training during the formative preschool years, or a problem of birth order, of parental neglect, or of fatherless homes.

The physical-coordination school suggests solutions ranging from reliance on exercises, such as bouncing on trampolines, jumping rope, walking balance beams, and bouncing basketballs, to the extreme of surgical correction, such as removal of adenoids or altering eye muscles. The proponents of a chemical view suggest measures such as the careful supervision of diet, food without preservatives, and massive doses of vitamins, tranquilizers, and sea-sickness pills. Theorists who attribute dyslexia to an intrapsychic problem suggest solutions ranging from individual counseling and play therapy to family analysis.

But human behavior cannot be reduced to a single cause. It is disheartening indeed to find parents, teachers, and educators first attempting to deny that dyslexia exists at all, and then reversing field and not only accepting the problem but seeking a single magical cure. Recently a somewhat cynical educational psychologist commented that, in the last decade, all the people who sold used cars, bait-and-switch real estate in Florida, and bust-development machines have moved into the dyslexia business. In fact, as a teacher you may be questioned in depth by anxious parents or school boards as to which single remedy is best—the "talking" typewriter, the sensory-deprivation booth, the color-coded alphabet, underwater swimming, behavior modification, organized crawling, or wall-to-wall trampolines?

Both theory and research evidence, of course, strongly suggest that no single technique will produce cures. In fact, the remedies are something less than spectacular, consisting of multisensory tutoring and massive amounts of human support. If some pupils cannot employ the usual channels for processing symbols, then an educational program needs to include a broader array of techniques and experiences. Multisensory programs allow the child quite obviously to use all the senses—see the letter, trace it in sand, cut it out of cardboard, say it out loud, pick it out of magazine ads and street signs, and touch it in block form.

The techniques really come down to "good" instruction—namely, an array of alternatives to help children learn the code. The same "solutions" apply to helping pupils learn to produce symbols. Since regular writing is difficult and at times torturous, other channels can be employed. In addition to paper and pencil, fat crayons, and chalk and blackboard, pupils can also be "allowed" to tape-record reports, give oral reports in class, or use a typewriter.

Employing multiple techniques is, of course, not enough. In learning new and difficult tasks, any pupil will need extra human support and encouragement—and this support is especially crucial for the dyslexic child. Signs of impatience, despair, and discouragement by a teacher are quickly transmitted to a child afflicted with word blindness, and such a child will be hyperalert to teacher feelings. Positive human support is necessary to create a low-anxiety atmosphere that will help the pupil take risks and not feel it necessary to cover up his or her difficulty. Some dyslexic children learn magnificent social skills to prevent a teacher from finding out that they can't read or write. Probably the best tutoring in this instance would be from older children and adults who themselves have struggled with the problem. Given support, encouragement, and a multisensory approach, the word-blind children do learn to read.

---

a pupil who is functioning far below potential as a result of some kind of neurological or other specific mental impairment. A low achiever, on the other hand, is a student of marginal general academic ability. To confuse the two clearly reduces the validity of the category.

Thus, the present picture appears quite troubling. The categories of LD (37 percent), MR (18 percent), and ED (8 percent) include a total of 63 percent, or almost two-thirds, of all handicapped children. Yet research indicates that the accuracy of such labels is very uncertain at best and highly unreliable at worst, thereby reducing validity. If only 25 percent of those classified MR are accurately diagnosed, and the other two categories of LD and ED are somewhat arbitrary, the basic ground is shaky indeed.

Some recent proposals seek to remedy the classification problem by combining categories. If you hear special educators talk about cross-categorical specialties, what they mean is that LD, MR, and ED have been combined. Now the problem is to develop sufficient difference in assessment to improve the reliability and validity of assigning children to this new and broader grouping. It may strike you as somewhat ironic that most accurate special-education assessment is for the deaf, blind, or orthopedically handicapped—all areas of the lowest incidence. These areas, as well as speech handicaps, are also ones where the difficulty is most obvious. Thus, the misclassification of special-education students is the greatest, unfortunately, in the areas of high incidence, which are also the ones where the greatest damage can be done through misdiagnosis.

An example of misclassification can be seen in results from a very large urban system. The rosters indicated that the system had three times more black students assigned to MR classes than any other school system in the country. For this to occur, either a huge concentration of retarded people all lived in a single city through some fluke or the method of assignment was at fault. Investigation has shown that the method was the cause. A major flaw in the use of MR, ED, and LD categories is that a disproportionate number of minority pupils are often classed as deviants. The label stigmatizes even when accurate; when inaccurate, it not only stigmatizes but leads to negative self-fulfilling prophecies. Research has shown consistently that minorities are the groups most often misclassified. In one study the MR label was applied to 16 percent of the school's minority population. A careful reassessment of the children indicated 2 percent were accurately classified. In the words of Maynard Reynolds, "Racial and ethnic minorities often deeply resent the high rates of classification of their children as 'retarded,' 'disturbed,' or 'maladjusted.'"[11] In the cases cited, the resentment appears more than justified.

As a result of the disproportionate placement of minority students in special-education classes, professional special education is a topic of great current interest. A recent national commission recommended a completely new approach to assessment. The first step, when a child isn't keeping up, would be to assess the learning environment in the classroom, carefully reviewing the teaching methods, materials, and classroom atmosphere. Also, pupil achievement would not be measured by traditional nationally normed achievement tests, nor would pupil ability be assessed through the standard IQ method. Nationally normed achievement tests measure only about one-third of the content of a given grade, which stacks the deck against a child as a measure of current classroom learning. The problems with IQ tests have already been noted. In the words of Samuel Messick (vice-president of research for the Educational Testing Service), "An individual assessment of the pupil would be permitted only after deficiencies in the learning environment had been ruled out."[12] Thus, a careful look at the quality of instruction would become the first step. As a second step, a new method of assessment that emphasized actual problem solving or "work samples" would be followed. Basically, testing would be used only as a last resort; otherwise, the pupil would be unnecessarily "exposed to the risks of stigma and misclassification in referral and individual assessment."[13] The final step, after ruling out the classroom environment and using a careful and comprehensive valid assessment of learning ability, would be to consider the special class placement *temporary*, no more than one year at a time. The reason for such a time limit on assignment to segregated special classes is simply that the longer a pupil remains out of the mainstream, the less the probability of the pupil's returning. In the words of another Educational Testing Service official, T. Ann Clearly, "The problem is the special education classes. There would be no controversy about testing if kids blossomed when they were put into special education classes.[14] But in such classes there is often "a sharply reduced curriculum and little cognitive demand."[15] Once in, the child is too often permanently assigned.

Judge Francis Peckham presided over a now famous court case (*Larry P. v. Riles*). After an exhaustive examination of placement practice and the learning environments in a large urban district, he pronounced that the special classrooms were "dead-end classrooms."[16] The doors, once closed, seemed permanently sealed.

To give you a greater personal sense of the effects of misdiagnosis, we present a brief case study drawn from the case files of a famous child psychotherapist.

Dibs: A case of misdiagnosis   Virginia Axline, a gifted child psychotherapist and author, has provided a dramatic case study of a little boy, Dibs. From parental description and nursery-school behavior, it appeared as if Dibs was grossly mentally defective. His parents reported that from birth on he was always remote, untouchable, slow to talk and walk, unable to play, and "striking out at people like a little wild animal."

The nursery-school teachers were baffled by him. The school psychologist had been unable to test him. The pediatrician had concluded he was "strange," perhaps mentally retarded, psychotic, or brain-damaged. No one was apparently able to get close enough to Dibs to find out the causes of his difficulties.

The parents themselves were both brilliant and successful yet terribly ashamed, fearful, and anxiety-ridden over their "problem" child. Deep down they believed that the awful truth was that Dibs was an "idiot."

The mother related an incident at home to Dr. Axline, in which she described a terrible fight between Dibs and her husband. The four-year-old had apparently hurled a chair at his father, kicking and screaming all the while, "I hate you." This was in response to the husband's direct comment to Dibs that he was babbling like an idiot. The mother reported to the therapist that she had said to her husband, "Dibs wasn't babbling like an idiot now. He said he hated you!" "Then, my husband sat down in a chair and actually wept! It was terrible; I had never seen a man cry before. I had never thought anything could cause my husband to shed a tear. I was afraid, suddenly terrified, because he seemed to be just as scared as I was. I think we were closer to each other than we have ever been. Suddenly, we were just two frightened, lonely, unhappy people with our defenses crumpled and deserted. It was terri-ble—and yet a relief to know that we could be human, and could fail and admit that we had failed! Finally, we pulled ourselves together and he said that maybe we had been wrong about Dibs. I said I would come and ask what you thought about Dibs." She looked at me with an expression of fear and panic in her eyes. "Tell me," she said. "Do you think that Dibs is mentally defective?"[17]

Dibs was "defective" only in the sense that he had suffered enormous emotional deprivation. For whatever reason, neither parent had been capable of forming a warm, supportive, nurturing early environment for him. In the language of a psychiatrist who interviewed the family, Dibs was "the most rejected and emotionally deprived child" he had ever seen.

In the case study itself, Dr. Axline describes the emotional reeducation she provided for Dibs, as well as the assistance to the parents so they could maintain the gains. Dibs gradually yet dramatically emerged from his shell into the world of human relationships and in the author's words, "was able to be a child." The work stands both as a moment of high drama and as a reminder of our basic human needs for supportive relationships to encourage healthy psychological development—an essential first step to becoming a person. The word "Dibs" is a common expression in England for "self."

An Alternative Classification Procedure

Test interpretation is a critical process, for it indicates how we make meaning and judgments. We certainly need a more comprehensive system of educational diagnosis for all children and particularly for those currently being classed as "special." Evelyn Deno, an eminent theorist-practitioner in this field, has developed a system that respects both the complexity of the problem and the need to employ careful assessment in the service of the children.[18] Rather than viewing the problem from society's perspective first, she suggests we start with the fundamental needs and rights of children. In this way we can keep our educational priorities in mind. The system is also based on a positive assessment concept designed to uncover the areas of positive educational potential. Thus, rather than generalizing from one negative aspect of a child's functioning, the system seeks to differentiate general functioning into a series of elements. This helps to prevent classifying children into negative categories. Instead, the children can be grouped into one of seven levels of educational environments, from regular classes to "total" care. The critical point, however, is the dynamic commitment in the plan to always move children upward in the system as far and as fast as possible. Thus, assignments are at first functional to the level of activity the child brings to the environment. The educational goal of any particular level, then, is to prepare the child for the next level up, so to speak; none of the levels, two through seven, is regarded as a permanent placement.

Alternative Educational Environments: Promoting Development

Evelyn Deno's system clearly implies the need for differential service. The diagnosis problem, as we indicated, involves broad assessment procedures in all areas of functioning. The critical assumption, however, is not the initial prescription; instead, it's the developmental program. From this point of view, the various categories of handicapping conditions are, at best, only immediate and temporary stations for the child. Growth is determined by interaction. The labels are dangerous since it's so easy to assume that the problems are safely locked up inside the child. The frameworks of Jean Piaget, Jerome Bruner, J. McV. Hunt, and Robert White suggest the following educational assumptions:

1. Special-education pupils develop through the same sequence of stages as "normal" pupils but at slower rates in the areas of their handicaps.

2. The growth of these children thus depends on the same set of principles applicable to "regular" children, namely, (a) a rich, stimulating, abundant early environment (Hunt); (b) an active versus passive learning environment, including a heavy emphasis on practice and participation from the early years onward (Piaget and Bruner).

3. Careful educational preparation is needed for stage growth and transition to the next stage up. This includes the process of *equilibration*, Piaget's term for a construction

match between the child's functioning stage and the learning environment—for example, a rich stimulating sensory environment during the very early years. Developmental growth, as we have noted, depends on interaction between the child and the environment. The opposite of this developmental assumption is the isomorphic view—that the learning problem is a deficit locked up inside the body of the designated child.

A number of studies, including a classic one by Maria Skodak and Harold Skeels,[19] the Perry Preschool program (see Chapter 3), and one by Sandra Scarr and Richard Weinberg,[20] indicate rather clearly that intellectual functioning and general development can be positively influenced by a rich, stimulating early environment. Skodak and Skeels demonstrated that cognitive functioning could be dramatically increased for young children by modifying an extremely barren orphanage environment. The Perry Preschool program showed the positive effects of a stimulating preschool environment, while Scarr and Weinberg showed the positive effects of modifying early-home-care environments. Whether the actual environment was an orphanage, a nursery school, or a home, the principles were the same—namely, that significant

Several studies conducted during the last thirty-five years all clearly indicate that intellectual functioning and general development can be positively influenced by a rich, stimulating early environment.

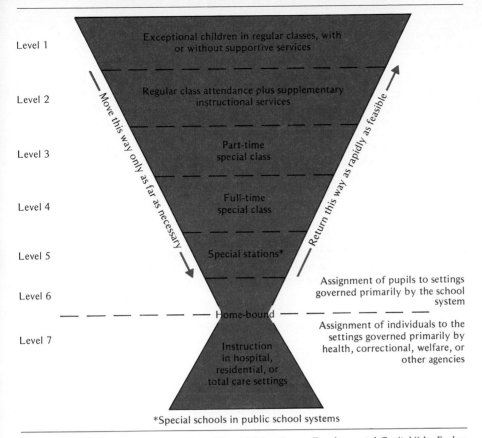

Level 1 — Exceptional children in regular classes, with or without supportive services

Level 2 — Regular class attendance plus supplementary instructional services

Level 3 — Part-time special class

Level 4 — Full-time special class

Level 5 — Special stations*

Level 6 — Home-bound

Level 7 — Instruction in hospital, residential, or total care settings

Move this way only as far as necessary

Return this way as rapidly as feasible

Assignment of pupils to settings governed primarily by the school system

Assignment of individuals to the settings governed primarily by health, correctional, welfare, or other agencies

*Special schools in public school systems

The "Cascade" classification system. From "Special Education as Developmental Capital," by Evelyn Deno, Exceptional Children, 37 (1970): 229–237. Copyright by The Council for Exceptional Children. Reprinted with permission.

increases were found in cognitive functioning as a result of "active" learning, positive interaction, and developmental-stage equilibration. This is simply a means of placing the explanations for positive growth in developmental language. In all these studies, many preschool children were initially classified, on the basis of an IQ test, as retarded or slow learners.

INTERVENTION PROGRAMS

Increasing the Accommodative Capacity of Classrooms

As mainstream programs increase, it is obvious that the educational environments will need careful preparation, including attention to teacher attitudes and the use of imaginative materials and methods. Studies have shown patterns of teacher behavior—namely, discomfort, anxiety, and stress that teachers experience when dealing with children who are different. We noted earlier that in some urban classrooms white teachers were not responsive to the needs of black children: Teachers engaged in less eye contact, more negative statements, more punitive behavior than toward white children. Whether mainstreaming succeeds, then, will depend on the ability to teach teachers to become more responsive to the fundamental needs of all children. In the special-education literature this is referred to as the need to increase the accommodative capacity of regular classrooms—to broaden the learning environment so that all pupils are genuinely included in positive learning activities. For example, it does little good to legalize racial integration in a school, only to have the school operate as a segregated institution with students eating separately, occupying different spaces in the same building, participating in separate activities,

MARIA MONTESSORI

Maria Montessori was on the forefront of change and innovation throughout her entire life. Born in 1870, she was raised in a conservative European atmosphere in the small Italian town of Chiaravelle. Her aspirations, however, led her, upon the completion of the equivalent of a secondary-school education, to seek admission to the prestigious University of Rome for the study of medicine. It was literally unheard of at the time for a woman to pursue a medical career—there were simply no woman physicians in the entire Italian nation. Such barriers, however, could not deter Montessori. Her brilliance of intellect, combined with personal drive and dedication, soon won the respect of the all-male college. At the age of twenty-four, she became the first woman physician in the country.

Her interest in practicing general medicine, which at that time consisted largely of treating symptoms, soon waned. She began to ask larger questions and shifted more toward the problems and needs of retarded children. The streets of Rome were inhabited by urchins, many of whom were regarded as insane. Montessori's clinical intuition, however, suggested that the difficulty might not be medical insanity. Careful observation of these children gradually created in her a conviction that the problems experiences by these waifs were not medical but rather pedagogical. The children, many from the most economically depressed areas of the city, were growing up under the worst possible conditions. Grinding poverty created devastating learning atmospheres during their early formative years.

She continued to challenge the existing views of her day by establishing a special school for the so-called insane children. At twenty-nine she became the school's director, created new learning materials, and applied her theories to the classroom, while studying the techniques of Edouard Seguin and Jean Marc Itard. She soon revolutionized the entire educational approach for such children; many were able to learn to read and write, using her highly structured materials and multisensory procedures. Montessori's children became the first generation to be what we now call "mainstreamed,"

in that they were placed in regular classes with normal children. This demonstrated rather dramatically that previously designated insane or retarded children were capable of learning under appropriate conditions.

Her work continued to expand in scope as she became increasingly interested in the general learning problems of all children, not just those of emotionally disturbed or "slum kids." She began to realize that learning was dependent on the interaction between the child and the environment. David Elkind, a contemporary American expert in cognitive-developmental theory, has noted that this concept of Montessori's was highly similar to some of Piaget's later theories.[a] She viewed development as occurring in a sequence of stages or "sensitive periods," as she called them, and she felt that such development proceeded by leaps and bounds followed by periods of integration. She used the phrase "growth explosions" to denote the qualitative shifts to new cognitive stages.

Of course, Montessori's other obvious similarity to Piaget was what Elkind termed her genius for empathy with children. Without doubt, this sensitivity, which enabled her to understand both the thoughts and feelings of young children, was the central ingredient, the *sine qua non* of her educational leadership.

Above all else, Maria Montessori throughout her entire life was com-

being treated separately by school rules and teachers. In the same way, if previously separated special-education pupils are mainstreamed only to be resegregated once again, changing the form but not substance will produce a perpetuation of the status quo.

Jack Birch at the University of Pittsburgh has summarized a series of studies in mainstreamed school districts. The cluster of positive attitudes of regular teachers was "the most effective force for excellent special education." He summarized the cluster of attitudes as follows:

mitted to educational practice. Whereas Piaget focused mostly on discovering how children learn as an interesting theoretical question, Montessori always viewed every problem with an eye to practical application. She was a bridge between theory and practice; she both *described* how children learn and *prescribed* teaching methods to accomplish developmental goals. Thus, she attempted to synthesize a theory of learning and a theory of instruction. From her naturalistic observations of how young children learn, she developed her now famous prepared environment. She wished not to accelerate growth or force children to grow up overnight but rather to develop maximally their own competencies within each stage of growth. The environment, if carefully matched to the child, provides the nourishment for such growth. Naturally, as seems to be the case with all major innovators, some of Montessori's "disciples" have misunderstood her intentions and have created some lock-step environments that do not serve children well. For Montessori development involved the matched environment of repetitive learning and multisensory materials, as well as spontaneity and empathy. Children do not learn in prescriptive educational straitjackets.

Her long life was devoted to increasing our theoretical and practical knowledge of child development, for both the normal and atypical child. In her lifetime she addressed many audiences: the teacher, the educational researcher, the curriculum-materials developer, and the parent. By the time of her death at age eighty-two, Montessori had become a powerful voice for children, and her pioneering efforts had opened the way for continuing educational practice.

---

[a] Elkind, D. (1970). *Children and adolescents* (p. 104). New York: Oxford University Press.

---

1. Belief in the right to education for all children

2. Readiness of special-education and regular-class teachers to cooperate with each other

3. Willingness to share competencies as a team in behalf of pupils

4. Openness to include parents as well as other professional colleagues in planning for and working with children

5. Flexibility with respect to class size and teaching assignments

6. Recognition that social and personal development can be taught, and that they are equally as important as academic achievement

He also noted that in the school districts that successfully "mainstreamed," including elementary and secondary levels and across disciplines, three factors stood out:

1. There was genuine appreciation of the team work with the special-education teachers, particularly the help the regular classroom teachers received with the children already in their rooms.

2. Regular classroom teachers found that special-education pupils were usually no more difficult to include in their classes than some children already there.

3. The spirit that "all the children are in the same school system" was expressed time after time.[21]

Developing the Requisite Teaching Skills

In addition to the obvious importance of teacher attitudes, we also need to consider the other side of the coin, new teaching skills for the classroom itself. It would do the teacher little good to have highly positive attitudes toward exceptional children, but not have the requisite teaching skills to help them. We noted earlier that the critical developmental assumptions are:

1. Exceptional children can develop through the same Piagetian stages (especially sensorimotor, preoperational, and concrete), in a manner similar to regular children, yet at slower rates.

2. Interaction with a rich, stimulating environment and active learning will promote growth.

Special-education studies have demonstrated the critical importance of positive teacher-child interaction in promoting intellectual growth.

Educational researcher David Hunt has shown repeatedly in a key series of studies that it is important to match the educational environment with the stage of development of the child.[22] Pupils who are functioning at relatively low levels of conceptual thinking tend to learn most adequately in a highly structured teaching environment. Thus, in elementary schools, as pupils are attempting to master the initial stages of concrete thinking, Hunt's work would definitely support carefully structured teaching. The educational tasks assigned should be (1) carefully explained, (2) relatively brief, (3) monitored quickly, (4) systematically varied, and in addition (5) should involve learning through multiple senses.

At first, this may strike you as overmanaging the child, shutting out the possibility of creativity and being too preplanned or programed. If you view it from the child's position, however, it may not seem as negative. Children starting school at low conceptual levels can be confused easily by ambiguity. Also, they may be afraid to ask for clarification, especially if they see that other children apparently understand the directions. Under such conditions children may revert to lower-stage thinking. If you were just on

the threshold of learning to think concretely and became confused, anxious, and unsure of an educational task, it would be understandable to fall back into an earlier mode of thought, namely, preoperational thinking.

From an educational standpoint, the careful use of a structured approach to teaching is legitimate as a means of helping so-called slower, or lower-conceptual, children to master some initial tasks. However, we wish to avoid suggesting that all problems of retardation or other types of exceptionality can be "cured" through high-structured learning. Although there may be some individual cases of dramatic improvement within a group of children previously segregated in special classes, those will remain the exception. In the nineteenth century in this country an early pioneer in special education, Edouard Seguin, unfortunately suggested that slow learning and retardation could be stamped out. With training and responsive environments all children could be normalized. Such overly optimistic hopes, of course, created a backlash of disappointment when reality indicated that improvement was slow and limited. However, we need not expect that retarded or slow-learning children are capable of becoming geniuses. Instead, the goal of the educator is to stimulate development. Small gains, in the long run, may in fact be the most significant and long-lasting.

FROM DIAGNOSIS TO TEACHING

Assuming we develop a more valid base for classifying the handicapped, particularly in reducing the overassignment of minority children, what are the teaching implications for you? Just how different is it to teach a handicapped child? What knowledge of special education and teaching strategies do you need? What are the special learning characteristics of the child so designated?[23] These questions are central to mainstream teaching. If there are nine handicapping conditions, are there nine different teaching strategies?

Martin Haberman, former dean of the University of Wisconsin at Milwaukee, has done a careful examination of the mainstream problem, but from the teacher's point of view.[24] He has reviewed both the variety of special-education techniques and the curriculum materials needed for special-education pupils who are now being mainstreamed. Also, he has examined the procedures and strategies that are common to all effective teachers. As a result he has presented a series of estimates as to how much special content and strategy you'll need, as well as general procedures for all children. When you look at Table 21.2, you may be quite surprised and, we hope, encouraged by his conclusions.

For example, the table estimates that from 5 to 10 percent of the time you will need to employ new materials and from 5 to 10 percent of the time, special methods of communications. With visually impaired students this would mean giving them access to books in Braille, having them use a tape recorder for answering an essay exam, setting up the room to minimize changes in furniture placement, and having them sit close to the front of the room. Many visually impaired students have some residual vision. Hearing impaired students would need a different set of materials, the use of a signer (a person adept at signing your words to the pupil), and similar accommodations to their special needs. For the orthopedically handicapped the room would be set up to reduce barriers to mobility for a wheelchair and the

TABLE 21.2   EFFECTIVE TEACHING STRATEGIES FOR MAINSTREAMED PUPILS (SUMMARIZED BY MARTIN HABERMAN)

APPROXIMATE PERCENTAGES OF TIME SPENT IN ACTIVITY	TEACHING ACTIVITIES FOR WHICH "HELP" MAY BE SOUGHT BY CLASSROOM TEACHERS LEARNING TO MAINSTREAM
5%–10%	Using special materials that are new to the teacher. This involves becoming familiar with materials and equipment and being shown how they operate.*
5%–10%	Communicating with students who have special handicaps (e.g., hearing, visual). This involves receiving straightforward directions.†
5%	Special methods of teaching. There is a *very* small body of special teaching behaviors for working with handicapped students that teachers can learn through observation and develop through practice (i.e., usually supervisory procedures).‡
75%–85%	Engaging in normal classroom teaching practices that are, in large part, effective with all children.§

* Maynard C. Reynolds and Jack W. Birch, *Teaching Exceptional Children in All America's Schools* (Reston, Va.: The Council for Exceptional Children, 1977), pp. 569–571 and p. 632.
† Ibid., pp. 562–563 and pp. 630–631.
‡ Ibid., pp. 565–569 and pp. 633–636.
§ Ibid., pp. 303–304.

From M. Haberman, "Principles of In-Service Training for Implementation of Mainstreaming in the Public Schools," in D. C. Corrigan and K. Howey (Eds.), Concepts to Guide the Education of Experienced Teachers, *1980, p. 60. Reprinted by permission of the Council for Exceptional Children.*

playground would have a lowered hoop for basketball. In one sense these are small changes, but they make a substantial difference to an individual student. Try maneuvering in the average school room or getting to the bathroom in a wheelchair, and you'll understand at an experiential level how different the world of a wheelchair user can be on things we take for granted.

In the area of special teaching methods, as Haberman notes, there is a very small body of unique approaches, involving perhaps 5 percent of the teaching time. Many educators would argue that even these special methods are not that unique. In any case the special-education resource teacher or school psychologist can provide you with the current recommendations. The consistent use of a time-out room for a hyperactive child, the close monitoring of individualized seatwork with frequent positive reinforcement for an MR child, or the use of different standards in judging penmanship for palsied children represent some examples of somewhat specialized teaching methods. Probably the most significant special technique is more psychological than pedagogical—what psychologists call "learned helplessness."

Learned Helplessness: A Common Characteristic

Some years ago a theorist, Martin Seligman, discovered a particular type of personality response that was common to many types of people who had been excluded from full participation in the mainstream of society.[25] Although Seligman originally focused on migrant workers, the economically poor, and ethnically different people, his theory can also be applied to handicapped children, many of whom suffer from a similar kind of exclusion and resultant stigma. His central point is that such people learn to appear helpless. They acquire an external set of behaviors to give an impression that they are not competent. Seligman stresses that these responses (giving up quickly, tears, refusal to try) have been *learned*. Research has shown that parental attitudes and practices often impede growth for handicapped children. Although it is a complex story, reduced to its simplest terms, parents tend either to reject or overprotect such children.[26] Parental anxiety

and guilt result in the parents' quite unintentionally fostering a dependency. However, do not make the mistake of simply blaming the parents, any more than you should blame teachers (remember Rosenthal's studies) for negative expectations. Remember that the syndrome is learned, and it can be unlearned. In dealing with learned helplessness it is most important, especially at the outset, to employ a careful set of behavioral strategies. Find some positive behavior of the child that you can positively reinforce, and do not under any circumstances positively reinforce helplessness when an activity is well within the child's ability. These two rules go together; unless you follow both, you will quickly undo your gains. You will probably find this whole process extremely difficult at a personal level. The child has spent years learning the process. It is as if individual competence has been frustrated, so the child now becomes competent in getting others to wait on him or her. In some cases the act is very convincing, having been polished through many performances. Such children can make you feel guilty and perhaps even heartless. At such times it's important to review your own role. They need your support to nurture their growth, but that does not mean you should do for them those things they can learn to do for themselves. Dealing with your feelings of compassion and concern for a child struggling with a handicapping condition may well be your most difficult experience as a teacher. As your own experience grows, you will gain more confidence in your ability to identify areas of positive accomplishment to reinforce and become even more consistent in avoiding reinforcing the appearance of helplessness.

In the long run you will see the gradual emergence of the child's positive competence drive. The first sign may be most dramatic. The handicapped child lets you know, "Look here, I can do this myself." That's when you'll realize you have made progress—as an educator for all children.

TEACHING STRATEGIES FOR MAINSTREAMING

As Table 21.2 clearly suggests, the greatest need in mainstreaming is the development of competent general teaching strategies. In this realm certain approaches need emphasis. These procedures are not unique to special-education pupils; they are useful with all children. Yet they are not used often enough in general and so must be underlined here as a system of instruction.

Also, by way of background, one of the major difficulties in developing teaching strategies for mainstreamed pupils has been the lack of diversity in teaching methods employed in the separate special-education classes prior to the new law. In fact, criticism of the profession of special education itself has increased substantially in the past decade. As more research is done, the weaknesses in the old methods of classification become more apparent, thus emphasizing the need for better and more valid classifications, especially in the high-incidence areas.[27] So too with teaching. There has been almost a complete reliance on behavior modification as the only method for such high-incidence areas. The difficulty from our view is simply the exclusion of other methods for teachers. A highly structured and simple-task approach is helpful (indeed the next section will provide an extensive outline of a behavior modification system that is most appropriate), but effective teaching for special-education children cannot begin and end here. Richard Snow, one of the originators of ATI (attribute-treatment interaction), has commented on the weakness of a singular approach: "A truly adaptive instructional system is needed, not a new blanket panacea chosen because it produces some average improvements."[28]

As you read these recommendations, keep in mind that the various elements can become a system. We do not advocate any one as a "blanket panacea," a single and final solution. The system includes (1) precise teaching, (2) cooperative learning, (3) tutoring, (4) social skills training, (5) matching and gradual mismatching.

Precise Teaching

Substantial work has been done in a method of precise teaching as a means of providing high structure for children newly mainstreamed. Essentially, the method is derived almost directly from learning theory and Skinnerian principles. The specific advantages of the method are that

it allows the learner to focus on a structured task, proceed at his or her own pace, receive positive reinforcement for accomplishments, and build up feelings of being a successful learner. The overall process, then, represents a method of tailoring educational tasks to fit each child, or as it's sometimes called, individualizing instruction. A discussion of the key elements involved in setting up this process follows.

Select a manageable task   The task to be learned by the child needs to be very specifically defined. Thus, the educational objective should not be too cosmic. To become more human, to appreciate American civilization, to be spontaneous, and so on are all too ambiguous as manageable tasks for precise teaching (see Chapter 10). Instead—and this may sound hopelessly pedestrian to you—it is important to identify a highly specific task: learning to count from one to ten, to recognize vowels, to read ten single words without an error, or similar highly structured learning activities. We should also note that this approach is useful not just in special-education classes but in almost any new learning situation, especially where the ambiguity of

Individualization of instruction requires that all educational activities be easily available to all children.

FIGURE 21.1 Behavior contracts for pupils who are not yet readers.

Contract		
What I Do	My Count	What Happens
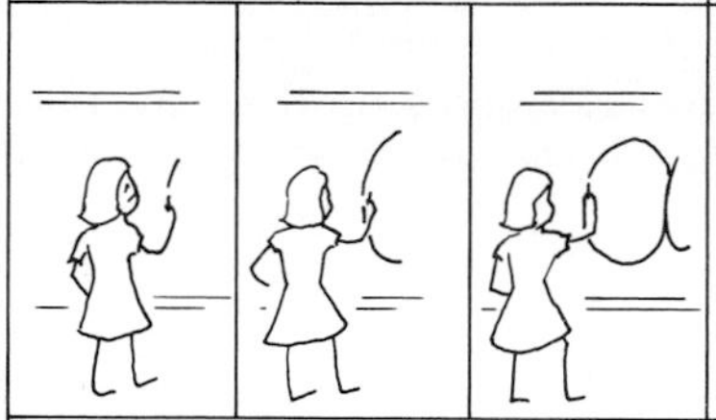	1 2 3 4 5 6 7 8 9 10 11 12 13 14 15 16 17 18	5 = ☆ ☆ ☆ ☆ = 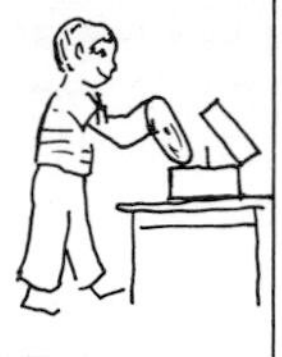

Teacher: ________________
Student: ________________
Dates: ________________

Contract		
What I Do	My Count	What Happens
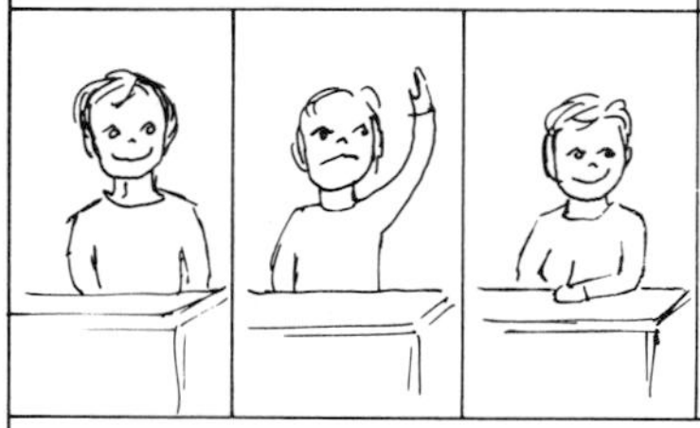	1 2 3 4 5 6 7 8 9 10 11 12 13 14 15 16 17 18 19 20	Each day = get 00000 Lose 0 for each talk out. End of day (L) 00 = 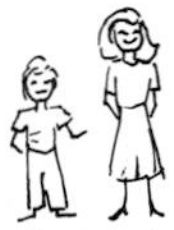 help teacher

Teacher: ________________
Student: ________________
Dates: ________________

From B. Dollar, Leadership Training Institute, University of Minnesota, Minneapolis. Used with permission.

a task may generate anxiety. Thus, the first problem is to pinpoint the specific area. Some examples of specific areas are:

1. *Subject areas.* Multiple mistakes in oral reading, faulty knowledge of the multiplication table, erratic completion of homework assignments, not enough divergent products in art work, and so on. (These must be described in behavioral terms—that is, in terms of something you can see and count with a very low level of inferences.)
2. *Deportment areas.* Hitting others, out-of-seat behavior, shouting out, not talking, never volunteering, excessive profanity, poor attendance, too much staring out of the window, and so on. (Be careful in picking out topics here. We don't want to turn all pupils into "goody two shoes.")
3. *Personal areas.* Negative feelings toward self, putting self down, overly apologetic, hostile feelings, not speaking up for self, never trying a new activity, and so on.

Set up a contract with the pupil The contract should specify who will keep track of the counting, how the chart is to be set up, and how the count is to be kept. Contracts can be developed in almost any area and can even employ pictures to describe the activities for nonreaders.

FIGURE 21.2   A behavior contract for pupils who can read.

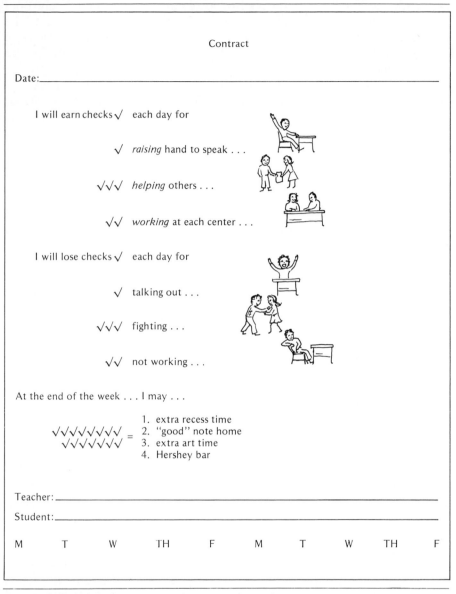

Contract

Date:_____

I will earn checks √   each day for

       √   *raising* hand to speak . . .

     √√√   *helping* others . . .

      √√   *working* at each center . . .

I will lose checks √   each day for

      √   talking out . . .

     √√√   fighting . . .

      √√   not working . . .

At the end of the week . . . I may . . .

√√√√√√√
√√√√√√ =   1. extra recess time
2. "good" note home
3. extra art time
4. Hershey bar

Teacher:_____

Student:_____

M   T   W   TH   F   M   T   W   TH   F

From B. Dollar, Leadership Training Institute, University of Minnesota, Minneapolis. Used with permission.

For example, in the contracts depicted in Figures 21.1 and 21.2, the positive behavior and desired reinforcements are described pictorially.

Other more sophisticated contracts naturally are possible and may specify more complex behaviors. Also, other methods of keeping track of the counting are available. The important point is that the record be visible to the pupil so that he or she can see on a cumulative basis how the score is mounting. This feedback is essential to the system. You could have pupils keep paper charts and graphs, use a plastic grocery-store counter, or have them make a leather bracelet containing small movable beads on strings of pipe cleaners. The one thing to avoid is asking them to keep track of the behaviors in their heads.*

---

* The classic research of George Miller has shown that humans in general can keep about five to seven discrete pieces of "knowledge" in their consciousness at one time. After that point, unless we employ chunking, we become easily confused (see Chapter 11).

Negotiate a significant "award"   There is a debate among behavior theorists as to whether just seeing a line on a chart "improve" is sufficient. In general, with younger pupils the more concrete the reinforcer, the better. There are thousands of funny stories about erroneous choices of reinforcers. For example, one teacher had pupils collect red chips for not speaking out of turn, then exchange five red for one blue, collect two blues and exchange for one gray, and exchange one gray for extra recess time. The children wouldn't exchange blue for gray. They didn't like the color.

It is certainly permissible to discuss the choice of reinforcers with the children. Also realize that you don't have to select conventional reinforcers, like a candy bar, gold stars, or extra recess time. Other possibilities might include open discussion time with you—setting aside a few moments of "special time" between an adult and a child can be an unusually powerful reinforcement. Remember that the quality of time, not quantity, is the crucial aspect. A few moments of focused individual attention can be most meaningful to a child, and for that matter to an adult too!

In setting up the contract, specify rewards for positive behavior. For example, if a student is in constant motion, the contract should reward time spent at his or her desk. As we noted in the preceding chapter, positive reinforcement is both more effective and more humane than punishment. Conversely, if you set up the contract so that the pupil loses privileges for disruptive behavior, you will find that the pupil will become less cooperative in general and more negative toward you in particular.

A final point on the reinforcement schedule is to make sure that the reinforcement itself follows close on the heels of the desired contracted behavior. Long delays between accomplishment and reinforcement are ineffective, in spite of what we may think about building character through self-denial and discipline. B. F. Skinner has commented that a person would never learn to play the piano if he or she had to wait a week to hear the note played. In baseball parks, electric scoreboards explode the very moment a home-run ball lands in the seats. The opera audience does not wait a month to reward an outstanding aria. A doctor is congratulated on the spot after a successful operation.

Don't employ the method too broadly   Try the method in single areas for relatively brief periods of time. It would be an obvious mistake to bombard a child with an endless series of contracts—too much of a good thing, so to speak. Thus, if we have children "charting" in all their subject areas, in a series of personal-management domains, and in extracurricular activities, the entire method of contracting may soon become aversive. The pupils will feel trapped, hemmed in, and rebellious. And that is not an invitation to ask them to keep track of that too!

Naturally, the point of contracts is to help pupils become successful in mastering a variety of tasks. They can provide positive motivation to help children focus their energies, receive positive feedback, and develop a sense of personal mastery in learning. The chart obviously should be used to help a child see how he or she is improving. Each child compares present performance only with his or her past performance. It would be destructive to have children compare themselves with each other, since the whole point of precise teaching to individualize instruction would be lost amid a flurry of competition. If I initially don't know how to read and then learn to recognize *cat*, *hat*, *bat*, and *sat*, that achievement should be regarded as significant in its own right. I should not be asked to compare my progress with that of another pupil who's learning to distinguish cases in Latin.

Cooperative Learning

We have provided a discussion on the use of the cooperative approach in Chapter 18, which will not be repeated here. It is important to remember that the cooperative method means mixing regular and special-education children together. For example, two researchers, Ray McDermott and Jeffrey Aron, set up a video recorder to examine teacher-pupil interaction in recently mainstreamed classes. Unfortunately, the teachers tended to isolate the four or five "new" special-education pupils in each class as a separate group in their classrooms. Thus, instead of four reading groups, there would be five, with similar groupings for math and other small-group activities. As you can see, almost from the start the new pupils were resegregated and clearly identified as different. To make matters worse, when the amount of teacher time was calculated from the video, it became apparent that the pupils in the segregated group had received almost no instruction. The special-education pupils were interrupted forty times in a thirty-minute reading group, whereas the top group of readers was interrupted only two times in the same interval. Thus, time-on-task virtually disappeared for the special-education pupils. The source of the interruptions was either the pupils in the top group or the teacher! The researchers observed, "Almost two-thirds of the time in the reading lesson is spent in either getting a turn or waiting for the teacher to attend to the group."[29]

Student Teams–Achievement Divisions   Robert Slavin of Johns Hopkins University has done a series of studies on actual classroom achievement when special-education children are mainstreamed. The learning tasks are set up as small-group activities with group problem solving. He calls one method the Student Teams–Achievement Divisions (STAD). The students are divided into groups of four or five, with high- and low-achieving students in each. After introducing the lesson content for the week through either direct or indirect teaching methods, the teacher hands out worksheets to each group. The students then quiz each other on the material, have a small-group discussion, and engage in a variety of activities. The final quiz scores within each small group are averaged and extra points are assigned during the semester for "improving" students in each small group. Slavin finds that this protects the slow learner from becoming a dead weight, or in baseball terminology, "an automatic strike-out." Figure 21.3 shows how the weekly team scores are posted. Often the overall rankings shift from week to week.

The advantage of this approach, according to Slavin, is that it reduces destructive competition. Conventional approaches to grading basically lead to an unequal distribution of positive reinforcers. A few excellent students receive all the positives; the rest do not. This does not happen with the cooperative approach, even though the so-called top students are recognized individually as well as through the team efforts. Most important, of course, are the learning outcomes for the special-education students. Rather than being allowed simply to "be," the students show both academic gains and social acceptance gains. Also, and in some ways this may be the most important point of all, the achievement of the other students does not decline; it improves. "This is critical; few schools would use a program designed to aid mainstreamed students if it did not also improve (or at least not retard) the achievement of the rest of the class."[30]

Tutoring

Individual tutoring has a long tradition as a teaching method. Studies have consistently found that effective tutoring is the single most valuable instructional tool in all of teaching. Benjamin Bloom has called it the "two sigma problem."[31] Tutoring yields achievement that is two standard deviations *above* the level of conventional group instruction. In Bloom's study, the average tutored student ranked above 98 percent of the students in the controlled classes.

Since most studies of tutoring were not done with exceptional children, we can't be sure whether the benefit for them would be as great. (Perhaps it would be greater.) We can say, however, that some overall benefit would accrue to mainstreamed children. We also need to note that the study was done with trained tutors. Placing an exceptional child with an untrained tutor does not guarantee success. Under appropriate conditions, however, working with students on an individual basis will promote their learning more effectively than any other technique or even combination of techniques.

But another question needs to be asked: How can teachers employ tutoring for mainstreamed students when they have to teach all the other students as well? The answer is that it's impossible if the teachers must do the tutoring. But if other students (or community volunteers) can be used as tutors, the problem is solved. Research quite clearly shows that children, teenagers, or volunteers can learn fundamental tutoring skills and that such tutoring improves the academic performance and attitudes toward school of the students helped.[32] This means that regular students can participate as tutors for mainstreamed children to help such children learn and prevent them from falling behind.

FIGURE 21.3   Slavin's newsletter: Student Teams–Achievement Divisions.

SPOTSYLVANIA ELEMENTARY SCHOOL

Issue No. 5
March 21, 1981

CALCULATORS OUTFIGURE CLASS!

The Calculators (Charlene, Alfredo, Laura, and Carl) calculated their way into first place this week, with big ten-point scores by Charlene, Alfredo, and Carl, and a near-perfect team score of 38! Their score jumped them from sixth to third in cumulative rank. Way to go Calcs! The Fantastic Four (Frank, Otis, Ursula, and Rebecca) also did a fantastic job, with Ursula and Rebecca turning in ten pointers, but the Tigers (Cissy, Lindsay, Arthur, and Willy) clawed their way from last place last week to a tie with the red-hot Four, who were second the first week, and first last week. The Fantastic Four stayed in first place in cumulative rank. The Tigers were helped out by ten-point scores from Lindsay and Arthur. The Math Monsters (Gary, Helen, Octavia, Ulysses, and Luis) held on to fourth place this week, but due to their big first-place score in the first week they're still in second place in overall rank. Helen and Luis got ten points to help the M.M.'s. Just behind the Math Monsters were the Five Alive (Carlos, Irene, Nancy, Charles, and Oliver), with ten-point scores by Carlos and Charles, and then in order the Little Professors, Fractions, and Brains. Susan turned in ten points for the L.P.'s, as did Linda for the Brains.

This Week's Rank	This Week's Score	Overall Score	Overall Rank
1st – Calculators	38	81	3
2nd – Fantastic Four ⎤ Tie	35	89	1
2nd – Tigers ⎦	35	73	6
4th – Math Monsters	40/32	85	2
5th – Five Alive	37/30	74	5
6th – Little Professors	26	70	8
7th – Fractions	23	78	4
8th – Brains	22	71	7

TEN-POINT SCORERS

Charlene	(Calculators	Helen	(Math Monsters)
Alfredo	(Calculators)	Luis	(Math Monsters)
Carl	(Calculators)	Carlos	(Five Alive)
Ursula	(Fantastic Four)	Charles	(Five Alive)
Rebecca	(Fantastic Four)	Susan	(Little Professors)
Lindsay	(Tigers)	Linda	(Brains)
Arthur	(Tigers)		

* * * * * *

From Slavin, R. E. (1980). Using Student Team Learning, *rev. ed. Baltimore, Md.: Johns Hopkins Team Learning Project. Used with permission.*

Also, such tutoring programs are becoming widely available.

But are we short-changing regular students by having them spend time tutoring other students? Naturally, if students were expected to spend fifteen to twenty hours per week tutoring, it would reduce the time they have for their own tasks. But if the time involved is reasonable (one to four hours per week), tutoring does not adversely affect the student tutor; in fact, it has the opposite effect. Some studies have shown that student tutors actually improve their own level of achievement at a greater rate than those they tutor. Some students have shown psychological gains as well. Student tutors exhibit higher rates of maturity, leadership, and empathy (concern for others) than peers who did not tutor. A carefully run tutoring program, then, benefits both groups. For those tutoring mainstreamed children, it is especially important to provide systematic training. Otherwise, volunteer student helpers may end up with more negative attitudes to exceptional children than they had prior to the experience.[33]

The objectives of tutoring are similar to those of cooperative learning, but the academic gains for tutoring are more clear-cut. Both methods reduce invidious competition. Neither method impairs the achievement of the normal-progress students.

Social Skills Training

You may wonder why a section on teaching effectiveness in a mainstreaming context would focus on social skills training as a special objective. The problem is simply that handicapped children are different from their peers not only in learning achievement but even more so in social skills. Because of both past isolation and current lack of interaction with normal peers, exceptional children often lag behind in rudimentary social abilities. Numerous studies have found that mainstreamed children unfortunately are not necessarily accepted socially by their peers. The base rates of interaction are low. The exceptional child is often ignored, or allowed to just "be."

Social role-taking refers to a process central to Erik Erikson's concept of personality development in stages—namely, the ability to understand where another person is "coming from," or a kind of interpersonal perspective taking. It is an ability that develops from interaction with other people. We aren't born understanding relationships; our role-taking ability grows slowly. Studies have shown that exceptional children lag behind peers on social role-taking.[34] During adolescence the difference increases. For example, prior to adolescence deaf children are approximately only 5 to 10 percent behind on estimates of social and emotional maturity; with the onset of adolescence that figure climbs to 20 percent.[35] Similar shifts are reported with other types of exceptionality. An important aspect of the exceptional child's interpersonal development, then, is being ignored.

The results also suggest something else. Without some planned programs, mixing regular and mainstreamed together produces negative effects on social interaction. Virginia Bruininks has shown that learning-disabled students received the lowest peer-status ratings of all groups in school. Perhaps the most upsetting finding was that learning-disabled students were unaware of their low social status.[36] They did not apparently "understand" that they were acually being ignored and thus weren't aware of the need to improve their social skills to gain some acceptance. For their part, the regular children were content to avoid the "others" as much as possible. We mentioned earlier that

Public Law 94-142 was based on the concept of the least restrictive environment for such children. The irony is that, especially during adolescence, mainstreaming can result in a more restrictive social environment.

Although you obviously cannot alter the social environment of an entire school, by employing some techniques such as social skills training, cooperative learning groups, and individual tutoring, you can reduce some of the isolation. You can also search out counselors and support their efforts to improve the social skills of the children and teen-agers. A recent and extensive review points out that some methods are effective in helping exceptional children fit into the school environment.[37] Also programs such as peer counseling have been shown to be effective as a means of socialization. In general, this aspect of development has been sadly neglected during the mainstreaming process.

Henry Dupont, who reviewed the studies demonstrating the increasing gap in emotional development of special-education students, suggests quite accurately that nearly all such children desperately need more adequate and responsive teaching-learning environments. The vocational adjustment and job success of these pupils are most directly related to their social-emotional adjustment. Social skills and interpersonal competence apparently are central ingredients of success after school. As a result, Dupont draws this conclusion: "All exceptional children need more acceptance as persons of individual worth. They also need an education that helps them develop higher levels of emotional-social maturity."[38] This is as true for the gifted as slow learners (see the accompanying box).

Matching and Gradual Mismatching

This strategy is mostly a reminder of Snow's point at the outset of this section. Effective teaching for special children requires a variety of methods, not one "blanket." In Chapter 13 we suggested that matching and gradual mismatching were in fact central to the process— or the art—of teaching. In David Hunt's sense, then, the same rules apply to mainstreamed students. Especially if you suspect that a partic-

CONTEMPORARY ISSUE

Giftedness: The Road to Elitism?

To some degree, unusually gifted or talented pupils represent a small yet special resource for the country. However, for a variety of reasons the public schools have exhibited almost a paralyzing ambivalence toward programs for such children. Our schools have been characterized as swinging from cool to cold on the question of giftedness. Apparently, it somehow seems undemocratic to admit that occasionally a particular child may be in a completely different league from the rest of the pupils, as a result of unique talents.

The fear of elitism also tends to accompany such a view. After all, so the critics argue, Plato, who distrusted democracy, suggested in *The Republic* that gifted children receive special consideration. Such treatment could be considered unfair to other children, rather like robbing Peter to pay Paul. The vision of a small elite cadre of a master race creates a shudder in the minds (and hearts) of most of us. The movie *The Prime of Miss Jean Brodie* explored just this kind of vision. In the movie, Miss Brodie calmly explains her goal of

shaping and directing the minds of "her" girls—the *crème de la crème*! In this view, the cream of the crop will lead, while the rest of us will meekly follow our betters.

Yet, is such a vision—or nightmare—the inevitable outcome of some kind of enriched program for those few who are enormously talented? If we admit that such children do exist, must it mean the creation of an antidemocratic master cadre? Obviously, the answers to such questions are crucial. As it stands now, with barely a handful of school programs in existence, very little is being done. Unfortunately, it is not always the case that such children will survive and thrive no matter what is done or not done for them. Although many do survive the educational experience, they are simply turned off by an unstimulating lock-step curriculum. Probably the greatest difficulty in all this is what happens to the individual teacher. Without policy or delineated programs, the teacher is usually left with a "just do your best" comment. Imagine what it might

be like if you're teaching in the third grade, following a nicely packaged age-graded curriculum, and you find a modern-day John Stuart Mill in your class, who has read and understood most of the Harvard Classics, has composed complicated musical scores, and has begun to work out new forms for democratic government—all prior to grade one!

The problem is obvious. We do need to rethink our approach to education. On the one hand, it is clearly important not to turn our schools into breeding grounds for antidemocratic elitism. On the other hand, what of our educators' credo that states our goal, namely, to stimulate and nurture the development of each child? Aren't unusually gifted children included in this credo?

At the present time there are three general approaches to the education of the gifted—enrichment, acceleration, and separation—each with proponents and with equally strong opponents. Enrichment involves giving gifted children who remain in regular age-graded classrooms additional

ular student is functioning at a very concrete, or even preoperational, level in Piaget's scheme (low CL in Hunt's scheme), then it is clearly most appropriate to match with high structure and all the elements of that approach. You also need to watch academic performance for signs of growth toward more independence as a learner. Watch for possible differences in levels of functioning in different subject areas or in different parts of the same subject. The major mistake to avoid is assuming that a child who may be classified as a slow learner is slow in all areas. Because none of the common assessment methods really tap all the different components

of what we commonly call "intelligence," be alert to any variation in school performance. By adjusting the teaching strategy, then gradual mismatching, you will increase the probability of developmental growth. Stages of development are not permanent classifications.

THE INDIVIDUALIZED EDUCATION PLAN

With these five strategies in mind, we now turn to the question of mainstreaming and lesson planning. In general, Madeline Hunter's system

experiences, special projects, and independent studies.[a] The critics say this is a poor compromise and only a minor adjustment; it doesn't meet the needs of gifted students. Acceleration involves a type of pull-out approach. In areas of gifted achievement—for example, math—the student leaves the regular class to attend an advanced class, usually with older children. Critics quickly point out that such an approach might help develop mathematical thinking but it might be very awkward interpersonally to be the only eleven-year-old in a high-school class. Separation involves a type of ability grouping, such as clustering all the students with an IQ of 135 or above in one class. In other words, a special-education classroom is created for the profoundly gifted. Critics immediately comment that such placement is really segregation but in a slightly different form. These critics also note that homogeneous grouping has never been shown to be effective

as a method of educational treatment.

Does it help to turn to research? Only partially. Recent meta-analyses show that the accelerated approach yields superior gains when compared to the other methods. The difficulty is that the outcome measures are focused only on academic achievement.[b] What may be happening psychologically to such gifted children has not been examined in any depth since the original studies of Lewis Terman some fifty years ago.

At this point then it may be safe to conclude that special programs for gifted and talented students remain controversial. The accelerated, or pull-out, approach does result in higher academic performance. The results of the other methods are much less clear-cut. However, the other effects of accelerated instruction have not been studied. Perhaps the main recommendation at the moment is to proceed with cau-

tion. The quality of the research in this area is not impressive, particularly in its attempts to assess the psychological or self-concept effects of special education on the gifted.[c] Indeed it is possible to view the research base in this area as neither particularly gifted nor talented. From a developmental view, the question is quite broad. How do we as educators "match and mismatch" with gifted students, being sure to interact in such a manner as to promote intellectual, interpersonal, personal, and value growth?

---

[a]   See Clark, B. (1983). *Growing up gifted.* Columbus, Ohio: Merrill. The book reviews actual classroom practice regarding enrichment, acceleration, and separate experiences.
[b]   Kulik, J. A., and Kulik, C-L. (1984). Synthesis of research on effects of accelerated instruction. *Educational Leadership, 42*(2), 84–90.
[c]   See Horowitz, F. O., and O'Brien, M. (Eds.). (1985). *The gifted and talented: Developmental perspectives.* Washington, D.C.: American Psychological Association.

---

is the most effective method for instructional planning. However, as more and more special-education students enter the regular classroom, the range of individual differences does increase. In order to ensure that the newly mainstreamed are not lost in the shuffle, the law includes a provision for an individualized education plan (IEP), which is basically a lesson plan for one child at a time.

The plan is created by a team made up of (1) the teacher, (2) the psychological assessment specialist, (3) the special-education resource consultant, and (4) a school administrator. Its purpose is to set out specific learning objectives in a timetable and to identify how the outcomes are to be evaluated. Perhaps the most unique feature of this approach is that the plan must be accepted and approved by the parent. When

first proposed, this feature of the IEP met with some resistance from school professionals, since in effect they must share the authority for the plan with parents. Also, further underlining the importance of this new approach, the parents had the right to bring in their own specialists, such as an independent psychological consultant and even a lawyer. After an initial period, however, the IEP approach has been largely accepted. School personnel and parents have found common ground in working out realistic goals and strategies for specific children. The plan starts where the learner is currently functioning and outlines the details. Each plan is reviewed every six months and includes:

1. Current academic performance level

2. Goals and objectives

3. Specific services to be provided

4. The designation of school personnel and their roles

5. Where and on what schedule the service will be provided

6. An evaluation plan

In the light of some ten years of experience, the IEP is no longer seen as a radical change in educational philosophy but rather as a useful method to prescribe manageable learning objectives for children who otherwise might be overlooked in the fast pace and complex environment of a regular class. The document does protect the child's interests and serves as a reminder of his or her individual needs. You may find it initially awkward setting up IEPs. With so many points of view represented, the first few conferences will be somewhat confusing and perhaps even frustrating. After a while, though, you will see that an IEP is just a lesson plan that is very concrete and specific. You will have a clearer sense of what you can accomplish plus access to a resource team to help with the implementation. You will also find that, as your confidence increases, you will provide more and more suggestions for goals and methods to improve the classroom performance.

THE CASE FOR MAINSTREAMING

In 1975, just prior to his death, Nicholas Hobbes, an eminent educational psychologist and clinician, headed a national commission charged with the responsibility of examining the problems of special-education classification systems. In a work significantly titled *The Futures of Children*,[39] Hobbes advanced the thesis that a comprehensive educational plan is required to classify children according to the services they need rather than the capabilities they lack. Special education and regular education essentially need the same point of view—namely, to create and emphasize educational programs that start where the learner is and then stimulate and nurture positive development. Both new skills and positive attitudes are needed for educational success in this area. For too long we have been satisfied to follow policies that have too often been designed to exclude or segregate significant numbers of children not only from the mainstream of schooling but from life as well. When so-called retarded children are placed in regular classrooms containing effective accommodative capacities, the pupils make as much educational progress as they would if they remained in separate classes (sometimes more). In addition to "academic" learning, such pupils all gain socially: Their self-concepts become more positive, less stigmatized, and less characterized by self-hatred and self-contempt.

A key factor in the entire concept of mainstreaming is the phrase *"increasing the accommodative capacity* of all classrooms to respond to a broad range of *individual differences."* A responsive humane environment with positive regard for all children and sets of manageable learning tasks represents an appropriate learning atmosphere for *all* children. In other words, we can either say that special education becomes less "special" or that all education becomes more special and significant for each child.

SUMMARY

Traditional educational practices for dealing with exceptional children involved remolding their characters so that they fit in society, excluding them from a society in which they did not fit, or segregating them from other so-called normal children. Under a new policy, mainstreaming, legislation requires that previously excluded groups of children now enter regular classrooms under the dictum that children should be educated in the least restrictive environments possible.

Nine designations of exceptionality have been set up; however, problems of accurate diagnosis and effective placement are substantial. The rate of error in diagnosis is highest in the categories that include the most children—mental retardation, learning disability, and emotional disturbance. As a result, traditional methods of dealing with exceptional children cannot be relied on. New approaches, such as Deno's system of graded educational environments that stress movement up as far and as fast as possible and other educators' emphasis on active learning and short-term, temporary placements for the exceptional, offer more promising alternatives.

The question of teaching strategies for special-education students is also important. Haberman has demonstrated that teaching strategies that are effective for "regular" students are just as effective with exceptional children; only a few procedures are needed in addition. Teachers must especially guard against fostering and maintaining a sense of learned helplessness so common among handicapped students.

The most useful teaching methods that can also be used with special-education students are: (1) precise teaching, (2) cooperative learning, (3) tutoring, (4) social skills training, and (5) matching and gradual mismatching. These strategies, taken as a whole, would help increase the accommodative capacity of regular classrooms and hence increase the learning potential of all pupils.

In using these methods with exceptional children, teachers can benefit their pupils most by also employing an individualized education plan (IEP). The plan is formulated by a school services team and is then revised according to student progress. Careful attention to teaching strategies can help the mainstreamed student progress both academically and socially, as he or she gains a more positive self-concept.

KEY TERMS AND NAMES

remolding
exclusion
segregation
mainstreaming
Public Law 94-142
handicapping condition
Maynard Reynolds

dyslexia
Maria Montessori
Martin Haberman
learned helplessness
precise teaching
Student Teams–Achievement Divisions
individualized education plans (IEP)

REFERENCES

1. Bakan, D. (1971). *The slaughter of the innocents*. San Francisco: Jossey-Bass.

2. Dormer, S. (1975). The relationship of physical handicap to stress in families with an adolescent with spina bifida. *Developmental Medical Child Neurology, 17,* 765–776.

3. Lee, H. (1962). *To kill a mockingbird* (pp. 31–32). New York: Popular Library.

4. Blatt, B. (1958). The physical, personality and academic status of children who are mentally retarded attending special classes as compared with children who are mentally retarded attending regular classes. *American Journal of Mental Deficiency, 62,* 810–818.

5. Baroff, G. S. (1974). *Mental retardation: Nature, cause, and management*. New York: Wiley.

6. Reynolds, M. (1972). *Exceptional children in regular classrooms*. Minneapolis: University of Minnesota, Department of Audio-Visual Extension.

7. Salvia, J., and Ysseldyke, J. (1981). *Assessment in special and remedial education*. Boston: Houghton Mifflin.

8. Reynolds, M. C. (1984). Classification of students with handicaps. In E. W. Gordon (Ed.), *Review of educational research* (pp. 63–92). Washington, D.C.: American Educational Research Association.

9. Grossman, H. J. (Ed.) (1983). *Classification in mental retardation*. Washington, D.C.: American Association on Mental Deficiency. See also Design for Change (1983). *Caught in the web: Misplaced children in Chicago's classes for the mentally retarded*. Chicago, Ill.: Design for Change (220 South State Street, Suite 1616, Chicago 60604).

10. Wood, F., and Lakin, C. (1979). *Disturbing or disturbed?* Reston, Va.: Council for Exceptional Children.

11. Reynolds, Classification of students with handicaps (p. 77). Of course, there is no guarantee that such a cross-categorical grouping as LD, ED, and MR will be universally accepted. In fact, one leading special educator has predicted a parental uproar from the LD groups. "Disbelievers are encouraged to ask leaders of their local LD group for reactions to a suggestion to combine LD and MR. However, please do not cite me as the originator of the idea." Reschly, D. J. (1984). Beyond I.Q. test bias. *Educational Researcher, 13*(4), 17.

12. Messick, S. (1984). Assessment in context: Appraising performance in relation to instructional quality. *Educational Researcher, 13*(3), 5.

13. Messick, Assessment in context, 8.

14. Clearly, T. A., quoted in Reynolds, M. R. (1984). Classification of students with handicaps. In E. W. Gordon (Ed.), *Review of educational research* (p. 78). Washington, D.C.: American Educational Research Association.

15. Fuin, J. D., and Resnick, L. (1984). Issues in the instruction of mildly mentally retarded children. *Educational Researcher, 13*(3), 9–11.

16. *Riles* v. *Larry P.* (1979). San Francisco Federal District Court, Judge Robert Peckham C-71–2270 RFP.

17. Axline, V. (1967). *Dibs* (p. 90). Boston: Houghton Mifflin.

18. Deno, E. (1970). Special education as developmental capital. *Exceptional Children, 37*, 229–237.

19. Skodak, M., and Skeels, H. M. (1949). A final follow-up study on one hundred adopted children. *Journal of Genetic Psychology, 75*, 85–125.

20. Scarr-Salapatek, S., and Weinberg, R. (1975). The war over race and IQ. *Psychology Today, 9*(7), 80–82.

21. Birch, W. J. (1974). *Mainstreaming* (p. 94). Reston, Va.: Council for Exceptional Children.

22. Hunt, D., and Sullivan, E. (1974). *Between psychology and education*. New York: Dryden.

23. Ysseldyke, J. E., and Algozzine, B. (1982). *Critical issues in special and remedial education*. Boston: Houghton Mifflin.

24. Haberman, M. (1980). Principles of in-service training for implementation of mainstreaming in the public schools. In D. C. Corrigan and K. Howey (Eds.), *Concepts to guide the education of experienced teachers* (pp. 53–64). Reston, Va.: Council for Exceptional Children.

25. Seligman, M. E. P. (1975). *Helplessness*. San Francisco: Freeman.

26. Chess, S., and Gordon, S. (1984). Psychosocial development and human variance. In E. W. Gordon (Ed.), *Review of educational research* (p. 44). Washington, D.C.: American Educational Research Association.

27. See Chess and Gordon, Psychosocial development and human variance (p. 29).

28. Snow, R. (1984). Placing children in special education. *Educational Researcher, 13*(3), 12–14.

29. McDermott, R. P., and Aron, J. (1978). Pirandello in the classroom: On the possibility of equal educational opportunity in American culture. In M. C. Reynolds (Ed.), *Futures of education for exceptional students* (p. 57). Reston, Va.: Council for Exceptional Children.

30. Slavin, R. E. (1983). *Cooperative learning* (p. 100). New York: Longman.

31. Bloom, B. S. (1984). The 2 sigma problem: The search for methods as effective as one-

to-one tutoring. *Educational Researcher, 13*(6), 4–16.

32. Sharpley, A., Irvin, J., and Sharpley, C. (1983). An examination of the effectiveness of a cross-age tutoring program in mathematics for elementary school children. *American Educational Research Journal, 20*(1), 103–111. See also Foster, E. S. (1985). *Tutoring: Learning by helping.* Minneapolis: Educational Media. And also Tindall, J. A. (1985). *Peer power: Becoming an effective peer helper.* Muncie, Ind.: Accelerated Development.

33. Sprinthall, N. A., and Blum, M. (1980). Peer and cross age teaching: Promoting social and psychological development in mainstream classes. In M. C. Reynolds (Ed.), *Social environment of the schools.* Reston, Va.: Council for Exceptional Children. See also Sprinthall, N. A. (1980). Psychology for secondary schools: The saber-tooth curriculum revisited? *American Psychologist, 35*(4), 336–347. The article discusses the positive effects of such role-taking programs in general.

34. Perry, J., and Krebs, D. (1980). Role-taking, moral development and mental retardation. *Journal of Genetic Psychology, 136*, 95–108.

35. Dupont, H. (1978). Meeting the emotional-social needs of students in a mainstream environment. *Counseling and Human Development, 10*(9), 1–11.

36. Bruininks, V. (1978). Actual and perceived peer status of learning-disabled students in mainstream programs. *Journal of Special Education, 12*(1), 51–58.

37. Gresham, F. M. (1981). Social skills training with handicapped children: A review. *Review of Educational Research, 51*(1), 139–176.

38. Dupont, H. (1978), Meeting the emotional-social needs of students, 11.

39. Hobbs, N. (1975). *The futures of children.* San Francisco: Jossey-Bass.

GLOSSARY

Jerome Bruner has said that the student must have a background of facts, "the stuff of learning," before discovery learning can take place. The glossary that follows helps provide the "stuff" for creative thinking in educational psychology.

Listening to lectures or reading text material, the student new to the field often becomes dismayed over the number of technical terms and seemingly endless jargon. But the forbidding jargon is an attempt to be precise. In order to understand the more global concepts in educational psychology, the student must master the tools of the trade, the methods and terms used by educational psychologists in communication with each other.

The glossary entries define specific terms, outline broad theoretical positions, or provide a brief biography of some of the significant persons in educational psychology. Every entry is a self-contained unit, giving complete information. Though there is some cross-referencing, this has deliberately been kept to a minimum. Where essential, you are directed to one or two additional entries in order to develop a complete thought. The number in parentheses at the end of each entry indicates the chapter in which the concept is discussed.

Accommodation

Concept used by Piaget in his discussion of cognitive development. Accommodation is the adjustment the individual makes when incorporating external reality. Piaget uses this concept in conjunction with *assimilation*, which is the individual's ability to internalize and conceptualize his or her environmental experiences. Accommodation is the individual's response to the immediate and compelling environmental demands that have been and are being assimilated. *See also* Assimilation. (5)

Achievement Motivation

A possibly intrinsic motive to achieve just for the sake of achieving, rather than the achievement being in the service of some other motive. Research shows that the most important single ingredient in achievement motivation is a feeling of self-directed competence. (19)

Acquired Motives

Motives that are based on the activation of psychological needs, such as approval, affection, power, and prestige. Such motives are said to have been learned. (19)

Active School

Based on Jean Piaget's ideas, the concept suggests that learning will be enhanced through active, or "hands on," experiences in combination with thoughtful reflection. Piaget's dictum states, "To know by heart is not to know." Passive memorization does not necessarily mean that the pupil has really learned or understood the concepts. (5)

After-Only Experimental Design

See Experimental Design.

American Question

According to Jean Piaget, any question about how to accelerate cognitive stage growth. Piaget suggests that Americans may be preoccupied with a concern for developmental teaching programs that are designed to speed up the naturally unfolding stages of cognitive growth. Some recent programs of infant stimulation are examples of Piaget's concern. (5)

Anal Stage

Second of Freud's psychosexual stages of development. During this stage, the child takes great pleasure, first in the act of defecating, and later in the act of withholding the feces. This stage usually takes place between the ages of eighteen months and three years. The first part of this stage is called the "anal expulsive" stage, which later develops into the "anal retentive" stage. Freud says that the way in which the child is treated during this stage (toilet training, etc.) makes a permanent imprint on the later adult personality. (6)

Anastasi, Anne (1909–)

A past president (1971) of the American Psychological Association, Anne Anastasi has written on a wide variety of subjects in the field, ranging from the psychology of art to the nature-nurture controversy. She is best known, however, for her work in statistics and test construction. A firm believer in IQ tests, she feels that discontinuing the IQ test would be like asking a physician to throw away the thermometer just because children who are ill register an undesirable deviation from the norm. In her 1958 paper "Heredity, Environment and the Question 'How?' "

Anastasi put the nature-nurture controversy in perspective. Instead of asking which component, heredity or environment, contributes more to the child's development, the better question is *how* heredity and environment interact in the development of behavioral differences. She also cites the importance of early experience on intellectual growth and development. (15)

Approval (Need for)

A social or acquired need for being accepted and positively evaluated by other persons. The need for approval is thought to be based on the individual's desire, learned in infancy, to be loved by his or her mother or primary caregiver. (19)

Artificial Intelligence

The simulation of human thinking by the use of a computer program. Programs attempt to parallel the human thought process. Artificial intelligence is based not only on our current understanding of how humans think but also on the fond hope that through the use of the program as a model our current understanding of thought processes will be increased. (11)

A/S Ratio

The A/S ratio is a concept developed by D. O. Hebb, the Canadian physiological psychologist. Hebb developed the ratio by comparing the amount of brain space devoted to association areas to the amount devoted to sensory areas. As he went up the phylogenetic ladder, from rat to monkey to humans, Hebb found an ever-increasing A/S ratio. Rats, with their lower A/S ratio, are more sensory-bound, whereas humans, with a higher A/S ratio, are capable of far more varied and greater amounts of learning. (4)

Assimilation

Concept used by Jean Piaget in his theory of cognitive development. Assimilation is the process of taking within, or internalizing, one's environmental experience. Assimilation is used by Piaget in conjunction with the concept of accommodation. Piaget believes that assimilation is a spontaneous process on the part of the child *See also* Accommodation. (5)

Attitudes

A *learned* predisposition to respond either positively or negatively to persons, situations, or things. Attitudes carry a strong emotional component and therefore can never be neutral. When a negative attitude is generalized to include an entire group of people, it is called a "stereotype." This can be destructive to the holder of the stereotype as well as to the group about which it is held. It can be especially destructive to the minority group member's self-image. (18)

Attribute-Treatment Interaction (ATI)

Framework, devised by David Hunt, that suggests that effective teaching should be a match between the developmental stage characteristics of the learner and both the process and content of the teaching program. At different conceptual levels (CLs), students have different needs regarding the amount of structure a teacher should employ and how concrete or abstract concepts being presented should be. Effectiveness requires starting where the learner is, then gradually removing the structure and increasing the abstractness of the concepts being taught. The term "stage" in Hunt's system refers to the currently preferred learning style rather than any sort of permanent classification. (13)

Ausubel, David (1918–)

Educational theorist who has contributed, among other things, the concept of advanced organizers to a model of teaching. His system involves providing learners with a clear set of objectives in advance of the presentation in order that they become oriented to the planned goals of the lesson. This model forms the basis for much of what is called the "direct instruction" approach. (12)

Authoritarian Leadership

Style of leadership in which the individual holding the leadership position retains all the decision-making power. (18)

Autokinetic Effect

A visual effect produced when a small but stationary pinpoint of light in an otherwise darkened room *appears* to move. Since the light remains physically stationary, and since the perceived movement is only apparent, the autokinetic effect has been used to further our understanding of how group norms emerge. Experiments using the autokinetic effect have been performed by social psychologist Muzafer Sherif. (18)

Bandura, Albert (1925–)

Originator of social learning theory, which suggests that learning may take place not just on the basis of straight reinforcement principles, but also as a result of a process called "modeling." Bandura insists that people may learn new responses simply by observing the behavior of others. (10)

Bayley, Nancy (1899–)

Developmental psychologist and author of the famous Berkeley Growth Study. Bayley was the first woman ever to win the American Psychological Association's Distinguished Scientific Contribution award. Bayley's major findings have been that:

1. IQs are not constant.
2. IQ variability is greatest during the first few years of life.
3. Intellectual growth may continue throughout life.
4. The components of intellect change with age level. (4)

Becker, Howard (1928–)

Investigator of the relationship between the social class of the teacher and pupil attitudes. He found many teachers from the lower-middle class had difficulty accepting students from either lower or higher socioeconomic levels.

BEEP

The Brookline Early Education Project, set up by Burton White and others. The purpose of the project was to enhance psychological development of children from eight to eighteen months of age. (4)

Before-After Experimental Design

See Experimental Design.

Behavior Genetics

A fairly new discipline within the field of animal psychology, concerned with the effects of genotype on behavior. Specifically, the behavior geneticist studies the effect of genetic differences on behavioral differences *within a population*. The method of study typically used is that of selective breeding and/or the use of inbred animal strains. An example would be Robert Tryon's study (1940) in which maze-bright and maze-dull rats were selectively bred and then compared over several generations according to their ability to run a maze. It must be pointed out that behavior genetics *is not* allied with the now discredited instinct theory. (3)

Behavior Modification

A system for changing behavior based on the principles of conditioning. The term "behavior modification," or, "behavior mod," is usually applied either to the classroom or to a patient undergoing therapy. When desirable behavior is exhibited, it is followed by a reinforcing stimulus; when undesirable behavior is emitted, it is followed either by no reinforcement (extinction) or, less commonly, by punishment. It is important when using this system that: (1) goals be defined precisely *and in behavioral terms,* and (2) the conditioning schedule be followed with absolute consistency. (10)

Behaviorism

A school of thought in psychology usually considered to have originated in the work and writings of John B. Watson. In 1913 Watson outlined the behaviorist position in his paper "Psychology as the Behaviorist Views It." Watson argued there against the use of introspection in gathering psychological data. He considered observable behavior the only valid data in psychology. According to Watson, any concepts, like mind or consciousness, that have mentalistic overtones must be purged from the field of psychology. The most famous current spokesperson for this tradition is Harvard University's B. F. Skinner. (8)

Binet, Alfred (1857–1911)

Originator of psychology's first modern intelligence test (1905). In assembling his test, this French psychologist set up a series of intellectual tasks, as opposed to the sensorimotor tasks previously used by Sir Frances Galton. Binet also introduced the concept of mental age as the basis for scoring his later tests (1908). The original Binet test items were later used as the basis for the famous Stanford-Binet intelligence test (1916), published in the United States by Lewis M. Terman. The test was scored on the basis of a ratio between one's mental age and one's chronological age. This ratio, multiplied by 100, is known as the Intelligence Quotient, or IQ. *See also* Intelligence Quotient, Stanford-Binet Test. (16)

Blatt, Moshe (1945–)

This graduate student of Kohlberg's was the first to try out value-reasoning programs with school students. He found that students can gradually develop more complex thinking ability through carefully guided and extensive discussions of moral dilemmas. (7)

Bloom, Benjamin S. (1913–)

American educational psychologist and professor at the University of Chicago and Northwestern. He is most widely known for his work in two important areas in educational psychology:
1. Bloom sought to describe systematically the classroom teacher's educational goals, and methods for achieving those goals. This work is called his "taxonomy for educational objectives."

2. Bloom also published the now classic *Stability and Change in Human Characteristics* (1964), which outlined an early-experience position regarding intellectual growth. Bloom maintained that there is a decreasing positive effect from a beneficial environment on intellectual growth as the child gets older. Three-year-old children profit far more from enriching experiences than do seven- or eight-year-old children. (4)

Bonding

A process occurring between mother and child, seen by some to be similar to imprinting. Bonding requires direct physical contact between the mother and child and must occur within the baby's first three days of life. It produces a strong emotional attachment between the two. Failure to form this bond has been hypothesized as the cause for later episodes of child neglect and even abuse. (3)

Bornstein's Infant Intelligence Test

Intelligence test used on six-month-old babies and based on how long it takes a baby to process information about moving stimuli. Marc Bornstein discovered significant correlations between his infant test scores and the IQ scores on Wechsler scales taken four years later. (16)

Brainstorming

A technique for generating new ideas in which individuals get together in a group and are urged to interact freely and call out any idea, no matter how seemingly bizarre. Brainstorming is used in many businesses, especially in areas where creativity is important, as in an advertising agency mapping out a new campaign. The actual research on brainstorming, however, casts some doubt on its effectiveness, with regard to both the number of new ideas and the quality of the ideas produced by the group. (18)

Bruner, Jerome S. (1915–)

Researcher of such varied subjects as propaganda techniques, the effect of need on perception, and most important, how people obtain knowledge and how they develop intellectually. In 1960, Bruner founded Harvard's Center for Cognitive Studies, and although he didn't invent cognitive psychology, he went a long way toward making it systematic and consistent with the rules of science. Perhaps Bruner's most famous statement is that any subject can be taught effectively in some intellectually honest form to any child at any stage of development. He stresses discovery learning and communication at three levels: enactive, iconic, and symbolic. (9)

Cattell, James McKeen (1860–1944)

A pioneer in the field of intelligence testing. Cattell, an American, studied both in Germany under Wilhelm Wundt and in England under Sir Francis Galton. He brought the message of European psychology back to America, and in 1888 he was appointed to the first professorship in psychology anywhere in the world. As Galton had done previously, Cattell devised a series of sensorimotor tests (auditory range, visual range, reaction time, etc.), designed to measure human intellectual potential by testing people's sensorimotor equipment. Cattell taught for many years at Columbia University, and on his illustrious list of students are the names E. L. Thorndike, R. S. Woodworth, and E. K. Strong.

Cattell is credited with fathering the mental-testing movement in the United States, and in fact it was Cattell, in 1890, who first used the term "mental test." (2)

Cell Assembly

Concept used by D. O. Hebb in describing cognitive growth. The cell assembly defines the action of a group of brain cells, organized into a coherent unit, and enabling the young child to learn at an ever-increasing rate. The child learns slowly and ploddingly when operating at the single-cell level, but after cell assemblies are formed in the brain, the child's learning speed increases dramatically. (4)

Character Education

Education to develop character through inculcation and brainwashing. Researching has shown it to be ineffective; rather, character appears to develop in stages as more democratic and humane values are incorporated. (20)

Charisma

Term used in describing a leader, or a leadership trait or quality, as in a charismatic leader. An individual who has charisma is thought to possess a kind of animal magnetism or hypnotic appeal. The power of a charismatic leader is seen by some as being almost mystical in its spellbinding appeal. When a charismatic person enters a room, the room is supposed to be suddenly charged with excitement. (18)

Chi square (χ^2)

A statistical test of significance used to determine whether or not frequency differences have occurred on the basis of chance. Whenever the researcher is interested in the actual number of cases (frequency of occurrence) that fall into two or more discrete categories, chi square becomes the appropriate statistical test. It is considered to be a nonparametric test since no population assumptions are required for its use. The basic equation is:

$$\chi^2 = \frac{\Sigma \ (f_o - f_e)^2}{f_e}$$

where f_o denotes the frequencies actually observed and f_e the frequencies expected on the basis of chance. (17)

Chomsky, Noam (1928–)

American psychologist interested in cognitive growth through language development. Chomsky has severely criticized the typical American learning-theory explanation of language as the result of straight conditioning. Chomsky insists that the conditioning model of language development simply doesn't fit with the facts. Children learn the use of language far more quickly than the conditioning theory can explain. Chomsky explains this rapid rate of language development on the basis of a built-in capacity for language acquisition. That is, a baby enters the world genetically prewired, or born with biological givens that direct the course of language development. (9)

Chromosome

Long, threadlike bits of protein. Each cell of the human body contains twenty-three pairs. Egg and sperm cells, however, carry only twenty-three chromosomes, or just half the number contained in other body cells. An infant receives half of its chromosomes from each parent at conception, twenty-three from the sperm cell and twenty-three from the egg cell, thus achieving its full complement. (3)

Chunking

The grouping together of several separate items in order to aid in their recall. Remembering digits that have been grouped in threes is an example of chunking. It is easier to retrieve the number 103, than the separate numbers one, zero, and three. (11)

Clark, Kenneth B. (1914–)

Noted black educator, psychologist, and professor at City College of New York. Clark's 1950 report on the effects of segregation in the schools was used extensively by the Supreme Court justices in their historic 1954 decision declaring segregation in public schools unconstitutional. Clark has worked and written in a wide variety of areas within the fields of educational and social psychology. (18)

Classical Conditioning

Term used to describe conditioning techniques introduced by Ivan P. Pavlov. It is the pairing of a conditioned stimulus with an unconditioned stimulus over long numbers of trials until the conditioned stimulus alone has the power to elict the conditioned response. During the conditioning trials, the conditioned stimulus acts as a signal that the unconditioned stimulus will follow, and the organism thus eventually learns to respond to the conditioned stimulus alone. In Pavlov's basic experiment, a dog was conditioned to salivate to the sound of a tone. The tone was presented (conditioned stimulus), followed by meat powder (unconditioned stimulus), until the dog began salivating just to the tone. (8)

Cognitive Dissonance

Concept introduced by social psychologist Leon Festinger. Individuals prefer to maintain a state of equilibrium among their various attitudes, beliefs, and behavior. Inconsistency between thoughts and actions sets up within the individual a state of cognitive dissonance, an uncomfortable state that the individual attempts to resolve by changing either his or her actions or beliefs. It is far more comfortable, and thus desirable from the individual's point of view, to attain cognitive consonance over cognitive dissonance. (18)

Cognitive Learning

The view that learning is based on a restructuring of perceptions and thoughts occurring within the organism. This restructuring allows the learner to perceive new relationships, solve new problems, and gain understanding of a subject area. Cognitive learning theorists stress the reorganization of one's perceptions in order to achieve understanding, as opposed to the conditioning theorists who stress the importance of associations formed between stimuli and responses. Gestalt psychology has been oriented toward the cognitive view of learning. (8)

Cohesiveness

A concept introduced by social psychologist Leon Festinger. Cohesiveness describes those positive forces that hold a group together and prevent its deterioration. Cohesiveness is one of the few truly group concepts in social psychology. It can be thought of as the cement that binds the group together, or the attraction of the group for its members. Group cohesiveness can be increased by (1) friendly interaction, (2) cooperation, (3) increased group status, (4) an outside threat, or (5) democratic rather than authoritarian leadership. (18)

Competence Motivation

Theory developed by the personality theorist Robert White. White feels that all humans, and even some animals, have a basic drive to achieve competence as a way of developing control over their environments. People have a need to be competent in some area. Of course, as competence increases, so too does enjoyment. Competence is a key concept for many educators, and is viewed as being synonymous with personal mastery and self-direction. (6)

Computer-Assisted Instruction (CAI)

Use of the computer, especially the microcomputer, as a "private tutor," constantly monitoring a student's progress and allowing a student to proceed at his or her own rate. The program, or software tutorial, may take a student through a discrete lesson unit and during its running allow many choices. A student's error, if it occurs, automatically triggers a program review of the material not fully comprehended. (10)

Concept Formation

In the information-processing model, the processing of data by identifying certain characteristics of incoming information and then organizing the information in such a way as to provide encoded meaning. (11)

Conceptual Level

Applied to teachers, David Hunt's concept that teachers process experience at different levels, according to their stage of conceptual development, and behave in the classroom accordingly. At the least complex level, stage A, teachers tend to view knowledge as fixed truth and pupils as passive memorizers of rote facts. At a more advanced level, stage B, teachers perceive their role as more interactive, and they emphasize a combination of goals, including promoting pupil development. Teachers functioning at the highest level, stage C, exhibit the broadest variety of teaching methods keyed specifically to pupil needs and their levels of understanding. *See also* Hunt, David. (13)

Concordance Rate

Term used in behavior genetics to denote the percentage of co-twins exhibiting a specific phenotypic trait. (3)

Concrete Operations Stage

A stage of thinking, according to Jean Piaget, that is characteristic of the period from ages seven to eleven.

At this stage thinking is based on specifics and literal-mindedness. The child using this mode of thought is objective and logical, but almost too literal-minded. The child wants facts and wants the facts to be specific, but he or she cannot separate facts from hypotheses during this stage. (5)

Conditioned Reinforcement

Sometimes called "secondary reinforcement," it describes the situation in which a previously neutral stimulus acquires reinforcing power by being repeatedly associated with a primary reinforcer. The sequence of events for establishing conditioned reinforcement is as follows: (1) response; (2) neutral stimulus, such as a light or buzzer; (3) the primary reinforcer, such as a pellet of food. In the classroom conditioned reinforcers might be good grades, prizes, promotions, and generalized social approval. The use of tokens by behavior-modification proponents is another example of conditioned reinforcement at work in the classroom. (9)

Conditioned Response

Term used both in classical conditioning and in operant conditioning. In classical conditioning, the conditioned response is the response being elicited by the conditioned stimulus. The stronger the conditioning, the greater the magnitude of the conditioned response and the shorter its latency. In Pavlov's experiment the conditioned response was the dog's salivation to the tone.

In operant conditioning, since the response must precede the reinforcer, the conditioned response is defined not in terms of magnitude or latency, but in terms of either the rate of the response or its resistance to extinction. For example, a strongly conditioned operant will occur far more rapidly than one that has been only weakly conditioned. Also, a strongly conditioned operant will be far more difficult to extinguish. (8)

Conditioned Stimulus

In classical conditioning, the previously neutral stimulus takes on the power to elicit the response through association with an unconditioned stimulus. For this to occur, the conditioned stimulus must precede the unconditioned stimulus on enough occasions that it will come to serve as a signal that the unconditioned stimulus will follow. In Pavlov's experiment on conditioning the dog, the tone was used as the conditioned stimulus. The tone was consistently followed by the meat powder, until the dog began salivating to the tone alone. (8)

Conditioning

Process of learning whereby stimuli and responses become associated through training. There are two general types of conditioning, classical and operant. In classical conditioning a conditioned stimulus is presented, followed by an unconditioned stimulus. Conditioning is exhibited when the organism learns to respond to the conditioned stimulus alone. In operant conditioning the operant is allowed to occur and then is followed by a reinforcing stimulus. Operant conditioning is exhibited when the rate of responding increases over the original, preconditioned rate. (8)

Confluence Model

A theory of intelligence proposed by R. B. Zajonc (rhymes with science) that proposes a strong relationship between the number of children per family and that family's overall intellectual level. The model predicts that the more children there are in a family and the closer together they are in age, the lower the IQs of all the children. (16)

Conformity

Term used in social psychology to describe the fact that individuals in group situations tend to behave in a uniform way. Group pressure acts on the individual to force him or her into acting in accord with the rules and norms of the group. Important studies in this area include: (1) Muzafer Sherif's study, in which individuals formed a common estimate of how far (autokinetic effect) a light appeared to move; (2) Solomon Asch's study, in which a naive subject's estimate of the length of a line conformed to the group's estimate, even though the group was obviously wrong; and (3) Stanley Milgram's study, in which subjects who believed they were severely shocking their lab partner were less apt to deliver high voltages when acting in a group situation than when acting alone. (18)

Congruence

One of the three necessary and sufficient conditions (the others being empathy and unconditional positive regard) for the promotion of learning, according to Carl Rogers. By congruence, Rogers means total and complete honesty. To promote learning, the teacher must be "real" and honest in dealing with students. Teachers can't go through the motions of liking students. A teacher without congruence should probably try a different line of work. (12)

Conservation

Term used by Jean Piaget in his theory of cognitive growth and illustrated by the idea that water from a tall, thin glass can be poured into a short, wide glass *without changing the amount of water involved.* According to Piaget, the concept of conservation is typically acquired by a child reaching the stage of concrete operations or operational thinking (at about the age of seven). (5)

Control Group

In experimental research the comparison group, or the group that ideally receives zero magnitude of the independent variable. The use of a control group is critical in evaluating the pure effects of the independent variable on the measured responses of the subjects. (17)

Correlation

A numerical statement as to the relationship among two or more variables. A correlation is said to be positive when high scores on one variable are associated with high scores on another variable, and low scores on the first variable are associated with low scores on the second. A correlation is said to be negative when high scores on the first variable are associated with low scores on the second, and vice versa. Correlations range in value from +1.00 to −1.00. Correlations that fall around zero indicate no consistent relationship among the measured variables. In psychological research a correlation is usually based on taking several response measures of *one group of subjects.* (15)

Criterion-Referenced Test

A test scored on the basis of how an individual's performance compares to an arbitrarily fixed standard of performance. Most teacher-made tests are criterion-referenced. (15)

Critical Periods

Concept used by Konrad Lorenz and other ethologists to define certain age periods in the organism's life in which learning can occur more easily than in any other age period. For example, Lorenz found that goslings imprint on moving stimuli only between hatching and an age of about thirty hours.

The concept of critical periods was also used in describing human growth and development by Myrtle McGraw in her study of the twins, Johnny and Jimmy.

The critical period hypothesis is usually used by those psychologists who favor an early-experience position on growth and development. *See also* imprinting. (4)

Cross-Sectional Research

Type of post-facto research, sometimes used to obtain data on possible growth trends in a population. The researcher selects a sample (cross-section) at one age level—say, twenty-year-olds—and compares these measurements with those taken on a sample of older subjects—say, sixty-five-year-olds. Comparisons of this type are often misleading in that today's twenty-year-olds may have had very different environmental backgrounds (educational experience, for example) than would the sixty-five-year-olds. *See also* Longitudinal Research. (17)

Curiosity Motivation

An inborn motive that is satisfied not by food, drink, or praise but simply by getting the answer. Harry Harlow feels the curiosity drive is fundamental and primary in monkeys and humans. (Why else would a child take apart the watch just to find out what makes it tick?) Daniel Berlyne, another theorist who posits the existence of curiosity motivation, believes that there is an optimum level of curiosity arousal that is a function of brain excitation. (19)

Democratic Leadership

Style of leadership in which the decision-making power is shared by members of a group. (18)

Deoxyribonucleic Acid (DNA)

Rather large organic molecules located in the chromosomes (which lie in the nucleus of every one of the body's cells). These molecules act to direct the body's growth and development. DNA has been called the building block of genetic organization and, along with RNA, makes up the chemical composition of the gene. Geneticists say that DNA acts as a blueprint for the formation of certain enzymes that guide the development of the organism. The coded information stored in the DNA molecule is transmitted to other parts of the cell by the RNA molecules. (3)

Dependent Variable

In any antecedent-consequent relationship, the consequent variable that measures output. In experimental research the dependent variable is the possible effect in a cause-and-effect relationship, whereas in correlational research it is the measure being predicted and is called the "criterion variable." In psychology the dependent variable is typically a response measure. (17)

Deutch, Morton (1920–)

Social psychologist who has studied, among other things, the issue of cooperation versus competition. Deutch believes that schools should be less competitively organized and that students will reap significant benefits from more cooperatively managed classrooms. (19)

Developmental Method of Discipline

A method of classroom control that matches discipline to the developmental stage of pupils. Depending upon the stage, the teacher may use physical restraint, behavior modification, peer pressure, contracts, or democratic decision making. There are humane as well as inhumane aspects to how each of these techniques can be implemented. (20)

Developmental Model

In teaching, the model that suggests that the teacher's role is to stimulate the natural growth process of all pupils. The developmental framework assumes that each child has a basic learning potential, and the teacher's role is to arrange the most appropriate learning environment in order to nurture that growth. Since by definition teaching cannot be value free, a goal for the professional development of each teacher is to become increasingly reflective about teaching while "doing." Teachers can then reduce the amount of pupil stereotyping and improve their attitudes. (14)

Developmental Stage

A growth and/or behavior organization category that satisfies the following four criteria:
1. It is qualitatively different from the preceding stage.
2. It represents a new and more comprehensive system of organization.
3. It occurs in a maturationally fixed sequence.
4. It is age-related within general confines. (5)

Deviation IQ

A technique for measuring intelligence based on calculating the percentage of individuals in each age category achieving a given score and then assessing how far a certain individual's score deviates from the mean score for the age group in which he or she belongs. The IQ score is thus determined on the basis of age standards and is considered to be norm-referenced. (16)

Dewey, John (1859–1952)

The philosopher and psychologist best known for his educational philosophy of "learning by doing." At the time of this pronouncement by Dewey, American education was still in the grip of the formal-discipline theorists, educators who were convinced that children should sit quietly in a classroom and "strengthen their minds" through the study of a classical curriculum. Dewey attempted to change this traditional method of education by creating learning environments in which children engaged actively in learning. To some extent, Dewey anticipated the ideas of Jean Piaget and the open classroom. Dewey's curriculum came to be known as "progressive education" and was incorrectly translated by many into meaning totally unguided education.

Before moving to Columbia, where he spent most of his professional career, Dewey was involved with the functionalist school of psychology at the University of Chicago. (1)

Discovery Learning

Term used by Jerome Bruner to describe a form of learning that results not from rote memorization or conditioning but from the active exploration of alternatives on the part of the learner. Bruner maintains that the learning attained through discovery is more meaningful and long-lasting than that from memorization. (9)

Discrimination

A term used by learning theorists to describe the ability of an organism to respond to one stimulus and not to respond to another similar stimulus. Ivan Pavlov first demonstrated this phenomenon by conditioning dogs to salivate to a given conditioned stimulus—say, a 2,000-cycle tone—while not salivating to a similar stimulus—say, a 1,900-cycle tone. This was accomplished by continuing to reinforce (with the unconditioned stimulus) the presentation of the 2,000-cycle tone, while withholding reinforcement of responses following presentation of the 1,900-cycle tone.

B. F. Skinner has identified essentially the same phenomenon in the area of operant conditioning. Skinner reinforces a response that occurs in the presence of a given stimulus (S^D), while extinguishing the response when it occurs in the presence of the similar stimulus (S^Δ). (9)

Distribution

A statistical term defined as the arrangement of measured scores in order of magnitude. Listing scores in distribution form allows the researcher to notice general trends more readily than the unordered set of raw scores would allow. A frequency distribution is a listing of each score achieved, together with the number of individuals receiving each score. In graphs of frequency distributions, the scores appear on the horizontal axis (abscissa) and the frequency of occurrence appears on the vertical axis (ordinate). (15)

Dizygotic (DZ) Twins

Fraternal twins resulting from eggs that are fertilized at the same time but that are not identical. Thus, DZ twins are no more alike genetically than any set of brothers and sisters. (3)

Dominant Gene

Gregor Mendel's term for the unit of heredity whose characteristics are expressed when paired with a like gene or with a recessive gene. Recessive gene characteristics are not expressed unless paired with a like gene. (3)

Double-Blind Study

A method used by researchers to eliminate experimental error. In a double-blind study neither the individual conducting the study nor the subjects are aware of which group is the experimental group and which is the control. This prevents any unconscious bias on the part of the experimenter, or any contaminating motivations on the part of the subjects. If a subject knows that he or she is in the experimental group, that subject may simply try harder. (17)

Drives

Parts of the motivational cycle that are really just activated needs. Drives always result in some observable change in behavior. (19)

Dual-Code Theory

The information-processing theory that suggests that information in long-term memory may be encoded both verbally and visually. Verbal representations, however, play the major role. (11)

Dyslexia

A common learning disability, particularly for males, sometimes called "word blindness." The person so afflicted may reverse letters and numbers, so that *dog* becomes *god* and 759 becomes 597. Many adults have learned to cope with this difficulty and have become successful in spite of the handicap. Effective instruction involves a combination of personal support, intensive tutoring, and fostering a positive outlook. Also, some alternate homework assignments may be employed from time to time. (21)

Early-Experience Position

A position taken by those researchers and theorists who stress the crucial importance of an individual's early environmental experiences in determining later adult characteristics. The early-experience proponents typically argue that the child goes through various time periods when certain cognitive and other skills can best be learned. Attempting to develop these skills either too early or too late can result in wasted effort on the part of the teacher and possible permanent damage to the student. (4)

Ebbinghaus, Hermann (1850–1909)

The father of the experimental study of learning. Ebbinghaus spent many hours memorizing long lists of nonsense syllables. Later he would relearn the lists, and he measured his retention capacity on the basis of how much more quickly he could learn the lists the second time. This technique is known as the method of savings. He drew two major conclusions from this work:

1. Forgetting occurs at an uneven rate, most of what is forgotten being lost very quickly.
2. In learning new material it is more efficient to space the practice sessions rather than mass them together. (8)

Elkind, David (1931–)

Researcher who has demonstrated the difference between concrete and formal operations in thinking. In discussing Stonehenge, for example, concrete thinkers are more impressed by a long list of facts than a theory to decide whether it was a fort or a temple. Elkind has also described the extreme forms of egocentric thinking, such as the imaginary audience and the personal fable, that young adolescents often use.

Embryo

The second stage of prenatal development, which for the human begins at two weeks after conception and lasts until about eight weeks after conception. During this stage the heart begins beating and sex organs, hands and feet, and all the internal organs are formed. At the end of the embryonic stage, the organism may be clearly identified as human. (3)

Empathy

The ability to realize, understand, and appreciate another person's feelings, or the ability to experience and "feel" the world through another person's eyes. Also, one of the three necessary and sufficient conditions for the promotion of learning, according to Carl Rogers. The other two are unconditional positive regard and congruence. (12)

Enactive Representation

Stage of cognitive development and method of communication introduced by Jerome Bruner. During this, Bruner's first, stage of development, the child thinks and communicates with "wordless messages." Young children understand things best at the action level: A chair is to sit on, a spoon is to eat with, and so on. Even adults may, and perhaps should, revert to this level of thinking when learning a new skill, especially a motor skill. An adept ski or tennis instructor often will ask the student (child or adult) to imitate his or her actions physically, rather than just teaching at the verbal level. (9)

Encoding

In the information-processing model, the creation of memory traces, or abstractions based on the salient features of the incoming information. The encoded information, which represents the external object or event, can thus be used for storage. (11)

Engram

Term used, usually by the physiological psychologists, to denote the hypothesized physical location of memory. (11)

Epigenetic Principle

Erik Erikson's notion that human beings have an inherent or inborn tendency to grow. It represents the ground plan for personality development through the psychosexual stages he describes. Each stage involves the resolution of opposite tendencies; successful resolution involves acquisition of a sequence of virtues—hope, will, purpose, competence, and fidelity—from birth through adolescence. (6)

Equilibration

Term used by Jean Piaget to describe the motivational force for arriving at an adjustment between the twin concepts of assimilation and accommodation. Equilibration makes it possible for the child to go on to new, higher-level assimilation and accommodation. (5)

Erikson, Erik H. (1902–)

German-born personality theorist who studied under Sigmund Freud at the Psychoanalytic Institute in Vienna. Erikson has been in the United States since 1936, and he has taught human development at Harvard University. Although his theory of personality development has its obvious roots in psychoanalytic theory, it is definitely not just "warmed over" Freud. His theory describes stages of personality development extending throughout life, though there is special emphasis on childhood. The focus is always on the normal and healthy personality. Erikson sees development progressing through eight stages, each typifying a particular crisis. Through the attempt to resolve these crises, the healthy personality emerges. (The stages are sequential, and when a healthy adjustment to a particular crisis does not occur, it is even more difficult to resolve a similar crisis at a later stage.) The mature personality should have a sense of identity, and although the climax of this search occurs during adolescence (identity crisis), residues of the conflict can emerge throughout life. (6)

Ethology

The study of the behavior of organisms in the organism's natural habitat. Unlike experimental psychologists, who often study animal behavior in artificial, laboratory situations, ethologists (like Konrad Lorenz) study behavior in the animal's natural environment. Ethologists have introduced such terms as *innate releasing mechanism* and *imprinting* into the working vocabulary of psychologists. *See also* Lorenz, Konrad. (2)

Exclusion

Method of dealing with those who do not conform to social expectations of normalcy by exile, physical avoidance, or even murder. (21)

Experimental Design

Techniques used in experimental (EXP) research for creating equivalent groups of subjects. There are three basic experimental designs:

1. *After-only*, in which subjects are randomly assigned to control and experimental conditions, and the dependent variable is measured only after the introduction of the independent variable
2. *Before-after*, in which a group of subjects is used as its own control, and the dependent variable is measured both before and after the introduction of the independent variable

3. *Matched-subjects,* in which subjects are matched or equated, person for person, on some relevant variable or variables. (17)

Experimental Group

In experimental methodology the group(s) which receive some level of exposure (other than zero magnitude) to the independent variable. (17)

Experimental Research (EXP)

Research conducted using the experimental method, where an independent variable (stimulus) is manipulated in order to bring about a change in the dependent variable (response). Using this method, the experimenter is allowed to make cause-and-effect inferences. Experimental research requires careful controls in order to establish the pure effects of the independent variable. Equivalent groups of subjects should be formed, then exposed to different treatment conditions, and then observed to see if response differences can be observed. (17)

Extinction

Term used by conditioning theorists to describe a forgetting process in which the stimulus-response associations are eroded. In classical conditioning extinction occurs when the conditioned stimulus is presented without being followed by the unconditioned stimulus. Extinction is then defined when the magnitude of the conditioned response returns to zero. In operant conditioning extinction occurs when the conditioned operant is allowed to occur without being followed by a reinforcing stimulus. Extinction is defined when the rate of responding returns to its preconditioned level (operant level). (8)

Extrinsic Motives

Those motives that are driven by the push of external reinforcers. Such motives are often considered necessary to initiate the learning process. *See also* Intrinsic Motives. (19)

F ratio (ANOVA)

Statistical test of significance developed by Sir Ronald Fisher. It is also referred to as *analysis of variance.* The test is designed to establish whether or not a significant (or nonchance) difference exists among several sample means. Statistically, it is the ratio of the variance occurring between the sample means to the variance of the scores occurring within the sample groups. A large *F* ratio, that is, when the variance between is larger than the variance within, usually indicates a nonchance or significant difference. (17)

Factor Approach

A mathematically based model of intelligence in which correlational statistical methods are used for determining the components of intelligence. Among the most widely known factor approaches are those of Charles Spearman (two-factors), Louis Thurstone (seven factors), and J. P. Guilford (120 factors). (16)

Fear of Success

A basic fear that may be due to the perceived unpleasant side effects brought about by being overly successful. Women appear to be especially prone to this condition due to a conscious or unconscious belief that success may make them appear to lose their femininity. (19)

Fetus

The third stage of prenatal development, lasting from the eighth week after conception until birth. The fetus is definitely a behaving organism, and its behavior can be studied. (3)

Flanders, Ned (1918–)

American educational psychologist known primarily for his work on defining teacher effectiveness. Using the concepts of direct and indirect teaching, Flanders found that despite various subject matters, different grade levels, and different school settings, teachers using indirect teaching styles were producing higher levels of student learning than were direct teachers. (12)

Formal Discipline (Theory)

Early educational theory that stressed a curriculum designed to discipline the mind. The theory rested on the assumption that the mind was like a muscle and must be systematically exercised until it became so strong it could learn and understand almost any new material. Subjects such as logic, Latin, and Greek were included in the curriculum, not because they were thought to have any immediate practical use, but because they would strengthen the mind. The theory of formal discipline originated in ancient Greece and remained in vogue until the early twentieth century. It was finally challenged by three psychologists, William James, E. L. Thorndike, and Charles Judd, whose independent studies in the area of positive transfer refuted the formal discipline position. *See also* Transfer. (1)

Formal Operations Stage

A stage of cognitive development, according to Jean Piaget, occurring during early adolescence. The period of formal operations (eleven to sixteen years) is the last of Piaget's stages and is characterized by the youth's ability to develop full, formal patterns of thinking based on abstract symbolism. The youth is able to reason things out logically at the abstract level, develop symbolic meanings, and generalize to other situations. This is the highest level of thinking and, according to Piaget, must await the maturation of certain structures in the brain for its full development. (5)

Four-Way Agenda of Teaching

The four elements that are always interacting during the process of education. They include: (1) student characteristics, (2) the subject matter, (3) teaching strategies, and (4) teacher characteristics.

Frank, Lawrence K. (1890–1968)

The researcher who reviewed a wide variety of cross-cultural methods of childrearing and found that too often adults attempt to remold children as if they are midget-sized adults. (6)

Freud, Sigmund (1856–1939)

Perhaps psychology's single most famous figure, who originated the school of thought called "psychoanalysis." A physician in Vienna, Freud treated patients with "nervous disorders" during the day and wrote down his thoughts and observations at night. From these observations and his own genius for speculating came the theory of psychoanalysis. It stated that all behavior is motivated and that the motives are usually hidden from the individual, thus causing much behavior to appear to be irrational. The basic source of energy for these motives is the libido, or pleasure-seeking drive. Freud described the personality as being composed of three structural components: id, ego, and superego. Most human anxiety results from inner conflict among these three components. Adult personality disorders can always be traced to and found to be directly caused by childhood trauma and anxiety. *See also* Psychoanalytic Theory. (6)

Frustration-Aggression Hypothesis

Neil Miller and John Dollard's theory to explain aggressive behavior. The hypothesis states that aggression results from environmental causes. When a person is frustrated, or experiences goal blockage, aggressive behavior results. (18)

Functional Autonomy

Concept introduced by Gordon Allport and used to explain the great number of human motives for which no biological needs seem present. A means to an end becomes an end in itself, and an acquired motive comes to function independently (autonomously). The resulting motive comes to have a life of its own and is no longer dependent on its biological base. (19)

Furth, Hans (1920–)

A leading contemporary Piagetian theorist interested in the interaction between "new" learning and "old" learning. He used the example of the young German boy and the church that looked like a house to point to what he called a "knowledge disturbance." He traced the process of such knowledge disturbances to show how a child gradually develops more complex cognitive structures to take in new and strange information. (5)

Gage, Nate (1917–)

One of the first educational researchers to accumulate a series of studies on teacher effectiveness. He was able to create the first scientific basis for the art of teaching and to show that different modes work better at the secondary than at the elementary level. (12)

Galloway, Charles (1930–)

One of the first researchers to study teaching from the nonverbal perspective of body language. He demonstrated that clusters of teacher nonverbal behaviors either facilitate or impair student learning so that teacher actions in the classroom may speak louder than words. (12)

Galton, Sir Francis (1822–1911)

Considered to be the "father of intelligence testing." Galton put together the first series of tests designed to measure intellectual ability. Although his tests seem somewhat naive by modern standards, his emphasis on the relationship between sensory ability and intellect foreshadows much of today's research on the importance of sensory stimulation in determining cognitive growth. Galton assumed that intelligence was dependent on the quality of the human sensory apparatus, and so his tests measured such abilities as reaction time, visual and auditory range, and sensory acuity. Galton firmly believed that one's sensory apparatus was largely inherited. Thus, the testing movement, from its very inception, sided with nature in the nature-nurture debate. Galton emphasized individual differences, and more than any other person, set psychology on the road to quantifying its data. (2)

Gene

The fundamental unit of analysis in genetics. The gene is a tiny particle that contains hereditary information. Genes are located in the chromosomes of each of the body's cells and are composed of rather large organic molecules called "nucleic acids." (3)

Genetics

The study of the rules and lawful relationships of heredity. Geneticists are interested in how inherited characteristics are transmitted from generation to generation. They study both the continuity and the variation of traits across generations. The first studies in genetics were those of Gregor Mendel (1860s), who determined that the color of flowers could be predicted from one generation to the next. Thomas Hunt Morgan (1910s) studied the fruit fly and suggested that genes are arranged in the chromosomes in an ordered sequence. James Watson and Francis Crick won the Nobel Prize in 1962 for their pioneering work on genetic composition. A subfield in genetics, called *behavior genetics*, is of special interest to psychologists since it studies the effects of genotype on behavior. *See also* Behavior Genetics. (3)

Genotype

The genetic properties of the organism, often latent (as opposed to the phenotype, which is always expressed). A brown-eyed individual may carry a gene for blue eyes (genotype), but since the gene for brown eyes is dominant over the gene for blue eyes, that particular genotype would not be expressed. (3)

Gestalt Psychology

A school of thought maintaining that the organized whole, configuration, or totality of psychological experience should be the proper object of study. Founded in Germany by Max Wertheimer in the early 1900s, gestalt psychology's first interest was in the field of perception. Later, under Wolfgang Kohler's direction, studies were done in the area of learning, and, under Kurt Lewin's direction, in the area of motivation. Gestalt psychologists tend to emphasize cognitive processes in the study of learning. They stress that true understanding occurs only through the reorganization of ideas and perceptions, not through memorization or conditioning. *See also* Wertheimer, Max. (8)

Gilligan, Carol (1936–)

Researcher who has charged that Lawrence Kohlberg's stage theory of moral development and scoring system is biased against women. Extensive reviews of the research literature, however, have failed to support her position. (7)

Goddard, Henry H. (1866–1957)

Early psychologist and strong hereditarian who researched the Kallikak family and concluded that intelligence was as directly controlled by heredity as was eye color. Goddard studied at Clark University under the tutelage of G. Stanley Hall and was the first psychologist to translate the Binet intelligence test into English. (2)

Great-Leader Theory

Theory that leadership is a function of personal traits rather than the social situation. Great leaders possess just the right blend of looks, personality traits, and intellect to be almost automatically thrust into power roles, regardless of the times in which they live. (18)

Greene, Maxine (1917–)

A philosopher of education who conceptualizes the teacher's role as a "stranger"—that is, he or she is to be with pupils in the classroom but also apart from them in order to nurture their growth toward freedom. She is the leading exponent for a positive existial theory for educational practice. Self-direction and democratic values represent her dual goals for teaching and learning. (1)

Group Dynamics

A subfield of social psychology that studies the processes that create and maintain group life. Group dynamics has as its goal the systematic understanding of group functioning, the discovery of general laws concerning group properties, and the application of those laws to enhance group life. Generally there are two broad positions within the field of group dynamics—the basic research wing and the applied wing. (18)

Group Tests of Intelligence

Tests sometimes called "paper-and-pencil tests" designed to measure large groups of individuals at a single sitting. Originally devised during World War I and called the "Army Alpha test," the group test became immediately popular, both because of its ease of administration and low cost. Many psychologists believe the group tests to have less validity than the individually administered tests. (16)

Guilford, J. P. (1897–)

A specialist in the area of statistics and measurement theory, Guilford has constructed, through the use of factor analysis, a model of the "structure of intellect." Guilford concluded that intelligence is not just a single trait but is made up of a series of distinctly different modes of thought. He has grouped similar modes together into appropriate categories, and his famous phrase "the three faces of intellect" suggests that intelligence can be separated into three categories: operation, content, and product. Each of these three categories contains a further series of dimensions. So far, he has identified a total of 70 separate traits of intelligence (out of a possible 120 traits provided for by his model). Among the traits identified so far are those responsible for what is usually called "creativity." (16)

Guthrie, Edwin R. (1886–1959)

Behaviorist and learning theorist in the tradition of John B. Watson. Guthrie believed that all learning could be explained on the basis of a single law—the law of contiguity: Learning resulted from the contiguous association of stimuli and responses. He also believed that forgetting was entirely the result of retroactive inhibition. (8)

Haberman, Martin (1931–)

Investigator who examined the variety of teaching strategies that research has found to be effective with mainstreamed children. Surprisingly, he concluded that between 75 to 85 percent of the time, teachers should use regular teaching strategies that are effective with all children. There is only a very small body of highly specialized teaching methods specifically appropriate for special-education children. (21)

Halo Effect

The fact that people who are viewed positively on one trait tend also to be thought to have many other positive traits. Advertisers depend on this effect when they use famous personalities to endorse various products. Teachers must guard against the halo effect in assigning grades. A poor grade in reading, for example, should reflect the student's poor level of reading achievement and not the teacher's unfavorable impression of the student's personality. (17)

Handicapping Conditions

A physical, mental, emotional, or other condition recognized by Public Law 94-142. The law specifies nine categories and says that education must be provided for all those in these categories until graduation from high school or until the age of twenty-one.

Recent study has shown that about 92 percent of the handicapping conditions are grouped into four types of a high incidence: (1) learning disability, (2) speech problems (e.g., stuttering), (3) mental retardation, and (4) emotional disturbance. All other handicapping conditions total just over 6 percent and include multiple handicaps, physical impairment, deafness, visual impairment, and deaf-blind conditions. The main difficulty with this classification is that the validity and accuracy of the diagnosis is lowest in the areas of high incidence and vice versa. (21)

Harlow, Harry F. (1905–)

An American psychologist who has spent most of his professional career at the primate lab of the University of Wisconsin. Harlow's research, usually on rhesus monkeys, has shed light on many important topics in psychology. Perhaps his three most famous studies were on: (1) surrogate mothers—in which frightened young monkeys preferred cloth-covered, cuddly surrogates rather than wire-framed surrogates that delivered food; (2) learning sets—in which monkeys solved oddity problems by developing solution rules or strategies, rather than on the basis of either insight or the slow accumulation of stimulus-response associations; and (3) curiosity drive—in which monkeys exhibited a motive to manipulate novel items in their environment, despite the fact that no primary reinforcement was presented. (19)

Hartshorne, Hugh (1885–1967)

Researcher who, together with Mark May, studied the process of value inculcation with a large sample of children in the 1920s. The results exploded the myth that values could be ingrained in children. Hartshorne and May found almost no relationship between character-training programs and how children behaved in tempting situations. (7)

Hawthorne Effect

A major research error that is due to response differences resulting not from the action of the independent variable but from the flattery or attention paid to the subjects by the experimenter. Typically, the potential for this error is inherent in any study using the before-after experimental design without an adequate control group. Any research, for example, in which subjects are measured, then subjected to some form of training, then measured again, should be viewed with suspicion unless an appropriate control group is used—that is, an equivalent group that is measured, then *not subjected to the training,* and then measured again. Only then can the researcher be reasonably confident that the response differences are due to the pure effects of the independent variable. (17)

Head Start: Perry Preschool Program

A longitudinal study of the effects of Head Start, a government-funded preschool program designed to enhance the intellectual potential of disadvantaged children. Measures were taken on nineteen-year-old youths who as children had been in the Head Start program, and these were compared with measures taken on a control group of youths who had not attended Head Start. In virtually every measurement category, Head Start was found to have produced positive effects, ranging from an increase in academic achievement to a decrease in criminal activity. (4)

Hebb, Donald O. (1904–)

Canadian physiological psychologist Hebb who, in *Organization of Behavior* (1949), revolutionized psychological thought, especially in the United States. In this work Hebb dared to infer the existence of some possible physiological correlates of behavior. He stated that there was a relationship between intelligence and the way brain cells are organized. This organization occurs first at the level of cell assemblies, then as phase sequences, and finally in the total organization of the brain cells. Hebb also proposed a distinction between Intelligence A and Intelligence B, the former being one's innate potential, and the latter, one's present ability level on the intellectual growth continuum. *See also* A/S Ratio *and* Cell Assembly. (4)

Heritability

The proportion of the total variability of a given trait in a population that is due to genetic as opposed to environmental factors. Heritability is expressed as a value, running between 1.00 and zero. Thus, regarding measured intelligence, if all the variation in IQ scores in a given population was due to genetic factors, the heritability of IQ would be 1.00. If all the variability was due to environmental factors, the heritability would be zero. The concept of heritability applies only to a particular population of a single generation under one set of environmental conditions. (16)

Herrnstein, Richard (1930–)

Harvard psychologist who has been critical of the environmental explanation of intellectual growth. Herrnstein insists that American psychology has overlooked the importance of genetic factors in determining intelligence. He has also expressed reservations about the value of early-intervention programs such as Head Start. (4)

Hidden Agenda

Basic teacher attitudes toward the instructional process, perceptions of students, and self-knowledge that have been found to have a major influence on student learning. The influence can be either positive or negative. (14)

Homozygosity

An organism (diploid) that carries identical alleles at one or several genetic sites. (3)

Horner, Matina (1939–)

Professor at Harvard University and, since 1972, president of Radcliffe College. Horner achieved almost instant recognition in the area of the psychology of women's attitudes and motives. She contends that society often conditions women both to expect and want to fail. Since motivational differences between the sexes are a result of social pressures, then educators must revise their ideas, practices, and policies concerning young women in schools and colleges. Horner's own career is a model of academic achievement. (19)

Hunt, David (1926–)

Researcher who, in applying developmental concepts to teachers and pupils, classified both groups according to conceptual level of development (CL). Hunt found that pupils' learning styles varied by CL stage according to preferences for the amount of structure provided. He also found certain teaching patterns (labeled A, B, and C) that were reflective of the CL stages of teachers. Teaching effectiveness was partly defined as the ability to "read and flex" with pupils and was correlated particularly with the higher conceptual levels. (13)

Hunter, Madeline (1927–)

Theorist who outlined a systematic approach to lesson planning. Hunter suggested a sequence of (1) anticipatory set, (2) stated objectives, (3) input, (4) modeling, (5) checking, (6) guided practice, and (7) independent practice. It is not necessary to use all these steps, but independent practice should be used as a guide to assessing the quality of the final product, and modifying a plan. (13)

Hypothesis of Association

Research hypothesis that states that two or more measured variables will be found to correlate with each other not just in the measured sample but also in the population being represented by the sample. (17)

Hypothesis of Difference

Research hypothesis that states that two or more groups of subjects will differ on measures of the dependent variable. This difference is assumed to occur not just in the samples being measured but also in the population represented by the samples. (17)

Iconic Representation

Jerome Bruner's second stage of cognitive growth and mode of communication, the first stage being the enactive level. At the iconic level, objects become conceivable without resorting to muscular action. The child can now visualize an object or concept. He or she possesses an image which no longer depends on action. The use of pictures and diagrams illustrates the iconic mode of communication. (9)

Imprinting

A special form of learning that is acquired early in life, usually during a very specific time interval, that is triggered by a releasing stimulus, and that is not reversible. Konrad Lorenz demonstrated this phenomenon by presenting himself as a moving stimulus to a group of newly hatched goslings. The goslings then imprinted on Lorenz himself and followed him around as though he were the mother goose. *See also* Critical Periods *and* Lorenz, Konrad. (2)

Independent Variable

In any antecedent-consequent relationship, the antecedent variable. Independent variables may be manipulated or assigned. A manipulated independent variable is a deliberate alteration of the environmental conditions to which subjects are being exposed by the researcher. An assigned independent variable is a categorization of subjects on the basis of some preexisting trait measured by the researcher. Whether the independent variable is manipulated or assigned determines whether the research is experimental (manipulated) or post-facto (assigned). In experimental research the independent variable is the potential causal half of the cause-and-effect relationship; in correlational research, it is the measure from which the prediction will be made and is thus called the "predictor variable." (17)

Individual Differences

The fact, first noted scientifically by Sir Francis Galton, that people tend to differ on a whole host of measured traits. Investigators disagree regarding the causes of these variations in abilities, traits, and performance measures, but there is no question as to their existence. (15)

Individualized Education Plans (IEP)

A plan of instruction, mandated by Public Law 94-142 for all children classified in any category of special education. A team establishes a series of educational goals and time tables for each child. The plan is reviewed on a regular basis. At each point in the child's schooling, he or she must be placed in the least restrictive environment that is consistent with achievable educational attainments. This may vary from a regular classroom to other environments that offer much greater structure, such as a self-contained special class or even a special residence. (21)

Inductive Fallacy

An error in logic resulting from overgeneralizing on the basis of too few observations. The inductive fallacy results when one assumes that all members of a class have a certain characteristic because one member of that class has it. It would be fallacious to assume that all Mongolians are liars on the basis of having met one Mongolian who was a liar. (15)

Information Processing

Theory of learning and remembering that is based on the computer as a model. Information is seen as flowing into and within the organism. The sense organs respond to incoming information, and it is passed along and encoded in the memory and nervous system. The encoded information may then be stored and processed and finally retrieved and acted on. As with the computer, there is information input, storage and/or processing, and output. (11)

Innate Releasing Mechanism (IRM)

An innate stimulus-response pattern, similar to an instinct, whose mechanism is built into the central nervous system. Thus, the IRM is a neurologically organized response or set of responses triggered by specific external stimuli, such as the male stickleback fish being induced into a set of attacking responses when presented with the color red. (2)

Insight

A suddenly realized solution to a problem, sometimes called the "A-ha! phenomenon." Introduced by Wolfgang Kohler, the concept of insight is used to explain the apparently spontaneous appearance of a solution to a problem. Insight results from the reorganization of ideas and perceptions, rather than from simple trial-and-error behavior. The concept of insight is used typically by gestalt psychologists. (8)

Instinct Theory

A now discredited theory that attempted to explain behavior by simply describing it and then calling it "instinctive." For example, humans were seen as going to war because of an "aggressive instinct," or forming groups because of a "gregarious instinct," or even twiddling thumbs because of a "thumb-twiddling instinct." Instinct theorists committed a logical error called the "nominal fallacy." *See* Nominal Fallacy. (2)

Intelligence

Widely varying definitions—from Wechsler's "global capacity of the individual to act purposefully, to think rationally, and to deal effectively with his environment" to E. G. Boring's positivistic definition of intelligence as simply that which an intelligence test measures. The problem with intelligence as a concept is that it cannot be directly observed. It must be inferred from behavior. Rather than *being intelligent*, one can be viewed as acting intelligently.

As a hypothetical construct, intelligence has come to mean higher-level thought processes, or intellectual abilities, as opposed to Sir Francis Galton's original notion of acute sensory powers. Statistical studies of intelligence utilize the concept of measured intelligence, which is the score received on a standardized intelligence test. *See also* Intelligence Quotient. (16)

Intelligence Quotient (IQ)

Originally, a measure of intelligence calculated by dividing a subject's mental age by the chronological age and multiplying by 100. That is, $IQ = MA/CA \times 100$. This is called the "ratio method" of obtaining IQ.

More recently, IQ has been computed by the deviation method. One's deviation IQ is defined by one's relative standing among peers. The deviation IQ is computed on the basis of how far one's score deviates from the mean score obtained for the entire group of individuals of the same chronological age.

This technique is based on the standard, or z-score, concept and assumes a normal distribution for each age group. (16)

Intrinsic Motives

Those motives that are sustained by internal factors—for example, the need for self-satisfaction. Learning that is based on intrinsic motivation has been found to be longer-lasting than that based on the more transitory push of external reinforcers. *See* Extrinsic Motives. (19)

Introspection

A technique used for ferreting out psychology's data by having a subject look within himself or herself and then report all feelings, sensations, and images. This technique was the basic method for obtaining data in the days of Wilhelm Wundt and the structuralist school of psychology. J. B. Watson, the founder of behaviorism, attacked the use of introspection as being too subjective for an objective, scientific discipline like psychology. The technique is rarely used in psychology today. (8)

Invariant Sequence

The notion, in developmental theories of the acquisition of values, that development occurs in stages arranged in a sequence that moves in only one direction. Further, these stages cannot be skipped. The growth process is thus seen as a sequence of steps that must be taken one at a time. (7)

James, William (1842–1910)

America's first, and probably most revered, psychologist. James spent his entire academic lifetime at Harvard University, first as a student and later as a professor. Though he received an M.D. degree, James carved out his career in academe, being a professor of both psychology and philosophy. In 1876 he created and taught the first psychology course ever offered in the United States. In 1890 he published *Principles of Psychology,* a book that still provides today's reader with a relatively modern version of psychology, so great was his vision. Later, in his famous "Talks with Teachers," James turned his attention to the classroom teacher and pointed out that the entire enterprise of education is determined by the performance of the teacher in the classroom. James is credited with originating the school of functionalism in psychology, a school of thought interested not so much in what the elements of consciousness are but in what they are for. (1)

Jensen, Arthur R. (1923–)

Researcher and professor of educational psychology whose special interest is IQ. Jensen's 1969 article "How Much Can We Boost IQ and Scholastic Achievement?" created a big stir in educational psychology because of its pronounced emphasis on genetic factors in the development of intellect. Jensen has been especially criticized for one of the implications of his article, namely, that the difference between the tested IQs of black and white children is a result of the genetic inferiority of the black children. (16)

Joyce, Bruce (1930–)

Theorist who conceptualizes effective teaching methods as a repertoire of different teaching models. Joyce suggests that teachers should deliberately employ a variety of modes. Exclusive reliance on any one mode will lead to boredom for both pupils and teachers. (12)

Just Community

System, developed by Lawrence Kohlberg and Ralph Mosher, in which a subgroup of high-school students is organized on the basis of Stage Five principles. The students and staff jointly determine and carry out all school rules. Research indicates that such communities have had some success in dealing with the usual problems of discipline and that levels of academic achievement increase while drug use and absenteeism decrease. (20)

Kallikak Family

Case name (taken from the Greek words for good and bad) for a family that was studied in great detail by Henry Goddard during the early years of this century. Goddard traced back two branches of the Kallikak family, both branches having originally been created by the Revolutionary War soldier Martin Kallikak. One branch, the "good Kallikaks," resulted from Martin Kallikak's marriage, while the "bad Kallikaks" were a result of Martin's affair with a barmaid. Goddard found that the two branches were significantly different in virtually every way, especially in regard to intelligence: Most good Kallikaks were superior and most bad Kallikaks retarded. This "good seed–bad seed" account is regarded as totally fanciful by today's students of genetics. (2)

Kohlberg, Lawrence (1927–)

Psychologist whose Ph.D. thesis, written at the University of Chicago, outlined a theory of how moral reasoning develops in children. His theory of moral development states that children proceed through a series of developmental stages—preconventional, conventional, and postconventional. Like Jean Piaget's theory of cognitive development, Kohlberg's theory sees moral development occurring in an invariant sequence, with each stage qualitatively different from the preceding stage. *See also* Moral Development. (7)

Kohler, Wolfgang, (1887–1967)

One of the founders of gestalt psychology. Having been a student of Max Wertheimer's at the University of Frankfurt, just before World War I, Kohler spent the war years in the Canary Islands, where he performed gestalt psychology's most famous animal-learning study. He discovered, while studying an ape, that some learning occurs on the basis of insight rather than solely on the basis of the slow accumulation of specific associations. Insight, or the "A-ha!" phenomenon, is learning that occurs suddenly as a new relationship among perceptions is discovered. *See also* Insight. (8)

Law of Effect

One of E. L. Thorndike's main laws of learning. It states that when an association between a stimulus and response is followed by a satisfying state of affairs, the association (or connection) is strengthened. When the association is followed by an annoying state of affairs, it is weakened. In brief, reward strengthens and punishment weakens any connection between stimuli and responses. In a later version of the law, Thorndike soft-pedaled the importance of punishment as a weakening agent. Thorndike's law of effect is considered by many psychologists to be the cornerstone on which B. F. Skinner built his system of operant conditioning. (8)

Law of Exercise

One of E. L. Thorndike's three main laws of learning. It states that the more frequently a stimulus-response connection occurs, the stronger the resulting association and, hence, the stronger the learning. The law was later amended to incorporate the importance of the consequences of the action; thus, practice without knowledge of results is not nearly as effective as when the consequences become known to the learner. (8)

Law of Readiness

One of E. L. Thorndike's three main laws of learning. It states that learning occurs when neurological conduction units are primed or ready to conduct. The reference here is to momentary readiness rather than maturational readiness. (8)

Learned Helplessness

The appearance of helplessness that is characteristic of some handicapped children. The term, from Martin Seligman, suggests the need for teachers to pay careful attention to such children in order to prevent them from being caught in the syndrome, especially since some of the children can be expert performers. Setting reasonable objectives in a firm yet supportive atmosphere will avoid reinforcing learned helplessness. (21)

Learning

A very general term referring to a process that leads to a relatively permanent change in behavior resulting from past experience. Thus, such activities as acquiring physical skills, memorizing poems, acquiring attitudes and prejudices or even tics and mannerisms are all examples of learning. Learning may be conscious or unconscious, adaptive or maladaptive, overt or covert. Although the learning process is typically measured on the basis of a change in performance, most psychologists agree that an accompanying change occurs within the nervous system. Though there are a great many theories and explanations concerning learning, there is general agreement regarding its definition. (8)

Learning Curve

A graphic presentation of learning performance, with the measure of learning being plotted on the vertical axis and the amount of practice on the horizontal axis. Though learning curves take many shapes, depending on what is being learned and under what conditions, the classical or ideal curve is negatively accelerated. That is, acceleration (improved performance) becomes less and less as the amount of practice increases. When there is no further increase in performance, the curve levels off into a plateau. (10)

Learning Sets

Concept developed by Harry Harlow and used as a modern explanation for the gestalt term *insight*. Harlow insists that what the gestaltists had viewed as insight does not come about as a sudden reorganization of perceptions but rather occurs on the basis of learning how to learn, or the learning of general rules. The learning set does not occur "in a flash" but takes many trials and much experience in which to develop. The concept of learning sets is also in opposition to the straight stimulus-response learning model in that the learning set involves developing a learning strategy rather than the slow accumulation of stimulus-response associations. A learning set is a form of nonspecific transfer. (10)

LM (Logico-Mathematical) Learning

Concept developed by Jean Piaget to describe a form of learning that results not from the physical environment acting on the learner but from the actions of the learner on the environment. LM learning is the result of an individual's continuous experience of organizing and reorganizing actions—a process that leads to the goal of understanding. Piaget says that LM learning is internally motivated. The discovery of a new relationship is self-rewarding. *See also* P Learning. (9)

Locus of Control

Concept that identifies the type of personal control used by an individual. When the locus of control is internal, individuals view themselves as personally in charge of their own destinies. When the locus of control is external, the person feels he or she is at the mercy of external circumstances. (18)

Long-Term Memory (LTM)

In the information-processing model, the second of the two main storage systems. Information that is in short-term memory may, under certain conditions, be passed along for processing and consolidation into a more permanent storage site, long-term memory. Long-term memory has the potential for holding encoded information for a lifetime. (11)

Longitudinal Research

A type of post-facto research in which subjects are measured repeatedly throughout their lives in order to obtain data on possible age trends in growth and development. Lewis Terman's massive study of growth trends among intellectually gifted children is an example of this research technique. The study, begun in the early 1920s, is still in progress today and is still providing psychology with new data. Longitudinal research requires great patience on the part of the investigator, but the data obtained are considered to be more valid than those obtained via the cross-sectional approach. *See* Cross-Sectional Research. (17)

Lorenz, Konrad (1903–)

Austrian ethologist and winner of the Nobel Prize in medicine in 1973. Lorenz has long insisted that to understand animal behavior one must study the animal in its natural habitat, not in the artificial confines of the laboratory. In 1937 Lorenz first described the phenomenon of imprinting, a form of learning that dramatically illustrates the interaction of heredity, environment, and time in the determination of behavioral characteristics. Lorenz was able to revive the long-discredited instinct theory and, by carefully analyzing the biological mechanisms involved, to make the theory scientifically respectable. He is currently the director of the Max Planck Institute in Germany. *See also* Imprinting. (2)

McClelland, David (1917–)

Harvard psychologist interested in achievement motivation. McClelland has studied the problems of underachievement, from the point of view of both the individual and the entire society. His studies indicate that the achievement motive, or "achievement syndrome," is composed of three major factors:

1. The ability to compete with some standard of excellence in mind
2. The ability to take moderate risks
3. The ability to make use of concrete feedback (19)

Mainstreaming

Placement of persons who might be classified as handicapped within the "mainstream" of society. Exceptional and/or retarded children are not placed in special classes but are kept in regular classrooms. Mainstreaming has been the policy since passage of Public Law 94-142. (21)

Massed Learning

Learning that occurs in massive doses, without a break, as opposed to spaced learning. Studies show that for many activities, especially motor activities, massed learning is less efficient than spaced learning. (10)

Matched-Subjects Experimental Design

See Experimental Design.

Matching and Mismatching

Method of teaching that involves discovering a student's cognitive stage of development, matching content and structure to that stage, and gradually introducing mismatches to stimulate development one stage up. Teachers should be alert, though, to the fact that some pupils may experience anxiety when new material is introduced or when going through developmental transitions. Also, some pupils may be "advanced thinkers" in certain subjects, though not in others. Watching for such variability in pupil responses can guide teachers in changing the level of structure when necessary. (13)

May, Mark (1891–1973)

See Hartshorne, Hugh.

Mean

A statistical measure of central tendency, found by adding all the scores in a distribution and dividing by the number of scores. It is also called the "arithmetic average." (15)

Measurement

The assigning of numbers to observations according to certain rules. The rule used to assign the numbers determines which scale of measurement is being employed—nominal, ordinal, interval, or ratio. (15)

Measures of Central Tendency

A statistical term used for describing the typical, middle, or central score in a distribution of scores. Measures of central tendency are used when the researcher wants to describe a group as a whole with a view toward characterizing that group on the basis of its most common measurement. The researcher wishes to know what score best represents a group of differing scores. The three measures of central tendency are the mean (or arithmetic average), the median (or the midpoint of the distribution), and the mode (the most frequently occurring score in the distribution). (15)

Median

A statistical measure of central tendency found by identifying the middle-most score in a distribution of ordered values. (15)

Mediation Theory

The theory that a covert associative response may occur between the overt stimulus and the observed response. The mediation is, therefore, an hypothesized internal association between a stimulus and response. (9)

Menarche

The time of the first menstruation, which signals the onset of puberty and/or adolescence among females. The girl who is secure in her sexual identity and has had adult support and guidance is less likely to feel anxiety when reaching this important developmental milestone. (3)

Mendel, Gregor (1822–1884)

Austrian monk whose work with the flower color of garden peas led to the theory of genetics that states that some genes are dominant and some recessive. When paired with a recessive gene, the dominant gene is the one whose characteristics will be expressed. (3)

Mental Age

Term first used by Alfred Binet as the unit for measuring intelligence. Binet defined mental age in terms of the age at which a given number of test items are passed by an average child. If, for example, the average six-year-old could correctly answer a certain number of items, then any other child correctly answering the same number of items would be assigned at least a mental age of six. (16)

Milgram, Stanley (1933–1986)

Researcher who has studied, among other subjects, human aggression and conformity. In one series of studies, Milgram asked subjects to deliver increasing amounts of electric shock to another person. He found that almost two-thirds of those tested were willing to risk killing someone they perceived to be a fellow subject. When tested in groups, however, only about 10 percent of the subjects pushed the shock lever all the way. Milgram interpreted this behavior on the basis of the liberating effects of conformity and group pressure on individual behavior. Milgram was a professor of social psychology at the City University in New York. Milgram's experiments also demonstrated the relationships between Kohlberg's stages and moral development. Most subjects at the conventional and preconventional levels were willing to follow orders and administer seemingly painful electric shocks. (7)

Miller, Alan (1938)

Researcher who has reviewed a large number of studies that support the idea that pupils at more complex conceptual levels benefit from indirect instruction while those at lower levels need more direct methods. Thus, teacher methods and content should vary in accord with pupils' attributes. (13)

Milwaukee Project

A program directed by Rick Heber whose aim was to increase the intellectual abilities of slum-raised children, born of low-IQ parents. Working with the children almost from the day of birth, Heber's staff at the Infant Education Center was able to increase the IQs of these culturally deprived children by what appear to be significant amounts. (4)

Mnemonic Devices

Memory aids used to increase retention powers. Mnemonic devices typically utilize one of the following learning strategies: (1) visual imagery, (2) rhyming, and (3) associations with past learning. Using the word *HOMES* for recalling the names of the Great Lakes (Huron, Ontario, Michigan, Erie, and Superior) is an example of a mnemonic device based on association with past learning. (11)

Mode

A statistical measure of central tendency found by identifying the most frequently occurring score in a distribution of scores. (15)

Modeling

Concept used in Bandura's social learning theory. Learning can occur not only through response conditioning but also through modeling, which is the imitation of the behavior of others. Learning by modeling can occur even when the imitative responses are not themselves being directly reinforced. *See also* Social Learning Theory. (10)

Monozygotic (MZ) Twins

Identical twins that have identical genetic backgrounds. They result from the fertilization of a single egg, which then divides. This provides for two individuals having precisely the same genetic makeup. (3)

Montessori, Maria (1870–1952)

Italian educator, psychologist and physician. Montessori was one of the first theorists to stress the developmental nature of humans in an evolutionary setting. Her approach to education was based on her work first with mentally retarded children and later with the culturally deprived children living in the slums of Rome. Her educational technique, now called the Montessori Method, stressed sensory training in a prepared environment. She insisted on the importance of early experience in cognitive development, and although her approach was rejected by most American behaviorists, it is now receiving renewed attention by serious educational psychologists. (21)

Moral Development

The process whereby children come to adopt guiding principles of right and wrong and achieve the ability to resist the temptations of unacceptable conduct. The view that morality develops in a series of growth stages originated in the work of Jean Piaget, who believed the development of moral stages was similar to cognitive development. One of the leading current spokespersons for this view is Lawrence Kohlberg, who sees moral development occurring in a series of stages: preconventional, conventional, and postconventional. Like Piaget, Kohlberg describes moral development as occurring in an invariant sequence, with each stage qualitatively different from the preceding stage. *See also* Kohlberg, Lawrence. (7)

Moratorium

Erik Erikson's term for a stage of identity formation during late adolescence. It is thought to be a time for possible experimentation, which precedes a commitment to an adult career. (6)

Motivation

A general psychological term used to explain behavior initiated by needs and directed toward a goal. Motives may be biogenic, stemming from tissue needs within the organism, or acquired, learned through interaction with the environment, especially the social environment. Almost all personality theorists have developed their own lists of important human motives, and great debates have occurred over which motives are of greatest importance or which can rightfully be called universal. Among learning theorists, Jerome Bruner makes much of the principle of motivation, assuming that almost all children have a built-in "will to learn."

Motivational Conflicts

Conflicts that result when individuals seek a number of goals, one (or some) of which may be antagonistic to others. Those conflicts that most affect the lives of school-aged children are: (1) the need for independence versus the need for dependence, (2) internal sexual needs versus society's demand to leave those needs unsatisfied, and (3) internal feelings of aggression versus society's rules that such feelings not be directly expressed. (19)

Motives

Activated needs (drives) that are directed toward or away from some specified goal. (19)

Nature-Nurture Controversy

Debate over which component, nature (heredity) or nurture (environment), is more influential in determining behavior. In psychology the behaviorists consistently argued on behalf of nurture, and the intelligence testers favored nature. Educational psychology has long been the battleground on which this issue has been fought, since the psychologists primarily concerned with the issue were the learning theorists (largely behaviorists) and measurement practitioners. (2)

Need Hierarchy

Theory proposed by Abraham Maslow that suggests that humans place their needs on the following universal, order-of-importance scale: (1) physiological needs, (2) safety needs, (3) love needs, (4) esteem needs, and (5) self-actualizing needs. (19)

Needs

The part of the motivational cycle seen as deficits that lie within the individual. These may be physiological (e.g., the need for food) or psychological (e.g., the need for approval). (19)

Negative Discipline Techniques

Inhumane methods of classroom discipline, such as brute physical force, aversive conditioning, and scapegoating, that do not generally produce long-lasting results. (20)

Negative Reinforcement

Any stimulus, the *removal* of which increases the rate of responding. If a rat is in a cage with an electrified floor grid and the electricity is turned off only after the rat presses a lever, the rate of the lever-pressing responses will tend to increase dramatically. Unlike punishment, which reduces response rates, negative reinforcement often increases response rates even more quickly than positive reinforcement. (9)

Negative Transfer

When the learning of A inhibits the learning and retention of B. For example, learning to type by the hunt-and-peck method may create bad habits that make the later learning of touch typing more difficult. (10)

Negatively Accelerated (Intellectual) Growth Curve

A graph of the relationship between intellectual growth and age. Benjamin S. Bloom suggests that this relationship is negative—that is, as a child increases in age his or her potential for continued intellectual growth decreases. (4)

Nominal Fallacy

A logical error resulting from the attempt to explain an event on the basis of a redescription of that same event. Saying that sleeping pills work because they have dormative power, or maintaining that people fight because they have aggressive instincts are examples of the nominal fallacy. The instinct theorists of the early 1900s built an entire system on the soft sands of the nominal fallacy. (2)

Nonverbal Behavior

Body language. Based largely on the theory of Charles Galloway and some research by Robert Rosenthal, the teacher's nonverbal behavior represents an important avenue for the transmission of teacher expectations. Galloway has shown how nonverbal behavior can promote or reduce pupil learning. Rosenthal has shown how his test (Profile of Nonverbal Sensitivity) can identify the channels for communicating how teachers really feel about their pupils. (12)

Norm-Referenced Test

A test scored on the basis of how an individual's performance compares to the average performance of the group to which the individual is being compared. Most of the nationally standardized tests are norm-referenced. (15)

Normal Curve

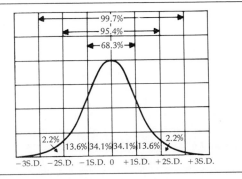

A frequency distribution curve in which scores are plotted on the horizontal axis (x), and frequency of occurrence is plotted on the vertical axis (y). The normal curve is a theoretical curve shaped like a bell, where (1) most of the scores cluster around the center, and as we move away from the center in either direction there are fewer and fewer scores; (2) the

scores fall into a symmetrical shape, each half of the curve being a mirror image of the other; (3) the mean, median, and mode all fall at precisely the same point, the center; and (4) there are constant area characteristics regarding the standard deviation. (15)

$$O = H \longleftrightarrow E \longleftrightarrow T$$

One of psychology's basic principles, which states that the organism is a product of heredity interacting with the environment interacting with time. (3)

Occam, William of (1300–1349)

British-born philosopher and Franciscan monk who warned that explanations are dangerous when they carry excess meaning. He believed that unnecessary assumptions should be avoided in order that explanations be kept as simple and straightforward as possible. This principle is now called the "law of parsimony," and the concept of "shaving away" excess meaning is now referred to as using "Occam's razor." Although primarily an empiricist, Occam tried to guide theorizing toward an objective approach that avoided both "woolly-headed" rationalism and "narrow-minded" empiricism. (1)

Operants

Responses, according to B. F. Skinner, for which the original stimuli are either unidentified or nonexistent. The consequences of operant behavior can be observed, even though the stimulus is not known. For example, if a rat presses the lever in a Skinner Box and this results in reinforcement, an increase in operant rate will be observed despite the fact that no stimulus could be identified as initiating the original bar press. In operant conditioning, reinforcement is contingent on the operant first being emitted. The organism must in some way "operate" on the environment in order that the reinforcement will follow. Operant responding at one time was called "instrumental" responding by some psychologists. (9)

Operant Conditioning

Form of conditioning described by B. F. Skinner in which the free operant is allowed to occur and is followed by a reinforcing stimulus that is, in turn, followed by an increased likelihood of the operant occurring again. For optimum conditioning the reinforcing stimulus should follow the operant immediately. The rate of responding for a conditioned operant may jump dramatically over the preconditioned rate (operant level). (9)

Operant Level

The original, or preconditioned, rate of operant responding before any reinforcing stimuli have been introduced. If a rat happens to press the lever in a Skinner Box four times an hour (without being reinforced), the operant level for that response is established at four per hour. Thus, the operant level is the rate at which the free operant is typically emitted prior to conditioning. (9)

Oral Stage

First of Freud's psychosexual stages of development. During this stage, the baby lives through and loves through its mouth. This stage occurs between birth and about age eighteen months and permanently affects the child's later feelings of independence and trust. (6)

P (Physical) Learning

Form of learning described by Jean Piaget that results from the action of the physical environment on the child rather than the actions of the child on the environment. Piaget's P learning (physical event acting on the learner) is very similar to B. F. Skinner's concept of operant conditioning. *See also* LM (Logico-Mathematical) Learning. (9)

Paired-Associate Learning

A method used in the study of verbal learning and memory. A subject is presented with a list of word pairs (blue–moon, red–dog, play–toy, etc.) and is then tested by being asked to repeat the second word of the pair (response) each time the first word (stimulus) is introduced. This is by far the most common technique employed in the study of verbal learning, since many psychologists believe the learning of item pairs is a fundamental process in thinking and memory. (9)

Path Analysis

A statistical technique for determining the possibility of a causal sequence among a series of time-ordered, correlated variables. Although not as definitive a proof of causation as the use of experimental methodology, path analysis is a long step forward from the naive extrapolations of causation that some of the early researchers made from simple bivariate correlations. (17)

Pavlov, Ivan (1849–1936)

Russian physiologist who won the Nobel prize in medicine in 1904 for his work on digestive activity in dogs. His lasting fame, however, resulted from his observation that dogs salivated not only when meat powder was placed in their mouths but also when stimuli occurred well ahead of time (for example, when they heard Pavlov's footsteps coming down the stairs to the laboratory). Pavlov coined the phrase "conditioned reflex" to describe this phenomenon. Pavlov attempted to relate these behavioral observations with the neural activity in the brain; for example, he introduced the concept of "cortical inhibition," which he believed important in producing sleep. Though most modern psychologists consider his theory of neurological activity as something of a historical curio, his laboratory findings on conditioning are still of great importance. Pavlov's system of conditioning is now generally called "classical conditioning." (8)

Pearson Product Moment Correlation (Pearson *r*)

Statistical test introduced by Karl Pearson for showing the degree of relationship between two variables. It is used to test the hypothesis of association, that is, whether or not there is a relationship between two sets of measurements. The Pearson *r* can be calculated as follows:

$$r = \frac{\Sigma\ XY/N - (\bar{X})\ (\bar{Y})}{\text{S.D.}_x\ \text{S.D.}_y}$$

Computed correlations range from + 1.00 (perfect positive correlation) through zero to − 1.00 (perfect negative correlation). The further the Pearson *r* is from zero, whether in a positive or negative direction, the stronger the relationship. The Pearson *r* may be used for making better-than-chance predictions but may not be used for directly isolating causal factors. (15)

Percentile

The percentage of cases falling at or below a given score. Thus, if an individual were to score at the 95th percentile, that individual would exceed 95 percent of all persons taking that particular test. If test scores are normally distributed, and if the standard deviation of the distribution is known, percentile scores can easily be converted from the resulting *z* scores. (15)

Performance IQ

Term used by David Wechsler to describe the nonverbal component of intelligence. Wechsler believed that the Stanford-Binet test was too heavily loaded with verbal items, and thus when constructing his own test, Wechsler included a section designed to tap visual-motor abilities. The Wechsler IQ tests are scored on the basis of verbal IQ, performance IQ, and full-scale IQ. Scores in each of the three categories are computed. (16)

Periodization

Stages through which the brain passes in developing. This growth appears to parallel the Piagetian stages of cognitive development. As yet, there is no evidence to support the idea that learning cannot take place during the transition periods of periodization. (5)

Peterson, Penelope (1949–)

Researcher who has investigated attribute-treatment interaction (ATI). Peterson has shown the positive effects of systematically varying the amount of structure in teaching according to levels of pupil ability, anxiety, and attitudes toward learning. (13)

Phallic Stage

Third stage of personality development in Freud's theory of psychosexual development. During the phallic stage (ages three to seven years) the child focuses on the genital area. Conflict results as the child projects its sexual desires on the opposite-sexed parent and feels the fear of retaliation from the like-sexed parent. The conflict is resolved at about age seven when the child identifies with the like-sexed parent. The major crisis for the child during this stage is over the struggle for sexual identification. (6)

Phenotype

The observable properties or the inherited traits that are expressed in the organism. (3)

Physiological Motives

Motives that are based on the activation of physical needs, such as the need for food, water, sleep, sex, and warmth. (19)

Piaget, Jean (1896–1980)

Swiss psychologist who spent most of his adult life studying cognitive development. Through carefully detailed, hour-by-hour observations of the developing child, Piaget formulated a theory of how children learn to know or form concepts. Piaget stated that children learn concepts only as they go through a series of developmental stages that are sequential in nature and biologically based. Thinking processes are a biological extension of newborn motor processes. Piaget's developmental stages are: (1) sensorimotor (birth to two years), (2) preoperational or intuitive (two to seven years), (3) concrete operations (seven

to eleven years), and (4) formal operations (eleven to sixteen years). (5)

Plus One

The concept that students can understand reasoning keyed to their present stage and can also gradually be attracted to reasoning that is slightly more complex than their current level (one stage higher, or plus one). They show almost no understanding of reasoning two or more stages higher, however. (7)

Polygenic Inheritance

Inherited traits that result from the combination of large numbers of genes, as opposed to traits, such as eye and hair color, determined by a single pair of genes. (3)

Positive Discipline Techniques

Humane methods for classroom discipline that are geared to the developmental stage of pupils. (20)

Positive Reinforcement

Any stimulus that, when added to the situation, increases the likelihood of the response recurring. A pellet of food may be a positive reinforcer to a hungry rat only if it can be observed that the rat emits the same response (pressing the lever in the Skinner Box) in order to get another pellet. In the classroom positive reinforcement may be provided by primary reinforcers, such as milk, cereal, or candy, or by conditioned reinforcers, such as gold stars, high grades, or social approval. (9)

Positive Transfer

When the learning of A aids in the learning and retention of B. For example, learning the rules of algebra makes the later learning of the principles of physics more efficient. (10)

Post-Facto (P/F) Research

A type of research that, while not allowing for direct cause-and-effect conclusions, does allow the researcher to make better-than-chance predictions. In such research subjects are measured on one response dimension, and these measures are then compared with other response or trait measures taken on the same subjects. (17)

Precise Teaching

Teaching technique used on newly mainstreamed children. Precise teaching provides maximum structure in the learning environment and utilizes behavior modification in order to aid students in mastering a variety of educational tasks. (21)

Preferred Style of Learning

The current system of problem solving preferred by a student at his or her stage of conceptual development. David Hunt believes that this learning mode is not fixed, nor is it a permanent classification. With appropriate matching and mismatching of material and methods, pupils can be encouraged to grow conceptually and increase the complexity of their thinking. (13)

Premack Principle

A principle of behavior modification introduced by David Premack. Premack states that behavior that occurs at a naturally high rate of frequency may be used to reinforce behavior that occurs at a naturally low rate. The establishment of high- and low-frequency responses must be done through careful observation. (10)

Preoperational Stage

The second of Jean Piaget's stages of cognitive growth (from ages two to seven). It is really the beginning of symbolic thinking and frees the child from the thinking of the sensorimotor period that is so directly tied to immediate experience. Oral vocabulary increases by a huge amount, and the child exhibits little concern over the accuracy or even the reality of perception. Imaginary friends, animals that talk, and very "tall" stories mark the period as one of freewheeling creativity. (5)

Proactive Inhibition (PI)

The disruption of information retrieval due to interference from other encoded and stored information. When learning task A and then later learning task B, the encoded information of A works forward to disturb efforts to retrieve the encoded information of B. In effect, old learning is preventing the recall of new learning. (11)

Profile of Nonverbal Sensitivity (PONS)

Robert Rosenthal's measuring instrument to assess the ability to identify aspects of nonverbal communications. The PONS measurement results have indicated that most adults in this culture are not aware of their own nonverbal behavior. The correlation between self-awareness and accuracy was zero. (14)

Programed Instruction

An arrangement of instructional material in a step-by-step sequence designed to lead the student to a specified goal. The material being presented is broken down into small units called frames. There are two general approaches to programing: (1) linear programs, in which all students go through the entire program, and the frames gradually increase in difficulty; and (2) branched programs, in which the student skips forward or backward in the program (the order of the frame presentation varies) as a result of the success or failure experienced in responding.

Programed instruction can be in book form, or it can be presented through the use of a teaching machine and/or computer. The concept of programed instruction is credited to B. F. Skinner. (10)

Protein Synthesis (in memory)

Part of a physiological memory theory that sees permanent memory as the result of RNA's role in synthesizing new brain protein. The new protein is assumed to contain the memory and is thus seen as the ultimate engram. *See* Engram. (11)

Psychoanalytic Theory

Theory of human behavior and method of treating mental illness presented by Sigmund Freud at the turn of the century. The theory attempts to give a rational explanation for irrational thoughts and responses. Psychoanalytic theory states (1) that all behavior is determined by specific motives; (2) that most human motives lie at the unconscious level, and therefore people are unaware of the reasons for most of their own behavior; (3) that neurotic symptoms result from an individual's inner conflicts; and (4) that inner conflicts are a product of childhood trauma and anxiety. The technique is based on the therapist revealing to the patient the source of his or her anxiety and helping the patient to thus achieve insight and emotional release. *See also* Freud, Sigmund. (6)

Psychological Defenses

Anna Freud's concept that adolescents employ various mechanisms, such as displacement, reversal of affect, and withdrawal, to ward off threats to their developing sense of self. These are considered relatively normal methods, while regression, asceticism and being uncompromising may indicate serious psychological problems of adjustment. (6)

Punishment

A method for controlling behavior through the use of aversive stimulation. Punishment, though not itself causing the extinction of a conditioned response, does severely reduce the rate of responding *while the punishment is in force*. Punishment should not be confused with negative reinforcement. *See* Negative Reinforcement. (10)

Qualitative Development

The notion in stage theory that cognitive growth and maturation occur in a sequence of qualitative transformations in a manner similar to the change from an egg to caterpillar, to butterfly. Each change leads to a major shift to a more complex system of thinking. (5)

Quantitative Development

Theory of intellectual development that sees growth occurring in a linear fashion. Cognitive growth is assumed to be based on steady additions to the intellect, not on any changes in the structure of thought. (5)

Random Sample

A selection in which everyone in a population that is being researched has an equal chance of being selected. This helps to ensure that the sample will be representative of the population from which it was selected. (15)

Range

A statistical measure of variability, found by subtracting the lowest score from the highest score. It measures the entire width of a distribution. (15)

Recessive Gene

Gregor Mendel's term for the unit of heredity whose characteristics are expressed only when paired with a like gene; those characteristics are not expressed when paired with dissimilar (dominant) genes. (3)

Rehearsal

In the information-processing model, the critical component of intentional learning. It consists of practice or repetition and is perhaps the key method whereby incoming information may become permanently encoded and stored. (11)

Reinforcement

Any stimulus that increases the likelihood of a response recurring. Reinforcement, as a Skinnerian concept, should not be confused with reward, feelings of pleasure, or any other concept with subjective or mentalistic overtones. Reinforcement may be used in either classical (respondent) or operant conditioning. In respondent conditioning the unconditioned stimulus serves as the reinforcement. In operant conditioning the presentation of any stimulus following the emitted response can be considered a reinforcement *if it results in a higher response rate*. *See also* Positive Reinforcement *and* Negative Reinforcement. (9)

Reliability

The consistency of a measuring instrument over time. A reliable test, for example, tends to produce roughly the same results when used repeatedly under the same conditions. (15)

Remolding

An early method of dealing with children who did not fit in with adult perceptions of normalcy by physically transforming them. (21)

Respondent Conditioning

B. F. Skinner's term for classical conditioning, in which a conditioned stimulus that has been paired several times with an unconditioned stimulus comes to evoke the conditioned response. (9)

Respondents

Name given by B. F. Skinner to those responses that are sometimes called "reflexes." Respondents are those responses that may be automatically elicited by a specific unconditioned or unlearned stimulus. Respondents are also called "unconditioned responses." *See also* Unconditioned Response. (9)

Retrieval

In the information-processing model, the output end of the memory process. Retrieval is the utilization of stored information and must be not only available but also accessible to the individual. (11)

Retroactive Inhibition (RI)

The disruption of information retrieval due to interference from other encoded and stored information. RI occurs when the learning of new material (task B), works backward to prevent the recall of older material (task A). Encoding new information thus hampers efforts to retrieve information already in storage. (11)

Retrograde Amnesia

The loss of memory for events just prior to a head injury, usually producing a loss of consciousness. (11)

Reynolds, Maynard (1922–)

A national leader in the mainstreaming movement who has been critical of the use of a single IQ test for diagnosis and placement of retarded pupils. Reynolds has also shown how the common approaches to special-education classification often penalize students from minority backgrounds and lead to negative self-fulfilling prophecies.

Ribonucleic Acid (RNA)

Molecules located in the chromosomes that carry the hereditary instructions contained in the DNA to other parts of the cell. RNA can be thought of as the "builder" that translates the DNA "blueprint" into a finished product. (3)

Risky Shift

Concept from social psychology suggesting that persons in a group situation are less cautious and more prone to risk taking than are persons who are alone. The group situation apparently allows individuals to become less conservative and more willing to take chances regarding both attitudes and behavior. (18)

RNA Theory (of memory)

Theory of memory based on chemical changes occurring within the organism. The life-controlling nucleic acid RNA (ribonucleic acid) is seen as being, if not the physical site of the memory itself, at least part of the chain of events leading to the physiological formation of memory. (11)

Rogers, Carl (1902–)

Founder of the client-centered, or nondirective, approach to personality. Rogers challenged the orthodox psychiatric and psychological treatment techniques in vogue when he started practice. He felt that psychiatrists often harmed their patients more than they helped them. Rogers insisted that all persons have a natural tendency to grow in healthy directions and that the role of the therapist is to provide conditions whereby the patient (or client) can fulfill his or her destiny of self-actualization. The famous Rogerian triad of unconditional positive regard, empathy, and congruence became the crucial ingredients in the helping process. Good teaching, like good counseling, is based on this same triad. Classroom interaction should be based on the development of equal and genuine relationships. (12)

Role

Term used by social psychologists to denote the dynamic aspect of status. Role is the behavioral repertoire associated with an individual's status—the bundle of responses available to a person as a result of his or her niche in society's prestige hierarchy. Society *expects* individuals of a given status to act in certain ways, and the individual feels obliged to act according to society's expectations. *See also* Status. (18)

Rosenthal Effect

Concept introduced by Robert Rosenthal, who found that teachers often form expectations about the performance of students, and the students then respond on the basis of a self-fulfilling prophecy. If a teacher assumes a child to be intellectually inferior, the teacher treats the child in such a way as to reinforce inferiority. The child thus begins to act in accordance with the teacher's expectations. (14)

Saber-Tooth Curriculum

An educational spoof that clearly points out the current debate over educational goals: Should we teach specific skills (how to scare away fierce tigers with firebrands) or general abilities (how to be courageous)? Educational leaders often take extreme positions on teaching goals that fit the examples taken by the tribal elders in this mock history. (13)

Schedules of Reinforcement

According to B. F. Skinner, the arrangement of reinforcers on the basis of either time elapsed or number of responses emitted. Responses that are reinforced periodically, rather than each time they are emitted, tend to be conditioned more strongly and are thus more resistant to extinction. The major schedules of reinforcement are: (1) continuous, (2) fixed ratio, (3) fixed interval, (4) variable ratio, and (5) variable interval. (9)

Segregation

A method of dealing with children who do not conform to societal perceptions of normalcy by providing separate facilities, such as residential schools in remote areas. (21)

Sensitive Period

A time period when an organism is susceptible to a change in behavior due to certain environmental stimulation. The sensitive periods typically occur early in the organism's life and tend to produce behavior changes that are relatively long-lasting. The process of mother-infant bonding is said to occur only during the baby's first three days of life.

Sensorimotor Stage

First stage of cognitive development, according to Jean Piaget, in which the child learns to distinguish himself or herself from the external environment, begins to notice and follow objects in the environment, and develops the rudiments of trial-and-error learning. This stage lasts from birth to age two years, and the child operates at the level of raw, immediate stimulation as experienced through the senses. An important milestone during this stage is the development of the concept of object permanence, the thought that objects still exist even though they are not, at the moment, being seen. Piaget insists that mental processes are developed directly from inborn motor processes. The child's ability at birth to make certain motor responses forms the basis for the cognitive processes that come later. (5)

Sensory Register

In the information-processing model, the first stop for incoming information. When information first impinges on sensory receptors, there is a brief moment when it is held as raw, unprocessed information in the sensory register. It is the "buffer" or "way-station" situated between the external environment and internal memory. (11)

Shaping (Successive Approximations)

Technique used by B. F. Skinner to encourage the acquisition of new conditioned operants. The learner is differentially reinforced for making ever-closer approximations of the behavior being conditioned. (10)

Short-Term Memory (STM)

In the information-processing model, the first of two main storage systems. Sometimes called "working" or "active" memory, it may only encode about seven separate items. Estimates of how long information may be retained in short-term memory vary from about twenty seconds to over a minute. (11)

Significance

A statistical term indicating that the results of the study are not simply a matter of chance. Researchers talk about significant differences and significant correlations, the assumption being that chance has been ruled out (on a probability basis) as the explanation. (17)

Skinner, B. F. (1904–)

Psychology's most important and honored behaviorist, Skinner is the originator of the system of operant conditioning. Using E. L. Thorndike's Law of Effect as a starting point, Skinner has shown that conditioning can take place when responses are allowed to occur and are then followed by reinforcing stimuli. Reinforcement is thus contingent on the fact that the response (operant) has been emitted. Skinner's emphasis is on response analysis. He is not concerned with what goes on inside the organism but is concerned with specifying the environmental conditions associating with and affecting the organism's response repertoire. Skinner's most notable contributions to education are the techniques of programed instruction and behavior modification. (9)

Snarey, John (1948–)

Investigator who used cross-cultural studies to determine whether Lawrence Kohlberg's system of classifying moral development was as universal as originally claimed. He found that Western and non-Western urban cultures were similar in the sequence of stages Kohlberg described, but tribal and/or feudal cultures exhibited a different pattern. (7)

Snow, C. P. (1905–1980)

Popularizer of the idea that science and the humanities are separate cultures, or distinct world views. The differences are often found in how the objective psychological scientist and the subjective educational practitioner' view the world of schools and classrooms. (1)

Social Facilitation

A concept from the field of social psychology used to explain the fact that in some circumstances individuals perform more quickly when in a group situation than when alone. Social facilitation is most pronounced in the case of fairly simple mechanical tasks. The more difficult and the more intellectual the task, the less the effect of social facilitation. (18)

Social Inhibition

The fact that individuals, in some circumstances, perform less well when in the presence of other people. This is especially true when the tasks being performed are perceived as being difficult by the individual being measured. The opposite of social inhibition is called "social facilitation." (18)

Social Learning Theory

Theory, proposed by Albert Bandura, suggesting that a large part of what a person learns occurs through imitation or modeling. Bandura's major concern is with learning that takes place in the context of a social situation where individuals come to modify behavior as a result of how others in the group respond. Social learning *does not* require primary reinforcement. (10)

Social Psychology

The study of individual behavior in the context of the social situation. Social psychology analyzes the ways in which people affect and are affected by other people. Major topics in the field include conformity, cohesiveness, status and role, attitudes and attitude change, social perception, and group structure and leadership. (18)

Socialization

Process by which an individual learns and internalizes society's rules and norms, thought by social psychologists to be brought about through societal pressures to conform. (18)

Spearman, Charles E. (1863–1945)

English psychometrician and psychologist who proposed that intelligence was not a simple unitary process but could be separated into an underlying general factor (*g*) and a series of very specific factors (*s*). Among the *s* factors were such things as verbal ability, math ability, and even musical ability. Spearman used a statistical approach, mainly correlational, to segregate these components of intelligence. (16)

Spontaneous Recovery

The fact that a conditioned response that has been extinguished will, after a brief time, tend to recur on its own. The conditioned response returns, despite having been extinguished, with no additional conditioning trials. (9)

Standard Deviation (S.D.)

A statistical measure of variability that is based on how far *all the scores* in a distribution vary from the mean. A large S.D. indicates a group of heterogeneous measures, whereas a small S.D. indicates homogeneity. (15)

Stanford-Binet Test

Intelligence test developed by Lewis M. Terman in 1916 while he was at Stanford University. The Stanford-Binet test was an American revision of the original Binet test, first published in France in 1905. It has since gone through numerous updates and revisions but is still considered to be more "verbally loaded" than its Wechsler counterparts. The Stanford-Binet, like the Wechsler, is an individual test of intelligence. (16)

Status

Term used in social psychology to define an individual's niche in society's prestige hierarchy, or the individual's standing in a social system. The behavior expected of an individual of a given status is called his or her "role." *See also* Role. (18)

Stimulus Generalization

Term used in conditioning to describe a situation in which a previously neutral stimulus similar to the actual stimulus used in the training procedure takes on the power to elicit the response. In classical conditioning the neutral stimulus is similar to the conditioned stimulus, whereas in operant conditioning the neutral stimulus is similar to the discriminated stimulus S^D. (9)

Stimulus-Response Theory

A theory that stresses the importance of the build up of stimulus-response *associations* in defining learning. Most behaviorists adhere to stimulus-response learning theories, the major exception being E. C. Tolman. The leading stimulus-response theorists are E. L. Thorndike, Ivan Pavlov, J. B. Watson, Edwin Guthrie, C. L. Hull, and B. F. Skinner. Stimulus-response theorists stress the importance of nurture in the nature-nurture debate. Most theories of learning during the first half of the twentieth century, especially in the United States, were stimulus-response theories. The cognitive-gestalt position, however, was *not* based on a stimulus-response theory. (8)

Stimulus Variety

Variation, at all sensory modes, of stimulus inputs. Stimulus variety was seen by many early-experience theorists as the crucial ingredient in intellectual development. J. McV. Hunt states that the more the child hears, sees, and touches, the more he or she will want to hear, see, and touch, and the more intellectual growth will occur. (4)

Storage

In the information-processing model the organism's internal memory. When information is stored it may persist over time. Currently, theorists refer to at least two storage components, short-term and long-term. (11)

Structure

Part of Jerome Bruner's theory of instruction, which states that any given subject area can be organized in an optimal fashion (structured), so that it can be transmitted to and understood by almost any student. Bruner feels that if a subject area is properly structured, then "any idea or problem or body of knowledge can be presented in a form simple enough so that any particular learner can understand it in a recognizable form." (9)

Student Crushes

A common problem for secondary-school teachers involving an inappropriate emotional attachment on the part of a student for a teacher. Using Anna Freud's framework, teachers can understand the need to handle such feelings without encouraging the fantasy. (6)

Student Teams–Achievement Divisions

A system created by Robert Slavin to promote mainstreaming. He integrates special-education and regular-class children and sets up achievement groups (teams) composed of a mix of students. By offering a variety of rewards, the system increases both group and individual achievement. It does not drain resources from the "regular" pupils to meet the needs of special-education children. (21)

Summerhill School

English boarding school whose curriculum and way of life is based on the permissive orientation of its founder, A. S. Neill. The school stresses the free expression of ideas without the rigors of required exams or the demands of required class attendance. (4)

Symbolic Representation

The third stage of cognitive development and method of communication introduced by Jerome Bruner, the first two being the enactive and iconic levels. At the symbolic level, the child is able to translate experience into language. Words can then be used for communication and for representing ideas. Symbolic representation allows us to make logical connections between ideas and to think more compactly. (9)

t Test

Statistical test used to establish whether or not a significant (nonchance) difference exists between two sample means. It is the ratio of the difference between two sample means to an estimate of the standard deviation of the distribution of differences. That is, the t ratio is equal to $\bar{x}_1 - \bar{x}_2$, divided by the standard error of difference. (17)

Teacher Enthusiasm

According to research by Jacob Kounin and Barak Rosenshine, the characteristic of being "with it" and alert that has been shown to have a consistent positive relationship with student behavior. (12)

Teacher Expectations

A teacher's attitudes toward student learning and achievement. Numerous factors have been found to influence teacher acceptance of pupils, including social class, ethnicity, gender, rearing in a single-parent home, personality, and academic achievement. Some estimates suggest that as much as 50 percent of current teachers hold one or more stereotypes and provide children with less than optimal learning opportunities in the classroom. (14)

Teaching Machine

A device used to present an instructional program one step (or frame) at a time. The student either writes in answers or presses a button corresponding to the correct alternative. The advantages of the teaching machine are: (1) The student can proceed at his or her own pace; (2) the student receives immediate feedback; (3) for many students the machines are intrinsically motivating. *See also* Programed Instruction. (10)

Terman, Lewis M. (1877–1956)

Professor of psychology at Stanford University (1910–1942) and deviser of the Stanford-Binet IQ test. The American revision of the original Binet intelligence test was published in 1916. Terman standardized the test on American schoolchildren, and he introduced so many new items that it was virtually a new test. He scored the test on the basis of IQ (intelligence quotient), rather than mental age as Binet had done. Terman is also noted for his long-term study of intellectually gifted children (IQs of 140 or higher), which proved that a high IQ does correlate with many traditional measures of success, both in school and in later life. (16)

Terminal Behavior

Concept used by experts in the field of behavior modification. Terminal behavior defines the educational goals for the class as a whole or for individual students. It defines these goals in objective, behavioral terms. Rather than using what they consider to be vaguely stated goals like "understanding," the behaviorists insist that the goals describe specific behaviors that will result when the objective is attained. For example, students can be said to have learned how to multiply when they can recite the multiplication table with no errors. (10)

Thelen's Seven Teacher Images

Different self-images of teachers described by Herbert Thelen as representing common teacher self-perceptions. The images include the teacher as Socrates, town-meeting manager, master to an apprentice, general, business executive, coach, and tour guide. These self-images are based not on the needs of children but on those of the adult teacher. (14)

Theory and Practice

The twin pillars of educational psychology. The discipline represents a bridge or connector, between psychology as the science of human behavior and the profession of education. (1)

Thorndike, Edward L. (1874–1949)

One of America's most renowned educational psychologists. Thorndike studied at Harvard under William James and later taught at Columbia Teacher's College. Early in his career, Thorndike did important laboratory studies of learning, using animals as subjects. From the results of these studies he constructed the first internally consistent learning theory. He created three major laws of learning (the Law of Readiness, the Law of Exercise, and the Law of Effect) and many subordinate laws. Thorndike believed learning occurs in a trial-and-error fashion and thought of learning itself as the result of a buildup of connections between stimuli and responses. He insisted that educational psychology must utilize the scientific method in establishing its own "book of knowledge." (8)

Thurstone, Louis L. (1887–1955)

One of the developers of the factor approach to the understanding of intelligence. Thurstone originally gave sixty different tests of special abilities to large groups of children and then separated out those test scores that correlated highly with each other. He discovered that out of the original list of seemingly separate tests, there were only seven underlying correlated groupings (or "primary abilities"): verbal comprehension, word fluency, numerical ability, spatial visualizations, associative memory, perceptual speed, and reasoning. (16)

Time-Out Room

A separate room for handling extremely difficult children by segregating them from other students for a relatively short period. Excessive use of such a room can become aversive, making the technique ineffective. (20)

Token System

A system of reinforcement used by proponents of behavior modification, in which tokens of varying point values are awarded to students for fulfilling specific behavioral objectives. The tokens (conditioned reinforcers) may be different colored pieces of cardboard or poker chips that the student may earn to achieve some desired prize or privilege. The system is said to have two main advantages: (1) It maintains a high daily rate of desirable responses, and (2) it teaches delayed gratification. (10)

Tolman, E. C. (1886–1959)

Creator of "purposive behaviorism," a bridge between rigid behaviorism and doctrinaire gestaltism. Tolman was a behaviorist to the extent that he accepted observable responses as psychology's basic data, but he insisted that, far from being random or based on trial and error, learning was purposive, or goal-directed. He agreed with the gestaltists that persons learn by forming cognitive maps of their environment. People can form hypotheses, see relationships, and then respond on the basis of these cognitive maps, rather than respond solely on the basis of a conditioned stimulus-response connection. Tolman's system is called an "S-S (sign-significate) theory" rather than an "S-R (stimulus-response) psychology." (8)

Transfer

What occurs when the learning of one activity influences the learning of a second ability. If the learning of A facilitates the learning of B, it is called positive transfer. If the learning of A inhibits the learning of B, it is called negative transfer. (10)

Trivia in the Classroom

A teacher's rapid-fire series of questions to students calling for rote-memory answers. A series of classroom observation studies dating back as far as the early 1900s and extending to the 1980s has indicated that too often this is the common mode of teacher-pupil interaction. (1)

Two-Stage Memory Theory

In the information-processing model, the theory that memories are encoded and stored in at least two stages—in short-term memory, which lasts from about a few seconds to up to a minute, and in long-term memory, which may last over a lifetime. (11)

Unconditional Positive Regard

Concept used by Carl Rogers in dealing both with clients in therapy and with students in the classroom. Unconditional positive regard means accepting persons for what they are, without passing judgment, and without exacting any condition for full acceptance. According to Rogers, this is one of the three necessary and sufficient conditions for the promotion of learning, the other two being empathy and congruence. (12)

Unconditioned Response

A reflex response or, in Skinnerian terms, a respondent. An unconditioned response is any response that can be elicited automatically by the presentation of a certain stimulus, without any training or learning. The term is used in classical conditioning, and in Ivan Pavlov's original experiment the unconditioned response was salivation to the stimulus of meat powder being placed in the dog's mouth. (8)

Unconditioned Stimulus

Any stimulus that will elicit a given response automatically, without any training or learning. The term is used in classical conditioning, and in the case of Ivan Pavlov's own experiment, the unconditioned stimulus was meat powder placed in the dog's mouth. (8)

Unconscious Motivation

Freudian view that most of a person's behavior is motivated by forces of which the person is unaware—irrational needs that lurk beneath the level of conscious awareness. (19)

Validity

The extent to which test instruments are true indicators of what they purport to measure. A valid history test, for example, should measure a person's knowledge of history, not his neatness, penmanship, or spelling ability. (15)

Variability Measures

Measures that give information regarding individual differences, or how persons vary in their measured scores. The two most important measures of variability are the range and the standard deviation. (15)

Variable

Anything that varies *and can be measured*. In experimental research the two most important variables to be identified are the independent variable and the dependent variable. The independent variable is a stimulus, is actively manipulated by the experimenter, and is the presumed causal half of the cause-and-effect relationship. The dependent variable is a measure of the subject's response and is the presumed effect half of the cause-and-effect relationship. (17)

Visual Cliff

The perceived drop-off at the edge of any steep place. Research has shown that the newborn of many species, including human babies, will avoid the "deep" side of a specially built platform. This seems to show that depth perception is innate rather than learned. (3)

WAIS (WAIS-R)

Wechsler Adult Intelligence Scale—individual IQ test developed by David Wechsler (along with the WISC or WISC-R—Wechsler Intelligence Scale for Children—and the WPPSI—Wechsler Preschool and Primary Scale of Intelligence). All the Wechsler tests are administered by a trained examiner to one person at a time. All the tests yield three scores: a verbal IQ, a performance IQ, and a full-scale IQ. Wechsler believed that many of the intelligence tests of the day were too heavily laden with verbal items, and, to correct for that, the Wechsler tests all include a performance section that tests an individual's visual-motor abilities. Wechsler tests use the deviation IQ method of scoring. In the hands of a skilled examiner, the WAIS can be used as a projective test for ferreting out a subject's personality traits. *See also* Intelligence Quotient. (16)

Walberg, Herbert (1937–)

A leading educational researcher who has applied the technique of meta-analysis to the study of teaching effectiveness. Walberg has been able to outline the relative importance of a variety of teaching strategies. Most important is providing positive reinforcement, followed by other methods such as giving cues and feedback, promoting cooperative learning, and establishing a positive classroom atmosphere. Other relevant factors are time on task, the incidence of higher-order questions, and use of advance organizers. (12)

Watson, John B. (1878–1958)

Founder of behaviorism, and, at one time, psychology's most vocal critic of subjectivism, mentalism, and especially the technique of introspection. Watson was a strong believer in the importance of environment (as opposed to heredity) in shaping virtually all human behavior. He also believed that learning resulted from a buildup of stimulus-response connections, or what he called "habits." He was a strong advocate of Ivan Pavlov's concept of classical conditioning and utilized this method in his study of the acquisition of fear in the baby, Albert. Watson taught psychology at Johns Hopkins and later spent many years working for an advertising agency in New York. *See also* Behaviorism. (2)

Wechsler, David (1896–1981)

America's premier psychologist in the area of intelligence testing and test construction. Beginning in 1939 with the publication of the Wechsler-Bellevue test, Wechsler introduced a series of individual IQ tests—the WAIS or, since its revision, the WAIS-R (Wechsler Adult Intelligence Scale), the WISC or, since its revision, the WISC-R (Wechsler Intelligence Scale for Children), and the WPPSI (Wechsler Preschool and Primary Scale of Intelligence). Wechsler defined intelligence as "the global capacity of an individual to think rationally, to act purposefully, and deal effectively with his environment." All the Wechsler tests report three separate scores: a verbal IQ, a performance IQ, and a full-scale IQ. (16)

Wertheimer, Max (1880–1943)

Founder of the gestalt school of psychology (in the early 1900s). Wertheimer had criticized the structuralists and their insistence that all psychological phenomena should be analyzed into the smallest possible parts. He felt that the whole was more than just the sum of its parts. In order to understand psychological phenomena, one had to study all the parts together in their particular *Gestalt*, a German word meaning whole, or totality of configuration. Wertheimer's first studies were in the area of perception, especially the perception of apparent movement. Later he became interested in education and the principles of learning.

He insisted that educators should teach for "understanding" rather than relying on repetition and rote memorization. *See also* Gestalt Psychology. (8)

White, Robert (1904–)

Harvard psychologist who has suggested that one of humankind's most fundamental motives is based on a strong personal desire to master the environment. White calls this the "competence" motive and believes it to be an intrinsic one that may even have survival value for the species. (19)

Wundt, Wilhelm (1832–1920)

German psychologist and founder of the structuralist school of thought. Wundt created the world's first laboratory of psychology at the University of Leipzig in 1879. He believed that psychology should devote itself to the study of the basic elements that make up conscious experience. To ferret out these individual elements, Wundt used trained subjects who looked within themselves and reported all their most fleeting and minute thoughts, feelings, and sensations. This technique of looking within the self is called "introspection." Wundt's goal was to take psychology out of the field of philosophy and give it a sense of scientific respectability. (8)

z Score (Standard Score)

A number that results from the transformation of a raw score into units of standard deviation. The z score specifies how far above or below the mean a given score is in these standard deviation units. The normal deviate, z, has a mean equal to 0 and a standard deviation equal to 1.00. (15)

Zeigarnik Effect

The fact that in some situations, persons are more apt to remember unfinished tasks than those they have completed. Memory is enhanced by the thought of the job still left undone. (19)

Zygote

First of the prenatal stages of development. The zygote is formed at conception and results from the fertilization of an egg by a sperm cell. The zygote floats freely within the uterus (for about two weeks) and finally attaches itself to the uterine wall. (3)

PHOTO CREDITS

Chapter 11

260: Robert Eckert/The Picture Cube. **262:** Thad R. Wiseheart. **264:** Bob McCormack. **265:** Wally Huntington. **267:** Eugene Richards/Magnum. **271:** Ambassador College. **277:** *The Andover Townsman.* **279:** *Left & right,* Joel Gordon.

Unit 3

285: Charles Harbutt/Archive.

Chapter 12

286: Charles Harbutt/Archive. **290:** Courtesy, Herbert Walberg. **291:** Courtesy, CBS, Inc. **294:** Al Parker/Far West Lab. **296:** Wally Huntington. **302:** Carl Rogers. **304:** Wally Huntington. **307:** Instructional Materials Production Center, North Carolina State University.

Chapter 13

312: Mark Antman/The Image Works. **316:** Courtesy, University News & Information Office, University of Chicago. **322:** Marshall Henrichs.

Chapter 14

334: Susan McElhinney/Archive. **336 & 338:** Wally Huntington. **342:** Courtesy, Harvard Office of News & Public Affairs. **354:** Courtesy, BBC Picture Publicity. **359:** Marshall Henrichs.

Unit 4

361: Arthur Grace/Stock, Boston.

Chapter 15

362: Arthur Grace/Stock, Boston. **364:** Marie Geggis. **377:** Brown Brothers. **380:** Photo by Tommy Weber, courtesy of Fordham University.

Chapter 16

384: Joel Gordon. **388:** Historical Pictures Service. **389:** Anne Kaufman Moon/Stock, Boston. **390:** Historical Pictures Service. **392:** Culver Pictures. **394:** Wally Huntington. **396:** Courtesy, David Wechsler. **397:** *Left & right,* Psychological Corporation, New York, NY. **398:** Rosemary Good. **399:** Thad R. Wiseheart. **401:** Jean Speiser, UNICEF Photos. **403:** Marshall Aronson. **407:** Courtesy, Sandra Scarr.

Chapter 17

414: Sarah Putnam/The Picture Cube.

Unit 5

431: Elizabeth Crews.

Chapter 18

432: Marc & Evelyne Bernheim/Woodfin Camp & Associates. **434:** Marshall Henrichs. **436:** Thad R. Wiseheart. **437:** Anne Kaufman Moon/Stock, Boston. **440:** Marshall Henrichs. **442:** Bruce Anderson. **452:** Wally Huntington. **454:** Photo by Raimondo Borea, courtesy, Clark, Phipps, Clark & Harris, Inc.

Chapter 19

460: Paul Fortin/Stock, Boston. **465 & 469:** Thad R. Wiseheart. **470:** Educational Ventures, Inc. **473:** Courtesy, Harvard Office of News & Public Affairs. **474:** Thad R. Wiseheart. **475:** Harry F. Harlow, University of Wisconsin Primate Laboratory. **476:** Jim Carroll.

Chapter 20

486: Elizabeth Crews. **489:** Marshall Henrichs. **491:** Bob Henriques/Magnum. **500 & 501:** Instructional Materials Production Center, North Carolina State University. **502:** David S. Strickler

Chapter 21

510: David S. Strickler/The Picture Cube. **515:** Marshall Henrichs. **520:** *Left & right,* State Historical Society of Wisconsin. **524:** *The Boston Globe.* **526:** Reverend William J. Codd, S. J. **528 & 531:** Marshall Henrichs.

INDEX

ABOUT THE AUTHORS

Norman A. Sprinthall is Professor and head of Counselor Education at North Carolina State University. He has also held professorships at the University of Minnesota and Harvard University. He earned his bachelor and masters degree from Brown University and his doctorate from Harvard. Dr. Sprinthall is listed in *Who's Who in America,* was elected a fellow in two divisions of the American Psychological Association, and holds membership in the American Educational Research Association and the American Association of Counseling and Development. He has served on the editorial boards of many journals and has written numerous works, including another Random House text, *Adolescent Psychology: A Developmental View.*

Richard C. Sprinthall is Professor of Psychology and Director of Graduate Studies at American International College. After earning his undergraduate degree from Brown, he received his masters and doctorate from Boston University. Listed in *Who's Who in American Education, American Men and Women of Science,* and *Contemporary Authors,* he is also a member of the American Psychological Association and the American Statistical Association. In addition to the current volume, he is the author or coauthor of other major textbooks and several journal articles.